# Letters of H. P. Lovecraft

## LETTERS TO FAMILY AND FAMILY FRIENDS
## VOLUME 1

*H. P. Lovecraft's childhood home at 454 Angell Street,
Providence, Rhode Island*

# *H. P. Lovecraft*

---

# Letters to Family and Family Friends
## Volume 1: 1911-1925

## Edited by S. T. Joshi and David E. Schultz

Hippocampus Press

---

New York

Published by Hippocampus Press
P.O. Box 641, New York, NY 10156.
www.hippocampuspress.com

Hippocampus Press logo designed by Anastasia Damianakos.
Cover art © 2020 by David C. Verba.
Cover design by Daniel V. Sauer, dansauerdesign.com

First Edition
1 3 5 7 9 8 6 4 2

ISBN 978-1-61498-247-0 vol. 1
ISBN 978-1-61498-301-9 vol. 2
ISBN 978-1-61498-302-6 set

# Contents

# Introduction

At first glance it may not seem as if H. P. Lovecraft was a "family man," but in many ways his family remained an emotional and financial bulwark for the whole of his life. His parents, Winfield Scott Lovecraft (1853–1898) and Sarah Susan ("Susie") Phillips Lovecraft (1857–1921), were married on 12 June 1889 and settled in the Boston area, although Lovecraft himself was born at his family home at 194 (later 454) Angell Street in Providence, R.I. But the Lovecrafts probably moved back to Boston within a few months of the birth, residing in various Boston suburbs as Winfield pursued his career as a "commercial traveler" (not a door-to-door salesman, but one who sold to wholesalers) for Gorham Silversmiths, a leading business based in Providence. But Winfield had some sort of nervous breakdown in the spring of 1893; he was brought back from Chicago to Providence in a straitjacket and confined for the rest of his life at Butler Hospital. He died of general paresis (a form of syphilis), and we are obliged to believe Lovecraft's comments that he had little remembrance of his father aside from a few quirks of temperament and the old-fashioned clothes he wore. Lovecraft did, however, claim that his Anglophilia derived in large part from Winfield, whose grandfather had emigrated from England.

Not a great deal is known about Susie Lovecraft, although the research of Kenneth W. Faig, Jr., and others has unearthed a number of facts that allow us to paint a rough portrait of her life and character. Born in Foster, R.I., she was educated at the Wheaton Seminary in Norton, Mass., for at least the period 1871–72, and at some point apparently made the acquaintance of the poet Louise Imogen Guiney (1861–1920). Lovecraft states that he and his parents spent the entire winter of 1892–93 in Guiney's home in Auburndale, Mass.; no confirmation of this stay has emerged, but in the absence of contrary evidence it must be provisionally accepted. Susie indulged her son in some of his early interests, notably the *Arabian Nights* as well as chemistry and astronomy.

Given that Lovecraft was no more than two and a half years old when Winfield was stricken, it is unlikely that there was any correspondence between father and son, even though Winfield did travel widely to pursue his career. After his death, Susie brought young Howard back to 454 Angell Street, and it was there that the major male presence in Lovecraft's childhood emerged—his maternal grandfather, Whipple Van Buren Phillips (1833–1904), a dynamic businessman whose far-flung ventures resulted in both the creation and the loss of several fortunes. It was Whipple who, in 1881, had supervised the building of the 454 Angell Street house, a rambling three-story structure that Lovecraft adored and in later years yearned to reclaim. In the

1890s Whipple was extensively involved in a project to build a dam across the Bruneau River in Idaho, an ambitious undertaking that was made more challenging when the dam was twice washed away.[1] The resulting financial setback may have contributed to the cerebral hemorrhage that Whipple suffered in the spring of 1904. He died on 28 March.

Whipple did engage in sporadic correspondence with his grandson while he was in Idaho in the 1890s; several letters to Lovecraft are extant, and it does appear that Lovecraft himself wrote back (one letter by Whipple is a response to a joint letter written by Lovecraft, his mother, and his aunt Annie E. P. Gamwell). These letters provide interesting glimpses of the precocious toddler, although in many ways they are of greater interest in reflecting Whipple's wide travels (the letters are written variously from Omaha, Nebraska, Grand View, Idaho, and Scranton, Pennsylvania). Whipple's charming nicknames for his grandson ("Skimper," "Punky") are indicative of how fond he was of the young Lovecraft; and his amusing comment in the letter of 19 June 1894 that Lovecraft should be a "good Boy and *wear trousers*" appears to reflect the fact that Susie kept her son in "frocks" well beyond the time when most mothers would have allowed their male children to don normal boys' clothing. Susie is reputed to have wished for a daughter, and she apparently sought to maintain that fantasy as long as she could viably do so.

Whipple's death necessitated the departure of Lovecraft and his mother from the beloved 454 Angell Street house. By this time, both of Lovecraft's aunts, Lillian D. Clark and Annie Gamwell, had married and moved out of the house. Susie and Lovecraft were forced to move into a double house at 598 Angell Street (the other side of the house is 600 Angell Street), a few blocks to the east. Lovecraft claimed to despise the cramped quarters of the house, but eventually he came to cherish it as a bastion of security; it proved to be the residence he occupied the longest during his life, a full twenty years. His own childhood and adolescence were troubled. His schooling at the Slater Avenue School had been sporadic, as he attended only for the years 1898–99 and 1902–03 (private tutors had instructed him in the interim). Now, having lost his grandfather and looking forward apprehensively to uncertain prospects at Hope Street High School, Lovecraft later claimed that he actually contemplated suicide.[2] But he refrained, and to his surprise he found high school enjoyable. Both at Slater Avenue and at Hope High he developed any number of friends, including the brothers Chester and Harold Munroe, Ronald Upham, Stuart Coleman, and Kenneth Tanner; but no correspondence—if there ever was any—survives from these individuals.

---

1. See further Kenneth W. Faig, Jr., "Whipple V. Phillips and the Owyhee Land and Irrigation Company," *Owyhee Outpost* No. 19 (May 1988): 21–30.
2. HPL to J. Vernon Shea, 4 February 1934; *Letters to J. Vernon Shea, Carl F. Strauch, and Lee McBride White* 221–22.

But Lovecraft failed to graduate from high school. He had in fact only attended for three years, 1904–05 and 1906–08; he had apparently sat out nearly the entirety of the 1905–06 term. The causes of the "nervous collapse"[3] that he claims to have undergone in 1908 are unclear; possibly Lovecraft—who had already been making a name for himself as an astronomer, having published articles on astronomy in two separate local papers in 1906–08—was unable to deal with the realization that, because of his weakness in mathematics, he would never become a professional astronomer. The result was a retreat into hermitry for the period 1908–13. The hothouse atmosphere of 598 Angell Street, where Lovecraft lived alone with his mother, can only be imagined. She herself was becoming increasingly disturbed, both through financial worries and perhaps through horror at the loathsome fate of her husband, which she must have known was the result of sexual irregularities (presumably Winfield's frequenting of prostitutes well before his marriage). She may have transferred this loathing to her son, now entering adulthood. It was apparently around this time that Susie told a neighbor, Clara Hess, that Lovecraft did not like to be seen in public because he was so "hideous."[4] Whatever the objective truth of such an assertion (Lovecraft was frequently mortified at the presence of ingrown facial hairs, which he regarded as a disfigurement), it is a remarkably uncharitable thing for a mother to say about her son.

But Susie's and Lovecraft's isolation continued even after Lovecraft tentatively emerged from hermitry in late 1913. He had been reading popular magazines such as the *Argosy* and the *All-Story*, and the romantic tales of one Fred Jackson, frequently published in the *Argosy*, so incensed the prudish Lovecraft that he wrote a fiery letter to the editor. Later this controversy flowered into a poetic duel between Lovecraft (who wielded a satirical pen honed by thorough familiarity with the verse satire of John Dryden and Alexander Pope) and some of his opponents, including an Englishman living in Tampa, Florida, named John Russell. The controversy was noted by Edward F. Daas of the United Amateur Press Association, who invited Lovecraft to join the organization. Lovecraft did so in April 1914.

Even so, Lovecraft was slow to come out of his shell, at least in person. Although he wrote prodigiously—poetry, essays, editorials, and (beginning in 1917) weird fiction—for the amateur press, he rarely ventured out of his house to meet any of them. Some of them came to him: W. Paul Cook came to Providence in 1917 to look up Lovecraft, as did Rheinhart Kleiner in 1918, 1919, and 1920. Lovecraft seemed to take pride in noting that, as late as 1915, he had yet to set foot outside the states of Rhode Island, Massachusetts, and

3. HPL to Bernard Austin Dwyer, 3 March 1927 (*MWM* 432).
4. Cited in August Derleth, "Lovecraft's Sensitivity" (1949), in *Lovecraft Remembered*, ed. Peter Cannon (Sauk City, WI: Arkham House, 1998), 34.

Connecticut[5] (in fact, he would not do so until 1921).

But then, to his apparent shock, Susie took ill in the spring of 1919. She herself had some kind of nervous collapse, brought on by financial worries about her talented but economically clueless son, and was confined to Butler Hospital, where she would remain until her death on 24 May 1921. It was just at this time—coincidentally or not—that Lovecraft began venturing somewhat further afield. Meetings of amateur journalists in Boston in 1921 afforded Lovecraft the opportunity to meet his friends and colleagues outside the confines of 598 Angell Street, and they resulted in several revealing letters that Lovecraft wrote to his mother. Anomalously, these are typed, not handwritten, perhaps to make it easier for Susie to read them. The two surviving letters may come across as a bit stiff and formal, but Lovecraft's deep if conflicted affection for his mother is unquestionable. It is, however, characteristic that he makes early mention of his perceived disfigurement ("The new suit, worn for the first time, was a work of art, and made me appear as nearly respectable as my face permits—and even the face was almost at its best"). One in fact wonders how Susie reacted to these letters. Lovecraft himself once stated that she did not care for his involvement in amateur journalism: "Of amateurdom her opinion was not high, for she had a certain aesthetic hypersensitiveness which made its crudeness very obvious and very annoying to her."[6] This may have reflected a class consciousness on Susie's part, as she apparently regarded herself as a member of Providence's informal social aristocracy and may have felt that many amateurs were, for all their intellectual gifts, not "well-bred." Her contrasting responses to the appearance on her doorstep of the rumpled W. Paul Cook in 1917 and the suave and polished Rheinhart Kleiner in 1918 (Susie almost prevented Cook from entering the door, whereas she welcomed Kleiner warmly) point in this direction.

Whether he knew it or not, Susie's death liberated Lovecraft from an increasingly oppressive familial presence; it may have made the rest of his life and career possible. When she had to be confined in Butler Hospital in 1919, his younger aunt, Annie Emeline Phillips Gamwell (1866–1941), moved into the house to take care of her nephew, although his elder aunt, Lillian Delora Clark (1856–1932), was frequently at the house. They—as well as Susie—are perhaps to be blamed for not encouraging Lovecraft more forcefully to train for some kind of white-collar employment, even of a humble sort, so that he could support himself by some other means than writing, especially given that he had adopted the eighteenth-century attitude of writing as an elegant amusement that should be practiced without any thought of remuneration. This lack of employable skills resulted in a lifelong poverty that became quite dire, not only for him but for his aunts as well, with the passing of the years.

---

5. HPL to Maurice W. Moe, 1 January 1915 (*MWM* 47).
6. HPL to Winifred Virginia Jackson, 7 June 1921 (*SL* 1.138).

Lillian, the oldest child of Whipple and Robie Phillips, was also educated at Wheaton Seminary and completed her education at the Rhode Island Normal School. She was a schoolteacher prior to her marriage to Dr. Franklin Chase Clark (1847–1915) on 10 April 1902; they had no children. Her marriage resulted in the emergence of a new and welcome male figure in Lovecraft's orbit, as Dr. Clark seems to have taken a strong interest in his nephew's budding attempts at writing, both prose and poetry. Clark, like his nephew, had long been fascinated with classical literature and had prepared unpublished translations of Virgil and other Latin poets. No correspondence between him and Lovecraft survives, perhaps because Clark rarely left Providence and therefore had no occasion to write to him on his travels. When Clark died, Lovecraft lost nearly the last male figure of that generation.[7] Lillian perforce had to look for work, and she is listed in the 1920 census as an occupant (as housekeeper) at 135 Benefit Street, a house that Lovecraft would later use as the setting of "The Shunned House" (1924). She must therefore have moved out of 598 Angell Street during this time (apparently 1919–20), but later she returned there.

Annie, the fifth and youngest child of Whipple and Robie Phillips, was educated in Providence and married Edward Francis Gamwell (1869–1936) on 3 June 1897; Lovecraft served as usher at the wedding. They had two children, Phillips Gamwell (1898–1916) and Marion Roby Gamwell, who lived only five days in February 1900. Edward was an editor of various newspapers in Cambridge, Mass., notably the *Tribune* (1901–12); Lovecraft states that it was this journalistic work on his uncle's part that inspired him to begin the *Rhode Island Journal of Astronomy* in 1903.[8] But Annie divorced Edward sometime prior to the death of Phillips, who perished of tuberculosis on the last day of 1916. Phillips's death appears to have shaken Lovecraft, for he had become quite close to his cousin. He observes that Phillips, when he was twelve years old (i.e., in 1910), had "blossomed out as a piquant letter-writer eager to discuss the various literary and scientific topics broached during our occasional personal conversations,"[9] and Lovecraft attributes his fondness for letter-writing to four or five years' correspondence with Phillips. It is therefore most unfortunate that no correspondence between the two survives.

The bulk of this book contains Lovecraft's letters to Lillian and Annie from 1921 to 1935, when he engaged in increasingly wide travels up and down the Eastern Seaboard and as far west as Cleveland. It is no accident that these letters begin in 1921, for this was when his burgeoning personal

---

7. He had never been particularly close to his maternal uncle, Edwin E. Phillips (1864–1918), especially after Edwin had dissipated much of Whipple's assets in 1911 through bad investments.

8. HPL to Rheinhart Kleiner, 16 November 1926 (*SL* 1.39).

9. HPL to Maurice W. Moe, 5 April 1931 (*MWM* 303).

and literary ties with amateur journalists led him to wander farther and farther afield. Trips that summer to his childhood haven, the Great Meadow Country Clubhouse in Rehoboth, Mass., and to New Hampshire to see Myrta Alice Little are notable for their mere existence, given Lovecraft's expression of severe depression following his mother's death only a few months earlier. But his travels became far more extensive the next year, as his desire to see Alfred Galpin and Samuel Loveman took him to Cleveland in August and then to New York in September and October, where he stayed with Sonia Haft Greene (1883–1972), the dynamic businesswoman he had met at the annual convention of the National Amateur Press Association in Boston in 1921 and who in 1924 would become his wife.[10] In spite of his own perceived social ineptitude, Lovecraft was perennially amazed that his friends and colleagues sought out his company and fêted him like a celebrity. It is poignant to read, in his letter to Annie of 9–11 September 1922: "Can you imagine Grandfather Theobald in good health, with very little facial bother, up in the daytime, going about from one interesting thing to the other, & with something to look forward to the next day? It seems incredible, yet nevertheless that's me!" Lovecraft was dimly becoming aware that the influence of his mother had been a largely deleterious one, and that his emergence from her shadow was the best thing that could have happened to him.[11] While he had respect for and devotion to his aunts, they were not in a position to dictate the terms of his life in the way his mother was.

The letters to Lillian and Annie quickly became a sort of diary—not merely of his travels, but of the most minute particulars of his daily life. As early as his letter to Annie of 13–16 September 1922 he is writing: "This is a letter & a diary combined!" This tendency only increased with the passing of time, and especially when Lovecraft abruptly eloped with Sonia in March 1924 and moved into her apartment at 259 Parkside Avenue, Brooklyn.

The fact that he made such a move without consulting his aunts could not have sat well with them. Regrettably, direct evidence of their views—on Sonia, on Lovecraft himself, or on any other subject—is all but unavailable; for although it is abundantly clear that both Lillie and Annie (especially the former) wrote to Lovecraft regularly, especially during his New York years (1924–26), not a single piece of correspondence from Lillian, and only one

---

10. HPL had first visited New York, at Sonia's behest, in April 1922. That visit is not chronicled in any surviving letters to HPL's aunts, but an extensive report can be found in a letter to Maurice W. Moe dated 18 May 1922 (*MWM* 84–100).

11. Cf. "The Thing on the Doorstep" (1933): "Edward [Derby]'s mother died when he was thirty-four, and for months he was incapacitated by some odd psychological malady. His father took him to Europe, however, and he managed to pull out of his trouble without visible effects. Afterward he seemed to feel a sort of grotesque exhilaration, as if of partial escape from some unseen bondage" (*CF* 3.328).

from Annie (dated 12 June 1935), survives.[12] So their views on the many issues connected with their nephew's life, work, and relationships can only be
inferred from what Lovecraft himself says in his own letters.

But there is some reason to believe that Lillian in particular was not keen
on Lovecraft marrying Sonia, and this attitude may in large part account for
why he did not alert her as to his intentions until 9 March 1924, six days after
the wedding had taken place. Up to this point, he had merely suggested in
various postcards that he was making one more visit to New York (and later to
Philadelphia, their honeymoon site) analogous to his previous visits. Annie may
have been somewhat less hostile to Sonia; she had joined her nephew for part
of Lovecraft's extensive stay in Brooklyn in September and October of 1922,
and as a more socially engaged woman she may have been more temperamen-
tally aligned with Lovecraft's new wife, with her outgoing and gregarious temperament. But as the couple settled down to married life, initially with high
hopes for both financial and personal success, only to find those hopes dashed,
Lillian may have been inclined at numerous points to say, "I told you so."

The nearly 250,000 words of letters that Lovecraft wrote to Lillian and
Annie during his two years in New York are an astonishing chronicle that allows for unprecedented insight into Lovecraft's daily habits, his association
with his many friends in the metropolis, and his shifting attitudes as his initial
thrill at being in the nation's center of art, culture, and publishing—as reflected in his wonder-filled letters of 1922—degenerates into defeat and depression as he finds himself unable to secure employment in spite of his high
intellect. Sonia had apparently made the imprudent decision to leave her high-
paying job at Ferle Heller's, a major department store in New York, to establish her own hat shop, which promptly failed; this "has created something of
a shortage in the exchequer," as Lovecraft notes ruefully to Lillian on 1 August 1924. It was at this time that he was compelled to seek employment of
whatever sort—including such unlikely positions as working for a bill-
collection agency and a lamp-testing firm—but it all came to naught, largely
because of his lack of prior work experience. On top of this, Sonia's health
gave way in the fall (perhaps echoing, in Lovecraft's mind, his own mother's
sudden collapse in 1919 as a result of financial worries), so that she had to go
to the hospital for a few days and then stay in a rest home in New Jersey.
Lovecraft was forced to become self-sufficient in maintaining himself, and he
takes great pride in learning how to cook simple meals, in keeping the place
well dusted, and even in playing chess with his wife in the hospital.

The situation could not last, and it didn't. Letters to the aunts come to a
sudden end for the last month of 1924, chiefly because Lillian spent the entirety of that month with the couple to deal with the crisis. The upshot was

---

12. There are envelopes of two other letters (postmarked 18 June and 21 July
1935) at JHL, but the letters themselves are nonextant.

that Sonia relocated to the Midwest (first Cincinnati, then Cleveland) to secure employment in various department stores. Since Sonia's spacious (and expensive) apartment at 259 Parkside was no longer needed, as she would be visiting New York only at wide intervals, Lovecraft was situated in a one-room apartment (with dressing alcove) in Brooklyn Heights, near where Samuel Loveman (and also the poet Hart Crane) lived. He had wished to move to Elizabeth, N.J., which he had visited earlier in 1924 (it led to the writing of "The Shunned House" in October), but he initially professed satisfaction with the apartment at 169 Clinton Street. At this time, Brooklyn Heights was somewhat down-at-heels, and Lovecraft gradually realized that the move was an unfortunate one. His apartment was plagued with mice; his landlady, Mrs. Burns, was stingy with the heat (in large part because she herself was forced to deal with a nationwide coal strike from September 1925 to February 1926); his neighbors seemed an unsavory lot; and, to cap the indignity, on 24 May 1925 he was robbed of nearly all his clothing along with other materials (including an expensive radio that belonged to Samuel Loveman) when thieves broke into the place through the dressing alcove and absconded with the goods while Lovecraft was sleeping in the main room.

Lovecraft was initially devastated by the blow, given his slender finances (he was at this time being almost entirely supported by money sent to him by Sonia, along with small and irregular payments from his aunts), but as early as 28 May he was already joking about the incident, writing an amusing letter to Lillian that expatiated on the loss:

> Alas for the robes of my infancy, perennial in their bloom, & now cut off—or snatched off—in the finest flowering of their first few decades! They knew the slender youth of old, & expanded to accomodate the portly citizen of middle life—aye, & condensed again to shroud the wizened shanks of old age! And now they are gone—gone—& the grey, bent wearer still lives to bemoan his nudity; gathering around his lean sides as best he may the strands of his long white beard to serve him in the office of a garment!

This mock-lament is accompanied by a hilarious drawing of Lovecraft wearing nothing but a barrel and with hair down to his ankles.

What followed was a somewhat manic quest to secure new suits that were both inexpensive and sufficiently conservative in cut and design. Lovecraft's long, meticulous accounts of his quest come to sound like the actions of someone afflicted with obsessive-compulsive disorder; but over the course of months he managed to restore his wardrobe (four suits—two light in weight [for summer] and two heavy in weight [for winter], two light in color and two dark), and along the way became a fairly shrewd bargainer with the merchants he was dealing with. When he purchased a splendid suit that he labelled the "Triumph," he actually wished to mail it to Lillian to show off the new acquisition, but she must have demurred.

With Sonia out of the picture, his aunts became an increasingly essential lifeline—a concrete link to the hometown that he now clearly regretted leaving so hastily. His reservations are crystallized in the poignant line in the story "He" (written in August 1925): "My coming to New York was a mistake." That story itself portrays a character seeking out antiquarian sites wherever he could find them, and Lovecraft had long been doing exactly that. He now undertook an even more exhaustive quest for such remains of colonialism—rather few and far between in a metropolis so devoted to speed and modernity—throughout the five boroughs. A certain number of these (for example, the houses on Charlton Street in lower Manhattan, which he referred to as "New York's best preserved Colonial thoroughfare") are no longer extant, but other important landmarks such as the Jumel Mansion (1765), the Bowne house in Brooklyn (1661), and others are still present. Lovecraft even found a rich treasure-house of antiquities, as well as scenic beauty, in such unlikely places as Garden City and Hempstead, in Long Island. These treks, often conducted on foot over many miles, are all chronicled minutely in his letters to his aunts; and it becomes clear that they served as a means of momentarily forgetting the miserable state of his existence. That his letters had, indeed, become definitively diary-like is indicated by the existence of an actual diary for 1925 (see *CE* 5.149–76) that manifestly served as an *aide-mémoire* to his letters to Lillian and Annie.

In the absence of Sonia, Lovecraft's friends served an even more central function in preventing him from descending even further into depression. This was the heyday of the Kalem Club—a group of friends whose last names all began with K, L, or M. Its chief members—George Kirk, Rheinhart Kleiner, Arthur Leeds, Frank Belknap Long, Samuel Loveman, Everett McNeil, James F. Morton—met weekly, first on Wednesdays, then on Thursdays. At some point a schism emerged because McNeil was irritated that Leeds was slow in repaying a small debt to him, and separate "McNeil" and "Leeds" meetings developed on alternate weeks. McNeil was the loser in this dispute, because the other members did not care much for his querulous temperament; but Lovecraft always attended every meeting. The hosting of the meetings rotated among the members, and Lovecraft took pride in being a good host. He even went to the effort of purchasing a 49¢ aluminum pail to fetch hot coffee from a nearby delicatessen, which he would then serve in his best china. Lovecraft never uses the term "Kalem Club" in his letters to his aunts, referring simply to "The Boys" or "the gang"; but it was clear that he was the central figure in these gatherings, holding forth with effortless erudition on all manner of subjects. But the meetings were also vital to his own psychological well-being. At one point he expressed irritation that the constant gallivanting around the city with the "gang," or lounging in various cheap restaurants or Automats (self-service cafeterias scattered throughout the metropolitan area), was a distraction from his literary work. Indeed, in his first seventeen months in New York he only wrote a single story ("The Shunned House") and a handful of poems, most of the latter written to order for gatherings of an amateur journalism group in Brooklyn, the Blue Pencil Club. But in spite of his resolution to cut down on his socializing, he does not seem to have made much headway. When, in November 1925, W. Paul Cook asked him to write a treatise on weird fiction, Lovecraft did become more disciplined; and his work on "Supernatural Horror in Literature" (not completed until he had returned to Providence) may also have led to a small resurgence in his writing of weird fiction, as testified by "Cool Air," written in February 1926.

Given his general misery in New York, it is not surprising that Lovecraft's racial attitudes flared up occasionally during this stressful period. This is the greatest black mark on his reputation, and certain individuals today have tendentiously seized upon it in an attempt to deny him any standing at all as a writer or thinker, in spite of his unquestioned merits as a creative artist and philosopher and his immense influence on the subsequent course of weird fiction. What these hasty and ahistorical critics overlook is the fact that these attitudes were very likely imbued in Lovecraft from a very early age, and by both familial influence and by the general influence of his culture in a conservative New England that did not look favorably upon the immense influx of immigrants in the later nineteenth and early twentieth centuries. The very fact that Winfield Scott Lovecraft, in one of the hallucinations he experienced during his seizure in Chicago in 1893, maintained that "three men—one a negro—in the room above [were] trying to do violence to his wife" suggests that Winfield was a racist, susceptible to age-old white fears of blacks' sexual potency, especially as purportedly directed toward white women; and he could well have inculcated his views into his infant son. Recent research indicates that racial attitudes are all but fixed in individuals from as early as the age of five and subsequently become very difficult to alter or eradicate.

Lovecraft's initial visits to New York, in 1922, exposed him to a cosmopolitan milieu for the first time; and it is not surprising that he expressed astonishment, even horror, at the presence of so many diverse individuals on the street. He had led a very sheltered life up to this point and had not even explored the slums of his native Providence; but his sudden witnessing of the dismal tenements of the lower East Side of Manhattan stunned him as a kind of cosmic aberration. These sentiments are not expressed in letters to Lillian, but during his two years in New York he makes many statements on the subject; and the fact that he did so, openly and unashamedly, makes it abundantly clear that Lillian herself must have shared his attitudes to some degree. However, a notorious letter of 11 January 1926 about Jews may perhaps have given even Lillian pause; for in a subsequent letter he notes:

Incidentally—don't fancy that my nervous reaction against alien N.Y. types takes the form of conversation likely to offend any individual. One knows when & where to discuss questions with a social or ethnic cast, & our group is not noted for *faux pas*'s or inconsiderate repetitions of opinion. I don't think I fail to appreciate the genius & good qualities of the entire assemblage, for every member of which I entertain unaffected respect.

Indeed, Frank Belknap Long, who met Lovecraft on an almost daily basis during his years in New York, has testified that "during all of those talks on long walks through the streets of New York and Providence, I never once heard him utter a derogatory remark about any member of a minority group who passed him on the street or had occasion to engage him in conversation"[13]—an inexplicable circumstance if one believes that Lovecraft was "obsessed" with the issue of race. Manifestly, his racial sentiments were at this time largely the product of his own wretchedness in a city he had come to loathe. The overriding question was how, or whether, he would be able to get out of the nightmare he found himself in.

An extraordinarily poignant letter to Lillian written on 8 August 1925 betrays the depths of Lovecraft's despair. She had apparently felt that her nephew's clinging to the possessions he had brought from Providence—books, furniture, and the like—were a "burden," leading Lovecraft to retort bitterly:

> I see no possibility of ever encountering a really congenial milieu or living among civilised people with old Yankee historic memories again—so in order to avoid the madness which leads to violence & suicide I must cling to the few shreds of old days & old ways which are left to me. Therefore no one need expect me to discard the ponderous furniture & paintings & clocks & books which help to keep 454 always in my dreams. When they go, I shall go, for they are all that make it possible for me to open my eyes in the morning or look forward to another day of consciousness without screaming in sheer desperation & pounding the walls & floor in a frenzied clamour to be waked up out of the nightmare of "reality" to my own room in Providence.

It is difficult to imagine Lillian's response to a letter in which her nephew comes fairly close to an explicit wish for self-destruction. There is no follow-up to the discussion, but one must believe that Lillian at this time began to think of how Lovecraft could be summoned back to Providence. The invitation did not occur until March 1926; was it that Lillian was uncertain whether Lovecraft would simply abandon his wife and come running back to his hometown with his tail between his legs? Whatever the case, that is exactly

---

13. Frank Belknap Long, *Howard Phillips Lovecraft: Dreamer on the Nightside* (Sauk City, WI: Arkham House, 1975), 227.

what Lovecraft did. His letters of the period are unprecedented in their nearly incoherent enthusiasm.

The move occurred on 17 April 1926, Sonia accompanying him as he settled into a second-floor apartment at 10 Barnes Street, just north of Brown University. Lillian had taken an apartment on the first floor. Where Sonia fitted into the new arrangement was by no means clear. At some unspecified date she made a bold proposal to the aunts:

> I suggested that I would take a large house, secure a good maid, pay all the expenses and have the two aunts live with us at no expense to them, or at least they would live better at no greater expense. H. P. and I actually negotiated the rental of such a house with the option to buy it if we found we liked it. H. P. was to use one side of it as his study and library, and I would use the other side as a business venture of my own. At this time the aunts gently but firmly informed me that neither they nor Howard could afford to have Howard's wife work for a living in Providence. That was that. I now knew where we all stood. Pride preferred to suffer in silence; both theirs and mine.14

There need be no criticism of the aunts for their attitude. They were acting in accordance with the social conventions they themselves had absorbed throughout their entire lives; and those conventions prohibited them from countenancing a "tradeswoman" wife for their nephew. They may have descended to shabby-genteel status, but they still regarded themselves—and were likely regarded by their friends and acquaintances—as members of the Providence aristocracy. Whether the fact that Sonia was a Ukrainian Jew had any bearing on the matter is unclear; probably it did. If Lovecraft himself is to be criticized for anything, it is for apparently standing by spinelessly while his aunts made this decision for him—a decision that he must have known (as Sonia certainly did) would essentially end their marriage. She did not pursue divorce proceedings until early 1929, but their breakup was inevitable.

Lovecraft's subsequent letters to his aunts almost exclusively take the form of travel diaries. Indeed, when in May 1929 he was robbed of the "black enamel-cloth case" he habitually carried, he particularly lamented the loss of "the 1929 diary with the record of all my spring travels & all my addresses written in it. However, I can reconstruct the diary from the letters & cards I have written home." Without these letters (especially those to Lillian), we would know very little of Lovecraft's surprising return to New York for a week or so in September 1926—apparently at Sonia's request—and another visit in the spring of 1928, when Sonia was setting up a new hat shop in Brooklyn and asked for her husband's assistance in getting it off the ground. On both these visits it becomes evident that Lovecraft had largely reverted to

---

14. Sonia H. Davis, *The Private Life of H. P. Lovecraft*, ed. S. T. Joshi (West Warwick, RI: Necronomicon Press, rev. ed. 1992), 20.

the kind of "guest" status he had assumed in 1922. A remarkable letter to Annie, dating to 17 September 1927, shows Lovecraft expatiating on the wonders of Newport; and his account of specific structures in that colonial city was manifestly written by memory. Other 1927 letters, mostly to Lillian, tell of his widening explorations in various corners of New England, including Newburyport, Haverhill, and Gloucester in Massachusetts and Portland, Maine. In 1927 and 1928 he visited Vermont, and on the latter trip he made the acquaintance of the picturesque rustic Bert G. Akley, whom he later transmogrified into Henry Wentworth Akeley, the protagonist of "The Whisperer in Darkness" (1930).

Indeed, it appeared that every successive year's travels expanded upon those of the year before, so that in 1929 he descended down the Eastern Seaboard to New York, Norfolk, Williamsburg, Richmond, Fredericksburg, and elsewhere, then back up to upstate New York, where he visited Bernard Austin Dwyer. In 1930 he made two epic treks—to Charleston to the south and Quebec to the north—interspersed with another visit to Dwyer in West Shokan, N.Y. In 1931 he managed to get all the way down to Key West, Florida, while also going through Charleston and spending much time in St. Augustine and Dunedin, Florida, where he stayed with the weird writer Henry S. Whitehead.

It is somewhat strange that no letters to Lillian (or, for that matter, to Annie) covering his 1932 travels survive, for Lovecraft once again undertook extensive explorations of New Orleans, Chattanooga, Natchez, and elsewhere in the South. But he was summoned home in early July by an urgent message from Annie stating that Lillian was in the terminal stages of atrophic arthritis. Lovecraft was at this time staying with Frank Belknap Long and his family in New York, but quickly caught the train back to Providence. He was present at her bedside when she died on 3 July 1932.

There is no question of Lovecraft's deep attachment to Lillian, as his hundreds of letters to her are sufficient to establish unequivocally. And his moving words to other correspondents about her passing are heartfelt:

> The vacuum created in this household is easy to imagine, since my aunt was its presiding genius and animating spirit. It will be impossible for me to get concentrated on any project of moment for some time to come—and meanwhile there intervenes the painful task of distributing my aunt's effects ... whose familiar arrangement, so expressive of her tastes and personality, I dread to disturb.[15]

So now the Lovecraft/Phillips household was reduced to two members, Lovecraft and his Aunt Annie. For some months they continued to maintain separate rented quarters; but in the spring of 1933 he states that "my aunt & I

---

15. HPL to Maurice W. Moe, 12 July 1932 (*MWM* 327).

had a desperate colloquy on family finances,"[16] with the idea of consolidating their households. On this occasion luck was with them; for they stumbled upon a large apartment at 66 College Street, just south of the John Hay Library of Brown University and owned by the university, that offered a rate of only $10 a week—about the same as what each had been paying separately. On top of that, the house was a quasi-colonial structure, built c. 1825 (Lovecraft thought the house dated to c. 1800). Aunt and nephew moved in on 15 May 1933. It would be the last residence Lovecraft would occupy.

A few months before the move, on March 11, Lovecraft saw his ex-wife Sonia for the last time, when she asked him to join her in the exploration of the quaint colonial towns of Farmington and Wethersfield, Connecticut. They had not been entirely out of touch, as the existence of "European Glimpses" (1932)—a travelogue about Sonia's recent tour of Europe, revised or ghostwritten by Lovecraft—attests. But after their less than cordial meeting in Connecticut (at the end of their first evening together, she had said, "Howard, won't you kiss me goodnight?"; he had replied, "No, it is better not to"), Sonia recognized that her relations with her ex-husband were over. About two years later she moved to California; just before the move she reports that she took Lovecraft's letters to her to a field and "set a match to them."[17] This must be one of the most painful utterances that a student of Lovecraft could ever read; for she had earlier noted the gargantuan extent of their correspondence, especially during their courtship, when "H. P. [was] writing me about everything he did and everywhere he went, introducing names of friends and his evaluation of them, sometimes filling 30, 40 and even 50 pages of finely written script."[18] As a result, only a single postcard from Lovecraft to Sonia now survives.[19]

Lovecraft's subsequent letters to Annie were largely restricted to minutely written postcards written during the Christmas seasons of 1932–33, 1933–34, and 1934–35, when he fell into the habit of venturing to New York (in spite of his aversion to the cold), staying with the Longs, and visiting his many friends in the metropolis. Matters take a more serious turn in the spring of 1936, when Annie was hospitalized. Lovecraft told his various correspondents that she had become afflicted with a particularly severe case of the "grippe" (an antiquated term for the flu) that he himself had suffered that winter; but in fact, Annie had breast cancer and was to undergo a mastectomy. The entire episode—which required her to be hospitalized for more than two weeks at Jane Brown Memorial Hospital and then spend additional weeks recovering at a private rest home—must have put a severe strain on the pair's finances, as the strange document that Lovecraft wrote at this time

---

16. HPL to Donald Wandrei, 21 February 1933; *Letters with Donald and Howard Wandrei and to Emil Petaja* 300.
17. Davis, *Private Life* 23, 24.
18. Davis, *Private Life* 18.
19. This document will be printed in a forthcoming *Miscellaneous Letters* volume.

demonstrates. This peculiar diary—written in installments that he would evidently bring over to Annie for her to read and digest—is chilling in its bland recounting of the extreme economies he was forced to undergo, especially in the matter of his diet. He unearthed canned goods remaining from his 10 Barnes Street days and, even though he found some items (such as some "earthy" cocoa) unappetizing, he nonetheless felt duty-bound to consume them. Is it any wonder that he at times "felt so tired that I was compelled to rest instead of going to the bank as I had planned"?

A somewhat pleasanter result of Annie's hospitalization was Lovecraft's accidental acquaintance with some of her friends, resulting in some delightful letters of a sort we rarely find among his correspondence. The most interesting of these acquaintances was Marian Frederika Bonner (1883–1952), who worked at the Providence Public Library but, more significantly, lived at the boarding-house at 53–55 Waterman Street, directly behind 66 College, where a bevy of cats sunned themselves on the roof of a shed. Lovecraft continued to write to Bonner long after Annie had come home, and his letters record his unaffected devotion to those cats (whom Lovecraft, living as he did on Brown's "fraternity row," identified as members of the K.A.T. fraternity), as they bear quaint drawings of cats and other tokens of light-hearted wit. The letters also become surprisingly revelatory of his many and diverse interests, from eighteenth-century literature to weird fiction to the charmingly mundane details of his daily life.

Much less is known of the other correspondents with whom Lovecraft communicated at this time: Bertha Rausch and Mayte E. Sutton. Rausch (b. 1863?) was the wife of Anthony J. Rausch (b. 1852). Lovecraft's one letter to her is addressed to "Mrs. Anthony Rausch, 159 Prospect St., Providence, R.I." On the envelope Annie Gamwell has written: "The letter my dear Howard wrote to Mrs. Rausch when I was ill—She was so pleased with it & saved it & brought it to me after my beloved Howard's death." As for Sutton (1879–1968), she lived at 100 Spring Avenue in Troy, N.Y. She stated in a letter to August Derleth that she had corresponded with Lovecraft "for nearly ten years,"[20] but Lovecraft's first extant letter to her dates to the fall of 1933, when, shortly after moving into 66 College Street, Annie had broken her ankle and took months to recover. He speaks of meeting Sutton and her daughter, Margaret Morgan, on his visit to New York during the Christmas period of 1932–33, but his comments suggest that he found them rather tiresome and strove to avoid direct contact. Nonetheless, Lovecraft continued writing to Sutton until as late as 1936.

---

20. Mayte E. Sutton to August Derleth, 5 March 1938 (ms., Wisconsin Historical Society). In this letter she also states that she has only one extant letter from HPL (presumably the one dated 6 August 1936, surviving in AHT). Presumably she returned the other letter (2 November 1933) to AEPG after HPL's death.

H. P. Lovecraft's relations with his mother and wife may have been troubled, but the devotion he exhibited to his aunts when they shared living space with him is touching and sheds valuable light on his character. It may well be, as Maurice Lévy stated, that Lovecraft preferred this kind of relationship because it was "discrete, competent, and *nonconjugal.*"[21] But he himself wrote to Maurice W. Moe in 1929 (presumably at the conclusion of his divorce proceedings): "And yet I didn't find matrimony such a bugbear as one might imagine. With a wife of the same temperament as my mother and aunts, I would probably have been able to reconstruct a type of domestic life not unlike that of Angell St. days, even though I would have had a different status in the household hierarchy."[22] There is no reason to doubt this assertion; and the bitter grief that Annie displayed in the years following the death of her nephew on 15 March 1937 demonstrates that Lovecraft's affection for his aunts was fully reciprocated. We wish there was more documentary evidence of the relations between Lovecraft and his close relations—his father, his mother, his aunts, his grandfather—but what remains, even if it is nearly all from Lovecraft's side, makes it undeniable that the Lovecraft/Phillips family, for all its financial and other difficulties and its ingrained New England reserve, was a tightly knit group who relied on one another in more ways than they themselves could have enumerated.

—S. T. JOSHI & DAVID E. SCHULTZ

*A Note on the Text*
The letters in this volume are derived almost entirely from handwritten or typed manuscripts found at the John Hay Library. R. H. Barlow, Lovecraft's literary executor, appears to have made a point of urging Annie E. P. Gamwell to donate letters to her and to Lillian from their nephew to the library, as these are among the earliest documents to have been accessed in the H. P. Lovecraft Papers. The letters clearly passed through Barlow's hands at some point, as they were donated to the library after his initial deposit of Lovecraft manuscript material in March–April 1937 (some letters bear his notations, as he evidently copied Lovecraft's notes on envelopes and then discarded the envelopes). Some critical letters—including the one announcing his marriage to Sonia (9 March 1924)—are found only in the Arkham House Transcripts. Annie or Barlow must have sent these letters to Arkham House for transcription; why all were not returned is unknown. Whereas Lillian seems to have been diligent in preserving her letters and postcards from her nephew (only a few letters to her can be specifically identified as nonextant), Annie seems to have been less careful, and numerous letters that Lovecraft mentions to Lilli-

---

21. Maurice Lévy, *Lovecraft: A Study in the Fantastic,* tr. S. T. Joshi (Detroit: Wayne State University Press, 1988), 23 (emphasis in original).
22. *MWM* 207.

an as having been written to Annie do not survive. Lovecraft's letters from Lillian and Annie (and there must have been many of these) must have been destroyed by Lovecraft himself, as he was habitually short of space.

No letters from Lovecraft to his grandfather, Whipple Van Buren Phillips, survive, but several charming letters from Whipple are extant. The few extant bits of correspondence Lovecraft to Sonia (before they were married) will be included in a separate volume.

The editors are grateful to Sean Donnelly, Stefan R. Dziemianowicz, Kenneth W. Faig, Jr., Christopher Geissler of the John Hay Library, Perry Grayson, Donovan K. Loucks, M. Eileen McNamara, Christopher O'Brien, J.-M. Rajala, Peter Ruber, and Jordan Douglas Smith for their invaluable assistance in the preparation of this volume. Special thanks to go Martin Andersson for his care and attention in examining the book at a late stage.

*Abbreviations*

| | |
|---|---|
| AHT | Arkham House transcripts of Lovecraft's letters |
| ALS | autograph letter, signed |
| ANS | autograph note, signed |
| JHL | John Hay Library, Brown University |
| NAPA | National Amateur Press Association |
| TLS | typed letter, signed |
| UAPA | United Amateur Press Association |
| | |
| *AT* | Lovecraft, *The Ancient Track* (2013 ed.) |
| *CE* | Lovecraft, *Collected Essays* (2004–06; 5 vols.) |
| *CF* | Lovecraft, *Collected Fiction* (2015–17; 4 vols.) |
| *LL* | Joshi and Schultz, *Lovecraft's Library* (2017 ed.) |
| *MWM* | Lovecraft, *Letters to Maurice W. Moe and Others* (2018) |
| *OFF* | Lovecraft, *O Fortunate Floridian!* (2007) |
| *SL* | Lovecraft, *Selected Letters* (1965–76; 5 vols.) |
| *WT* | *Weird Tales* |
| | |
| AEPG | Annie E. P. Gamwell |
| FBL | Frank Belknap Long |
| HPL | H. P. Lovecraft |
| LDC | Lillian D. Clark |
| The Man from Genoa | Frank Belknap Long |
| MFB | Marian F. Bonner |
| RHB | R. H. Barlow |
| SSL | Sarah Susan Lovecraft |

*Howard Phillips Lovecraft, with parents Sarah and Winfield*

# Letters to Sarah Susan Lovecraft

[1]　　[ANS, JHL]*

Thu., Nov 30, 1911.

Dear Mother:—

3:30a-m

If, as you start toward Lillie's festive spread,
You find me snoring loudly in my bed,
Awake me not, for I would fain repose,
And through the day in quiet slumbers doze.
But lest I starve, for lack of food to eat,
Leave here a dish of Quaker Puffèd Wheat,
Or breakfast biscuit, which, it matters not,
To break my fast when out of bed I've got.
And if to supper you perchance should stay,
Thus to complete a glorious festive day,
Announce the fact to me by Telephone,
That whilst you eat, I may prepare my own.

H. P. Lovecraft

[2]　　[TLS, JHL]

598 Angell St., Providence, R.I.
February 24, 1921

My dearest Mother:—

I was greatly pleased to receive your letter, and thank you in addition for the small primroses,—which still adorn this apartment—the Weekly Review, the banana, and that most captivating cat picture, which I shall give a permanent place on the wall.

The Amateur Journalists' Conference of Tuesday, February 22, was a most distinguished success in every way, and gave me the most pleasant day I can recall since childhood. The new suit, worn for the first time, was a work of art, and made me appear as nearly respectable as my face permits—and even the face was almost at its best.[1] In short, the excellence of my attire permitted me to be absolutely unconscious of my appearance—to forget that I was visible, as it were—which is the secret of all genuine enjoyment in public. Every plan materialised with clockwork success. I was feeling well, planned for the 12:25 train, and caught the latter without hurrying. Being an enthusiast about railways and

---

*[Note by Sarah Susan Lovecraft:] Written on Thanksgiving day By HPL when I went to Lillie[']s to dinner & he was asleep—

travel, my enjoyment began at once; and I watched the countryside whirl by with a feeling of old-time satisfaction, remembering my more frequent rides of other days. The train reached Boston on time, and I strolled leisurely to the Quincy House, which I reached in time for the very first of the programme. The attendance was large and distinguished, including Willard O. Wylie, Nelson G. Morton, W. Paul Cook, W. V. Jackson and mother, Mrs. Miniter, Mrs. Sawyer, George Julian Houtain, Mrs. S. Lilian McMullen (Lilian Middleton), J. B. Lynch, Mrs. Bertha Grant Avery (exceedingly prominent in amateurdom from 1880 to 1890), Charles A. A. Parker, Annie Cross Ellis (prominent professional newspaper woman whose son, Willard T. Ellis, is also an amateur), Mrs. K. Leyson Brown (the kindly old lady who was in Providence last December), and many others—including two especially promising prospective members, a young physician with a tenderly cherished chin-beard, and a very bright college youth, editor of the weekly magazine of Boston University. I have mentioned only a few, who possess distinguishing qualifications. The entire attendance was far too large to count. The proceedings were conducted in two large rooms; one assembly hall fitted with rows of chairs and a desk, and one banquet-hall, with appropriately arranged tables.

The afternoon session, opening at 2 p.m. and presided over by Nelson Glazier Morton, was primarily a symposium of speeches and papers on the subject "What Have You Done for Amateur Journalism, and What Has Amateur Journalism Done for You." Absent members were first heard from, their papers being read by chosen members who were present. Samuel Loveman's paper was very poetic—he had asked me to read it, but Mrs. Miniter (in charge of the programme) thought she had better assign it to Mrs. McMullen, who had not felt equal to preparing a paper of her own. Mrs. McM. read it with great success—but not without having to ask me beforehand how to pronounce the name of the neo-Platonic philosopher Plotinus! I think the reason Loveman had wished me to read it was because it contained classical names. My own remarks were received with a surprising amount of applause, which naturally gratified me immensely.[2] In fact, the flattery of these Bostonians is something extraordinary! Each formal paper was followed by discussion, so that nearly three hours were consumed by this symposium. Following this, a musical programme was rendered with great success, the chief ingredient being the McMullen-Adams song, "The Bumble Fairy", which you played the other day. Mrs. McM was reluctant to sing it, not possessing a voice quite up to her own standard of excellence; but her scruples were entirely unnecessary, since the rendition proved phenomenally pleasing. I was immensely glad to hear the piece played properly, and found that in my own crude picking out I had not correctly interpreted the *time*. This Ernest H. Adams is certainly a composer of the greatest possible ability, and I think Mrs. McM is singularly fortunate in her opportunity to write words for his airs. Neither suffers by comparison with the other—it is an ideal "team".

Mrs. McMullen was very glad to hear that you liked "The Bumble Fairy", and bade me thank you for your favourable opinion. It appears to me that she is destined for professional prominence at an early date—sooner perhaps than many amateurs of even greater genius, such as Winifred V. Jackson and Samuel Loveman. And yet in the end little Alfred Galpin will outstrip them all! Two reporters from Boston papers were present at this session, and I suppose I shall later be sent the press reports of the event—if they amount to anything. A curious situation was produced by the divided associational interests of the gathering. The overwhelming majority were adherents of the rival or National Association (which is, of course, now friendly with the United), but the Jackson–McMullen–Theobald group formed a compact minority of purely United enthusiasts. This group remained as an unbroken unit throughout both afternoon and evening, the line of demarcation appearing most clearly when the possible new members were approached in regard to affiliating with amateurdom. The Nationalites presented all the advantages of their society, but we lost no opportunity to insist on the superior merits of the United, with its more serious educational purpose and more exclusive literary standard. I think, though it was three against the whole majority, that the United element won; for both of the brilliant prospectives were studious and serious-minded young men, and seemed impressed with the United arguments. If we did not "land" the college youth, I think Galpin can do it by letter. All this rivalry, however, was conducted with the utmost good humour. Mrs. Sawyer, for the National, insisted that her society was larger and older—that the United was merely a smaller, later society. To this I replied that the analogy of organic nature held good—the National was the crude, primitive, coarsely organised monster of prehistoric times—the dinosaur or pterodactyl of amateurdom; gigantic in size and anterior in date, but forced in the course of evolution to give way to the later-comer of smaller size but incomparably greater intelligence—the United, corresponding to mankind. This bit of biological repartee seemed well received, judging from the hilarity it caused. Miss Jackson writes that Mrs. Miniter is still debating whether or not to include it in the paper about the conference which she is preparing. Mrs. M. deems it humorous, but hesitates to record such an attack on the antique and boastful National, of which she has been a member since 1883. Actually, it would not be a bad idea if the prospectives should join both associations. They would soon find out which suited them the more! Cook and Houtain are "on the fence" associationally— they never commit themselves as partisans of either one or the other.

The banquet opened at 6 p.m., with Willard Otis Wylie, veteran amateur and prohibitionist, as toastmaster. The tables were arranged in the form of a letter "E", with Toastmaster Wylie at the head—at the base of the middle stroke, to use the alphabetical analogy. All the real veterans—members prior to 1890—sat at this rear table. I was on the lower stroke of the "E" as part of the United group, with W. V. Jackson to the left and Mrs. McM. to the right.

Houtain and those connected with the coming National campaign were on the upper stroke of the "E"—farthest from me, though Houtain's voice made it very easy to catch every word of his brilliant conversation! The courses were five in number—oysters, tomato soup, fish, chicken and potato, and a kind of pudding which no one near me could exactly name, but which was very toothsome with its fruity sauce. I need not say that I glided gracefully and easily over courses 1 and 3 without consuming very much!! At such times I languidly occupied myself with a biscuit and olives. Miss Jackson found a pearl in her oyster, at which Mrs. Sawyer, the premier humourist, remarked wittily that the other United leader, Theobald, had found a stone in his olive! To this I replied that the difference between the two "finds" corresponded very well with the difference in value of Jacksonian and Theobaldian poetry! The waiters were in full dress suits—which is more than can be said of the banqueters themselves, although such an exquisite Outlet product as mine sure-ly *ought* to receive some sort of honourable mention![3] Discussion at the banquet proved mainly political—at least, in my immediate vicinity, since the row just across the table from me contained a gentleman inclined to Wilsonism, and an old lady who did not quite know whether she ought to be a socialist or not. I hardly need outline the nature or political complexion of my replies and ar-guments—which were seconded by the rest of the United group. It may be relied upon that conservatism, Great Britain, Mr. Harding, and the Republi-can party, were defended against all the assaults of idealism and radicalism!

Finally the speechmaking session arrived. I had prepared a set speech on my designated subject, "The Best Poet", a copy of which I am enclosing for your perusal.[4] I did not, however, read it from the manuscript; since I found that all the preceding speakers were making wholly impromptu flourishes. I waited till the last moment for my decision, and was soon glad of my choice; for to my own astonishment I was able to make an extemporaneous address (around the same synopsis as the manuscript, but filled with immediate allu-sions) which evoked fairly thunderous applause. Afterward I was still further surprised by the compliments I received, for no less than five persons, includ-ing the Toastmaster, told me that it was the best speech of the evening. Hou-tain told me never to read from MS. again—that I was a born public speaker! All of which is rather amazing to me, since I am a hermit who had never be-fore addressed a banquet. The enclosed set speech, as I have intimated, will give you an approximate idea of the tenor and sequence of my remarks. Ac-tually, I introduced many embellishments. When I spoke of not naming the *really* best poet because of modesty I received an interjected bit of applause coupled with laughter at the attempted humour. At this I paused, and pref-aced my further remarks by saying (in the manner of vaudeville monologue artists) "Now that the tempestuous laughter and applause of this large and intelligent audience have subsided, I will continue—" Probably my freedom from embarrassment, which Houtain said was unusual in one who had never addressed a banquet before, was due to that immaculate Outlet suit. To think I owe a post-prandial triumph to a set of Jews! Pardon the egotism which doubtless animates this narration—I thought the incident might interest you, since such a role is so diametrically opposite to my usual secluded routine. I hear indirectly that I shall be written up quite extensively and favourably in Mrs. Miniter's paper, "Aftermath".[5]

After the banquet followed another session of discussion and song. Lynch, who has no sense of proportion and who unabashedly sang his "Starry Night in Ireland" directly after Mrs. McM's exquisite "Bumble Fairy", begged me to sing, recalling my performance at the less formal gathering last September.[6] Anglo-Saxons, however, have a sense of fitness and dignity; and I gently declined the insistent invitation. At this final session I found opportunities for some interesting conversation with Cook, Wylie, and Houtain, and also prepared a message from the Conference to President Galpin of the United, which I induced everyone to sign. The youth thus received the homage of a throng all of whom are his elders, most of whom are old enough to be his parents, and some of whom are old enough to be his grandparents! At 11.00 a session of the keenest enjoyment to all came to a close. Houtain had expected to take my train, but found to his amazement that his ticket was for the 11:40 Boston and Albany train instead of the 11:45 N.Y.N.H.&.H. train. He had arrived only just before me—thus making a journey six hours long each way, just to attend the Conference. As I departed, I was overwhelmed with invitations to attend a gathering on March 17—how I wish there were free transportation betwixt Providence and Boston!!

The walk back to the train was uneventful, as was the homeward ride as far as Attleboro. At the latter metropolis, however, the train gracefully stopped just east of the station and remained quiescent for the space of nearly two hours! No one seemed to know what the matter was, most guessing that poor coal had reduced steam pressure; but in the next night's paper I found the answer. The 11:08 Philadelphia express, which had gone out ahead of my train, had suffered a slight wreck—in which no one was even shaken up—and had blocked the main line completely. But a path was finally cleared, so that I reached the Union Station at 3:00 a.m. and reached 598 Angell at 3:30. It had been a notable day—not for ten or fifteen years can I recall any experience equally delightful. Surely the Conference justified all the time, money, and planning bestowed upon it for weeks to ensure its success.

I showed my new paternal watch to all who had been with me at Newton Centre when its predecessor had caused me so much trouble. Its appearance was highly praised, and my word regarding its timekeeping qualities was taken without reservations—so much so that Mrs. McMullen, who had to leave before the formal dispersing, asked me the time as the evening advanced. It has not varied a second since November, when I first adopted it, and I have never let it run down. It is odd how much more care one takes of a really nice thing. I was constantly letting my other watches run down—I knew they were cheap, coarsely made affairs. But now I am punctiliousness itself, conscious of the real worth and elegance of my horological heirloom.

My daytime record is very good lately—so much so that I am using this machine quite extensively. I had an $8.10 cheque from Bush the other day—it is not quite all he owes me, but he is always as prompt and conscientious as he can be.

I gave A.E.P.G. the address of the pastor whom you mentioned—or rather, I gave the name of his church. I am glad to know that your new tooth ordeal will not be comparable to the first one—that must have been intensely nerve-shattering.

But I will not exhaust your eyesight with additional text—this close typing makes a letter seem shorter than it really is.

With all good wishes, I remain

Yr most aff: Son & obt: Servt:

H. P. L.

P.S. At the Conference I saw to it, by setting an example, that *W. Paul Cook* received the loudest & longest applause. Despite his impenetrable cloak of modesty & his humble exterior, he has done more for amateur journalism than any other one person in its history.

## Notes

1. HPL refers to his persistent problem of ingrown facial hairs, which he considered disfiguring.

2. "What Amateurdom and I Have Done for Each Other" (*CE* 1.271–73).

3. HPL refers to The Outlet, a long-established department store in downtown Providence.

4. This speech apparently is nonextant.

5. *Aftermath* was an occasional paper that Miniter produced following amateur conventions. HPL refers to the forthcoming final issue of November 1921. See Edith Miniter, *Dead Houses and Other Works*, ed. Kenneth W. Faig, Jr., and Sean Donnelly (New York: Hippocampus Press, 2008), 149–70.

6. At a gathering of amateur journalists in Boston on 5 September 1920, HPL had read his essay "Amateur Journalism: Its Possible Needs and Betterment" (*CE* 1.259–62). Evidently he also sang at this event, although no account of his singing survives.

[3]     [TLS, JHL]

Thursday, March 17, 1921.

My dearest Mother:—

I was glad to receive your letter of Sunday, and must thank you exceedingly for the Reviews, apples, and beautiful picture of the Taj Mahal, which reminds one of the fabulous Oriental edifices in Lord Dunsany's tales. Just now I am taking a breathing spell before plunging into a fresh sea of Bush work—he has sent a new rush order which ought to bring in a considerable sum, but I shall not begin it tonight. One needs a fresh start to cope with his impossibilities! He enclosed in his order a new circular about himself and his work, with a new picture which looks almost human. I think I will send it out for you to see, asking that you return it eventually. The fellow has improved in aspect, and certainly has a formidable-sounding list of lecture subjects; but is, if possible, worse than ever as a "poet". He is humanity's prime enigma—sublimely inscrutable!

My trip of a week ago was a brilliant success—I can scarce recall another time so enjoyable in years. The old green tie I used is not a *bright* green, but it filled the technical requirements. I would not have worn a bright one in public even had I possessed it! I found that others followed the same course— none of the visitors had on anything in the least Irish or conspicuous! The journey to Boston was pleasing and uneventful, and the sunny nature of the day made it even more delightful than the trip of last month, when clouds hung overhead and slush encumbered the ground. The landscape was spring-like enough to attract the artistic eye, and I beheld many an agreeable rural scene as the train—an accomodation—rolled from village to village. Arrived at the South Station, I took subway and car to Allston and was soon at the now familiar 20 Webster Street. The house was decorated with streamers of green paper in honour of the departed Celtic saint, and the presiding hostesses, Mesdames Miniter and Sawyer and W. V. Jackson, were attired in green habiliments with green paper ribbons incorporated in their coiffures. Ere long the house began to fill with guests, more or less verdured for the occasion though not conspicuously so. They were for the most part persons whom I have described before, although several new faces visible. The new recruit, Dr. Joseph Homer and beardlet, was present; and he proved to be a man of more learning and philosophical insight than I had suspected at the conference. He is an agnostic, and admirer of Samuel Butler; and I think that Galpin and I can make quite an amateur of him before we are through. His ideas are for the most part exactly like ours. In point of numbers, the gathering was the largest save the Conference, and it would be impossible to catalogue all present. Fortunately, 20 Webster is an immense house. The delegates were finally seated in a circle around the principal parlour, and the assemblage placed in charge of Mrs. Annie Cross Ellis; who called for literary contributions in order of seating, beginning with the venerable Mrs. K. L. Brown (the lady who was in Providence last December), at her right. Contributions were rather mediocre till Nelson Glazier Morton was reached, but he furnished some comic verses which in my humble opinion form the cleverest bit of light rhyme amateurdom has seen for a long time. I felt then that he would win the prize—whatever it was—and he did. It was a green pasteboard "shtovepoipe" hat of the sort which Hibernians are popularly supposed to wear on

St. Patrick's day. The next contribution of merit, a dialect playlet, was presented by an elderly lady, a Mrs. Choate, who was formerly a professional reader or reciter. The best contribution from a purely literary point of view was from Mrs. McMullen, but it was a serious poem and therefore not a popular prize-winner. Interesting in a prosaic way was the paper of a Miss Noyes—a school-teacher and one of those who founded the club in 1890—touching on actual travels in Ireland. No contribution was given by W. V. Jackson, who had nothing Irish on hand and who cannot—or thinks she cannot—write anything to order. By this time the circle was nearing its end, and Grandfather Theobald was called upon. Extracting from my pocket the fatal manuscript, I proceeded to horrify the assemblage with my spectral "Moon-Bog", rendered with all the rhetorical effect needed to heighten the terror, though prefaced by a few impromptu comic remarks. From the amount of applause received, I judge that it was not wholly a failure, though probably only about half the company really liked it. After me came only the chairman herself—Mrs. Ellis—and she read an original story which was absolutely the worst I have ever encountered in amateur journalism. It was hardly more than a collection of later Victorian stock phrases and situations, and for a long time I fancied the intent was satirical—on the order of Leacock's Nonsense Novels in Harpers.[1] But it was all meant seriously, as I finally saw. The next day it was the standing joke of the household, and laughter was evoked merely by quoting a sentence or two from it. But the audience was admirably polite, and the good lady saw not a single trace of levity in her amused hearers. There now followed a period of general discussion, during which the affairs of the universe were settled as conclusively as they are always settled at literary convocations. I was impressed anew that the bearded Homer is a "find", and that he will play an important part in amateur affairs in the future. Our philosophical colloquy drew about us rather a large circle of wide-eyed listeners; two or three of whom may have understood some of the words we used. At this point refreshments were announced, and the company divided into small groups scattered all over the house at sundry small tables. Since mine was a United rather than National group, literature rather than amateur politics formed the topic of discussion. The fare was so well suited to me that I could not have chosen better myself—cheese sandwiches, stuffed olives, and other delicacies agreeable to my palate. Since I was the only out-of-town guest, and was staying all night, no attempt at observing a time schedule was made; and the company did not disperse till 11:30. The occasion had been a brilliant one, and thenceforward my chronicle deals with placid conversations rather than public performances. Mrs. Sawyer retired at once, but W.V.J. and Mrs. Miniter are like myself somewhat given to the enjoyment of nocturnal quiet; so that the conversation did not terminate till 1:30. Mrs. M. had exhumed an amateur book I have been anxious for five years to see—Ernest A. Edkins' "Amenophra"—and the Poe-like contents furnished ample material for discussion. Thereafter I retired to the spacious apartment assigned me—the very room occupied by Houtain last July—and surprising to relate, drifted off into a dreamless and restful slumber from which I did not emerge till 9 a.m.

Friday morning dawned sunny and pleasant, and I arose quite refreshed. As I emerged into the inhabited sitting room I found two gifts awaiting me— a copy of Hervey's "Meditations" printed in 1778, which Mrs. Sawyer said she thought I would appreciate on account of my antique tendencies, and a large and artistic wall card containing the Jacksonian verses (which I revised in 1916) "The River of Life". The verses were professionally purchased by the card publishers, and form an excellent professional opening for the authoress. A.E.P.G. likes them so well that she has ordered another card to give someone as a birthday present—probably the cards will prove popular. A breakfast whose central features were bacon and muffins now appeared, and was disposed of without disaster. Adjournment was now made to an upper library, where there ensued continuous conversation on every imaginable literary, philosophical, and amateurical topic. All three Allstonians, W.V.J.— Miniter—Sawyer (Mrs. Jackson was absent on a visit) are exceedingly brilliant and well-informed, though inclining each to a different province. Miss Jackson is, as readers of her verse scarce need to be informed, a master of the imaginative and the poetic; having probably the most substantial endowments of original genius of anyone in amateurdom, and in addition a manner as refined and restful as that of Kleiner. Mrs. Miniter is without a doubt the leading fiction writer of amateurdom, having excelled in grim, realistic stories since her entrance in 1883. She is not in sympathy with imaginative work, but achieves her effects by the close and relentless observation of detail. Her spirit and methods are very close to those of the ultra-modern school, although she was using them ages before that school came into being. She writes professionally, and has one published book. Mrs. Sawyer, though widely read, makes less claim to literary achievements than the others; being noted chiefly for a scintillant and inimitable humour which is employed on all occasions both in speech and on paper. Such a perpetual fountain of wit is quite remarkable, and is much more acceptable to amateurdom than the dull and heavy effusions of less gifted but more ambitious scribblers. All are skilled in that pleasing and Houtain-like flattery which so cheers the spirits of an obscure author; though the apparent flattery of W. V. J. appears to be really the result of a deficient critical sense, since I found my worthless poetical attempts predominating in her old scrap books which date back to a time when their inspection by me was probably never anticipated. I am glad that at least one or two readers have found my trash worth preserving, though that fact does not blind me to its actual want of merit. Loveman, more analytical and more deeply read than Miss Jackson, is a critic whose judgment can better be relied upon. In cataloguing the inhabitants of 20 Webster Street one should not forget the maltese feline gentleman who goes by the appellation of "Tat"—a word coined in the dim past by the eldest of the now grown, wedded, and departed Sawyer boys. Tat has a reputation for wildness and fear of strangers, but before I left he permitted me to pick him up, and sat contented in my lap, purring sleepily. He is exactly the colour of my new Outlet suit, so I would not have minded his shedding—but as it happened, he did not shed. I am told that I am the first stranger to succeed in holding him—but cats are my especial province, anyway! Thus the hours passed imperceptibly in discourse of varied kind, an inexhaustible diversity of topics presenting themselves though I endeavoured not to prove boresome by continuous conversation. Subjects tended to change according to audience—thus Mrs. Miniter seemed mainly interested in the past history of amateurdom, Mrs. Sawyer in present amateur controversies, and Miss Jackson in general literary and poetical matters. The chronicle of a conversation, however varied, is of necessity dull; hence it would be impossible to convey the interest of the occasion. At about 6.00 dinner was served, though it did not interrupt the flow of words and ideas. Later was still more of conversation, varied by the writing of a joint letter to W. Paul Cook, all four sections of which were read aloud, assembled, and mailed by me when I departed. I was shown many amateur books which I had not seen before, together with several meritorious unpublished manuscripts; and it was hard to believe that a day of fourteen hours had passed when my faithful paternal watch proclaimed the advent of the eleventh hour. Departure was now necessary—by reason of N.Y.N.H.& H. time tables, if not merely for the sake of courtesy and mercy after so long a series of lectures on my part—and I prepared to make my adieus. The apparent genuineness of the insistent requests that I repeat the trip, make me hope that my conversation did not exhaust all patience; though railway fares will deter me from journeying as often as the kindly Allstonites urged me to do. Final details of the trip include an uneventful ride to the South Station, an equally uneventful ride to Providence, and a quiet journey up to #598, which I reached at 1:30 a.m. The trip had been long and delightful, yet I suffered no ill effects and am calmly back in my customary routine.

I note the Guiney poem by Thos. Jones with great interest—I had cut the same piece from a Transcript of A.E.P.G.'s to send you, but you were ahead of me![2] There is an excellent account of Miss Guiney in a Literary Digest I have—I will endeavour to find it and send it out by L.D.C., who is now here. (Please return Digest.)[3] Miss G. was referred to at Allston during my sojourn—for years W.V.J. has sent me every clipping she has found pertaining to her; in fact, I believe you have seen most of them. Guiney poetry is not of the variety I most value, however. I can perceive its excellence, but prefer art requiring less interpretation. The greatest bards have been the simplest— Homer, Virgil, and Shakespeare require no subtle searching in order to be comprehended and appreciated. Even Keats, who I believe was Miss G.'s particular idol, dealt more in crystally clear images than in learned riddles and cryptical adumbrations.

I am glad you saw "David Garrick", though sorry it kept you awake afterward. I saw the Albee Co. present it several years ago—the year Jack Hess was trying to break into the company. Jack was absurdly awkward in the required costume—fortunately for him he had no lines to speak. Churchill had the part of Garrick, and needless to say, acquitted himself with great credit. I also saw this play in moving pictures with Dustin Farnum as Garrick.[4] This was one of the finest scenic productions I ever saw—the eighteenth century and Dr. Johnson's day mirrored without flaw or anachronism. In matters of scenery the moving picture can of course leave the stage far behind; though this hardly atones for the lack of sound and colour. I have been hoping that the collegians would present their Dunsany plays at the hospital, so that you might see the work of this literary giant—if they do, pray do not fail to attend!

I am glad that your dental matters are progressing, and hope the new teeth can finally be adjusted to fit without hurting. I transmitted your dental suggestion to A.E.P.G., but do not think she has acted upon it. The first pulling is no doubt approached with all the trepidation that attends a venture into the unknown.

Concerning hats—I will think about snowy straws when the sun climbs a bit higher in the zodiac. My 1916 and 1917 "lids" are still capable of taking on a semblance of respectability under proper treatment, and since shape is more important than hue, it would be no disaster if I skipped another season. I had almost rather have a new felt hat in the autumn—my 1917 hat is good, but its surface lacks that freshness which one finds in less archaic millinery. However—the one former crying need, a new winter suit, is certainly fulfilled in glorious fashion, as you will see when some suitable spring day affords the opportunity!

I shall soon have a couple of amateur papers to send—a November United Amateur and Galpin's long-awaited Philosopher.[5] These things are frightfully slow in materialising, yet they always come in time to save the amateur world from disintegration. How great a boon is amateurdom! More than one of its devotees would perish of ennui and monotony but for its ever-varied and enlivening influence.

But I must close, subscribing myself as
   Yr most aff: Son & obt: Servt:
     H. P. L.

## Notes

1. The *Nonsense Novels* by Canadian humorist Stephen Leacock (1869–1944) was a series of novelettes that were published as a book in 1911. A series of four "New Nonsense Novels" appeared in *Harper's Magazine* (July–October 1920).

2. Thomas S. Jones, Jr. (1882–1932), "The Vigil: Louise Imogen Guiney," *Boston Transcript* (12 March 1921); *Step Ladder* 4, No. 1 (December 1921): 6.

3. [Unsigned], "Louise Imogen Guiney," *Literary Digest* 67 (27 November 1920): 35–36.

4. *David Garrick* (1869), a play by British dramatist Thomas William Robertson (1829–1871). HPL also refers to the actors Berton Churchill (1876–1940) and Dustin Farnum (1874–1929), who starred in a silent film of the play (Pallas Pictures, 1916), directed by Frank Lloyd. J. J. (Jack) Hess later became Director of Publicity and Marketing for the RKO circuit.

5. Galpin published only one issue of the *Philosopher* (December 1920).

# Letters to Lillian D. Clark and Annie E. P. Gamwell

## 1921

[1]     [ANS postcard][1] [HPL and Rheinhart Kleiner to LDC]
[Postmarked Boston, Mass.,
6 July 1921]

Excellent convention making up for lost Kleiner visit. We are going to Museum of Fine Arts this afternoon.

H P Lovecraft
Rheinhart Kleiner

*Notes*

1. *Front:* Tremont St., Boston, Mass.

[2]     [ALS] [HPL to AEPG]

598 Angell—
8 / 19 / 21

Dear Aunt Annie:—

I received with great pleasure your cards of 8th & 11th inst., & take my pen in hand to indite a long-deferred response. Bush still hangs on—though I have taken a breathing spell during the last three or four days.

According to your cards & description, Chocorua must indeed present a pleasing variety of scenic embellishments.[1] The Old Man is highly interesting, but I dislike his long chin—which reminds me unpleasantly of my own ugly visage, & of the visage of a once notorious politician named Wilton—or Wilson—or something like that—who kept his country out of war for two years & out of good sense for eight years.

Under separate cover I am sending some recent amateur matter of which I have duplicates. If it be of no interest, the waste basket is always at hand. As the weeks drift by I shall have more of this rubbish to send—two *United Amateurs* dated May & July, & a *Conservative* dated June. The latter will contain my "Quest of Iranon", plus a group of sombre Jackson poems selected by no less a literary titan than the nigger Bill Braithwaite—the *Boston Transcript* coon, & not his vanished feline namesake across the street from here.[2]

Wednesday I went to the country for a day of quiet—meeting for the first time the prominent United member Mrs. Renshaw, who is visiting with the relatives of a friend in Newton Centre—106 Tyler Terrace. The trip was marked by a train-missing which complicated the preliminaries, but failed to interfere with the main programme. Mrs. Renshaw's Northern sojourn is of a week's extent, & she had arranged to meet as many amateurs as possible. The Hub Club meeting was yesterday, but on account of the increasing political gap between the (Nationalite) Hub element & the United, she set Wednesday as the day for conferring at length with the United element—W. V. Jackson, Miss Hamlet, Mrs. McMullen, &c. Naturally, the United day was my day! The conference was to be held at 3 p.m. at the Curry School of Expression on Huntington Ave. near the village square—just across the street from Mr. Copley Plaza's boarding house where I heard Dunsany lecture in 1919. This hour would have been very convenient for me; but Miss Hamlet, who had also been notified, asked me to precede the event with a Dorchester call— since she did not care to attend the session for fear of meeting some of the National members whom she detests so thoroughly. Alas for the complexity of local feuds! To include Dorchester—which I was not especially anxious to do, but which I attempted through dislike of slighting so urgent an invitation—I should have taken an early train; but some tangle (slowness of clock & long wait for car) caused me to miss the 11:00, & to fall back therefore upon the 12:25. Reaching Back Bay at 1:44, I proceeded to Dorchester for a brief call of courtesy—when lo! I found that my tardiness had set awry a disconcerting amount of preparation which had been made, all unknown to me, in my honour. It seems that the Hamlets had arranged a flying motor trip to Quincy to see poor Mrs. Bell the impoverished invalid, & that they had waited for me until just six minutes before my belated arrival; finally departing lest they disappoint their aged hostess. As a matter of prosaic fact, my loss of this trip caused me no very profound grief; but the Dorcastrians seemed amazingly disappointed. The aunt, Mrs. Thompson, insisted on calling up Miss H. at the Quincy City Home, & Miss H. appeared to view the exploded schedule as little short of calamitous. Considering my insignificance, such concern was of course flattering—but I could not politely leave the telephone & proceed to Copley Square till I had consented to make another Boston trip before Labour Day, for which the Hamlets wish to prepare some picnic or special event to make up for the present fiasco. Such super-hospitality is very pleasing—but it does not pay any railway fares! Incidentally—Miss H. has taken upon herself the humane task of trying to rescue Mrs. Bell from the institution which so humiliates her. She is trying to look up Bell relatives—the family is old & prominent—& to interest the Unitarian church to which Mrs. B. belongs. A worthy task, though possibly a futile one.

Having finally broken away from Dorchester & attained Copley Square, I at last met in person the celebrated leader of United affairs whom I have known by letters for seven years—Mrs. Anne Tillery Renshaw of Rocky Mount, N.C., & Washington, D.C. In aspect stout & homely, she is in conversation pleasant, cultivated, & intelligent; with all the force of mind & speech becoming a philosopher, poet, & professor of English, drama, & public speaking. I found that the conference had been deferred till evening, when the locale would be transferred to the residence of Mrs. M<sup>c</sup>Mullen at 53 Morton, where we were to have dinner. At the School of Expression the only amateurs were Mrs. Renshaw & her travelling companion Miss Crist—a colourless young woman who acts as her secretary, typist, & general caretaker; reminding her when she leaves her handbag behind or fails to put on her hat—for Mrs. R. has all the absent-mindedness of genius. It is the older sister of this Miss Crist—a Mrs. Wurtz—with whom Mrs. R. is visiting in Newton Centre. The conversation consisted almost exclusively of philosophical argument, in which Mrs. R. has all the facility & urbanity of James F. Morton Jr. At about 4:45 the session adjourned to Newton Centre, but there was no cessation of the argument—which proceeded unimpeded along Dartmouth St., in the Trinity Place station, in the B. & A. circuit train, & during the walk from the Newton Centre station to the Wurtz mansion. Nor did it stop there save for the brief time allotted to those introductory civilities whereby I was made acquainted with the family—which includes some prepossessing members of from four to seven. After a short argument at this temporary halting-place, the expedition proceeded to 53 Morton St., which I have of course seen before. Here I met Mrs. M<sup>c</sup>Mullen, & had the honour of breaking to her the pleasing news that she has won the United's 1921 Poet-Laureateship. Galpin had told me, but had neglected to inform the Laureate herself! Mrs. Miniter was also there—the only National member to venture into such an exclusive United stronghold. Dinner was excellent—beefsteak (well done), mashed potato, corn, & accessories; & for dessert cake, tea, & peaches. After this non-essential digression the evening assumed more of the aspect of an ordinary amateur gathering, the company being augmented by the arrival of W. V. J., Miss Crist, Mrs. Wurtz, & a neighbour of Mrs. M<sup>c</sup>Mullen's whose name has slipped my memory but who ought to be remembered for the menagerie which she brought with her—two large collie dogs, & the most exquisite *kitten* I have beheld in aeons. Mrs. M<sup>c</sup>Mullen averred that the latter small gentleman was brought especially in my honour, my liking for the feline species being well known in amateurdom. He was a greyish person of infinitely handsome features & longish hair, & a bushy tail suggesting a drop or two of Angora blood. Around his neck was a quaint collar with tiny bells; & as he gracefully moved, his antics pleased both eye & ear. He must have been about two or three months old—a good double handful in size—& he remained in his Grandpa Theobald's lap during most of the evening, chewing my vest buttons or fingers according to his youthful taste. Musical features were introduced, & the kitten pricked up his ears in vast & attentive interest, whilst the dogs dozed in a positively bourgeois fashion. Mrs. M<sup>c</sup>Mullen played & sang her "Bumble Fairy", & Mrs. Renshaw sang two songs (of which she wrote the words) in an excellent contralto, with Miss Crist as accompanist. I inflexibly refused all requests for song, & categorically denied the accusation of W. V. J., Mrs. Miniter, & Mrs. M^cMullen that I could sing. My voice is a monstrosity which must be used with circumspection & discrimination—it will do for a reckless throng of which George Julian Houtain is a bellowing constituent, but not for a small & refined assemblage in the drawing-room of a real musician.[3] So I let Mesdames Renshaw & M^cMullen bear off all the honours. The amusing thing of the evening was to see the pro-National Mrs. Miniter coping with a United majority for the first time in her life. Usually she has her Hub Club behind her, placing United partisans in the minority. This time she has had a taste of United supremacy—although the arguments & repartee never transcended the limits of utmost courtesy & urbanity. The United–National cleavage in Boston is doubtless augmented by the removal of the Jacksons from the Webster St. Epgephian Temple[4] to an humble but independent habitation at 79 Myrtle St., Beacon Hill, in Boston proper. There is now no strong United leader amongst the Hubites. However—amateur politics was by no means the sole topic of conversation. Pure literature, grammar, technique, ancient balladry, & the Irish situation (the M^cMullens are loyal British subjects & Protestants from Ireland) all received attention; & even D. V. Bush & remunerative endeavour were discussed. Mrs. Renshaw, who had evidently acquired some of that flattering tendency which is inherent in the air of country villages like Boston, insisted that I ought to write a text-book on English—offering to see to its publication & introduce it in classes at Research University, where she is now head of the English Department.[5] This rather reminded me of the high-flown pipe-dreams of Alnaschar[6]—but another of her commercial suggestions was really practical so far as appearances go. This latter was a plan for me to correct & criticise by mail a number of English themes each week—the exercises of Mrs. R's classes at the University. Such a procedure would, if the price were sufficiently high, be rather less horrible than Bush work—but there was no time that evening to discuss details. Plans with financial features usually fall through, so I am not yet planning what make of automobile I shall purchase with the fortune gained from text book authorship & associate professorship! At 11:10 the meeting dispersed; so, bidding adieu to the kitten & the others, I sought once more the village & the dee-po. The train did not fail me, & ere long I was back in the city—just in time to get drenched by a sudden rain which caught me as I was walking from the Red Bridge night car to #598. I attained mine own roof at 1:20 a.m., as usual.

Such was my latest excursion into the outside world. Less geographically extended & socially diverse, yet fuller by far of reminiscent magic, was another excursion of a week & two days before; in which the star figure was none other than the best friend of my youth—Deputy Sheriff Harold Bateman Munroe! On Monday, August 8, as I was splashing in the tub at 9:30 a.m. after a long & opportune sleep on the top of my downy resting-place, a telephone call arrived from H.B.M. Not for anyone else would I have left the genial billows of my artificial sea, but H B M is H B M—so I made haste to answer as soon as possible. Nor was my fraternal devotion without its reward! The call was nothing less than an invitation to renew for a day's span that lost & happy youth of fifteen years ago, & to traverse in H B M's new camouflaged Ford—purchased last April—those rural Massachusetts byways about which we gaily & carelessly disported when we were young men. It seems that H B M had some business to do in Taunton—soliciting orders for Brown Bros.—& had decided to make the trip a social & retrospective event as well. I dressed as quickly as possible, & did not force H B M to wait long when he arrived in his new but humble machine. He is the same old Harold—just as he used to fit his bicycle up with all accessories, cyclometer, horn, luggage rack, &c, so has he now equipped his Ford with every conceivable device & improvement, bringing the total cost up to $675.00. He has a self-starter, speedometer, &c &c &c—making the flivver typically Munrovian. We first went to his new East Providence home—which is exceedingly attractive—& there he had to take on as a passenger an elderly cousin of his wife's, who was going on a visit to Taunton. This lady, however, was admirably quiet & unobtrusive; so that as we sped out along the Taunton Pike through remembered scenes, exchanging anecdotes & reminiscences as old men will, we quite forgot that there was anyone in the seat behind. The old pike had changed very little. True, there were some ugly new hovels of Italian & Portugese swine, & some of the old farmhouses were re-painted. Also—an old mill about which we used to play has tumbled down with wormy decrepitude. Yet the spirit of the antique fields & groves is changeless, & as we viewed the familiar stone walls & peasant cottages we were transported back to those far, dim days when we last gazed upon them. Rehoboth Village dreams on as of old in the immutable & perpetual twilight of its hoary arching oaks. Not a shingle on any house seems to have changed since the Revolutionary War—for in so drowsy a place the very process of repair & replacement is vague & imperceptible. Finally we reached Taunton, where all was as of old. Taunton is a sort of enlarged edition of Rehoboth Village, with nothing new or altered. Whilst a few features may have changed since the Revolution, I fancy that the Civil War found its cobbled streets & low buildings stone for stone & brick for brick as they are today. Still—there is a modern dee-po built in 1865, the last year of the war, a Soldier's Monument having the aesthetic—or unaesthetic!—earmarks of the 'seventies, & a court house whose modernity is absolutely obtrusive—1884!! Much time was wasted in Taunton over the inessential trivialities of mere bourgeois trade—Harold stopped at several factories, including the extensive Whittenton Mills north of the town, but secured only one small order—and further waste was made by a needless stop at a cafeteria for nourishment—H B M is the same old eater! But finally we left trade & Taunton behind, & rattled along the pike toward the greatest adventure of all—a pious pilgrimage to the tomb of our dead youth—Great Meadow Hill & the old clubhouse! As we undulated over the hilly macadam ribbon between the meadows we speculated upon how much we would find of the crude tar-papered edifice which we deserted eight years ago. Harold thought that only the "chimbly"—built of great stones by honest old James Kay, now dead—would be standing. I, however, believed that we would still find the walls of the *newer* part—the addition we built to the original woodman's hut, which was larger than the hut itself. Thus did we speculate as we turned from the pike into the narrow rutted road at Wheeler's Corners, jogging over the indescribable washouts & hummocks that used to force us to dismount in the old cycling days. The new-cut forest of 1909, which gave us a vast horizon & panorama when we discovered the spot, had now grown up again; & tall young maple-trees & tangles of underbrush now enshrouded the site of the clubhouse. Through the foliage we saw the antique "chimbly" (that was James Kay's pronunciation!), & thrilled at the thought that at least one memorial of the old times remained—a sort of monument or headstone to our buried youth & hopes. Then through an opening in the new-grown trees we beheld the long-deserted spot in full—and lo! upon our eyes dawned the one sight that neither of us had dared expect—*the old Great Meadow Country Clubhouse intact, in all the solid perfection of the old days!* We drew near, looked long, & tried the door. Aside from a broken lock, all was as ever, for in drowsy Rehoboth even relentless Time sometimes nods & lets a few years slip by undevastatingly. There had been no decay, nor even vandalism. Tables stood about as of yore, pictures we knew still adorned the walls with unbroken glass. Not an inch of tar paper was ripped off, & in the cement hearth we found still embedded the small pebbles we stamped in when it was new & wet—pebbles arranged to form the initials G.M.C.C. Nothing was lacking—save the fire, the ambition, the ebulliency of youth in ourselves; & that can never be replaced. Thus two stolid middle-aged men caught for a moment a vision of the aureate & iridescent past—caught it, & sighed for days that are no more.

On the way back—the long way over which we used to sing "Sweet Elaine", "Dreaming", & "Down in de Co'nfield"[7]—we speculated upon the possibility of *reviving the G.M.C.C.* & holding monthly meetings with Ronald Upham & Stuart Coleman in the antique way. Harold seemed quite captivated with the idea—which he himself proposed—& I am sure that no better substitute for our departed youth could be devised. But that was a week & four days ago—so H B M has no doubt forgotten all about it now. He does not miss youth as I do. For him the dull routine of adult life is perfectly adequate—yet I would trade any two of my adult & intellectual Boston "sprees" of today for one short hour as a boy of 17 or 18 with the old "gang"—just carefree "fellers", talking, laughing, & singing—or trying to sing. Verily,

Grandfather Theobald is getting very old now; he nods of an evening, & babbles of the past as he sits by the fire.

But speaking of trips & the hectic diversions of society—verily, the old man is getting to be a positive worldling & confirmed traveller! For since I commenced this interminable epistle, **still another** invitation hath 'arriven'! This time it is New Hampshire & Haverhill again—Miss Little inviting me to make a second trip Thursday, stopping over *two* nights.[8] I think I shall accept, for the ancient quiet of that Boreal region is inimitable, & a call on honest old Smithy can be included. I shall take my valise, & carry a planisphere & prism binoculars for use in observing the sky from the unrivalled hill which I described to you. I shall likewise take a camera, snapping not only my hosts but the quaint fire-&-accident recluse of 408 Groveland St. if he will let me—to say nothing of Tom.[9] And I may also combine with this trip the trip to Dorchester previously mentioned—complying with courtesy, yet saving the railway fare!!

It is now past midnight—and officially the 20th according to civil time. (By astronomical time it is still the 19th until the following noon.) At 9 a.m. I will be one more milepost nearer the welcome sepulchre which yawns for my grey head. 31! How I wish those numbers read backward, giving me the youth & the optimism of 13! I yet recall the happiness of Aug. 20, 1903, when I attained that age—the balmy evening in the yard at #454 under the trees with my telescope, seemingly secure in a prosperous environment, & fresh with the wonder of gazing up through space at other worlds. And my old niggerman was leaping in & out of the shadowy bushes, occasionally deigning to let his Grandpa Theobald pick him up, put his green shining eye to the telescope, & show him the cryptical surfaces of remote planets—where for all we know the dominant denizens may be lithe, quadrupedal, sable-furred gentlemen exactly like Nigger-Man himself![10]

Amateur affairs jog on as usual—I have just rejected an honourable mention & silver medal in the essay contest of the National, since I wish to hold no honours outside the United.[11] It may antagonise Houtain—but he must understand that I am not like Cook, & that no amount of flattery can alienate me from mine own association. But flattery is getting to be omnipresent— our own Moe has just issued a new paper, in which he absurdly lauds my letter-writing to the skies! United prosperity seems to be increasing. Contributions to the fund are ample, & Galpin has shewn unwonted energy. He is back in Appleton after six marvellous weeks at the U. of Wis.—whither he will return next month to finish his collegiate education. No more one-horse Lawrence stuff for the wise & citified Alfredus![12] I wish I could pay that kid a visit—if my travelling increases, perhaps I shall!!

With best wishes for your enjoyment of the arctic state which I shall revisit next week, & trusting to receive the annual birthday epistle,

I have the honour to subscribe myself as

Yr most aff. Grandfather & obt Servt
L: Theobald Jun.

P.S. Omitted the matinee this week on account of trip. L.D.C. will accompany me next week—the day before I depart on my long journey. Seats all purchased.

## Notes

1. Chocorua is a small community in east-central New Hampshire. Mt. Chocorua is part of the White Mountains chain. At the southern base of the mountain is Chocorua Lake.

2. There was no issue of HPL's amateur journal, the *Conservative*, between July 1919 and March 1923. Braithwaite was rumored to have been Winifred Jackson's lover. He cited dozens of her poems in his annual *Anthology of Magazine Verse*.

3. HPL refers to the fact that, at a meeting of the Hub Club in Boston at which George Julian Houtain was present, HPL had actually sung. See SSL 2.

4. HPL refers to a home at 20 Webster St. in Allston, MA, where Miniter and Charles A. A. Parker lived, and where they and other amateur journalists would congregate. They produced a journal, *Epgephi*, to which HPL occasionally contributed.

5. Some fifteen years later, Renshaw herself undertook such a task, requesting HPL's revisory assistance. The result was *Well Bred Speech* (1936), in which much of HPL's work was ultimately omitted.

6. In the *Spectator* No. 525 (13 November 1712), Joseph Addison tells a tale (which he found in Antoine Galland's French translation of the *Arabian Nights*) of Alnaschar, a petty merchant who deals in glassware. One day Alnaschar became so involved in a daydream about attaining fantastic wealth from his business that he inadvertently kicked over his glassware, shattering it and destroying its value.

7. "In the Golden Autumn-Time, My Sweet Elaine" (1905), words by Richard H. Gerard, music by S. R. Henry; "Dreaming" (1906), words by L. W. Heiser, music by J. Anton Dailey; "Massa's in de Cold Ground" (1852), words and music by Stephen Foster (the first line of the chorus is "Down in de cornfield").

8. HPL's first visit to Myrta Alice Little in New Hampshire occurred on 8–9 June 1921.

9. 408 Groveland Street in Haverhill, MA, was the home of C. W. Smith. Tom was Smith's cat. See HPL's poem "Sir Thomas Tryout: Died Nov. 15, 1921" (*AT* 160–61).

10. Nigger-Man was HPL's cat—the only pet he ever owned. The cat ran away when HPL's family moved from 454 Angell Street to 598 Angell Street in 1904. HPL used the name for the cat in "The Rats in the Walls" (1923).

11. See Kenneth W. Faig, Jr., "The Unknown Lovecraft II: Reluctant Laureate," in Faig's *The Unknown Lovecraft* (New York: Hippocampus Press, 2009), 91–135.

12. HPL refers to Lawrence College in Appleton, WI, where Galpin began his collegiate career.

[3]      [ALS] [HPL to AEPG]

Hampstead, N.H.,

(Westville P.O.)

Aug 27, 1921

Dear A.E.P.G.:—

Behold! I am in your new state of New Hampshire—though not very far in it, since the Massachusetts line looms near. I arrived Thursday, called on Smith & visited museum of Haverhill Historical Society yesterday, & will return today to the city; incidentally passing through Attleboro & Boston on the train. It is one of the best trips, without doubt, that I have yet taken; & I have even slept well.

The greatest event was the visit to the Historical Society, which is housed in a museum attached to the ancestral mansion of the director. The latter place is itself a museum—all the more interesting because it is the natural collection of a family rather than the artificial collection of an institution. The director—a Mr. Leonard Smith,—is an elderly man of vast refinement & scholarship. Yesterday was not a visiting day, but since the Littles are personally acquainted with important personages of the society, we were allowed to go through the collection. Mr. Smith—as delightful in a patrician way as C. W. Smith is in a plebeian way—personally guided the tour, showing his house & landscape gardens as well as the museum. On the grounds is another small house—the oldest in Haverhill—built in *1640*.[1] It is the oldest house I have ever seen or entered.

Another new experience was picking *strawberries*—& in late August. I had never before seen these well-known commodities in the process of growth.

I took with me field glasses & planisphere with the aim of observing the nocturnal sky from the "Pinnacle"; but though I indeed climbed that elevation by a flashlight's flickering rays, an adverse fortune beclouded the heavens with mist ere I attained the peak!

But now permit me to thank you most abundantly for your delightful birthday letter, and for the inexpressibly appropriate gift, than which nothing could have pleased me more. Of all portraits that is the one which I most wished, & the framing is exquisite. It is now propped up on my table, & will presently adorn the wall in the most artistic & accessible location I can discover. Again accept the gratitude of an old man!

I trust that your part of New Hampshire is as pleasant as this part—which I need not describe anew, having done so last June. It is necessary only to say that the district seems as remarkable in its scenic attractiveness as in the unfailing courtesy & abounding hospitality of all its inhabitants.

With renewed expressions of gratitude,

Yr most aff: Nephew & obt Servt

H P L

## Notes

1. The John Ward House is located on the property of the Haverhill Historical Society. At the time, the structure was thought to date to the founding of Haverhill as the home of Haverhill's first minister, John Ward. It has since been determined that the eastern half of the wooden-framed building dates only to 1720, the western half to 1800. The building had been removed from the site in 1882 and returned in 1906 when acquired by the museum.

# 1922

[4]    [ANS postcard][1] [HPL to LDC]

[Postmarked Dover, N.H.,
25 May 1922]

Went to Dover with Littles in automobile—farthest north I ever was in my life! Scenery is splendid—beautiful New England towns with no foreign trace. Exeter is lovely beyond description, Portsmouth is thoroughly Colonial. Boston tonight. H.P.L.

P.S. Have *seen* state of Maine—bringing total up to seven.

*Notes*

1. *Front:* The Old Corner Central Sq. Dover N.H.

[5]    [ANS postcard][1] [HPL to LDC]

[Postmarked Gloucester, Mass.,
26 June 1922]

Here it is! Saw it yesterday but did not jump in. Caught train safely & everything developed finely. Fine room in pleasant house—same house Mrs. G. stays at.[2] Meals at boarding house in main village square. Magnolia is delightful—combines country & seashore. Tramped all day yesterday without getting tired. In evening walked to Gloucester & rode back in omnibus. Slept well, & am doing writing today. May stay a week. Took some pictures yesterday.
      Yr aff. Nephew & obt Servt
               H P L

*Notes*

1. *Front:* Rafe's Chasm, Magnolia, Mass.
2. Sonia Greene accompanied HPL on this trip.

[6]    [ANS postcard][1] [HPL to LDC]

[Postmarked Gloucester, Mass.,
30 June 1922]
*June 29*

Spent this morning on the rocks whilst pearl-grey mists surged out of the sky to mix with the sea. Over the cliffs one might see only an abyss of milky vapour, as if it were the void beyond the edge of the world.

Will not return, in all probability, till morning of Wednesday, July 5—will thus gain holiday here. Trust you are forwarding letter mail—I'm anxious to know how Galpin & Loveman like each other!

Yr aff. Nephew & obt Servt

H P L

Notes

1. *Front:* The Pond on the Road to the Station, Magnolia, Mass.

[7]      [ANS postcard][1] [HPL to LDC]

[Postmarked Gloucester, Mass.,
1 July 1922]

Got up this morning at 4 to see sunrise over ocean. Clouds interfered, but fairly good effect was obtained. ¶ Heard from Galpin—he is enraptured with Loveman. ¶ That Bush letter was a cheque for Morton—no rush orders or other nuisances, thank Heaven! ¶ Am having great time—will not be home till Wednesday *night*—coming on my usual 11:45 from Boston.

Yr aff. nephew & obt Servt

H P L

Notes

1. *Front:* Shore Road, Magnolia, Mass.

[8]      [ANS postcard][1] [HPL to LDC]

[Postmarked Gloucester, Mass.,
1? July 1922]

Here on a solitary shopping tour—had glasses tightened, & optician charged nothing at all. A generous village! Have been exploring mystical & antique waterfront, savouring of a century ago. Great place!

Yr aff. nephew & obt Servt

H P L

Notes

1. *Front:* [Sailing ships at sea.]

[9]      [ANS postcard][1] [HPL and Sonia H. Greene to LDC]

[Postmarked Newport, R.I.,
16 July 1922]

No—this is not Rafe's Chasm! I haven't seen this awesome spectacle, but fancy that Magnolia can afford better. Wish you were along—Grandpa.

---

So do I.

Sincerely yours
Sonia

*Notes*

1. *Front:* Purgatory, Newport, R. I.

[10]    [ANS postcard][1] [HPL to LDC]

[Postmarked New York, N.Y.,
26 July 1922]

I crossed Hell Gate Bridge on the train, but instead of leading to H——, it led safely to the Pennsylvania Station! Am at 259 Parkside, alive & conscious. I transmitted your regards to the hostess, who sends hers in return. More later. Cold doing tolerably. H P L

P.S. I send along my own regards as a matter of course!

*Notes*

1. *Front:* Hell Gate Bridge, New York City.

[11]    [AHT] [HPL to LDC]

9231 Birchdale Ave.,
Cleveland, Ohio
August 4, 1922

My dear Aunt Lillian:—

As to mine own voyages and travels—the cards covered the N.Y. preliminaries fairly well. Concy Island is a quaint place—especially one section where the fantastic buildings are illuminated with myriads of electric lights, giving the effect of some weird Dunsanian city beyond the East. The play Thursday night was excellent—Galpin had recommended it from reading the book. It is produced by the same select "Theatre Guild" which produced "John Ferguson",[1] and forms without a doubt the best drama now in the metropolis. I enclose programme. Friday I did nothing in particular—but bought my Cleveland ticket, and read Mencken in Prospect Park. Saturday, at six thirty p.m., I boarded the "Lake Shore Limited" at the Grand Central, and was soon whirling up the Hudson amidst the resplendent Palisades and Catskills.

I had expected to seem rather clumsy and inexperienced in sleeping-car procedure—I had an upper berth, and knew nothing of the technique—but by a judicious combination of guess-work, deduction, and observation I managed to "get by" without drawing the least bit of notice to my ignorance. I dressed and undressed in my berth—some feat!

Having rested surprisingly well, I awaked in Pennsylvania and settled down to await the momentous Clevelandic arrival. The train was one and one-half hours late, but at ten-thirty (or I should say, *nine-thirty*, since Cleveland does not use daylight time) the suburban 105th St. station was reached. Meanwhile I had been intensely interested in watching the Ohio landscape from the window. It is quite unlike—and inferior to—New-England, having vast level stretches, sparser vegetation and foliage, and different types of architecture. (Flatter roofs, etc.) The villages are insufferably dismal—like "Main St."[2] They have no ancient features, and totally lack the mellow charm and scenery which make New-England villages so delightful. I was glad that my destination was a large city!

At ten-thirty I alighted from the train, and immediately perceived a lank, altitudinous, hatless form loping cordially toward me. Mutual recognition? I'll say so! The Kid is *exactly* like those recent Madison pictures, and he says I am exactly like my own snapshots. Some meeting! I exclaimed spontaneously— "So this is my Son Alfredus!" And he responded, "It sure is!" We shook hands till paralysis threatened to set in, and then began to talk an incessant stream. Are we congenial? I'll tell the world! The Kid is utterly delightful— exactly the same as he is on paper, and as fascinating a companion as Harold Munroe into the bargain. We have not been out of each other's sight a second since we met, except when sleeping, and it will certainly be a melancholy event when I have to bid him *au revoir* on the fifteenth at midnight. At that hour he goes to Mackinac to join his father in a sail around the Great Lakes, whilst I go to New-York. After our ecstasy of greetings, Alfredus guided me to a neat and inexpensive lunch counter. (Where we have since taken most of our humble but excellent meals). The blessed child insisted not only on paying for his Grandpa's refreshments, but on carrying the old gentleman's heavy valise as well. Some boy! Subsequently we proceeded to our joint hangout— 9231 Birchdale—which is just around the corner from Loveman's house. The neighbourhood is very good, and the cottage very pleasant. My room is diagonally across a hall from my grandson's. We rise about noon, eat twice a day, and retire after midnight—a routine forming a sort of cross betwixt normalcy and Theobaldism. This is A. G.'s ordinary schedule when not in school. After Saturday Alfredus and I will be sole masters of the house—the family is going away for a week, leaving us in undisturbed possession. Probably we shall sing and shout to our heart's content—and dance clog dances in the parlour if we want to! But we shan't break any windows or spit tobacco on the floor. Heigho—but this is the life!

After settling down at 9231, we proceeded around the corner to Loveman's place—The Lonore Apartments—which is an excellent place. S. L. was on hand, looking ten years younger and ten times more cheerful than last April, and full of flattering compliments for the Old Gentleman. His mother, a kindly and excellent person, and his genial brother—with the automobile—were on hand, and presently took us for a ride of sightseeing. Loveman's room is a veritable museum—filled with antiques and books of rare vintage. His devotion to all the arts is well attested by a profusion of art books and an unrivalled collection of classical records for the phonograph. Before he and Alfredus are through with me, I shall probably be half-civilised—they feed me large doses of art, music, and literature. The automobile ride gave me a chance to become familiar with Cleveland and its suburbs—it is a rather attractive city whose chief characteristic is *breadth* in parts and entirety alike. The streets are very broad, houses set far back from sidewalks, and the whole spread out over an immense area. Despite a population of about a million, (it is the fifth city of the U.S.) there are no subways or elevateds; and the atmosphere of provincialism subtly lingers. The climate is not as good as that of the East. In the daytime the heat is actually oppressive—even to *me* (!!!)—and one drinks glass after glass of water. Not till the evening breeze comes in from Lake Erie is there a clearing of the general discomfort and stickiness. I am glad I brought along an ample shirt supply—much of which is now in the capable Mongolian hands of one Sam Lee on Superior St., for purposes of rejuvenation. . . . . . Sunday evening we met the rare book dealer George Kirk—a friend of Loveman's—and the quartette of us explored the excellent Cleveland Art Museum in Wade Park.

Monday morning Alfredus and I loafed around Loveman's room—looking at rare books and pictures, and hearing phonograph records. We saw the hideous drawings of Loveman's friend Clark Ashton Smith—grotesque, unutterable things,—and I took some over here for subsequent study. Just as samples, I will enclose a few—which *please return with care,* (send them in the enclosed envelope, which is large enough). Did you ever see anything more ghoulish? Smith is a genius, beyond a doubt. By the way—speaking of geniuses—"Gordon Cresset" is indeed a myth, though Loveman has a very bright seventeen-year-old protege named Clarence Wheeler, on whose personality he based the myth. I have seen Wheeler—a nice little fellow, but no Galpin. Monday afternoon Galpin and I went out to the suburbs to see George Kirk, who showed us an infinity of rare books and plates, and who has a delectable black angora cat named "Hodge" (after Dr. Johnson's)[3] which sat in my lap and purred all through the visit. Later Kirk, Galpin, and I took a long scenic walk through "Forest Hills"—the Rockefeller Estate, which is used as a public park. The scenery is very beautiful, and quite transported the Westerners, though it is not nearly so attractive as Quinsnicket. We are going again some time *by moonlight.* Monday evening Loveman, Galpin, and I went to the Public

Library and watched a thunderstorm gather, burst, and fade away. There are very few long rains in Cleveland—storms are short and sudden.

Tuesday we called on Loveman in the book shop where he works—a very inviting place. Later we read in Rockefeller Park, and in the evening Loveman organised a party to see the most lavish cinema show in town—a party consisting of himself, a friend named Baldwin, Kirk, young Wheeler, Galpin, and myself. It is odd to see a really sumptuous and artistic theatre devoted to moving pictures—but such is Cleveland.

Meanwhile a strange transformation had taken place in the aspect of Grandfather Theobald! That I had become tanned and thinner, was only to be expected—but who could have expected the rest? Moved by the oppressive heat, and by the constant and rejuvenating companionship of youth, I proceeded to imitate my grandson in the following details:

(a) I left off my vest and bought a belt—a fine new kind with my initial on the buckle; which has no perforations, but adjusts to *any* circumference.
(b) I bought some *soft* collars (yes, really!) and have worn them continuously.
(c) I commenced going *hatless* like A. G.—using a hat only on formal occasions.

Can you picture me vestless, hatless, soft-collared, and belted, ambling about with a boy of twenty, as if I were no older? I will have Alfredus take a snap shot to prove it! One can be free and easy in a provincial city—when I hit New York again I shall resume the solemn manner and sedate vestments befitting my advanced years, but for the present I have cast aside the eleven years which separate me from His Imperial Kidship! The face is doing finely, and I am altogether free from melancholy—positively cheerful, in fact. What I need in order to be cheerful is the constant company of youthful and congenial literary persons.

Wednesday Galpin and I loafed and read around Rockefeller Park, and in the evening prepared to attend a feast given in our honour by the local amateur journalists. Some of the latter could not be present, but Dowdell and Harry E. Martin were there, together with an interesting Sicilian musician named Raoul Bonanno, who sings for Victor records. The dinner—spaghetti—was at an Italian restaurant; a very interesting place. This was my first meeting with Martin, (former Professor of English Literature at Mount Union College, Alliance, Ohio) and I like him immensely. The Kid and I are going to see him next week—he lives in the western suburbs and wants to show us more of the country in his automobile. He has also asked us to inspect the sumptuous bank building—Guardian Trust Co.—where he works. After dinner Bonanno had to leave, but Dowdell insisted on taking the rest of us to the vaudeville theatre with which he is connected. It is of very mediocre quality, but on this occasion was amusing because of Dowdell. He had instructed the comedians to name, casually, each one of his guests during the performance—and it was done ingeniously. One man asked 'how to spell HARRY' (E. Martin), whilst another addressed a colleague as 'SAM'. The name 'LOVECRAFT' was brought in on a pun, and toward the end of the show a singer said he was about to sing 'a pathetic little ballad by AL GALPIN'! Dowdell is a pleasant fellow, though wholly unintellectual. Probably we shall not see him again during our local sojourn. He is, as you probably know, now president of the National Ass'n.

Thursday was a day of literary loafing, during which Galpin and I did not get a glimpse of Loveman. Friday we met an unusual character—an artist named William Summers,[4] who looks exactly like a backwoods farmer and eats with his knife. In the evening a party consisting of Galpin, Loveman, Kirk, Wheeler, and I visited Gordon Park, which fronts on Lake Erie. There were heavy breakers, giving a perfect impersonation of the ocean except for the salty air. Saturday I took my suit to be pressed, meanwhile wearing the light grey trousers *and a coat of Galpin's*. I looked so rejuvenated in this outfit that I had A. G. take my picture in it—the film will be ready Tuesday. In the evening we met at the bookshop another of Loveman's friends—a musician named Hatfield[5]—and later took a sightseeing stroll through Central Ave.—the negro quarter. It was like exploring a gorilla-peopled jungle. Sunday we loafed, visited the museum, and went to see George Kirk and his books. We are now the sole occupants of 9231 Birchdale—the family having gone away for a week, leaving the whole place in Galpinio-Theobaldian hands. Will we have a good time? I'll say so! Tuesday evening we are going to hold a reception for the whole gang—Kirk, Wheeler, Martin, Loveman, Summers, etc. etc.—acting the part of hosts and native Clevelanders to perfection!

With every good wish, I have the honour to subscribe myself
Yr most aff: nephew and obt. Servt.
H. P. L.

*Notes*

1. St. John Ervine (1883–1971), *John Ferguson* (1915), a powerful play about religious faith by a leading Irish playwright of the period.

2. HPL alludes to the best-selling novel by Sinclair Lewis.

3. Samuel Johnson (1709–1784) was devoted to a cat named Hodge.

4. Actually William Sommer (1867–1949), who would become a leading Modernist painter.

5. Gordon Hatfield, a gay man and a friend of Hart Crane. HPL later wrote of him: "Dear, dear! how he used to sit cross-legged on the floor at Eglin's, little white sailor's cap tucked gracefully under one arm, sport shirt open at the neck, gazing soulfully up at Samuelus and discoursing of arts and harmonies of life! I'm afraid he thought me a very crude, stupid, commonplace, masculine sort of person" (*SL* 1.281–82).

[12]      [ALS] [HPL to LDC]

9231 Birchdale Ave., N.E.,

Cleveland, O.,

August 9, 1922

My dear Aunt Lillian:—

I was exceedingly glad to receive your letter of the 6th with enclosures. So H B M has a son & heir at last, to carry on the glorious name of Munroe! I must send him a card of acknowledgment soon—it will surprise him, coming from Cleveland. The cuttings are interesting—too bad I was not in Gloucester late enough to hear the bells! When I get to Brooklyn I will ask Houtain if the explosion was in his Home Brewery!

Alfredus is certainly Alfred the Magnificent, Great, Generous, Learned, & everything else distinguished. In short, he is the most absolutely splendid kid imaginable. He is at this moment clicking on his typewriter across the hall, & shouts to me to send his regards to you. We are the sole occupants of the house now, & are having a great time. [Did I tell you in my last letter that the family is away, leaving us in full possession?]

I am glad the *Home Brews* came. You need not send any more copies, for they are on sale here.[1] Alfredus bought one the other day—what a miserable mess it is! I have not received the $20.00 Houtain owes me, but he will pay me when I am in New York. I received a letter from him recently—possibly you did not notice the envelope, since it was faintly printed. He was not angry after all—merely frightfully busy. He is anxious for me to come to see him.

As for the kind of time I am having—it is simply great! I have just the incentive I need to keep me active & free from melancholy, & I look so well that I doubt if any Providence person would know me by sight! I have no headaches or depressed spells—in short, I am for the time being really alive & in good health & spirits. The companionship of youth & artistic taste is what keeps one going! The programme of the past few days is much like that of the days previously chronicled, but last night was rather unusual. We held a meeting here of all the members of Loveman's literary circle, at which the conversation covered every branch of aesthetics. I have often spoken of "Allston flattery",[2] but the Cleveland article is more enthusiastic still! It gave me a novel sensation to be "lionised" so much beyond my deserts by men as able as the painter Summers, Loveman, Galpin, &c. I met some new figures— Crane the poet, Lazar[e], an ambitious literary student now in the army, & a delightful young fellow named Carroll Lawrence,[3] who writes weird stories & wants to see all of mine. Loveman persuaded me to deliver my scene from "Richard III", & it was received with surprising applause—just as if I could really act! All the circle say they like my stories—which duly inflates me with pride. I am learning to appreciate music—Galpin has given me a record of a Chopin nocturne, played by De Pachmann,[4] which was especially potent in evoking imaginative images—here's hoping I don't break it on the way home.

Tonight Galpin, Crane, I, & a fellow I have not yet met are going to a concert held in the art museum building. Great days!!

I am sorry you miss me—though much flattered that you should do so! I wish that you & A E P G could be here—this city is much more intellectually alive than Providence, where all artistic manifestations are confined to artificial & quasi-Victorian society groups. (But don't tell A E P G that I concede any point of superiority to a non-Providential city!) My money is holding out amazingly, because both Galpin & Loveman, to say nothing of Kirk, insist on playing the host with unlimited generosity wherever we go. However—all Paradises must eventually be lost, so that before many weeks I shall indeed be stagnating in accustomed hibernation. I shall get to N.Y. Wednesday or Thursday—depending on whether or not I take the Niagara Falls trip[5]—& after a reasonable period of metropolitan sightseeing will again hit the homeward trail. After so ample & varied a glimpse of the outside world I certainly ought to have some material for literary production during the quiet months!

I am indeed glad that A E P G was so much benefited by her briefer outings—as I told her when writing yesterday. She sent the Magistris cheque for my signature—which I duly affixed.[6] You can send me the receipt pad if you think I ought to send Magistris a receipt immediately. A.E.P.G. thought I might need to keep the money—but I didn't. Galpin even makes me send my laundry with his, free of charge. He is a splendid grandson!

The weather here has indeed been propitious. Long rains are very rare, & of the brief one-or-two-hour storms we have had very few. It is now decidedly cooler than during the first sweltering week, but not enough so to be unpleasant. I have had no colds & no headaches—which reminds me that I am indeed sorry you have had a relapse of your cold.

All the letters forwarded seem to have arrived safely. I have, however, very little time to answer them; since my grandson is always proposing something or other to do. This may be an appropriate time to get rid of about twenty uninteresting correspondents! As to railways—I am watching them with care, yet all seems well. If I get stranded, I'll hire an aeroplane, or something of the sort!

But the hour of the concert approaches, & I must lay down my pen for the nonce. How did you like the Clark Ashton Smith drawings—do you think they beat my yarns for sheer horror? Last night Summers raved over them—& he is a real artist.

With every good wish, among which is the wish that you were here enjoying the respite from lethal monotony, I remain

> Yr. most aff. nephew & obt Servt
>> H P L

P.S. The *face* is practically *well* at present! Only a few hairs have to be picked, & I shave regularly every 2 or 3 days!

[P.]P.S. I enclosed the Cleveland snap-shots in my letter to A E P G—ask her to show them to you. More copies later.
[P.]P.P.S. Have just dropped a message to Harold.

## Notes

1. HPL's serial "Herbert West—Reanimator" had just concluded in *Home Brew* (February–July 1922).
2. See LDC/AEPG 2n4.
3. HPL recruited Lawrence into the NAPA in the fall of 1923.
4. Vladimir de Pachmann (1848–1933), renowned Russian-German pianist who specialized in interpreting Chopin.
5. HPL probably did not go to Niagara Falls. In his letter to LDC of 13 June 1930, he writes that "Doane's Falls, in the woods of Royalston [MA]" was the "greatest waterfall" he had ever seen.
6. HPL refers to the semiannual mortgage payment of $37.08 made by Mariano de Magistris for a quarry owned by the Phillips family in the western part of Providence at 44 Leander Street.

[13]      [AHT] [HPL to LDC]

259 Parkside Ave.,
Brooklyn, N.Y.
August 31, 1922

My dear Aunt Lillian:—

Monday I went over to Houtain's, where some amateur matters of the greatest moment were discussed. I had not intended to be active in amateurdom this year; but such are recent developments, that I may shortly make a political move well fitted to startle the entire fraternity and jolt my ungrateful colleagues in the *United*—of this more later.*[1] Kleiner joined the party for dinner, and the session lasted well into the evening. Houtain has grown so fat since April that I hardly recognised him—he weighs 228 pounds and has three well-defined chins!!

By the way—I hope you received the apple pie which Mrs. Greene sent you. It is of her especial original brand, which undoubtedly eclipses any other I have encountered. I mailed it myself at the Flatbush Post Office, Tuesday morning, and was told it would reach you the next day.

Sept. 1, 1922

At the above point I had to drop my pen in order to keep my engagement with Kid Long. We had a great time—"doing" the Fine Arts Museum in greater detail than Loveman and I could follow last April, and getting

---

*Later—I probably shan't make the move after all!

caught in such a beastly thunder-storm that we had to take a taxi back to his house. The Longs are all splendid—their house is upset with painters and decorators, so they dine out at an exclusive uptown cafe; the St. George, on Broadway. Each meal-time they insist on my going with them, and likewise insist on paying all expenses. . . . Really, I never knew the world held so many generous people till I started on my travels! I am trying to show my appreciation by presenting the Kid with a book which he wanted very much— Beckford's "Vathek". It is hard to get nowadays, but Mrs. Greene knows N.Y. bookshops very well, and assisted me in securing a small and inexpensive, yet exquisitely artistic copy through E. P. Dutton Co. I shall mail it tonight to little Belknap at Atlantic City—he will go into ecstasies over it. And yet it is a cheap return for all the lavish hospitality his family have shown me. Long Senior is a splendid chap—he is fifty-four years old, but hardly looks thirty-five. I discovered to my great interest that his father—the Kid's grandfather—was the Engineer who erected the Statue of Liberty! He was Col. Long of the U.S. Army, and on account of his great skill was selected for the task.[2] The Longs have a splendid model of the statue, given to him by his subordinates and engraved with his name, as well as several letters from the artist Bartholdi, and the French and American flags which draped the Statue at the dedication ceremony. Col. Long was a typical West Pointer, who served valiantly in the Civil War and was later distinguished in peace-time military affairs. He was gruff but kindly—I have seen a picture of him holding small Belknap (aged five) on his knee, and he looks the proud grandparent to perfection. Belknap barely remembers him, but the memory is full of affection. Last night Belknap and I added the final touch to the "Francis Bardon" hoax we are playing on Galpin. Did I tell you about it? In friendly revenge for Galpin's "Gordon Cresset" hoax, Belknap when in Maine invented a fictitious old man—Francis Bardon—whose age is 125, and who knew Poe intimately. It fooled Galpin for ten minutes, though Loveman and I were not for a moment taken in. The matter rested till last Tuesday, when Belknap and I decided to revive it. Then we both wrote enthusiastically of "Bardon's" arrival in New York—we pretended he was with us on all our trips. And to cap the climax, we (or rather I) wrote a fake Poe poem which we said was an unpublished piece given us by Bardon. It is called "To Zara", and the Kid thinks it is really Poe-esque. Of course, it won't really fool Alfredus; but it will give him a rather amusing quarter of an hour.

—Extra! Special! The postman just arrived with the latest bunch of forwarded mail, and guess who that Auburn, Cal. letter was from? CLARK ASHTON SMITH, the author of "The Star-Treader", "Odes and Sonnets", "The Hasheesh-Eater", etc., and the artist who drew the unutterably hideous pictures I sent you! I had written him at Loveman's suggestion, but never thought he would answer. He's a good fellow—he has seen one of my stories ("Beyond the Wall of Sleep", which Loveman sent him), praises it effusively,

and wants to see more. I shall accomodate him, you can bet! Did I tell you—
or A. E. P. G.—that I have both of his already published works? Galpin
(generous little divvle!) gave me "The Star-Treader", whilst George Kirk (benevolent soul!) gave me "Odes and Sonnets" (deluxe edition, price $6.00) out
of his regular stock. As you know, Kirk is a bookseller . . . Smith is a genius.
As a poet he is on par with Loveman, and as an artist he is alone in his field.
He is going to give me his new book when it is out. I have lent "Odes and
Sonnets" to little Longlet, and the child is transported with Smith's devastating horror. By the way—Longlet himself is an absolute master of stark, crawl-
ing terror. He has told me some of the plots that are floating about in his
head, and I vow that they surpass anything of mine. He has the most hideous
nightmares—often he screams in his sleep so that his mother has to wake
him up—and each nightmare is worthy of development as an artistic and macabre phantasy.

Yr aff. nephew and obt. Servt.—<br>H. P. L.

## Notes

1. HPL became interim president of the NAPA on 30 November 1922 following the
resignation of William J. Dowdell. He served until the end of the term in July 1923.
2. Charles O. Long (1845–1904), superintendent of the Statue of Liberty.

[14]     [ALS] [HPL to AEPG]

259 Parkside Ave.,<br>Brooklyn, N.Y.,<br>Septr. 9, 1922<br>to " 11 "

My dear daughter Anne:—

How do I do? Great, I'll tell the world! Can you
imagine Grandfather Theobald in good health, with very little facial bother,
up in the daytime, going about from one interesting thing to the other, &
with something to look forward to the next day? It seems incredible, yet nevertheless that's me! The arrival of Mortonius Augustus has increased the delights of the season—we now have a literary gang much like that in
Cleveland. Yesterday Morton & I went over to Long's—the kid is just back
from Atlantic City—& had a marvellous afternoon of literary & philosophical
debate. Felis, the kid's glossy & ornate coon cat, sat purring in my lap whilst
Democritus, Epicurus, Aristippus, Lucretius, Plato, Aristotle, & other sages
filled the air. In the evening Morton, Longlet, & I went to the 44th St. Theatre—after dining at a cafeteria—to see the cinema version of "The Count of
Monte Cristo" . . . . which was histrionically & mechanically good, but which
was very clumsily adapted from the original novel.[1] A duel scene in a court-

room, near the end, was so crude & anticlimactic that the more enlightened part of the audience could not repress perceptible snickers. Among the snickerers were the literate trio above mentioned. After the show we all had fruit sundaes & saw one another to our respective subway or elevated entrances. The kid—who is as un-geographical as Kleiner—got lost on 34th St., & I had to set him aright. How did I know the way? Absurdly simple & obvious, my dear Watson! By the *moon!* Astronomy, after all, has its practical side! But everyone finally reached home safely—I must hire out as a guide to the highways, by-ways, & Broadways of New-York! This afternoon Mrs. Greene & I are going to see a matinee of a play containing something of Poe-esque hideousness—"The Monster", at the 39th St. Theatre.[2] Let us hope that it may prove sufficiently ghoulish & unutterable to be of at least mild interest. Tomorrow the Longs dine here—as do also Morton, & an authoress named Winifred Harper Cooley—the latter being a daughter of the famous suffragette Ida Husted Harper, & the best—or approximately best—friend of Mrs. Greene.[3] She was Laureate Judge of Poetry in the National Association this year. Yes—it's some crowded social calendar! I forgot to mention that Thursday evening we went to see a comedy called "Kiki" at the Belasco Theatre—moderately clever, but hardly destined for immortality.[4]

Is Providence still the metropolis of the world? Sure it is! The only trouble with Providence is its *inhabitants*—backward & unimaginative bourgeois types who go to church, revere the gods of commerce & the commonplace, & find their utmost limit of aesthetic & intellectual expansion in mock art-clubs & tame lectures wherein gossip of the day & social pageantry form the real motive forces. Estimable Philistines—worthy folk—correct & solid citizenry—but still living in the anaesthetic 'eighties of the nineteenth century. . . . . . . . . .

Later—at this point I had to make a break for the matinee; & wonder of wonders, I wasn't late! However; I would have been, had not Mrs. G. issued several carefully timed reminders. The play was *absolutely great*—crude in spots, of course, & with the conventional American happy ending—but withal conceived with a true appreciation of the horrible & ghastly. The author, Crane Wilbur, is a former cinema actor; but he does much better as a playwright. On the screen he was of the super-handsome & posing sort; but with brain, pen, & ink he's all right! The play concerns a lonely house by the sea where terrible things happen—automobiles are wrecked & persons disappear. The owner of this sinister abode is a mad doctor who needs live specimens for certain experiments—there is one unutterable scene in his vaulted cellar dissecting room. It reminded me of my own "Herbert West"—but enough! You must positively see the play when it hits the Shubert-Majestic . . . . I will compel you to go if you won't go voluntarily! It's a bird, I'll inform the cosmos!

Speaking of unmentionable horror—I recently struck a bargain of most delectable quality . . . . Ambrose Bierce's best book of hideous tales, "Can

Such Things Be", in good condition at a second-hand bookstall on 59th St for only one dollar! It is now out of print, & used to cost $2.50 when it was in print. I have always wished to own it, & now I do . . . my idle moments are spent in its re-perusal, & Mrs. G. also likes its ghoulish & macabre contents. Bierce was a great man, & is becoming more & more appreciated. I think I told you that Loveman is about to publish his letters, with a brief original introduction.

About Mortonius & the Cantabridgian *Tribune*—I am hoping with all the hopes in my system that he gets the editorship![5] The paper is now controlled by several persons; two of whom are anxious to secure him, & confident that they can persuade the rest. He will try to make it something unique & superior—though of course instituting all changes gradually. Among his plans is that of helping to introduce to the literary world the poetry of Samuel Loveman & Clark Ashton Smith, & the prose of a very obscure writer named Lovegrove or Lovecrab or something like that . . . . . a queer old fellow who writes horrible stories. It certainly seems strange to run across the *Cambridge Tribune* from two angles so distinct & separate—but after all, life is only one coincidence after another. Morton is splendid—I must see more of him during the ensuing days. I'll vouch for his capability as a *Tribune* editor!

I am glad you are free from the Foster family for a few festive days at least. What a nuisance the Victorian bourgeoisie is, anyway! I trust you had a good visit at Drownville, (I won't use that perniciously modern name of West Barrington!) & that the Westport extension was equally pleasant.

As to the school business—I'll wager you'd have been a more intelligent secretary than the trained automaton who was secured; but if the outcome was a relief to you, I won't object violently. Scholastic folk are funny—Galpinius despises all of 'em, & says that a teacher is one of the lowest forms of animal life . . . . He's afraid he'll have to be one himself!

Mrs. Renshaw didn't show up that day she was expected—now watch me charge her double for Research U. work if she sends any! She is the most negligent of mortals—you doubtless recall her custom of forgetting to put full postage on heavy envelopes.

I am glad you like the Brooklyn pie—you ought to see the rest of the cuisine here! Positively, I never before encountered such a uniformly high standard of the table in any private home. Everything is just as exceptional as the pie—even the fruit is selected with scientific scrutiny, so that one gains a higher respect for such supposedly common articles as the pear or the apple. And oh, boy—the *cheese!!* The enclosed label represents a brand possessing absolutely unique virtues—mild, but with a flavour & individuality little short of the poetic! It comes in tinfoil'd triangles packed in a flat circular box—a small box, but costing eighty cents! In this world one usually gets what one pays for.

As to vacations—Mrs. Greene was to have one this week, but business conditions made it necessary to postpone it till the middle of next week. Such assiduous application to industry would kill me in a fortnight—it's a wonder she stands it for interminable periods! By the way—on account of this new postponement, I shall defer my departure another week or so. Mrs. G. says that she has hardly had a visit from me yet, since her only free days are Sundays & Saturday afternoons. We shall explore several museums hitherto unvisited, see at least one play, ("Whispering Wires"—circular enclosed)[6] & inspect the mediaeval French chapel brought across the ocean in dismantled form by the sculptor George Grey Barnard, & reassembled stone by stone on his studio grounds in northern Manhattan.[7] Believe me—it's a great programme! Being up, about, & interested in things agrees with me—I have almost forgotten what a headache or fit of melancholy is like!

Speaking of ills—I hope L.D.C.'s finger is recovering. She mentioned having Dr. Cooke about it, & I trust he displayed adequate skill. The causes of such things are often obscure—but that does not make the result any less painful!

As for Houtain—my letter to L.D.C. described my meeting with him. I have *not* collected my cash yet, but may see him again, & am hoping for the best. He owes me twenty simoleons—for four of the stories. . . . . . . . Later still—9:30 p.m. A neighbour's boy—Harold Moran, aged 13, has just been in, accompanied by "Fluffy", the most fascinating jet-black coon cat I have ever seen. He has been sitting in my lap most of the evening—Fluffy, not his young master! The latter, though, is a bright little fellow—he entered high school at twelve, & writes excellent poetry. I shall introduce him to Galpin, Long, & Davis—the latter being of exactly the same age. He seemed exceedingly interested in one of Davis' pyrotechnic & colourful epistles which I showed him.

*Monday Morning*

Well—I must finish this elongated document some time, & I find myself in the mood as I wait for the hour to start for Belknap's joint. We're going to "do" a few museums today—probably a group very far uptown. Tomorrow comes another trip with both Kid Belknap & Mortonius—it's a great life! Mrs. Greene has just received your letter to her, which she appreciates & values most intensely. She bids me tell you that her delay in answering your last was due to a devastating pressure of business, & that she hopes to indulge in a session of Gamwellian epistolary composition very soon.

Yesterday's banquet came off finely, although the senior Longs could not be present on account of duties arising from the illness of Mrs. Long's father. Belknap was there, as well as Morton & the learned Mrs. Cooley. The latter is clever but boresome—I don't wonder that she often gets on Mrs. Greene's nerves. After the repast—a most marvellous meal prepared by Mrs. G. alone since the negress disappointed her & failed to appear—a programme of literary reading & discussion took place. I read my "Doom That Came to Sarnath" & "The Tree", Belknap read his "Eye Above the Mantel", Mrs. Greene read her "Four O'Clock" & one of the other Magnolia horror-tales not yet revised,[8] whilst Morton read Loveman's great unfinished poem, "The Hermaphrodite", which Alfredus & I copied in Cleveland. Mrs. Cooley, who admires disinterested art despite her literary professionalism, considered some of the pieces very notable. She has met *Ambrose Bierce*—years ago.

In the evening "Fluffy" called again—this time accompanied by Mrs. Moran, his master's mother. The Moran family are quite intelligent—at least, as much so as devout Roman Catholics can be. They would enjoy your church & pastor—St. Sebastian's, & Father Craig. Guests left in the following order—Mrs. Cooley, Kid Long, Fluffy & Mrs. Moran, & Mortonius. As before, James Ferdinand stayed till after 1 a.m., long after the retirement of our magnanimous hostess. We discussed everything under the sun, specialising on Persia, amateur journalism, niggers, & the *Cambridge Tribune*. If Jim doesn't land the *Tribune* job, he may go to Persia as a government adviser—his Bahai interests give him influence. He prefers the *Tribune,* though—he says he would rather edit this weekly than any other in the country.

But hark! The clock tells me that I must beat it for Belknap's or I shall be late—probably I'll be late anyway.

I gave your regards to Mrs. Greene, & am instructed to forward similar protestations in return. She hopes she can see you in N.Y. during the winter—& I can assure you that the hospitality of 259 Parkside is *some* hospitality!

Well—more next time.

Yr aff: nephew & obt Servt

H P L

## Notes

1. *The Count of Monte Cristo* (Fox Film Corp., 1922), directed by Emmett J. Flynn; starring John Gilbert, Estelle Taylor, and Robert McKim. Based on the novel by Alexandre Dumas *père.*

2. Crane Wilbur (1886–1973), *The Monster* (1922), a horror drama directed by Joseph M. Gaites and starring Walter James, Frank McCormack, and Marguerite Risser. It was adapted for a 1925 silent film.

3. Winnifred Harper Cooley (1874–1967), author of *The New Womanhood* (1904) and other works. Daughter of Ida Husted Harper (1851–1931), author of *History of the Movement for Woman Suffrage in the United States* (1907) and a leading advocate on the subject.

4. *Kiki: A Character Study* (1921), adapted by David Belasco (1853–1931) from the play *Kiki* (1920) by André Picard (1874–1926), directed by David Belasco, starring Lenore Ulric, Gertrude Bond, and Harry Burkhardt. It ran for 233 performances at the Belasco Theatre.

5. AEPG's ex-husband, Edward F. Gamwell, was editor and proprietor of the *Cambridge Tribune* (1901–1912). Morton was not hired as editor.

6. Kate McLaurin (1885?–1933), *Whispering Wires* (1922), playing at the 49th Street

Theatre; directed by J. C. Huffman and John Harwood; starring Malcolm Duncan, Gaby Fleury, and George Howell.

7. The Cloisters, at Fort Tryon Park in the far northern tip of Manhattan. The complex includes portions of four medieval abbeys brought over piecemeal from France. Construction began in 1917 and was completed in 1939.

8. Probably "The Horror at Martin's Beach."

[15]     [ANS postcard][1] [HPL to LDC]

[Postmarked Brooklyn, N.Y.,
12 September 1922]

Your delightful letter recd. Will answer in a day or two. Have been persuaded (very easily persuaded!) to prolong visit about a week more—Long & Morton have innumerable sights to show me, & Mrs. Greene wants me to see several plays. Yesterday I picked up some marvellous book bargains in a shop on 59th St. Hope your finger is doing well. More later—

Yr aff: nephew & obt Servt
H P L

P.S. Mrs. G. sends regards.

*Notes*

1. *Front:* The New York Public Library, New York City.

[16]     [ALS] [HPL to LDC]

259 Parkside Ave.,
Brooklyn, N.Y.,
Septr 13, 1922
— 16, —

My dear Aunt Lillian:—
                As my preceding card indicated, I was indeed pleased to receive your letters of the 4th & 8th. Would that you could be here to participate in the ceaseless round of pleasant activity & intellectual encouragement which has for the time wholly banished my ancient melancholy! My recent programme will be found outlined in an epistle which A.E.P.G. will shew you—since that was written, events have progressed in the same brilliant way. One wonders whether one can be actually awake—it is odd to welcome the next day instead of dreading it! But days filled with congenial & varied discussion, & enlivened by learned youth, are ever welcome. Sunday occurred the scholarly gathering here. Monday Long & I explored the American Museum of Natural History—examining it in far greater detail than did Kleiner & I a couple of weeks ago. Long appreciates science & nature more

than Kleiner does—he is a marvellous kid, far above the average "amateur journalist" type. In the evening I introduced him to a new phase of activity— browsing among the second-hand book shops. Curiously enough, he had never before investigated such a place, & was utterly unfamiliar with East 59th St., their principal Manhattan habitat. Needless to say, he was transported by the bargains he found; & has resolved to prove a steady customer of these erudite emporia. He picked up some magnificent bargains, as did I—one of my prizes is the first edition of Ingram's authoritative life of Poe—which you must surely read. The bookshops of New-York vastly surpass those of both Providence & Boston; abounding in desirable volumes, & having prices almost incredibly low. Some of the books I obtained, cost only *3⅓* cents—that is, were quoted at three for ten cents. The two-volume Poe biography was $2.00—a rare find at that small price; and for *15¢* I picked up a complete edition of Pepys' Diary in one large volume—it lacks covers, but has the full text well printed & intact. But enough of these sordid & mundane commercial details! Yesterday—Tuesday—Morton & I went over to Long's for dinner; the family's first home dinner since the renovation of their flat. They have a new servant—brighter than her predecessor—& all went very well indeed. After a period of discussion & repartee, which Mrs. Long said reminded her of the epigrammatic paradoxes of Oscar Wilde & Whistler, the gang adjourned to Morton's chaotic apartment in Harlem. I had never before seen Morton's abode, & naturally I was interested. He dwells in a street now overrun by *niggers* of the cleaner & less offensive sort—decayed, but still retaining the outlines of its former beauty. There are pleasing trees on both sides, & the architecture of the houses is highly prepossessing. No. 211—the Morton mansion—is an old brick single house owned by an elderly eccentric named Edwin C. Walker; a spacious & unkempt edifice, thick with dust, & with half the rooms unused. Morton's room is on the top floor, reached by dark & winding stairs, & is remarkably neat though atrociously dusty. Morton is not only his own chambermaid, but his own cook; as many objects attest. The principal contents of the room is *books*—every wall* lined with them from floor to ceiling, & all arranged in the most logical order conceivable. There is here nothing of the disorder found in James Pyke's collection.[1] On the whole, I believe that Morton's library is the best I have ever seen possessed by a private individual—it is infinitely well-chosen, & of amazing amplitude. Besides books, there are many rare minerals & choice pictures; to say nothing of shelves of carefully filed papers, & albums containing a record-breaking stamp collection. The place is fascinating—I shall visit it repeatedly, in response to Morton's hyper-cordial invitation. He has lent me several books, including a scarce copy of Colman's famous comedy (produced in Dr. John-

---

*N.B. On the wall of Morton's room is a framed MS. of "My Country, 'Tis of Thee", in the original handwriting of its author—his grandfather.

son's day) "The Heir At Law". I plan to make Morton a present—"The Poets & Poetry of America";[2] which he lacks but desires, & which I saw for sale cheap in a 59th St. bookshop. I did not buy it Monday because I have a copy myself. After the Mortonian session I met Mrs. Greene downtown, had dinner at the St. Regis, & attended the mystery play "Whispering Wires" at the 49th St. Theatre—the same place at which we saw the fantastic "Chauve-Souris" last April.[3] The drama was very good—cleverly written & intelligently acted—though of course not as spectral & sinister as "The Monster" (cf. my letter to A.E.P.G.) Today I am writing preparatory to going over to Long's again—we are as inseparable as Galpin & I in Cleveland—and in the afternoon we shall join Morton for a tour of the Jumel Mansion (Gen. Washington's headquarters during the Revolution) & of an interesting group of uptown museums at 150th St. & Broadway.

*Next day—Sept'' 14*

Yesterday's programme was great—we liked the Jumel Mansion so well that we stayed there all the afternoon & deferred the Museum trip till Friday . . . . . . . that is, Morton & I liked it, though Belknap professes to be bored by my beloved 18th Century. The place is entrancing—situated on Washington Heights, on a bluff above the Harlem River, & commanding an expansive view of what was in its day a magnificent panorama. Now, the view is polluted by city edifices & unsightly railway yards—but once it consisted only of blue water, green fields & forests, occasional white houses & steeples, & gently rolling hills—a pastoral scene of ineffable beauty. One of the old spires remains, & I permitted my fancy to restore the original scene as it must have been in 1740 or 1750, before ever the Colonies thought of treason & rebellion against His Majesty's Government. The mansion is in excellent condition, & replete with relics of Gen. Washington & his day—flags, uniforms, furniture, arms, watches, newspapers, & utensils & devices of every description. It was a breath of my own era of periwigs—there was a register for visitors to sign, & I signed it "H: Lovecraft, Gent., Providence-Plantations, in Rd: Island"—just as I signed the register in the old Sawyer place in Merrimac last May. On the wall of one of the rooms was a framed MS. of "My Country, 'Tis of Thee" in the original handwriting of Morton's grandfather—which duly edified the equally gifted grandson.[4] Great old boys—both of 'em! Today Morton is busy, & Kid Long & I intend to spend the whole afternoon exploring old bookshops in 59th St. May Heaven guard my purse in the face of such temptation! Belknap is going to take along a suitcase full of old books which he wishes to get rid of either by sale or by trade. If he can strike a good bargain, I may try the same thing with some of the superfluous junk in the attic—though Providence shops have not such a good variety of books to trade in return. 59th St. is surely the centre of the booklover's universe—anyone who can walk along it between Lexington & Madison Avenues with-

out spending money is a hero & deserves a medal! . . . . . Postman just came
with a big package from Galpin*—books for everybody! The generous little
divvle is making presents on a large scale—Smith's "Star Treader" for me, an
art book for Kid Belknap, & Leonard's translation of Lucretius for Mrs.
Greene—with whom he is trying to make up after his rudeness of last spring.
Leonard is his English professor at the U. of Wis.—a scholar of note. I'll take
Belknap's book over to him this morning when I go—which, by the way, the
clock tells me will have to be darned soon. Dinner will be early, since his
mother is going out for the afternoon.

Speaking of social events—I am glad that you are having your share of
them. The Woods expedition must have been interesting—was the portrait
good? I am sorry that your finger has proved troublesome, & hope that Dr.
Cooke's skill has by this time relegated the affliction to the domain of the remote past. My own health is amazingly good—face well-behaved, strength
equal to my programme of walking, hours & meals normal, & best of all, spirits bright & cheerful. I am not even bald yet, though I shall be glad to employ
whatever preventive against that disaster you may have discovered or devised.

As to weather—there has been very little continuous rain, so that sightseeing has suffered hardly any impediments. And when it has rained, I have
been safely dry beneath the protecting shade of a borrowed umbrella. Today
is ideally sunny—which reminds me anew that I must beat it for Kid Belknap's house—quite a subway trip from Brooklyn to upper Manhattan. Well—
s'long . . . see you later!

*Late the same night*

Had a fine trip with Belknap—went up to the old Jumel Mansion again
(it didn't bore him as badly as he said!) & had a talk with the pleasant 77-year-
old who presides over the front hall. He remembers the locality back in 1855,
when it was all open country, & gave us many hints as to other points of Colonial & Revolutionary interest. Later we walked north to Highbridge—that
stately piece of antique masonry which Poe so loved, & which he used so often to visit in the evening twilight alone & pensive. It was after a walk there
that he composed "Ulalume"—but I fear Belknap & I will not achieve anything so classic as a result of our pilgrimage! Parts of the adjacent shore are
still rustic—there is one idyllic lane which Gen. Washington may well have
known when he occupied the mansion on the heights. Later still we went
down to 59th St. & raided the bookstalls. Belknap got $4.00 for his suitcase
full of books, & spent only 40¢ on a paper-covered edition of "Salammbo".
Profitable transaction! I had previously obtained the same book for half the
price, though! And for 15¢ I obtained the *one* important Poe work I have nev-

---

*That package he sent to 598 is *sandalwood*—I know not in what form—which
The Kid picked up in a Japanese curio shop on Mackinac Island.

er before possessed—the philosophical study "Eureka". My good fortune was ensured by the existence of a broken set. However—I didn't buy up the whole street. I preferred to leave something for next time.

*Saturday Morning*

This is a letter & a diary combined! Yesterday Belknap, Morton, & I explored the group of museums at 150ᵗʰ St. & B'way; concentrating our attention on the Hispanic Museum, which contains many priceless specimens of Spanish painting, sculpture, cartography, & bookmaking, & the Numismatic Museum, which has the best collection of ancient & modern coins in the United States. We also took in the Spanish church in the same neighbourhood—a strange Popish affair redolent of the Middle Ages & the Inquisition. Later Mortonius left us, & Belknap & I revisited the 59ᵗʰ St. bookstalls—where he picked up Ransome's critical study of Wilde for 60¢, & I found a small Holbein art book for 25¢, which I shall send as a gift to Galpinius. Possibly I mentioned that ever since the Cleveland trip Alfredus has been enthusiastic about pictorial art. In the evening I met Mrs. Greene, & we proceeded to the Capitol Theatre—Broadway & 51st St.—which is without doubt the most sumptuous moving-picture show in existence. The building is vastly proportioned, & decorated with a wealth of luxurious frescoes, columns, mirrors, statues, paintings, & the like. Vistas of marble stairways & corridors strike the eye at every turn, & there is a profusion of neatly uniformed ushers whose courtesy & intelligence seems [*sic*] impeccable. The orchestra is titanic—it must contain a hundred men, & is directed by a musician of considerable standing—M. Erno Rappee—evidently a Frenchman.[5] Admission is 85¢ to the parquet, 55¢ to the balcony—very small, considering the excellent programme. On this occasion the main film was that weirdest of all "Sherlock Holmes" stories—"The Hound of the Baskervilles"—& in my opinion the production was excellent.[6] I enclose the programme, which may interest you. After the theatre we explored that quaint & artificial colony of half-baked would-be aesthetes called "Greenwich Village", which centres around Washington Square & Fourth Street, having supper at an eccentric place called the "T.N.T. (Tea and Tea) Shop" in Macdougal Street. This is one of many oddly furnished eating places in which an effort is made to achieve "Bohemian" atmosphere & colouring. Seedy & superficial philosophers sit about tables & benches in the feeble yellow light, smoking, eating, & pretending to discuss literature. They move about from place to place with an air of self-conscious informality, & doubtless fancy that they are "just too intellectual for anything." There is only one waiter, a Japanese, & he lives up to his official title chronologically as well as vocationally. Nobody minds the delay, however, since the favourite pastime of the assembled *intelligentsia* is to loaf. The food—when it finally did arrive—was not at all bad.

Today Morton, Kleiner,* Belknap, & I are going to visit the Brooklyn Museum with its adjacent Japanese garden. Tomorrow we shall endeavour to arrange a programme with Kleiner in it. Some trip! This burg is certainly well populated with active & congenial amateurs!

In my last letter I told you about the fake Poe "poem" which I wrote as part of the hoax for Galpinius prepared by Belknap & me. The result was more than we ever expected, for although of course Alfredus did not believe Poe wrote the piece, he praised it to the skies as a work of art, & devoted a long paragraph to an analysis of its "good points", "tranquil beauty", &c. &c. He fancied we had copied it from the obscure works of some standard poet—probably Arthur O'Shaunessy[7]—a vast joke considering the fact that it was thrown together spoofingly in fifteen minutes' time by one whom Galpin deems anything but a poet! We are stringing the kid along a while—giving him the impression that Belknap wrote it. The piece itself is as follows—one of Poe's favourite subjects handled in close parody of his manner:

TO ZARA

Inscribed to Mifs Sarah Longhurst†

By Edgar A. Poe
June 1829

I look'd upon thee yesternight
Beneath the drops of yellow light
That fell from out a poppy moon
Like notes of some far opiate tune.
I look'd & sigh'd, I knew not why,
As when a condor flutters by,
And thought the moonbeams on thy face
Timid to seek thy resting-place.
O sacred spot! Memorial bow'r!
Unsuited to the mocking hour
When winds of myrrh from Tempë's lake
Stir soft, yet stir thee not awake!
Thy clear brow, ZARA, rests so fair,
I cannot think death lingers there;
Thy lip as from thy blood is red,
Nor hints of ichors of the dead;

---

*11 a.m.—I just called him up, & he says he'll be able to meet the gang at 2 o'clock in front of the museum.

† a mediocre authoress of the 1830 period—author of "Lost, Lost Rosa Belle".

Canst thou, whom love so late consum'd,
Lie prey to worms—dissolv'd, entomb'd?
And he, whose name suffus'd thy cheek
With ecstasies thou couldst not speak;
Will he in fancy hold thee ever
Fair as thou art, decaying never,
And dreaming, on thine eyelids prefs
A tribute to thy lovelinefs?
Or will his fancy rove beneath
The carven urn & chisell'd wreath,
Where still—so still—the shroud shall drape
Grotesque, liquescent turns of shape?
No, ZARA, no! Such beauty reigns
Immortal in immortal fanes;
Radiant for ever, ever laden
With beams of uncorrupted Aidenn,
And naught that slumbers here tonight
Can perish from a lover's sight.
Where'er thy soul, where'er thy clay
May rise to hail another day,
Thy second soul, thy beauty's flame,
The songs of passionate lutes shall claim;
Pale, lovely ghost—so young, so fair,
To flutter in sepulchral air—
To flutter where the taper dies
Amidst a mourner's choking sighs!

I note with regret the encroachments of commercialism upon familiar Providence scenes—such intrusions in a purely residential district are ever to be deplored. However—all things change .... Providence won't know me any better than I'll know it when we meet! And anent that meeting—my card told you of the pushing forward of the date. Positively, I never saw such universal & profound cordiality as that which I have struck during this trip! Mrs. Greene says she hates to hear my departure even alluded to, & wishes that the matter could be reversed by your coming to N.Y. instead of my going go Prov.; & small Belknap entreats me to be as slow as possible in leaving him to his accustomed desolation—he told Mrs. Greene over the telephone that 'he can't see enough of me'! And Morton & Kleiner—bless my soul, but they are flattering in their utterances! Moreover, fancy who has just written, asking me to meet him if convenient in N.Y. at the Victor Hotel, 37th St. & 5th Ave., on Saturday, Sept. 23, (one week from today) 1922? None other than that John Russell, the Florida Scotchman who in 1913 conducted the *Argosy* controversy with me which led to my discovering amateur journalism![8] I had never thought to see him in the flesh, although I have corresponded to some extent with him; & the present chance is wholly accidental—he has been home to Scotland & is returning by way of New York. The odd thing is, that he has no idea I am in N.Y.—his suggestion is that I make the trip from Prov. especially to see him—which would be a bit expensive & unlikely. I should like to meet the man whose verses elicited the satires from which Daas recruited me, & I have half a mind to do it—I'll let you know. It's so darned congenial here that I hate to break away—but I am a philosopher, & accept with stoical imperturbability every circumstance & dispensation of fate. However—what I'd advise is your coming along here & mixing in the festivities!!! You'd find Belknap a little angel—he's second only to the immortal Alfredus. By the way—lest you wonder what I am wearing in lieu of the straw hat which became obsolete yesterday, let me assure you that my almost-bald head is safely covered with grey felt. When I saw the approach of the "bell-ringing" season I intended to be on the safe side & send to you for my brown felt—but Mrs. Greene said it would be foolish to make you take the trouble of wrapping (or crating) & mailing a paltry *$2.85* lid; & insisted that since her persuasion has detained me, she ought to furnish the incidental appurtenances! I remonstrated to no avail—& finally gave in, since the plea not to cause you bother was quite unanswerable. However—I was firm in specifying that the dome-piece be no more than a two-eighty-fiver—as a result of which firmness I am now sporting a conservative dark-grey rotunda of the humble & accustomed "Truly Warner" brand . . . . I chose grey in order to be different from last year. It really looks good, in my opinion—before long I'll shew it to you & see what you think of it. If I recall aright, it will be a fine match for my grey winter suit . . . . . . a suit, by the way, which I'll be glad to don in a month or less. This blue outfit is worn absolutely threadbare—being up & about sure is hard on clothes!

I'll send the straw hat back by parcel post—it ought to be good for at least the first half of next summer. My new books I shall send by express (unless post is cheaper), & there will probably have to be a third package consisting of laundered material—my valise would never hold a third of the junk which must accompany (or precede or follow) me in my wanderings! I shall have some borrowed books as well as my own—Long, Mrs. Greene, & Morton are all lending me volumes which I have wished to read but cannot find in the Prov. Public Library.

Bush—bah, what a pest he is! I have done considerable stuff for the poor fish lately, & have received some distinctly helpful cheques; but he remains the premier nightmare of this terraqueous spheroid! He's getting dissatisfied with Morton's work, & insists on my personal revision—which gives me the ticklish task of telling James Ferdinand to maintain a higher standard—ugh! I hope I won't offend him. I'll have to hint gently & tactfully—& anyway I won't just now. Tomorrow will do. When Morton really tries, he can do better work than I can.

But the hour of 1:30 approaches, & I shall soon hear the infant Longlet's ring* at the door. More anon! Yr. aff: nephew & obt Servt

H P L

P.S. John Clarke sent his $4.00—covering interest up to Aug. 28.⁹ You might send me a blank receipt if convenient—also his detailed address, though I suppose simply "Seekonk Mass." would be enough.

[On envelope:] P.S.—Eleventh hour—Just recd. your letter of the 15th—delighted! Will answer soon.

H P L

Fine trip today—the 16th. Explored Bklyn Museum much more thoroughly than before. Tomorrow Kleiner & I will have a sightseeing tour.

## Notes

1. James Tobey Pyke (1858–1935) was for a time HPL's neighbor, residing next door to 598 Angell Street. By January 1916, Pyke had moved to East Providence (see "Introducing Mr. James Pyke," *Conservative,* January 1916; *CE* 1.97). HPL published some of Pyke's poetry in his *Conservative.* See also HPL's poem "To the Rev. James Pyke."

2. A celebrated anthology edited by Rufus Wilmot Griswold.

3. *Le Chauve Souris* (The Bat), a touring revue originating in Moscow and directed by Nikita Balieff.

4. "My Country, 'Tis of Thee" (also known as "America") was written by Samuel Francis Smith (1808–1895), a Baptist minister, using the tune of the British national anthem. His daughter, Caroline Edwards Smith (b. 1843), was Morton's mother.

5. Ernö Rapée (1891–1945), Estonian-born conductor. He was the musical director at the Capitol Theatre (1645 Broadway) from 1919 to 1923. He later conducted the Radio City Symphony Orchestra (1932–45).

6. *The Hound of the Baskervilles* (Stoll Picture Productions, 1921), directed by Maurice Elvey; starring Eille Norwood, Catina Campbell, and Rex McDougall. Based on the novel by Sir Arthur Conan Doyle.

7. Arthur O'Shaughnessy (1844–1881), minor British poet associated with the Pre-Raphaelites.

8. Russell was a British amateur journalist living in Florida and infrequent associate of HPL. When HPL wrote a letter to the *Argosy* criticizing romance writer Fred Jackson (published in the September 1913 issue), Russell was one of many to protest—but his protest (published in the November 1913 issue) was in verse, leading HPL to respond with the *Ad Criticos* poems. After a year of sporadic exchanges, the editor of the *Argo-*

---

*speaking of ringing—how's this for a coincidence? The telephone started that very second—Mrs. Greene called up to tell me to invite the whole gang to dinner tonight. High society stuff, I'll say!

*sy* asked the two writers to reconcile, and they did so in an item published as "The Critics' Farewell" in the October 1914 issue, containing HPL's poem "The End of the Jackson War" and Russell's "Our Apology to E. M. W."

9. It is unclear what this payment was for. Perhaps HPL's family had another mortgage, possibly acquired through HPL's uncle Edwin E. Phillips.

[17]       [ANS postcard][1] [HPL to LDC]

[Postmarked Brooklyn, N.Y.,
15 September 1922]

Basking amidst the past—my favourite diversion! Am on page 7 of my letter to you—you'll see it soon. Yesterday Long & I visited Washington's Headquarters & walked to Highbridge, Poe's loved rural haunt. It is not *quite* urban yet— one finds a lingering trace or two of the ancient countryside. More anon.

Yr aff: nephew & obt Servt
H P L

*Notes*

1. *Front:* Washington's Headquarters 1776, 130th Street and Edgecombe Avenue, New York.

[18]       [ANS postcard][1] [HPL and FBL to LDC]

[Postmarked Brooklyn, N.Y.,
20 September 1922]

Here's a cat I'd like to have around the house! Am exploring N.Y. Zoölogical Garden with my grandson Belknap—having a great time. Will write soon.

Yr. aff: nephew & obt Servt
H P L

Frank Belknap Long, Jr.

*Notes*

1. *Front:* 1357 B Jaguar "Señor Lopez" / New York Zoological Park.

[19]       [ANS postcard][1] [HPL, James F. Morton, and FBL to LDC]

[Postmarked New York, N.Y.,
23 September 1922]

Here's the coach I'm coming home in—will specify date later. Exploring out-of-the-way musaea & other cryptical urban arcana under expert & erudite guidance.

Yr aff: nephew & obt Servt
H P L

And permit me to introduce the cream of New-York's intellectual elite—

James F. Morton, Jr.

Frank Belknap Long, Jr.

[Note by HPL on front:] This extraordinary museum visited Sept[r] 22, 1922[.]

## Notes

1. *Front:* The Beekman Family Coach, The New York Historical Society.

[20]     [ALS] [HPL and Sonia H. Greene to AEPG]

[24 September 1922]

[Darling,—

Ten minutes after your special to Howard I am rushing this off to you. Gee! I'm so glad you can come! For the length of time you can stay, can be decided on after you get here.

It doesn't make any difference about my own lack of time just now— because Howard and Belknap and maybe Morton can take you to places of interest in the daytime and you can rest comfortably in the evenings talking to me, while Howard can go out if he wishes or remain with us.

And on Saturday evening and Sunday the three of us can have a perfectly lovely time[.]

My Dear, I do hope you can stay a long time! Who knows? I'm a regular female Micawber—something unexpected may happen—pleasureable [*sic*] and beneficial so that you can remain here.

I just can't wait until you get here.

With eager and pleasureable anticipation

I am

Lovingly Yours

Sonia]

All hail! I can't resist adding a word in support of the plea that you hit the big town before I depart.[1] Now's your opportunity—so forget hesitancy & beat it hither! You'll never have another chance to see the sights under so expert a guide as myself (note the egotism I am acquiring!)—I know the old burg from A to Z, & with the special localised knowledge of a recent sight-seer rather than the diffuse, indefinite knowledge of a mere native. I am free all day—as no one else hereabouts seems to be—& I will guarantee to show you practically everything worth seeing, no matter how brief your sojourn is forced to be. And incidentally—as Galpinius would say—*$%# that snappish old termagant Mrs. Foster!![2] Chuck her if you can! You will like this burg immensely—it contains about everything under the sun; even sylvan rusticity & provincialism, which one may find on isolated Staten Island. As for the inhabitants—you already know our benignant hostess, & Belknap cannot fail to captivate you. The kid is deliciously bright, refined, gentle, & unspoiled—he reminds me in many ways of P. G.[3] Morton you will find pleasantly impressive, & Kleiner you already know. Moreover—you cannot fail to be captivated by little Belknap's marvellous coon cat, "Felis"—one of the most artistic & intellectual persons of his kind whom I have ever met.

I shall answer your delightful letter soon—this is just a hurried & ecstatic line to urge you to share my phenomenal sojourn here.

As to my grey best winter suit—I would indeed appreciate it, if sending it would not be too much trouble. I haven't needed it yet, but cold days are all too close . . . bah, how I hate autumn & winter! Moreover, this blue rag-bag is becoming positively frightful in its threadbareness—I vow, 'tis almost past respectability, though Belknap still assures me he is not ashamed to be seen in my company. I can tell you with much certainty that the Outlet is going to have a customer next April!!

And by the way—along with the suit, would you mind sending

(a) 2 pairs of stockings

(b) The least disreputable pair of *thin* gloves which you can find in my top bureau drawer?

Everything else is in prime condition, but my incessant *walking* plays the very deuce with stockings. My new roof will harmonise well with the suit—I selected a grey one with just that intention. The vest of the suit needs alteration around the neck, but there's a tailor next door.

But I'll subside for the present, deferring a complete epistle till I have more leisure. Dinner is imminent, & Kleiner is coming for that occasion. . . . . This reminds me—expect some swell feeds when you get here. Greenesque cooking is something absolutely unparallelled—after a few doses of it, Fosterian fare will never seem the same again.

I like N.Y. so well that I am going to lug some of it home with me. Yesterday I bought the Woolworth Building & the Statue of Liberty from a smooth-tongued & smartly dressed young man whom I met down town. He was very pleasant. I paid 25¢ for the Woolworth Bldg. & 10¢ for the Statue of Liberty—& took them away in my pocket. I shall use them for paperweights or mantelpiece ornaments . . . . Or perhaps I shall set up the W. Bldg. in the business district, so that our skyline may no longer be dominated by that asinine Christian Science Church!

As for Bush—don't worry! I am doing his work right along, & he now owes me $11.74, which I expect any day. There is enough work for a regiment! Some pieces he insists that I revise personally, since he says Morton's work is not so good. I am making experiments in raising rates—even unto $1.00 per *8 lines*. I'll say it's worth it, too! I can do Bush work better here—the atmosphere of animation stimulates the mental processes.

Well—so long . . . & come along!

Yr aff: nephew & obt Servt
H P L

## Notes

1. AEPG did in fact join HPL in New York for a time.

2. Apparently AEPG's landlady.

3. Phillips Gamwell, HPL's deceased cousin.

[21]     [ANS postcard][1] [HPL to LDC]

[Postmarked Brooklyn, N.Y.,
26 September 1922]

Am going to write you presently—but just now I can't resist bragging about the book bargain I secured yesterday—Ovid's Epistles, *in black-letter*, printed in **1567**, when Shakespeare was only 3 yrs old . . . for only $2.00! ¶ Am waiting for word from A.E.P.G. as to whether she can share the last days of this delectable metropolitan sojourn. Wish that *you* could! // Yr aff: nephew & obt Servt

H P L

P.S. Attended a dinner last night at which the poet Clement Wood, the editor of the N.Y. Times,[2] & J. F. Morton Jr spoke.

## Notes

1. *Front:* Astor Trust Building, Fifth Ave. at 42nd St., N. Y.

2. Clement Wood (1888–1950), American poet, biographer, and activist. HPL refers erroneously to Adolph Ochs (1858–1935), publisher of the *New York Times* (1904–35). See LDC/AEPG 22, where he cites Ochs by name.

[22]     [ALS] [HPL to LDC]

259 Parkside Ave.,
Brooklyn, N.Y.
Sept[r] 29, 1922

My dear Aunt Lillian:—

        In replying to your recent & highly appreciated epistles, let me first thank you for sending the suit & minor accessories. The bundle arrived last night, & all the contents was in good condition. I donned the suit immediately—it was certainly a relief to be suitably dressed after weeks of existence in a pitiably threadbare disguise. As I wrote A.E.P.G., the Outlet is certainly going to have a determined customer next spring! The gloves seem all right to me—perhaps I shan't need them at all, but it gives one a sense of security to have them in one's pocket.

I am indeed sorry that you cannot think of getting here to share the conclusion of this epochal sojourn. Failing that, pray do your best to induce A.E.P.G. to make the venture! You cannot imagine the idyllic delight of such a visit—every possible consideration, superb cuisine, & unceasing variety in amusements, excursions, & conversations. Better reconsider & try it!

As to my recent programme—I believe the last chronicle left off Saturday, Sept. 16, with a hasty exterior P.S. telling of the afternoon's trip with Kleiner, Belknap, & Morton. That evening Kleiner & I investigated the principal antiquity of this section—the old Dutch Reformed Church—& were well repaid for our quest. Parkside Avenue, be it known, is not part of the original town of Breucklin—or Brookland—or Brooklyn—as the Long Island metropolis is variously known, but is a remnant of the early Dutch village of *Flatbush*, which was engulfed about a quarter of a century ago by the expansion of the great city. Most of the original village edifices have long been destroyed, & replaced by blocks of shops & apartment houses; but some benign fate has preserved the ancient village church, whose ivy-twined belfry & spire still dominate the local sky-line. This venerable congregation was founded in 1654 by the honest & simple Holland burghers who settled the region. In 1698 a second & more elegant church replaced the original structure—British rule had brought prosperity, yet the villagers still adhered to their Dutch speech & manners. Then, in about three-quarters of a century, came the lamented rebellion of the colonies, with the unfortunate victory of the rebels & the secession of all His Majesty's Dominions south of Canada. Alas! Time passed; & in 1796, under the newly-welded government of the United-States, the worthy Flatbush burghers built a third & still more substantial church on the ancient site—the graceful structure of Georgian outlines which stands to this day. But though they adopted the artistic architecture of the conquering Saxon, they themselves remained unalterably Dutch. Around the old pile is a hoary churchyard, with interments dating from about 1730 to the middle of the nineteenth century. Nearly all the stones bear inscriptions & epitaphs in the Dutch language—beginning with the characteristic "Hier lygen", which analogy makes quite easily recognisable to the devotee of English graveyards. Up to about 1815 or 1820 the Dutch tongue predominates. Here & there an English inscription tells of a family looking forward to the changing order of things; & now & then an English *name* reveals the beginning of that gradual intermarriage which has today completely fused the Dutch & English colonists into one native stock—a stock, alas, now menaced in its turn by the appalling tidal wave of modern inferior immigration. As I viewed this village churchyard in the autumn twilight, the city seemed to fade from sight, & give place to the Netherland town of long ago. In fancy I saw the cottages of the simple Dutchmen, their small-paned windows lighted one by one as evening stole over the harvest-fields. And I reflected upon the vanity of mankind, which seeks even after death a tawdry fame in carven stone & marble. Here were slabs chiselled with care, that all the world might know the virtues—real or fictitious—of those who sleep beneath; slabs designed for the eyes of the future, yet through fate's triumphant irony couched in a fading speech which today no passer-by can read! So, too, may be the pompous legends which adorn our own sepulchres & mausolea—transient hieroglyphics which succeeding ages & succeeding races of conquerors will labour in vain to decipher. Sic transit gloria mundi! This ancient churchyard is, in a sense, a discovery of my own; since none of the local amateurs had ever visited it, or so much as suspected that any Dutch cemetery remained in the country. Kleiner & I have since examined it again— also in the twilight, when small birds flew down in great numbers out of the sky & pecked at the ancient grave-earth as if imbibing some hideous species of nourishment. I would like to have understood the mocking chatter of those birds, as they hopped about on the graves of forgotten burghers, or flew to shelter beneath the shadowy eaves of that old & ivied church . . . . . . From one of the crumbling gravestones—dated 1747—I chipped a small piece to carry away. It lies before me as I write—& ought to suggest some sort of a horror-story. I must some night place it beneath my pillow as I sleep . . . . who can say what *thing* might not come out of the centuried earth to exact vengeance for his desecrated tomb? And should it come, who can say what it might not resemble?[1] At midnight, in many antique burying-grounds, shadows steal terribly about; shadows in periwigs & three-cornered hats, & tattered, mouldy knee-breeches that flap about crumbling bones. They have no voices, but sometimes do hideous deeds *silently*.

But to continue the chronicle—on Sunday the 17th, Kleiner & I took a long tour of exploration. We met at Borough Hall, Brooklyn, & thence strolled to the waterfront, where we beheld with melancholy interest the squalid edifice which marks the almost-abandoned Fulton Ferry. In the old days, before the advent of bridge & subway tube, Fulton Ferry was a gorgeous & bustling depot of commerce & fashion. The smart ferryboats, plying almost every moment, bore impatient crowds, liveried equipages, & laden drays; whilst the Brooklyn ferry-house, with its niched & pedestalled statue of Robert Fulton, was considered the last word in architectural magnificence. Today the crowds, the equipages, & the drays are gone. One old ferryboat, battered & wheezing, still makes a trip or two per day for old time's sake. The ferry-house still stands—bizarre, Victorian, unpainted, & hopelessly decrepit. Poor Robert Fulton—tarnished with the years—maintains his vigil . . . . but old waterfront denizens say his face is overcast with a look of sadness which he lacked in the old days, when he was newly set up for the admiration of prosperous throngs. Eheu! Tempora mutantur, et nos in illis![2]

From Fulton Ferry we walked over Brooklyn Bridge to Manhattan. The bridge, too, is getting old; & is closed to all non-rail vehicles save the horse-drawn. As a result, its once crowded driveways are almost deserted—for the much-discussed revival of the horse is confined to the dapper hansoms & victorias whose drivers hold forth in the opulent Central Park & 5th Ave. region. It is possible that Brooklyn Bridge may soon be torn down to make way for a more modern structure—a replacement which will occasion much sentimental regret amongst those who cherish old things. Strongly as it was designed, it has not the absolute imperishability of those European bridges which stand for uncounted centuries.

From Brooklyn Bridge we strolled through the narrow, hilly, & winding streets of New-York's ancient lower end. These thoroughfares date from Colonial times, though most of the buildings are rather less archaic—averaging about 75 to 100 years in age. There is much of the old atmosphere present, & occasionally one finds a *really* old place, like Fraunce's [*sic*] Tavern, where Gen. Washington bade farewell to his victorious horde of rebels on Decr. 4, 1783. Kleiner & I knocked at the tavern door, but did not find the landlord at home . . . . Perchance, as a friend & host of Gen. W's rebel army, he was disinclined to grant his hospitality to as loyal a Tory & subject of His Majesty as myself.

Thence we took a ferry boat to Staten-Island, the one thoroughly rural area within the corporate limits of greater New-York. The place is idyllic—sleepy villages, old houses, quaint streets, & unpolluted countryside. We landed at St. George, & made a trolley trip to Port Richmond, which lies so close to the New-Jersey coast that one might easily throw a stone thither. Curiously enough, I have not yet set foot in New-Jersey. In antique Port-Richmond there is a church built in 1766, with many venerable graves around it. Whilst exploring this place, Kleiner & I came on a half-hidden gate amid the trees behind the building—opening which, we encountered a deserted & forgotten cemetery; whose interments all antedate the Civil War. It is a ghoulish place; lonely, neglected, & unseen from the outside world—hilly, darkened by the shade of trees, & overrun with weeds, tall grass, & climbing moss. The moss has almost obscured the inscriptions on most of the gravestones. Under the church runs a hidden stream, echoing spectrally in the masonry vaults along its course. One fancies bats & daemons not far off. Staten-Island, despite its proximity, is still amazingly independent of New-York; many of the simple rural denizens never having been to the metropolis whose towering skyline they behold across five miles of intervening water. Last year, whilst on a trip there, Kleiner met an old man who boasted of his *one* visit to the city—shortly after the Civil War. But athwart this Arcadian isolation falls the chilling shadow of metropolitan absorption. If, as threatened, the subway system is extended to Staten-Island; the region will immediately be exploited by unpoetic real-estate men, and where now quaint village streets ramble, & stone-walled meadows gleam in the morning sun, there will rise row on row of cheap flats, shops, & cottages—destroying the flavour of American individuality & tradition, & substituting the mechanical tawdriness & grossness of mongrel urbanism. Alas for the pleasing hills & vales, meads & groves, farms & villages of our fathers! It was evening when Kleiner & I left this agrestic isle—we would have stayed longer, & watched the starlight over still pastures, had not Kleiner been forced to keep a city engagement at 8 o'clock.

Monday I went up to Belknap's as usual, & we later strolled about the walks & glens of Central Park's northern end. This tract, wherein is preserved the original primitive topography of Manhattan, would be a veritable Tempë if it were not for the annoying presence of herds of plebeian children.

Tuesday afternoon Belknap & I visited the Bronx Zoölogical Gardens; which we vastly enjoyed, both as regards natural scenery & imported animals. We observed with a philosophic smile that instinct of kinship which causes negroes to be fascinated with the great apes. Before the chimpanzee cage; gazing with rapt interest, & unconscious of the time, we noted two huge, jet-black buck niggers; one of them—curiously enough—in army uniform with a very businesslike trench helmet. Later we sat on a bench and discussed *Bush work,* which Belknap thought he might try for a while. I revised some from a current job then & there—& Belknap abandoned his plan when he saw what nerve-racking business it was. He said he wasn't sure he *could* do it—& that even if he *could,* he *was* sure he *wouldn't.* This reminds me that a very welcome Bush cheque came today—he is now paying just *three times* the former *highest* rate, & doing it cheerfully. I told him that only at this high price could I guarantee my own personal service—he doesn't like Morton's work so well, & asked me to do as much as possible myself. I now get *$1.00 per 8 lines*—very convenient for a traveller seeing the big town, I can assure you! In the evening Mrs. Greene & I went to see "The Serpent's Tooth" at the Little Theatre on 44th St.[3] It was rather good,—epigrammatic & smart—though the sophisticated quality was marred by an incongruous strain of conventional sentimentalism & bourgeois psychology. I will enclose the programme.

Wednesday found me at Belknap's again—sometimes I fear I impose on the Longs by being with them at dinner practically every day, but they protest so violently that I don't impose, that I cannot but believe them! Surely their hospitality is of the first order—New-York eclipses all other cities in the spontaneous cordiality & generosity of its inhabitants—at least, such inhabitants as I have encountered. I thought the Bostonians were flattering, but the Gothamites are more complimentary still! One day when I thought I had another engagement (with Russell, who didn't show up, after all!) but later found I hadn't, & telephoned Belknap that I was coming to see him; Mrs. Long said his face positively lighted up with pleasure when he heard the news of my coming. My head sure will get turned! But anyway—to turn from egotistical reflections to objective facts—I went to Belknap's Wednesday, & we later formed an expedition for other regions. First we admired the scenic grandeur of the "mall" in Central Park, lounging long on the cliffs overlooking the lake. Then I took the kid down to the Vesey-St bookshop section, which he had never before seen. This is where Loveman & I secured our bargains last April. Belknap, having sharper eyes than his old Grandpa, picked up a book which I would have given much to have seen first—"Tales of Mystery",[4] composed of extracts from the most celebrated horror novelists of the 18th century—Walpole, Mrs. Radcliffe, Lewis, &c. He will later lend his prize to me—just as I am lending him my own prizes. Belknap sure is a great kid— I think I shall kidnap & adopt him, along with Galpinius! Some twins!

Thursday—the 21st—Belknap & I rested from our strenuous bookbuying; lounging about his house, planning stories, & finally taking a mild stroll through the south end of Central Park. We have now seen the whole park— & an excellent tract it is . . . or would be, but for the presence of the common herd. I prefer Prospect & Bronx parks, on the whole.

Friday we again had the august Mortonius with us, & a darned good time did we make of it; visiting a museum which, although previously unknown to all three, turned out to be the finest thing of its kind in the United States! I refer to the N.Y. Historical Society, where reposes the coach whose picture I sent you. It is a magnificent treasure-house of all sorts of early Americana— duelling pistols, household articles, maps, prints, portraits, &c . . . even the fragments of that statue of His Majesty George III which stood in Bowling Green, N.Y., & which was demolished in 1775 by the local rebels. I saluted reverently this symbol of my lawful sovereign. But the American material is only part of the show! For example—there are three mummified *bulls* from Egypt, 4500 years old, & the only things of their kind in the U.S. Also—there is the finest collection of Italian, Dutch, & Spanish Renaissance painting in the United States—original canvases by Titian, Murillo, Velazquez, Hals, Holbein, Giorgione, Da Vinci, &c. &c. . . . . . Galpinius would go wild at the spectacle, as indeed he did when I wrote him about it. But the carelessness with which these masterpieces are hung, is little short of criminal. All the lighting is bad, & the most valuable painting of all—Titian's famous "Execution of St Lawrence"—is placed on a wall in the basement, unprotected & open to the destructive work of thief or fanatic. If some monomaniac ever slashes or otherwise mutilates this priceless thing, the museum can thank itself, for lack of suitable guarding!

Saturday, the 23d, I expected to meet the traveller John Russell at the Hotel Victor—but my inquiries both then & since proved fruitless. In case he missed his steamer, & will still be here later, I'll occasionally call up the hotel—Fitzroy 0307—I have the number by rote! I shouldn't like to miss him if we are in the same city. Russell failing, I called up Belknap; & was soon beneath his hospitable roof. Later we started on a tour of exploration of lower Manhattan; ascending the Woolworth Building—an experience new to Belknap—& gathering impressions along the waterfront. In the Woolworth Tower many souvenirs are on sale, & I could not resist buying a couple—a model of the Woolworth Building (a *bank* for dimes—no doubt commemorative of the Woolworth fortune, made in ten-cent-stores) for 25¢, & one of the Statue of Liberty for ten cents. I hope the dime-bank will teach me thrift in my old age . . . . so far I haven't put anything in it! The waterfront was tame after Gloucester—there were no sailing ships present, & the sailors seemed merely tough rather than picturesque. They dress in cheap "store clothes" instead of the pea-jackets, bandannas, & sashes of marine fiction. We discussed the advisability of hiring the most sinister-looking crew we could pick, & organising a pirate expedition to the Spanish Main; but finally decided that the specimens we saw were not quite murderous enough to serve as our merry men.

Sunday I had my hair cut—the second time in N.Y. It was, in my opinion, a good job . . . . . the lord knows it ought to be, at **65 cents!** Kleiner came over for dinner, & general discussion long reigned. Later Klei & I went for a walk around Flatbush, whilst Mrs. Greene prepared some hats for a customer of the evening—she sometimes makes exceptionally artistic hats herself, aside from the work of the establishment. Good profit—just now she's getting $60.00 for a couple whose raw material cost only $20.00. Forty simoleons for labour which isn't in the least repulsive . . . . apparently millinery work beats Bush work! The Kleinero-Theobaldian ramble was as delightful as all such rambles are, & led us to a spot neither had seen or dreamed of before. In the midst of an ordinary-looking façade of shops along Flatbush Ave., we descried a low, arched opening labelled "Albemarle Arcade". Attracted by the title & uniqueness, we entered—& lo! After passing through we emerged into the most delightful conceivable replica of a lazy, beautiful, London side-street of 200 years ago! Our Orchard Ave. (north side) isn't in it with this fascinating walk—ancient architecture, knockers, iron railings, fanlights, brick sidewalks, spreading trees,—in short, the complete early Georgian scene faithfully reproduced for modernity. I wish this type of architecture were more widespread! In the evening I went alone to a local amateur gathering at the Sheepshead-Bay bungalow of Ernest A. Dench. Mrs. G. didn't go because of the hat business—the customer was expected to call—& Kleiner didn't go because he wasn't invited. He is on the Houtain side of the local feud, & therefore not in the inmost councils of the standard club element. The feud, by the way, progresses merrily. Houtain is reorganising the ancient "Gotham Club" as a rival to the existing "Blue Pencil Club"— & they'll probably fight till they've killed each other off! It is a very absorbing fight, although no one is able to remember what it all began about . . . . a most trivial detail! With my boasted geographical sense, I found Dench's place without difficulty—though it's a wonder I could distinguish it with the naked eye. Positively, it is the smallest dwelling I have ever beheld—the rooms are about the size of packing-boxes. It is said that a meeting of 23 amateurs was once held there—though I can't see where Dench ever stowed 'em all. Possibly he edged them in sidewise, & left a few outside. New-Anvik[5] was a palace compared to this joint—I'll wager the house isn't any bigger than our

Great Meadow Clubhouse in Rehoboth! This time the company was small—Dench, his wife, his sister-in-law, his father-in-law, Mortonius, & a quiet, pleasant author of 60 years' age, named Everett McNeil. You can find McNeil in "Who's Who"—he specialises in boys' books, has had 11 books & countless short stories published, & lives for picturesqueness' sake in the celebrated slum district called "Hell's Kitchen", which lies around 10th & 11th Aves between 30th & 50th Sts. I like McNeil—but on this occasion my attention centred in the family *cat*, which I held all the evening. This feline gentleman is a personage of some importance—as witness the enclosed card of invitation to the club festivities of tomorrow night, which I expect to attend! A lunch was served at midnight, & at 2 a.m. the revellers dispersed. This time-schedule reminded me somewhat of my own hours—though my nocturnal habits are generally matters of "upness" rather than "outness". Morton, McNeil, & I rode in on the subway together, & I hated to leave 'em at the Parkside station, as I had to do at 2:30.

Monday . . . . yes, you guessed it! Up at Belknap's again! I know the upper Broadway & Riverside Drive section as well as Brooklyn—& it's some section, too. This time we organised another bookstall raid—on the hitherto unvisited 4th Ave. district. And oh, boy! what luck I had! For only two plunks I grabbed a *black-letter* Ovid, printed in **1567**, when Bill Shakespeare was a 3-year-old toddling around his father's house in Stratford! It is the oldest book I have ever owned, & probably older than any other owned by an amateur—Loveman had a 1483 book, but sold it during his period of poverty. Morton admits he has nothing as old. The English is delectably pre-Elizabethan—get this sample:

> The heauie ſtepdame Iuno by hir fraude
> And friende Euryſtheus, purpoſde to destroye
> Alcides: for the Prince of Mycene lande
> Stirde him to conquer Monſters. But with laude
> And life he ſcapt away, nor had annoye
> By any beaſt the Champion tooke in hande:
> Bulles, Dragons, Dogges, and Semitaurs he ſlewe,
> And aye more greane his gotten glorie grewe.

In quoting, I have purposely chosen a mere "argument" in Roman type—since the black-letter of the text proper is too darned hard to copy by hand. This is, I think, the greatest bibliophilic treasure I have ever acquired—& the price is almost a joke for an imprint of that period. I also bought a good edition of Wilde's Poems, & an 18th century classic called "The Farmer's Boy", by Robert Bloomfield. (First American edition, 1803.) In the evening I attended the first fall meeting of Morton's beloved "Sunrise Club"—a thirty-year-old organisation devoted to oral discussion of literary, social, & political subjects. Mrs. Greene is a member, but did not attend this meeting because she is bored by the poet who formed the chief orator—Clement Wood. Morton persuaded me to attend, & I found it mildly interesting. The company was rather good—a moderate sprinkling of evening clothes—& the chicken dinner was excellent. The scene was the Café Boulevard, 41st St. & Broadway, & the attendance—about normal—must have exceeded a hundred. I sat beside Morton, at Table 13. Houtain was there, & I told him I was coming to see him some evening; but could hardly dun him for my twenty on such an occasion as this. The subject, opened after a dinner of some four or more courses, was literary censorship—a question on which I am fairly neutral, with a leaning toward a moderate middle course. Wood & most of the speakers, including Morton, were antis; but none of them save Morton gave any substantial argument. Wood was facetious & irrelevant—one "culchawed" & mellow-voiced idealist was unconsciously comic—all had to refer back to Morton for solid facts & convincing arguments. The pro side had as its leader the editor of the *N.Y. Times*—Ochs. Its logic was not notable until a fellow named Rinn stepped into the breach—& unfortunately his poor taste in language & method obscured the importance of what he had to say. Intellectually Morton leads them all—& this reminds me that some of my praise has reached him indirectly through Gamwellian channels—a Miss Spencer of Cambridge wrote him that her friend Mrs. Gamwell had a nephew who admired him & delighted in his company!

Tuesday dawned bright & fair—& as usual I hit the trail for Belknap's. We had made an engagement to visit McNeil in his Hell's Kitchen studio, & in due time we proceeded to keep it. Hell's Kitchen is the last remnant of the ancient slums—& by ancient I mean slums in which the denizens are not sly, cringing foreigners; but "tough" & energetic members of the superior Nordic stock—Irish, German, & American. The slinking Dago or Jew of the lower East Side is a strange, furtive animal—with the coming of his kind the Bowery ceased to be picturesque, for his crimes are of the treacherous secret kind—he uses poison instead of fists, automatic revolvers instead of bricks & blackjacks. But west of Broadway the old toughs have made their last stand. True, they are not the blithesome, omnipresent ruffians of yore—but in spite of their relative tameness they still make it very unpleasant for brass buttons & blue coats. Policemen are likely to have bricks dropped on their heads, or to be beaten by roving gangs—last year one was shot. Squalor is extreme, but not so odorous as in the foreign districts. Churches flourish—for all the natives are devout & violent Roman Catholics. It was odd to see slums in which the denizens are Nordic—with shapely faces, & often light hair & blue eyes. Nowadays we associate evil with dark foreign features—but McNeil assured us that any one of these cherubic blond youths could use language calculated to make strong men faint, & could on occasion beat up a cop or stab a plain-clothes-man with the utmost nonchalance & savoir faire. Irish are in the majority—the raw material of the Tammany vote. M<sup>c</sup>Neil lives on the fifth floor of a squalid tenement at 543 West 49<sup>th</sup> St., in a plain but neat apartment lined with books & pictures. He is writing a novel about Hell's Kitchen, & can obtain from his windows all the local colour—& odour—he can possibly use. Cordial was the entertainment accorded Belknap & me. M<sup>c</sup>Neil, though quiet, converses excellently; & after a time he conducted us on a walk through the teeming streets of the locality. Finally we returned to his flat, where he treated us to coffee & crackers & lent me a book of his which he thinks I might like— "The Lost Nation". I haven't read it yet, but I think it will prove clever in idea & careless in style. M<sup>c</sup>Neil should guard his English more closely.

Wednesday we formed a trio—that now indissoluble triumvirate of Belnapius, Mortonius, & Theobaldus. Dinner at Belknap's, then an expedition to the scenes & impressions of the past—the northwest corner of Manhattan Island where, only 12 miles from the teeming region of skyscrapers, still remains the last scrap of genuine *countryside* in the world's most populous borough. First—suburbs & survivals. At the corner of Broadway & 204<sup>th</sup> St., in a region building up with sad rapidity, stands the last Dutch farmhouse on Manhattan Island*—the Dyckman Cottage. Long ago did the last of the Dyckmans leave its homely shelter, but a society has preserved it as a museum; so that it still broods amidst its neat Dutch garden, its lawns, walks, & shrubs; white, solid, & comely as of yore, & furnished with appropriate articles. Its general outlines are not unlike those of an average New-England farmhouse of similar period, but many subtle differences are noticeable. The shape of the roof, the plan of the grounds, the doors whose upper & lower halves open independently, & the singular arrangement of the rooms, with Dutch ovens & a semi-subterranean "winter kitchen" reached by a flight of stairs so cramped that one must bend one's head to descend—all these things are distinctively of the Netherlands, & not found in our own English Colonial homesteads. About the premises was the most attractive *black cat* conceivable. I held him during most of my stay, & he assured me that he is descended from the very best cats of Amsterdam, his family having been purely Dutch except for one ancestor, Tomas Le Chat, who came from Brussells [*sic*] in 1596 & is said to have been the grandson of a noted cat of Paris. Leaving the Dyckman place, we set out for the wilds of the Inwood section—the narrow strip immediately bordering on Spuyten Duyvil creek, Manhattan's northern boundary. It lies, geographically, between Dyckman & 212th Sts., but aesthetically it is part of the immemorial past—of antique New-England, & of that Old England which is the mother of all placid beauty. Here is a forest primeval, with winding paths, gigantic trees, & not a mortal in sight. Suddenly, at a turn of the path, one sees far below in a valley the blue waters of Spuyten Duyvil, & of the Hudson beyond. On the banks are the huts & nets

---

*The Van Cortlandt Mansion is not on the island, but in the Bronx.

of fishers, & at small piers boats ride wistfully at anchor. The pastoral simplicity of the picture is beyond description—one would swear it was a quiet fishing village on the coast of Maine or Massachusetts. Another turn & we are in the ancient forest again. From the main path a byway leads—following it, we come upon a small farm where poultry-guarding dogs bark warningly at us. The illusion is perfect—we are in the agrestic past, the first of His Majesty's subjects to penetrate this Dutch region. As for the New-York of subways & skyscrapers—pouf! it is a myth; a dream! For us are the green fields & quaint farmsteads of the New Netherlands. Another turn, and lo! a silent, narrow, country road winding up from a valley concealed by a bend. It is rutted from farm-wagons, & bordered by stone walls & shrubbery. Here & there is a modest farmhouse—with lights just appearing in the windows, since evening is falling. Down in the valley, where so little is distinguishable, the village lights begin to twinkle. Night has come to Innwood, [sic] & the cows are home. The thrifty burghers are saying their prayers after the harvest toil, & their lights will not stay long. Longer, though, will burn those distant lights from the wooded crest beyond the village; for on those heights are His Majesty's soldiers, manning the breastworks of Fort George against the Continental rebels. God Save the King, & preserve his Dominions! One cannot see New-York from here—there is a milestone put up in 1769 on the Broad-Way, which says "12 miles to New-York"...... It was with reluctance that "The Three Musketeers" quitted this Arcadian spot. Heavy-footed, we walked through suburban streets to the Dyckman St. station of the Broadway subway line. A delightful half-moon shone, but shone sadly where steam-shovels rent the weeping fields to prepare cellars for future apartment houses. Let us hope that the Inwood forest may be acquired by the municipality as a park, before it shall have been desecrated by the vandal hand of progress & real-estate industry!

Thursday I remained indoors, reading & writing. I am reading voraciously—more in a week than I do in a month at home. Today—Friday—I have also stayed in. I have oceans of correspondence to attend to, & when Belknap is free I neglect it! He is just now occupied with collegiate cares—he entered Columbia yesterday—but tomorrow he & I will explore Van Cortlandt Park; possibly in the company of young Paul Livingston Keil, whom I previously neglected to look up, but to whom I have now dropped a card. Keil is a nice kid, but not very literary—which makes him of only moderate interest. He is religious, poor child! Tomorrow night I shall attend the B.P.C. meeting at Sheepshead Bay. Each member (or visitor) is supposed to read an original essay entitled "An Interesting Trip"—a subject whose schoolboyish immaturity makes me laugh. I don't know whether I'll write a serious essay or give 'em some kind of satirical spoof—maybe I'll copy some of the purple passages in this very epistle & save labour! Some of the clubites are tediously bourgeois—they make Mrs. Greene tired—but they are excellent & well-meaning, & Kleiner & Morton make the meetings worth attending. Mrs. G. isn't going—a business engagement serves her admirably as an excuse for escaping a dull evening.

Galpin has been "put wise" to the "Zara" hoax, & vows he was sincere in praising the piece. Now he knows that I wrote it, he is less enthusiastic about it—blessed little divvle! I wish he were here in N.Y., to share excursions with Belknap, Morton, & me—he will settle there permanently a year from next June, when he gets his A.M. at the University. Belknap, though, wants him to make it next June; & to study for the degree at Columbia. Alfredus & I correspond by return mail, as of yore—he is positively the greatest human being I have ever encountered or ever will encounter . . . . a fact no less apparent because of the merits of small Belknap. I wish they were both my sons! Recently I heard from young Lawrence, the Cleveland horror prodigy. He is very fluent & enthusiastic, but lacks the genius of either Galpinius or Belnapius. His letter shews a somewhat childish sentimentality, whilst his story—though splendidly ghoulish—is markedly immature in development, phraseology, & tonecolour. Among other things, it lacks a definite climax. None of us save Galpin gets a word from Loveman—he is deep in the preparation of his Bierce book, which is announced for early appearance.[6] Belknap & I may send him a spoofing telegram tomorrow—a night letter. I have written the hideous poet Clark Ashton Smith again—on re-reading his nightmarish sonnets I am almost inclined to agree with the overenthusiastic Alfredus when that child calls him "America's greatest living poet". Smith asked to see my stories, & I have sent him several—here's hoping he likes them. I wish I could get some of his ghoulish drawings—the kind I sent for you to see last month.

So the old Narragansett is waking up in memory of the days when it was Providence's finest! Good work! But for elegance it will have to go some to catch up with the Biltmore. No doubt it will continue to be chosen as the seat of flower-shows & the like, since it is so much a part of local life & history. In Providence the name "Narragansett" will always mean more than "Biltmore"—just as "Prov. Opera House" will always mean more than "Shubert-Majestic".

I am glad your finger has recovered, but sorry it incommoded you at all. Don't worry about *work*—the less anyone does, the better . . . . and I practice what I preach! Thanks for the extra underclothing suggestion—all I needed were stockings, & I now have them. The grey suit is welcome indeed—you ought to see how worn out that blue thing is! It is kind of Belknap not to be ashamed to have me with him in public when I wear that archaic rag-bag! My new hat goes finely with the grey suit—that's why I chose a grey shade—& when I wear my grey tie, it's quite unanimous except for shoes & stockings . . . . and a dusty road will soon make it perfectly unanimous! As for *overcoats*—brrr! . . . but I hate to think of overcoat weather!

About domestic overhauling—I shall certainly try to get rid of a lot of junk upon my return. Since I am leaving amateurdom, I will send oceans of old papers to Moe—who is having a renewed spasm of activity—or to my dear friend, opponent, & successor Fritter—who is at least as good as an ash dump. The current *United Amateur* is a bit interesting—the Haughton clique, hating to give me any credit, tried to suppress that Rhoades letter treating of the winning stories. It is due solely to the influence of Daas & Campbell that it was published. I am glad Rhoades thinks so well of my junk—we *Howard Phillipses* have to hang together! Little Longlet certainly deserved his honourable mention—he is a genuine artist, & the more I see of him the more I realise it. He was pleased at the honour he won.

About my "reform" anent the daylight question—I wouldn't expect too much after the stimulus of the trip & the constant & animated companionship of youth have faded. The good effects will no doubt remain more or less—but it takes a darned lot to make me able to do effective literary or revisory work in the glare of solar radiance. My creative thinking, at least at home, is more or less dependent on the genial Welsbach[7]—& the small, dark hours are just the proper time for spooks! However—time will tell. I doubt if it would be well to move the typewriter into the parlour, because (a) it's more expensive to heat, & (b) I need my library of books & papers around me. I can see, after a fashion, in my room—& the evenings are long in winter anyway. Winter—grrr! I hate to feel it coming! Hunter's Moon . . . Hallowe'en . . . . Bleak winds over the barren moors . . . . . End of the Harvesting . . . . . Cattle huddled in their byres . . . . The first snow . . . . The leafless trees sighing in the cold night . . . . ugh!

About my homecoming—A.E.P.G.'s programme will have a lot to do with that. I was delighted when she suggested the possibility of an escape to N.Y., & Mrs. Greene was positively transported! I only wish that you could join the gang—you'd sure like to meet Belknap & Morton. I want to hang on as long, at least, as A.E.P.G. does, & act as her guide to Gotham's wonders— I'll be freer for that work than anyone else, & my metropolitan knowledge is of the kind most useful to the sightseer. As my letters indicate, this is sure *some* burg—with interesting things of every conceivable variety.

I'll pack my Providence-bound merchandise safely enough—leave it to me! I'm not hurrying about it now, since I want the books available for consultation & exhibition as long as I'm here. Watch me knock those Blue-Pencil mediocrities cold tomorrow night by springing that 1567 book on 'em! The first thing I'll send home is my straw hat—which is remarkably well-preserved considering its continuous Clevelando-Noveboracan wear. Next will come the blue rags which were once a suit—just now I may need 'em occasionally on warm days. And last of all, immediately preceding my insignificant self, will be the literary loads—owned & borrowed. After I get back, I must rearrange shelf space—providing for an immediate library better suited to my present pursuits. At present, my books are arranged in conformity with the tastes of my later 'teens—with physics & chemistry usurping much space which might be allotted to literature & belles-lettres generally. I shall try to sell many books—if Belknap got $4.50 for a few college manuals, I ought to be able to make some sort of a trade with Gregory!

Oh, by the way—apropos of nothing—is my old grey wrap fit for another winter's wear? If not, I might pick up some sober monastic robes here cheaper than in Providence, & send 'em on by express. I'll let you decide. If memory plays no tricks, my pontifical vestments have a lot more fringe & lacework than the ordinances of the Holy Catholic Church provide for!

I hope this overgrown 22-page epistle won't bore you—or blind you! This is the sort of thing I shoot at Moe & Galpin—do you think I try their patience too severely? Probably I was incited, in this especial case, by your kind praise of my former descriptive communications; or perhaps by the excellent writing conditions created by a newly cleaned pen & a fresh bottle of ink. My old ink has almost spoiled—I find I make a mistake in purchasing large quantities. Henceforward I shall obtain 10-cent bottles, & obtain them often. Do you notice the superiority of this ink over that I have been using? Anyhow, it makes writing a darned sight easier for me!

But I must close—I enjoyed your letters immensely, & shall enjoy relating this whole visit to you at length when I see you. Better come along with A.E.P.G.—it's less of an effort than it seems, especially if you take a parlour-car! I have transmitted your regards to my benign hostess, & in turn transmit her most affectionate regards toward yourself. She has also sent you her regards in a night-letter to A.E.P.G. anent the eagerly anticipated visit. Hoping, then, that you can manage to survive this document; I have y$^e$ honour to subscribe myself as y$^r$ most aff: nephew & ob$^t$ Serv$^t$

H P L

P.S. Thanks for the various amusing & appropriate cuttings. Anent the straw hat cartoon—I've seen several battered lids along the streets lately, probably the work of toughs who knocked belated specimens from the heads of the unprogressive!

## Notes

1. HPL used this incident as the basis for his story "The Hound," written in October 1922.

2. "Times change, and we change with them." An ancient Latin saying.

3. Arthur Richman (1886–1944), *A Serpent's Tooth* (1924), produced by John Golden; starring Howard Freeman, and W. Graham Browne, and Leslie Howard.

4. Ed. George Saintsbury. HPL ultimately did acquire a copy.

5. New Anvik was a "little village" that HPL and his boyhood friends Harold and Chester Munroe erected in a vacant lot adjacent to 598 Angell Street. The name was derived from a boys' novel by Kirk Munroe. See HPL to the Gallomo, 3 September 1920; *Letters to Alfred Galpin* 95.

6. HPL refers to Loveman's edition of *Twenty-one Letters of Ambrose Bierce.*

7. Welsbach was a manufacturer of electric lighting fixtures.

[23]      [ALS] [HPL to AEPG]

259 Parkside—<br>
Oct<sup>r</sup> 3, 1922

My dear Daughter:—

           I take my pen in hand to shoot off a word prior to your felicitous advent to this thriving suburb of West Providence. Believe me, you've got *some* welcome awaiting you! I scarcely need say how glad I shall be, but it would not be out of place to delineate the ecstatic enthusiasm with which my benevolent hostess anticipates your arrival. She has hung new curtains at most of the windows; purchased additional plants, with pedestals to hold them, for the garnishing of the rooms; & will, upon *definite* news of your coming, obtain a new double mattress to adapt her now single parlour couch for two tenants. When your journey seemed doubtful, she was visibly depressed; & now that it seems certain, her spirits have soared to the empyrean. Not many guests, I am sure, are so eagerly hailed; & you should feel duly flattered by so great a tribute to your personality! Mrs. G's only regret is that L.D.C. cannot accompany you—a regret which I share. See if you can't induce her at the last moment to come along—parlour-car travel is not at all strenuous, I am told.

           Let me know, by letter or telegram, just when you will arrive—& try to select a train arriving at the Grand Central instead of the Pennsylvania Station. The latter is not a terminal, & consequently is more confusing as regards meetings. At the G.C. one knows on which track a train will arrive. I will certainly be on hand as an infallible guide; & if the hour is in the evening, Mrs. G. will be there also. But don't select a late train on that account—I can serve just as well alone, for by this time I know New-York better than she does herself. I guide little Belknap around his native town on all occasions, & we never get lost!

           About calling on my revered relatives—I fear that would be rather a bore; since so far as I know, they are prim, pious, conventional, unimaginative folk—the sort who get so fearfully on my nerves. Still, since they are kinsfolk, it might do no harm to look them up some rainy day when there's nothing else to do—I'll leave that till you get here, & perhaps we'll give 'em a duty call together.[1]

           Anent Bush—he lately sent me a nice cheque, & agreed to pay my highest price for guaranteed personal service—$1.00 per *8* lines. That's something like! It will be easier to tackle his bally nonsense when I reflect that each 8-line stanza brings me in one solid iron man! For Mortonian work he'll pay $1.00 per 16 l. Speaking of Jim Ferdy—he recently had a letter from his mother, in which she said that a friend of hers, Miss Mary Spencer of Cambridge, had a friend named Mrs. Gamwell, who had a nephew who was visiting N.Y. & taking great pleasure in Mortonian companionship! How's that for diffusion of news? Only a congenital detestation of the trite prevents me from uttering the venerable platitude anent the microscopic dimensions of this terraqueous globe!

I trust you continue to enjoy the village gossip of Higginson's L & L.[2] Too bad Mrs. Foster doesn't appreciate Boston—it's so deliciously quaint, artificial, & out-of-the-way! You'll find New-York more like Providence— quite civilised, in fact, for its size. Read my latest epistle to L.D.C. for current data anent the big town—I believe I therein chronicled most events up to last Friday evening.

Continuing that chronicle—Saturday I dined at Kid Belknap's & we went up to Van Cortlandt Park, near the New York–Yonkers boundary. Here stands the ancient stone mansion of the Van Cortlandts, built in 1748, & still in perfect preservation as a museum a la Pendleton House. Just as the Dyckman Cottage (vide epistolam Clarkianam) reflects the life of the Dutch middle class, so does the Van Cortlandt Mansion reflect that of the Dutch gentry— the lordly patroons with their manorial grants from the Dutch West India Company & the Holland States-General. Jacobus Van Cortlandt was a gentleman of taste, & it was a delight to linger about the stately rooms of his tasteful abode. The parlour is furnished in the English manner, but other rooms reveal the Netherlandish origin of their inhabitants—the dining room has captivating tiles, & rows of plates & steins; whilst an upstairs room, wainscoted & provided with a huge fireplace, transports one for the nonce to Amsterdam itself. We neglected to get post cards of this appealing place—a deficiency which we will amend when you & I go thither next week.

In the evening I attended a meeting of the Blue Pencil Club at the Dench home, on Sheepshead Bay. Mrs. Greene did not attend—she is frightfully bored by the commonplace bourgeois members of the club, despite their determined & occasionally fawning efforts to hang on to her as long as they can. I am more tolerant, since I regard all human beings as futile & pitiful creatures—anyway, Morton & Kleiner make the meetings worth attending. There were about 20 present—& I don't see how Dench ever packed them all into his sardine-box of a bungalow. The literary subject assigned by the director in advance amused me considerably—since it was that hackneyed old standby of the fifth grade—"An Interesting Trip". At first I thought I wouldn't bother with the thing at all; but later I wavered, & at the last moment concocted something in haste—mainly a transcript of what I wrote L.D.C. about the Flatbush churchyard, the Dyckman Cottage, & the Inwood forest. I cast it in 18th century prose after the manner of The Spectator, & stuck on a Latin motto from Lucretius for good measure. Lucretius is very well represented in this house at the moment, & all due to my Alfredus-child; who gave an original Latin copy to me, & a translation (by his learned English

professor William Ellery Leonard) to Mrs G. The piece was very well received—in fact, the audience told me I would have won the prize had not my
lack of membership made me ineligible. In another competition—a general-
information question-match devised by Morton & modelled after the ancient
spelling-match—the non-membership barrier did not exist, & I had the honour & good-fortune to win. After 16 questions everyone had tripped up save
old Grandpa Theobald! The meeting lasted till 2 a.m., & I did not hit the hay
till 4—a very Providence-like relapse!

Sunday little Belknap came over here for dinner, & we had a delightful
stroll through the "Old Fashioned Garden" in Prospect Park. Belknap is a
great kid—I am sure you will find him incomparably likeable. He is dark,
small, radiantly handsome, tastefully dressed, & infinitely appealing. He is
gentle, & a trifle bashful, without being in the least effeminate; & his taste,
genius, & scholarship mark him out as a coming literary figure. He is very retiring, & has almost no close friends & no correspondents except Galpin,
Loveman, myself, & our newly-discovered titan Clark Ashton Smith. He does
not move in local amateur club circles, since he shares Mrs. Greene's boredom at the mediocrities forming the B.P.C. Morton & Kleiner, though, he
likes exceedingly—although he does not see them except with me. He is a
poet, dreamer, & fantaisiste; & shares my tendency toward nightmares. Sometimes his nocturnal screams are so loud that his mother has to awake him.
The kid is now 21, though he looks about 15.[3] He is trying his best to grow a
Poesque moustache—at least that is what his mother says. I thought at first
that he had merely been eating Hershey's Chocolate! Galpin & Belknap have
become the closest of correspondents. Being utter antitheses, they are infinitely congenial. Two delightful little divvles, bless their hearts! I hope they
can meet in person next year. Belknap has transferred from N.Y.U. to Columbia College, & is urging Alfredus to transfer from U. of Wis. & take his
M.A. at Columbia. By the way—Saturday Belknap showed me over the Columbia campus after our return from Van Cortlandt Park. It is a fascinating
place, crowning a park-like & precipitous Acropolis known as Morningside-
Heights. From a neighbouring telegraph office we sent a night-letter chiding
Loveman for his epistolary neglect of us—he telegraphed a reply the next
day, saying that his silence was due to hard work on his books—letters of
Ambrose Bierce & critique on the writings of Edgar Saltus[4] . . . . . But I ramble. Let us return to Sunday—when, as I said, Belknap was over, & we
strolled in Prospect Park. After dinner—at 3 o'clock—Morton & Kleiner
came over; & all hands took a walk among the venerable antiquities of Flatbush. In the graveyard I chipped another piece from a hoary tombstone . . . I
must summon from their deeps the ghouls of midnight! Later the gang had to
split—Morton & Kleiner sought a lunch room, whilst I guided small Longlet
to the nearest Interborough Subway on Nostrand Ave. The kid has a strange
idea that the Interborough makes better time than the B.R.T.—though I infi-

nitely prefer the latter because of its immense & spacious cars.[5] The cars of N.Y. are all fascinating—some of them are probably the *oldest* in use in the United States . . . . . even including Boston, with the possible exception of those pieced-together horse-cars that rattle out Huntington Avenue.

Monday—yesterday—I was mostly indoors reading & writing, though I took a village shopping stroll with Mrs. G. in the early evening—ordering some stuff in expectation of your visit. Today I have been cleaning up reams of accumulated correspondence—though most of the stupid amateurs will be dropped from my list.

Now for the love of Pegāna *come,* & stay *as long as possible!* You'll have a record-breaking welcome, & Mrs. Greene surpasses all precedent as a cordial, congenial, & considerate hostess. As for the sights of the town—I'll show you all of 'em with bells on! So pack up, tell Mrs. Foster to go to Halifax, N.S., & meet me Friday afternoon in the Grand Central! So long!

Yr most aff: grandfather & ob[t] Serv[t]

H P L

P.S. Mrs. G has just come in—she sends all sorts of regards, & begs you not to fail to show up on Friday!

[P.]P.S. Don't forget—don't buy any hat or coat till you get here. Mrs. G. can put you next to all sorts of special bargains & opportunities to get really high-grade & artistic stuff.

## Notes

1. It is not clear what relations HPL is referring to. He mentions a paternal aunt, Emma Jane (Lovecraft) Hill (1847–1925), wife of Isaac C. Hill (1849–1932), living in Pelham, NY, in Westchester County, just north of New York City (*SL* 1.5).

2. LDC must have been reading Henry Lee Higginson's *Letters and Journals* (1921).

3. Long (b. 1901) was in fact twenty-two at this time. HPL had actually written "22," but then crossed it out and wrote "21."

4. Loveman's study of Edgar Saltus was scheduled to be published, but never appeared.

5. HPL cites some of the overlapping subway lines in New York City: the Interborough Rapid Transit Company (IRT), the Brooklyn Rapid Transit Company (BRT), and the Independent Subway System (IND). The BRT went bankrupt in 1919 and became the Brooklyn-Manhattan Transit Company (BMT).

[24]      [ANS postcard][1] [HPL to LDC]

[Postmarked Brooklyn, N.Y.,
7 October 1922]

Will write in a day or two—just now I'm wading in *Bush!* Hope A.E.P.G. told you all about the sights of N.Y. . . . . . wish you could come—I'd be careful of your voice! ¶ Going to Writer's Club tonight—great institution—will tell you about it. Later B.P.C. & Sunrise meetings. Did A E P G tell you of my 12-mile walk at & after the Columbus Day picnic? Great stuff! Will be heading toward hibernation in a couple of weeks or so—don't despair!

Yr aff nephew & obt Servt

H P L

P.S. Overcoat here safely. Thanks!

## Notes

1. *Front:* Drawing Room / Van Cortlandt Museum.

[25]     [ANS postcard][1] [HPL and others to LDC]

[Postmarked Brooklyn, N.Y.,<br>8 October 1922]

Showing A.E.P.G. the big town! Better come along & join the party. Recd. your interesting letter & will answer soon. Be sure to see Robert Mantell—in "Richard III", if possible.[2] A.E.P.G. saw art museum yesterday—wish you could!

Yr aff nephew & obt Servt H.P.L.

S.H.G.
A.E.P.G. & L: Theobald, Jun.
Frank Belknap Long, Jr.
James F. Morton, Jr.

## Notes

1. *Front:* Papyrus Capital—Egyptian, XXX Dynasty. The Metropolitan Museum of Art.
2. Robert B. Mantell (1854–1928), Scottish-born Shakespearean actor. HPL recalled seeing Mantell and Fritz Leiber, Sr., in several Shakespeare plays performed at the Providence Opera House (*SL* 5.350).

[26]     [ANS postcard][1] [HPL and others to LDC]

[Postmarked Brooklyn, N.Y.,<br>12 October 1922]

Have been wearing A.E.P.G. out! Today the following:

Fraunces' Tavern
Cunard Bldg.
Museum Nat. Hist.
Van Cortlandt Mansion—(vide over)
Columbia College
Dinner at Belknap's

And more on subsequent days! This is the life—better come & join the gang!
Will write soon.—THEOBALDVS

| A.E.P.G. | Frank B. Long, Jr. |
|---|---|
| S.H.G. | Mrs. F. B. Long. |

## Notes

1. *Front:* Van Cortlandt House.

# 1923

[27]     [ANS postcard][1] [HPL to LDC]

[Postmarked Boston, Mass.,
9 February 1923]

Did Royall Mansion at Medford yesterday afternoon. Great! Hub meeting fine—stayed at Parker–Miniter's—today Salem & Marblehead, then back to Boston & dine with Cole.

Yr aff nephew & obt Servt  H P L

*Notes*

1. *Front:* State House, Beacon Hill, Boston.

[28]     [ANS postcard][1] [HPL to LDC]

[Postmarked Salem, Mass.,
9 February 1923]

Where can you beat this architecture? Having great time in archaic Salem. Now for Marblehead!

Yr aff nephew & obt Servt  H P L

*Notes*

1. *Front:* Salem Court House.

[29]     [ANS postcard][1] [HPL to LDC]

[Postmarked Boston, Mass.,
10 February 1923]

Here's a house that could serve well for some amateur journalists—especially of Columbus, Ohio.[2] ¶ Revelling in the past, but homeward bound now. I'll see you before you see this!

Yr aff nephew & obt Servt

H P L

*Notes*

1. *Front:* The Old Spite House, Marblehead, Mass.

2. A "spite house" is a house deliberately built to block a view or in an ugly manner to irritate neighbors. The Old Spite House in Marblehead was built in 1716 by Thomas

Wood. HPL was at this time having disputes with amateur journalists in Columbus, especially the Woodbees led by Ida C. Haughton.

[30]      [ANS postcard][1] [HPL to LDC]

[Postmarked Boston, Mass.,
12 April 1923]

Just blew in—the old village looks placid in the sunset! Trip uneventful—I dozed most of the way. Wish I didn't have this infernal overcoat! Don't upset th' old room too much!
Yr aff: nephew & obt Servt  H P L

*Notes*

1. *Front:* Faneuil Hall, Boston.

[31]      [ANS postcard][1] [HPL to LDC]

[Postmarked Salem, Mass.,
13 April 1923]

Meeting rather good.* Was glad in evening that I took overcoat! Old Salem today—but have left overcoat at Miniter–Parker domicile. Fine day—& the antique realms look as well as ever. More later.
Yr aff nephew & obt Servt  H P L

*Notes*

1. *Front:* Old Narbonne House, Salem, Mass.

[32]      [ANS postcard][1] [HPL to LDC]

[Postmarked Haverhill, Mass.,
14 April 1923]

See how this old bimbo looked before he trained the trick alfalfa on his chin!
Yr aff nephew & obt Servt  H P L

*Notes*

1. *Front:* Birthplace of John Greenleaf Whittier.

---

*But Cole wasn't there!

[33]     [ANS postcard]¹ [HPL and Edgar J. Davis to LDC]

[Postmarked Newburyport, Mass.,
15 April 1923]

Behold the quaintness amidst which I & my great-grandson are sojourning!

Yr aff: nephew & obt Servt

H P L

And the other—

E. J. Davis

Notes

1. *Front:* State Street from Charter Street, Newburyport, Mass.

[34]     [ANS postcard]¹ [HPL to AEPG]

[Postmarked Marblehead, Mass.,
6 July 1923]

Hotels all exorbitant! Leslie $26.00 a week up—Oceanside (on the neck) $35.00 uniform—Glover Inn $25.00 uniform. ¶ But in a quaint & modest house on a hillside on Front St. lives old Mrs. Bixby, widow of the artist who designed the Town Seal of Marblehead, who will give a plain but nice room for *$8.00* per week. Address—126 Front St., Marblehead. ¶ Yr aff nephew & obt Servt H P L

P.S. TRAGEDY! I've lost my fountain pen!

Notes

1. *Front:* Old North Congregational Church, Marblehead, Mass.

[35]     [ANS postcard]¹ [HPL and Sonia H. Greene to LDC]

[Postmarked Providence, R.I.,
17 July 1923]

See Grandpa's visage on t'other side—I'm almost that bald now! Summering at the Pier—sounds well, but in truth the bally place is a half desert waste!

Yr aff nephew & obt Servt

H P L

I wish you were with us.

Sonia.

Notes

1. *Front:* Old Man's Face, Point Judith, Narragansett Pier, R.I.

[36]     [ANS postcard][1] [HPL to LDC]

[Postmarked Boston, Mass.,
13 August 1923]

Nearly exhausted Moe showing him Salem, Marblehead, & Boston, but he is still alive & on the way to N.Y. & civilisation. I am going to Portsmouth N.H. tomorrow—home that night or later—may write again. Moe is a fine fellow—wish he could have stayed longer.

Yr aff nephew & obt Servt  H P L

[P.S.] Mrs. Renshaw didn't show up.
[P.P.S.] Saw Moe's family in Boston
[P.P.P.S.] Moe said you & A E P G were the most interesting persons he met

*Notes*

1. *Front:* Bunker Hill Monument, Charlestown, Mass.

[37]     [ANS postcard][1] [HPL and James F. Morton to LDC]

[Postmarked Marblehead, Mass.,
15 September 1923]

Well, here we are! You simply must see this place! And this time I have a sage companion whom I can't fatigue! Meeting excellent—another one tomorrow. Don't know when I'll be home, but you'll see me Tuesday anyway. Yr. aff. nephew & obt Servt

H P L

May I join in sending greetings? I look forward to meeting you next week.

James F. Morton, Jr.

*Notes*

1. *Front:* The Old Spite House, Marblehead, Mass.

[38]     [ANS postcard][1] [HPL and Sonia H. Greene to LDC]

[Postmarked Boston, Mass.,
27 November 1923]

Having great time in Marblehead. Tomorrow Cambridge, Medford, Isaac Royall mansion &c. Home *Thursday,* when you are commanded to attend a Thanksgiving dinner with the undersigned.—Grandpa

and S H G.

*Notes*

1. *Front:* Old Lafayette House, Marblehead, Mass.

# 1924

[39]     [ANS postcard][1] [HPL to LDC]

[Postmarked Brooklyn, N.Y.,
4 March 1924]

See the Gothic! Arrived safely—& great literary talk is in the air! Miss Tuck-er,[2] who is extremely pleasant & apparently quite influential, thinks she may be able to get me a *permanent literary position* soon!! ¶ Philadelphia tomorrow—dream of Colonial magnificence! Wait till you get kidnapped & taken all over these routes! ¶ S H G sends all kinds of regards & says she'll MAKE you come here!

Yr aff nephew & obt Servt  H P L

P.S. Spent all morning at *Reading Lamp* office—more later.
[P.]P.S. Send along all the "Corners and Characters"![3]

*Notes*

1. *Front:* St. Patrick's Cathedral, New York.

2. Gertrude Estelle Tucker (1885–1949), an editor associated with *The Reading Lamp*.

3. "Corners and Characters of Rhode Island" was a long-running column in the [Providence] *Evening Bulletin* written mostly by George D. Laswell.

[40]     [ANS postcard][1] [HPL and Sonia H. Greene to LDC]

[Postmarked Philadelphia, Pa.,
5 March 1924]

Love and best wishes from S.H.G.

Here be the dead ones—just like the dead ones that still inhabit this passè but captivating ex metropolis. Queer place, & worth a good tour—we took it in via rubberneck bus—folder of which I'll send later. You ought to see this stuff—you must make this side trip after you get to N.Y.

Yr aff nephew & Obt Servt
H P L

*Notes*

1. *Front:* Old Swede's Church, Philadelphia, Pa.

[41]      [ANS postcard][1] [HPL to LDC]

[Postmarked Philadelphia, Pa.,
5 March 1924]

Here is a great old building that they don't show on the rubberneck tours. In an ineffably picturesque locality, far back from the street & reached by fascinating court betwixt ancient buildings. Kleiner thought it especially appealing when here, & once sent me a picture of it. Let's see all the Corners & Characters that Laswell grinds out!

Yr aff nephew & obt Servt  H P L

*Notes*

1. *Front:* Carpenters' Hall, Philadelphia, Pa.

[42]      [ANS postcard][1] [HPL and Sonia H. Greene to LDC]

[Postmarked Philadelphia, Pa.,
5 March 1924]

More corners & characters! Great old colonial town with many houses (see over) like those of New England & New York, but others (vide travelogue to come) absolutely distinctive, & moulded by German & Quaker influences. Yr aff nephew & obt Servt

H P L

Hope to see you in New York soon. S.H.G.

*Notes*

1. *Front:* "Cliveden," The Chew Mansion, Germantown, Philadelphia, Pa.

[43]      [ANS postcard][1] [HPL to LDC]

[Postmarked Philadelphia, Pa.,
5 March 1924]

Here's a house older than any which Laswell can get to! Older than any in Boston, though surpassed in age by the earliest houses of the Salem-Marblehead region. Got here Tuesday, spending Wednesday lapping up antiquities. Back to N Y tonight—then some museums—& then, let's hope, the job! Big letter will follow—also a set of Philadelphia pictures &c. Yr aff nephew & obt Servt  H P L

*Notes*

1. *Front:* William Penn Cottage in Fairmount Park.

[44]     [AHT] [HPL to LDC]

259 Parkside Ave.

Brooklyn, N.Y.

March 9, 1924

My dear Aunt Lillian:—

I need not say how glad I was to receive your delightful letter and the accompanying matter. But pray don't feel lonesome, since you are most certainly coming right along hither yourself! Bless my old bones! Dost fancy the Old Gentleman would transfer the family seat without sending for his first-born daughter? You will feel better and more active here—I wish you could behold Grandpa this week, getting up regularly in the daytime, hustling briskly about, and even being able to replace a vast amount of facial tweezer technique with honest, simple, and rapid gilletting. And all this with a prospect of regular literary work—my first real job—in the offing!

Meanwhile—and here prepare for revolutionary news—there is no need to worry about my securing an adequate room, or being well taken care of (doddering patriarch that I am) until you arrive. 259 Parkside is pretty homelike with the fine Colonial secretary cleared out and devoted to my use, and will be still more so when all my things—and yourself—reach here.

By this time the drift of this ponderous epistle will have begun to make itself clear. The selection of 259 Parkside as a *permanent* residence, rallying-point, and successor to 454 and 598 is in truth the only maturely logical and thoroughly common-sense solution of the problem created when finance disrupts the Old Homestead and forces aged Theobald to "give over" his listless midnight mooning and helpless hermitage for a more active life.

That more active life, to one of my temperament, demands many things which I could dispense with when drifting sleepily and inertly along, shunning a world which exhausted and disgusted me, and having no goal but a phial of cyanide when my money should give out. I had formerly meant to follow this latter course, and was fully prepared to seek oblivion whenever cash should fail or sheer ennui grow too much for me; when suddenly, nearly three years ago, our benevolent angel S.H.G. stepped into my circle of consciousness and began to combat that idea with the opposite one of effort, and the enjoyment of life through the rewards which effort will bring.

At the time, this doctrine seemed to me singularly impracticable; for how could I ever maintain—or even begin—a programme of activity and achievement when engulfed by the uninspiring seclusion surviving from a weak and nerve-racked childhood and youth? How, I wondered, could anyone so sensitive to environment ever keep up and apply himself to a career of genuine labour without the constant stimulus of vigorous, understanding, and sympathetic literary companionship—the companionship which adds to an enlivening energy the rarer and more potent boon of perfect psychological comprehension?

Such were my reflections—reflections all the more marked when Magnolia, N.Y., etc. showed me how marvellously I actually did rally in response to companionship of the right kind; companionship which I saw no way of securing permanently as the incentive to an active life, and which therefore only seemed to emphasise the difficulty of breaking away from the tentacles of ingrained inertia and oblivion-seeking.

But meanwhile—egotistical as it sounds to relate it—it began to be apparent that I was not alone in finding psychological solitude more or less of a handicap. A detailed intellectual and aesthetic acquaintance since 1921, and a three-months visit in 1922 wherein congeniality was tested and found perfect in an infinity of ways, furnished abundant proof not only that S.H.G. is the most inspiring and encouraging influence which could possibly be brought to bear on me, but that she herself had begun to find me more congenial than anyone else, and had come to depend to a great extent on my correspondence and conversation for mental contentment and artistic and philosophical enjoyment. Being, like me, highly individualised; she found average minds only a source of grating and discomfort, and average people only a bore to escape from—so that in our letters and discussions we were assuming more and more the position of two detached and dissenting secessionists from the bourgeois *milieu;* a source of encouragement to each other, but fatigued to depression by the stolid grey surface of commonplaceness on all sides and relieved only by such isolated points of light as Sonny Belknap, Mortonius, Loveman, Alfredus, Kleiner, and the like.

S.H.G. was not tardy, I believe, in mentioning to you and A.E.P.G. sundry phases of her side of this mutual indispensability; but as a follower of the unsentimental tradition, reluctant to be spoofed about a matter which was truly more rationally psychological than sentimental, I was naturally more conservative in giving estimates of my side—although of course I freely extolled the revivifying effects of my Magnolia and Parkside visits, and of S.H.G.'s various visits to the Providence or Eastern New-England area.

With a congeniality so preponderant, and having such a vital bearing on the progress, activity, and contentment of those concerned, one might well wonder why some permanent programme of propinquity was not arranged over a year and a half ago. Radical events, however, do not develop hastily; no matter how sudden their conscious and immediate planning, or their final occurrence, may seem to be. You know Theobaldian reserve, Theobaldian conservatism, and Theobaldian adherence to the old order of things until some *deus ex machina* roughly descends to override all indecision and precipitate an abrupt turn of affairs. In this case finance, pessimistic weighing of all life against cyanidic oblivion, sheer inertia, reticence, and a blind clinging to the hibernatory past as represented by uncommercial daytime sleeping at 598, all united to maintain a listless *status-quo.* Then dawned the inevitable need of doing something definite—the need to "get up and get" industrially, or to make good my ancient plan of shuffling off to a Swan Point subterranean repose.[1] The old sleep was over, and unless I wished to face a new and voluntarily eternal sleep I must secure the settled and bracing environment which can electrify a fat, ambitionless, and drowsing senile shuffler into a real man and professionally capable entity.

New York! Of course! Where else can one be alive when he has no vitality of his own and needs the magic spur of external inducement to active life and effective toil? And Parkside? Seemingly sudden, yet where else should one go when that is the seat of the greatest encouragement, inspiration, and congeniality? A "room" somewhere might be all very well—but how stupid to accept clumsy makeshifts when a real *home* was waiting, with all the care, kindred taste, regard, and incentives for waging the battle of life that a weary, sensitive, and otherwise spiritless Old Gentleman might wish? Of course there is always the financial question—bogie of the bourgeois—which naturally deferred any suggestions of mine till it was rationally laid to rest amidst the full, free, logical, and sanely un-attitudinized discussion which preceded the move. Parkside was there, and would be paid for just the same whether or not shared by the aged Theobald. That same Theobald, moreover, would come not as a burden but as the filler of a lonely void and the bearer of aesthetic and intellectual congeniality to one who had not found this quality in others. More still—and this was his own point—he would of course contribute to the common fund as much as he safely could . . . and easily as much as he would otherwise pay for a "room"; adopting a more responsible basis when warranted by substantial earnings. In short—for artificial prides and hackneyed notions was substituted the rare and revered principle of comfortable adjustment and intelligent co-operation.

At this point—or earlier—or a minute later—you will no doubt ask why I did not mention this entire matter before. S.H.G. herself was anxious to do so, and if possible to have both you and A.E.P.G. present at the event about to be described. But here again appeared Old Theobald's hatred of sentimental spoofing, and of that agonisingly indecisive "talking over" which radical steps always prompt among mortals, yet which really exceeds the fullest necessary quota of sober and analytical appraisal and debate. Wandering discussion, incredulous exclamations, sighs of "I never would have thought it", and all that sort of thing are infinitely exhausting to a sensitive personality after calm reason has had its leisurely reflection and expression, and made its logical decision. It hardly seemed to me that, in view of my well-known temperament, anyone could feel even slightly hurt by a decisive and dramatic gesture sweeping away the barnacles of timidity and of blindly reactionary holding-back. The step, once well considered, was for each an individualistic one; and the news will be broken to the amateur circle only after this more important message has been completed. Even Little Belknap yet remains to be called up by his Old Grandpa!

So, epochal and stupefying as it sounds, (pray don't faint, or I shall feel that all the preceding paragraphs of artistic preamble have gone for naught!) the unbelievable is a reality. Old Theobald is a householder at last, and (hold in readiness the smelling-salts) a bona-fide partner with that most inspiring, congenial, tasteful, intelligent, solicitous, and devoted of mortals and co-workers, S.H.G., in the venerable and truly classical institution of Holy Matrimony!

### (RECESS FOR RECOVERY OF POISE)

Yes, my daughter, the Old Gentleman has brought you a new mother at last! Gradual and sudden at once . . . for backed as it was by a mature evolution of years, and long dreamed of vaguely, academically, and objectively as a possibility for some remote future, the imminent certainty scarcely crystallised till the final week; when the actual "brass tacks" of moving and settling came up with a coldly realistic insistence not to be denied.

After the cataclysmic springing of the *idea,* the *events* cannot but be somewhat anticlimactic to relate—yet it were barbarous to frustrate the natural demands of human curiosity.

I missed the 10:09 train Sunday, but got the 11:09, and after a pleasing journey blew into the Grand Central (instead of the Pennsylvania as planned . . . . . . I sent a corrective telegram) at 3:40 p.m.; there met by S.H.G. We at once proceeded to 259, where Miss Tucker of *The Reading Lamp* was a guest, and there the whole programme and future were zestfully discussed with an intensely interested and sympathetic auditor. Miss T. is of old Baltimore stock, and is a figure of much influence in N.Y. literary circles. (Sample of her stationery enclosed.) She has taken a most keen liking to S.H.G.L., and will do anything she can to promote the progress of all connected with that prepossessing deity. She believes that my stories, and my essays as exemplified by letters to S.H., are of singular merit; and is considering most seriously their publication in book form. Meanwhile she has every expectation of getting me a job in some publishing house—a job which my newly-acquired helpmate will see that I reach each morning punctually and in good order. The chicken dinner was superb—as all S.H. dinners are—and I was not too fatigued by the week's efforts to appreciate it. Post-prandial discussion was congenial and appropriate, and included Miss Tucker's interested and not altogether unamused perusal of Friend Henneberger's epistles. (It's all right, by the way, about that telegram stuff. Henny has his manuscript by this time, gawd bless him!)

The following morning—the eventful *third of March*—all three started out for a busy day . . . . busy? Believe an Old Married Man! The morning was spent at the *Reading Lamp* office, where Miss T. got some idea of what I can do at various literary tasks. Then S.H. and I went to a Dago joint in thirty-somethingth street and absorbed a fine *spaghetti* dinner. After that—and here note the dawn of decisive events—we beat it by subway to the Brooklyn borough hall, where we took out a marriage license with all the cool nonchalance and easy *savoir faire* of old campaigners . . . . . migosh! but you'd ought to have saw me! Brigham Young annexing his 27th, or King Solomon starting in on the second thousand, had nothing on me for languid fluency and casual conversation! The bimbo that handed out the papers has been to Providence, and is quite an admirer of Waterman St. . . . . . . which he knew by location but not by name.

Then for the ring! S.H. having discovered that plain gold bands are old stuff, we gave the once-over to some rather more contemporary baubles of kindred import. Through business connexions S.H. obtained some reduced quotations at a small shop, and (although she first selected a white gold trifle of inexpensive aspect) I induced her to blow in eighty-five fish for something worth one hundred fifty—platinum with twenty-four diamond chips—whose expense I shall defray (as befits an arrogant and masterful spouse) from my next Hennebergian influx. Yes—there was a nifty li'l' case, and everything!

We now prepared for the historic spectacle of the execution; wishing to face Fate sprucely and jauntily, and die game! S.H. patronised a manicure in order that the eighty-five-berry-worth-one-hundred-fifty finger-hoop might be lived up to, and I condescended to get both a haircut and a shoe-shine. Then, having reconvened, we hopped a taxi (real sports—don't care how much they spend!) and proceeded to the *Place de la Guillotine.*

And what was the place? A hades of a question to ask an old British Colonial ever faithful to His Majesty, King George the Third! Where was it that Richard, Lord Howe, Admiral of His Majesty's fleet, worshipped from 1776 to 1783—and where H. R. H. the Prince of Wales (later the Prince Regent and finally King George IV) was a communicant whilst a midshipman with the fleet? Where, indeed, can one find most strongly Old Theobald's traditional and mythological background—a background intensified by the marriage of his parents in Boston's venerable St. Paul's? (1820) Yes—of course you guess'd it! St. Paul's Chapel, Broadway and Vesey St., built in 1766, and like the Providence 1st Baptist design'd after St. Martin's-in-the-Fields! GOD SAVE THE KING! (Booklet under separate cover.)

In the Church St. parsonage we hunted up the resident curate, Father George Benson Cox, who upon inspecting the license was more than willing to perform the soldering process. Having brought no retinue of our own, we availed ourselves of the ecclesiastical force for purposes of witnessing—a force represented in this performance by one Joseph Gorman and one Joseph G. Armstrong, who I'll bet is the old boy's grandson although I didn't ask him. With actors thus arranged, the show went off without a hitch. Outside, the ancient burying ground and graceful Wren steeple; within, the glittering cross and traditional vestments of the priest—colourful legacies of OLD ENGLAND'S gentle legendry and ceremonial expression. The full service was read; and in the aesthetically histrionic spirit of one to whom elder custom, however intellectually empty, is sacred, I went through the various motions with a stately assurance which had the stamp of antiquarian appreciation if not of pious sanctity. S. H., needless to say, did the same—and with an additional grace. Then fees, thanks, congratulations, inspections of Colonial pictures in Father Cox's study, and farewells! Two are one. Another bears the name of Lovecraft. A new household is founded!

We had intended to depart for Philadelphia at once, but the fatigue of the preceding heavy programme prompted us to defer this melilunar pilgrimage till the morrow. On that day we notified some of S.H.'s non-amateur friends of the change, and received their ecstatic congratulations; good Mrs. Moran, down-the-hall neighbour and mother of the stamp-collecting and erstwhile cat-owning boy, being especially delighted. The name "Greene" on the door directory and mail box was suitably transmuted to "Lovecraft", and the *nouveau regime* in general given a visible and appropriate recognition. Incidentally—mail, express, and freight destined for this domicile need no longer be "in care of" anybody! Anything addressed to "H. P. Lovecraft" or (miraculous and unpredictable appellation) "Mrs. H. P. Lovecraft" will henceforward reach its recipient without additional formalities.

Tuesday afternoon we did get started for Philadelphia, leaving from the magnificently Roman Pennsylvania Station which I missed the Sunday before by missing the 10:09 Wash'n Express. Of the details of the trip, and of the unique personality of sprawling and antique Philadelphia, I shall say more in the travelogue with which I shall answer A.E.P.G.'s appreciated letter. Here, lest I bore you with a superposition of treatise upon treatise, I will simply outline the salient itinerary. Arriving at the Quaker City at six p.m., we stopped at the Robert Morris hotel—a new but reasonably inexpensive hostelry which performs the marvel of harmoniously combining a Gothic exterior with a Colonial interior. Signing the register "Mr. and Mrs." was easy despite total inexperience! Being obliged to get some typing done instantly, we finished the evening at the only public stenographer's office in town which was then open—that at the Hotel Vendig, where for a dollar we obtained the use of a Royal machine for three hours. S.H. dictated whilst I typed—a marvellous way of speeding up copying, and one which I shall constantly use in future, since my partner expresses a willingness amounting to eagerness so far as her share of the toil is concerned. She has the absolutely unique gift of being able to read the careless scrawl of my rough manuscripts—no matter how cryptically and involvedly interlined![2]

The next day we "saw Philadelphia right" in the double trip of the Royal Blue Line rubberneck wagon. (Vide enclosure). Of that more anon—but I may here remark that the town of William Penn is one of the most distinctive and interesting I have ever seen, (tho' dull to inhabit continuously) and one which we must inspect more minutely later on. It is only two hours from

N.Y., hence can hardly be called inaccessible. You have seen the cards—and you will see the travelogue soon. I send under separate cover a complete Independence Hall set, from which you may gain at least a fair idea of that noted edifice's magnificent colonial interior. That evening we had to do typing again at the Vendig—truly, a most practical and industrious honeymoon—and late at night we returned to N.Y., putting in the remaining days writing; since on Monday S.H.'s vacation will be over, whilst I myself (incredible as it may sound) may have to be ready for business engagements of one sort or another.

Such is the epic, down to date! Could any fate for Old Theobald be better? I await with eagerness the congratulations I know you and A.E.P.G. will extend, and only wish you were both here now to observe the new menage, and to see Grandpa up brightly every day and amazingly free from facial trouble. The latter improvement is almost *miraculous*—I have had no severe probings and comparatively few pullings; the vast majority of hairs coming naturally to the surface and causing so little trouble that I can retain them and reduce most of the question to a short genuine shave every other day. Really, astounding as it appears, I honestly believe that the face will form scarcely any handicap to my future industrial efforts, as I had feared it would before migrating. Please send the tin box with all my Gillette blades—for I am now able to put them to a very good and cheerfully optimistic use!

My general health is ideal. S.H.'s cooking, as you know already from me and from A.E.P.G., is the last word in perfection as regards both palate and digestion. She even makes *edible* bran muffins! She is also a fresh-air specialist, and as great an insister on carefulness and remedies as you are with the camphor discoids—already she has deluged me with a nose and mouth wash, and has made me heal with vaseline the cracked lip which was open all winter—to say nothing of the place where I skinned my shin slipping downstairs that time last week—when I tripp'd on a trip to the attic. And—*mirabile dictu*—she is at least *trying* to make me stick to the Walter Camp exercises known as the "Daily Dozen"! The headache prescription came safely, and I shall get a bottle of my Old Reliable—although so far I haven't had a headache since the wearing off of the one induced by the Houdini–Henneberger rush. Decidedly, Old Theobald is alive as he was never alive before!

So much for that. Now to get you folks in on the celebration! You—and this is already an irrevocable dictum of Fate—are going to live here permanently. No negative decision will be accepted, and if you don't come voluntarily you'll be kidnapped! And that goes for A.E.P.G. too, whenever she isn't otherwise in demand industrially. Tell her to come along for her sojourn here just as though there were a "room" to look for. It's all the better—for now she will have no responsibility, and all the time can be devoted to sightseeing at a leisurely rate. You likewise must do some sightseeing when you get here—and at a rate doubly leisurely. One sight a day—and the Old Gentleman won't permit you to get tired!

Don't worry about space—there will be ample room for all when the household plan is readjusted. The present artistically impeccable scheme will continue only till after the reception we shall give the assembled amateurs—then the existing dining-room (which A.E.P.G. can describe to you) will become my homely and homelike study, cluttered with the possessions and atmosphere of a conservative Old Gentleman; whilst any number of other easy metamorphoses will be made to adapt the apartment to the entire House of Phillips.

Later discussions will develop just what pieces of furniture should or shouldn't be sent on from 598. I have the secretary now, but believe I shall want Dr. Clark's table for my precious cabinet and typewriter—and of course there are myriad other indispensables like the morris-chair, favourite pictures, library table, and so on. The *bookcases,* Pegāna be prais'd, will furnish *no problem at all!* There is space for every one, including the one upstairs, and what cannot go into my study will go easily into the large L-shaped hall. Send them all on in one grand load as soon as the reception is over and we get the space ready for them.

As for this same reception—S.H. is absolutely set on the attendance of both you and A.E.P.G., even if you children have to make a special trip. She'd be glad to assist on the expense of this extra journey if you would let her—and I don't see why you shouldn't. Since it's her own particular and individual wish . . . . . heartily seconded, of course, by the Old Gentleman. I always told you she was stuck on you children independently.

Meanwhile there are a few things I should like right away—and in mentioning this I must not omit thanks for the Belknap book and the dual express shipment, both of which have already arrived, after some petty vicissitudes on the part of the latter. Of the following list the *first two* items are *very important,* and connected with the literary business brought up by Miss Tucker—at whose office, by the way, I am bidden to call at four p.m. tomorrow, bearing as much of my published and unpublished work as I have in N.Y. The others can follow more at leisure, being connected with comfort, atmosphere, and the like, rather than with commercial opportunity.

LIST

1. The tin box on the middle shelf of the glass-doored cabinet, bearing all my unpublished manuscripts.
2. The pile of magazines on and under the tabouret, including the complete file of *Weird Tales* and the *Home Brews* with my two serials.
3. My new wrap or dressing-gown.
4. My calendars—daily Dickens, colonial doorway, and Paul Revere's Ride.

5. My *old* Webster's Unabridged, from the east (clock-bearing) book-case, and my red Stormonth's Dictionary from the south bookcase, on a lower shelf, at the very end next the table.

6. My postal scales.

7. The tin box of Gillette blades.

8. When convenient—the precious cabinet with all its contents.

I note what you say about the typewriter, and shall await with philosophical equanimity the motions of honest Neilan. It's all right about the case. We'll arrange with some neighbour to receive the shipment at any time when these diggings are left untenanted, and thus avoid the delay experienced with the previous twain of consignments. The blue suit, too, will be welcome; as will the grey when it is cleaned—although of course there's no hurry about that. By the way—apropos of saving and shipping—I want my blue *jumbo cup,* whose capacious depths have dealt me out so much nourishment, and which has become so much a part of my essential background! You will recall that you gave me that in the beginning.

I'm delighted to hear of the frame for the powder-horn picture—and as soon as convenient I'd like that and the 1762 panorama . . . . . together with the box of Old Providence material. When I begin the rounds of the museums with the gang, I shall want to be able to show some comparative data on my own native village! But wait till I take you through the museum of the N.Y. Historical Society in Central Park West, and show you the Beekman coach and the maps of early New York, and all the rest. I'll make a regular Manhattanite of you if you'll promise not to acquire the local pronunciation and say "woild", "hoit", etc.

I appreciated the Peter Randall house, and have no doubt but that its owner was of the clan for whom Randall Square was named. Soon, I trust, I shall receive the usual three extras; for this is an especially captivating scene. I vaguely know this house by sight, though I have not given it the detailed study it deserves. Future Corners and Characters are eagerly awaited.

But I must begin to think of closing, else you will deem the length of this epistle excessive even in view of the titanic tidings it contains. Announcements of the Big Event are now being engraved, and although I consider such matters personal rather than social and public, I'll be glad to send on any quantity which you may desire for distribution. No doubt the zest of the gregariously curious demands the sop of a neatly graven notification—tissue paper, double envelope, and all—even though these selfsame worthies don't give a damn about me beyond the circumstance that I'm a distant relative of John Jones's second wife's uncle's eighth cousin-in-law's step-brother's great-aunt. There'll be a copper plate—so that even if we don't have enough placards in the first batch, we can have as many more finished up as you can find a use for. In any case, there's no hurry.

Well—as Sandusky phrases it—that's that! Here's hoping the news isn't giving you and A.E.P.G. too great a jolt, and that you'll recognise amidst the surprise how miraculous a salvation the whole thing is for an erstwhile aimless Old Gentleman who always needs a bomb set off under him to make him move. It looks as if there weren't any more need to worry about Ancient Theobald's future, for if there's anything in him, he's surely got a lifelong assurance of the sort of care, companionship, and environment needed to bring it out.

And so I conclude—awaiting first your congratulations and later your presence. S.H. sends an overflowing fount of regard and affection to both you and A.E.P.G., and adds her urgent voice to the chorus of demand that you come hither first for the reception (date of which we'll supply) and then permanently. If I've overlooked anything essential in these pages, pray forgive it and find an explanation in the bewildering and inordinate length of so important a document.

With every sort of love and good wishes, and hoping to see you soon, I have yᵉ honour to subscribe myself

Yr most aff: nephew and obt Servt

H P L

## Notes

1. HPL refers to the Phillips plot at Swan Point Cemetery in Providence.
2. HPL refers to the fact that, in leaving Providence on 3 March, he lost the typescript of his story "Under the Pyramids" (ghostwritten for Harry Houdini) in the train station. He had the autograph ms. with him, and he and Sonia were obliged to spend the evening typing it in order to deliver it to *WT* on time.

[45]     [ANS postcard][1] [HPL to LDC]

[Postmarked New York, N.Y.,
10 March 1924]

More corners & characters! How did you like the news? Up at 7:00 this morning—& dressed & out exactly one hour later! Took walk in Central Park, & am now at the Metropolitan Museum, where I'll be until 3:45. At 4 I go to the *Reading Lamp* office. Will look up Hohokus dope tonight, so as to qualify as guide for A E P G tomorrow.

Yr aff nephew & obt Servt  H P L

## Notes

1. *Front:* Old North Dutch Church, N.Y.

[46]      [ANS postcard][1] [HPL to LDC]

[Postmarked New York, N.Y.,
10 March 1924]

Egyptian stuff! That Houdini–Henneberger job has set me off on the most exhaustive survey of Nilotic antiquities that I ever made. I missed a vast lot in 1922. You must see this museum little by little—there's enough in it to keep a real connoisseur busy for months, devoting each day to one detail. And you should see the Egyptian obelisk in the park nearby!
Yr aff neph & obt Ser
H P L

[P.S.] Just got lunch in the museum cafeteria. Pete! How they soak you! Outside next time!

## Notes

1. *Front:* Painted Wooden Horse and Rider. Egyptian. XVII–XVIII Dynasty. 33494. The Metropolitan Museum of Art.

[47]      [ANS postcard][1] [HPL to LDC]

[Postmarked New York, N.Y.,
10 March 1924]

Can't break away from Egypt! The collection here is titanic—greater than I ever realised from my previous surveys. If I'm not a fully qualified Egyptologist by this time, I'll resign from my position as Director-General of Antiquities at Cairo! I'm going to send you an envelope of other material—& I guess I'll get duplicates for A.E.P.G. ¶ Yr aff nph & obt Ser
H P L

## Notes

1. *Front:* Painted Limestone Group. Egyptian. XVIII Dynasty. 34306. The Metropolitan Museum of Art.

[48]      [ANS postcard][1] [HPL to LDC]

[Postmarked New York, N.Y.,
10 March 1924]

Here is what our French friends were doing in the line of decoration when we were perfecting our Colonial interiors. You'll note the same elements of Georgian design, though executed on a more sumptuous scale. I frankly prefer the Anglo-American Colonial—though my decision may be biassed. ¶ Yr aff nephew & obt Servt

H P L

*Notes*

1. *Front:* Library, Detail, Hôtel de Gaulin, Dijon. M.M. 987. French, Louis XVI / 1770–1780 (?) / The Metropolitan Museum of Art.

[49]     [ANS postcard][1] [HPL to LDC]

[Postmarked New York, N.Y.,
10 March 1924]

More French—18th century.
    Now to beat it for the Reading Lamp office!
Yr aff nephew & obt Servt

H P L

*Notes*

1. *Front:* Salon, Hôtel de Gaulin, Dijon. M.M. 990. French, Louis XVI / 1770–1780 (?) / The Metropolitan Museum of Art.

[50]     [ANS postcard][1] [HPL to LDC]

[Postmarked New York, N.Y.,
10 March 1924]

Just through with *Reading Lamp* interview. Miss T. thinks a book of my anti-quarian & other essays would be quite practicable, & urges me to prepare at least three as samples at once. Also, she thinks she can get me a contract with a chain of magazines to write minor matter to order. And more—as soon as my MSS. arrive, she wants to see all of them, with a view to a weird book. Yr aff & obt H P L

[P.S.] What Miss T. wants in the way of essays is quaint stuff with a flavour of the supernatural.

*Notes*

1. *Front:* 33297. The Tomb of Perneb. The Metropolitan Museum of Art.

[51]     [AHT] [HPL to LDC]

259 Parkside Avenue, Bklyn, N.Y.,
March 18, 1924

My very dear Daughter Lillian:—
                    Your letter was a long-awaited pleasure, and
I need not say with how great delight I perused it! Yes indeed, Grandpa The-

obald is most staidly settled in the routine of placid matrimony; and anxious to see his eldest daughter an integral part of the new household. Try like the dickens to get to the reception, for S.H. says that she hardly feels like having any really organised reception unless you can be present. That would be just a preliminary trip—after which you could attend to the final migratory details before coming here permanently. As for the latter—bless me! we won't hear of any such thing as a negative! This is no ordinary bourgeois household where conflicts of interest and authority, and all that sort of thing, develop. It is the transferred Phillips centre—the reincarnation of 454 Angell Street— and would not be in any sense complete unless presided over by the logical head of the clan! This is no spoof—I can't begin to say how much real delight and sense of background and affectionate solidity your presence will bring! And this wish is not merely my individual one—which may indeed be taken for granted—but the combined wish of both members of the firm, and as intense in the new partner as if she had been a charter member! Bless my old bones! Do you suppose I would ever have planned any domestic arrange-ment, or looked ahead with pleasure to any domestic arrangement, which did not include my daughter L.D.C.? Later we expect to have larger quarters; but meanwhile you will find this flat larger than you have imagined, and amply capacious enough to accomodate our presiding genius. The present dining-room will become a homelike combination of my study and a sleeping room; and the present bedroom, quiet and independent with its oaken door and per-fect detachment, extends you a welcome as a permanent inhabitant—either with the present white Colonial furniture, or with any furniture of your own which you may prefer for old association's sake. Remember—this is 454 transplanted, and you are expected to dignify it with the intangible element of Phillips atmosphere which it cannot otherwise obtain! Be a sport—don't dis-appoint us!

About the announcements—the engraved cards ought to come today, and the envelopes are already here and addressed. Of Providentians I have remembered Harold, Ronald, and Eddy[1]—the only ones I think would be re-ally interested. I have also, of course, addressed one to Chester in Asheville.[2] To my unseen Pelham kinsfolk I have addressed two—one to Mr. and Mrs. Hill and the other to Mr. and Mrs. Lyon.[3] A.E.P.G. didn't give me any list of others, but as I said before I'll either send you some blank envelopes to mail to whom you please, or mail them myself to any names you may submit to me.

Thanks prodigiously for getting the Dexter and powder-horn pictures framed—you can imagine the eagerness with which I await them! All the goods sent either by express or by A.E.P.G. arrived safely, and formed a most welcome series of consignments. With my vivid calendars hung on the wall, and my old Remington merrily clicking, this spot seems very much like home; and I am certain you will have a distinct sense of homecoming when you ar-rive here!

Thanks also for the extra "Corners and Characters", and for the cuttings of Pawtucket antiquities. The Daggett house is a great asset—as is the Slater mill …… which reminds me that the date attributed to the latter in the cutting is wrong. For 1671 should be substituted the much less impressive 1791—a fact which becomes very obvious when one reflects closely upon the history both of the region and of the textile art in these Colonies. Future "Corners and Characters" will be welcomed regularly—and I shall get Eddy to send them to me after you are here.

A.E.P.G., as you already know, arrived safely and happily; and has been in town twice since her sojourn in the wilds of Hohokus. She spent last Friday in antiquarian exploration with me, and on Sunday was a Parkside guest; partaking of one of S.H.'s superb dinners, and receiving from that benign divinity an exquisitely tasteful quota of headgear. It being S.H.'s birthday, A.E.P.G. brought a fine bunch of flowers and an appropriate card. Tomorrow she will be in N.Y. again—taking dinner with S.H. and me at a delectable French restaurant in 50th Street (where we also dined Friday), and later participating in more exploration—probably the Poe cottage in Fordham. Pretty soon I hope to be taking you over the same routes—not so intensively, however, as to fatigue you.

I hope to be working soon on the tentative chapters of the weird book, and am meanwhile inspecting a contract for the handling of work which Miss Tucker has submitted for approval. I think I shall make two amendments before affixing my signature—one to exempt collaborated writing from the scope of the document, and the other to ensure non-alteration on the part of the Tucker–Allen firm. The latter provision would stipulate that my original manuscripts be used as typed by me, "down to the last comma and semicolon", as I told Baird when sending my first stories to WEIRD TALES. By the way—could you send me the *duplicate* copies of WEIRD TALES now on the top of my bedstead? Miss T. wants to shew some of these things around when marketing my work, and I don't wish my best file copies soiled or frayed or perhaps lost. Have you purchased the latest issue with "Arthur Jermyn" (here called *The White Ape*) and "Nemesis"? There are two misprints in the latter, as follows:

> Stanza Three, last line—for *water* read *waters*.
> Stanza Five, last line—for *curs'd* read *cursed*.

I am quite flattered at the advance notice given "Hypnos", and hope that the public may receive it as favourably as the editorial staff did. You will note the absence of "The Eyrie" in this issue—which no doubt marks the passing of the Baird regime. And of course you will observe Eddy's story[4]—on which I trust you will congratulate him when you see him about the book and furniture question.

March 19.

...... Since beginning this letter many intermissions have occurred, and many things have arrived from 598. Thanks for all the BULLETIN matter, which is of extreme interest, and pray don't fail to send all similar matter as it appears. The old Morris homestead is delectable, and very familiar to me from actual observation. The South Main Street place, also, is a dream of golden yesterdays—although the accompanying article is wrong in calling it "one of the few remaining houses of that kind in the neighbourhood". As a matter of fact, this district is especially rich in Colonial structures, the skyline being practically solid with them on both sides of the street—but the fact that most of them have been raised over modern shops conceals their nature from the superficial glance. The Market Square view is a reprint of one which appeared not long ago, but I am exceedingly glad of the additional duplicate. The various small cuttings were all interesting—that museum idea is not a bad one, for many have pointed out the pernicious psychological effect of the so-called "museum hush".

The announcements have now arrived, and were mailed yesterday. Just after the mailing came a letter from Hohokus in which A.E.P.G. pointed out some social niceties (such as saying only "Mr. and Mrs. Brown"—no initials—on the inner envelope) which we neglected to observe; but I trust that not many will adjudge us boors for the manner in which we did send the things. A.E.P.G. says she will attend to the Providence and Phillips-family mailing—but you may think of names that she will forget, so I'll send you a list of those she selects, and you can add ad libitum. Cards plentifull [*sic*] abound.

We had our first callers yesterday—Mrs. Adams of Plainfield, N.J., and Mrs. Myers of Cambridge,[5] who is visiting Mrs. Adams before sailing for Paris for six months. They seemed very favourably impressed with the new household, and S.H. assures me that I did not appear altogether ridiculous as a host. We have now sent invitations to several amateurs to come over next Sunday—among them Small Sonny-Boy, who will no doubt be properly knocked out by the announcement! Today I am going to meet A.E.P.G. at noon, take her uptown to Budry's restaurant where we will both meet S.H. for lunch, and subsequently take her somewhere sightseeing—probably the Poe cottage in Fordham. Wait till I get you here! I'll show you all this and more!

As to literary stuff—Henneberger made a special trip to Murfreesboro, Tennessee to show my new story to Houdini, and the latter took to it marvellously—writing me a note at once, which I answered at his New York address, 278 West 113th St. This morning Houdini answered in a most cordial note, promising a longer reply soon, and asking me to call on him. He seems to be a very pleasant person in a mildly commonplace way, and I am sure that I shall enjoy meeting him—and his library.

But it is from Henneberger that the startling thing came—the thing which has aroused vast excitement in this placid and newly-founded household. This honest but uncouth worthy writes that he is making a radical change in WEIRD TALES, and that he has in mind a brand new magazine to cover the field of Poe–Machen shudders. This magazine, he says, will be "right in my line", and he wants to know if I would consider moving to Chicago to edit it! My gawd, Pete, bring the stretcher! It may be a flivver, but S.H. is urging me to take it up if it definitely materialises and is accompanied by the requisite guarantees. She would be willing to move at any time, for the millinery world of Chicago is as promising as that of N.Y. To me, however, such a break away from Colonial scenes would be little short of tragic; and big though the proposition would be if genuine, I would not consent to such a move without previously exhausting every sort of rhetoric in an effort to persuade Henneberger to let me edit at long-distance from N.Y. The trouble is, that the darned thing might fail after a few issues, leaving me stranded in uncongenial Western scenes … you can bet that I'll look sharply into anything of the sort before I consider it seriously! But it may be all hot air anyway. I shall see Henneberger soon, for he means to visit N.Y. And he says he is sending me a cheque this week. (GLORIOUS REALITY!!! March 21—I held this epistle over to copy the travelogue for Moe, Sechrist, et al., and in the interim Henneberger's cheque came—for ANOTHER HUNDRED!!!!) The Houdini story may appear without my name, for Henny is so dull that he doesn't see how a collaborated work can be written in the first person—he expected third, and indulged in several saline tears because I didn't write it thus!

I don't envy you the breaking-up job, but later on we'll collaborate on a programme of elimination. I fancy poor Eddy will take much furniture off your hands—heaven knows he needs it, for his barren dump is the most meagre and destitute place I ever beheld! I must write him shortly, and attend to some of his manuscripts which I promised to revise. The longer I wait, the busier I'll be; hence early action means best results!

And now for a few remarks on the Corners and Characters I have been seeing, both in Philadelphia and New-York. The Philadelphia trip was richly repaid in sights, even though we could not include all the objects we wished to observe. The route thither leads over a flat, ugly, and somewhat marshy New-Jersey countryside, pleasantly broken here and there by the spires of some Colonial town. Elizabeth and New Brunswick, as seen from the train, are especially replete with eighteenth century architecture; and I design to visit both later on for detailed exploration.

Philadelphia, two hours from New York, does not at first impress the traveller. Having attained a maximum of prosperity in the Victorian age, its business section is saddled with a plethora of "Butler-Exchanges" architecture—which in progressive cities like New York has long ago been superseded by skyscraper types and revived Colonialism. But a certain distinctiveness of atmosphere is at once manifest—a distinctiveness which quickly tells the visitor that he has entered a new zone of American civilisation, wherein the familiar conditions of New-England and New-York are subtly modified by proximity to the vast and stable South. Leisure and easy slipshodness are everywhere conspicuous and niggers abound in a proportion surprising to the thorough Northerner. Philadelphia is an ancient town in negligee—a vast, slow, sprawling organism a little frayed at the edges; dimly lighted, lacking in tone and smartness, but withal dignified by a sense of background and maturity which compels respect and finally admiration. It has curious uniquities and local customs, some captivating, some disconcerting. Old houses have reflectors attached to the front windows to show the inhabitants of the second story who is standing on the low porchless steps before the front door . . . . at night the streets are flushed with water from a curious kind of high-pressure tank on wheels, whose titanic hose emits violent streams which send hapless pedestrians to cover in the alcoves of shop doors . . . . . the electric lighting is very dim, so that Providence is spruce and brilliant by comparison . . . . . at the centre of the town is the vast Victorian City Hall, blocking the intersection of two main thoroughfares and forcing vehicles to detour by side streets, though allowing pedestrians to pass under great stone arches and through a quaintly quiet inner court where numberless pigeons feed and lazy niggers loaf . . . . . .

The town was founded in 1683 by William Penn on the bank of the Delaware River, in territory given him by a royal charter of Charles II in 1680, and having thin previous settlements of Dutch and Swedes. This date is very late for a Colonial town; Portsmouth, Newburyport, Salem, Boston, Plymouth, Newport, New Haven, and New York being by that time well-established and prosperous, and Providence having just appeared as a rising seaport, due to the building of Pardon Tillinghast's wharf at Towne and Transit Streets. Penn being a Quaker and a theorist, his city was laid out with much greater regularity than was the case with towns of more natural and spontaneous growth—indeed, there was from the first a certain artificiality comparable to that of the city of Washington, or that of very modern cities. This design was aided by the even surface of the ground, and the absence of multitudinous streams and other topographical features which usually prompt picturesque irregularity in ancient settlements. Even the most venerable parts are of chessboard precision; so that although many narrow and alluring courts and alleys are found, there are scarcely any of the steep, curving, and boldly fantastic effects which one encounters in Providence, Old Boston, or lower Manhattan. With the growth of the city, the settled area extended westward from the Delaware to the tributary Schuylkill, as Providence's east side gradually extended toward the Seekonk; so that the entire inter-river peninsula is now thickly built up, with generous overlappings even beyond the Schuylkill. On both sides of that stream, and united by several bridges, is the wild natural expanse of Fairmount Park, containing the 1876 Centennial grounds and having an undulating surface which contrasts agreeably with the plainness of

Philadelphia in general. Germantown, north of Old Philadelphia but now part of the greater city, was at an early date the abode of German gentlemen of taste; and to this day retains some of the finest Colonial doorways in America. Penn's own house, the first brick edifice in the region, was built in 1682 before the formal laying out of the town. It is still standing, tho' remov'd from its original location to Fairmount Park, where I beheld it in all its Quaker simplicity—a simplicity which precludes even the classick doorway which such a structure might be expected to have.

The central position of Philadelphia in the area of the Colonies, the solid and enterprising character of the Quaker inhabitants, and the personal genius of the celebrated Dr. Franklin, who had early emigrated thither from the Province of the Massachusetts-Bay, all combin'd to impart to the town a prosperity of phenomenal swiftness and magnitude; so that before the middle of the eighteenth century it was the recognis'd metropolis of America, and the seat of numerous publick institutions both learned and philanthropick, secular and religious. Dr. Franklin, whose immortal experiments in the capture of electrical fire were here conducted, succeeded in divesting the people of much of their Quaker primness and narrowness; and little by little a gay and wholesome social life sprang up, whilst architectural skill rear'd to the sky a pleasing array of rich and tasteful structures. In 1731 the Library Company of Philadelphia founded the first publick library in these Colonies, thus setting an example which other towns were all too slow to follow.

By the time of the late unfortunate rebellion against His Majesty's government, Philadelphia had become built up in an extremely definite and distinct fashion, wherein the Quaker spirit of the founders blended very agreeably with the newer atmosphere of progress and prosperity. Some of the houses were of the general American urban type of the period—small brick facades, backward-sloping roofs, and one or more dormer windows overlooking the street. Of this style is the celebrated abode of Miss Betsey Ross, still standing, where the permanent Colonial flag was first design'd and fashion'd. More, however, had a peculiar form and aesthetick of their own; being arrang'd in long solid blocks of red brick, with white marble steps, arched doors faced with marble, and windows with marble lintels and keystones. There were no porches, but merely flat facades with low flights of steps, railed on one side, as the sole jutting feature. To glimpse a typical street of these houses, a ravine with solid red cliff walls and innumerable white flights of steps projecting out from the flat marble-faced doors, was to feel oneself unmistakably in Philadelphia—tho' the town of Baltimore is said to have had effects not altogether dissimilar. Occasional mansions in the suburbs were of more ambitious type, and parallelled fairly well the New-England and New-York houses of similar quality. The publick buildings, moreover, were rich to the point of lavishness; their survivors yet furnishing some of the finest models of Colonial architecture in America.

On this occasion, lacking the time for leisurely exploration, we condescended to employ the sightseeing omnibus of the Royal Blue Line, which touches at the principal points of interest and furnishes a good basis for a general orientation to the town. The route was very ample, and the lecturer singularly intelligent; so that in a single afternoon we obtained a clear perspective and vivid impression of those images and touches of colour peculiarly Philadelphian.

One's introduction to colonial Philadelphia is, in a fashion, especially dramatic. Working east along busy Victorian Chestnut Street, one spies suddenly on the right, beyond the dingy neo-Romanesque and baroque shop facades, the warm red brick of the old days. A few more steps and the eye is confronted by as magnificent a row of Georgian publick buildings as any antiquary could ask for—Congress Hall, built in 1790, and housing the Federal government when Philadelphia was the nation's capital; Independence Hall, or the Old State House, famous for its part in the regrettable insurrection of 1775–1783; and the U.S. Supreme Court House, built in 1791 and now housing a notable collection of relicks. To circumnavigate this splendid Colonial array, viewing it from all angles and especially from the square to the south, whence many other colonial buildings may be seen, is to live again in that subtle atmosphere of the urban eighteenth century, of which so few perfect specimens now survive. The effect is marvellous—elsewhere one may find the spirit of the Colonial village and small town, but only here may one grasp to the fullest extent the soul of the Colonial *city*—mature and populous when the third George sate upon our throne.

Independence Hall is the largest and by far the finest of this group of buildings. At present it is tripartite, with a great central structure and two wings; the latter built shortly after the revolution, and the former, or Independence Hall proper, erected by Andrew Hamilton, Esq. for the Pennsylvania Assembly in 1734. The belfry and steeple were completed in 1751—being now restored after removal in 1781. The interior of this edifice is without doubt the finest example of Colonial carving and panelling I have ever beheld, with the sole possible exception of the New-York City Hall (1812). It were futile to try to describe, save in prose-poetry, the massed effect of the exquisite cornices, pilasters, wainscots, doorways, staircases, mantels, columns, and other decorative details; all of the purest Georgian tradition, and gleaming whitely as a perfect background for the delicate furniture and absorbing relics with which the place abounds. Among these latter things are the desk of the President of the Congress, the well-known Liberty Bell, formerly hung in the belfry but now especially display'd on the ground floor in a hall, a sofa of General Washington's and a chair of Chief Justice Jay's, the silver inkstand and sand-shaker us'd in preparing the seditious so-call'd Declaration of Independence (well known, beyond a doubt, to our friend Stephen Hopkins!), and many notable paintings, among them works of the Philadelphian Benjamin West, and of his still greater pupil, the Rhode-Islander Gilbert Stuart. The rear doorway of Independence Hall, surmounted by a mightily tasteful triple window, is a delightful specimen of Dorick art as employ'd in early colonial design.

Another vastly interesting building is Carpenters' Hall, set back from Chestnut Street at the end of a little colonial court (like Harding's Alley) some distance east of the Independence Hall row of buildings. This structure, commenc'd in 1770 but not finish'd till much later, hous'd the first treasonable Continental Congress in 1774; at which event General Washington and other rebels knelt and pray'd, under the false impression that Boston had been destroy'd by bombardment. We examin'd the interior of this place, but found it not to be compar'd to Independence Hall; though it holds some historical relicks of no small interest. Its exterior is very fine, including a red brick facade, classick doorway, and gleaming white belfry.

Being now in a very ancient section of the town, we henceforward encounter'd Colonial reliquiae in rapid succession. Christ Church Cemetery, containing all that is mortal of Dr. Franklin (whose parents' graves I have frequently beheld in the Granary Burying Ground, Boston), is a favour'd haven of the antiquary; nor is the neighbouring Quaker Meeting House to be despis'd. The home of Mrs. Ross, who made the rebel flag, is a pleasing type of modest colonial city residence, whilst Christ Church (built 1727) represents the utmost extreme of Georgian ecclesiastical magnificence with its bold outlines and severe but sumptuous details of ornamentation. It is the etching of that church in Col. Shepley's museum which first recommended Philadelphia to me.[6] Other churches, which we had not time to examine, are Old Swedes' (1700), St. Mary's, (1763), St. Peter's, (1761) St. Paul's (circa 1765), and the Old Mennonite (1774). Altogether, I believe that Philadelphia has more Colonial churches than any other town in these provinces.

Other parts of the tour lay through modern and semi-modern sections of doubtful interest, but expectancy was always maintain'd at a high pitch by the possibility of glimpsing, down some obscure side street, occasional vistas of the Old Philadelphia with its rows of brick colonial facades and marble steps and facings. These vistas are surprisingly numerous considering the size and growth of the town, and even extend to sections of such prominent main thoroughfares as Arch Street. They are, it is true, devoid of the beautiful doorways which we New-Englanders know as Colonial; but they carry the particular and authentick flavour of Quaker, half-German Philadelphia, and are as truly characteristick of their locale as the gambrel roof is of our own locale. Repeated glimpses of them transport the observer back to the days of Robert Morris, Benjamin West, and the great unrest preceding the revolution; with the shrewd, gifted, and benign shadow of old Dr. Franklin over all. One sees them most solidly, perhaps, in the present nigger quarter—which was of course a most respectable and unimpeachably Caucasian district in Colonial times. Blot out the black faces, and you have here a picture of days as effective for its region as anything Marblehead can furnish!

Fairmount Park, through which we drove, is thickly dotted with fine Colonial estates—the country-seats of ancient Philadelphia gentry. Many of these we saw in alluring glimpses over low hills or betwixt the boughs of vast and venerable trees, and although we stopt at none of them, their memory is ineffaceable. The leisurely life of the old Pennsylvania province, and the mature, serene opulence of the Colonies' richest dominion, was mirrored and impressed upon us to the full; till my fancy populated every rural shade with coaching or fox-hunting squires, and every urban doorway with periwigg'd gentlemen knocking or bidding adieu.

Of the non-colonial impressions I gather'd, perhaps the strongest were furnished by Girard College—whose main building is the finest Corinthian temple I have ever seen—and Horticultural Hall, one of the old 1876 exposition buildings, which now houses such a titanic collection of giant tropical vegetation that the spectator fancies himself in the heart of the Amazon country. Girard College was founded by the will of the wealthy Philadelphia merchant Stephen Girard, a Frenchman by birth and an eccentrick by nature. It was design'd for the instruction of orphan boys, and for fear of contaminating influences, the founder specify'd that it shou'd be encircled by a wall twenty feet high, within which no minister or ecclesiastick of any denomination whatsoever shou'd ever set foot. Since a wall of twenty feet wou'd obviously suggest a prison, the executors of the will (which was as perversely binding as Ebenezer Knight Dexter's)[7] circumvented the provision by placing ten feet of the wall *underground.*

Such, then, was Philadelphia, as view'd all too shortly. I design to explore it again at some future date when my exchequer may be less straiten'd, on which occasion I shall include Germantown, with its many fine Georgian remains, and perhaps Valley Forge, so celebrated in the annals of the nation. Returning by a late train to New-York, we reluctantly put the Colonial past behind us; until I brought it again to view through Manhattan's own captivating antiquities, which I shew'd to A.E.P.G. on Friday, March 14th., during the course of a delightful afternoon's trip.

This latter trip was one on which I shall take many visiting amateurs in future, and to which I hope soon to introduce you. It includes Colonial sections of New-York whose very existence is unsuspected by the throng, and leaves ineffaceable memories of the gay and tasteful town of the 1770's, when Lord Howe worshipp'd at St. Paul's, and the Prince of Wales was nearly drown'd whilst skating on Collect Pond. We had dined with S.H. at Budry's French restaurant in 50th St., and had ridden down Fifth Avenue atop one of the numberless omnibuses—past Madison Square with its Diana-topp'd Garden, its Metropolitan Tower, and its Flatiron Building, past shops of seedier mien, and finally past the late-colonial dignity of lower Fifth Avenue, with its brick residences and stately churches—including that of your friend Percy Stickney Grant.[8] Then, emerging into ancient Washington Square with its vast marble arch of Roman design, we alighted at the terminus of the line, in the midst of that Little Old New York which is as Georgian and quaintly flavoured as the best of Benefit Street, Beacon Hill, or Marblehead.

Washington Square, the nucleus of an outlying town or village known as Greenwich, which was overtaken and engulfed by the expanding city in the early nineteenth century, has been successively a meadow, a potter's field, a parade-ground, and a residential square. With certain inessential exceptions, it was all built up before the close of the colonial architectural period; and to this day it retains the true elder atmosphere. Once fallen into slums, it later became the lurking-place of undesirable "artists" and "Bohemians"; but is now in process of reclamation, with the mansions on the north side already restored to pristine aristocratic dignity. These mansions, as we viewed them, glowed mellowly in the afternoon sun; with quiet brick facades and austere stone doorway-pillars which suggest the best traditions of Anglo-American refinement, reticence, and mature cultivation. They are like the row of houses in Benefit Street just beside the Athenaeum—with that savour of Georgian London which adds the last touch of desirable background. To the east, the building of New York University does not detract from the general atmosphere. Westward open several colonial streets, later to be described, and sustaining the tradition in full. To the south are some of the really oldest houses of all—genuine pre-revolutionary structures reminiscent of the days when Admiral Sir Peter Warren, Bart.—hero of Louisburg as naval aide to Sir William Pepperell, and finely portrayed in the Portsmouth N.H. Athenaeum—acquired his large holdings in the neighbourhood. Sir Peter, as curious antiquaries know, became very great indeed, and now lies in Westminster Abbey. Here and there are modern structures, such as a Baptist church and attached hotel which interested A.E.P.G. because some relative of ours—one Frank Lawton[9]—once resided there. But these are gladly overlooked by the lover of the past. The real antiquary drinks in the quiet colonial doorways, well-kept or decrepit, admires the replicas of the neo-colonial houses, and lets his fancy trickle dreamily down the Georgian vistas of such debouching streets as Fourth and MacDougall. Georgian yesterdays . . . . . rattle of coaches and smoke of homely chimney-pots . . . . avaunt, Corruption! begone, Modernity! Old England's wraith is stronger than all your realities, because she is the mother of all the virtue that is here! GOD SAVE THE KING!

We thence work'd south along McDougall, observing as we did so some splendid Colonial houses and doorways viciously defaced by the vandal paint and bizarre signs of such "Bohemian" pseudo-artists as have not yet been driven out of the neighbourhood. These houses are still intact; and will, thank the gods, some day be restored to proper condition as so many others have been. The district now became a tortuous Italian slum, especially around

Bleecker Street, but the traces of colonial habitation were so numerous that A.E.P.G. was reminded of our South Main Street. As we threaded the labyrinthine ways, we became impress'd with the fact that New-York, as well as Philadelphia, has a colonial architecture all its own; differing in many details from that of New-England on the one hand, and from that of Pennsylvania on the other hand. The majority of the houses are small and made of brick, with sloping roof and dormer windows much like those of the non-Quaker Philadelphia type—i.e., the type of the Betsey Ross house. Their doorways, more classic than the prim portals of Philadelphia, are yet very remote from the elaborate New-England fanlighted kind; and are mark'd by certain unmistakable characteristics. Usually they are sunken in the facade, surmounted by a transom instead of fanlight, reached by a short double-rail'd flight of steps (or sometimes the sidewise double flight and flanked by slender columns, usually of the Ionick or Corinthian order. Sometimes these columns stand as single sentinels, one on each side, but more often they occur in pairs, or in groups of one free and one engaged column—the latter frequently exchanged for a pilaster. The transoms are supplied with traceries as rich as those of our fanlights; though I will own that the fanlight's geometrical form lends itself to more graceful designs. In colour the doorways vary greatly. As with us, white is in vast favour; but the proportion of dark green or almost black woodwork is very high. The quality of the workmanship is just as high as that in our New-England doorways—for these delicate products have outlasted a century and a half of weathering and often of slum decadence. I cannot recall any Providence doorway typical of this school, though in Boston one may find a few on Beacon Hill.

Curving Minetta Street, whose prospective restoration was described in the *Tribune* last winter, has not yet felt the hammer of the repairer; hence still presents a distinctly squalid aspect—which vanishes, however, at a certain angle when the sensitive fancy half-swoons at the beauty of the colonial design, and refuses to see more than that quaint loveliness which the periwigg'd designer intended so many years ago! It is a genuine Pomander Walk—in possibilities if not in actuality—and I am glad to know that the plans for its renaissance are so thorough and binding. When finished the restored houses will be leased only with the stipulation that they be kept in colonial form.

And now we fared still southward—here and there verging toward the west as some new colonial vista beckoned us. Certainly, we were "doing" Old Greenwich most thoroughly; though one district did remain for me to discover on a lone subsequent excursion. The climax was Charlton Street—New York's best preserved Colonial thoroughfare. How can I describe it? It was perfection! Little Old New York—the New York of the 1780's—surviving in full and amazing splendour, with gleaming white doorways, polish'd knockers, jaunty dormer windows reflecting the sunset, and quaint gables enticingly silhouetted against the purpling east with its background of smoke! The past incarnate—Old Greenwich reflected as faithfully as Benefit Street reflects Old Providence, with every distinctive feature emphasised and glorified! We paused, admired, and marvelled—face to face with antiquity, and half-listening for the rumble of the stage coach with mail for sleepy, steepled Providence, many-gabled Boston, gambrel-roof'd Salem, and remote, chimney-potted Newburyport, where the little boys laugh at the latest antick of Lord Timothy Dexter![10]

But did I say that Charlton Street was the climax? I look ahead and doubt! Surely there was no anticlimax in what followed—the walk through Prince Street with its decaying occasional colonialism, down Broadway with the titanick Woolworth tower in the exact foreground, looming from purple to gold against the southern sky as the setting sun transfigured it with Midas-touch, and the rapt exploration of the City Hall, whose magnificently vaulted colonial interior is a poem eclipsing even Independence Hall in Philadelphia! That City Hall! Hurry up and come to see it! It is a dream of Rome join'd to London and season'd with New York! Finished in 1812, it is an immortal triumph—and for those who like history there is a superlative governor's chamber with a table that General Washington used.

It was now twilight, but we meant to squeeze the day dry; hence still kept on. This time we struck west around story'd old St. Paul's—so signally recognised by your obt. Servt.—examining the ancient stones in the churchyard, and even entering to hear the melodious beginning of the evening prayer. There brooded the old vaulted roof, the classick pillars, the lofty venerable pulpit, and H. R. H. The Prince of Wales's arms—aloft just as they were during the occupation by His Majesty's forces under Lord Howe! GOD SAVE THE KING! Quitting the fane, we glanc'd down archaick Vesey-St., where small-paned windows told of many yesterdays, and descended Broadway to Trinity Church, at whose hoary graves we gaz'd with a sense of background and reverence. Turning east, we now descended the narrow chasm of Wall Street, that we might ponder on other olden scenes in the gentle dusk. We curved through century-trodded ways, and in the gloaming paused by the mellow India-House in Hanover-Square—blest stronghold of British subjects in the elder times. How restful is that quiet scene! So strong is its appeal to my fancy, that I cannot see or hear the ugly clattering elevated overhead! Shades fell . . . . and still we wander'd. More ancient houses, odd musty warehouses, queer old corners . . . . and finally the trim brick walls of the Queen's Head Tavern—vulgarly known as Fraunces'. Within I could swear I heard the revelry of jolly burghers and red-coated half-pay officers of His Majesty . . . . . but perhaps it was only dream. At any rate, we mov'd on toward Bowling Green and the Battery, brooded a moment over the heaving, immemorial sea and the statue of Liberty outlined against the coming night, and struck up Broadway in search of a restaurant and of the Hudson Tunnel which would bear A.E.P.G. to Hohokus. A day was over, and one more devotion had arisen to the gentle, unfading spirit of the colonial past.

My latest expedition occurred on the very next day, and was prosecuted alone. The telling need not be long, for the trip was limited; but I may mention the discovery of vast colonial areas in the western part of Greenwich Village around Sheridan Square, and my first trip east around the Astor Place region, where I saw the celebrated Cooper Union, and had my long-awaited introduction to that delectable Georgian church of 1795—St. Mark's-in-the-Bouwerie. This edifice is of noble proportion and design, though its outré pedimental decoration and general stucco finish make it less classick and impressive than noble St. Paul's. Its region is very appealing—an oasis of gentility in the midst of repellent slums—and on another occasion I propose revisiting the spot, and pushing north as far as Stuyvesant Square. In all these rambles I find myself infinitely aided by that little leather guide book which A.E.P.G. gave me [for] Christmas. Ironically enough, she left hers at 598 and has to depend on mine . . . . bread cast upon the waters.

March 20.

And now another intermission has occurred, punctuated by the arrival of my magazines etc., by express, and by my receipt of your appreciated post card. Yesterday A.E.P.G. was in town again, but we confined our pilgrimages to a survey of possible markets for the carven chess-men, and a hasty glance at some of the treasures of the Metropolitan Museum. She gave me the enclosed list of persons to whom wedding announcements were to be sent, and I hastened to fill the order. I am sending it to you to avoid duplication in case you have any other names to suggest. These persons have now received their cards, but if there are any others (as I don't believe there are), I will gladly supply anyone whom you may name. You will see by this epistle that the typewriter *did* arrive. So did everything else, wherefor I am mightily grateful. Now follow them yourself, and all is perfect! Congratulations have begun to arrive from amateurs—notes today from Kleiner and Sonny-Boy, both of whom I hope to see Sunday at the amateur reception which A.E.P.G. will likewise grace. S.H. transmits an inundation of affectionate regards, which merges gracefully with the cosmos of similar matter that I am sending on my own hook. More later from me, and written matter from you always welcome till you get here in person! Then—what a lark!

Yr most aff: Nephew & obt Servt: H. P. L.

## Notes

1. Presumably Harold Bateman Munroe, Ronald K. Upham, and C. M. Eddy, Jr.
2. Chester Pierce Munroe, who had relocated to Asheville, NC.

3. For the Hills, see LDC/AEPG 23n1. HPL also refers to David Lyon (d. 1945, aet. 71) and Ida (Hill) Lyon (d. 1951, aet. 77). Mrs. Lyon was the daughter of Isaac C. Hill and Emma Jane (Lovecraft) Hill, sister of Winfield Scott Lovecraft.

4. "The Ghost-Eater" (*WT,* April 1924).

5. Hazel Pratt Adams (1888–1927), an amateur journalist from Massachusetts. She was elected president of the NAPA for 1923–24. HPL wrote the elegy "The Absent Leader" following her death. Denys P. Myers (1884–1972) and Ethel May Johnston Myers (1882–1971) were friends of HPL in Cambridge, MA, associated with amateur journalists in the area.

6. The private library of Colonel George L. Shepley (1854–1924) was housed at 292 Benefit Street, in a house erected in 1921. HPL visited the library in 1923 (see *SL* 1.268). It is no longer extant. HPL refers to it in *The Case of Charles Dexter Ward* (*CF* 2.221).

7. Ebenezer Knight Dexter (1773–1824) was a wealthy Providence businessman. By the terms of his will, his property was bequeathed to the city for the building of Dexter Asylum, a home for the poor. It was built in 1828 and operated for more than a century; in the 1950s the property was purchased by Brown University for the building of an athletic complex (now called Aldrich–Dexter Field).

8. Of the Church of the Ascension in New York City.

9. Frank Lawton of Washington Square, New York City. Whipple V. Phillips's cousin Mary Brayton Phillips (1833–1918), daughter of his uncle Whipple Phillips (1797–1856), married Louis DeMotte Lawton (1833–1899) and removed to Delavan, IL. It is unknown whether Frank Lawton was related to this family.

10. Self-proclaimed "Lord" Timothy Dexter (1747–1806), an eccentric businessman who wrote *A Pickle for the Knowing Ones* (1802).

[52]     [ANS postcard][1] [HPL to LDC]

[Postmarked Brooklyn, N.Y.,
19 March 1924]

See the sort of neo-Colonial buildings we have in Flatbush! ¶ Am about half through a letter to you, which you will receive shortly. ¶ Various parcels &c. arriving safely. Thanks! ¶ Had an exciting letter from Henneberger, who liked my story, & asks me if I would consider moving to CHICAGO to edit a *new* magazine of weirdness which he is about to found!!! He is coming to N.Y. soon, so I shall have a talk with him. And Houdini has cordially asked me to call at his home here—in 113th St. More anon. Yr aff nephew H P L

[P.S.] Going to meet A E P G at noon, & shew her more of the town.

## Notes

1. *Front:* Irving National Bank, Flatbush and Linden Avenue, South, Flushing, Brooklyn, N.Y.

[53]     [ANS postcard][1] [HPL to LDC]

[Postmarked Brooklyn, N.Y.,
28 March 1924]

Letter follows—but I am dropping a line to supply an omission which A E P G says she has made in her list of desiderate articles. ¶ I *do most emphatically* want the glass-doored cabinet in my room! It will be almost invaluable, & takes little space. Also—don't forget any little old-fashion'd things like the trunk & the pen rack & the little lion paperweight & the Milton bust, &c. &c. In haste,
Yr aff & obt
H P L

[P.S.] And send the carpet-cover'd box full of letters!

*Notes*

1. *Front:* Vista of Woolworth Building.

[54]     [AHT] [HPL to LDC]

259 Parkside Ave., Brooklyn, N. Y.
March 30, 1924

My dear Daughter Lillian:—

          I duly received all your communications, and was indeed glad to hear from you . . . . . though I shall be gladder still when I can persuade you to be here permanently in person! The vital questions of packing and shipping were very generously answered for me by A. E. P. G., but I will append a few notes and supplements here in case anything failed of perfect explicitness.

          Imprimis: despite my previous plan to discard picture frames, I think it will be best to ship all the paintings in their present settings—including the great painting which you gave me and which is in storage. There is room for them all in present form, and the new frames can be obtained at leisure. A list of pictures, aside from smaller ones already decided upon or to be mentioned later, would run about as follows:

                    The vast forest picture now in storage
                    The Foster farm in crayon—in my room
                    The castle over the dining-room mantel
                    The duck in same room
                    The fox in same room
                    Your autumn view to match the fox
                    The stag in the parlour
                    The roses by my mother
                    One of the Fra Angelicos (hoping you safely guard the other)

Of smaller pictures, I might mention the moon view over my globe, all my little bas-reliefs (including Dante and Reynolds' cherub after all), all my cat pictures, the framed evolution chart, the Dr. Clark elegy, the pictures of Phil over my clothespress door, pictures of my father and mother, the large picture of Grandpa in the drawer of the west dining-room bookcase, the fancy picture of my mother in the attic room, the Old Providence and powder-horn views, the two Langdon house views—doorway and whole house (the colonial ones), the picture of St. Paul's, Boston, in the front hall . . . . and such others as your judgment may suggest. The Clough view in the parlour can be sold, as also (albeit with regret) the pastels in the dining-room.

And here are a few notes on odd sundries . . . . . things that it has recently occurred to me to include in the catalogue of necessary articles, A yardstick, if there is one; all the soft collars in my bureau drawer; my pole and clothes hangers from my clothespress; my brown felt hat, my old straw hat, and my brand new straw hat as carefully packed away; all my overcoats, new grey summer suit, old oxford winter suit, best thin alpaca coat, summer wrap, bedroom shoes, bath sandals; all blankets and bedding, especially the ancestrally woven blankets . . . . . but I guess you know all of this anyway!

Proceeding to answer your questions and consider your suggestions—yes, we'd like a few pots and pans, and I *do* want my room clock besides the old red parlour clock. The double bed mattress here is 74 by 53 inches in size, and we would appreciate anything in the mattress line which may conform to these dimensions. All china and silver will be eminently acceptable. No—I don't believe the musician busts or Barye lions are distinctive enough for a Colonial household; but be sure to send the little paperweight lion you gave me, which is genuinely piquant and artistic and not in the least hackneyed. Yes—all lace curtains and kindred objects will be highly in order. And I trust the Putney establishment will make favourable terms anent barometer and smaller telescope. The large telescope I must have.

I am not, I assure you, insensible of the trouble and strain of packing at your end—or of the disconcerting ordeal of unpacking at my end! The truck plan seems ideal to me, though A.E.P.G. finds the quoted rate rather high as compared with that quoted by a Boston firm for moving her friend's goods from Boston to Hohokus N.J.

One thing just occurred to us—yesterday afternoon A.E.P.G. and I did some shopping around here, and found that our beloved Hershey's chocolate buds cost seventy or seventy-five cents per pound in this locality, whereas they are only about forty-nine or fifty at Gibson's in Providence! Now if you are going down town before the final assembling of the load, you might slip in a pound or two of these pleasing commodities at their Rhode Island price, which would certainly effect a most welcome saving on a highly desirable article!

Your detailed catalogue of articles for transportation proved an invaluable aid. A.E.P.G. hath return'd it to you by this time, and I trust she was perfectly explicit in her additions, erasures, and annotations. The bulk of the list represents exactly what I went—and I assume that you recall all the other little things—like the green case and other brush of the brush-and-comb set—which I mentioned as indispensable at the time of the general classification. Don't forget the calendar with Paul Revere's Ride . . . . colour and quaintness are the keynotes!

I need not say how grateful I am for all the "Corners and Characters". Eventually I shall subscribe regularly for the BULLETIN—especially after you get here—as I hope you will—and I shall need other means of keeping track of Rhode Island affairs. If Laswell ever publishes a book of his drawings I must certainly have it, for Old Providence has become one of my chief interests.[1] The account of the old Deacon Taylor house gave me occasion for some mild crowing—for you will recall my insistence that it must have been built before 1800 despite the evidence which you had of its later origin. In this sketch it is stated that the house was built betwixt 1775 and 1800, and my own guess is that 1775 is considerably nearer the mark. The lines of the whole house, and especially of the doorway, fairly shout an origin far anterior to the suave and elaborate forms of the post-revolutionary period. Laswell handles this scene magnificently—the view is truly one of his best. As to the Old Pidge House—you will recall my mention of its process of repair last summer, as I saw it from the car when going to Pawtucket in quest of the Daggett house. I am overjoyed to know it will be a public museum, and hope to explore its wonders some day. The Arsenal, too, makes a delightful picture; though it is of course not in the strictest sense Colonial.

I am glad you enjoyed Wilde's "Decay of Lying", and trust you did not fail to read Dunsany's "A Dreamer's Tales" as well. I have just read Dunsany's new book of short plays, "Plays of Near and Far", and find it delightful, though perhaps a trace less vivid than the Dunsany work of yore. Yes—the realists get to be a bore after a while—though personally I think the romantic writers are an even worse bore. Most of my reading now is of the weirdest description—in preparation for my book of essays of supernatural survivals in America. I have found oceans of profound and terrible material at the main 42nd St. library, and only yesterday got Huysmans' hideous "Down There" (La Bas) at a private circulating library in Flatbush. Vivid stuff—and Morton has lent me still more from his own collection.

I am glad you purchased WEIRD TALES, and hope you made due allowances for the two misprints in "Nemesis". The magazine is now under its new editor, Farnsworth Wright, and he has just accepted Sonny Belknap's story "The Desert Lich" with high compliments.[2] In his letter to Belknap he mentioned my stories with extravagant praise—saying that I am the greatest short story writer since Poe, or something like that (Belknap read the extract over the telephone, so I can't be sure till I see him tomorrow)—though of course the word of a mediocre commercial editor has no literary weight.

Yes—the assemblage of March 23 came off successfully, with a somewhat paler echo yesterday. On the former occasion I greeted my small grandchild Belknap in person for the first time since Nov. 6, 1922, and since then I have seen him nearly every day. We all dined at Longs' last Wednesday evening—around a candle-lit table pleasantly suggesting my eighteenth century. Last Tuesday I attended the Writers' Club, where I heard an exceedingly acute address on Shakespeare by the celebrated Will Irwin,[3] who had enough new material to teach something to even the most erudite of his hearers. As a casual anecdote I may remark that at the general breaking-up it was my fortune to be helped on with my overcoat by none other than the distinguished speaker himself . . . . . to whom, however, I refrained from offering a tip! Thursday the circle of "The Boys" met at McNeil's, where the session was highly enjoyable despite the absence of Small Belknap. It was after one a.m. when we broke up, and we look forward eagerly to our next meeting—which will be held here. On Saturday S.H. and I were to have gone to the Blue Pencil meeting; but on account of fatigue and a cold on her part we refrained. The next morning we rather regretted our absence, for it seems that the meeting had been something of a party in our honour, with a carefully prepared speech by Mortonius, and the presentation of a wedding gift—a magnificent set of glassware—by the club as a whole! When apprised by telephone we duly apologised and appreciated—and A.E.P.G. and I went after the gift, which was at the place of the meeting, the home of a Miss Collier in another part of Brooklyn. Another striking wedding gift was from Mr. and Mrs. Eugene Smythe—Mrs. Smythe being the opera-singer Mme. Machat, who is a childhood friend of S.H.[4] This gift is a clay calendar disc from 1000 to 3000 years old, dug up from the prehistoric ruins of Mexico, and bearing the characteristic astronomical and artistic devices of the ancient Aztec or Toltec civilisation. Smythe is a splendid chap—a government entomologist having a position something like Sechrist's, but rather more important. He and his wife were among the guests here yesterday, and I was interested to see his portfolio of drawings—for he is, despite his maturity, beginning to take up art in a serious way. Another present was from Mrs. Winifred Harper Cooley, the writer and lecturer; and consisted of a copy of the celebrated new play of New-England life—"Icebound", by Owen Davis.

When you get the breaking-up work well disposed of, I shall hope to see you thinking about a migration hither on your own part—for a royal welcome and unending piquant sights await you! A.E.P.G. is at Mount Vernon today, but I hope to have a chance before long to show her some scenes and antiquities she has not seen before—the previous days having been hampered by a recurrence of her hoarseness which makes her averse to intensive sightseeing. She has bade her adieux at the Gillets', and is now staying here at Parkside—though she may spend tonight with her afternoon's hostess Miss Ray.[5] Tomorrow evening S. H. wants to take her to the Gamut Club, whilst I shall probably attend The Writers—unless Belknap and I find something more interesting to do. Grandpa's nice boy is looking stouter, but his health is still very frail, and now complicated with a heart trouble which makes his mamma scold him when he climbs steps needlessly or over-exerts in any way. He's a great kid—and he has duly initiated me into the workings of the great public library at 42nd street.

I had a piquant note from Eddy today, and must answer it soon. My correspondence and amateur work, however, have had to be greatly neglected on account of this rush order for three chapters of a book of American superstition. Miss Tucker probably failed to realise the vast amount of preliminary reading necessary to approach such a theme with even a shadow of the adequate background—but I am determined to try my best. It is, of course, essentially a gamble; for no one can tell whether a publisher will want it till after the three trial chapters are done; but on the whole I think the magnitude of the stakes justifies the hazard. Besides—now that I am started I really want to write the thing for its own sake!

The most revealing and stupefying book among those I have been reading is "The Witch Cult in Western Europe", by Margaret Alice Murray, which was published in 1921 and reviewed with great attention by Burton Rascoe in the *Tribune*. In this book the problem of witchcraft superstition is attacked from an entirely new angle—wherein the explanation of delusion and hysteria is discarded in favour of an hypothesis almost exactly like the one used by Arthur Machen in fiction [marginal note?: The Three Impostors]—i.e., that there has existed since prehistoric times, side by side with the dominant religion, a dark, secret, and terrible system of worship nocturnally practiced by the peasants and including the most horrible rites and incantations. This worship, Miss Murray believes, is handed down from the squat Mongoloid peoples who inhabited Europe before the coming of the Aryans; and reflects the life and thought of a barbarous culture in which stock-breeding had not yet been supplanted by agriculture. This latter feature is clear from the dates of the two great nocturnal feasts and orgies . . . Roodmas, or April 30, and Hallowe'en, or October 31—dates having a connexion with nothing whatever in agriculture (unlike such agricultural festivals as Easter, Harvest-home, etc.), but corresponding with uncanny fidelity to the breeding-seasons of the flocks and herds. Buttressed by an amazing array of sound documentary evidence taken from witchcraft trial reports, Miss Murray unhesitatingly asserts that the similarities and consistencies in the testimony of witch-suspects cannot be explained on any assumption save one which allows for a certain amount of actuality. In her mind, practically all the confessions treat not of dreams and delusions, but form highly coloured versions of real meetings and ceremonies conducted in deep woods and lonely places betwixt midnight and dawn, attended by secretly initiated peasants stolen thither one by one, and presided over by local cult-leaders clad in animal skins and called the "Devils" of their particular branches or "Covens". The hideous nature of the cult-rites is amply attested—and the whole subject takes on a new fascination when one reflects that the system probably survived to comparatively recent times. Miss Murray has no difficulty in tracing the cult's presence in the Salem witchcraft of 1692, and ventures to name the Reverend George Burroughs as "Devil" of the particular branch or Coven involved. Cotton Mather thus stands vindicated, and displayed as the suppressor of a movement involving the most loathsome and offensive practices. Another point of interest is the association of Joan of Arc with the witch-cult—a circumstance which makes one weep less at her fiery martyrdom. The use of this newly unearthed lore in a study of American superstition will be quite new, so that I really believe my book will have some degree of interest if it is ever suffered to materialise!

But I must close. All hands transmit abundant regards and expressions of affection, and I shall await most eagerly your letters and later on your presence!

Yr. most aff: nephew and obt: Servt: H. P. L.

## Notes

1. Laswell did not publish a book of his drawings, but he did issue a selection of his columns with illustrations in *"Corners and Characters of Rhode Island"* (Providence, RI: Oxford Press, 1924).

2. *WT,* November 1924.

3. Will Irwin (1873–1948), American author and journalist best known for an article ("The City That Was") on the San Francisco earthquake and fire published in the *New York Sun.*

4. Laya Machat, American opera singer of Russian descent.

5. Anne Gardner Ray (1955–1940?). Her parents lived in Rochester, NY, at the time George Lovecraft and his family lived there.

[55]     [ANS postcard][1] [HPL to LDC and AEPG]]

[Postmarked Brooklyn, N.Y.,
28 May 1924]

Well, I hope you don't think the Old Man is dead! Started a letter last Monday, & am now on page 13, but got sidetracked by sundry immediate concerns. ¶ Visited this cottage with Belknap a couple of weeks ago. ¶ Have some interesting news to tell regarding real estate in Westchester county—the most idyllic & Novanglian Colonial countryside I have ever seen! ¶ Letter in a day or two. Yr aff & obt
H P L

[P.S.] Saw David V. Bush last Saturday!

*Notes*

1. *Front:* Poe Cottage, Bronx, N.Y.

[56]     [ANS postcard][1] [HPL to LDC]

> [Postmarked Brooklyn, N.Y.,
> 26 June 1924]
> Wednesday

My dear Daughter:—

Yes—by all means keep the travelling rocker! It's a favourite of mine, & exactly fits me! I meant to drop a line sooner, but was hoping to make it a letter—which I shall send shortly. ¶ Shall be all ready for the miscellaneous material next Monday, when A E P G tells me it will arrive. ¶ Can you get "The Golden Ladder"[2] at Gregory's? Among the cuttings I'm going to send is something about the Jumel Mansion. ¶ I've just read "Visible & Invisible", a new collection of weird stories by E. F. Benson, *one* of which is magnificent! ¶ More anon.

Yr aff parent & obt Servt  H P L

P.S. The Eddy cat has gone to another & a better world, by advice of a veterinary & the Animal Rescue League!

P.P.S. Can you send extras of Greene house, John Carter Brown House, & Sullivan Dorr house?

[P.P.P.S.] Thanks for Peleg Rhodes h.

[P.P.P.P.S.] Tell A E P G all the cheques came safely.

*Notes*

1. *Front:* Blank.

2. HPL refers to *The Golden Ladder* (New York: Harper, 1924), by bestselling writer Rupert Hughes (1872–1956). It is a historical novel about Eliza Bowen (1775–1865), a Providence-born woman who married Stephen Jumel (who in 1810 purchased the home now known as the Morris–Jumel Mansion, which HPL frequently visited) and later married Aaron Burr. See also Margaret L. Oppenheimer, *The Remarkable Rise of Eliza Jumel* (Chicago: Chicago Review Press, 2016).

[57]     [ANS postcard][1] [HPL to LDC]

> [Postmarked Englewood, N.J.,
> 7 July 1924]

New-Jerseying for the afternoon—equipped with big game rifles for the mosquitoes. (Joke, vintage 1830)

Love from Sonia!

And more of the same from
    Yr aff: father & obt Servt
        H P L

## Notes

1. *Front:* Dyckman St. Ferry Drive, Englewood, N.J.

[58]    [ANS postcard][1] [HPL to LDC]

> [Postmarked Newark, N.J.,
> 23 July 1924]

Still on the trail of the colonial! This church was built in 1787, & there's another here built in 1810. Newark is quite a town, but the antiquities are far apart & hard to find. ¶ Will write soon. ¶ Can I have extras of the Market House, Old Stone house, & Franklin Hotel in the Corners & Characters? Yr aff nephew & obt Servt H P L

## Notes

1. *Front:* First Presbyterian Church, Newark, N.J.

[59]    [AHT] [HPL to LDC]

> 259 Parkside Ave.
> Brooklyn, N.Y.
> August 1, 1924

My dear Daughter Lillian:—

    I trust that my occasional cards have helped to dispel the impression which my extended epistolary silence may have created, that Grandpa Theobald is altogether dead and buried! Truth to tell, the death and burial are only partial, and occasioned by the bustle and strain of the industrial quest which tense finances have served to accelerate. The non-materialisation of sundry literary prospects, coupled with the somewhat disastrous collapse of S.H.'s independent millinery venture, has created something of a shortage in the exchequer; so that it seemed advisable for me to investigate whatever commercial prospects of any kind might offer themselves—but the results thereof to date have been conspicuously negative. Positions of every kind seem virtually unattainable to persons without experience, and the enclosed matter—representing only part of the total attempts made—tells the tale of a quest which has so far failed to pay for the ink and shoe-leather consumed. What came nearest to materialisation was the Newark venture—whose interesting amplitude has led me to devote a separate envelope to it. As you will note, it began by my answering an attractive advertisement and receiving an attractive reply. I telephoned to Newark immediately upon receiving the first Ott letter, and made an appointment for the next day—Wednesday, July 23. The opening proved to be for canvassing salesmen to introduce the service of the Creditors' National Clearing House, a Boston firm with a Newark branch, whose specialty (vide enclosed sales approach as revised by me) is the collection of slightly overdue accounts before they develop into bad debts. The sales manager, Mr. Ott, seemed to welcome my affiliation; and although there was no salary—only a commission on sales, with a prospect of a permanent district position if a certain amount of business was done in three months—I decided to give the thing a trial . . . especially since all other positions seemed unattainable. Accordingly I took home contracts, application for bond, and the like, and the next day returned to Newark, where I presented the filled-out blanks and received a briefcase full of selling material which I was to study before reporting for final details at a salesmen's meeting Saturday morning. The situation, on investigation, seemed clear; so much so that I revised the main line of approach (vide enclosed) in order to marshal the facts effectively. On Saturday the 26th I attended the salesmen's meeting, absorbed points from veteran salesmen, and was introduced to the head of the Newark branch, a crude but well-meaning fellow named William J. Bristol, who seems to display traces of a Levantine heritage. My revised version of the "selling talk" created something of a sensation in a mild way, and I had the satisfaction of hearing myself mentioned at the meeting—when Mr. Ott announced to the assembled multitude that my text was to be adopted thereafter as the regular sales formula of the house! But the actual struggle began on Monday, when I set out to canvass among wholesalers whose names, as per Ott's suggestion, I had culled from a telephone business directory. One of the enclosed documents—the rough draught of my day's report to Ott—tells the salient features of this fruitless and exhausting day. Much energy spent, but nothing gained. By the time fatigue supervened to cut the labour short, I had reached a pretty definite opinion that I lack the magnetism, or brass, or whatever wizardry it may be, which forms the essential part of an effective canvasser. But, having been told by a veteran that retailers are easier than wholesalers, I returned to the fray on Wednesday, after my joints and muscles had progressed somewhat on the road to retained normalcy. This time I covered the main business district of Brooklyn, but with results scarcely better than before. The dealers were more courteous, but not a whit more inclined to discussion. Only two—an optician and a tailor—cared so much as to hear the distinctive features of the collection service or to have printed matter left with them. Obviously, I was not progressing very rapidly toward the nonchalant and insolent successfulness of the born canvasser! On Thursday—yesterday—I (together with one other novice, a dashing and prepossessing young ex-officer in the A.E.F. named Edward Hutchings) had an appointment to meet the head of the branch in Manhattan, and to be taken around on a specimen canvassing tour with an expert, so that subtle points of experienced salesmanship might be picked up. The meeting-point was the Fulton St. entrance of the Hudson Tubes (about which A.E.P.G. can tell you), and Hutchings and I were promptly on hand at the designated hour— nine-thirty a.m. He had had slightly better success than I, but was very dissat- isfied with his progress and intimated the likelihood of his early resignation. Our conferees—Bristol and a breezy veteran salesman named De Kay—were over half an hour late; but treated us to a free open car ride up Broadway to the New York sub-branch—the office of a Mr. D. Costa, who takes orders from the Newark territorial headquarters. There many details were discussed, but the "roughneck" nature of the proposition became more and more evi- dent—especially since it developed that most successful canvassing lies among the so-called "needle trades"—i.e., garment industries which are al- most wholly in the hands of the most impossible sort of persons. The party then split for the specimen tours; De Kay taking Hutchings and Bristol taking me. I had not walked far when my guide became very candid about the tone of the business, and admitted that a gentleman born and bred has very little chance for success in such lines of canvassing salesmanship . . . where one must either be miraculously magnetic and captivating, or else so boorish and callous that he can transcend every rule of tasteful conduct and push conver- sation on bored, hostile, and unwilling victims. I will own that I was marvel- lously relieved to be able to resign my arduous burthen without serving the week's notice which had been stipulated in the contract—and I was still fur- ther pleased at the deference and cordiality which honest Bristol displayed. For no sooner was the canvassing proposition out of the way, than he began to tell me something of his future plans, and to intimate that he may be able to co-operate with me quite extensively some time in revisory and other ways. He is (though he asked me not to mention it) dissatisfied with his present managership, and anxious to re-enter the insurance business, where his main experience lies. When he does that, he said, he may be able to offer me some proposition of really feasible nature; for in such a case he would need the as- sistance of a gentleman . . . his own crudity being painfully in his conscious- ness, and forming in his opinion a serious handicap to his success in higher lines of commercial endeavour. As a beginning, he is having me revise (or ra- ther, write completely from oral hints) a letter of application for a general agency or district managership, which he means to send in duplicate to all the principal insurance companies of the country. With this approach in faultless rhetoric, he relies on his practical knowledge of the business to plead his cause after he has secured an audience with whatever powers may be. Here's wishing him success—his plight is a bit pathetic, taking into account the ceaseless struggle between unlimited ambition and a crudity of which he does not share David V. Bush's idyllic unconsciousness. He wants to improve his speech and oratory as well as his written style—but for this I have referred him to a better authority than myself—none other than good old Morton, who is a graduate and former instructor of the Curry School of Expression in Boston.[1] Heigho—it's a great life! I enclose the application letter I have prepared for Bristol. No use—if I have any forte, it's in the line of writing and revision. The best sort of position I'll ever get is one which employs my pen—and I trust in Time and the Gods to put such an opening in my path![2]

Yes, so far as finance is concerned, we have no bonanzas today! As I said, the independent millinery venture turned out badly; and S.H. has had great difficulty in finding another regular affiliation. A couple of weeks ago she was engaged by a large and prominent firm in 57th Street, the Bruck–Weiss Millinery, whose head is a dour, capricious, and uncultivated woman with more ability than conscientiousness. The salary was to be sixty dollars per week and the duties of great variety and importance. One of the first acts of the firm was to request from S.H. a list of all her tried and true customers, and a form letter to be sent to all of them, telling of the new affiliation and urging them to transfer their patronage to the establishment. This did not impress S.H. very favourably, but she nevertheless complied; furnishing a letter of admirable point and taste, which the firm was glad enough to adopt, multigraph, and distribute to those whom S.H. had listed. But lo! Only yesterday S.H. was notified that on account of slack trade she is to have a vacation for the next two weeks—a device, she is certain, for severing the connexion altogether, although the final dismissal will not come at once, but will arrive tardily and sneakily by letter or over the telephone. The "game", apparently, was to extract the list of names and the letter—wherefore S.H. was hired despite the fact that the sales force was evidently large enough before. Now that the desiderate matter is obtained, the victim may look out for herself! Such is modern business, as practiced by the rising and exotic commercial oligarchy of bad manners and vacant background into whose hands the apparel trade of this colourful and heterogeneous metropolis hath fallen! The immediate results for this household are alarming enough. Unless something arrives from somewhere, the overdue instalments on the Bryn Mawr property will furnish a pretty complication indeed—whilst as to immediate rent, grocery bills, and the like . . . . one may only bow ceremoniously to Pegāna's gods. We have considered cheaper living quarters; though of course as long as I decide to retain my own life, my books, furniture, and heirlooms will be with me. Mariano's semi-annual cheque arrived this morning,[3] and I shall proceed with proper caution to its cashing and dispersal. Meanwhile my economy is something to admire . . . if I do say it myself! I never spent so little in my life before, and am soundly laying the foundations of a strong and miserly character. When I do get gold, I shall be like Old Gaspard in the Chimes of Normandy, and keep it in leathern bags to take out now and then for admiration; letting it clink through my fingers and through my unkempt hair . . . if I have any of the latter left. Better be sure to keep me supplied with that hair tonic, lest I

have to spin my future doubloons and pieces of eight on a glabrous and reluctant hemisphere! But avaunt, dull care! Let me drown my worries in wa-
tered ink, or the clatter of Remington keys. I might remark, as a matter of
collecting discursive loose ends, that among the things we've done is to look
over houses with a view toward room-renting . . . . . and also that my underwear did come safely from the Boston Store, as I erroneously thought I had
mentioned on one of my inter-epistolary pictorial rectangles.

Ah, yes—it's about time for the diary now. I believe my last previous instalment was to A.E.P.G., and covered June the 30th, on which date the final
furniture instalment arrived. Well, the sun rose quite as usual on the following
day, apparently unmoved by the sudden augmentation of Flatbush's ligneous
wealth. At noon both S.H. and I went over to 'Ittle-Sonny's for lunch; and in
the afternoon the ladies confabulated indoors whilst Sonny and his Grandpa
strolled on Riverside Drive, and later stopped on a settee to read Wilde's
"The Critic as Artist". As A.E.P.G. can tell you, there's a delightful and
many-path'd park on the steep side-hill betwixt Riverside Drive and the adjacent railway tracks and shore. Were it not for the human herds who waddle
through it, it would be one of the choicest spots—or rather strips—on this
terraqueous globe. On the following day—July 2nd—S.H. and I went down
town on one of the last of our bonnet-bearing expeditions; incidentally meeting Kleiner quite by chance in 40th Street. That evening I went to a stag gathering at the Dench menage, held in honour of Leonard A. Merritt, of
Washington, D.C., Dench's amiable and pleasantly vacuous father-in-law.
This had previously been announced wrongly—but Kleiner gave me the
straight tip at that chance encounter I spoke of—thus enabling me to take in
an event which I had quite given up because of overstaying at Belknap's on
the day when I thought it was to occur. Anyhow, it wasn't as bad a bore as I
had anticipated, and Arthur Leeds and I quite forgot our dignity in an orgy of
song—both he and I being conspicuously well stored with the random bal-
lads of generations agone, when we were young and carefree. The next
night—July 3—marked a meeting of The Boys at Belknap's. As usual, the
programme was interesting; and this time diversified by interruptions made
for the purpose of listening to Democratic convention reports over the radio.
"ALABAMA—24 VOTES FOR UNDERWOOD . . . . . . GENTLEM . . . . .
OUR GRAN' AN' GLORIOUS NATIO . . . . . . THE GEMPMUN I WISH
TO INTRODUCE . . . . I AFFIRM THA . . . BLAH . . . . BLAH . . . . ." and
thus progresses the always fashionable middle-class sport of political evasion
and self-delusion. McNeil was absent—poor old duffer, he takes his Dutton
contract seriously and slaves incessantly on "Tonty of the Iron Hand" . . . . so
much so that Leeds has nicknamed him "Mac of the Iron Routine". After the
dispersal at two a.m., Kleiner, Leeds, and I walked down to 49th Street before
a final disintegration. The next day—the so-called glorious fourth of the Yankee rebels—S.H. and I devoted to open-air reading in Prospect Park. We

have discovered a delightfully unfrequented rock overhanging a lake not far from our own door; and there we while away many an hour in the pages of chosen friends from our well-stocked shelves. On this occasion my book was "Marius the Epicurean", and hers was your old acquaintance "The Conqueror", by Gertrude Atherton.[4] So great an impression did the latter volume produce, that upon our next trip down town we visited the impressive pyramidal tomb of Alexander Hamilton in Trinity Churchyard! Saturday, the fifth, this reading programme was repeated; and on Sunday we spent most of the day answering the help wanted advertisements in the Sunday papers. Monday the seventh, we dedicated to pleasure and travel—that is, after one business interview—meeting at Trinity about noon, paying our respects to Hamilton's grave, visiting the fine Colonial town house of President James Monroe (of Monroe Doctrine fame), which is now sunk in slum degradation and imperilled by new building plans (see enclosed picture), threading some Colonial alleys in Greenwich-Village, and finally taking the omnibus at Washington Square and riding all the way up to Fort George, where we descended the steep hill to Dyckman Street, took lunch in a humble restaurant, (that had a fascinating whitish kitten) and proceeded to the ferry. Here embarking, we crossed the spacious Hudson to the foot of the Palisades; changing to an omnibus which climbed the precipitous slope by a zigzag road arrangement affording some magnificent views, and which finally turned inland through a forest road lined with fine estates and terminating at the quaint and sleepy village of Englewood, N.J., which A.E.P.G. can describe to you. After that we rode down to Fort Lee (opposite 125th St.) by trolley, crossed to the ferry, and rode all the way home by various changes of open surface car. It was a great day, and gave us some fine sunset glimpses of the Woolworth and Municipal buildings as we changed cars at the Brooklyn Bridge on the homeward trip.

The next day—Tuesday the eighth—I spent the afternoon with Sonny, going to an excellent cinema show near his house. In the evening S.H. and I went down to Dench's at Sheepshead Bay, where a gathering was held for the out-of-town amateurs passing through on their way home from the N.A.P.A. Boston convention. Morton was there—having returned only that same day—but he could do no more than say "ave atque vale",[5] since the next day he was off again for points south, to attend an Esperanto congress in Arden, Del., and deliver a radio speech from a Philadelphia department store. It's a great life—ho, for the happy gypsy road! On this occasion I met for the first time the Michigan amateur Clyde G. Townsend (no relative of Delilah's, but a fine Nordic specimen with yellow hair and blue eyes!),[6] the prepossessing Alabaman W. Alvin Cook, my literary enemy Edna Hyde of New Jersey,[7] and an attractive young man named Albert Rader, from Lorain, Ohio, whose tempestuous experiences have recently preëmpted front page space in the *Evening Bulletin*. The days now following were exceedingly domestic, being devoted mainly to home work, local house-inspecting walks, and innocuous readings in the park. The one exception was Thursday evening, the tenth, when I celebrated A.E.P.G.'s birthday by attending the meeting of The Boys at Belknap's—the last held before Sonny's departure with his papa and mamma for Maine. This time we succeeded in dragging out good old McNeil, and but for Morton's absence would have had a full house. After the farewells in the early morning, Kleiner, McNeil, and I walked down town along Riverside Drive, whilst Leeds took the subway to meet an interesting young friend of his—a supernally intelligent Greek who keeps a restaurant and dabbles in the sciences, and who had promised Leeds a good meal at closing time in grateful payment for scholastic and intellectual aid furnished in connexion with some correspondence course he is taking. As our party traversed the Drive we beheld the aftermath of what must have been a very spectacular accident . . . . an overturned omnibus suffering mutely on its side, with its nose ploughed half way into a stately roadside tree. McNeil then confessed that he never dares to ride on one of those pesky modern contrivances . . . though we of sterner stuff despise life and safety, and continue to camp upon the racing roofs regardless of any base material considerations. After Kleiner and I dropped McNeil, we looked up Leeds at his protege's eating-house; and sure enough, there we found him, engaged in learned post-prandial discourse with the youthful proprietor, and rehearsing in detail the glory that was Greece. When we entered, they were classically agreeing that the Hermes of Praxiteles ought never to be brought to America. But the day was yet young! Another Hellene was there on a visit to his "ro'st-biff-kipp-caffee-butt'rrr-to'st" compatriot, and had with him a shining new motor-car, wrested from Fortune by that shrewdness to be expected in a cultural heir of the πολυμήχανος Ὀδυσσεύς.[8] Into this, upon a cordial invitation, all the motley company piled; proceeding to take a leisurely spin through the drives of southern Central Park with all the assurance of early evening. This done, and our Achaian allies bidden a ceremonious farewell, we were yet loath to break up! Kleiner being opprest by the pangs of an ever-recurrent hunger, we stopped at a neat little South American or Mexican restaurant at the entrance to the 49th Street subway station; where the sufferer assuaged his inward gnawings with a plate of Chile con carne—a highly spiced dish which I mean some day to investigate for myself. Our legion thereafter crossed the road to a less bizarre and extranational refectory, where we wound up on discussion of the cosmos and a cup of coffee apiece. At last we parted—in, or shortly prior to, the dawn's early light; staggering to the subway with riotously linked arms, and hiccoughing forth with all the abandon of caffeine-spifflocated souses the plaintive staves of that venerable psalm tune, "We won't go home till morning."[9] At about five a.m., having successfully dodged the traditional fusillade of conjugal flatirons and rolling-pins, I was with Hypnos, Lord of Slumbers. Friday the eleventh was domestic and quiet. So was Saturday, though diversified by a walk way down Flatbush Avenue in the evening—to a strange cinema called the Farragut. En route we discovered a delightful old English byway—a placid backwater of life, far from the bustling main road, whose houses followed the Elizabethan pattern, and whose lights were old iron lanthorns. Sunday the thirteenth was another advertisement-answering day—ugh!—and on the morrow I tried some personal replies to notices calling for such. It was a weary and detestable tramp—door to door, refusal to refusal—and by evening I was ready to change the subject, notwithstanding that I had managed to work in quite a little artistic and antiquarian sightseeing. I walked up Madison Avenue, where the choicest emporia of the rare and beautiful hold forth, and in great windows lost myself amidst antique vases and clocks, ship models and miniatures, and classically carven desks whereon have rested quill pens and lace-ruffled wrists. Then, too, I revisited the narrow and twisting Colonial sections of lower Manhattan, and spacious Sutton Place, up near the piers of the Queensboro Bridge, where wealth and taste have reclaimed one short section of dingy Avenue A, making it into a paradise of Georgian gardens and Londonesque facades, with quaint terraces overlooking the East River that rushes far below. A.E.P.G. will know the locality approximately if you tell her that it is within about three blocks of the Jane Teller Mansion which she and I visited—in 61st St. Another thing I visited that day was Chinatown—Mott and Dyer Sts., branching off from sordid Chatham Square. This I had seen after dark two years ago with Kleiner and Loveman; but I now beheld it for the first time by day. There are some interesting Oriental balconies, carved and gilded, but so few that one's expectations are invariably disappointed. Whilst I was absent Small Sonny called up to tell his Grandpa he was leaving for Maine. Tuesday came more local walking and house-inspecting—including a jaunt through green, shady ways in western Flatbush which remind one infinitely of such Providence sections as Cooke St. In the evening I did some Bush work—a sudden job to be included in a coming book. On Wednesday I took my Bush work along—together with the "Kasidah" of Sir Richard Burton[10]—for a day of hard work in the open. First accompanying S.H. to a business appointment which after all yielded nothing, I next proceeded to show her some of the sights I had myself seen on the previous Monday; including Madison Avenue and Sutton Place. Then depositing her on a homeward car, I took David V. and Sir Richard on foot to Central Park, where I spent all the afternoon wandering in green ways or sitting on rocks beneath rural shade; reading and revising, revising and reading. By evening I had worked up to the northern boundary, and had scaled the height whereon stands the old 1812 blockhouse. In returning I crossed into Morningside Park, scaled the heights beside the Cathedral of St. John the Divine, and emerged on the Columbia campus; taking the homeward train at Broadway and 116th St. And this brought us around to another Thursday—blest occasion! This time the meeting was at my favourite spot—right here—a place where it is not often held whilst Belknap is in town, since his mama doesn't let him go to Brooklyn at night. Now he was away, and we tough old fellows could meet where we pleased! Yet even so, McNeil was absent. Poor old Tonty! If it weren't for Leeds, who drags him out by force once in every so often, the good soul would vegetate in his slum tenement and never breathe the air of civilisation! Well, be that as it may, we had a darned good time. I dug up all my old New England Primers, Grandpa's "District School as it Was",[11] and sundry ancestral school books of marked archaism and naivete; and Morton and I gave selected readings illustrative of the elementary academic spirit of the early American culture—the unsophisticated culture of that pioneer period whose end we may place roughly in the thirties—though it survived longer in remote districts, so that Mr. Hoag remembers it well. Leeds read from a new story of his—something about strange adventure in Northern New Zealand—and at last, after the penning of a joint epistle to Tiny Belknap, we disbanded for the week .... tired but happy, and a good time having been had by all. The day after was domestic and uneventful. Saturday was equally so, save that just as I write these lines I have a curious notion that it was *this* instead of the *preceding* Saturday that we went to that distant cinema and saw that curious old English terrace in the gentle twilight when the ancient lamps flickered up one by one. That is the deuce of compiling a diary purely from memory and without notes, covering the better part of a month. One *will* get dates mixed! But there's no mixture about Sunday the twentieth—for that's when I wrote the batch of letters including the Newark one! Monday I was at home attending—or trying to attend—to amateur correspondence. Tuesday my Newark reply came—and I also received a disconcerting telephone to the effect that on the Saturday before—whilst participating in a B.P.C. hike which we did not attend—Kleiner had been struck by a motor and quite severely injured! I called up his house at once, and was relieved to learn from his cousin that he was, though painfully hurt, in no danger. He was confined to his bed, but would soon be up in a dressing-gown and able to receive individual guests. It seems that he had been hit by the fender, knocked down, and dragged some distance. Morton picked him up and carried him to the roadside, where it was soon seen that no bones were broken. The offending motorist, admirably contrite, carried him to the Jamaica Hospital, where several stitches were taken in a cut above his eye, and other wounds dressed in the milder fashion that they demanded. He was conscious throughout, and so stoically brave that his friends are according him new laurels of admiration. The motorist later conveyed him home, and generally displayed a deep concern and courtesy. After telephoning Kleiner, I also wrote him a cheering letter; including the following impromptu lines:

> Mechanick Force the gentle Poet feels,
> And Genius sinks beneath insensate Wheels;
> Unfeeling Matter, careless of its Way,

Rides down the Light that sheds PIERIA'S Ray.
But lo! from ev'ry Grove and Fountain run
Consoling Nymphs with healing Orison,
So whilst the dull Destroyer hides in Shame,
The Bard triumphant shines with brighter Flame!

In the late afternoon we had a call from a Mr. Bailey, connected with the Homeland Co. who sold us the Bryn Mawr land, and discussed with him the type of house we would wish if we ever got that far out of the morass of fiscal peril.[12] He was a naive and architecturally unlettered young fellow, and appeared vastly interested in what was said about pure Colonial design. I showed him my file of Corners and Characters, and most of my Colonial post cards as well. What these modern chaps need is to realise that even the best of modern so-called Colonial houses cannot begin to equal in simple classicism the average genuine specimen built in the eighteenth century. There is a tawdriness about modern taste which seems psychologically to inhibit the architect from sticking to the austere purity of real Georgian design. The next day—Wednesday—I went to Newark for the first time; taking the Hudson Tubes[13] which A.E.P.G. knows so well, and proceeding straight to my destination [. . .] the train—which after a time comes to the surface and runs over the P.R.R. tracks to the Park Place Station, Newark. On alighting in this large city (414,524 in the 1920 census) I was both puzzled and delighted at the air of straggling rusticity which prevails despite the indubitably large population. There is a great open common shadowed by the spire of a Colonial church— Trinity Cathedral, built in 1746, but extensively reconstructed in 1810, after a disastrous fire. No tall buildings are seen, and the people proceed about their business with a leisurely air difficult to associate with so extensive a place. The streets are, with too few exceptions, unpicturesquely broad; and there are not enough hills and alleys and curving courts to make the spot really fascinating. Even the modern features are unimpressive—suggesting Philadelphia rather than New York. Providence is so prodigiously superior both in scenery and antiquities, and in modern beauty and smartness, that no comparison is possible. It seems incredible that Providence, with its mature finish and spruce grace, should actually be much the smaller of the two. But Newark is not to be despised! Besides Trinity, there is the First Presbyterian Church of which I sent you a picture—built in 1787, and standing with its venerable rear churchyard directly beside the building (fragmentarily discernible in the view) where the Creditors' National Clearing House holds forth. Then there is an excellent Public Library, a well-equipped historical society, some alluring bookstalls, (one of which is in a Colonial house) and a few fine old specimens of domestic architecture—especially the Plume homestead, a magnificent stone gambrel-roofer of the middle eighteenth century; perfectly preserved, but (to my ineffable and impotent rage) about to be torn down to make way for some beastly modern thing. That is the vice of Newark—disregard for the past. Nearly all the connected blocks of Colonial houses have been swept away, so that by comparison Providence, Salem, or any New England town is a living leaf of the golden yesterday. On the next day—Thursday the twenty-fourth—I revisited Newark; and later paid a call on the invalid poet, whom I found in dressing-gown and slippers, hopping about with the aid of a cane, but uncowed and untainted in spirit. Having discussed with him all things ancient and semi-ancient, I returned home for a hasty supper and set off for McNeil's to a meeting of The Boys—a meeting which, naturally enough, my host of the afternoon could not consider attending. The programme was fairly interesting, and we disbanded with a resolve to carry the mountain to Mohammed on the following week, and hold the meeting at Kleiner's own residence—which is generally avoided by the timid members on account of the geographical difficulty of reaching a spot so enmeshed in the trackless labyrinth that is Brooklyn. Friday was a home day—spent largely in studying the preliminary part of my ill-starred mercantile venture. Saturday I attended the salesmen's meeting in Newark, later coming home and becoming properly transfixed with astonishment on receiving a telephone call from one whom I had fancied far away in Ovidian exile at the Tomi of Belgrade Lakes—LITTLE BELKNAP HIM-SELF! It seems that his mother, whose health is nearly as uncertain as his own, had been taken ill in Maine; developing a high fever, and seeming in general so upset that a return to New York was the only safe thing to plan. The return had benefited her, and she was now steadily recovering, but Belknap's nerves were still shaken with the strain of the sudden perturbation. As it happened, I had large news to impart to him . . . not only Kleiner's accident, about which he was properly sympathetic, but the coming advent to New York—perhaps within three weeks—of that arch-poet and aesthete, destined at once to step to the supremacy of our circle—SAMUEL LOVEMAN! Most of Loveman's friends, including George Kirk, Hart Crane, and Gordon Hatfield, are already in the metropolis; and he now means to follow—fortified by the virtual certainty of the literary success and recognition for which he has so long striven. His book on the late Edgar Saltus is about to be professionally published, and Saltus' widow is anxious to meet him and aid him in establishing himself as a standard literary figure. He certainly has all the congratulations and good wishes of our circle, and we have begun to pride ourselves on the higher literary tone which our hebdomadal discussions will assume under his influence. In a way, this will give a better showing to our aesthetic party, now represented only by Sonny and myself, as against the more Philistine faction which Leeds, Kleiner, McNeil, and Morton represent. Belknap, though, may be away when Loveman arrives; since the family plan to atone for their shattered Novangling by a trip to Atlantic City. But to resume the journal—on Sunday the twenty-seventh S.H. and I attended the B.P.C. meeting at Sheepshead Bay, and I was formally voted in as a member of the organisation. Ugh . . . now I'll have to pay dues! Kleiner was there with his cane—conveyed to and from the festivities by Ernest Adams, who has a motor. Discussion was interesting whilst it lasted, but we returned early to prepare for the coming strenuous day . . . . and dii immortales, what a day it turned out to be! Blue Monday! You will find elsewhere the harrowing chronicle of this industrious episode, but I may add that between breaths I unearthed some highly interesting Colonial houses on Brooklyn Heights—the region where the shore abruptly rises just opposite New York. Most of them are wooden, much like the town houses of Colonial New England, save that they have the New York type of door. All of which reminds me that I wish I could have seen a well-preserved series of Colonial doorways in Newark. Unlike most of the other towns of this region, Newark has no Dutch antecedents, but was founded in 1666 by Connecticut malcontents under Robert Treat. It ought, therefore, to have our New England characteristics rather than those vestigial Netherlandisms which distinguish the dominant reliquiae of this terrain as a whole. For one thing, the great triangular common or village green is an unmistakable New England inheritance. But I ramble. Tuesday morning I was laid up, and in the afternoon I went to see Little Sonny. His mother, he said, was comfortably sitting up; though I did not see her. Sonny and I settled the fate of literature betwixt us and parted early in the evening—with the understanding that The Boys meet up there on Thursday, August 7th, if Mrs. Long is well enough to stand the racket. Otherwise we convene at Morton's dump in Bantu and barbaric Harlem, our first meeting there, by the way. Wednesday was my retail canvassing experience—a pale rose and lavender repetition of the intensive ordeal of Monday. Enough is a sufficiency, as little Sandy puts it! In the evening S. H. and I dined out—getting a splendid roast chicken dinner at the Blue Bird Inn, a converted dwelling-house directly beside the Parkside Ave. subway station . . . . A.E.P.G. may recall seeing it. After that we walked in Prospect Park in search of a Quaker burying ground which we didn't find—although we wandered interestingly in the young dusk, and became picturesquely lost—as Grandpa and I used to get lost driving "Tom" in East Providence—on some unknown height whence we could behold New York harbour and the statue of Liberty. Yesterday—you see that I'm catching up with Old Man Chronos after all—I wound up my commercial business as indicated earlier in this twenty-volume tome, and attended the Boys' meeting at Kleiner's in the evening. It was a great old session—the high spot being the reading by Leeds of a hideous short story by Algernon Blackwood—"The Listener,"—from a volume which none of the rest of us had ever seen before. Kleiner himself was very chipper, though still wedded to his oaken staff to some extent. He expects to be with us next time, whether we convene at Sonny's or at Mortonius'. After the meeting Morton, Leeds, McNeil and I walked together to the De Kalb Ave. subway station, where we parted—I to go south, and the rest north—north, into the Arctic wastes of darkest Manhattan! So here we are! Today has been a home day, with reading (Plato's Dialogues) and letter-writing (if you call this a real letter) as salient landmarks. O yes—the package came a couple of hours ago, and I have been distributing the sundries in their respective habitats—silver, book, handkerchief, Corners and Characters, etc. . . . . . . . . Thanks!

  I am ever Yr most aff: Nephew & Obt Servt,

    H. P. L.

## Notes

1. Samuel Silas Curry (1847–1921) founded the School of Elocution and Expression (now Curry College) in Milton, MA, in 1879.

2. HPL alludes to a book by Lord Dunsany.

3. See letter 56n6.

4. *Marius the Epicurean* is a philosophical novel by Walter Pater. *The Conqueror* is a historical novel about Alexander Hamilton.

5. "Hail and farewell."

6. Clyde G. Townsend (1898–1966) was editor of the *Oracle* (to which HPL contributed the essay "The Omnipresent Philistine") and vice president of the NAPA in 1922–23 (when HPL was president). HPL also refers to Delilah Townsend (1870?–1944), an African American woman who was a servant at 454 Angell Street and in later years continued to do occasional work for HPL's aunts.

7. Edna Hyde (formerly Edna von der Heide) was coeditor of the *Inspiration* (of which HPL was assistant editor and to which he contributed the poem "Britannia Victura"). It is not clear why he refers to her as his "literary enemy," as he generally speaks favorably of her work in his various columns on amateur journalism.

8. "Resourceful Odysseus." See Homer, *Iliad* 2.173.

9. "We Won't Go Home Till Morning," a traditional tune adapted by several composers, including Stephen Foster.

10. *The Kasidah of Hâjî Abdû El-Yezdî* (1880) is a long philosophical poem purportedly translated from the Farsi by Sir Richard Burton (1821–1890) but actually written by him.

11. A book by Warren Burton. HPL refers to the fact that AEPG had given the book to HPL's grandfather, Whipple Phillips, who in turn gave it to HPL. See LDC/AEPG 100.

12. HPL refers to the fact that he and Sonia had, in May, purchased two home lots in Bryn Mawr Park, a development in Yonkers. But on 29 July HPL wrote to the Homeland Company: "Owing to financial difficulties of the most acute and unforeseen sort, I find myself unable at present to make the remittances now due on the property which I purchased last May at Bryn Mawr Park" (ms., JHL). Sonia managed to retain control of at least one of these lots for a few more years.

13. Subway lines beneath the surface of the Hudson River, connecting lower Manhattan and Jersey City, Newark, and Hoboken, NJ. Now called the PATH trains.

[60]    [ANS postcard]¹ [HPL to LDC]

[no postmark:
19 August 1924]

Fraunces' Tavern

Built 1719 as residence of Etienne De Lancey, Esq. Bought 1762 by Sam<sup>l</sup> Fraunces', from y<sup>e</sup> West Indies, & open'd by him as y<sup>e</sup> Queen's Head. Later call'd Fraunces' Tavern. Degenerated to miscellaneous commercial purposes in 19<sup>th</sup> century—in 1907 restor'd to exact form it had as a tavern in y<sup>e</sup> time of Gen<sup>l</sup> Washington.

H. P. Lovecraft eat here on 19th August 1924.

*Notes*

1. *Front:* Fraunces' Tavern / Broad and Pearl Sts. / New York.

[61]    [AHT] [HPL to LDC]

259 Parkside-Avenue

Brookland-Parish

Province of New-York

20th August, 1724

My dear Daughter Lillian:—

[. . .]

Thursday, August fourteenth, was spent in correspondence; the largest specimen going to A.E.P.G. in Holliston. In the evening The Boys met at Morton's—up in niggerville—and had a great time despite the African cast of the contiguous terrain. Everybody but Sonny was present, and all subjects under the sun were discussed. Afterward—about two a.m., Kirk, Leeds, and I walked all the way down town in the "burning moonlight" (as James Elroy Flecker phrases it in "Hassan"),¹ loitering around 49th St. and petting an amiable yellow cat till the imminence of dawn drove us timidly away, as is the wont of ghostly apparitions. Friday and Saturday were solid home days—except that on Saturday evening S.H. and I went to the cinema—The Linden—and saw an indifferent melodrama entitled "The Woman on the Jury".² Sunday we answered advertisements and hoped for the best, but Monday we decided to have some fun whilst life might last, so went to the American Museum of Natural History. Here we lingered over the illuminated bird displays (vide enclosed circular—they consist of stuffed specimens mounted amidst artificial scenery of the most elaborate description—ask A.E.P.G.), and noted in passing the famous dinosaur eggs discovered by the museum's Mongolian expedition.³ The latter were not impressive—being the eggs of a very small dinosaur, the ancestor of the later massive species. We also dwelt upon the antiquities of Peru and Mexico, indulging in infinite speculations on the sources of the strange Inca and Aztec civilisations. It is my opinion, that a thread of cultural homogeneity runs through all the various Indian groups, no matter how widely separated. The carved totem-poles of the Tlingit tribes of Alaska and British Columbia have true analogues in the grotesque monoliths of Yucatan and Cuzco, thousands of miles to the south; and I can even fancy a crude echo of the influence in the rough pictorial attempts of our own relatively undeveloped Eastern Indians—Iroquois, Mohegans, Pequots, Narragansetts, and the like. That the great centres of civilisation in Central and South America once had contacts with external cultures of Asia and Africa is highly probable; but despite this I think the central thread of their artistic tradition is indigenous—that is, spontaneous with all the copper-skinned hordes who entered the continent over Behring Strait before history, and whose successive dispersals gave rise to the several branches of the Indian race. We intend shortly to revisit the American Indian Museum high up on Broadway. After the museum, we took an 8th Ave. surface car down town, and dined in Italian style at the Milan restaurant in 42nd St. The spaghetti there is excellent, though I insist that S.H. herself can prepare a brand still more magical in its subtle appeal. After dinner, home. On Tuesday—yesterday—we continued our pleasure-seeking, interrupted only by the industrial recesses mentioned on the first page of this document. This time our programme was antiquarian, and we commenced at Fraunces' Tavern, (open'd in 1762 as The Queen's Head) an antient hostelry famed as the scene of General Washington's farewell to his officers in 1783. As when A.E.P.G. and I visited it in 1922, the door was open'd for us with great ceremony by a servitor in periwig and small-cloaths; and we at once proceeded to the oak-panell'd dining hall, where under the beaming eye of our portray'd host (for Saml. Fraunces' painting hangs over the mantelpiece) and in sight of a magnificent white Colonial archway in the corridor adjacent, we partook of a good repast (S.H. fried clams, H.P. spaghetti) in an atmosphere redolent of greater and earlier dinners—General Washington, Alexander Hamilton, Esq., Nathanael Greene of Rhode-Island, and the like . . . . . all of whom I cou'd clearly discern in spirit, with gleaming silver buckles and periwigs new-powder'd. After dinner we went up the white Colonial staircase to the museum floors aloft—the great hall where General Washington addressed his parting officers, and the third story, where are group'd some of the most interesting relicks I have ever beheld; including many letters writ in Providence during the late unfortunate rebellion of 1775–1783, and an unexcell'd assortment of Colonial Providence papers; embracing, of course, our friend John Carter's *Providence Gazette and Country-Journal,* containing the Freshest Advices both Foreign and Domestick; Printed at the Sign of Shakespear's-Head in Gaol-Lane, and sold by Stationers throughout Providence, and the Southern part of New-England. Likewise was there the Newport Mercury, and many another reminder of the smallest and greatest of American commonwealths. I regretted, however, to observe the absence of Roger Williams' watch, which was there as a loan two years ago. Much of this local material is due to the fact that the curator, a Mr. Drowne, comes of an antient Providence family. The tavern is now the property of the Sons of the American Revolution, having been restor'd from decadence by them in 1907. I enclose herewith a picture, which you may, with my compliments, add to your permanent collection. The neighbourhood wherein this edifice stands, is itself very antient. The slant-roof'd building next the tavern is itself late Colonial, and within a stone's throw are some of the oldest wharves, warehouses, shops, and private houses of the pre-Revolutionary town. Pearl Street was once, as you may recall from "The Golden Ladder", New-York's principal business thoroughfare; Broadway being the fashionable promenade of the freshly powder'd belles and beaux of fashion, much as the Fifth Avenue is today. All in all, our sojourn at the Queen's Head was most enjoyable, and we left it with reluctance at its closing time. I enclose a picture shewing its general aspect to very great advantage. As I think I have mention'd, it is now restor'd with utmost accuracy to its Revolutionary condition. N.B. I filch'd some pieces of sugar wrapped with General Washington's effigy; one of which I will try to insert in this bulky package. On the same evening, at six o'clock, our expedition arriv'd at old Greenwich-Village; resolv'd to wrest from that antient suburban town (now bury'd in the teeming metropolis) the beautiful secrets of its village youth, when trim brick houses with pillar'd doorways wound round and round, in and out, along the prettiest conceivable labyrinths of curving lanes. Greenwich, which I have before described to you, was a delectable Colonial town, and the seat of residence of Admiral Sir Peter Warren, K.C.B., whose fine portrait hangs in the Athenaeum at Portsmouth, N.H. Sir Peter in 1744 married Susannah, daughter of Etienne DeLancey, Esq., (who in 1719 built as his private home the structure sold in 1762 to Saml: Fraunces for a tavern, and just visited by our expedition!) and purchas'd for an estate much Greenwich land, having his house just outside the thicker part of the village, which centred round the present Sheridan Square and Washington Square—the latter then a training-ground new-reclaim'd from being a potter's field. Since Sir Peter's day much change has come—elevated railways have intruded, new wide avenues have been cut through, poverty has attacked many a fine doorway and facade, and slum foreigners and Bohemian decadents have replaced the sturdy English and Dutch villagers. But something of the old spirit has lingered in the antient lanes, and defied alike the forces of time, death, and decay. Greenwich still lives, and in it lives the eighteenth century. Ghosts of gilt-panell'd coaches and three-corner'd hats still flit around certain shadowy corners at twilight; and when candles shine out at evening from the myriad small-pan'd windows, one sees curious shadows of periwigs and lace cuffs on the mildew'd curtains. It is still the Greenwich that Lord Howe and the Prince of Wales knew; still the Greenwich that cheer'd General Washington and Gov. Clinton. Parts of

it—most of it, in fact—I had explor'd before; but recent reading had inform'd me of certain highly obscure and highly Colonial byways which I had
miss'd—so that on this occasion I was not only a guide, but an explorer
awaiting archaic revelations as new to me as to the rest of my party. Entering
the village from Broadway—down which we had ridden in an open car—we
stopped for a cold drink at a chemist's shop in a venerable wooden Colonial
house, on the south side of Washington-Square. Thence going westward, we
frequently darted down this lane and that in quest of some odd antediluvian
sight—finding many a Colonial doorway and once encountering a wooden,
peaked-roof'd house of the New-England Colonial type. One row of low
shops with bow-windows was irresistible! Alexander Hamilton may have
traded there—though I doubt if he would care to do so today. On the corner
of Washington-Square and McDougall-Street, in the iron-fenc'd yard of a colonial mansion, we beheld a fine plump black-and-white cat. A moment later
another appear'd—this one jet black, like my old nigger-man. In two more
moments a prepossessing tiger join'd the company; and by the time I had
stoop'd to stroke the haughty blackamoor, no less than six or seven had assembled; some friendly, some indifferent, and some frankly curious. It was a
feline convention; and, Khatist that I am, I made the most of it in purring and
intelligent conversation. In vain did my spouse seek to set me in motion . . . .
should not an old tomcat occasionally pause to chat with the furry cronies of
his youth? Finally, though, when I had sighted another cat—a black and yellow aristocrat perched on the outside of an ancient small-paned window—
and was about to begin a fresh discussion with him, S.H. dragg'd me away by
main force; checking resistance by pointing to counter-attractions ahead
. . . . . Colonial gables and distant Georgian chimney-pots in West Fourth
Street. So westward we went, pausing in the mellow golden sunset over more
than one idyllick Colonial corner remote from the tide of modern decay.
Sheridan Square has been spoilt—as Kleiner never ceases to lament—by the
extension of broad Seventh Avenue, but even at this point there is many a
noble survivor to evoke the atmosphere of Salem and Beacon Hill and Benefit Street and Thomas St. We now headed still farther west along Grove
Street, having on the horizon ahead the most delicious imaginable silhouette
of Colonial slanting roofs and dormer windows. Best of all, our approach did
not disenchant us; for most of the houses are well kept, and display a cheerful
synthesis of shining knockers and freshly painted classic doorways. At one
time a marvellous vision dawn'd on our right—a wooden house of the New-
England type, white with green blinds, and with all the fascination of Salem
brooding behind the small panes of the windows. Behind this was a white
house of similar date, but rather ruin'd by the owner's effort to make it look
*still older* by means of diamond-paned windows, which belong to the seventeenth century and not to the eighteenth at all. However, new wonders lay
ahead. In the aperture betwixt Nos. 10 and 12 Grove St., there opens the way

to a half-hidden but wholly delightful court, with shrubs and verdure in the centre, and a row of plain but neat and fetching Colonial houses in the rear— the whole exceedingly well-kept. At the end of the street is old St. Luke's Chapel—part of Trinity Parish—and around the corner in Hudson Street are numberless Colonial houses, still solidly preserv'd, though sunk to the uses of an Italian slum. Walking north to Christopher Street, we saw endless rows of Colonial houses in both directions; after which we turned in this thorough-fare to the east, doubling on our general direction, but retracing our way through a slightly different territory in search of the particular seats of quaintness we were seeking. One of these—Gay Street—I had beheld before . . . . and sunk to the steps of one of the ancient houses in an aesthetick transport as I did so. (On June 26). The others—Patchin Place and Milligan Place, were known to me only through books. On this occasion Gay Street came first; and my delighted breathlessness of June was repeated in full as we rounded into the quaint, curving little alley where city turmoil never reaches, and where the trimly huddled little Colonial houses with brick facades, small-paned windows, and knocker'd doorways are undergoing a cheerful process of restoration and renovation despite the unpleasing proximity of African habitations. Gay Street is the soul of the eighteenth century—not even Salem can surpass it, and Marblehead reaches a higher level only in magical Lookout Court. This, forsooth, is the Old Greenwich through which Sir Peter Warren us'd to drive—though I vow to God he had to leave his wide coach in trav-ersing this needle-like byway! Gentle dusk had now half-fallen, and the old lamp posts (which reign supreme in this antique corner of the world) began to shed mellow patches of soft yellow light. From Gay-Street we crossed to Sixth Avenue by the (ugly and Victorian) Jefferson Market, and thence rounded to the approach to Patchin Place—fam'd as a Colonial retreat, but never beheld by me. Imagine the anticipation with which I approached the revealing corner—WHAT marvels of the past lay in store for me in a few short steps more? And may Gad split me if the actuality was not full as pleas-ing as the anticipation! 'Zounds, Ma'am, but what lay spread before mine eyes! A lane of brick Colonial houses with iron-rail'd steps, shaded by slender occasional trees, and diversified by bits of nebulous greenery here and there . . . and at the end a high stone wall with vine-bearing trellis, lit by the solitary antique lamp-post whose pale beams cast alluring shadows of archaic things half of the imagination. I paus'd and looked, then paus'd and looked again— —. It was unbelievable—it was the living Georgian past, and my fancy peo-pled every doorway and window with periwigg'd and satin-coated forms. On-ly the promise of greater wonders could induce me to leave—but had not the guide-book said that Milligan Place, just around the corner off Sixth Avenue, was quainter and more wondrous still? So around the corner we went in the thickening dusk, and it was S.H. who first discerned the tiny opening betwixt two nondescript business places which actually marked the gate to the desiderate haven of antiquity. Even then I could scarce believe that a Georgian oasis could be tucked away so completely amongst the dingy stigmata of shabby modernity, but a neighbouring loafer of weatherbeaten face and incongruously good speech clear'd away my last doubt. This was indeed Milligan Place—so, diving and squeezing into the slight crevice betwixt the dingy modern shop buildings, we left the world behind and were confronted with a sight which will ever remain graven upon my recollection. Picture—only a step from the clanging elevated and vortex of metropolitan trade—a hushed triangular court with flagstone sidewalk, slender saplings here and there, urn and greenery in the widest open spot, single bracket lamp of the most ancient pattern affixed to the north wall, and straight ahead a curving line—surviving from forgotten days when the court was part of a longer alley and led to farther regions now closed—of idyllically simple Colonial doorways with ironrail'd steps and bronze knockers, beside which were small-paned windows now shedding the evening's first beams of candle-light! The hush of centuries was on the place—and not a glimpse of the outside modern world could invade these recesses so carefully guarded by towering three-story walls. Like Providence's old Arsenal Lane, it was a full and perfect fragment of an elder and vanished town; snatched away from the strident changing life around, and embalmed for ever with all the vivid fidelity of a Pharaoh's mummy lying intact in secret and millennial caves below the desert. It was Little Old New York—it was, and is! But one inner wonder more lay unreveal'd! Falling into a conversation with the chrysostomic gentleman of leisure above-mention'd, we learned much of local history;[4] including the fact that the houses in Milligan Court were originally put up in the late 1700's by the Methodist Church, for the poorer but respectable families of the parish. Continuing his expositions, our amiable Mentor led us to a seemingly undistinguished door within the court, and through the dim hallway beyond to a back door. Whither he was taking us, we knew not; but upon emerging from the back door we paus'd in delighted amazement. There, excluded from the world on *every* side by sheer walls and house facades, was *a second hidden court or alley,* with vegetation growing here and there, and on the south side a row of simple Colonial doorways and small-pan'd windows!! It was beyond words—it is still beyond words, and that is why I cannot do it justice here! Buried deep in the entrails of nondescript commercial blocks, this little lost world of a century and a quarter ago sleeps unheeding of the throng. Here stretch worn pavements which silver-buckled shoes have trod—here, hidden in cryptical recesses which no street, lane, or passageway connects with the Manhattan of today! Two dim lamp-posts illumined the scene—that elder and mysterious scene for which the uninitiated search in vain, though scouring every linear inch of New-York's visible streets. Transported, I paus'd to reflect and let my fancy run riot. What awesome images are suggested by the existence of such secret cities within cities! Beholding this ingulph'd and search-defying fragment of yesterday, the active imagination conjures up endless weird possibilities—ancient and unremember'd towns still living in decay, swallow'd up by the stern business blocks that weary the superficial eye, and sometimes sending forth at twilight strains of ghostly music for whose source the modern city-dwellers seek in vain. Having seen this thing, one cannot look at an ordinary crowded street without wondering what surviving marvels may lurk unsuspected behind the prim and monotonous blocks . . . . . Gad's death, if ever I get an unworried moment to write another story, I vow 'twill deal with some such embalmed street, or square as this nameless inner court within a court! I may only add, that this vanished area was once, like Milligan Place outside it, part of an open and accessible thoroughfare. Time closes up roads as well as opens new ones, and in this case a mushroom growth of Victorian buildings broke into fragments—some lost, some still remember'd—a little old lane that used to connect Amos Street with the Union Road. I have an idea that Patchin Place, open to West 10th St. on its south side, was once part of this lane; for its rear wall bears an extremely significant relation to the buildings which, on their other side, block the end of Milligan Place. Heigho! Sweet are the memories of yesterday! Most of the buildings of this colourful section are inhabited by authors and artists who appreciate them—a member, for example, of the celebrated Lippincott family dwelling in Milligan Place. The one drawback is the damp, congested, and somewhat odorous nature of the locality. I was so aesthetically transported that I had no active senses but sight and fancy; but S.H. averr'd that the whole neighbourhood was most intolerably tainted with decay'd fish, and was made quite faint before our final emergence to the "great open spaces" of Eleventh Street. This begins the homeward route. Dusk was now thick, but Eleventh Street lay tranquil and beautiful in the commingled twilight and lamplight. The houses in this thoroughfare seem to be of the 1820–1830 period, but they are all restor'd to Colonial splendour; so that in a recent contest, Eleventh Street was awarded the prize as the most beautiful highway in Greenwich-Village. At one place a spectral surprise lurks. Crossing Sixth Avenue on the way to Fifth, a clump of pallid slabs and shafts salutes the eye; and on the right, huddled behind an iron railing in the angle of a tasteful late-Colonial mansion, we behold a wan bit of isolated and deserted burying ground! It is the second of the ancient Jewish cemeteries, used from 1809 to 1825, and a successor to that still more antique one in New Bowery, which dates from 1656 and was mention'd in my recent travelogue to A.E.P.G. In this second necropolis, the stones are in English; and most of the startlingly palaeogean quality of the elder one is absent. Night had now completely fallen, and we proceeded to the Eighth Street subway station for a train home. It had been a great day, and gave me perhaps more of the ancient New-York than any other one of my numerous pilgrimages. The town is full of Colonial arcana, and in time I mean to unearth and revel in them all! Today has been a home day, and tomorrow The Boys meet at George Kirk's. You, too, must behold all the Colonial arcana eventually!

    With every sort of regards from both, and with the hope of an early reply, I am

        Yr. Most aff: Nephew and obt Servt.
        H. P. L.

*Notes*

1. HPL's memory is in error. The phrase "blazing moonlight" appears in a stage direction in Flecker's play. See *Hassan* (New York: Knopf, 1922), 166.
2. *The Woman on the Jury* (Associated First National Pictures, 1924), directed by Harry O. Hoyt; starring Sylvia Breamer, Frank Mayo, and Lew Cody.
3. Roy Chapman Andrews (1884–1960), American explorer and adventurer who became the director of the American Museum of Natural History, led a series of expeditions into the Gobi Desert and Mongolia in the early 20th century. He acquired the first-known fossil dinosaur eggs for the museum.
4. The scene is reminiscent of HPL's "He" (written on 11 August 1925), where a similarly "chrysostomic" (i.e., golden-tongued) gentleman expounds the history of the area to the narrator. But the courtyard in the story is based on one in Perry Street that HPL found in 1925 (see LDC/AEPG 74).

[62]　　[ANS postcard][1] [HPL to LDC]

        [Postmarked Brooklyn, N.Y.,
        27 August 1924]

One by one we slip! Here's some news that can't wait for a letter. Alfredus—Grandpa's little Galpinius-child—is *married!* The event occurred last June, but The Boy kept it a secret for a while—perhaps waiting to see whether or not it would turn out well. ¶ In a day or two I'm going to send you a delightful little book on Old New York. Yr aff nephew & obt Servt H P L

P.S. Belknap's back, & today George Kirk & I are going to see him.

*Notes*

1. *Front:* St. Paul's Chapel, New York City.

[63]　　[ANS postcard][1] [HPL to LDC]

        [Postmarked Staten Island, N.Y.,
        1 September 1924]

Spending Sunday amidst the Colonial rusticity of Staten Island, whose quaint villages are a cross betwixt East Greenwich, Bristol, Moosup Valley, & Newburyport. Will have another travelogue ready soon, describing today, & another Colonial trip in Manhattan made day before yesterday.

Yr aff: nephew & obt Servt
H P L

## Notes

1. *Front:* Main Street, Tottenville, S.I., N.Y.

[64]     [ANS postcard]¹ [HPL to LDC]

[Postmarked Perth Amboy, N.J.,
1 September 1924]

All hail! Having crossed Staten Island to Tottenville & seen the old Billopp House (1664), I've taken another ferry to Perth Amboy, N.J., one of the most archaic & Colonial towns I've ever seen. ¶ Look at this hotel! It is *new*—showing how perfectly they keep to the Colonial tradition here. ¶ Am about to explore more of P.A. Yr aff nephew & obt Servt  H P L

## Notes

1. *Front:* New Packer House, Perth Amboy, N.J.

[65]     [ANS postcard]¹ [HPL to LDC]

[Postmarked New York, N.Y.,
2 September 1924]

All hail! Returned from Perth Amboy, but still & always in the Colonial past! ¶ Another Clevelander has hit N.Y.—this latest acquisition being Edward Lazarre, [*sic*] a bright young chap whom I met often in 1922. I haven't seen him yet, but tomorrow he, Belknap, George Kirk, Morton (if we can get him) & I are coming up here to the museum for a grand aesthetick revel! ¶ Wish you could be here to take in all these sights!—Yr aff: nephew & obt Servt. H P L

[On front:] Heigho! The first things I look for in N.Y. are specimens of old New-England colonialism! This panelling will be on exhibition here next month in the new American wing now building.

## Notes

1. *Front:* 41760. American (Connecticut) 1760 (?) / Wall Panelling / The Metropolitan Museum of Art.

[66]     [ANS postcard][1] [HPL to LDC]

[No postmark
8 September] 1924]

Well, here's our good old friend Hamilton, beside whose tomb in Trinity Churchyard I so frequently pause to meditate! ¶ Your splendid letter recd.— will reply soon in diary form. ¶ Going up to Belknap's now. Then he & I are going over to Kirk's, where we will await a telegram from Loveman, who is expected today.

Yr aff nephew & obt Servt
H P L

Notes

1. *Front:* Alexander Hamilton—by Sharpless [*sic*]. The New York Historical Society. [The artist was James Sharples (1751/2–1811).]

[67]     [ANS postcard][1] [HPL to LDC]

[Postmarked New York, N.Y.,
10 September 1924]

At the Historical Museum—great place! Have been at an electrical laboratory interviewing a possible employer for a very lowly post in the lamp testing dept. He says I can have it *unless* a more experienced man applies between now & tonight. And I'll bet such an one *will* apply! That's Theobaldian luck. ¶ I wish N.Y. looked like this view today!
Yr aff nephew & obt Servt  H P L

Notes

1. *Front:* New York in 1794 / The New York Historical Society.

[68]     [ANS postcard][1] [HPL to LDC]

[Postmarked New York, N.Y.,
10 September 1924]

Stopped off at another museum! It's a gay life, I'll inform the empyrean! What's the use of living in a big town if you don't use the advantages thereof? I mean to soak up all the artistic & scientific stuff this burg has to offer!

Yr aff nephew & obt Servt
H P L

Notes

1. *Front:* Heads of Primitive Man.

[69]     [ANS postcard][1] [HPL to LDC]

[Postmarked New York, N.Y.,
18 September 1924]

Am ceasing answering advts for a while, to give Henneberger a chance to prove his business sincerity. ¶ He has—or says he has—hired me for his new magazine at a salary beginning at $40.00 per wk & later going up (HE SAYS) to $100.00.[2] I'll have to give him my undivided time, of course, but I'll lose nothing thereby, since the moment he stops paying I can stop working. First payment—a week from tomorrow. His plans sound more businesslike than ever before. Yr aff & obt H P L

[P.S.] They've just got a fine new cast of the skull of the Rhodesian primitive man up at this museum.
[P.P.S.] Henneberger introduced me to a fine young writer named Robert Coates who knows Old N.Y. well.[3]

## Notes

1. *Front:* Prehistoric pitchers from Pueblo Bonito, New Mexico.
2. The magazine in question was a humor magazine, the *Magazine of Fun*. It never got off the ground.
3. Possibly Robert M. Coates (1897–1973), who wrote for the *New York Times* and the *New Yorker* and published several novels and works of nonfiction.

[70]     [ANS postcard][1] [HPL to LDC]

[Postmarked New York, N.Y.,
18 September 1924]

At the museum again (I darned near *live* at such places!) waiting for 2:00 p.m., when I shall take the car down town to meet Loveman at 2:30 in front of the Public Library. He is going home soon—can't find work & doesn't like New York. We shall all be sorry to lose him. His Saltus book is about to be published in Philadelphia, & Mrs. Saltus is enthusiastic about it. Yr aff nephew & obt Servt

H P L

[P.S.] Belknap's college opens today—he's up there registering this noon.
[P.P.S.] The Boys meet tonight at Belknap's. Loveman will be there.

## Notes

1. *Front:* Bowls from San Ildefonso Pueblo used to hold the sacred corn meal.

[71]     [ANS postcard]¹ [HPL to LDC]

[Postmarked New York, N.Y.,
18 September 1924]

One museum a day isn't enough—have just crossed the sun-golden expanse of Central Park to the 5th Ave. side, & am taking in the Metropolitan! Eternal beauty! To immerse oneself in its strongest solution, & grow drunken with its poignant intensity, is the only way for a man of taste & sensitiveness to forget life & reality, & postpone the hour of self-sought oblivion! Am in a landscape mood today. Is this not an exquisite view? The French have an admirable eye for wild nature. H P L

Notes

1. *Front:* P. E. T. Rousseau / Edge of the Woods. / The Metropolitan Museum of Art.

[72]     [ANS postcard]¹ [HPL and Samuel Loveman to LDC]

[Postmarked Brooklyn, N.Y.,
18 September 1924]

And here's the *third* museum I've taken in today! This time Samuelus was with me. I hadn't been to this place for 2 years, & found it bless'd with many pleasing augmentations, including a series of alcoves typifying the COLONIAL rooms of various periods. Here is the only one which hath been immortalis'd by post-card portrayal—pretty neat, but nothing up to the Pendleton House.

Yr aff nephew & obt Servt  H P L

Best wishes and kindest regards from—
Samuel Loveman

Notes

1. *Front:* Dining room, Secretary House, 17th Century / Brooklyn Museum.

[73]     [ANS postcard]¹ [HPL and AEPG to LDC]

[Postmarked New York, N.Y.,
26 September 1924]

Communing with the Colonial past—as usual! Now that one daughter's here, I wish you were on the spot to complete the family circle!

Yr aff: nephew & obt Servt
H P L

Would like to buy this house—it's so homey & nice.
A.E.P.G.

## Notes

1. *Front:* The Old "Dyckman House" Broadway and 204th St., New York City.

[74]    [TLS] [HPL to LDC]

259 Parkside Ave., Brooklyn, N.Y.,
September 29, 1924
Finish'd Tuesday, Septr. 30.

My dear Daughter Lillian:—

'Tis hard to believe I have not writ you at length since my birthday, but such wou'd seem to be the case according to my records! Since then Daughter Anne has been here and gone, and I now hear a rumour that (O blessed possibility!) you may yourself be not far off ere long, since Mifs Ray of Mount Vernon desires your company exceedingly! Meanwhile let me acknowledge with gratitude the post cards, and the numerous consignments of clipt pictures; to say nothing of the "hair ile", which comes at an exceedingly timely juncture. I am returning the delightful Sterling poem, of which I have the duplicate. Sterling, as you probably recall, is the especial friend and patron of my gifted California correspondent Clark Ashton Smith.

Beginning with your cards and proceeding backward toward the letter, let me assure you that I did write to John T. Winterich—the editor connected with Roy Morrish, Esq.—as soon as I received his address.[1] The result— negative as usual—came in this afternoon's mail; and I will enclose it for your perusal. Meanwhile other prospects have been steadily considered, some of which I will expatiate upon later in this brief note. That concerning Henneberger, of which I sent you a post-card notice, has by no means vanished; and though delayed in the first week's pay, Henny absolutely promises me a full two-week quota of eighty dollars next Friday. I will enclose a copy of some of the things I am doing for Henneberger—it is very feasible work if it lasts.

So the large bedstead and parlour carpet went to the old Smithville Seminary! Very appropriate—and I am delighted beyond words to know that it was not seriously damaged by the fire of which I saw an account in the Bulletin. Such old semi-Colonial academies are rare nowadays, and I can but wish that some responsible school would purchase the building and maintain it in a suitable manner. The Pentecostal fanatics and freaks now in charge are unable to conduct it save in a fearsomely slipshod way—as you will doubtless recall from our trip there in 1906 with A E P G and Phil.[2]

About Frank Crane[3]—I do not think he has ever lectured on psychology in the Bush manner. He is a wearisome platitudinarian whose optimistic rubbish is widely syndicated and devoured by the middle classes, but I doubt if even the emptiest of his vapourings descends to the frankly charlatanic D. V.

Bush level. New York is just now in the throes of a "psychologist" epidemic, Bush having been followed at Carnegie Hall[4] by another of the same breed—a mild rival, as it were. Leeds went to hear one of his lectures, and witnessed an amusing incident when, after his declaring that the "power of thought" could think hair back on a bald head, someone in the audience asked why, if that were so, David V. Bush is bald-headed!

I hope you can get "Visible and Invisible". I was reminded anew of it when last Thursday night Morton read aloud to "The Boys" one of its best stories—"The Horror-Horn". But far ahead of this volume is another which I have since read—"The Listener, and Other Stories", by Algernon Blackwood. One of the tales in this book, "The Willows", is perhaps the most devastating piece of supernaturally hideous suggestion which I have beheld in a decade—Little Sonny is so enraptured by it that he declares he will never write another story in his life—Blackwood having said all there is to say in that field! I now possess "The Golden Ladder" permanently—a gift from the effusive Henneberger, who has also given me Hergesheimer's "Balisand" (by the author of "Java Head") and given S H (after asking her to name what she would prefer) Geothe's [*sic*] "Sorrows of Werther". Speaking of books—some other recent accessions to my library, coming either through gift or second-hand purchase, are "Eothen", a volume of strange travel,[5] the poems of Thomas Parsons, Herodotus complete in one translated volume, Irving's Knickerbocker History of N.Y., a modern illustrated history of N.Y.,[6] Hawthorne's "Mosses from an Old Manse", a volume of the Elizabethan dramatist Webster containing the famous and sanguinary "Duchess of Malfi", an abridged edition of the mediaeval chronicler Froissart, Thackeray's book on the 18th century essayists, and some fine 18th century material in five-cent paper form, including Mackenzie's well-known "Man of Feeling", and a fascinating description of London in 1731.[7]

All the cuttings interested me exceedingly, and I am sending some more in case they will interest you. That on Rhode Island is so inaccurate that it evoked an amused reply in the Bulletin, which possibly you noticed a week or two ago. Even the sedate Times nods now and then! The item on disappearing steeples I had already clipped and sent to Sechrist in the course of a discussion. It is an infernal shame that so characteristic a Georgian New-England feature should go, and I certainly hope the rising tide of disintegration can be checked. Few colonial steeples are built nowadays, though as I think I mentioned, one has lately gone up in Washington, D.C. Among my enclosures I will include a side-splitting bit which one of The Boys gave me, touching on the bad pronunciation of the mediocre New-Yorker. You are aware that such persons say "oi" when they mean "er"—as "woild", "skoit", etc., but you may not have realised that they also do the reverse—though perhaps not so universally—saying "er" for "oi", and thus perpetrating absurdities like "berl" for "boil". Such a New-Yorker would say "The Oil of

Joisey bought erl stock" if he were trying to say that the Earl of Jersey—Dunsany's father-in-law—bought oil stock. Never have I seen this dialectic idiosyncrasy so well displayed as in the accompanying spoof. Speaking of New York, I will enclose something about Pennell's recent etchings covering that place[8]—also a bit referring to a "Mount Vernon" which isn't the one you're going to visit. This Mount Vernon is a stone house in 61st Street near the river, also known as the Jane Teller house, and visited by A E P G and me last spring. Other cuttings I will enclose are connected with the excavation of Septimius Severus' home town of Leptis Magna in North Africa. You will recall Severus from "Andivius Hedulio"[9]—and the same book also gives an excellent picture of Roman life in Africa during the period when that part of the world was tremendously important, and "more Roman than Italy itself". Other cuttings are old Englisg [sic] scenes which appeal to me. The one relating to "Wuthering Heights" reminds me that you ought to read that novel by Emily Bronte—perhaps the greatest of all the literary products of the celebrated Bronte family.

But now I must begin my diary—which will extend to considerable length on account of the vast space covered. This time I have jotted down notes from day to day, so that the chronology will be somewhat less uncertain. We begin on my birthday, which I spent at the machine as you already know. The next day, Aug. 21, was likewise spent at home with pen in hand; but in the evening something started which indeed merits ample record! The Boys met at Kirk's, and a royal good time was had by all. Leeds brought a copy of that Little Old New York book[10]—the first I had seen—and the talk ran much on antiquarian matters. At 1:30 a.m. the meeting broke up, and we all started out—including our genial host, who resolved to walk as far as the farthest-walking of his guests. We dropped Morton and McNeil at the 104th St. elevated station, (Belknap being in Atlantic City) and Kleiner at the 103d street subway kiosk. This left Leeds, Kirk, and Grandpa Theobald as the surviving pedestrians. Down Broadway we walked, admiring the architecture and planning explorations. At Columbus Circle we turned into 8th Avenue, obtaining at an all-night orangeade booth the bottles of Private Stock which I later shipped to my daughters. Gay atmosphere! At 49th Street we dropped Leeds at his new hotel—the Ray—to which he had just moved from the Cort across the street. Then, cleared for action and with the evening yet young before us, Kirk and I resolved to "do" the Colonial town. Having a receptive audience, I proposed to show off the local Georgian antiquities as they should be shewn! We continued down Eighth Avenue with an air of expectancy. Hitherto we had encountered nothing colonial, since with rare exceptions all the town above 14th street dates from the 19th century or later. Around the twenties we saw an old house or two—survivors from the one-time Chelsea Village—but the "real stuff" burst upon us just below Fourteenth, where Eighth Avenue melts into ancient Hudson St. at a crossroads as quaint and old-world as that Soho view I am enclosing. This marks, of course, the entrance into Greenwich-Village; and is made still more interesting by the park-like triangular breathing space called Abingdon Square. Brick colonial houses were now numerous, and I pointed out to Kirk in the early morning stillness the characteristic features of the leading types of N.Y. colonial doorways. From Hudson we turned into Grove, where some splendidly preserved colonial specimens occur; and from there we entered the grilled iron gate of Grove Court, (ask A E P G about it) a delicious 18th century byway where bits of garden and occasional restored doorways lend an atmosphere which only a poet could describe. It is out of the vulgar world, and part of the fabric of tranquil and lovely dream. The flowers were sweet in the stillness, and graceful grey cats lent a touch of mingled beauty and eeriness. Thence we repaired to Gay Street (see former letter), whose curving unworldliness captivated Kirk, and afterward we crossed to Patchin and Milligan Places, and the nameless inner place of which I have already told you. If these ancient spots were fascinating in the busy hours of twilight, fancy their utter and poignant charm in the sinister hours before dawn, when only cats, criminals, astronomers, and poetic antiquarians roam the waking world! Kirk went into raptures, seeing them for the first time; and I, though I had seen them before, was not far behind him in enthusiasm. Truly, we had cast the modern and visible world aside, and were sporting through the centuries with the spirit of timeless antiquity! From this section—the "Jefferson Market" section of Greenwich Village,—we proceeded to that congeries of lanes known as the "Minettas", (see my long letter of last March) where night brought a thousand charms I had never anticipated. All the Italian squalor was faded into shadow, and I could fancy spotless periwigs and sedan chairs under the wan, waning half moon that struggled above the lines of antique gables. We explored some cryptical inner courts which I had never seen before, and where black recesses and bits of archaic moonlit wall formed pictures worthy of any etcher. From these we sought the broad colonial expanse of Varick Street, where endless rows of 18th century dormer windows and occasional gambrel roofs give an unrivalled mass picture of the New York known to Hamilton and Washington. At a small restaurant we stopt for a cup of coffee—it was near dawn now, but our spirits were yet fresh! The street lamps were still burning when we turned into ancient Charlton Street—best preserved of all the colonial thoroughfares, where spotless paint and gleaming knockers suggest the neat prosperity as well as the artistic inclinations of the Georgian householders. More raptures—and the dawn was grey when we entered Prince Street, crossed Broadway, and paused at the pitifully decrepit house where James Monroe died. This, one might fancy, was enough for any trip; but the fever of the explorer was upon us, so forgetting the hour we turned south toward the Brooklyn Bridge section, alternating between Mott and Mulberry streets in order to observe as many ancient houses as possible. This section was farm land in colonial times, so that all the old houses are farmhouses—crowded amidst the unending brick squalor of a populous slum. At Chatham Square we saw the ancient cemetery, and presently turned toward the picturesque antiquities of Batavia and Cherry Streets. In the latter narrow hilly way we found many wonders, including a marvellous hidden court where burns a venerable diamond-shaped lamp—the only one I have seen in N.Y. except the one in Milligan Place. Later ascending to Franklin Square, we passed under the piers of Brooklyn Bridge, observing the old sugar-house where rebel prisoners were confined from 1776 to 1783, (original house torn down, but one of the windows incorporated into the new building) and discovering a magnificent colonial section around Vandewater and New Chambers Streets—where gambrel roofs, curving iron railings, and all the appurtenances of the past abound. We now went down Pearl Street to Hanover Square and Fraunces' Tavern, incidentally drinking in the colonial houses and cross-street waterfront vistas which loomed along the way. After that we crossed Broadway to the west waterfront, noting the venerable edifices on every hand, and remarking especially the Planters' Hotel—the colonial building which Poe inhabited in its seedy old age—and Tom's Chop House, which has been open continuously since 1797. Of course we meditated in Trinity and St. Paul's churchyards, and admired the Georgian beauty of St. Paul's—both facade and steeple. Then, as a climax, we approached the City Hall (1812); whose classic beauty is immortal. The rosy dawn had broken whilst we were on Pearl Street, gilding the steeples of the Brooklyn shore across the glittering water. By the time we reached the city hall it was bright morning, and we gazed at the sun-splendid pinnacles of the Woolworth Building as seen through the arch of the Municipal building. This was the culmination. Glancing at the fine unfinished courthouse whose classic lines are apparently going to be spoilt by some tawdry addition above the pediment, we sought our respective home stations—parting at a little before eight by St. Paul's colonial clock. I reached 259 shortly before nine, went out to buy some groceries, and retired in expectancy of the evening's trip to colonial Sheridan Square to see O'Neill's play "All God's Chilluns".[11] This, of course, was Friday the 22nd. I awaked in time to accompany S H to the theatre, and we arrived so early that we had time for an antiquarian stroll around Patchin and Milligan Places. The play, which deals with the marriage of a low Irish girl to an educated nigger, went off very smoothly and capably—save that the mayor had forbidden the performance of the first act, which involved the participation of small children and the use by them of low language. This act was read from the stage by the director, who interspersed many appropriately sarcastic remarks of his own, reflecting on the intelligence of mayors and other annoyances. It seems that this ban has continued, since the act was still omitted when Belknap saw the play a month later. O'Neill is surely a great dramatist—perhaps the only American dramatist of note now living. The tragic symbolism of the theme in this play is admirably enhanced by such devices as the street songs of different periods, and by the prominence given to a Congo mask—one of the few primitive expressions of art which the negro has achieved. (These masks, by the way, are becoming quite the rage among the ultra-moderns, who are copying their technique in certain pictorial and sculptural works of their own.) The play let out early, and we were home before midnight. The next day I carried S H's hat sample case on a trip down town. On the way home we purchased a prepared welsh rarebit at a place near the 49th st. subway station, which we subsequently ate with vast relish. On this day also Belknap came home from Atlantic City—where, poor little man, he had quite a dangerous attack of fainting and heart trouble. He is having to be careful these days, though the doctors tell his mother that he will be all right in the end if he will only go easy now, and avoid every sort of violent exertion. Sunday the 24th was a home day—answering beastly advertisements, some of which I enclose. Monday noon I went up to Little Belknap's with George Kirk, where we had a splendidly interesting period of literary discussion. Was glad to see Sonny again! In the evening there called, accompanied by his wife, the Rev. George T. Baker, round-collar'd rector of St. Gabriel's Church, who betwixt genial smiles and puffs of unending cigars made an offer for the piano which S H had advertised for sale the day before. We let him have it for $350.00.[12] Next morning he called for it with a dray—on which he and I rode back to his house (quite near here), where he wrote me a cheque and a letter of identification at his bank. I then went to the bank at Church and Flatbush Avenues, got the cash, paid the grocer with $48.00 of it, and returned with the residue. The rest of the day I wrote letters—and commiserated with S H on the fearsome ankle sprain which she sustained in the 34th St. subway station that morning. I told her to get a doctor, but she wouldn't—and the sprain grew worse. Next day—Aug. 27—she did get the doctor—a capable chap named Donley, who had treated her before—and lay quietly with ice packs on the injured member. I wrote letters. The next day—after a second call from Donley and the adoption of some strapping—she went down town to a business interview with me as a crutch. After her interview I went to one of my own—with an advertiser named Woods, of whom I spoke in a previous letter either to you or A E P G. Then home and reading till evening, when I joined The Boys at Sonny's. This was a mild meeting, nor were there any all-night jaunts afterward! The next day—Friday the 29th—I went to see Woods again, and was sent with a note of introduction to his brother-advertiser Townley— whom also I have described in a Providence letter. After a somewhat unsatisfactory conversation with this latter personage, I embarked upon one of my lone tours of colonial exploration. Beginning near the lower end of Manhattan, I walked up West Broadway and enjoyed the occasional bits of colonialism. York Street presents an admirably quaint corner, whilst betwixt 434 and 436 W. Bway. is one of the most curious ancient courts I have ever seen.

Reaching Bleecker St., I walked west to 7th Avenue, where I looked about for new worlds to conquer. These worlds I found in the shape of a network of colonial streets I had never before observed. They are slightly south of Grove St.—Commerce, Bedford, and Barrow—and have some of the finest doorways and odd corners in all the town. At the corner of Commerce and Bedford there is a fine old gambrel-roofer, whilst at a bend in Barrow is a gorgeous pre-Revolutionary facade bent convex to follow the curve of the street. I now sought Perry Street, in an effort to ferret out the nameless hidden court which the Evening Post had written up that day. (I sent you the cutting.)[13] I found the place without difficulty, and enjoyed it all the more for having seen its picture. These lost lanes of an elder city have for me the utmost fascination, and I am constantly on the lookout for new ones. On my way back to the home subway I paused at Mulry Square—where 7th Ave., Perry St. and Waverley Place converge—to investigate the delicate greenery I had before noticed protruding above certain alluringly inviting high board fences. Marvel upon marvels! Upon peering over I discovered a series of entrancing old-fashioned gardens—with hollyhocks, flagstones, mossy stonework, and floral kettles swung from rustic tripods—which formed the back yards of the neighbouring ancient houses! That is the charm of an old and populous district—one never knows what deliciously incongruous mysteries may lie concealed behind the walls one observes. Saturday the 30th was a home day—reading and writing, not to mention arithmetic—but on Sunday I made up for this undue domesticity by taking an all-day jaunt to elder regions. Whoopee! The past for me! I embarked on the Staten Island ferry, and was soon in a land of quaint villages that might have been five hundred miles from any metropolis. St. George is a sort of Attleboro. Stapleton suggests East Greenwich. And there I took a wheezy accomodation train for Tottenville, on the far tip of the island, which when reached savoured of Pascoag. A short walk out of Tottenville, embowered among antique pines on the south shore and now in a state of vast decrepitude, is the old Billopp house, a stone pile built by the first British circumnavigator of the island about 1664. There is something both impressive and terrible in its steep and hoary gable—one could write a story about it. I talked with the owner, a crude man whose family have inhabited it for ninety years. He does not appreciate his habitat, though he knows it is popular with visitors from the outside world. From Tottenville I took the ferry to Perth Amboy, N.J., whose colonial skyline loomed beckoningly across the water. And what a town it turned out to be!! As the ferry drew near its mooring I saw that I had encountered something unusual, for the approaching waterfront was a quaint, dingy, huddle of eighteenth-century brick and wood buildings whose lines could not have changed since the days when Dr. Franklin and John Adams used to stop at Packer's Tavern on their coach and horseback journeys. What a skyline! Peaked and chimney'd gables, small-paned windows, fanlighted doorways, and over all one slant-roofed wooden edifice towering perilously on a rock ledge—where it must have towered since good Queen Anne sate on the throne! Another moment and I was on land, treading winding, narrow colonial ways up hill and down, and noting the little uniquities of the spot. Perth Amboy was never a large or prosperous place, but it was solid; and amidst the wooden houses was many a brick mansion. On the whole, it resembles New-England more than New-York—and must be much as Newark was before its oldest buildings were replaced. Of course the high spot was Packer's Tavern—gloriously reconstructed in modern times on strictly Georgian lines. You saw my card. I can see it yet—and wish that other towns could shew equally faithful reproductions of the style of the great days. Having given Perth Amboy a thorough exploration, I retraced my steps. The return ride across Staten Island in the sunset was very beautiful, the country reminding one of New-England. Twilight fell on the ferry trip back to New York, and I saw the lights come out one by one in the skyscrapers which make of Manhattan a thing of Dunsanian beauty. The Statue of Liberty was one of the earliest things to ignite— and it looked very picturesque with its flambeau tipt with flame. Monday Sept. 1st was a home day. Tuesday I had two fruitless business calls— Marwick, Mitchell & Co., and Townley—though the latter was out. Later I "did" the museums—historical and art—and drowned trouble in beauty. Meanwhile I had word that a new gang member [*sic*] was in town—Edward Lazare, the friend of Loveman and Kirk whom I had met in Cleveland in 1922. I made an appointment to meet him at 'Ittle-Sonny's next day. On that next day the meeting came off finely. Lazare was interesting, and seemed not a whit changed since 1922, though his army uniform was replaced by a blue civilian suit. He discussed life and letters with much intelligence, and I decided that he would make a fitting accession to our select circle of The Boys. This youth, the son of a French father and Irish mother, was educated as a strict Catholic, but is now a scientific atheist. He is only 22—slightly less, in fact—thus replacing Belknap as our official baby, although he has seen too much of the world to be a really shy and perfect child like Sonny. He does not write as yet, but reads and discusses literature with seasoned appreciation. He had hard work securing a position here, and has only just now landed a permanent berth . . . . in some automobile place. Thursday the 4th I had a talk with Woods, spent the afternoon reading in Prospect Park, and in the evening had Lazare to dinner, prior to taking him over to the Boys' meeting at Kleiner's. This meeting was a success as usual, and Lazare took well with the elder members. In the small hours I went home, where I remained for three days following, reading and catching up with my correspondence. On the evening of the third day—Sunday the 7th—I had a call from Henneberger, who was here on another business trip. Going over to his hotel, I had quite a talk with him; during which he told me of the new lease of life achieved by *Weird Tales*, and of the fine job he had in store for me. Monday I had a final interview with Woods, after which I went to Belknap's to pick him up on my way to Kirk's, where he and Lazare were assembled awaiting a telegram from the expected visitor of honour—Samuel Loveman. No telegram arrived, so we disbanded till another day after an interesting session of quadrangular discussion. Kirk lent me a new translation of de Maupassant (by Ernest Boyd),[14] the reading of which formed my sole activity of Tuesday. On Wednesday we again assembled to wait word from Loveman—even going down to the post office to see if any late word had arrived for Kirk in the General Delivery— but nothing doing! However, the expected did arrive! I was the first recipient of the tidings, and after a telephonic heralding Samuelus ambled over here in the evening to receive a hearty welcome. He was the same gentle aesthetic spirit as ever—not changed a whit in the two years since my last glimpse of him. His book on Edgar Saltus is coming out through a Philadelphia firm this winter, and he has already been extended many courtesies by Saltus' widow— who has given him valuable manuscripts and keepsakes of her late husband's. Oh yes—and I forgot to say that I had started the day with another fruitless business interview—with that electric company at the foot of 80th street. On Thursday I did some reading, and in the afternoon took charge of Loveman for a sightseeing trip. We visited a Brooklyn cluster of book and antique shops, obtained the magnificent view from Fort Greene Park, studied Brooklyn's colonial waterfront, and viewed the aristocratic street on the heights above the East River—Columbia Heights—where Loveman was to room across the hall from his old Cleveland friend Hart Crane—an egotistical young aesthete who has obtained some real recognition in the Dial and other modernist organs, and who has an unfortunate predilection for the wine when it is red. Columbia Heights—which you will find mentioned in the accompanying Pennell article—is one of the most delightful spots I have ever seen—with its harbour view, its quiet, and its little parklike spaces overlooking the water, where crystal fountains plash and odd flowers bloom amidst the greensward. From there we went to the always lovely Japanese garden near the Brooklyn Museum, and thence to 259 through Prospect Park. Here we had dinner, after which we started off to Little Belknap's to pick him up on our way to the Boys' meeting at Kirk's. No one but Sonny and I knew that Loveman had arrived, so that our entry to the gathering was to be a surprise. The Longs were all overjoyed to see Samuelus again—even haughty Felis purred—and the cordiality of the surprised Boys, after we reached Kirk's, was positively uproarious. After a period of literary festivity—during which Mortonius read Loveman's greatest poem aloud[15]—we all broke up; Samuelus coming home with me to sleep in the still unrented room before moving his things from his provisional hotel downtown to the Crane establishment. In the morning I bade Samuelus adieu, but soon followed him downtown to make a round of employment agencies. After a little of this, I started out on one of my lone explorations, having a mind to see Corlear's Hook—which tho' now immers'd in the maelstrom of East Side urban squalor, was in the eighteenth century a pleasing rural point of land, two miles from the town, where in a grove of elms and willows near the sea stood a restful old Dutch tavern which Washington Irving has immortalised in his tale of Wolfert Webber.[16] The road thither—Cherry St. for the most part,—is still lined with many ancient houses, and passes under the dank and impressively Roman arches of the Manhattan Bridge foundations. Here, and in the nearby Water Street, I found many survivals of elder life; including two of the very few remaining blacksmith shops in New York. Corlear's Hook itself is a sort of dreary open park, devoid of large trees, and scarcely suggestive of the old Dutch days. However, I felt that spirit of rest which descended psychically from my own 18th century; and sate down on a bench (as Wolfert Webber once sate on the bench before the tavern) to read. My book—lent by Belknap but recommended a year ago by Mrs. Miniter—was Elliot H. Paul's "Indelible", which has a marvellously faithful picture of Malden and the dreary north-of Boston suburbs. From Corlear's Hook I went to Rivington Street, and inland up this thoruoghfare, [*sic*] which is the heart of New York's densest and least Americanised Ghetto. This place was a revelation, for no other slum I had ever seen is just like it. Here exist assorted Jews in the absolutely unassimilated state, with their ancestral beards, skull-caps, and general costumes—which make them very picturesque, and not nearly so offensive as the strident, pushing Jews who affect clean shaves and American dress. In this particular section, where Hebrew books are vended from pushcarts, and patriarchal rabbins totter in high hats and frock coats, there are far less offensive faces than in the general subways of the town—probably because most of the pushing commercial Jews are from another colony where the blood is less pure. It is now definitely known that many allegedly Semitic types of today are not in reality Semitic or even white at all, but derived from Asiatic Tatar-Mongoloids who were Judaised by missionaries before their entrance into Central Europe from the Thibetan plateaux in the 8th or 9th century A.D. Of these are the queer-eyed, yellow-red, thick-lipped flat-nosed types seen in Providence's North End and in many parts of New York. These Rivington-Streeters are altogether different, and when they depart from the Semitic type, the variation is toward the Aryan rather than toward the Asiatic. I followed Rivington to the Bowery, where I branched north in search of a quaint cemetery which Kirk had discovered on a tour of the bookstalls. En route I saw some of the colonial houses of the one-time Bowery Village, including a fine brick gambrel-roofer on the corner of 1st St. and the Bowery. North from 1st street near here runs the quaint and microscopic Extra Place, which is held to be very picturesque, though I deem it inferior to the scenic spots of Greenwich Village. Behind a church, and visible only through an iron railing in Second Street, I found the cemetery I sought. It is a refreshing spot, with greenery, well-tended walks, ivy-grown walls, and all the appurtenances of

American village life, though wholly engulfed in alien nastiness. It is a bit of ruralism as completely fenced off from its surroundings as Dexter Asylum is fenced off from urban residential Providence.

> Where dwell that race beneath whose rule benign
>      The village rich in bliss and virtue grew,
> The moonlight shews us as its pencils shine
>      Above the mounds and tablets by the yew.[17]

North from here I found Cooper Square, on whose eastern side are some marvellous Colonial buildings. This is the northern part of Bowery Village, not far from the colonial steeple of St. Mark's-in-the-Bowery. Thence I returned home, to read and meditate upon the past. The next day opened inauspiciously, for S H had another stumble which aggravated her former sprain, and another doctor had to be called—this time the tried and true McChesney, who cured her of the great neuritis attack of 1922–3. At noon I went to see Henneberger, who promised great things, and insisted on presenting books broadcast to all the household. He wanted me, moreover, to accompany him to a horse race at Belmont Park; but a previous engagement saved me that boredom. This engagement began by meeting Loveman up at Sonny-Boy's, and was soon augmented by our triangular adjournment to Kirk's, where we found our host awaiting us in the company of Lazare, who was then rooming with him. Ere long Kleiner and Morton put in an appearance; and we finished the afternoon in an exceedingly festive manner. At six Sonny had to go home, and we all saw him to his door. Then the rest of us lunched at a place in Columbus Ave., and started to walk down town, incidentally stopping at every bookstall we saw. It was by this time dark, and as we crossed Central Park diagonally near its southern end we had some of the most beautiful vistas of lighted buildings which the fancy can conceive. Then came a tour of 59th Street bookstalls, after which Mortonius left us. Kirk, Loveman, Kleiner, Lazare and I remained to explore the antient places. It was midnight—and we took the subway to Prince Street to view James Monroe's old home. Some boys and youths were on the steps, singing to the notes of strange lutes or rebecs—a very colourful item, and not wholly spoilt by the fact that the tunes were jazz ones. Thence we walked through to Greenwich-Village, where Prince becomes Charlton Street, and where the colonial houses are bright and well-kept. Here Loveman was genuinely impressed by the Georgian quaintness of the sight—an impression deepened when we took him through the winding musteries [*sic*] of the Minettas, and around the cryptical blacknesses of Commerce, Bedford, Barrow, and Grove Streets to the idyllic little backwater of Grove Court. Then came Gay Street, Jefferson Market, and Patchin and Milligan Places—high spots, quickly followed by the bit of graveyard in 11th St., and the leafy shades of Washington Square. There we sat on a bench—Loveman obtaining a snatch of sleep—and watched the stately brick mansions on the north side with many a dream of Benefit Street, Salem Common, and Beacon Hill. After this we fared westward to the elevated, where after a bit of lunch—the third that evening, counting some coffee previously absorbed in Sheridan Square—we took the elevated for lower Manhattan. On the ride we digested what we had seen, and Samuelus opined what he afterward reiterated, that one of the quaintest features of all colonial New York is the number of cats seen at large. There was a charming maltese kitten in Minetta Place which I could hardly resist taking home in my pocket! We left the elevated at Park Place, walking directly out Park Row to Chatham Square, where we viewed the ancient cemetery and adjacent bits of quaintness. Some of the reeling toughs—and gutter-ensconced toughs—we beheld were interesting indeed, and revived memories of the wild days midway betwixt the colonial period and the present, when no well-dressed man was safe in the neighbourhood after dark. We now worked down to the waterfront and under the great piers of the Manhattan Bridge, intending to prolong our excursion to Fraunces' Tavern and the western shore; but fatigue on Loveman's part—for he has been semi-ill with bronchial trouble ever since arriving here— caused us to cut the excursion short at Franklin qsuare [*sic*] about 3:30 or 4 a.m. To retire so early was really a shame, but since we did not wish to continue without the guest of honour we grudgingly desisted and returned to our respective domiciles. Heigho! I bought a premature Sunday Times in Park Row, which saved my going out the next day. That day was one of gloom and nerves—more advertisement answering, which has become such a psychological strain that I almost fall unconscious over it! Monday the 15th I went in vain to a publishing house whither I was sent by one of the agencies I had consulted, and later visited other agencies—with as little result. After that, to get the taste out of my mouth, I made another lone exploring trip; this time covering the entire length of colonial Hudson Street, where some marvellous houses and corners still lurk unimpaired. Where Hudson, Watts, and Canal Streets converge to an open square, there is a surprising wealth of colonialism; embracing houses and shops of every kind, and a tavern still Georgian with its swinging sign. This oasis, however, is probably doomed by the coming of the Hudson River Vehicular Tunnel,[18] whose Manhattan portal is not far off, and whose litter and upheaval are now very much in evidence. Another splendid colonial centre is in King Street, with the adjacent parts of Hudson. I followed north to Fourteenth Street, lingered luxuriously amidst the antiquity of some of the neighbouring winding streets, and finally boarded the subway for home, to spend the rest of the day in study and meditation. On Tuesday S L called, and accompanied S H and me downtown, later leaving us to visit a bookstall. S H had a fruitless interview at the Saks shop, and we later attended to miscellaneous errands—bank, Scribners (where I am trying to get cash in place of the credit entered for me by Henneberger), a furniture shop where we enviously admired a splendid Queen Anne dining suite, a silk shop, and finally a boot and shoe emporium where S H found some high shoes to relieve her sorely tried ankle. The rest of the day I read deMaupassant. The next day Henneberger called up on business—he wanted me to turn out some samples of my adapting of jokes for his proposed magazine. This job kept me busy the rest of the day, and at night I had quite a pile ready. On Thursday, at 10:30 a.m., I called on Henneberger, and liking my samples enthusiastically he "hired" me on the spot as outlined on the post card I immediately sent you. Whilst at his room I met another writer on his staff—a fine young fellow named Robert Coates, who is the most perfect Celtic red-head type I have ever seen. Coates is translating some French for Henny, but is mainly a free-lance article writer, with a penchant for Old New York themes. He tipped me off to some quaint corners, although upon investigation I did not find them nearly so quaint as those I already knew. From Henneberger's I went on a tour of all the museums, seeing many curious things I had overlooked before—for example, in the Nat. Hist. Mus. there is a piece of rhinoceros horn in a case, which was used by one of the Popes to ward off disease in accordance with the ancient superstition about the medicinal virtues of the unicorn's tusk—with which the rhinoceros horn was confused. Also, I saw the new cast of the Rhodesian skull—a remnant of primitive man found in South Africa three years ago. My last museum was the Metropolitan, from which I departed at 2 p.m., having an appointment with Loveman at the library at 2:30. Arriving early, I made a detour along 42nd St. to buy a set of New York etchings I had long admired—duplicates of which I have just sent to you and A E P G. Loveman was on hand at the appointed time, and we proceeded at once to the Brooklyn Museum, where we enjoyed the exhibits in general, and the Chinese blue and gold porcelains in particular. Of especial interest to me was the series of colonial rooms on the top floor—each fitted out to represent a typical room of some particular sort at some particular period. Such was the antiquarian accuracy, that distinctions were drawn betwixt the late 17th century, and the several decorative subdivisions of the 18th century—a thing I have seen attempted nowhere else save at the Essex Institute in Salem. I sent you the only post card covering this department—though I hope they will have more printed eventually. From the museum we went to the Japanese Garden, where on a green bank beside a lilied pool spanned by arched bridges and fed by terraces of tiny waterfalls, we read from the manuscript of Loveman's Saltus book. This work is truly a masterpiece of creative criticism, and lives up nobly to Wilde's conception of "The Critic as Artist". Like Saltus or not, no one can fail to admit that the Lovemanic interpretation of him is a prose pastel—a study in colour and imagery whose sheer verbal beauty is sufficient excuse for its being. I am anxious to see the printed version, and hope sincerely that the publishers will belie the popular reputation of Philadelphia for somnolent delay! From there we proceeded to 259 by way of Prospect Park and the Botanic Garden, pausing to survey the colonial Lefferts house, and feeding the omnipresent squirrels with some nuts which Samuelus had purchased. We had dinner here, immediately after which we set out for Sonny's house where The Boys were meeting. This meeting was not large, since Kirk, Lazare, and McNeil were absent; but it was made interesting by readings from Loveman's Saltus book. Samuelus himself was not feeling well, and had to leave early; after which departure the conversation became distinctly less poetic in tone. We broke up about 1 a.m., and Kleiner, Leeds, Morton and I started to walk downtown. Kleiner had some uncomfortable new shoes, so dropt off at 72nd St. Morton deserted at the 53d St. elevated station. Leeds and I kept on to the subway station at 49th St. and 7th Ave., where we parted some time before dawn. The next day—Friday the 19th—I did some Henneberger work, and at 4:30 p.m. welcomed Loveman. He was feeling rather weak, however, so that he slept in the morris-chair most of the time, whilst I continued to work. After dinner he felt much better—perhaps due to the quinine which he purchased and took—and I accompanied him to his room in Columbia Heights, where I met the redoubtable Hart Crane, a little ruddier, a little puffier, and slightly more moustached than when I saw him in Cleveland two years ago. Crane, whatever his limitations, is a thorough aesthete; and I had some enjoyable conversation with him. His room is in excellent taste, with a few paintings by William Sommer (that elderly eccentric whom I described when I visited Cleveland), a choice collection of modern books, and some splendid small objets d'art of which a carven Buddha and an exquisitely carved Chinese ivory box are the high spots. Loveman's room is at the other end of the hall, with an outlook over the East River and a stupendous panorama of the Manhattan skyline. I nearly swooned with aesthetic exaltation when I beheld the panorama—the evening scene with innumerable lights in the skyscrapers, shimmering reflections and bobbing ship lights on the water, and at the extreme left and right, the flaming Statue of Liberty and the scintillant arc of the Brooklyn Bridge, respectively. But even this was not exactly the climax. That came when we went out on the flat roof (Crane and Loveman are on the fourth and top story) and saw the thing in all its unlimited and unglassed magnificence. It was something mightier than the dreams of old-world legend—a constellation of infernal majesty—a poem in Babylonian fire! No wonder Dunsany waxed rhapsodic about it when he saw it for the first time . . . . it is beyond the description of any but him![19] Added to the weird lights are the weird sounds of the port, where the traffick of all the world comes to a focus. Fog-horns, ships' bells, the creak of distant windlasses . . . . . visions of far shores of Ind, where bright-plumed birds are roused to song by the incense of strange garden-girt pagodas, and gaudy-robed cameldrivers barter before sandalwood taverns with deep-voiced sailors having the sea's mystery in their eyes. Silks and spices, curiously-wrought ornaments of Bengal gold, and gods and elephants strangely carven in jade and carnelian.

Ah, me! Would that I could express the magick of the scene! Crane is writing a long poem on Brooklyn Bridge in a modern medium, which may some time be printed in the Dial. But such is which. The evening advanced, and I went home. The next day—Saturday the 20th—was illuminated by news of A E P G's prospective advent. Samuelus and I met up at 'Ittle-Sonny's, and all three went on a grand tour of the bookstalls—this being the occasion when I picked up my Herodotus. Belknap picked up Cotton Mather's "Wonders of the Invisible World" for $1.50, which was adjudged the premier "find" of the afternoon. At 6:30 we dispersed, Samuelus coming here to dinner, after which he and I amused ourselves by making drawings of each other—results herewith enclosed. On this day I received a letter from Houdini—who was playing at the Albee and stopping at the Crown—offering to assist me in finding a position on his return to N.Y. I had given Eddy a letter of introduction to him, and the two had had some very exhaustive discussions, during which the magician expressed much eagerness to be of assistance to us both. I enclose the letter—which I answered, and to which I have just received a reply, asking me to telephone Houdini next Sunday or Monday, when he will be here before leaving for a vaudeville tour of the Pacific Coast. The next day—Sunday the 21st—I spent in desultory reading and excited anticipation of A E P G. Loveman came to dinner, and went down to the Hudson Terminal with me when the guest of honour's telephone call came. You can imagine how delighted I was to welcome my daughter—whom Loveman and I jointly escorted to 259, and to whom the former presented a copy of some verses he had just written on his old Grandpa Theobald.[20] I presume A.E.P.G. hath shewn these lines to you, but I'll make you an individual copy for permanent preservation. After Samuelus' departure, all hands retired and slumbered the slumbers of the moderately equitable. The next day—Monday the 22nd—I did some Hennebergian work, and in the afternoon fared forth with my daughter to the Long establishment, where Sonny and his mamma were very glad to see the amiable voyager. In the subway en route I did much Henneberger work on a small pad; thus sticking to my job despite my embarkation on ventures of pleasure. We stayed till well into the evening, then returned to 259 with a borrowed umbrella—for a drizzle of no mean proportions had sprung up. A E P G. purchased some rubbers at a shop near Belknap's. On Tuesday I did more work—both at home and en route. The route in question was a varied one, beginning when A.E.P.G. and I went down town to meet Loveman in front of the library. We alighted at the 40th street entrance of the Times Square subway station, walking through 40th street and admiring at close range the details of the exquisite black and gold American Radiator Building, which was designed by a Pawtucket architect. It is, in a sense, an experiment in a wholly new style—as Crane heatedly maintains—but its ethereal verticality clearly shews its legitimate descent from the Gothic. We met Loveman without hitch, and with him took the elevated uptown to meet Tiny Belknap at the Museum of Natural History. Sonny, too, was promptly on hand; and the four of us "did" not only the Nat. Hist., but the Historical Museum as well. We saw, among other things, the originals of those "Course of Empire" pictures which I sent you. At five the museum closed, and we took the elevated downtown again—Loveman alighting at 42nd St. to keep an appointment with Kirk, and A E P G and Sonny staying with Grandpa to be shewn the winding colonial ways of Greenwich-Village. The trio alighted at the Jefferson Market station of the elevated, crossing directly to Sheridan Square, and inspecting the Commerce–Barrow–Bedford–Grove tangle of ancient streets. A slight preliminary delay was the breakage of A E P G's bead string, and the hectic recovery of the larger precipitant beads from the pavement. A later pause came when Sonny had to telephone home to mamma like a dutiful child, that he would be later than he had promised. We now made the round of Gay Street, Patchin and Milligan Places, and the nameless inner place where primordial mysteries lurk. We have discovered, by the way, that the corridors of the houses in this cryptic recess lead through to Patchin Place, thus connecting up the whole curious outfit! On our return to Sheridan Square, Belknap took the subway home whilst my daughter and I dined on veal at a neighbouring cafeteria—the same one, by the way, where our gang had taken coffee during the small hours on the all-night session of Sept. 13–14th. After that, we walkt to Washington Square, whose stately edifices are never lacking in charm. A E P G pointed out to me something I had never noted before, but of which she had learnt from the Lawtonii—a memorial tree with bronze tablet opposite the house where the young war poet Alan Seeger lived in his childhood. Seeger, as you may recall from the verses I wrote on him, was a member of the French foreign legion, and died in action at Belloy-en-Santerre July 4, 1916.[21] After this, home. The next day A E P G met S H down town, whilst I took Samuelus to the Poe Cottage in Fordham. The old magick yet lingered about the spot and gave Loveman that sense of rest and domesticity whose absence from modern New-York disturbs him so gravely. Fordham, the site of the cottage, is close to the northern rim of the present New York with Bronx Park to the east and Van Cortlandt Park to the west. A crosstown surface car line connects all three, but up to this time I had never ridden on it—having seen the three places as separate sights, each on an excursion from central Manhattan. Now, however, I wished to shew Loveman the Van Cortlandt Mansion; so we boarded an open car westbound and prepared for sights as new to me as to him. And believe me, it was certainly worth the nickel apiece! The route takes one down a picturesquely precipitous descent with magnificent green hills rising in the foreground, and gives in general a delightfully bold and unusual study in semi-urban landscape. Having reached Van Cortlandt Park, we revelled in the stately atmosphere of old Dutch manorial life in the province. I have more than once, I think, described the mansion and its furnishings to you; hence need only say now that its charm was in every respect unimpaired. On emerging, we paused to rest on a bench in the resplendent sunken garden, which was gay with autumn blooms. Loveman slept a little—he has the power to nod off into slumber at odd moments—and refresht by this, fared downtown to meet Crane for a tour of literary centres. I went downtown also, making one of my lone tours of colonial exploration and looking up some of the quaint corners Coates had recommended to me. At eve I returned home, but finding to my dismay that I had forgotten to deliver a telephone memorandum to Samuelus, set out again at once for his abode in Columbia Heights—this time accompanied by my daughter Anne, to whom I wisht to shew the pleasing sights of that locality. The trip was very pleasant, and tho' our hosts were not in, (I later learnt that Crane had gotten hilariously drunk, and that Loveman had had to take him home amidst many an amusing incident) I took A E P G to the roof and displayed to her that superlative illuminated skyline which had so moved me on my former visit. She appreciated it fully, as she will no doubt tell you in person. Then home again. The next day—Thursday the 25th—I took A E P G on her first visit to the Poe Cottage, which she found exceedingly pleasing; not only as a reminder of the departed bard, but likewise as a specimen of very humble Dutch colonial cottage architecture. The house is very squat and cramped, yet withal possesses such a charm that I wish I dwelt there. We now decided to visit the zoölogical gardens at Bronx Park, hence took—in the opposite direction—the same crosstown car line which Samuelus and I had taken the day before. This part of its route was not so striking as the other part, yet included several objects of interest, such as the main square of Fordham village, which still retains its individuality despite its absorption by New York, and the grey Gothic buildings of Fordham College, a well-known Catholic university. Finally the greenery of Bronx Park hove in sight, and we alighted at the Crotona Gate—paying the admission demanded on pay days. Bronx Park is a beautiful undulating, wooded tract in which the animals are kept as far as possible in their natural environment. There are, of course, houses for them; but the cages in the rear run out to a great length, and include as much real scenery as possible. For example—the bear dens are situate in the most natural rock ledges imaginable; so that a minimum of the menagerie atmosphere is secured. It would be hard to say what the most interesting sight was. Ask A E P G. The reptiles—the pachydermata—the raucously screaming and chromatically plumed macaws and parraqueets—the unspoiled woodland walks suggestive of Quinsnicket—the terraced formal garden gay with riotous blooms—the bit of antique farmland with rolling meadow and stone byre near the main entrance—but who could relate it all? Ask A E P G or come yourself—preferably both! At twilight we emerged, taking dinner at a humble but clean eating-house on the Boston Post Road. I had a Yankee pot roast and apple-pie a la mode—good stuff—and AEPG, whilst sharing the same sort of dessert, chose some chicken something-or-other with potato salad. I then put her on the homeward elevated, whilst I took a strange crosstown line along 180th street—or was it 181st Street?—in an effort to cross the Bronx and connect with the elevated line touching Morton's neighbourhood—for it was Thursday, and James Ferdinand was to be The Boys' host. Usually one approaches him from downtown, but being on the northern rim, I wished to approach him from uptown. The street-car sped through a region I had never seen before—the old-time Bronx of Victoria's reign, where middle-class commuters held their own before driven out by the plague of foreigners. Here, in the gathering dusk, I saw ugly wooden houses reminiscent of Elmwood Ave.—with more than a touch of the Cranston St. atmosphere. Victorian seediness—hideous as hades, yet not without a certain fascination in its grotesque bizarrerie. In places the landscape is rather pretty; and once I glimpsed on the right a park set atop a rock ledge—labelled "Echo Park"—which I design to visit some day. But at last Jerome Ave. was reached, and I changed to the downtown elevated. This ride was uneventful, and before eight I was deposited at my destination in darktown, w'ere br'er Mo'ton done hang out. McNeil, Belknap, and Lazare were absent; but otherwise all hands were on deck, including Loveman. Our discussion was snappier than usual, on account of Samuelus' starting a heated protest (prearranged with Kirk) against the popular-reading tendencies of certain of our number—notably Leeds and Morton. Later on Morton read aloud "The Horror-Horn" from Benson's "Visible and Invisible", and we dispersed with a suitable sense of the hideousness of the cosmos. But did I say dispersed? I mean it only in part. Kleiner decamped with his usual promptness, but Loveman, Leeds and I walked with Kirk down to the latter's lodging place in 106th street, where we found young Lazare back from a successful quest for work, and shared a superlatively excellent cheese cake which Kirk had purchased at a bakery en route. Some time in the morning Leeds, Lazare (who is boarding in Brooklyn) and I took our departure—Loveman staying with Kirk because of fatigue. Leeds left at 50th St., Lazare at 42nd, and Grandpa jogged the rest of the way in dignified solitude. Home 4 a.m. The next day I took A E P G to the Dyckman Cottage, at Broadway and 204th St., which is without a doubt the most homelike surviving specimen of Dutch farmhouse architecture, furnishing, and grounds. I have told you about this place before—and what I haven't, my daughter Anne undoubtedly will; so that I need touch only on the high lights. I trust you received the card we sent—a card, however, which cannot begin to reflect the inimitable charm of the place. It is the old America embodied—the neat, clean, tidy, self-respecting old America which survives so feebly today amidst an heterogeneous welter! What broad-planked, spotless floors—what attics—what furniture, silver, and china—what kitchens and fireplaces—what lawns and groves and paths and gardens and arbours—and what a smokehouse whitely nestling in a hollow! Old times, old times! How I wish we could purchase the old place in Foster! Behind the Dyckman place is a dugout used by the common soldiers of His Majesty's forces from 1776 to 1783—and in it we saw the characteristically rude accomodations of the soldiery. We now took a surface car for the Columbia College or Morningside Heights region, arriving there somewhat before sunset, and observing the 1812 blockhouse (part of the same line of defences which included the blockhouse in Central Park) on the rock cliff at the northern end of Morningside Park. We had passed through dismal slums, but upon debouching into the park were at once transported to a faery mediaeval region—our path being about seven-eighths up the face of the Morningside precipice, with infinite space and skylines of steeples at the left below us, and a great stone wall of an hundred feet, with embrasures and buttresses, on our right, stretching up to the rim of the greenery and shewing above it the tops of the luxurious buildings in Morningside Drive. At last we ascended to the Drive itself by means of a serpentine series of stone steps, and after a look over the eastern valley from one of the parapets—where the Carl Schurz statue stands—turned into the Columbia Campus. This was as attractive as ever, but we soon quit it to wander south along Morningside Drive, and finally to enter the rambling yard of the unfinished Cathedral of St. John the Divine. This cathedral will some day be the mightiest thing of its kind in North America, but just now only a single apse and chapel are completed.[22] What I regret is the passing of the old building—a classick of brick and stone in the colonial style. It is yet intact, with antiquity shining from its small-paned windows; but when the new Gothick stonework is extended, it will be demolisht and totally ingulph'd. From here, darkness having fallen, we repair'd to Broadway in quest of an eating-house; and found on the corner of 109th St. a very agreeable French place, the Trianon, whose panelling and decorations are in the Gallick style of the Fourteenth Louis. Being shewn upstairs, we eat a dinner indicated on the accompanying bill of fare; paying one dollar each, with customary gratuity to the serving-man. The food was excellent, a special mention being due to the unpronounceable cheese dish which form'd our dessert, and which I have markt upon the card. A E P G will tell you about it. Thence we proceeded to 259, an enjoyable day having been had. The next day—Saturday the 27th—was markt in a melancholy way by the departure of AEPG despite every argument and obstacle I could offer. We visited the publick library in the afternoon, observing Stuart and Copley paintings, old English prints, and a great variety of displays of etchers', lithographers', and woodcut tools. When the dismal train hour drew nigh, we repair'd to a Childs' restaurant in 42nd street, where we were duly overcharged for an excellent meal of chicken croquette, peach shortcake, and coffee. Thence to the Grand Central—where we observ'd with interest the old locomotive DeWitt Clinton with its original train of stage-coach-like cars—first ever run on the N.Y. Central, preserved perfectly from 1831 to the present time. There were also marvellous miniature models of other old locomotives and types of car—a whole gallery devoted to this subject, which I had never seen before. At last A E P G had to leave—but I lingered on and took the elevator to the art galleries which this enterprising "dee-po" maintains. These galleries, of excellent construction and lighting, are designed to display the best work of modern American artists; and their entire contents is for sale. I observed some excellent items, especially a whole room panelled in the antient English manner, of which I enclose a circular for your permanent retention. I now return'd to Flatbush, went to the barbers', and return'd home. A Blue Pencil Club meeting was scheduled for the evening, and upon learning that S H would go, I set myself to work writing a contribution on the prescribed subject—"The Old Home Town". As you can well imagine, this theme is one on which I need but little urging to eloquence; so that after three-quarters of an hour I had produced the accompanying tribute to our Providence Corners and Characters.[23] I finished its preliminary revision in the subway en route to Sheepshead Bay—for the gathering was at Dench's—and had the satisfaction of seeing it voted the best contribution of the evening after I had read it at a somewhat boresome session. Kleiner and Loveman were not there, and I have yet to find out why. The next day I revised the verses still further, reducing them to the shape you now behold. The carbon is for your permanent retention—tell AEPG I'll make her another copy if she wants one. The next day—Sunday the 28th—was dragged out in advertisement-answering. Monday—the day I began this epistle but which has now become a yesterday—Henneberger called me up, and I had quite a talk with him at his hotel. He promises to pay me regularly after next Friday, and I can but hope that he will live up to his statement this time. The rest of the day— after a call at Scribners—was spent in writing—a pursuit which has also engrossed this present Tuesday. I am fearsomely behindhand in my correspondence—as a peremptory letter from Eddy, with self-addressed envelope, is at this moment reminding me! Tell AEPG that I shall write her soon, and meanwhile pray let me hear from both you children. S H received your epistle, and will answer when possible. She is still at the place where she has been the last few weeks, but feels that the situation is insecure, and is looking sharply for something more solid and promising. Did I say that Houdini has written, promising to find something for me? Probably I did—but I might as well transcribe in toto the note I received yesterday. (Monday)

Sept. 28, 1924

My dear Lovecraft:—

　　　　　　　　Received your letter and will be back next Sunday and Monday, October 5 and 6, respectively, before I leave for the coast.

Give me a ring on my private 'phone, Cathedral 8260, by all means, as I want to put you in touch with someone worth-while. In the meantime I am already spreading propaganda.

With kindest regards,

Sincerely yours,

HOUDINI.

Keith's Phila. Week Sept. 29.

Just at this moment your letter to A E P G has arrived! I've removed the Harding stamp for C. W. Smith, and am returning the residue to you. You can hand it to A E P G if you wish, or can transmit the equivalent of its contents orally. What delayed it was probably the postman's unfamiliarity with the name—which it probably took him a minute or two to connect with the name Lovecraft which reposes in the letterbox slot.

And now let me urge you to take advantage of that Ray invitation which Daughter Anne tells me about! Bless my soul! but I can't really begin to enjoy the sights here till I can shew them to you—one by one, in an easy fashion guaranteed to avoid overdoing and fatigue. I know you would find the museums and old houses and panoramas delightful—and if you saw them yourself you wouldn't have to wade through these repetitious wanderings and maunderings of a tedious old gentleman. . . . S H tells me that in my letters home I do nothing but say the same thing over and over again, and I guess she's right, for at my age one has very few interests, and these are all bound up in the past—one's own past, or the past of one's race and civilisation. So come along and be on the spot, avoiding long-winded second-hand cataloguing! There is plenty which I haven't seen myself—several things up in Westchester County where you will be, among which is old St. Paul's church with its antient graveyard at Eastchester, about which Mortonius hath told me so much.

But I must desist now, for if I don't mail this epistle soon, it can't get off till tomorrow. Pray write me whenever 'tis convenient, and come along in person if you can possibly arrange it. You must spend some of the time here, where a whole secluded room will be dedicated to your exclusive use, day or night. Did you receive the set of etchings which I sent Saturday? I am quite captivated by them, and could not rest easy till they were equally digested by all the family. They mirror the beauty of the modern city as no mere photographs could do—indeed, I am not sure but that in many cases they are more beautiful than the reality itself! And with which observation I will conclude in truth, subscribing myſelf ever Yr moſt aff: nephew and obt: Servt:

H P L

*P.S. Appendix.* S H & I are probably—unless we change our minds—going to a cinema show this evening.

## Notes

1. John T. Winterich (1891–1970) was managing editor of *Stars and Stripes* and, later, of the *Colophon*. Roy A. Morrish, Sr. (1886–1957) was the husband of HPL's second cousin, Ethel Phillips Morrish (1888–1987).

2. HPL apparently refers to a trip to Smithville (a village in the town of North Scituate, east of Providence) in 1906 with LDC, AEPG, and HPL's cousin Phillips Gamwell.

3. Frank Crane (1861–1928), a Presbyterian minister and author of a ten-volume series of booklets, *Four Minute Essays* (1919), and other books on religion and ethics.

4. For which see Kenneth W. Faig, Jr., "Lovecraft's Third Meeting with David V. Bush," *Lovecraft Annual* No. 8 (2014): 162–77.

5. By Alexander William Kinglake.

6. By Rufus Rockwell Wilson.

7 See Bibliography under Manoel Gonzales.

8. Joseph Pennell (1857–1926) was an American artist and author.

9. A historical novel by Edward Lucas White.

10. [Unsigned], *Little Old New York* (Poughkeepsie, NY: Oxford Publishing Co., 1910).

11. *All God's Chillun Got Wings* by Eugene O'Neill (1888–1953) was playing at the Greenwich Village Theatre (Seventh Avenue South near Christopher St.) from 15 May to 24 October 1924.

12. See the *Brooklyn Daily Eagle* (20 April 1924): "BRAND NEW Kranich & Bach upright piano, original price $900, will sell for $500 cash; beautiful new mahogany Colonial dining suite, 10 pieces, original $500, sale $250; two artistic mahogany armchairs and taborette to match, all hand-carved, original $117, will sell for $65; lovely large Corot print, beautifully framed, $25 sale price; absolutely no dealers. Apply Tuesday and evenings all week. H. P. Lovecraft, 259 Parkside ave., Brooklyn." See also LDC/AEPG 90, pp. 221–22.

13. "Little Sketches about Town," *New York Evening Post* (29 August 1924): 9. Rpt. in H. P. Lovecraft, *From the Pest Zone: Stories from New York*, ed. S. T. Joshi and David E. Schultz (New York: Hippocampus Press, 2003), 106. HPL used this locale for the setting of "He" (11 August 1925).

14. The critic and editor Ernest Boyd (1887–1946) was supervising a new translation of many of Maupassant's novels and tales. Volumes that had appeared by the time of this letter are *Boule de Soif and Other Stories* (1922), *The Sister of Rondoli and Other Stories* (1923), *Bel-Ami* (1923), *Little Roque and Other Stories* (1924), and *Day and Night Stories* (1924). Later volumes include *The Olive Orchard and Other Stories* (1925), *The Pedlar and Other Stories* (1925), and *A Woman's Heart* (1926).

15. I.e., *The Hermaphrodite* (1926).

16. "Wolfert Webber, or Golden Dreams," in *Tales of a Traveller* (1824).

17. "On a New-England Village Seen by Moonlight," ll. 25–28.

18. I.e., the Holland Tunnel, begun in 1920 and completed in 1927.

19. HPL refers to Dunsany's "A City of Wonder" (in *Tales of Three Hemispheres,* 1919), a prose-poem describing Dunsany's first view of New York as he arrived there by boat to begin his American lecture tour of 1919–20.

20. "To H. P. L." (dated 21 September 1924), in Hart and Joshi, *Lovecraft's New York Circle* 197.

21. HPL memorialized the American poet Alan Seeger (1888–1916) in the poem "To Alan Seeger" (*Tryout,* July 1918).

22. The cathedral of the Episcopal Diocese of New York is located on Amsterdam Avenue between West 110th and 113th Streets in Manhattan's Morningside Heights neighborhood. Designed in 1888 and begun in 1892, it is still unfinished.

23. I.e., the poem "Providence."


[75]    [ANS postcard][1] [HPL to LDC]

[Postmarked Elizabeth, N.J.,
10 October 1924]

Passing thro' quaint Colonial villages of Staten Island bound for ferry to ancient Elizabethtown, in His Majesty's Province of New-Jersey. More anon. ¶ You ought to see the veritable library of books I ordered at Scribners yesterday, Sonny helped Grandpa pick 'em out. ¶ Yr aff nephew & obt Servt  H P L

[P.S.] Your delightful letter rec'd!

## Notes

1. *Front:* The Old Town Square, Stapleton, S.I., N.Y.


[76]    [ANS postcard][1] [HPL to LDC]

[Postmarked Elizabeth, N.J.,
10 October 1924]

In Elizabethtown at last, but all the colonial houses I've seen so far are shabby. There are, however, a wealth of hideously decayed colonial houses on the shore of Staten Island—en route to the ferry that brought me here. These houses tend to have porches & pillars in front—not only the mansions, but the small places as well. And there are sinister willows & winding hillside lanes, & spectral wharves! Yr aff & obt H P L

[P.S.] Just noticed! An old gambrel-roofer, *raised up,* on the main corner of the town!

## Notes

1. *Front:* Elizabeth Ave., showing Court House, Elizabeth, N.J.

[77]     [ANS postcard][1] [HPL to LDC]

[Postmarked Elizabeth, N.J.,
11 October 1924]

Back in Elizabeth! Zounds, what a Colonial paradise I've discovered! Once I got a guide to the town, I found the *real* part of it; & it's a marvel of antiquarian survival comparable only to Salem. Moreover, it appreciates its old houses & scenes, & publishes a book on the subject—a copy of which I will send you. No other town so frankly antique, & so proud of its Colonial past, have I seen outside New England. It is, if I may use the term, self-consciously ancient. More later—just now I can only absorb & admire!
Yr aff nephew & obt Servt  H P L

*Notes*

1. *Front:* The Court House, Elizabeth, N.J.

[78]     [ALS] [HPL to LDC]

259 Parkside Ave.,
Brooklyn, N.Y.,
Novr. 4–5, 1924.
Finisht **Novr. 6**

My very dear daughter Lillian:—

Can it be that an entire month & more hath pafs'd since last I writ you? So saith the Old Farmer's Almanack, (of which I am monstrous eager to get the 1925 ifsue) & I am not dispos'd to contradict so venerable & reliable an authority; but I am confident that you will pardon me in view of the nerve-draining events mention'd in my letter to A E P G— the illness & hospital sojourn of my spouse, & the impending dissolution of this establishment in a maze of poverty & uncertainty. Of such is life— glorious life—compos'd—but being of haughty & imperial instincts, I will proceed to play blithely on the lyre whilst Rome burns.

Your letter—as usual—afforded me the keenest delight, & I have pored most appreciatively over all the pictures sent at various times. What splendid colonial structures Providence is acquiring! I am impressed with the new Olneyville Boys' Club—as drawn by that prince of sketchers, George D. Laswell. It was in the text appended to one of those views that I discovered the "George D."—some day perhaps I shall unearth enough material about this hero of mine to form a "Who's Who" biography!

Your description of the Temple of Musick at the Park fascinated me greatly. I already have views of it in my portfolio, but a first-hand account is much to be preferred. Providence is fortunate in having such a classic specimen, & I hope it will soon be immortalised in post-card form. After all, with the sole exception of the Gothick cathedral, contemporary architecture has no model to follow save the austere marbles of Greece & Rome. Classical antiquity said all there was to be said in line & mass—& he is best today who copies most faithfully. All the charm of my beloved Georgian-Colonial architecture is drawn from its free use & adaptation of Graeco-Roman ornament . . . . But I have said all this many times before, & with far less excuse!

Yes—the excavations at Leptis Magna are certainly epoch-making.[1] This is a rich period for archaeology—note in the envelope I sent ahead a cutting anent the new discoveries at Rome itself, in the forum of Augustus. Still another event is the unearthing of ancient Carthage—the real old Punic town of Hamilcar & Hannibal, & not the Roman town built later on its site—by a French nobleman. I'll send the cutting—a full page from the *Times*—when Belknap returns it. In this matter it is interesting to note that the explorer has chosen as his guide-book not any dry-as-dust tome on archaeology & antiquities, but the immortal romance of Gustave Flaubert—"Salammbo". Flaubert, with that romantic realism of which he is still reckoned the world's greatest master, studied Carthage for years before writing that tremendous novel, & when he did write it he put into it the very life & soul of that half-forgotten Punic Empire whose annals come down to us mostly through the one-sided medium of its Roman conquerors. He made Carthage live as Edward Lucas White in "Andivius Hedulio" makes Rome live, & so minute was his accuracy in describing the geography, architecture, institutions, & customs of the Punic scene, that he was able to refute triumphantly the attacks of all the archaeologists who—because he had delved farther than they & therefore differed from them on many matters—accused him of misrepresenting his subject. What an impressive vindication—his novel used as a guide & authority by one of the world's most eminent archaeologists!

But I digress. I wish I might have seen those shop windows—Alexander Hamilton & the Colonial mantel—but not seeing them, the next best thing is hearing of them. In turn, I wish I could shew you the museums here! Too bad you didn't get me that Breeches Bible—I'll wager Kirk or Loveman would have picked it up as a speculation if they'd heard of it. I've never seen one. There's a Vinegar Bible in St John's Church in Portsmouth N.H., but when I was there I couldn't get in—or rather, didn't know enough to go across the street & fetch the sexton.[2] Glad you liked the Baring-Gould book. I'm on the lookout for a chance to purchase it—as well as the same author's work on werewolves. He died only a few months ago at a very advanced age.[3] Thanks enormously for the sketch of the time-towers in the Journal window. The originals with their starry background must have made an impressive skyline, & I trust they received some measure of appreciation from the passing crowds.

So it cost $12.00 to repair your clock! Well—it's worth it! My old (ci-devant[4] kitchen) clock will not run, & I cannot keep the parlour clock going because its sound wears on S H's nerves, but I love to look at both of them.

Clocks have always attracted me, & there is nothing I want more than a banjo or hall clock of colonial vintage. Did you keep the library clock? It wouldn't run, but I somewhat hate to think of it in the ash dump! Yes—bring along the kitchen alarm clock unless you have use for it yourself!

This reminds me that I'd enormously like to see you here. There are myriad sights to show you, as A E P G can attest; & if your advent were haply to coincide with my domestic disintegration, I can assure you that your brain-power would be keenly appreciated—though I would not let you do any physical work of breaking-up after your summer ordeal of like nature & your vernal mishap to the back. After all, this place won't be a fraction as hard as 598 to disperse, since there are no vast attic accumulations.

But enough of practical things. Let us to the diary—which ought to begin about October 8, since my last homeward line was written to A E P G on the 7th, in the evening on a bench in Washington Square, after which I simply returned to 259, did some reading, & retired.

On Wednesday, the 8th, then, I did some letter-writing & departed in the late afternoon for 'Ittle Belknap's, where Loveman & I were invited to dinner before The Boys met there—our meetings having been changed to Wednesday on account of a college class which Sonny has on Thursday evening. On this occasion 'a good time was had by all'—especially after the gang arrived, & late was the hour ere we disperst. Kleiner, Kirk, Loveman, & Morton dodged off impatiently whilst Leeds & I lingered at the door talking with Belknap, so the left-behind pair went down town, sipped coffee at an all-night "Automat",* & parted about 2 a.m. in quest of the hay. The next day— Thursday the 9th—Belknap & I descended on Scribners' to use up that sixty-dollar credit of Henneberger's which I could not convert into cash. Sonny was there to help his Grandpa pick out good books, & I decided to choose one for him in partial repayment for the many dinners & courtesies I am receiving from his household. We secured a delightful clerk—a finely-bred young chap with an incipient red moustache who discussed intelligently & literarily all the authors we mentioned—& with his aid set about our pleasing task. Some of the books were more expensive than I had anticipated, but even so I managed to gather up a very respectable "five-foot shelf". The full list follows. Most of them came in two days, but those which Scribner did not have in stock (here marked with an asterisk) were delayed till a week ago— Wednesday, Oct. 29th. You may easily see what a treat I have:

---

*a restaurant where the food is arranged on plates in glass-doored pigeonholes along the walls. A nickel in the slot unlocks the door, & the plate of food is taken by the purchaser to one of the many tables in the great room.

*Books by Lord Dunsany*
*The Queen [*sic*] of Elfland's Daughter
*Fifty-One Tales
Five Plays
Plays of Near & Far

*Books by Arthur Machen*

| | |
|---|---|
| The House of Souls | The Secret Glory |
| The Hill of Dreams | The London Adventure |
| Far-Off Things | *Hieroglyphics |
| Things Near & Far | |

*Books on colonial material*
The Architecture of Colonial America—Eberlein
Furniture of our Forefathers—Singleton
Early American Craftsmen—Dyer
Old New England Churches—Bacon
Crooked & Narrow Streets of Old Boston—Thwing

*Miscellaneous*
*Episodes of Vathek—Beckford
Rome of Today & Yesterday—Dennie

*For Belknap* (his own choice)
The Thing In the Woods (new horror novel)—Harper Williams

---

Some haul? I'd never have ventured such a plunge if it hadn't been the only way to get the value Henneberger owed me. But I'm glad of it for all that! If any of these titles appeal to you, I'll be glad to make a loan! This choosing took us till about 4 o'clock, after which we went over to the west side slums for a call on honest old McNeil. McNeil doesn't come to our meetings any more because of a quarrel with Leeds over eight dollars which the latter owes him, so we hunt him up occasionally to have a chat for old times' sake. He has finished "Tonty of the Iron Hand", & the Duttons like it very much. He is now looking about for a new subject for a boys' book—which he will proceed to write according to the terms of his contract. We talked of things in general, Belknap leaving at six & I at eight. After that, home, reading, & retiring.

Friday the 10th, in accordance with a plan of long standing which a chance editorial in the *Times* (enc.) brought to fruition,[5] I started out on a tour of exploration whose focus was the antient colonial city of Elizabethtown, (now call'd Elizabeth) in the Province of New-Jersey. I went by way of Staten Island, taking the ferry from the Battery to St. George, & at that point taking the trolley line across the north shore of the island through antique Port

Richmond to the old Elizabethtown ferry, where in 1780 His Majesty's forces under Sir Henry Clinton crossed on a temporary pontoon bridge in their attempt to capture the town. I had been to Port Richmond before—with Kleiner two years ago, when I wrote you about the 1783 church under which a brook flows, & behind which is a hellish neglected graveyard. This time I did not stop to see these things, but kept on the car & changed from side to side to watch the antiquities which loomed on every hand. And how abundant those antiquities were! Shabby, dilapidated houses along the waterfront & on every grassy hillock, with here & there a village-like cluster leading inland. Their type is very local & distinctive, & markt by a great prevalence of pillared facades—with porch & Dutch curved roof join'd by great rows of square or classic columns extending up two stories as in the late southern plantation-houses. This arrangement exists not only in the spacious mansions, but with equal frequency in the humbler houses, where it possesses a certain touch of subtle incongruity. A touch of the sinister is supply'd by the paintlessness & *extreme* decrepitude of most of these places, some of which are uninhabited & lonely on their sparsely turfed sand banks. The whole effect is bleak & a bit terrifying—I shall never forget the hideously gnarled & grotesque willow trees, & the little steep lanes leading up forbidding hillsides. At last the ferry was reached, & I went across to the dingy wharf at Elizabethport. This is now a Polish slum, & lacking all knowledge of the city I had to take a car to the business centre to procure maps, guides, pictures, historic matter, & the like. At last, having rolled from pillar to post—stationery store, public library, & newspaper office—I managed to accumulate a fine array of data, including the historical guide booklet of which I sent you a duplicate. Thus armed, I did some quick studying; & finally proceeded to follow the routes prescribed by the booklet. Night fell all too soon, but there was a great moon; & I continued my quest in the spectral night. Never will I forget the sunset as it came upon me that day—I was on a scarcely used part of the old Essex & Middlesex turnpike, a road yet unpaved, & lined with the great elms & tiny colonial cottages that Genl. Washington knew. To the west stretcht the open fields & the primeval forest, & down over that haunted expanse sank the great solar disc in a riot of flame & glamour, painting the sky with a thousand streamers of weird & unimagined wildness long after the glowing edge had vanished beneath the trees & the hills. I returned to Brooklyn via steamtrain, Hudson Tubes, & subway in the late evening, but returned the first thing on the following day—anxious to study the town at leisure by sunlight, & with the background of geographical & historical knowledge which I had so extemporaneously acquired. On that second day I went both ways by the Staten Island & ferry route—which has vast inexpensiveness, to say nothing of vast picturesqueness, to recommend it.

Elizabethtown, as you already know from the book, was founded in 1664 & well built up at an early date, both with small houses & with mansions of taste & opulence. The largest & oldest part of the town is a little over a mile inland, on the narrow & curving Elizabeth river, & is reached from the ferry by an ancient road—King's Highway, now comprising Elizabeth Ave. & First Ave.—which is older than the town itself, having been laid out by the Dutch to communicate betwixt New-Amsterdam & the settlements in Delaware.

Landing at the ferry house, one walks a trifle south to King's Highway & commences the march inland—fancying oneself, perchance, part of a spectral column of His Majesty's invading troops under Clinton or Knyphausen.[6] Not far from the shore, in front of a branch library, is a boundary stone of 1694, which at once establishes connexions with the past which one is seeking.

Approaching the town by the gently curving road, we see more & more colonial houses; till at last, near Union Square, they become delightfully prevalent. At that point the highway bends considerably, dipping straight down to the gentle valley where the old town nestles through the ages. Straight ahead on the skyline looms the tall, slender steeple of the old Presbyterian Church—still the dominant feature of the city's silhouette—& all around it cluster the ancient gambrel roofs of the forefathers—good old English roofs, for Elizabethtown was never Dutch—wrapt in the blue haze of distance which is akin to elfin magick. Down we march to the main street—Broad—where still the houses of the past are thickly sprinkled. As we approach the First Church we perceive what a marvellous place it is—standing in the front yard & looking north we have on our left the great facade & mighty spire—magnificent later Georgian work—& beside & beyond it the ancient churchyard with crumbling brownstone slabs (instead of slate, as in N.E.) dating back to the sixteen-hundreds, long before the present edifice was built. Here sleep the fathers—their stones of varying workmanship, their names variously spelt. Crane, Craine, Hetfield, Hatfield, Hindes, Ogden—& so on. In the rear are willow trees & grassy banks & impressive tombs. Clad in mellow ivy is the old brick church, which was built in 1784 on the site of one burnt in 1780. To the north winds crooked old Broad street, still studded with colonial gambrels, though some of the ancient houses have been raised like those of our own South Main St. to permit of modern shops beneath. Adjoining the churchyard is the new parish house—brick, & on such severe colonial lines that it might well be deem'd contemporary with the church. All vistas beckon us, but we choose the southward road, across the quaint stone bridge which spans the narrow, winding river. And what a river! Down to its sloping banks of grass & moss stretch the yards of the most ancient houses, gay with the tangles of old-fashion'd gardens, & grim with the great snakelike willows that bend out from the shore & lean far over the tranquil stream. Sime or Doré would revel in the sight—as did I in my humbler & unproductive fashion. Beyond the bridge the land sinks to the east & rises to the west. I chose the latter course, where Washington St. meanders up betwixt incredibly archaic houses to a striking crest where colonial gables brood on every corner, & a great many-dormered gambrel-roofer silhouettes itself boldly against the polychrome sunset as a background in full keeping with the spirit of the place. Climbing this hill, it is well to follow Washington St. as it bends south to join the ancient Essex & Middlesex turnpike, passing another Georgian church & finally reaching the open country. Most of this country is now doomed by prospective real-estate developments, but one may still enjoy it as one cuts across the newly laid out & still houseless Bayway to Rahway Ave., an old-time road—part of the original King's Highway—on which are many mansions of noble refugees from France, chief among which is the "Old Chateau" of the Jouets, an impressive stone building in the middle Georgian manner, with two great wings. It is well here to turn north toward the town again, noting such alluring landmarks as the old De Hart house, perched on its high terrace & still displaying the airs & graces of 1766.

One now returns down the hill—eastward past the great gambrel-roofer & antediluvian chimneys by the river—& crosses Broad St., following the curving line of Pearl past many an archaic rooftree & garden, & past the old bridge to Elizabeth Ave., which spans another bend of the sinuous river. Pearl St. finally curves south, where it used to end among the marshes, though it is now being cut through to an entirely new factory district. At the old foot of the street, close to the open fields, stands the ancient Hatfield house, (1667) peaked & gabled in the earliest pre-Georgian manner, & probably forming today the oldest house in Elizabethtown if not in all New Jersey. You have probably read about it in the book—though I must warn you that the quaint well-sweep has vanished during the iconoclastic decade since 1914, when the little guide was printed. It is now interesting to retrace one's steps to the bridge at the bend in Pearl St., cross to Elizabeth Ave., & examine the ancient houses in the streets, lanes, & hidden courts nearby. The "old fort" in Thompson's Lane was built in 1734, & is still in good condition—a long brick house of plain lines—today inhabited entirely by niggers! The Andrew Joline house, built in 1735, is wholly hidden from the street by shops, but stands in a spectral courtyard, with its back on the river bank. And on the northeast corner of Bridge St. & Elizabeth Ave. is a terrible old house—a hellish place where night-black deeds must have been done in the early seventeen-hundreds—with a blackish unpainted surface, unnaturally steep roof, & an outside flight of steps leading to the second story, suffocatingly embowered in a tangle of ivy so dense that one cannot but imagine it accursed or corpse-fed. It reminded me of the Babbitt house in Benefit St.,[7] which as you recall made me write those lines entitled "The House" in 1920. Later its image came up again with renewed vividness, finally causing me to write a new horror story with its scene in Providence & with the Babbitt house as its basis. It is called "The Shunned House", & I finished it last Sunday night. After a taste of this uncanny waterfront it is well to turn up Spring St. to East Jersey, where abound the finest mansions of the early colonial time. As we turn the corner we notice across the street a splendid colonial public building whose red brick facade, white pillars, & keystoned, small-paned windows arouse in us the highest expectations. Breathless, we conjure up an hundred pre-Revolutionary British images as we strive to decipher the modest corner-stone. Then—ugh! Illusion drops with a 'dull, sickening thud'[8] as we find that the place is a brand new Jewish synagogue, built only last year! 1923—oi, oi! But *Newport* can boast a *really* colonial synagogue, built in 1763, when the Touros & Mendez's reigned supreme, & still in good condition not a stone's throw from old Trinity. One more step, & we regain the truly colonial with a vengeance, beholding on a high terrace the peaked pre-Georgian gabled Bon-nell house, built in 1682, & the second-oldest edifice in the town. Across the street is an ivy-clad specimen of the Early Georgian—the Ogden mansion, built before 1742, where from 1751 to 1757 dwelt Jonathan Belcher, Esq., His Majesty's Governor of the Province—a Massachusetts man who had gained considerable unpopularity when ruling his own Bay Province from 1737 to 1747. Returning toward Broad St. we find a multiplicity of colonial mansions; including the residence of Elias Boudinot (1750—now spoilt by an added French roof & used as an Old Ladies' Home) & the Barnet house (1763) where Gen. Winfield Scott later liv'd. In toward the centre of the town is the 2nd Presbyterian Church, a late Georgian building dating from 1821 & shewn on one of the cards I sent home—either to you or A E P G—& around the corner in Broad St. is old St. John's—an 1859 Gothick church, but with an ancient churchyard dating from 1702.

But lud, ma'am—I cou'd rave all night about Elizabethtown! Did I send you a postcard of the old Carteret Arms by the river—the red gambrel-roofer where the D.A.R. now holds forth? It was built in 1797, & has a fine panell'd interior. Elizabethtown in general has several architectural & other idiosyn-crasies of great distinctiveness. There is an unusual prevalence of gambrel-roof'd houses with a triangular pediment in front—standing out like a flat-tened gable from the lower pitch of the roof, as shewn in the view of the Car-teret Arms. Fine colonial *doorways* are very rare—these being a distinctively New England feature, whilst the builders of the middle colonies sought beau-ty rather in the proportioning of the whole mass. Life in the town is delicious-ly leisurely & provincial. There is no taint of New York & its nasty cosmopolitanism. All the people of substance are native Yankees, & though the factory sections teem with low Poles, they are not frequently met on the main streets. Niggers are quite thick in the byways of the town, & a curious custom shared alike by people, Poles, & niggers is the wearing of white caps or muslin kerchiefs by the housewives—mainly those of the petty middle class & lower. The whole atmosphere of the place is marvellously colonial. Of tall buildings there are absolutely none, & on every hand the ancient skyline is dominated by delicate steeples in the Christopher Wren tradition, that of the First Presbyterian being foremost & loftiest of all. Elizabethtown is a balm, a sedative, & a tonic to the old-fashion'd soul rackt with modernity. I must re-visit it & shew it to others—to you, I hope, in the near future!

The day after my second Elizabethan tour—Sunday the 12th—Loveman was here to dinner, & was greatly interested in my account of my travels. He will soon make a trip there himself, with Old Theobald as guide. After dinner we walked down to the Brooklyn Heights section to call on his friend Hart Crane in Columbia Heights, with whom he had stopped till he moved up to Kirk's in 106th St., Manhattan. The walk was very lovely—downhill from the heights on which the Brooklyn Museum stands, & with many a sunset vista of old houses & far spires. We reached the heights in the deep twilight, when the aërial skyline across the river had a charm peculiar to the hour—a perfect silhouette effect, since it was too dark for surface definition, yet too light to allow the contours to become merged into the black recesses of engulfing night. We found Crane in & sober—but boasting over the two-day spree he had just slept off, during which he had been picked up dead drunk from the street in Greenwich Village by the eminent modernist poet E. E. Cum-mings—whom he knows well—& put in a homeward taxi. Poor Crane! I hope he'll sober up with the years, for there's really good stuff & a bit of ge-nius in him. He is a genuine poet of a sort, & his excellent taste is reflected in the choice objets d'art with which he has surrounded himself. I would give much for a certain Chinese ivory box of his, with panels exquisitely carved into delicate pastoral scenes in high relief—every detail of landscape & foliage standing out with that absolute beauty & maturely assured perfection for which the best Chinese art is distinguished. After some conversation we all went out for a scenic walk through the ancient narrow hill streets that wind about the Brooklyn shore. There is a dark charm in this decaying waterfront, & the culmination of our tour was the poor old Fulton Ferry, which we reached about 9 o'clock, in the best season to enjoy the flaming arc of Brook-lyn Bridge in conjunction with the constellation of Manhattan lights across the river, & the glimmering beacons of slow-moving shipping on the lapping tides. When I was last there—in 1922 with Kleiner—the old ferry was still running, & the pensive wooden statue of Robert Fulton was looking down on the scene of decline from his niche in the front of the floridly Victorian ferry-house. Now even these things are gone. The ferry made its last trip on the 19th of last January, & the statue has vanished—presumably to adorn some museum—leaving a gapingly empty niche to brood over the spectacle of des-olation. Thence we returned to Crane's, threading more old streets, & inci-dentally looking up rooms for Loveman in Columbia Heights. There was one splendidly large room for $10.00 per week in an impressive brick mansion of the Rutherford B. Hayes period—presided over by an aged Mrs. Grey, who has seen better days. Loveman, however, didn't take it; & if I could afford that much rent I'd snap it up tomorrow. I can't, though—& I think I'll get in touch with Crane & ask him about the smaller $5.00-per-wk. rooms which he was likewise recommending to Samuelus.

Leaving Crane's about 10:30, Samuelus & I proceeded to the subway, crossed the river, emerged at Wall St., & prepared to finish that nocturnal tour of colonial sights which his fatigue cut short last September. We went down Wall to Pearl, turned in there, & subsequently marched past many a colonial doorway to Hanover-Square, which had in the still of the night regain'd something of its aristocratick British dignity of the 1760's. The ancient India-House greeted us with its carven facade & small-pan'd windows, & all that cou'd draw us away was the prospect of Fraunces' Tavern ahead. We came upon the tavern in the burning moonlight—the same round-disc'd moonlight which had laid witchery on the waters during my Elizabethan trips of the two days preceding—& paus'd in proper awe at the sight. There rose the antique walls in Georgian grace, whilst the swinging sign creak'd in a gentle wind—a gentle wind blowing down the ages with ghosts of red coats & white periwigs. Silence was our supreme tribute—& next day Loveman dropt me a postcard of sheer ecstasy at the spectacle. Thence we proceeded westward, turning up Broadway & later down Rector St., past the grave of Alexander Hamilton in ancient Trinity Churchyard. Rector led to Church, & Church to narrow Thames—down which we defiled reverently, saluting the tiny brick colonial houses on the north side. This brought us to Greenwich St., & the venerable brick facade of that colonial hostelry, the Planters' Hotel—a favourite gathering-place of travelling Virginia gentry in the old days. This place has its *Poe* memories, too; for when the bard landed in New-York from Philadelphia (whence he had come by train to Perth Amboy—an old town described in one of my former travelogues—& the rest of the way by boat) he found it in its decline—as Mrs. Morrison's cheap boarding-house—& obtain'd lodgment there for himself & his ailing wife prior to taking the Fordham cottage. That was in April, 1844; but since then the tavern hath been restor'd to its colonial outlines & something of its colonial dignity. From the Planters' we walkt north one square to Cedar St., up which we turn'd, observing the many colonial houses on the south side—one of which is Tom's Chop House, (open continuously since 1797) whose picture I sent you last summer. From Cedar we went up Church to Fulton, & up that to Broadway, admiring on our left the archaic churchyard & Christopher Wren steeple of noble old St. Paul's. It was now close on midnight, so with a lingering glance at St. Pauls' [*sic*] 1766 facade, & the 1812 grace of the marble City Hall across the park, we dove into our respective subways & concluded a performance of unalloy'd delight.

The next day—Monday the 13th—I went up to Sonny-Child's for lunch, & spent the afternoon revelling amongst the exotic curios which his opulent aunt—Mrs. William Symmes—had just brought him from Paris & London.[9] There were exquisite portfolios of de luxe colour'd views of Versailles & Fontainbleau, queer china dishes & pieces of silver plate, unusual & bizarre fabricks, & most attractive of all to the Belknap-infant, a peculiar pipe formed of a hollow block of polisht wood connected in hookah-fashion with a hard-rubber mouthpiece by a gaudy green rubber tube over six feet long. 'Ittle-Man hath since shewn it to all The Boys with every mark of proprietary satisfaction, & all agree that it is a most marvellous creation for a small boy to own! Late in the afternoon we all—Sonny, his mamma, his papa, & his Grandpa Theobald—took a 'bus ride far uptown, returning on the same vehicle without alighting at the terminus. The return trip was in the twilight, & after the Belnapii alighted at their 100th St., I kept on the stage-coach & rode down to ancient Washington-Square via Riverside Drive & 5th Ave., thence seeking the homeward subway.

Tuesday the 14th I read my principal book on colonial houses, & in the afternoon went to interview the man to whom Houdini had given me a letter of introduction—Brett Page, head of a newspaper syndicate service whose office is at the corner of Broadway & 58th St. Page was amazingly affable, & detain'd me an hour & a half in cordial conversation; but had nothing at all in the way of a vacant position. He said that just two sorts of places are fitted for me—assistant editorship of a trade paper, & readership or revisorship in a book publishing house. He advised me to ask Houdini for an introduction to a book publisher—which I shall do when my nerves permit me to indite a coherent epistle. In the evening I read more colonial material—as usual.

Wednesday the 15th I had lunch with S H downtown at that quaint basement cafeteria at Madison Ave. & 36th St. Riding home on the subway, I was struck with the memory of weird things I had seen at twilight in Elizabethtown, & other weird things of longer ago—& at once realised that I was about to write a story. During the afternoon I laid out the preliminary design, & discussed it in some detail when The Boys met in the evening at Kirk's. Morton was absent on account of the death of his mother, which had called him back to Massachusetts; but in spite of this fact we managed to have a tolerable time till about 3 a.m. Thursday, Friday, Saturday, & Sunday may be dispos'd of with much brevity; for I did nothing but write upon my story. It is longer than my average product, & needed much care; so that many drastic eliminations & rearrangements were perforce adopted before I could assemble it as a continuous bit of text. Sunday afternoon S H & I took a walk in Prospect Park, & in the evening went to the cinema, after which we bought some ice-cream at the corner candy shop & took it (i.c., not shop) home to eat. And we ate it.

Monday the 20th I was at Sonny's all day—for both lunch & dinner—& we discussed the story (then about ¾ done) at length; Belknap making several suggestions for re-proportioning, one of which I very gratefully adopted. In the evening I did considerable work on the story, starting for bed about midnight—but having to dress again in haste the very moment I emerged from the tub, on account of the sudden gastric spasms with which S H had been seized whilst resting in bed after a day of general ill-feeling. It was then that we called up the hospital, as related in my epistle to A E P G, & hastened down in a taxicab whilst the grim small hours brooded over the world. Tuesday the 21st I took many things to the hospital, returned home, & in the evening started out to meet Kleiner & Loveman downtown for a tour of the bookstalls. A subway tieup, however, delayed me hopelessly—train ahead had hot box, & power had to be shut off half an hour—so that I missed the appointed rendezvous at Union Square. Arriving there & finding myself alone, I toured the literary emporia independently; picking up several ten-cent bargains, the most striking of which was a play of the Salem witchcraft by Mary E. Wilkins.[10] I had a marvellously good & cheap dinner—lamb stew, apple-pie, & coffee—at a modest cafeteria in 8th St., (it all cost only 35¢) after which I returned home, read the Salem play, & retired.

The next day—Wednesday the 22nd—I made passable coffee from written directions furnisht by S H the day before, & rounded out breakfast with bread, cheese, & a 20-minute egg which I cookt with vast finesse. I then visited the hospital, taking books, papers, stationery, & an Eversharp pencil I bought as a gift to the patient, & subsequently went directly from there to a meeting of The Boys at Belknap's. This time Mortonius was present, bearing up well after his bereavement, & with a fine horror book he had pickt up in Boston—at Goodspeed's, in Park St. This volume—"The Door of the Unreal", by Gerald Biss, he lent me; & it turned out to be a very effective werewolf story. Sleepy Kleiner broke the meeting up at midnight, but Morton, Leeds, Kirk, Loveman, & I adjourned to a neighbouring cafeteria where we sate in grave discussion till 1:30. Then Kirk & Samuelus struck up north, Leeds took the subway south, whilst Mortonius & I walkt down to 72nd St. & across to Columbus Ave., where we climbed opposite sides of the elevated, gesturing grotesquely to each other across the tracks till—by an happy coincidence—opposite trains came at exactly the same time to engulf us & bear us away in our respective homeward directions, uptown & downtown.

Thursday the 23d I divided betwixt the hospital & home reading. Friday the 24th was much the same till evening, when instead of going home I went up to a special meeting of The Boys at Kirk's—a meeting called to ensure the attendance of nice, honest old McNeil, who on account of a financial quarrel will not attend when Leeds is present. Leeds borrowed $8.00 of him, & failed to return it when promised; a breach of faith which preys on the good old boy's simple Victorian mind, so that he won't recognise his erring brother till reparation is made. We find much ground for sympathy on both sides, & wish we could have both boys with us—but it has to be Leeds at the regular meetings, since McNeil is the one to make the break, & we can hardly tell Leeds to get out when he hasn't harmed the rest of us. This special meeting was very delightful—even though Mortonius was absent. Loveman played his new hundred-dollar radio set—bringing to our humble clubroom a very fair vocal rendering of "The Mikado"—& McNeil prattled amiably of life's simple things. At 1:30 we broke up—Kleiner taking the subway, whilst Kirk, (our host, who always accompanies his guests home as far as they will walk!) McNeil, & I embarked on a pedestrian journey down town. It was a great little walk down Central Park West, & toward the end a waning crescent moon arose. At 49th St. Kirk & I turned west with McNeil, & accompanied him to his lofty abode in "Hell's Kitchen", remaining & chatting till 5 a.m., when we adjourned to a cafeteria in Broadway near 49th St. En route to this latter place, we indulged in considerable astronomical speculation anent a curious *duplication* of the lunar crescent which both clearly observ'd without having had the least alcoholick preparation. In the cafeteria Kirk turned the conversation to philosophy—& time vanished in a thin grey mist. Dawn paled the east, & then gilded the peaks of the neighbouring skyscrapers; but we knew it not. Our minds were upon grave generalities; & since no officious waiter disturb'd us, we soared to the uttermost bounds of the cosmos whilst our gross clay sprawled in one-arm chairs along the tiled wall. Kirk is more intelligent than I had realised—for he is usually quiet & uncommunicative. In beliefs, he & I are exactly as one—for despite a stern Methodist upbringing he is an absolute cynick & sceptick, who realises most poignantly the fundamental purposelessness of the universe. At 9:30 we paused for breath, & sallied forth into the fresh morning air for a tour of antiquarian exploration. First we walkt to the old Jane Teller mansion at the foot of 61st street—the one which A E P G & I visited last April. It was very beautiful with the sun on its eastern end, & we lingered long before passing under the sinister masonry of the Queensboro Bridge in quest of Sutton Place—the reclaimed district of sumptuous neo-Georgian houses, courts, & gardens on a high terrace above the East River. Sutton Place, however, proved equally delightful; & in order to gain a view of the rear gardens which line the river out of sight of the street, we climbed perilously out along the face of the perpendicular cliff, clinging to the wire netting which bounds them for safety's sake, & finding precarious footholds in the crumbling earth of the bluff. Our pains were repaid, for we saw many colonial marvels in the way of walks & bowers; & one magnificent rear door of the Connecticut valley, broken-pedimented type. Thence we return'd to the busy streets; plodding along philosophically, washing our clayey hands at a convenient hydrant, & exploring an alluring car-barn in 8th Ave., where among more modern vehicles we found a splendid old converted horse-car (like the old Olneyville & Market Sq. white cars) used as a work-car. At Times Square we lunched at the Automat (vide sheet III, side 2) where Leeds & I lunched on a former occasion, my fare this time being macaroni, potato salad, cheese pie, & coffee. From this filling station we repaired to 40th St. to inspect the American Radiator Co.'s building—the new black & gold Dunsanian skyscraper design'd by the Pawtucket architect—& for the first time explored the interior. The basement is a dream of picturesqueness & spectral charm—crypt under crypt of massive vaulted masonry . . . . terrible arches on Cyclopean columns, black *things* & haunted niches here & there, & endless stone steps leading down . . . down . . . . down . . . to hellish catacombs where sticky, brackish water drips. It is like the vaulted space behind the entrances to some ancient amphitheatre in Rome or Constantinople— that, or some ghoulish tomb-nightmare not to be imagined save in visions of nameless drugs out of unfathomable Ind. We must take the rest of the gang there some time! Our next station was the 10 cent store, where we made a mild literary investment or two, (I got Montaigne's Essays for a dime) & after that we repair'd to Hetherington's drug store for some post cards. Next came the Grand Central Station, whose collection of ancient railway material (which I shew'd to A E P G on the day when I reluctantly consign'd her to the eastbound N Y N H & H) I wished to display to Kirk. He was much fascinated by the old "De Witt Clinton" & its train—the *actual* engine & cars run on the N.Y. Central in 1831, now preserved for ever in a mighty gallery—& the clever working models of engines old & new, arranged in cases near by. Then, at last, we began to think of concluding. Getting a chocolate sundae apiece at Hetherington's, we commenced the slow trek back to Fifth Ave., when there overtook us a final thrill in the way of a crowd & a political procession, the centre of which was none other than Theodore Roosevelt, Jr., (whose illustrious sire I beheld in Aug. 1912 at the Prov. Opera House) newly come home after a speaking tour of the provinces.[11] He was standing up in a motor, smiling, bowing, & waving a fedora hat at the assembled populace— looking considerably like the immortal Theodorus I, & sporting a neat but spreading bald spot just where my own is developing. Vivat Theodorus Rex! I'm beastly sorry he was defeated, even though Smith isn't at all bad. He must have to exercise considerable fortitude not to grow a moustache, wear a heavy-rimm'd pince-nez, & shew his teeth like the eminent departed! Better luck next time—here's to him!

By this time the diary date ought definitely to be changed to Saturday, Octr. 25. Kirk took a bus uptown at 5th Ave., whilst I follow'd Teddy II & the crowd to Times Square, where I took the subway to 259. There I bathed & brush'd up, & started out again at once for the hospital. At the latter place I had an interesting conversation with Dr. Westbrook, & stayed till the closing hour of 9 p.m., incidentally breaking a semi-engagement with Loveman to go to Newark & make a raid on the bookstalls there.

Sunday & Monday I put in hospitalling, also perfecting my household technique & coffee-making art. I kept the place finely swept & dusted, so that S H knew no difference from normal when she got back. Tuesday—after a spectacular success in cooking & preparing *spaghetti* according to directions from S H—I went to the hospital for my usual call, after which I went down town to meet Sonny-Boy at McNeil's, where we had planned to pay the old fellow a call. We found him out, however, hence changed our evening to one of bookstall touring—covering the 59th St. area of shops. Belknap picked up a fine thing of Walter Pater's, & an exquisite volume of Landor's poetry. I got a Gautier—with introduction by Edgar Saltus—for myself, & a copy of "The Castle of Otranto" for Mortonius.[12] After a dispersal of the expedition I return'd home to find awaiting me a letter from that brilliant Washingtonian, Edward Lloyd Sechrist, announcing his arrival in New York on the following Sunday for a week's sightseeing & visiting among friends, with headquarters at the historick old Brevoort House, 5th Ave. & 8th St, where Washington Irving & his literary coterie used to lounge about the lobby. I despatched an enthusiastick card of welcome, & prepared to enjoy the zest of congenial anticipation.

Wednesday the 29th the remainder of my Scribner books came, & I at once began the new Dunsany novel—"The King of Elfland's Daughter." Incidentally, I saw to the return & placing of the bedspring which **I**—self-sufficient housekeeper—had sent out to have mended. (price, 10 fish!) Later I assembled a great cargo of goods for S H—chessboard & men, &c. &c., & went downtown to negotiate some purchases—book on chess at Brentano's,[13] & pecan nuts at Park & Tilford's. I reached the hospital loaded, but soon dispersed my goods & chattels & began a laborious attempt to learn the game of chess anew after twenty years' total neglect. In the evening I set out for The Boys—at Belknap's—& found all possible hands present, tho' Mortonius was unhappily lost to the world through the agency of one of those new-fangled crossword puzzles which Leeds thrust upon his avid intelligence in an injudicious moment. Mortonius, by the way, won't be with us again till the meeting of Nov. 19 or perhaps Nov. 26, on account of that hideously exacting job of writing two medical books for a capable through inarticulate physician. I prepared the Boys for Sechrist's presence at the next meeting, & stuck till the last man flew; riding down on the elevated with Leeds after the usual exchange of gestures with north-bound Mortonius, & chatting in an 8th Ave. cafeteria till 3 or 4 a.m.

The next day—Thursday the 30th—I spent at the hospital playing chess & reading Dunsany. And on Friday—as related to A E P G—S H came home in time for a very quiet Hallowe'en party with only the discursive Mrs. Moran as a guest. Saturday I also chronicled to A E P G—yea, that and Sunday too, tho' perhaps I didn't mention that on the latter day I finished my story at one fell swoop & made a telephone engagement with Sechrist for 9 a.m. the following day.

Monday dawned bright, & Sechrist was over on time, bringing a portfolio of literary material & an album of South Sea photographs—for the home of his soul is tropick Tahiti, & his chief interest is Polynesian folklore. I was darned glad to see him, & after a time we started out to do the town, having made an engagement to call at Sonny's about 2:30 p.m. Deciding on the art museum—the Metropolitan—as a starting-point, we found ourselves so absorbed that we went nowhere else; but roamed the beauty-freighted halls in a continuous ecstasy of aesthetick appreciation. There is no one more sensitive to beauty than Sechrist—he found chief delight in the remnants of Minoan (or prehistoric Cretan) antiquities, & in the beautiful glassware of Cyprus—stained to a thousand elfin fires of iridescence by its corrosive immersion in the earth for thousands of years. I also discovered a series of French 18th century rooms—panelled & furnished with genuine Louis period wainscoting & furniture & decorations—which I had not seen before myself! The French 18th century was certainly exquisite with its lavish use of white & gold & marble—but I vow to God I prefer the plainer, severer, & more austerely classick British work of the same period—the age of Chippendale, Hepplewhite, & the brothers Adam. GOD SAVE THE KING! Going up to Belknap's via surface car across the park & elevated up to 99th St, we found the child in excellent health & spirits. He & Sechrist took to each other at once—kindred aesthetes—& read to each other many a specimen of written beauty. Sonny had the new *Weird Tales* with the cover design of his story,[14] (nothing of mine in it) & we all enjoy'd examining the distinguisht specimen. Finally Sechrist had to leave in order to keep an engagement, so Sonny & I rode down town with him atop a 'bus. He left at 45th St., but Sonny & I went down to Madison Square, bought another *Weird Tales*, & walked still farther down to 4th Ave. & 13th St., where we found Loveman at his post in Stone's rare book shop. He quickly left with us, & we all crossed over to a new lunch room—incredibly cheap but incredibly good, with an effusively friendly German proprietor—where Belknap & I watched Samuelus eat before we went home to our own dinners. At length we all walked through to the Colonial mazes of Greenwich Village, where Sonny & Loveman took the subway at the Christopher St. station & rode uptown together, whilst I walked observantly back to mine own subway, observing the Georgian doorways & dormers with the true antiquarian eye of old age. During the evening I played—or played at playing—chess with S H, & retired in all the mellow good-humour of continuous & consecutive defeat. On Tuesday the 4th ('tis now Thursday the 6th at 4 p.m.) I read Dunsany, wrote A E P G, & had a dinner of prime spaghetti with S H's magical brand of home-made sauce. The next morning I was up bright & early for my second appointment with Sechrist at 9 o'clock.

Sechrist came on time, & we lost not many minutes in getting embarked on our strenuous day of sightseeing. We telephoned Sonny—but the child had hurt his little foot on a steam pipe in the bathroom the day before, so couldn't be in on the walking, though he promised to get over to Kirk's—only a few blocks—for the evening meeting of The Boys. Sechrist & I stopped first at the Anderson Galleries, Park Ave. & 59th St., which A E P G will remember well, since she & I saw an auction there last March. A friend of Sechrist's—John M. Price—is employed there in an editorial capacity—preparing catalogues &c—& he shew'd us over the place most courteously. Price is a splendid young chap, though I don't agree with his politics, & he has invited Sechrist & me over to his house tonight—he lives in East 9th St., in colonial Greenwich. If he could help me find out how to apply for a position in the Anderson Galleries—as Sechrist thinks he might—he would virtually save my life! I could do the Anderson work very well—in fact, Loveman long ago suggested how well-suited such a job would be to me. I think I'll get over to Price's tonight if I can finish this letter in time—though Pegāna knows I need a haircut first, the last having been the day A E P G left—Septr. 27.

But to return to yesterday—Wednesday the 5th. After the galleries we took the East Side subway for the Poe cottage, incidentally discovering what none of our veteran N.Y. friends realised—that this subway is a *two-story* one, the express trains running in a sub-subway under the tube where the locals run. We reached the cottage at 1 p.m., & gloried in its simple outlines—for Sechrist, as you may recall from his enthusiasm for the Athenaeum & Mrs. Whitman's house[15]—is a true Poe enthusiast. Luck, however, was against us when we tried to enter; since unknown to me before, the cottage closes from 1 to 2, & we had no time to wait. So sadly we took the crosstown car for the Van Cortlandt mansion, finding that noble pile in its prime, & revelling in the Colonial atmosphere. Sechrist was born in his ancestral Colonial homestead in Maryland, & found boyhood memories in every piece of china, silver, pewter, or kitchen facility. He was so moved that he has vowed to write his brother—who still lives on the paternal acres—to take care in saving such pieces as modern unappreciativeness has consigned to the cobwebs of cellar or attic. He got several postcards, & is an avowed convert to Georgianism! From the Van Cortlandt we rode down to the Dyckman, where we repeated our experience & ecstasy. An added joy for me was a little grey-&-white kittie—a real Dutch Dyckman kittie—who purred contentedly in my arms during the entire tour of the place. You will recall that when I explored this house two years ago, I held a black cat, & fell down the cellar stairs with him. This time I didn't fall—though I stove in my hat (fortunately soft felt) against the low rafters on that same staircase!! From here we rode down to the N.Y. Historical Society's museum at 77th St & Central Park West, where Sechrist properly enjoy'd the Beekman Coach, old prints, relics of George III's statue, "Course of Empire" paintings, Renaissance masters, &c. &c. At 5 p.m. they chucked us out, so we rode down to Loveman's shop, picked him up, & went across to his new favourite restaurant where Kleiner joined us. Amidst the general introductions it was obvious that Sechrist fitted in magnificently with our gang; & we all regret poignantly that he does not live in New York. After dinner—where I tasted Hungarian goulash (stewed beef with pungent vegetables) for the first time, & also for the first time tried an apple "sprudel", (a sort of tart) which with a cup of coffee rounded out my meal—we all walked across town to Greenwich Village, where we delighted Sechrist by shewing him Milligan Place, the inner mystery, & Patchin Place by sickly, sinister, accursed lamplight. Tell A E P G—who has been there—that the little wooden florist shop has been torn out of Milligan Place, adding very much to its atmospherick charm. We then took the elevated up to Kirk's, where we played the radio, introduced Sechrist to Kirk & Leeds, & had the usual carefree good time. I lent Sonny "The King of Elfland's Daughter" & my own new story, desiring his verdict on the latter in its completed form. Sechrist's South Sea myths, tales, & photographs made a decided hit, & Kirk & Loveman busied themselves in offering advice anent the author's hitherto fruitless quest for a publisher. We broke up about 1 a.m., Sechrist, Leeds, & I riding down on the elevated. Leeds debarked at 53d St., whilst Sechrist & I continued to Christopher St., there alighting & walking through colonial Greenwich—including crooked Gay St.—to the venerable Brevoort. There Sechrist shew'd me the quaint interior—the quasi-Colonial staircases, the white panelling, the tiny cubbyhole lifts, the oddly varying floor-levels, & the plain, monastic rooms. He has #254, a tiny cubbyhole at the end of a corridor—but he pays $3.50 per day. The place is still expensive because of its atmosphere & traditions, & the exclusiveness with which it is still managed. It is one old-time institution which has *not* decayed with the years! Bidding Sechrist adieu, I returned home to find S H rather exhausted after an afternoon & evening visit to the Van Heules in Flushing—who have a new young man, several weeks old, added to the family since our call of last summer. S H took Mrs. van H. some of her magick spaghetti sauce, & in return Mrs. van H. has presented her with a dozen splendid white country eggs, one of which I hard-boiled & eat this morning.

Today S H has gone down town to attend to some financial business, & I have cooked my breakfast & washed the dishes as I did during her absence. Tomorrow Sechrist is coming again, & intends to bring a friend of his—a young woman whom he thinks S H will be interested to meet. This morning I have been immersed in science, reading that much-discussed prophecy as to future developments—"Daedalus", by Prof. J. B. S. Haldane of Cambridge (Eng.) Univ. Kirk lent it to me last night, & tonight I'm going to sub-lend it to Sechrist. After finishing "Daedalus", I commenced the final instalment of this epistle, which I shall now commend to the tender mercies of the U.S. Mail. More anon.

And hurrah for the election! I knew Coolidge would get it, but in local politics I was worried about the possible appeal that scoundrel Toupin might have on the Canuck herds of the Blackstone & Pawtuxet Valleys. With Aram & Jesse the state is saved—& I'm also darned glad Gainer got another term— the Thomas A. Doyle of the period![16]

Well—that's that. I'll tip you off to any new disasters, & would meanwhile be mighty darned glad if you found it convenient to visit these parts about this season. And now I'll take another chocolate bud (for which thanks) & subscribe myself

Yr aff nephew & obt Servt

H P L

P.S. 95% Ethyl alcohol is the good old pre-war stuff which you can't buy now. It's worth its weight in gold, tho' contraband. Hang on to it!

## Notes

1. Leptis Magna, known as Lebda to modern-day residents of Libya, was a prominent city of the Roman Empire. When Italy conquered Libya in the early 20th century, it dedicated huge efforts to the rediscovery of Leptis Magna.

2. The Breeches Bible (1579) is a variant of the Geneva Bible (1560), containing a variant text ("they [Adam and Eve] knew they were naked, and they sewed figge tree leaves together, and made themselves breeches" [Gen. 3:7]; the King James Version reads "aprons" for "breeches"). The Vinegar Bible (1717) contains an erroneous heading for Luke 20 ("The Parable of the Vinegar" instead of "The Parable of the Vineyard").

3. HPL presumably refers to *Curious Myths of the Middle Ages* and *The Book of Werewolves*. Baring-Gould died on 2 January 1924, 26 days short of his 90th birthday.

4. I.e., from or an earlier time; indicating that something once possessed a specified characteristic but no longer does so.

5. See "Ann Arbor and Elizabeth," *New York Times* (5 October 1924): Sec. 2, p. 4, about some interesting antiquities in the city.

6. Wilhelm von Knyphausen (1716–1800), commander of the Hessian auxiliaries (allied with Great Britain) during the Revolutionary War.

7. 135 Benefit Street. HPL calls it the Babbitt [*sic*] house because it was then owned by Mrs. C. H. Babbit. LDC was a paid companion to Mrs. Babbit around 1919–20 and is listed as a resident of the house in the 1920 census.

8. A common slang expression of the day, appearing in print no later than 1889.

9. For Cassie (Doty) Symmes (1872–1935), see David Goudsward, "Cassie Symmes: Inadvertent Lovecraftian," *Lovecraft Annual* No. 9 (2015): 130–35. HPL would later ghostwrite (for FBL) the foreword to Symmes's *Old World Footprints* (1928).

10. *Giles Corey, Yeoman.*

11. Theodore Roosevelt, Jr. (1887–1944), son of the president, was running for governor of New York. He lost the election (held on November 4) to the incumbent, Alfred E. Smith.

12. The Gautier volume is a joint publication of *Avatar* with Prosper Mérimée's "The Venus of Ille," under the title *Tales Before Supper. The Castle of Otranto* is a celebrated Gothic novel by Horace Walpole.

13. Probably David Andrew Mitchell (1883–?), *Mitchell's Guide to the Game of Chess* (Philadelphia: David McKay, 1915; *LL* 661).

14. The December 1924 issue of *WT* had a cover design illustrating FBL's tale "Death-Waters."

15. Sarah Helen Whitman (1803–1878), poet, essayist, and transcendentalist, lived at 88 Benefit Street (1783–92).

16. The Republican Calvin Coolidge won the presidential election of 1924 after taking over as president upon the death of Warren G. Harding in 1923. HPL also refers to Aram J. Pothier (1854–1928), governor of Rhode Island (1909–15, 1925–28); Jesse N.

Metcalf (1860–1942), U.S. senator from Rhode Island (1924–37); Joseph H. Gainer (1878–1945), mayor of Providence (1913–27); and Thomas A. Doyle (1827–1886), mayor of Providence (1864–69, 1870–81, 1884–86).

[79]      [ANS postcard][1] [HPL and Sonia H. Lovecraft to LDC]

[Postmarked Somerville, N.J.,

10 November 1924]

Have accompanied S H to her rustication near Somerville, & now, being about half way to Philadelphia, am going the rest of the way & absorb more fully than before the sights of the Quaker City. ¶ S H is coming back to N Y in a week to help me break up, so that you & A E P G won't have to bother to come. ¶ Under separate cover am sending samples of the two village papers here. Yr aff nephew & obt Servt  H P L
[P.S.] Lovingly S H L

*Notes*

1. *Front:* Washington's Headquarters, Somerville, N.J.

[80]      [ANS postcard][1] [HPL to LDC]

[Postmarked Philadelphia, Pa.,

11 November 1924]

Just blew in! This is a fine etching—wish I could find its fellows as mentioned or implied. Think I shall take S H's advice & stop at the Y M C A if there's any space left with them. I'd like to get 2 days here, for the place is a veritable mine of Colonialism. More anon—I saw some unbelievably ancient roofs from the train.
Yr aff nephew & obt Servt
H P L

*Notes*

1. *Front:* The Philadelphia Art Alliance Post Card Series No. 4. Broad Street in 1915—Joseph Pennell.

[81]      [ALS] [HPL to LDC]

Small hours—

Tuesday.

[11 November 1924]

My dear daughter Lillian:—

This isn't a real epistle—that will come after my return to 259—but merely a bulletin of my gay colonial exploring expedition of one. Let us eat, drink, & be merry, as I said tonight when inhaling my 15¢ baked beans & coffee at a Chestnut St. automat—for tomorrow we disintegrate!

But at that—I might as well bring the diary up to date. Since I'm to be a migratory bird without a home, why not start in practicing the technique, & see what I can do toward composition in a $1.50 Y M C A room?

I turned off the hot air Thursday evening just before I went down to meet Sechrist at the Brevoort. Well—I found him with a curious Welshman named Stanley Williams, who was born in Arthur Machen's country & knows all about the Roman camp, & Caerleon-on-Usk, &c. &c., but who has since roved most amazingly about the world—including the South Sea Isles. Williams has led a strenuous life—was once arrested by mistake for a bandit & taken from Los Angeles to Chicago for identification—& looks it . . . . red head, broken nose, &c. . . . but has found time to retain at least a few aesthetic interests. After a brief chat in Sechrist's room, we all went over to John M. Price's at the corner of 9ᵗʰ Ave & 14th St (on the fringe of Greenwich Village) where a small company of quasi-intellectuals were assembled for discussion. Price is a good chap, but many hopeless bores were present. One pale, languid youth named Ray Larsen quite amused me with his Grosvenor-Square Londonese drawl till I saw how sincerely he appreciated Machen. I questioned everyone anent positions—& a proofreader named Buck told of a large firm to which it might pay me to apply. A long trail, forsooth. The meeting dissolved at 12:30, but Price invites me to attend similar gatherings every Sunday at 4. He is, as I have said, a fine chap—the nephew of a professor in the University of Chicago. His wife is intelligent, but sharp-featured & a bit strident—not so prepossessing as he. After the meeting I piloted Sechrist, Williams, & Buck through my favourite Colonial haunts, reaching the Brevoort at 1:30—where Williams & I stayed till 2:30. Then home.

Friday I read & wrote & cleaned house, & at 8 p.m. Sechrist came over with the young woman he wished us to meet—a lumpish, inane sort of vegetable whose name I don't recall. He read finely from his Polynesian tales, & we genuinely regretted his departure—for he was not to call on us again before returning to Washington.

Saturday I did odds & ends & got my hair cut. Sunday Loveman came over for lunch, & at 4 p.m. accompanied us down to the ferry when we started, valises in hand, for S H's place of rustication in Somerville. She had secured the name of her prospective landlady from an advertisement in the paper, & further correspondence impressed her favourably. The place announced itself as a farm without frills*—& that is exactly what the patient desired to soothe her nerves. Our journey was accomplished without incident— across to Jersey City & by train to Somerville—& we were met at the station

---

*Room, with three lavish meals per day, $12.50 per wk.

by the eldest son of the hostess—Mrs. R. A. Craig—in a battered Chevrolet car. Soon we were whirling for moonlit miles over level roads, past fields where yellow farmhouse lights glittered, & occasional sheaves stood out picturesquely against the mellow sky. In twenty minutes we were at the Craig farmhouse—a large cement-block structure far from any main road, & commanding a plantation of 52 acres. Friendly dogs barked at our approach, & as we alighted we found Mrs. Craig in the doorway—a quiet, somewhat refined person of middle age, whose husband is a surveyor much away from home, & whose two sons are in high-school. We were shewn to a good sized & thoroughly neat room, informed as to bath facilities & the like, (the house has running water from an artesian well, & electric lights from its own dynamo) & introduced to the adult dogs—Ranger (a vocal creature of black & white) & his wife Sketch (of similar colouring but shorter hair)—both pointers, & reputed mighty in the chase. Next day we beheld their pleasing litter of small puppies in the cellar. That evening we ate an excellent dinner and took two walks by moonlight, accompanied by the dogs. S H liked the quiet, & hoped to sleep well—though she did not sleep as well as I. I stayed over, having a valise packed for my proposed extension trip to Philadelphia. Since Somerville is half way there, I thought it a good chance to save a separate trip & finish my explorations of the Quaker City & its colonial antiquities.

Next day—Monday—we were up at ten, ate the excellent food provided, & took a walk. The scenery is quaint & pleasing—distant purple hills, ancient farmhouse gables peering through trees, great red barns, & harvest fields made magick by rows of golden sheaves—though not so agreeably diversified as that of New-England. The roads are of hard earth, & give off a *reddish* dust on account of the peculiar sandstone of the region. Houses average from a quarter to a half-mile apart, & all the sparse population seems quite desirable. Mrs. Craig serves excellent food—including *pheasants* shot by those mighty hunters, her sons. The cook & waitress is middle-aged & half-witted, but knows her business. There are good books in the house, & the atmosphere is very quiet—no other boarders save a fat, unobtrusive woman with jangled nerves. In summer there are many boarders—but that does not concern us S H is not yet certain how long she will stay, but surely the place is not one to be lightly despised.

There are at least *seven cats*. Two adults, (maltese & tiger) two half-grown & delectably pugilistic kittens, (one yellow & one maltese) & three very little kittens—captivating handfuls of tender grey fuzziness with beautiful faces & great saucer eyes of yellow-green. I carried one in my pocket for a long time, & wish I could have taken him away!

After a hearty lunch of pancakes, syrup, & accessories, we started out on a walk of four miles to Somerville. I took my valise, for I was not to return. The countryside was very beautiful in the afternoon sun, & S H gained a healthy colour which she has long lacked. After two hours we entered the village—or city, as it prefers to be known—a quaint huddle of small buildings old & new, with much of the colonial, & a fine new courthouse of classick marble. Here we bought cards & papers, & absorbed the atmosphere of the place. I like it—despite the upheaval incident to the removal of a railway grade crossing. Twilight now deepened to dusk, & S H & I went to the railway station, where young Craig was to have his motor to meet his father at six—an arrangement offering S H convenient transportation to the farm. I took the 6:10 for Bound Brook—connecting for Philadelphia—bidding S H au revoir until Saturday, when she returns to 259 for a week to help in the packing up. She is very eager to superintend all this herself, averring that there is no need to bother you or A E P G. I have not yet decided where I shall go.

Such is which. I changed cars without a hitch, & was in Philadelphia at 9:10. Getting a return ticket to N.Y., I proceeded to the Y M C A, where I obtained a good room for $1.50 per day—taking it for 2 days. It has no water, but just around the corner is a splendid *shower-bath,* the first I have used since 1899–1900, when I went to the gymnasium at the old Prov. Athletic Assn.— where the Crown Hotel is now.

Having registered, I started on a nocturnal tour of the colonial past—in the older section toward the Delaware waterfront—& lud, ma'am, the wonders I found!! I never knew the town before! Mile on mile of Georgian houses of every sort—and in one place south of Walnut & east of Broad a labyrinth of Georgian alleys & peaked gables forming virtually another world—a piquant world of vanished yesterdays. Streets hardly wide enough for two men to pass—brick walls separated from the roadway with iron posts—vista on vista of antediluvian roofs—pillared doorways with shining knockers—but what's the use? I can't describe it as it suddenly burst on me when I rounded an obscure corner behind Ritz-Carlton. New York's Greenwich Village is tame in comparison—wait till day dawns, & watch me give the whole thing a brand new inspection! I also surveyed some of the ancient churches & their ghoulish yards—picking up just enough of the atmosphere to serve me in good stead during later voyages. Tomorrow I shall "do" Germantown, the opulent Colonial suburb, & perhaps some other distant region which promises well. Guide books are all around me—& I shall get even more Georgian data from the Public Library. Returning to the "Y" I saw Independence Hall under that eldritch moon, & took a light lunch at the Automat. Then I came hither, & here I am. Now for a bit of sleep—though first I'll mention that I *did* find the remainder of that set of Philadelphia etchings, & am now sending them along in the certainty that you'll find them interesting. I'll also send the leading paper—*The Publick Ledger*—which with the *Boston Transcript* used to share by syndication the astronomical articles of Prof. Upton in our *Journal* & *Bulletin.*

*Intermission for sleep*

9 a.m. Tuesday

Awake again, & ready for the colonial. Among the marvellous things I haven't seen but am about to see is Old Swedes' Church, built in 1701, which lies far south of any part of the town that the ordinary visitor knows. I also hope to see certain interiors—including the U. of P. Museum with its famous Assyrian & Babylonian antiquities. I have in my valise Eberlein's treatise on Colonial houses, & mean to know exactly what I am going to see. There must be many marvellous networks of alleys which I did not find last night—I am particularly anxious to find a picturesque Georgian inn yard alluringly illustrated in the book.

Well—I must be going if I'm to improve my time in this metropolis of leisure & good breeding. Philadelphia grows on one—it must be a great place to reside in. One colourful—though perhaps comical—element is the new uniform of the police as organised by the picturesquely vigorous Gen. Butler.[1] They have leather puttees & visible revolver holsters, & wear over their blue uniforms the most startling sort of snow-white "Sam Browne" belts & shoulder pieces. They walk mostly two by two—as if needing moral support for their crusade against the lawless & ill-mannered.

With which remark I take leave of the modern world, & plunge out into the red brick 18th century town of Dr. Franklin. GOD SAVE THE KING!

Yr affec: nephew & obt Servt

H P L

## Notes

1. Smedley Butler (1881–1940), a major general in the U.S. Marine Corps. In 1924 he was appointed Director of Public Safety by W. Freeland Kendrick, newly elected mayor of Philadelphia. He was therefore put in charge of the city's police and fire departments.

[82]    [ANS postcard][1] [HPL to LDC]

[Postmarked Philadelphia, Pa.,
11 November 1924]

Having a great time—new worlds of unbelievable colonialism unfold themselves in the archaic byways of this unsurpassable* town. You ought to see the collection of paintings illustrating American history in this building! The past lies unveil'd in one tremendous pageant. Nothing like it anywhere else. Yr aff nephew & obt Servt

H P L

*except by Prov.

*Notes*

1. *Front:* Congress Hall.

[83]     [ANS postcard]¹ [HPL to LDC]

[Postmarked Philadelphia, Pa.,
11 November 1924]

This church is a wonderful thing—*absolutely* unchanged inside & out—with high pews, boxlike pulpit, original bell & organ, &c. &c. I sat & meditated in the churchyard, & then went in; the organ putting me into such a mood of awe that I beheld in vision a fantastic procession of all the ancient periwigged worshippers.
Yr aff nephew & obt Servt
H P L

P.S. And there was the most friendly big yellow cat imaginable on a corner diagonally across the street from the church. I petted him suitably.

*Notes*

1. *Front:* Old St. Peter's Church, Third and Pine Sts., Philadelphia, Pa.

[84]     [ALS] [HPL to LDC]

*Wednesday Morning*
[12 November 1924]

My dear daughter Lillian:—

Philadelphia is marvellous! I am entranced beyond words! I must stay over another day—& meanwhile must keep the children posted on my doings. So here's a continuation of the diary which I mailed yesterday morning.

That morning was dull grey, but the spirit of colonial exploration brightened all things. Resolv'd to explore more intelligently, I repair'd to the publick library, where I was greatly help'd by the books, & by the advice of one of the attendants—an old lady descended from the best local families. This library is housed in a building of about the civil war period—quite in contrast to the modern structures in Providence, Boston, & New York—but the architecture is very conservative, & lacks the bad taste of most Victorian designs.

Having now a little expert knowledge, I plunged again into Colonial labyrinths, & revell'd in an intoxication of antiquity. One by one I lookt up the notable houses & doorways recommended by the best authorities; & though some of them had been torn down, a vast proportion were still there to reward my pious pilgrimage.

I return'd to St. Peter's—which I had seen by moonlight the night before—& meditated long in the grassy churchyard where the willows weep & rustic flagstones lead among the ancient graves. Then I enter'd the church, noted the colonial high pews & turret-like pulpit, & finally succumbed to the charm of the stately organ musick—reminiscent peals which awak'd a thousand ancestral memories of OLD ENGLAND. God save the King!

I now proceeded still further east—to Second St. & the old market, where my breath was fairly taken away by the sight which greeted me. Imagine an ancient street rising toward the south, with colonial gables & dormers on both sides silhouetted against a grey sky, & spreading abruptly to accomodate a large building in its very centre. That building—a trim brick bit of colonialism with massive white cupola, white lintels, & a white string course betwixt upper & lower stories—is the old Market House itself; & vary'd indeed is its long history. During the War of 1812 it was used as a recruiting station & known as Commissioners' Hall. Mere words cannot describe the peculiar effect of this singular scene. The region is squalid, but a strange charm inheres. Perhaps it is because *every* structure in sight is colonial; because these structures are all larger & more elaborate than the colonial survivals in other cities; because the quaint spire & gilded cross of St. Peter's towers up majestically at the extreme right; or because the rising ground limns the line of roofs & chimneys against the blank sky & thus adds a dramatick unity to the picture. Be all this as it may, there is a glamour profound & inescapable; & I felt queer impressions of previous familiarity steal over me—impressions involving visions of colonial farmers' wains, & the clatter of hooves as periwigged horsemen pushed their way through knee-breeched crowds.

Pausing in this vicinity only long enough to observe certain fine old houses & doorways recommended by the books I had consulted, I struck out for the north, & was soon at the corner of Dock St., before the splendid old Maritime Exchange with its semicircle of giant Corinthian columns above the first story, & its crowning skyward monument—a free adaptation of the famous choragic monument of Lysicrates in Athens. This is the work of Strickland, & I was very much imprefs'd a year ago by an etching of it in the Shepley library.

Not a stone's throw away is one of the earliest classick revival buildings in America—the old bank in Third St. with its Greek temple facade, erected in 1795. It is still a bank, & still in fine preservation, for which I am profoundly thankful. The only false note is a use of the popular American Eagle motif in the frieze—a thing which clashes with the Hellenism of the conception as a whole.

I now proceeded to the Independence Hall row of buildings, & once again stood awestruck at the beautiful interior carving, panelling, & proportioning of Andrew Hamilton's masterpiece. This time I also visited Congress Hall (the brick building on the right) & was infinitely delighted with the great collection of paintings illustrating typical scenes from American history. Before leaving this general vicinity I took appreciative glances at the old Doric-temple Custom House (1824) & Carpenter's Hall, after which I struck north to the Quaker meeting house & Christ Church cemetery, where I ponder'd long by the grave of the estimable Dr. Franklin.

Fired by the name of Franklin, I now turn'd northwest to find the venerable square that bears it; & at length arriv'd at a fine expanse of greenery surrounded by early 19th century mansions in a manner reminiscent of Washington-Square, in New-York. These mansions are now sunk to lodging houses, & the park & fountain are not unknown to bench loafers; but little physical deterioration has set in, so that reclamation would be easy. In the region just east of this, there is in progress a wholesale demolition of colonial houses to provide an approach for the titanic new bridge across the Delaware to Camden N.J. Now would be the time to pick up a carved mantel, doorway pediment, or bit of panelling cheaply—would that I were able to use such things in a colonial house of mine own!

I travers'd this region on my way to the northern reaches of Second St., where books had led me to expect several colonial inn-yards with brick & stone archways. I found only one of them—the ancient Black Horse—& even this was abandoned & boarded up. However, the walk well repaid me, since it led me through streets & alleys so solidly colonial that at times I had a dazed doubt of the reality of the scene—or of my own existence in this prosaic & decadent XXth century!

Next came Arch St. & the Betsey Ross house—which is a shop for souvenirs, with several rooms open to display the neat & tasteful panelling. Here I found one of those garrulous old antiquarians of whose species I am so fond—a quaint fellow like honest George Fuller of the Royall house at Medford—& he gave me some invaluable hints on local antiquities, including a sloping & particularly colourful Colonial alley which I lost no time in visiting.

Dusk had now fallen, so that I could take only the most cursory exterior glance at Christ Church (which I shall visit this morning) & the neighbouring alleys. Accordingly I boarded a southbound car in quest of Old Swedes' Church & the gruesome churchyard in front of it. This fane was built by those Swedish settlers who established themselves here before William Penn, & with whom the Dutch—under Petrus Stuyvesant—had such incessant warfare on account of the neighbouring Dutch settlements in Delaware. On the car I purchased a dime guide to the principal Philadelphia sights, out of which I have already culled a wealth of suggestions. I found Old Swedes' in the midst of a district as colonial as the rest of eastern Philadelphia, high on a banked terrace overlooking the railway yards & the waterfront. In the pallid light of feeble lamps the antique & curious spire loom'd up impressively, whilst the ghoulish headstones leer'd on every side. It was a cheering sight, & I design to revisit the spot by day if I can find the time.

Now edging back to the centre of things through many a cryptick & palaeogean alley, I indulged in a bean & spaghetti supper at a Thompson lunch, (the Y M C A cafeteria charges like the deuce) rounded off with a chocolate sundae at a neighbouring chemist's shop, & sought my humble room & quaint shower bath—pausing only to address & mail a few cards. I then mapped out with extreme care my prospective course of sightseeing, after which I sunk into the deep & restful sleep of honesty. Now I'm up again, showered, fed with a delightful kind of sandwich peculiar to Philadelphia of which I laid up a suitable stock, (vide enclosed label) & have written the foregoing mess of inanity. A good start—& now for the day & all its wonders!

More later, as I absorb new marvels to relate.

Meanwhile believe me

Ever yr most aff nephew & obt Servt

H P L

[85]  [ANS postcard][1] [HPL to LDC]

[Postmarked Philadelphia, Pa.,
12 November 1924]

Staying over another night! Today did Christ Church, Historical Society, &c. &c. & looked up some amazingly quaint odds & ends. Tomorrow I tackle the suburban mansions—colonial country-seats.

Yr aff nephew & obt Servt

H P L

[P.S.] Saw Penn's original wampum treaty with Indians at Hist. Soc.

*Notes*

1. *Front:* Ridgeway Library, Phila, Pa.

[86]  [ALS] [HPL to LDC]

*Wednesday Evening*
[12 November 1924]

My dear Daughter Lillian:—

I have often heard of the valiant attempts made by the Y M C A to provide a "homelike" atmosphere for the world's wandering boys, but never till tonight did I realise the extent to which these efforts are carry'd. Even telepathy must be involv'd, since at this moment someone in distant & lower regions is playing—in intention if not in achievement— upon a sonorous saxophone, & evoking all the domestick associations which come with memories of young Prescott Pierce & his harmonic divertissements! I have just taken a shower-bath, & am about to sum up the day on paper in wonted fashion.

As to this serious business call'd sightseeing—today's acquisitions have been more solid than sensational. Starting out in the morning, I made direct tracks for old Christ Church, which I found prodigiously enchanting both outside & inside, & in whose fascinating churchyard I paus'd long enough to ponder upon the mortality of mankind & the general decay of this age. This edifice is of much vaster grandeur than St. Peter's, with a lofty, snow-white, carv'd interior, & ornate stain'd glaſs in the great Palladian window of the apse which looks on 2nd St. The exterior is in splendid taste, & exhibits on a large scale that peculiarity of colonial brickwork which appears more frequently in Philadelphia than elsewhere, & which has been copied to some extent by local modern designers. I refer to the alternation of colour—black "headers" (ends) & red "stretchers" (sides)*—which was caus'd at first by the primitive kilns that overbaked & blackened the ends of the bricks whilst leaving the sides red & underbaked. This alternation appears strikingly when—as is frequent in Philadelphia—the bricks are laid in "Flemish Bond"—i.e., headers & stretchers alternating. Philadelphians seem to have liked it, since they employ'd it voluntarily long after they had more effective methods of baking—indeed, it is wholly a matter of choice in this case, since the bricks of Christ Church were imported from England. My attention being once call'd to the matter, I have notic'd prodigious numbers of Philadelphia structures with these alternating bricks—though I cannot recall any instance outside this town. I enclose a couple of very pleasing historical circulars—one for each of you children—of the church, of which I took a large supply for distribution amongst acquaintances. The little drawing is especially delightful—quite Laswellian in its grasp of the Georgian spirit.

From Christ Church I proceeded north amongst endless colonial alleys, finally taking to Front St. in quest of an house at 111 Spring which Dr. Franklin us'd to inhabit. Here occurr'd a disappointment—for the entire street is torn down to make way for the approaches of the new bridge to Camden N.J. Now taking the elevated north, I soon arriv'd at Penn Treaty Park—a green waterfront space hedg'd in by ugly factories, where in 1682, under a great elm which blew down in 1810, William Penn sign'd his celebrated treaty with the Indians that gave him the land by native sanction as well as Royal grant. There is a wharf here, & I obtain'd some fine views of the river, the Camden waterfront, & the adjacent shipping. After this I took the car in quest of the house where Poe lived during his editorship of *Graham's Magazine*—520 N. 7th St.—but found it remov'd—probably on account of the widening of Spring Garden St., which cuts through there. Disappointment #2!

Now, striking south, I made for Leary's famous bookstore in S. 9th St.,

---

*If these technical architectural terms were better known, what a field they would have offered to the jokesmiths of bicycle days . . . . . "He took a HEADER, & went to the hospital on a STRETCHER!"

about which Kleiner has raved ever since his discovery of it a few years ago. It is certainly an impressive place, with gallery on gallery of second-hand volumes, all accurately classify'd according to subject. There were several fine Rhode-Island items; but lacking the cash to obtain them, I went my way in peace.

My next stop was at the superb new colonial building at 13th & Locust—pure Georgian in every detail both inside & out—which houses the collection of the Pennsylvania Historical Society. Here I was long detain'd in a state of the keenest interest & excitement, for there spread around me in lavish array some of the most captivating relicks of elder times which I have ever seen. The whole life of the 18th & late 17th centuries surges back into existence amidst this multiplicity of intimate memorials—William Penn's razor—the original wampum treaty with the Indians—Robert Morris' strong-box—a ticket to the fashionable Meschianza—the architect's original plan of Independence Hall—a 1710 Bradford prayer-book—the sword presented by Louis XVI to John Paul Jones—but who cou'd catalogue it all? I wish you could see it! It was after four when I broke away, but I still had time to visit the bits of modern quaintness near Rittenhouse Square. Just off Ludlow St.—which runs west from 19th St. immediately below Market—is a green alley of tiny new cottages of multifarious colourations & self-consciously bizarre design—something like Washington Mews in N Y—called Lantern Lane. Farther south & west the quaint ideal has been followed with greater success; one small alley having sidewalk posts like those of the ancient Philadelphia alleys, & a court running east from 22nd St. below Walnut being develop'd in a fashion rivalling Flatbush's Albemarle Terrace—of which A E P G can tell you. This court is call'd the English Village, & extends back through lanthorn-topt gates to a rear wall of brick, where an house surmounts an arch thro' which vehicles may paſs. The effect is certainly redolent of Britiſh semi-rusticity—especially since the houses along the court are mostly of the peaked, gabled, plaster'd, Elizabethan sort, with one Georgian brick building to add the needed touch of variety & organick vitality. All in all, this English Village is quite a triumph—& I think it ought to be seen by every traveller in Philadelphia.

I now took the car for William Penn's house in Fairmount Park, which I saw last March, but which I wish'd to enter & explore. This is the oldest brick house in Philadelphia, & has the alternating red & black bricks which later became so typical of the town. Only the large front room is open to the publick, but this gives a fair idea of the proportioning, woodwork, & fireplace. The house formerly stood in Letitia-St., in the old part of the town near the Delaware, but was mov'd to the park in the 'eighties.

Twilight had now set in, & I saw that it wou'd be necefsary to postpone my tour of other houses in the park. Walking back over the Girard Ave. bridge & up the eastern shore a bit, I visualised the lay of the land, & plann'd my itinerary for the following day. I shall begin at the south & work north, later taking the park trolley to more westerly points acrofs the Schuylkill. Yet

unvisited are Chester, (S. of Philadᵃ·, & having an ancient Town Hall) Bartram's Gardens, the park mansions, & Germantown. How much of this I'll
be able to squeeze into tomorrow, Pegāna alone can say—but I'll tell you in
my next, which will doubtless bear the familiar Brooklyn-Flatbuſh poſtmark.
After my park ramble I took an inbound car, obtain'd a beef-pie-macaroni-
apple-pie-coffee dinner at the "Automat", (full cost 40¢—& splendid in flavour) laid in my breakfast supply of cheese & peanut butter sandwiches, (label enclosed—cost 10¢) dropt postcards to the family, & return'd to the Y for
bath & writing. Here I am still—& I mean to retire fairly early for a big day
tomorrow. The old town has captivated me utterly—I shall quit it with Reluctance, & recall it with Affection.

And so I will lay down my pen, promising to relate on a later occasion
such events as may befall me on the morrow. Trusting that you children are
both well, I will subscribe my self

Yr moſt affec: Parent & obt Servt<br>H P L

[87]     [ANS postcard][1] [HPL to LDC]

[Postmarked Chester, Pa.,<br>13 November 1924]

See this gem—1724! Have seen curious old Bartram house (1731) by the
Schuylkill, & am now trying to get back to Philadelphia in time to see Fairmount Park & Germantown before dark.

Yr aff nephew & obt Servt  H P L

*Notes*

1. *Front:* Old City Hall and Pennsylvania National Bank, Chester, Pa.

[88]     [ANS postcard][1] [HPL to LDC]

[Postmarked Philadelphia, Pa.,<br>14 November 1924]

Hooray! Up before daybreak to watch the sun rise over Philadᵃ· from the high
wooded banks of the Schuylkill (now Fairmount Park) where colonial country-seats dot the landscape & command a splendid view of the winding river.
¶ Have now gone to Germantown, which is wholly unlike Philadᵃ· & strongly
suggestive of New England save that stone is used more than wood as a
building material. Secured a guide leaflet at the historical museum—which is
housed in a fine colonial edifice. N.Y. tonight—alas! More soon.

Yr aff nephew & obt Servt  H P L

[P.S.] See the New-Englandish Colonial door!

*Notes*

1. *Front:* Philadelphia—Warner House, Germantown (Once occupied by Commodore James Barron in 1842.)

[89]     [ANS postcard]¹ [HPL to LDC]

[Postmarked Philadelphia, Pa.,
14 November 1924]

Well, what do you think of this! The old gentleman is staying over another day! Chester ate up so much of my time that I couldn't finish Fairmount Park before dark—to say nothing of Germantown. Wait till you hear of the splendid colonial country-seats I have seen—Benedict Arnold's among others. ¶ Decided to telephone Washington Van Dusen,² the local United member, this evening; & he invited me out to his home in Germantown. He is a nice little old man of aesthetic & historical tastes—he shewed me his oil paintings & gave me many valuable tips on seeing Germantown. More soon. Yr aff nephew & obt Servt  H P L

[On front:] This is far north, beyond where Van Dusen lives.

*Notes*

1. *Front:* Valley Green Inn, Wissahickon Drive, Fairmount Park, Philadelphia, Pa.
2. Washington Van Dusen (1857–1932), a poet. Author of *Songs of Life and Love Sonnets on Great Men and Women* (1929).

[90]     [ALS] [HPL to LDC]

259 Parkside Ave.,
Brooklyn, N.Y.,
Novr. 17, 1924
Finish'd Nov. 18

My dear daughter Lillian:—

Your telegram, of course, duly came; & by this time you have my reply. Let me assure you that we can handle the breaking-up entirely alone, so that you need make no trip which will drain your energy or imperil the perfect mending of your strained back. Rest while you require it, & save your trip till you feel capable of taking it for pure pleasure & without duties or responsibility—then, whilst you have headquarters at the Ray Mansion, I'll be eager to shew you the sights in proper & leisurely fashion! But just now, when your strength is doubtful & the atmosphere here one of upheaval, you had better take it easy. That is what S H says as well as I—she thought it rather barbarous of me to suggest your assistance at a time when travel will be such a burden to you.

We are both here, & endeavouring to decide on possible locations. Unless I can secure a position in N.Y., I wish to have my room in Elizabeth, N.J., where rent is less, & the atmosphere more colonial & American. Loveman, however, is seeing what he can do toward securing the influence of his employer—the bookseller Stone—in getting me a place in the Anderson Galleries, where Stone seems to have considerable "pull". I shall make my final decision toward the end of this week, & will then consider the apportionment of my effects. Your suggestions will all be adopted, & I am very grateful for them. In any event, there is nothing you need worry about; so pray think no more of harassing forced journeys—but wait till I am settled somewhere, & your back is wholly well, & then we will plan a session of really pleasant sightseeing! S H is nervous, but getting along without acute mishaps, & fully able to superintend the disintegration. She hopes we can vacate this month, but if not we will stay over another. It will be good in one way to be out—for the place is disconcertingly cold in this sudden approach to zero, & no independent exists for my Vulcan.[1] I will, of course, keep you fully advised as to developments.

S H did not care for the Craig farm on closer acquaintance; for the standard of immaculateness in housekeeping left something to be desired, whilst the company of the one other boarder—a nervous woman with alternating moroseness & loquacity—was not exactly inspiring. She therefore returned a day before she had planned—so that I found her here upon my arrival from Philadelphia. Just where she will next go for rest, she has not yet decided; but she hopes to find some place where she can obtain congenial lodgment in exchange for light services thus eliminating expense.

As to my diary—which ended Wednesday night with my return from a scouting expedition in Fairmount Park, Philadelphia—I may continue by noting that on Thursday morning I started out by trolley to explore some of the rural & suburban features near the Quaker town, beginning with the eccentric Bartram house in the Kingsessing district to the southwest beyond the Schuylkill. The route led through the Rittenhouse Square district which I had travers'd afoot the day before, & thence to the city's rim—where, on a high bank above the river & now surrounded by a cemetery, I saw the fine colonial mansion Woodlands, built by Wm. Hamilton, Efq., in 1770, & forming one of the earliest examples of the third & most delicate phase of Georgian architecture. In some respects this splendid house foreshadows the classical revival of the early 19th century, for on its south front is a lofty pillar'd portico of the Greek temple variety. But the car sped on, & I was soon at the Bartram house—an eccentric, home-made stone mansion constructed by John Bartram, the botanist, with his own hands in 1731. It lies back some distance from the road, & is reached through the fine botanick gardens laid out by the builder. The north facade is plain, but on the south side above the river there is a profusion of rococo ornament in stone, & three two-story Ionick columns—made of thinnish concentric discs piled up, & surmounted by huge & uncouth volutes. Bartram was quaintly peculiar, & his nature is reflected in the crudity & heterogeneity of his house. Ornamental stone panels are set here & there—both in house & outbuildings—& around the windows are curious German mouldings of carved stone. The doors are double—vertically so—& over one of the windows is the following pious inscription, placed there in panel form thirty-nine years after the building of the house:

> 'TIS GOD ALONE, ALMYTY LORD,
> THE HOLY ONE, BY ME ADOR'D
> JOHN BARTRAM 1770

The interior not being open for inspection, I walkt north a brief space & took a car for the adjacent small city of Chester—a kind of Taunton or Fall River—where stands a famous 1724 court & town house, the oldest building of its kind in the country. The ride led through a highly interesting region, & at one turn of the road I saw a fine old deserted stone mansion of the Middle Colonies type—with cornice extending round the gable ends—bearing a panel with the date 1760.

Chester I found very interesting. The Town Hall (of which I sent you a card) is quite unique; & bears traces of the Welsh influence paramount in this region. Opposite it—across the street—is a wooden inn where Gen[l.] Washington wrote his midnight report of the Battle of Brandywine, & where he later received congratulations as first President of the new republick. Around a stone pav'd court behind the Town House, are grouped the newer city hall & office of the *Chester Times,* both of pure Georgian design, & built of stone to match the 1724 edifice. Near by are many colonial houses, & altogether the scene is one to delight the antiquarian eye.

Returning to Philadelphia, I next set out for Fairmount Park, determin'd to observe before nightfall such colonial country-seats as lie on the eastern bank of the Schuylkill—reserving the rest for the morrow, when I wish'd to greet the dawn from the majestick hills of the western park. All these old mansions rise on or near the towering slopes beside the river, commanding the most agreeable prospects, & presenting the most engaging aspect. Beginning at the south I observ'd Lemon Hill, the residence of the celebrated Robt. Morris, the Fisher place, built in 1743, & Mount Pleasant—the ornate & magnificent structure of second-phase Georgian architecture, built in 1761 by Capt. John Macpherson & bought during the Revolution by the traitor Benedict Arnold. I have seen few houses more genuinely splendid & baronial than Mount Pleasant. It has a thorough sumptuousness, elegance, & majesty unknown in New-York, & but seldom attain'd in New-England. Would that I could get you a postcard of it . . . . but I have not succeeded in finding any. The hipped roof, doorway pediments, brick quoins, Palladian window mouldings, quadruple & arch-connected chimneys, & massive cornices all bespeak a heaviness which sacrifices nothing of grace, but which turns itself to advantage in creating an atmosphere of unparallelled dignity. Smaller outbuildings of similar ornamentation, design'd for servants' quarters, give the estate a profoundly manorial & almost southern cast; whilst the lawn down to the river (tragically broken by a railway track) adds the final touch of substantial elegance.

Going north, I observ'd & appreciated two more mansions of later date—Rockland, built in 1810, & Ormiston, whose valley prospect is unique & majestick. Beyond them lies Edgely, a middle Georgian specimen much defac'd with additions, Woodford, a magnificently rambling structure in the later colonial manner, & Strawberry Mansion—a wooden farmhouse rais'd to seigneural dignity by the addition of two huge square wings at the ends. These last three houses I explored in the twilight, guided by an intelligent man of middle age of whom I had askt directions, & who—as a matter of amazing coincidence—turn'd out to be a greater & more fully inform'd architectural enthusiast than I! He furnisht me with many pointers on Philadelphian antiquities, & explain'd to me the meaning of a peculiar metal device I had found on the front of many colonial buildings—an oval panel of the following nature:—I had speculated long upon its possible significance, & was now inform'd that it was the sign of a house which had subscrib'd to the *Fire Association* of the period—an organisation sponsor'd  by Dr. Franklin—& which was therefore entitled to the protection of the then newly-introduced fire-engines. The notion of an universal free fire department was unheard-of!

As dusk fell, I thankt my informant & proceeded to town, where I obtain'd a good 25¢ lunch—beans, cinnamon bun, & coffee—after which I telephon'd the local amateur Washington Van Dusen & started out for his place upon his cordial invitation. He lives in a modern double house in a fine Colonial neighbourhood—West Washington Lane, Germantown—& is a splendid old fellow with thin white hair, moustache of like hue & texture, & small, trim figure. He writes poetry & paints in oil, & is descended from the most ancient Philadelphia families. In historical matters he is quite an authority, & our talk was exceedingly congenial. He lives in one of the fields I had selected for particular exploration, & gave me many points on the colonial territory I was to traverse on the morrow—Germantown & vicinity. At last thanking him greatly, I departed at a reasonable hour & retir'd in anticipation of the morrow's sunrise expedition.

Friday morning I was up before the sun, for I wish'd not only to observe the gold & rose dawn from the hills beyond the Schuylkill, but also to have as long a day as pofsible, since my return to Brooklyn that night was financially imperative. Before taking the car for Fairmount Park I strolled in the gloom to the ancient Christ Church region, where in a network of ancient alleys I found the oldest house still standing in the town—a 17th century brick relic with steep slate roof & flat dormers. The pitch of the gambrel—as here illustrated—is a Swedish feature; this influence coming from the Swedes who had built farms along the Delaware before the coming of William Penn with his English & German colonists.

Now taking a westbound car & depositing my 8¢ token (as in Providence) with the sleepy conductor, I set sail for the Schuylkill & Fairmount Park. The waning moon was bright as I debark'd near William Penn's transplanted house & proceeded up Lansdowne Drive, & it shone beautifully on the white wood of Sweet Brier Mansion, a late-colonial & very New Englandish country seat whose lawn sweeps majestically down to the river.

I now walkt across the park & through the Cyclopean gates of the old 1876 centennial grounds—grey dawn overtaking the moonlight as I pass'd famous Horticultural Hall. It was definitely daylight when I climb'd George's Hill, & great bars of fire streaked the sky as I surmounted the crest & beheld the old Belmont estate with its 1750 manor-house & sweeping terraces descending toward the Schuylkill—beyond which the distant spires of Philadelphia stood out in an impressive panorama. This was, in more senses than one, the "high spot" of the pilgrimage. Sitting down at a table near the house, I began a letter to A E P G, during the course of which the flaming disc of the sun burst forth in [a] flood of glory.

I now cross'd a ravine, beheld a cottage which the poet Moore inhabited during his American trip of 1802, & proceeded to the northern limit of the park, where the Georgian mansion of Chamounix looks down from a pointed bluff upon limitless village-dotted valleys & the glimmering silken thread of the Schuylkill. There taking a car, I proceeded with several changes to Germantown, the destin'd seat of my most exhaustive explorations. I stopt at the very border in order to observe the early Georgian mansion of Stenton (1727) & its delectable old-fashion'd gardens which the Indian Summer had kept still in bloom.

Germantown is an ancient village once wholly distinct from Philadelphia, but overtaken as Providence has overtaken Olneyville, Boston Roxbury, or New York Flatbush. It was founded in 1683 by Germans whose peculiar religious sects (Dunkards, Mennonites, &c.) evoked persecutions by the Lutheran majority in Germany, & at first its sole language was the German. Architecturally it copied English influences at a very early date, so that few traces of a continental heritage are apparent. It did not, however, emulate its neighbour Philadelphia—& its houses remind one rather of New England save that they are of stone & that the larger mansions have cornices carried round the gable ends—a Pennsylvanian feature of Welsh origin. The life of Germantown is still its own—& though Philadelphia has engulf'd it, it still has its own newspapers, libraries, customs, & styles of building. It is a very fashionable suburb, but though the new residents are Philadelphians they have deferred to the local tradition & built stone mansions of the Germantown type instead of following the brick & marble trimming tradition of Philadelphia. Some of these new mansions lie on splendid hilly estates, & are so closely modelled on the old Georgian lines that one can hardly distinguish them from the many really old mansions which survive on every hand. The oldest part of Germantown is its main street, now call'd Germantown Ave. Here are endless rows of colonial houses—many with a striking history, since the place has seen varied & stirring events, including a prominent battle of the Revolution—of every sort of early architectural pattern; the whole having occasional suggestions of New England, & certain corners boasting a veritably Marbleheadish aspect! One goes north up a steep hill, & sees it before one—a great stone mansion atop a bluff to the left, & little white East-Greenwich like houses on the curving slope to the right. Then the procession begins, broken by a square, a park, & a white marble town hall just in procefs of construction, whose curving lines suggest the old Maritime Exchange of Philadelphia, & the Greek monument which in turn suggested the Exchange to the colonial architect Strickland.

In Vernon Park, where the Site & Relic Society maintains a fine historical museum in a colonial mansion, I obtain'd folders of the principal old houses; copies of which I have sent to both of you children. Of the objects there describ'd, I view'd all save the Rittenhouse homestead, Roset house, & Rock house. Particularly interesting were the Wister house, where the ends of the wooden beams project through the stonework of one of the gable ends, the Green Tree Tavern, the old German pre-Georgian manor-house of Wyck, oldest building in Germantown, the Mennonite meeting-house & churchyard, Keyser house, Washington Tavern, (a *wooden* house of perfect *New-England* gambrel outline) the Concord School, the Peter Keyser house, the Chew mansion, (of which you've seen a picture—it bears Revolutionary bullet marks, & has statues in the yard with heads knocked off by Revolutionary cannon-fire) the Lutheran school, (1740) the Academy, &c. &c. &c. . . . but space forbids a catalogue!!

At last I struck off abruptly westward, with the intention of obtaining a glance at that famous beauty-spot, the Wissahickon valley, which extends north from the east side of Fairmount Park & passes somewhat near Germantown. It is a deep, wooded gorge of prodigious scenic magnificence, at the bottom of which flows the narrow, limpid Wissahickon on its way to join the Schuylkill. Legend has woven many beautiful tales around this piny paradise with its precipitous walls, & even Quinsnicket Park must look to its laurels in comparison. A bridle path runs close to the water, whilst half-way up the eastern bank runs a footpath—narrow & in places perilous—which is the delight of the imaginative & beauty-loving pedestrian. The whole valley is part of Philadelphia's park system.

Traversing some luxurious avenues in the Mt. Airy district north of Germantown, I eventually hit upon a descending path which at once submerged me in a sea of perfumed pines. Down, down, down . . . interminably down past old farmhouses & bits of abandoned stone buildings . . . . dizzying descent like that of Ulysses, Aeneas, or Dante into Hades . . . . then ahead a glimpse of further abysses sudden & profound—poignant green, macabre brown, & distances vast & vertiginous, with a glint & a ripple in the far depths where sight faintly merges into imagination.

I clamber'd down the whole distance, & stood beside some bubbling rapids that diversified the generally placid stream. Above me on either side were precipices reaching into the sky, & arcades of green that shut out heaven & the world alike. Down there in the hush'd green twilight I paus'd to ponder, & finally set out along the foot path, whose insecure footings were now & then supplemented by steps, bridges, & railings. Midway in air—alone with the forest & the river gods! Fancy the riot of classick memories & fantastick visions that ingulph'd a born pagan & mythologist!! I am not sure yet whether it was a dream or a reality—but in any case it was ecstatically vivid! The part I saw was the merest fraction—yet advancing time forbade further lingering. Regretfully I climb'd up the slope at my left & enter'd the world again— plodding back to Germantown, getting an 11¢ lunch at a place near a car- barn, (cheese sandwich 6¢, coffee 5¢) & consoling myself with a glimpse of the old village in the twilight, with evening's first candles gently shining thro' the ancient fanlights & small-pan'd windows.

Such was the day. With dusk at hand & cash at an end, only the railway station remain'd; so boarding a car & winding up my affairs, I was soon in the Broad St. Station aboard the N.Y. train due to pull out at seven.

I regretted the departure, for Philadelphia has an atmosphere peculiarly suited to old gentlemen like me. None of the crude, foreign hostility & un- derbreeding of New York—none of the vulgar trade spirit & plebeian hustle. A city of real American background—an integral & continuous outgrowth of a definite & aristocratic past instead of an Asiatic hell's huddle of the world's cowed, broken, inartistic, & unfit. What a poise—what a mellowness—what a character in the preponderantly Nordic faces! Yet it has a real prosperity as well as a history, & is enjoying a building wave in which the uglier Victorian structures are gradually succumbing to new houses cast in judicious reproduc tions of the old Georgian manner. A great old town—shall I ever forget it? Those mazes of colonial brick alleys, that red & black brickwork, those pro- jecting eaves & corniced gables, those slanting cellar-doors & lateral foot-

scrapers, those iron sidewalk-posts, those panell'd double doors & semicircular fanlights, those zigzag brick sidewalks, those ancient needle-like steeples,
those F. A. house plates, those queer window reflectors—all these urban
things, with the glamour of quiet squares & venerable churchyards where the
ghost of Dr. Franklin wanders, & besides them the glorious countryside of
Fairmount & the Schuylkill, where ancient manor houses rest on their high
terraces & immemorial lawns whose feet the silver waters bathe. These, and
quaint Germantown, & the vale of the Wissahickon . . . That last is a hard
name to remember—at least for a stranger to remember—& I made many
blunders before pinning myself down to it through an impromptu mnemon-
ick couplet—

> Bright are the blooms I gaily pick on
> The piny steeps of Wissahickon!

Eheu—& now it is all miles away. But some day I may have the cash to
revisit it—inspiring hope!

The train pulled into N.Y. at 9:30, & I proceeded without delay to 259,
where I was surpris'd to find S H—arriv'd a day early. I unpackt, eat a spaghetti supper, & retir'd; the next day reading my accumulated mail, (among
which was a $5.00 cheque from the *Bulletin* for my verse) going with S H to
Dr. McChesney's, & accompanying her to a cinema show at the Albemarle.

Sunday I went with 'Ittle-Boy to the Metropolitan Museum, where the
new American Wing (vide enclosure) is just open; & there I revell'd in the incredible wealth of colonial material presented. It is a wonderful display—
room on room, each furnished to perfection in the exact style of some typical
place & period—panelled or paper'd, decorated, & fitted up with all the antiquarian precision of the Pendleton House. The mere *number* of such rooms is
impressive. 17th century apartments, low-pitch'd, with diamond-pan'd lattice
windows & ugly Puritan furniture—a whole hall with roof trussed with hand-
pegg'd beams after the manner of the Old Ship Church at Hingham Mass.—
18th century rooms of every sort, from cottage, town house, & mansion, &
having a geographical scope extending from New Hampshire to Maryland &
Virginia. Each period & subdivision of a period is there—you can tell the pre-
Georgian from the Georgian, & distinguish betwixt the first, second, & third
Georgian phases—tracing the rise of the delicate Adam influence in the late
18th & early 19th centuries, & watching its culmination in Bulfinch & the classick revival. And there is one room from Portsmouth, R.I.!! As to the furniture, china, & pewter & silver plate—one may only say that any type not there
is not worth seeing! Every type of Colonial life is represented except the
Dutch of New-York—that probably being omitted because the Dyckman &
Van Cortlandt mansions tell all there is to be told on that subject. Most surprising of all were the crowds—good old Yankee faces, too—which surged in

to see this new exhibit. I never saw such a run on a museum—for so dense were the streams of visitors that attendants had to form lines & regulate them like traffick policemen! At length our tour was over, & Belknap & I went up to the Kirk–Loveman roost in 106th St. where Kleiner was also expected. Here we had a great session of comment & discussion in spite of the fact that Kirk was feeling rather indisposed, & after Sonny's departure I read aloud my new story—to which the Child had appended some marginal suggestions for condensation.

The result was more gratifying than I could possibly have wish'd for— since not only did my audience observe no sign of senile decadence in my style, but instead waxed incredibly enthusiastick in affirming that it is the best thing I ever writ. Loveman in particular became quite rhapsodick in his praise, & made me promise *not* to follow Belknap's suggestions for abridgements in the first half. He took it so seriously that he begged me to type it before Wednesday, so that he may show it to one of the readers of the Alfred A. Knopf Co. (Arthur Machen's publishers) with whom he has some acquaintance. All of which would be highly flattering if it meant anything. I may type the darned mess, at that!

In the evening—Kirk not feeling like a trip—Loveman, Kleiner, & I went first to a neighbouring restaurant & then to the Double-R Coffee House in 44th St., where we sate & discussed aestheticks till a rather late period. Then home.

Today—Monday—I went up to Sonny's for lunch, argued all the afternoon with the Child on whether there is any standard of civilisation, & if so what—& later went out with him to inspect a quaint Elizabethan court (like the English Village in Philadelphia that I wrote of) which he had just discover'd off 95th St. It was delightful—& I held many pleasing memories of it as I rode home in the subway. Since arriving, I have been eating & writing. Tomorrow I hope to take S H to see that marvellous American Wing—'Gad's death, but it is a marvel!!

*Tomorrow—Tuesday*

This morning A E P G's special delivery letter came—& I hasten to add such comments as are evoked. Egad—but wouldn't it be great if you could see this Providence-like study before it is broken up! And yet, as I said before, I wouldn't for the world have you do anything to tax your energy or impair the recovery of your strained back. With the aid of the professional packer whose prices we have secured, we can probably vacate by the first of December; though if anything retards—such as difficulty in securing new quarters— we will of course stay over—though I would have to get the rent from Providence. This morning S H sold some of her own books for $20.00, & an appraiser came to look over the furniture which I am to sell—saying that his firm would not give anything for it, though private persons might give from

$25.00 to $30.00. The articles I have decided to part with—unless you advise to the contrary—are:

> Dining-Room table & chairs
> Ebony parlour chair with broken seat
> Round oak table with claw & glass ball feet
> Oak Office Chair—revolving
> Broken oak office table
> Semicircular cherry chair with green plush seat

How much I can ever get into any room which I might hire, the dim gods atop Pegāna are alone competent to predict. I *must* have the Dr. Clark table & chair, the cabinet, the typewriter table, the 454 library table, & several book-cases—to say nothing of some sort of bed or couch, & a bureau or chiffonier. A small room is impossible to consider—& for the sake of cheaper rent I would vastly prefer something out of town. Elizabeth, N.J. has my kind of atmosphere—old American background, & the leisurely aura of good breeding—& I shall investigate it unless some position suddenly shews up, which would necessitate my presence within subway radius of Manhattan. In that latter case, the neighbourhood of Brooklyn Heights—where Hart Crane lives, & which I shewed to A E P G—would appeal most strongly to me. Best of all would it be if—your Mt. Vernon visit being accomplished—you & I could find some means of co-operative housekeeping here which might once more light the Phillips home-fires, albeit on distant sod. The rents are high in New York—but Elizabeth is a deliciously old-fashion'd town where I am sure one might find more moderate facilities. Still, one has to think cautiously amidst the devastating tangle of problems & uncertainties which looms ahead on the path of the exiled & the impecunious!

But at any rate, there are a few days ahead in which one may breathe. Don't undertake anything which may prove a strain, & in any case be assured that we can pull through unaided. On Monday the 24th—when A E P G suggested you might be here—this room will still be in its old-gentlemanly Providence condition, & ample sleeping facilities for all will remain. Do not, however, come *as a duty;* but only if you would *genuinely* enjoy seeing this bit of transplanted Rhode-Island before its dispersal. We can "swing the job" independently; & if you would prefer to let your visit be one of unalloy'd & gradual sightseeing, pray time it with that programme in mind. All told, I will leave the entire matter to your own health & maturest judgment. I don't have to say how glad I will be to stage a family reunion, or how eagerly I will post down to the Grand Central to meet your train be it next Monday, a week from then, a month from then, or any time at all from then!!

So it stands. Nothing is compulsory—but on the other hand a record-breaking welcome is ready to be staged at any time at a moment's notice. Long live the House of Phillips!

As to latest news in the job-hunting business—Loveman telephoned this morning & informed me of a bookshop in 59th St. where his employer has some influence & where there may be need of a man in the cataloguing department. The name is G. A. Baker, & Loveman says he will telephone further details tonight. I am, naturally, sharply on the lookout; & am profoundly grateful for all these pains taken on my behalf. I'll let you know if any result ensues. Loveman said, by the way, that my new story keeps running in his head; & that he means to get in touch with the Knopf reader at the earliest possible moment. Be that as it may, I'm glad my style isn't going to seed; for writing after all is the essence of whatever is left in my life, & if the ability or opportunity for that goes, I have no further reason for—or mind to endure—the joke of existence.

And now let me thank you profoundly for the two delightful letters & absorbingly interesting enclosures! I have read all with the keenest apprecia-

tion, & have distributed the printed & pictorial matter in the appropriate corners & cubbyholes. That Kingstown article absorbed me—& made me wish
that in my day I had given Wickford a more careful examination. I have been
there repeatedly, yet noted the buildings with only a casual eye. The antiquarian matter is interesting—I'll send you some more on the archaeological activities of the Comte de Prohock[2] when Sonny returns the cutting I've lent him.
The *Sunday Journal* is splendid—I think I'll subscribe soon. I am especially
fond of the Providence views—& that old set of Rules for the Providence
Aſſembly is a delight. Enclosed are a few things from papers here—including
a brief & tragick item on what happen'd to the late-blooming flowers of Philadelphia the *very day* after I saw them in full splendour in the ancient gardens
of Stenton (1727).

As to the 'verse about the old Bowery village cemetery'—I must confess
that I don't recall what I sent! My old memory isn't what it used to be, & it's
an even guess whether—in describing the place—I inserted a quotation or
coined a bit of new doggerel. If there are quotation-marks, it's somebody's
else; if there aren't, it's mine—& that's all a forgetful old man can tell about it!

So you once thought of writing a story about the Billopp house! I saw
that place last August when I explored Staten Island & Perth Amboy, & will
show it to you if you come here. That Rindge N.H. anecdote is alluring—&
reminds me that the Munroes spent the summer of 1912 in West Rindge. I
used to receive endless letters from Harold with that postmark.

I envy you your Scituate ride & glimpse of the Lapham Institute—or
Smithville Seminary. I heard the old place had been damaged by fire, & am
glad to learn that the devastation was not profound. Would that it might be
saved for ever, & restored to that pristine grandeur it enjoy'd when Rhoby A.
Place sat side by side with the future president of the University of Michigan![3]

So you liked Visible & Invisible! I'm now reading another which Sonny
has lent me—"Great Ghost Stories", selected by Joseph Lewis French, containing several masterpieces by various well-known authors. Recently I picked
up a little book containing Gautier's "Avatar" & Merimee's "Venus of Ille",
translated by Edgar Saltus—the man whose work Loveman is popularising.
Both tales are very good, & I will lend you the book if you care for it. I also
have back the "Episodes of Vathek" which I lent Belknap.

I've seen "Told by an Idiot" advertised, but haven't read it.[4] I don't go in
for modern stuff any more, but have settled back on the classicks as the Perfect Old Gentleman. Don't miss "Wuthering Heights"—it's great, & I know
that Sonny will like it when he tackles it.

How unfortunate that the Sterling cutting was lost! When I can find the
other one I'll send it on, but just now my files are in a state of the most complete chaos. Slowly I am trying to classify my junk preparatory to removal—
'eav'n 'elp me!

I am glad to hear, for A E P G's sake, that the Ripley home is tasteful &

congenial. Here's hoping A E P G can hang on, for pleasing openings don't occur every day. S H has just answered a companion advertisement—elderly lady who wants a companion & will impose no other duties—but the competition will undoubtedly be strong—& the old lady may be another Maybell Paulina![5]

We've just examin'd that Valley Forge card & noted the likenesses mention'd. Good stuff! I wish we *were* there—but Valley Forge is one of the few places I didn't see even on my recent trip. It's over 20 miles from Philadelphia, & communication is both difficult & expensive. The same reason has also kept me from seeing the Wayside Inn at South Sudbury, despite my frequent sojourns in Boston.

But I must close, since the day advances & S H & I are going to the cinema to see "The Sea-Hawk"[6]—which I guess A E P G saw either at the Strand or The Modern. Loveman telephoned again, & says that the job prospect seems good—though I've heard that story before. Tomorrow I'll go & see this bimbo Baker—he's right in that marvellous row of 2nd hand bookstalls which I can't pass without spending all I have in my pocket . . . . fitting reciprocity if the place would turn around & put money in that selfsame pocket! Tomorrow night The Boys meet at Belknap's—I was sorry to forego their session last week, but Philly is Philly! The new member will be present—Wheeler Dryden, half-brother of Charles Chaplin—& we expect some amusing arguments when he expatiates in his effusive fashion on the high & purposeful mission of his art, &c. &c.—he is a quaint 19th century survival, but a dear boy & delightfully amiable soul for all that! ¶ Oh yes—did I say that *Weird Tales* had sent me proofs of the art headings for my next two stories? And have you seen Little Belknap's cover design?

¶ Well—the page is getting crowded. Let me 'see how things is', & I'll keep you duly posted. Let health & inclination be your guides!

Yr aff nephew & obt Servt
        H P L

## Notes

1. HPL refers to his gas stove.

2. HPL means the Comte de Prorok. See LDC/AEPG 145n6.

3. James Burrill Angell (1829–1916) was a graduate of and professor at Brown University and later the president of the University of Vermont (1866–71) and the University of Michigan (1871–1909). HPL owned a copy of Angell's *Reminiscences* (1912; *LL* 41).

4. A novel by Rose Macaulay.

5. Maybell Paulina Davis (Mrs. Theodore Waters Forest) of Providence, a graduate of Swarthmore (1878).

6. *The Sea Hawk* (Frank Lloyd Productions, 1924), directed by Frank Lloyd; starring Milton Sills, Enid Bennett, and Lloyd Hughes. A tale of adventure on the high seas.

[91]    [ANS postcard][1] [HPL to LDC]

[Postmarked Brooklyn, N.Y.,
20 November 1924]

Have just arranged to retain 259 another month, so *come ahead Monday* if the trip would be a pure *pleasure* excursion. ¶ Let me know train in advance if the jaunt appeals. ¶ For three weeks we can have a high old time seeing sights & postponing packing—S H may be here, or may possibly find some restful roosting-place in the country. ¶ Then—when you go to the Ray abode for your visit there—S H & I will attend to the rough stuff without incommoding you except by occasional polite requests for advice. How about it? Lemme know! Yr aff & obt H P L

## Notes

1. *Front:* Washington Arch, New York City.

[92]    [ANS postcard][1] [HPL to LDC]

[Postmarked Flatbush, N.Y.,
n.d.; 24 November 1924?]

Your card recd.—hurrah for Monday December 1st! Send all particulars as to train time &c., & watch for the brass band at the Grand Central! But be cautious about your health, & don't do anything the doctor doesn't freely advise! ¶ Hope you received my story—which you can read at leisure & return any time. Note the R.I. local colour! ¶ Will send a diary letter in a day or two, so that when you arrive you will be right in touch with things. ¶ See in the Bulletin that our cousin Joseph Vaughn is dead—suppose you'll have to attend his funeral Friday before coming here to mine.[2] ¶ That American Wing at the Museum is magnificent—I'll send you a bulletin of it if I can get a duplicate. ¶ Have just finished "The Time Machine" by H. G. Wells—it's pretty good. ¶ Yr aff nephew & obt Servt
        H P L

[P.S. on picture side:] This is a brand new imitation Colonial building.

## Notes

1. *Front:* First Church Parish House, Elizabeth, N.J.
2. Joseph W. Vaughn (1853–1924), son of Sarah Ann Place (1824–1911), older sister of HPL's grandmother Robie Alzada (Place) Phillips.

[93]     [ALS] [HPL to LDC]

259 Parkside Ave.,
Brooklyn, N.Y.,
Novr. 29, 1924

My very dear Daughter Lillian:—

Hurrah for the coming reunion!! Send us a wire when you decide on the train—then sing ho for a delirious (tho' divided & deliberate) round of sightseeing, antiquarian & otherwise. The fort is still held, & you'll see the Providence Room in fullest splendour—including that clock whose telepathic photograph you obtained through the cryptical processes of etheric radiation.

And as for the diary—I wrote on Novr. 18, & thereafter went to see a cinema of "The Sea-Hawk", which was quite uniformly excellent. The next day—Wednesday—I went down to see about that bookshop position, but found it had been unexpectedly filled—though Loveman & his employer think they may be able to find another opening somewhere. During the afternoon I did much reading in my study, & in the evening went to Belknap's for a meeting of The Boys—at which the attendance was disappointingly slender. Loafing along downtown with Leeds, I reached home in the small hours— less saturated than usual with tobacco, because fewer smokers had been present. The next day I read all the morning, & in the afternoon took S H to see that magnificent new American Wing at the museum—for the cutting about which from the *Sunday Journal* I most sincerely thank you. This time I obtained the illustrated bulletin of the exhibit, which you shall shortly see. In the evening I did more reading—some day I may really become tolerably well-inform'd. The next day—Friday the 21st—Morton came over for lunch, & I read him my new story—which he liked exceedingly. He has just taken a civil-service examination for a most important post—curator & absolute head of a new general museum to be established in Paterson, N.J., a manufacturing city about an hour's ride from here. The questions were very abstruse, & he slipped up on one or two of them; but he still has great hopes of landing the coveted prize. It will be a great thing if it goes through—Morton will automatically become one of the most leading of the leading lights of Paterson, & will have the complete guidance of what will ultimately develop into one of the nation's genuinely important museums. All of The Boys are wishing him luck, & we have all applied for positions as janitors, office-boys, &c—under him in the event of his success. Later on Friday Morton, S H, & I went down to some municipal place in Brooklyn, where we met honest Mrs. Moran—she & Mortonius being needed to supply technical points in the naturalisation process of S H, as persons who have known the latter for over five years. As it happens, the trip was made in vain, since the appointment ought to have been definitely arranged in advance; but Mortonius & Mrs. M. did not complain—being basically good-natur'd souls. In the evening I began the typing of my story—hateful job—& retired at an hour of unsanctified lateness. The next day—Saturday the 22nd—Grandpa's birthday[1]—I completed the typing of the tale, & S H read it aloud to me in order to eliminate all typographical errors. During the evening we played chess—S H being uniformly the victor. On Sunday I wrote letters, read a fine book on "Literary N.Y." which Kleiner lent me,[2] & went to the cinema with S H to see that mediaeval film "Yolanda",[3] which has recently been shewn in Providence. The plot was inane, but the architectural effects were splendid—giving stupendous vistas of Gothick & Romanesque construction. On Monday the 24th I took S H to see the Historical Society Museum, (which you & I will presently be exploring) & she was properly delighted with the colourful reliquiae of other days—to say naught of the Renaissance paintings on the upper floor. When the museum closed at 5 p.m., we walked all the way down town (from 77th to 42nd St.) & had a stupendous Italian dinner at the Milan restaurant—where we have dined twice before. I ate for the first time the celebrated Italian dish called "ravioli", (meat enclosed in pastry, with tomato sauce) with which I was suitably enraptured, & which S H promises to make for me on a not far distant day. That evening I read H. G. Wells' "Time Machine", which Sonny had obtain'd from the library for his Grandpa to read, & which was thoroughly entertaining in every detail. The next day—Tuesday the 25th—I took S H to the Bronx Park Zoölogical Gardens, which A E P G will remember, & at which S H found the reptiles the most interesting of all the exhibits. When closing time came, she proceeded homeward, whilst I stopped off down town to meet the Belknap lambkin at honest old McNeil's. Sonny was there, but McNeil was not at home; so the Child & I went over to the publick library & read some of Lafcadio Hearn's posthumous work as recently collected & published by Albert Mordell under the title "An American Miscellany". At 7:30 we left—Sonny to attend an evening class at college, & Grandpa to haste home to a sumptuous dinner & a reading of Huysmans' "En Route"—an exaltation of the aesthetic side of monasticism which Sonny lent me, & which held me so riveted that I stayed up till most un-monastic hours to finish it. On Wednesday I began the two-volume history of N.Y. by Rufus Rockwell Wilson which I am still reading, & digested the text between trips outside to various dealers in toothsome edibles in connexion with the Novanglian feast of the morrow. We had meant to have Morton as a guest, in addition to the Kirk–Loveman pair; but found at the last moment that he had a prior engagement with the members of the Blue Pencil Club. Sonny & his family were booked with relatives in Atlantic City. For dinner on this "night before" we had several luscious foretastes of the coming banquet—including boiled & roasted chestnuts . . . . which would have delighted the heart of my epicurean old Nigger-Man of 21 years ago! Finally I went to the meeting of the Boys— up at the Kirk–Loveman ranch—& found all the active members present. As long as Belknap was there, discussion stayed literary; but later (under the malign inspiration of Mortonius, who has lately fallen hard for the season's latest folly) the gang drifted off into the infertile silences of crossword-puzzle solving—so that the only audible features of our protracted small-hour vigil were grunts such as "23 vertical", "13 horizontal", "word of 17 letters beginning with X & meaning cloudy in the attic", &c. &c. &c. Have you ever tackled any of these popular futilities in the *Bulletin?* The first I heard of them was just a year ago, when honest (or more or less honest) Eddy shew'd me one in the *Boston Post.* To what devastating proportions hath grown the blight which then arose so quietly, as a cloud in the northwest no bigger than a man's hand! On this occasion I presented Belknap with the book which I got for him at Scribner's a couple of months ago, but which I kept until I might have a chance to read it. It is an excellent horror story by someone I never heard of before—Harper Williams—entitled "The Thing in the Woods", & dealing with the superstitious Pennsylvania countryside. There is more than a hint of obscure lycanthropy—but read it for yourself when you get here! On the flyleaf I wrote the following dedication to the Child:

> Belknap, accept from *Theobald's* ſpectral Claw
> Theſe haunting Chapters of dæmoniack Awe;
> Such nightmare Yarns we both have often writ,
> With goblin Whiſpers, and an Hint of **IT**.
> Till ſure, we're like to think all Terror's grown
> A ſort of private Product of our own!
> Leſt, then, our Pride our ſober Senſe miſlead,
> And make us copyright each helliſh Deed,
> 'Tis ours to ſee what ghastly Flames can blaze
> From Spooks and Ghouls that other Wizards raiſe!

At about 2:30 a.m. the meeting dissolved, with Morton's crossword puzzle still unsolved. Loveman went to bed, but Kirk—as usual—set out to walk as far as his hardiest guest would walk. We saw Mortonius to his elevated & Leeds & Kleiner to their subway—then Kirk & I started out on one of our famous all-night jaunts. In the dark of the moon—with only malign Astarte to blink down upon us in our limbo of planetary souls—we crossed Central Park via the reservoir path, entered 5th Ave. at an odd spot by jumping down a sheer wall taller than we are, & proceeded down 86th St to the East River—through slum territory which was once the beautiful & agrestick village of Yorkville. Ere long, however, we struck something which is still fairly agrestick & mildly beautiful—the nocturnal expanse of East River Park on the bluffs above Hell Gate, where Washington Irving used to visit the first John Jacob Astor in his now vanisht colonial country-seat, & where yet remains the archaic Gracie Mansion, (1813) recently opened as a municipal museum, & not yet visited by me during open hours. There's a trip ahead for us—as new to me as to you, though Belknap & I got in a moment last April before it was fully fitted up. We now strolled southward along the shore, which gradually changed from a park to a hideous district of factories, coal-pockets, & gas-houses. In time the Queensboro Bridge drew near, & from the shadow of its massive piers we saw the old stone mansion which A E P G & I visited last spring. Then came magically restored Sutton Place with its neo-Georgian splendour—after which we worked inland & across to the west side, going down 9th & 8th Avenues through Chelsea Village to Greenwich, & pausing only for a cup of coffee at a corner refectory where a somewhat spifflocated gent tried vainly to establish a convivial friendship with us, & where I tried with slightly greater success to establish a less spirituous friend-ship with two of the cutest little kittens I ever saw—roguish little divvles who darted about nimbly & airily in pursuit of the tails of themselves & of their proudly purring mamma. Thence our course led to the tangled village lanes of Greenwich; which we enter'd at Abingdon Square*, & gradually travers'd in the direction of the Minettas. Dawn had now come; & as we approacht the hidden congeries of winding alleys which was our destination, we observ'd how great a progress had been made upon that labour of restoration of which I read in the *Tribune* these two years gone. One by one the Italian families are being cleared out, & their erstwhile rookeries scoured, fumigated, painted, & remodelled into at least a fair semblance of the colonial dignity they lost a century ago. An inner court, long closed, has anew been open'd up; & will once more form an abode of gentry, with a park-like space in the centre. The restoration is still but incipient; but when completed, the region will com-mand a high rental & possess a Georgian charm even greater than that of its nearest existing analogue—broad Charlton Street, with its rectilinear proces-sion of graceful dormers & pillar'd & knocker'd doorways. Heigho for the past! But all this N.Y. stuff seems sadly tame after the marvels of antique PHILADELPHIA.

As the sun rose, Kirk & I wheeled around through McDougall St. to Washington Square, crossing that Salem-like haunt of brick & granite dignity with appropriate reverence, & proceeding (after a hurried & delighted glimpse of the sunken gardens behind the artists' studios in Washington Mews) to the 8th station of the B.M.T. Subway. Here we said farewell—with promises to meet in six hours & a half by the festive board of 259. The hour being 7 o'clock, & the sun being up, we may well adopt this point as a transition to a new day; & say that on Thursday the 27th I rode home, retir'd, rose again at 12:30 noon, & at 1:30 p.m. welcomed Loveman & Kirk to the collation. And what a classick repast! Enchanted soup—apotheosised roast turkey with dressing of chestnuts & all the rare spices & savoury herbs that camel-

---

*so nam'd from the daughter of one of the great citizens—Admiral Sir Peter Warren, K.C.B.—who marry'd the Earl of Abingdon.

caravans with tinkling bells bring secretly from forgotten orients of eternal spring across the deserts beyond the Oxus—cauliflower with cryptical cream-ing—cranberry sauce with the soul of Rhode-Island bogs in it—salads that emperors have dreamed into reality—sweet potatoes with visions of pillar'd Virginian plantation-houses—gravy for which Apicius strove & Lucullus sigh'd in vain—plum pudding such as Irving never tasted at Bracebridge Hall—& to crown the feast, a gorgeous mince pie fairly articulate with mem-ories of New-England fireplaces & cold-cellars. All the glory of earth subli-mated in one transcendent repast—one divides one's life into periods of before & after having consumed—or even smelled or dream'd of—such a meal! And the coffee—with the narcotic incense of Araby & the sanctity of the holy Ka'ba in it—& the lemonade—for whose piquancy exotick & flow-ering groves in scented tropicks have yielded up their life-blood! But all things must end—& all stomachs have a limit of distensibility. I was askt if I had all I *wanted,* & I reply'd that I had all I *could hold.* Afterward—in the torpor which follows such orgies of nourishment—I read to the guests some of my stories which they had not before heard, & shew'd them the choicest treasures of my collection of colonial postcards. When sufficiently bored, they took their cer-emonious departure—in turn inviting me to be with them on the following Saturday night, when they will entertain a literary man of some prominence— Allen Tate,[4] of *The Nation,* whom they want me to meet with a view of gradu-ally getting my stories before suitably influential & conceivably appreciative eyes. That Saturday night is tonight—which reminds me that I shall have to cease this chronicle at 6:30 sharp if I expect to be bathed & dressed & up at 106th St. by 8:30, the designated hour. I shall be rather interested to see this Tate, of whom I've heard before. But the departure of the Samuelo-Georgian contingent did not end the day. Just as we were relaxing in negligee to read a few chapters of our respective books in hand before retiring, the doorbell rang to announce a surprise call from four of the Blue Pencil circle—Morton, Kleiner, & Mr. & Mrs. Dench. Hastily restoring our exterior finish, we admit-ted them—& I went out for some cake, which to the accompaniment of an excellent decoction of the Chinese herb served to allay the ravening appetites of those who had but too soon forgotten the internally vanisht glories of a noontide gorge. Conversation was far from dull; & when at midnight the del-egation dispers'd, the day was unanimously adjudg'd quite the reverse of un-interesting. On Friday the 28th I was put in a good humour by the arrival of a six-dollar cheque from *Weird Tales*—covering the lines "To A Dreamer" which appeared in the November issue. This unsolicited compliance with the promise to pay during month of dated publication has to some extent restor'd my confidence in the enterprise; & leads me to rejoice that I have seven sto-ries accepted, which ought to give me $25.00 or more each month, beginning with the end of January. A E P G's cheque also came—twin life-savers! As the day developt, S H & I went down town & took a pedestrian jaunt in the neighbourhood of 5th Ave., after which we returned to partake of the bygone feast's last lingering echoes. Later I spent some time in giving my colonial postcards a somewhat better classification, & finally I finisht the first volume of the N.Y. history which is still engrossing me. The hours being now small, an interval of slumber punctuates the diary; which reopens today—Saturday the 29th—to the accompaniment of genteel reading & refined epistolary composition. So far, so good. The rest is futurity—though the several passages immediately following will display such industry as I can manage to exercise before 6:30 p.m.

And now pray let me exprefs my unaffected gratitude for the letters & cuttings of recent date! I am somewhat tantalised by your reference to a box of turkey—as well as by a reference of A E P G's to an Old Farmer's Almanack—since neither has so far put in an appearance; but I know the tardinefs of 3d & 4th class mail service, hence am unterrified by disquieting apprehensions. The *Sunday Journal* & cuttings *did* come—for which a world of thanks!

All the Rhodinsular matter I inhaled with accustom'd avidity—rejoicing especially in the School of Design's new museum. Did you hear the McFee address? I presume you recall his "Casuals of the Sea".[5] The picture of the R.I. windmill is indeed absorbing—I have seen one of them with mine own eyes whilst on the way to Newport, & possess an excellent postcard of it. I doubt if they are of Dutch origin as here stated—it seems to me that they were built by the regular Yankee settlers to supply the lack occasion'd by the absence of vigorous streams on the island of Aquidneck. The removal of this structure to the Province of the Mafsachusetts-Bay is in some degree regrettable. Ford has set a bad precedent for wealthy antiquarians, since distinctive architectural remains ought to be viewed on their own natural sites. Rhode-Island wou'd do well to guard its colonial treasures, & ensure their perpetual survival within the bounds of our own commonwealth. By the way—as I continue to stuff cuttings into this place & that, I am strengthen'd in my resolve to get a set of neat portfolios which will accomodate all my floating treasures in orderly & classify'd fashion. I have seen just what I want at the 5 & 10 cent store.

In turn, I am enclosing a few items of interest, all to be returned. The cat essay in "Mann Hatton's" *Evening Post* column[6] is an absolute reflection of mine own sentiments—& an excellent corroboration of that William Lyon Phelps article which we read last winter & which I am still preserving as a crushing blow to all mistaken logicians who uphold canine supremacy over my beloved felidae.[7] The home of Alexander Hamilton, as illustrated in another cutting, is still unvisited by me; since I did not know till lately that it is still standing. Perhaps you & I will see it together for the first time! In the book I am reading, there are described as still existing (in *1902,* however) some old *Dutch* houses in Pearl St.—& it is also said that the warehouse at 73 Pearl St. is built on the still surviving stone foundations of the New-

Amsterdam Stadt Huys—matters which I shall investigate with considerable assiduity despite Kleiner's assertion (on sundry authorities) that the last bit of urban Dutch work vanished during the 1860's. Another ancient place I have not seen—though I have known of it—is the venerable Schenck house; a peaked-roof'd affair describ'd in the enclosed cutting, & built from the timbers of an old privateer during the governorship of Petrus Stuyvesant.

Returning to practical & boresome things—the furniture is not yet sold, & dealers seem disposed to give little or nothing for it. I don't think I will dispose of the semicircular chair—as you say, it is in perfect condition, & not in the least unattractive. When you get here, we can decide what to advertise—& all that. Of course I shall retain all silver & crockery—the barrel down cellar has never been opened. Linen & bedding will be intact; & if S H needs the living-room couch herself, I will get as cheap an one as I can find. I have been wondering about the phonograph cabinet—S H has a Victrola but no cabinet, & I have a cabinet but no Victrola! Which, as it were, or as one might say, is of the most use to whom?!?! Possibly I'll trade my cabinet for a little stand of hers on which I now keep my typewriter at present—but I shall keep my records intact in case I ever have a phonograph again, for S H has no use for my light-&-airy musical lowbrowism & leanings toward light opera. Yo-ho! We sail the ocean blue, & our saucy ship's a beauty! And—to change the subject—as for my ship model, I think I'll tote it in me own 'ands whithersoever I may wander. The packer & moving-man, yclept James A. Perry, is scheduled for Dec. 26—notice of departure given to the Kingsway Realty Co. on the 15th preceding. It ought to go off fairly smoothly once we decide on a roost where Grandpa can hang out—& unless I get some sort of immediate situation I fancy that the atmosphere—& rents—of Elizabethtown, in His Majeſty's Province of New-Jersey, wou'd be admirably fitted alike to my temper & my purse. We must take a trip thither before arriving at any irrevocable decision—but I know you will share my liking for it. Don't hustle or overtax yourself—& I'll promise not to lay out too strenuous itineraries for you. S H will probably be on hand to sustain her share of the domestick burthen, since the unaccountable delay & uncertainty of her insurance company has kept from her the cash needed to secure a lodging-place in the country. Much as she needs an actual rest, she is having to satisfy herself with the minor advantage of merely staying home & avoiding the maddening, enervating crowds of rushing & slithering human vermin in the subway & downtown district. She wishes that $A E P G$ could join us all on Christmas, so that the day before the dispersal we might have a veritable Phillips feast in the old Providence Room—a Yuletide feast of her own cooking, wherein she promises to eclipse even the unbelievable splendours of the Thanksgiving banquet! Such a farewell feast before a collapse is not without an excellent Providence precedent—the Rhode-Island cotton plunger Daniel J. Sully having given one in his pillar'd Brook St. mansion before the shattering of his brief bubble of speculative wealth. As to finances—we have calculated that one more cheque for *$75.00* from A E P G will float us through December to whatsoever ignominious haven the dawn of 1925 may bring. After that, the deluge!

I am infernally sorry that you are being put to all this trouble of acquiring clothes & other accessories on my account—but believe that you will at least have the compensation of seeing some darned interesting things! I'm glad you had a good holiday repast at Shepard's Colonial—where A E P G, S H, & I ate last year—& only wish that you & A E P G could have timed it to eat together. Hope the funeral won't bore her too badly—there may be some colonial slate slabs in the cemetery.

Speaking of burials—I'm glad you found "The Shunned House" worth reading. Loveman veritably throws fits over this bit of cheerful morbidity, & vows he'll bring it to the attention of a publisher's reader. I'm enjoying the flatter'd sensation till some actual reader punctures the crystal bubble.

All litterateurs have their troubles. Poor Eddy is down & out again, as you may see by the enclosed epistle—which you might return, since I haven't answered it. He has his "Deaf Dumb & Blind" back *without* any revision from me—in answer to the very peremptory telegram which I enclose for your amusement. A tough case, these easy-going tassels on the fringe of literature! Just now I'm trying to get back the book I lent that poor fish Hancock[8]—one postal has brought no results, so I'll try a more drastick line with a return address in case his P.O. Box is a blind alley. Poor devil—some time ago he cancelled his club address—no doubt chucked for non-payment of dues!

More anon. Drop us a line & watch for the reception committee with flying flags, right at your car & seat! Whoopee!!

Yr aff nephew & obt Servt

H P L

P.S. Pray tell A E P G that I'm about to answer her vastly appreciated communications.

## Notes

1. Whipple Van Buren Phillips was born on 22 November 1833.

2. Apparently Charles Hemstreet (1866–?), *Literary New York: Its Landmarks and Associations* (New York: G. P. Putnam's Sons, 1903).

3. *Yolanda* (MGM, 1924), directed by Robert G. Vignola; starring Marion Davies, Lyn Harding, and Holbrook Blinn. A film about Princess Mary of Burgundy.

4. Allen Tate (1899–1979), later to become a celebrated poet and essayist, was a friend of Hart Crane who at this time was working as a freelance writer for the *Nation*. It is not clear that HPL's planned meeting with him ever took place.

5. William McFee, *Casuals of the Sea* (1916), a novel about life on the sea. McFee (1881–1966) was a British writer of sea stories.

6. "Mann Hatton" was the pseudonym of Russel Crouse (1893–1966), a playwright best known for his collaborations with Howard Lindsay, including *Anything Goes* and *Life with Father*.

7. William Lyon Phelps (1865–1943) wrote about cats in his "As I Like It" column in *Scribner's Magazine* 75, No. 1 (January 1924): 116–22. HPL cites this article in "Cats and Dogs" (1926; *CE* 5.189).

8. Ernest La Touche Hancock (1857–1926), a minor poet, journalist, and short story writer, and author of *Desultory Verse* (1912). Cf. HPL's reference to the "old-time wit & columnist La Touche Hancock (once a shining light on the old N.Y. Sun), who eventually drank himself to death" (HPL to J. Vernon Shea, 14 February 1934; *Letters to J. Vernon Shea, Carl F. Strauch, and Lee McBride White* 234).

[94]     [ANS postcard][1] [HPL to LDC]

[Postmarked Brooklyn, N.Y.,
31 December 1924]
Wednesday—
9 p.m.

Half-settled! All goods moved today, & you ought to see this room!! Effect is splendid—reminds one of 454—wait till you see the finished product!! ¶ S H went to Cincinnati a day early—today 4 p.m. ¶ Now I'm going up to The Boys' & watch the old year out. ¶ More anon. Hope you're feeling better.

Yr aff: nephew & obt Servt
H P L

*Notes*

1. *Front:* Blank.

# 1925

169 Clinton St.,

Brooklyn, N.Y.,

Jany 22, 1925

My dear daughter Lillian:—

Needless to say that I received your card with the greatest pleasure, & that I hope to see you in person this week with better health & an infinite capacity for sightseeing.

Just now the principal sights will be found in the *sky*, hence I am mailing you some data on the eclipse of Saturday morning, which will be total at Mt. Vernon, (cf. Yonkers data on card) & which you must not under any circumstances miss. The dark film is of just the right consistency to look through, & the accompanying information is correct—though phrased in a more or less immature style. Be posted early if it is clear. Watch the onward creeping of the moon's dark disc, & the final onrush of its shadow over the earth. Then, when the precious second of totality arrives, cast aside the dark screen & behold with unhampered vision (either naked eye or opera or field glass) the marvellous spectacle of corona & prominences. It will last about a minute where you are. Soon a flash of light will appear, & the dark glass must be resumed as one watches the slow withdrawal of the lunar screen from the shining surface. The Boys will view the sight from some good point in Yonkers—meeting at 6:00 a.m. at Van Cortlandt Park & faring northward by trolley or foot as the gods—or the schedule—may determine.

Since your departure I have been perforce very active, owing to the liveliness of events within the circle. The day after seeing you to the Grand Central I welcomed S H to 169, where she took the room you had lately vacated. In the afternoon we visited 259, calling on Mrs. Moran & getting some accumulated mail; & later we explored Greenwood Cemetery, finally returning to 169, where S H fixed enamel cloth in the washroom & generally aided in promoting the habitability of the place. The next day—Monday the 12th—S H transacted business downtown, meeting me for dinner at the Taormina (that Italian restaurant in Clinton St.) & accompanying me to Loveman's over the icy pavement to see his room. The trip fatigued her, hence she used a taxicab for her return—with myself, Loveman, & George Kirk as companions. After her retiring, the residue of the party discussed the universe & finally sallied forth to a cafeteria, where Kirk & I learned for the first time that the following Wednesday—the date of The Boys' meeting at Loveman's—would be our host's 38th birthday! After leaving S L at his airy domicile &

starting on a walk over Brooklyn Bridge & up through Chinatown to the north, Kirk & I decided to surprise Loveman with a birthday gift—as which, after much deliberation, we chose a *bookcase,* plus several cheap decorative accessories to brighten & domesticate his room. I went home with Kirk, &— omitting sleep from the programme—accompanied him downtown again in the morning. We then proceeded to 169, whence we set out for the Fulton St. (Bklyn.) second-hand furniture district. After a hectic afternoon's search we found exactly what we wanted—a tall, black-walnut, glass-doored affair with two drawers beneath the shelves—& purchased it, together with two pale green glass candlesticks. Later S H insisted on sharing in this gift to the extent of a third. The bargain sealed, we arranged for delivery on the morrow & parted—I hastening downtown to meet S H for an Italian dinner & a trip to Jolson's Theatre, (7th Ave & 58th St) where we saw the splendid musical play "The Student Prince"—an adaptation of the well-known "Old Heidelberg", which the Albee Stock Co. played in 1910.[1] That night I put a new ribbon in my typewriter & copied a lecture which S H was to deliver on the following Tuesday to a club of the executives of her store. In the morning I received telephone calls, & telephoned Houdini about some Hippodrome seats which he had offered me for his current performance—obtaining fine places for Thursday night. Later I had a call from Richardson—the law lecturer in this house who knows the Burwells—& lent him a *Weird Tales* & Clark Ashton Smith book. Later still Kirk & I made a round of the 10¢ stores in quest of ornaments for Loveman's room, returning with a heavy load of vases, pictures, candlesticks, Japanese bowls, & the like—which I placed as artistically as possible in the room, whilst Kirk went down town to capture Loveman & hold him at a restaurant till his apartment was ready. I joined the party at last—as did Morton—& when we finally reached S L's eyrie we found Leeds & Kleiner already arrived. Loveman's surprise was complete & ecstatic, & the event was by all adjudg'd a thorough success. After the meeting Kirk, Kleiner, Leeds, Morton, & I went to my regular Tiffany cafeteria, after which Leeds & Morton accompanied me home—to see my room for the first time & to depart properly impressed. The next day I spent at Small Sonny's—taking both lunch & dinner there, & in the meantime going with the child to see the MS. collection at the 42nd St. library. He was entranced by the autographick specimens, & lingered long over the Keats lock of hair. Catalogues were on sale, & we obtained a couple. During this session Belknap insisted on planning a gift for Loveman to rival what The Boys had already given collectively; & at my suggestion hit upon *writing materials,* which the poet sadly lacked. In the evening I joined S H at the Hippodrome—a pleasantly immense house—& saw Houdini go through the same tricks he shewed in Providence about 1898. Then to a restaurant for a bite, & home. Friday I saw S H off for Cincinnati at the Grand Central, & immediately afterward started buying a desk outfit for Loveman as Sonny's gift. This I fixed with great care in his room, (I have the key to his house) after which I hastened home to entertain a special meeting of The Boys with Kleiner, Kirk, Loveman, & honest old McNeil. "Mac" saw the room for the first time, & expressed suitable admiration. Then, after a period of discussion, we all adjourned to Loveman's; where upon lighting the light our host beheld the well-appointed table with pens, paper, blotters, & the like, which Belknap & I had prepared to surprise him.[2] His rapture was of appropriate magnitude, & after a pleasing session we dispersed for the night. I say *dispersed*, though in truth I accompanied Kirk home to his roost in 106th St., where after a short sleep in our clothes—he on the couch & I across the bed—we embarkt upon a further extension of our gang's aesthetick renaissance; the decorating of his room to match in taste the apartments of Loveman & myself. Saturday was a hectic round of the shops—both Harlem & Brooklyn—on Kirk's behalf; & in the evening we parted laden with vases, candlesticks, sofa pillows, steins, Japanese panels, & the like—which Kirk bore to his room whilst I returned to 169 for slumber. Sunday noon I was at Kirk's again, & by 4 p.m. had the room as tastefully decorated as its rather mediocre character permitted. Kirk realised that he would have to get a finer room if he wished to enjoy really beautiful surroundings, & I advised him to migrate over here to Brooklyn Heights, where he might have the benefit of an impressive background of bygone splendour. But as things were, the improvement was vast enough to delight & astonish Belknap, Kleiner, & Loveman when they came over; & we passed a most enjoyable evening there & at the "Double-R" Coffee-House in 44th St. downtown. On this occasion Kirk shewed his generosity by giving me a prodigious load of long ($8\frac{1}{2} \times 13$) typewriter paper which formed part of the vast stock he has on hand. It is not exactly my size, but its quality is excellent, & it will last me for years unless my activity multiplies beyond all reason. Surely a mighty cash saving! Monday I rose late, & accompanied Loveman on a tour of Fulton St. (Bklyn.) bookshops. Here we obtained some unbelievable bargains, though Loveman insisted on treating me to those I wanted most. Among my "hauls" are the first edition of Fitzhugh Ludlow's "Hasheesh-Eater" (a reprint of which I have always envied Kleiner) & an 1800 copy of Walpole's "Castle of Otranto" on large paper, with long s's, & with a fine set of engraved illustrations coloured by hand. The later evening I spent at Loveman's, emerging to find the world immers'd in the beginning of a very ponderable snowstorm. The next day I also rose late, & dined at the Tiffany with Loveman & Kirk. Then, after a brief bookstall tour, we all returned to 169, to discuss aestheticks & interview Mrs. Burns regarding vacant rooms in the house—for here all of our congenial band ought to congregate. Incidentally, we found the second Burns boy delightfully artistic in an embryonick way—an incipient art student with sensitiveness so well developed that he became highly enthusiastic at the loan of some Aubrey Beardsley material. The interview itself terminated beyond all expectation—for directly above me (beside the small room you had) is a tasteful & delicate chamber with fireplace, mantel, & pier glass—roughly a counterpart of my own, & commanding a rental of ten dollars weekly. With quick but well-considered readiness Kirk took the room, paid his first week's quota, & became my next-floor neighbour—a sudden step no less surprising because long advised! Later at night we dispersed, & I accompanied Kirk to his place to inaugurate the disintegration there. He has many rare books, & the process consumed all night & the next day, punctuated by a sleeping interval & trips in search of truckmen. The goods, however, were finally packed, & a man engaged to bring them today. At any moment they will arrive—& 169 will have its second aesthete's den! Meanwhile at 8 p.m. Kirk & I went over to 'Ittle-Child's for the weekly meeting, where all were present, & indulged in piquant discussion plus some magnificent Welsh Rarebit which Mrs. Long made especially for the occasion. Only small Sonny himself—who hates cheese—was unable to appreciate the tid-bit. I have now return'd home, rested, & taken my pen in hand to attack some heavily accumulated mail. This epistle is the first—& I hope soon to be able to supplement it with oral discourse. Telephone any day when you think you can come on the morrow, & I'll be ready with the cordial reception committee at the appointed hour. Mrs. Long is eager to see you again, & you must meet my new neighbour Kirk, whom curiously enough you have never seen. I enclose his picture, & will add the information that he is Loveman's best friend, a rare book dealer by profession, 26 years of age, of old American stock—Scotch with a dash of Pennsylvania Dutch—& a distant relative of the poet Edward Rowland Sill.[3] Also—if you can sidetrack your plan to meet A E P G in Providence before her Daytonian departure—S H would be ecstatically delighted to see you on her next N.Y. sojourn, which begins a week from next Tuesday—Feby. 3—& lasts for three days.

And now don't forget the eclipse! I shall tell A E P G to go somewhere to the south—Bristol, East Greenwich, Newport, or even Auburn if she is not particular about long duration. The Bulletin predicts cloudy weather, but one can't rely on such things, so that my expectancy is still keen.

Hoping to see you soon, I am ever

Yr moſt aff: nephew & obt Servt

H P L

[On envelope:]
P.S. Please let A E P G see this epistle & the Kirk photograph.
P.P.S. Your letter just arrived—what an infernal shame the cold hangs on! Thanks for the cuttings. ¶ Kirk has just come & the moving men are clattering merrily upstairs! More anon.

## Notes

1. *The Student Prince* (Jolson's 59th Street Theatre, 2 December 1924–18 May 1926), a musical (music by Sigmund Romberg; written by Dorothy Donnelly). Based on *Alt Heidelberg* (1902) by Wilhelm Meyer-Foerster (1862–1934).

2. For the occasion, HPL wrote two poems, "To Samuel Loveman, Esq., upon Adorning His Room for His Birthday," and "To Saml Loveman Esq., with a Belated Present of Some Stationery" (*AT* 174–75).

3. Edward Rowland Sill (1841–1887), American poet best known for "The Fool's Prayer" (1879). His *Poems* appeared in 1902.


[96]     [ANS postcard][1] [HPL to LDC]

[Postmarked Brooklyn, N.Y.,
25 January 1925]

Did you see the eclipse? Five of us—Morton, Kirk, Leeds, Dench, & I—went up to Yonkers & had a magnificent view of the entire thing from the summit of a high hill. Corona was splendid, & planets were brilliantly visible. We suffered from the cold, but the experience was worth it! ¶ On our return trip we stopped at the famous Philipse Manor House, of which the oldest part was built in 1682. A fine old man shewed us through, & we bought a book with the history & description of the place in detail. ¶ Hope to see you soon, & learn how you fared during the eclipse.

Yr aff neph & obt Servt  H P L

[P.S.] Hope A E P G went south of Roger Williams Park!

## Notes

1. *Front:* Times Building.


[97]     [ANS postcard][1] [HPL to LDC]

[Postmarked Brooklyn, N.Y.,
2 February 1925]

Waited for your message Friday, but am glad you're not going so soon after all, since S H *will* be in town tomorrow (Tuesday the 3d) owing to a change of plan. She may be able to stay only a couple of days, but I hope you can see her—I guess we'll telephone you when she arrives, so that you can arrange to come. She has been in the hospital once more, but a treatment of the nasal cavity enabled her to tide over till warmer weather, when the septum or antrum operation will occur. ¶ My chairs have come at last from the repairer—am sitting in one now! ¶ *Weird Tales* has just sent a $35.00 cheque,[2] & Mariano's $37.08 came in the same mail! ¶ Blue Pencil meeting Saturday night wås dull, but I composed some comic verse for it.[3] ¶ And my hair is cut!! Found a local barber excellent despite unpromising exterior. ¶ More anon. ¶ Yr aff neph H P L

P.S. C. M. Eddy Jr. has just blown in!! On business in N.Y. to see Houdini & some editors.

## Notes

1. *Front:* Gilbert Stuart Homestead. Rhode Island Artist Famous for His Paintings of George Washington.
2. For either "The Festival" (January 1925) or "The Statement of Randolph Carter" (February 1925).
3. "My Favourite Character."

[98]     [ANS postcard][1] [HPL to LDC]

[Postmark illegible;
9 February 1925]

Glad to receive both cards. Meant to write yesterday, but had to shelve everything in favour of my annual Hoag verses, which I'd completely forgotten to write. The birthday is Feby. 10, & I was forced to do some tall hustling—but I got the copies off in time to the proper papers. I'll send you the text soon.[2] ¶ Glad you arrived safely in spite of seat competition. S H also found her berth sold to somebody else—it's getting to be a habit! She had some eye trouble Thursday night & went to a specialist whom Dr. Long recommended—I'll be glad to hear how she stood the journey. ¶ I'll remember the aluminum dish business & tell Kirk. ¶ Eddy got home safely & has got me a copy of "Our Police"[3] for $2.00 at his uncle's shop. Wish I'd kept ours! Yr aff neph & obt Servt H P L

P.S. Going up to Belknap's today for lunch & afternoon.
P.P.S. Fine article in Tribune by Librarian of John Carter Brown Library.[4]
[P.P.]P.S. And *Morton has got his museum job!*

## Notes

1. *Front:* Childs / The Rendezvous of the Elite / On the Boardwalk at Coney Island.
2. "To Mr. Hoag on His Ninety-fourth Birthday, February 10, 1925." The poem appeared in the *Troy* [NY] *Times* and the *Tryout,* but may have appeared in other papers in the area of Troy, NY.
3. A book about the Providence police force by Henry Mann.
4. Lawrence Counselman Wroth (1884–1970), "A Manuscript Portolan Atlas in the Boston Public Library," *New York Tribune* (8 February 1925): 15, under "Notes for Bibliophiles," ed. Leonard K. Mackall.

[99]     [ALS] [HPL to AEPG]

169 Clinton St.,<br>
Brooklyn, N.Y.,<br>
Feby 10, 1925

My dear Granddaughter:—

'Tis with pleasure that I seize an opportunity when I may write a Floridan without undue & bitter envy—for today is one of a series of springlike days which have (despite misty skies) quite removed the poignant pain-madness of the eclipse period, & have caused more than one window to stand open beside the torrid superfluities of closed radiators. Of your journey I read each descriptive word with the keenest of attention, & pored long over the illustrations displaying your ochraceous & palm-shaded abode, & your benign & ebon pastor. Surely railway service in the south is not belied by the many jests related of it—& I am quite prepar'd to believe the classick tale of the group at a Georgia station awaiting a train, & cheered by the heralding advent of the engineer's dog, whose custom it was to gallop blithely ahead of the engine. Your mention of Macon interested me, since 'tis the home of that simple & once pious amateur journalist John Milton Samples of *Silver Clarion* fame, with whom I used to correspond in more expansive days. Poor John! he thought Macon was a real town—& perhaps he thinks so now. But it must be funny to see the dismal swampy meadows & the squalid cabins oozing brack folks big & little. The separation of people & niggers at the stations is an excellent idea—which ought to be practiced on the Harlem subway trains here—& it would please me always to alight at the quaint & picturesque town of WHITE. Too bad you have nothing Colonial about you—see if you can't stop at *Charleston, S.C.* on your return trip—that's a veritable mine of Georgian antiquity.[1]

Speaking of antiquity—I enclose two cuttings shewing the diverse fate of two colonial buildings in The City. One is bound upward as a State House annex—hurrah!—& the other downward into oblivion—alas! I shall hate to see that Eddy St. corner house go, for it preserved something of the air of the elder Westminster St. about it. Now may Heaven preserve the similar house at the corner of Clemence St., the brick house where Mumford's Restaurant is, & the good old Arcade—which latter has just changed hands & is about to undergo interior alterations.[2] Note the enclosed speech by H. Anthony Dyer relating to the preservation of Colonial reliques.[3] And whilst I am enclosing— see the article in Sunday's *Tribune* by our new John Carter Brown librarian— the pleasant chap who was so cordial to Mortonius & me a year ago last September. And I hope you got the Amer. Wing postcards!

Your letter to S H arrived just after her departure hence, & I promptly remailed it. She was very grateful for the solicitude you expressed in other communications, & bade me tell you so. She also bade me describe to you in detail the hats & scarf she sent you, fearing that some tradesperson might substitute inferior goods in the parcel. I will henceforth strive to reproduce from notes what she said, trusting that you can unriddle whatever my ignorance hath obscured: (Hat I) Large navy blue canton crepe top, straw underfacing, tea-coloured leaves half-way around crown, 2 tea-roses of chiffon in front, hat a little longer over right shoulder than over left, manufactured by Herbel. (Hat II) Large ombre-shaded hat, wood-colour underfacing & side crown, full trimming of flowers from side to side across hat. If head size is too small, place on knee & stretch with both hands. Manufactured by Herstein. (Scarf) Manufactured by Weil—if you like it, you might return two others sent on approval. She also mentions having telegraphed you anent these matters.

Oh, yes! And day before yesterday I wrote my annual birthday tribute to Mr. Hoag, whose 94th birthday falls today. It was rather late, but I had been hurried & lost in extraneous activity—& when I did get to it I hustled! Here is the result—poor no doubt, but the best one could do at short notice, & after having covered the same subject seven times before:

To Mr. Hoag
Upon his 94th Birthday, Feby. 10, 1925

Deep in the purple heaven,
 High by the clouds o'erfleec'd,
Carol the gods at even,
 Praising their elder priest.
Joyous above their altars,
 Chanting in tones of yore,
Writing in crystal psalters,
 "SCRIBA is ninety-four!"

Sprites of the lofty mountain,
 Gnomes of the nether caves,
Nymphs of the limpid fountain
 Where the green alder waves;
Tritons from antique ocean,
 Elves from the torrent steep,
Join in the glad devotion,
 Eager your day to keep!

True is the love they shew you,
 Grateful the hearts they bear,
Conscious of what they owe you—
 You, who have drawn them fair!
Never their debt ignoring,
 Look they for boons anew,

Knowing their loftiest soaring
    Rests with your lyre, & you!

So have they gladly granted
    All that they have to give;
Orpheus' sweet art transplanted,
    Sibyl's long days to live;
Voice that is always golden,
    Born of a soul sublime,
Gentle, serene, & olden,
    Safe from the rust of time.

Long may their kindness leave you
    Here in your native bow'rs,
Here where fond eyes perceive you,
    Here where your songs are ours!
Long may your lips enlighten,
    Genial & happy still,
Scribe whom the years but brighten,
    Scribe of the shining quill!

---

Oh, yes—*& Morton has landed his museum job!!!* We are all ecstatically jubilant, for at one fell swoop it puts the good old boy into just the intellectual, social, & financial niche he should always have occupied! We hope his migration to Paterson won't rob us of his presence at meetings—he will be a regular householder now, I fancy, for Kleiner tells me that his settling down will be preceded by his marriage to the colourless Miss Merritt.[4]

As for the diary—I see I last writ you on the 27th January, completion of the epistle forming the conclusion of the day. On Wednesday the 28th, the weather having abated, L D C did come to town after all; & I had the pleasure of piloting her through the Metropolitan Museum in greater detail than formerly, including a thorough examination of the American Wing. We then dined at the St. Regis, (L D C—veal chop & baked apple, H P L veal chop & charlotte russe) after which I reluctantly saw L D C off at the Grand Central on a Mt. Vernon train of the good old N Y N H & H which made me think of the Bristol & Fall River trains. As I rode home in the subway the old stations filtered through my mind:

        Providence
        East Providence
        Kettle Point
        Silver Spring
        Squantum

Vanity Fair (formerly Hauterieve)
Pomham
Riverside
Bullock's Point
Crescent Park
West Barrington (properly Drownville)
Nayatt
Barrington
Hampton Roads
North Warren
Warren
East Warren (Parker's Mills)
Touisset
Ocean Grove
South Swansea
Brayton Point
Brayton
Fall River
South Warren (Green's Landing)
Bristol Highlands
Poppasquash Road
Franklin St. (old station)
Church St.
State St.
Constitution St. (ferry)

Shortly after my arrival at 169, the Boys began to gather for the meeting, of which I was host. All were present except 'Ittle-Sonny, & Kirk (a copy of whose new professional letterhead I will enclose) aided nobly in purchasing & serving refreshments—pastry & coffee—giving my new blue china & Japanese tinware its *baptême de feu*. (N.B. I washed all the dishes myself!) Discussion was fairly brisk, & rendered quite amusing by the efforts of Wheeler Dryden (Charlie Chaplin's half-brother) to comprehend the theory of philosophick determinism—his principal argumentative *bete noire*. After the meeting, which lasted till about 3 a.m., all hands dispersed & went early to bed. The next day—Thursday the 29th—I went up to Sonny's for lunch & the afternoon, spending much of the time in reading & discussing Synge's "Riders to the Sea". In the evening I returned to 169, where I found Loveman & Kirk assembled in the latter's room. Thence we fared forth to a fascinating curio shop around the corner, where Kirk bought a quaint old cane (which proved too short, & which he later gave young Edward Lazare) & Loveman became enamoured of a bronze Buddha which he later bought. (L D C has seen it) Later we lunched at the Tiffany cafeteria—where we played with the most captivating black-&-white kitten imaginable—after which I returned home to read & write. Friday I was up late, & went to Flatbush to rouse the indolent furniture-mender who had two chairs of mine. (He delivered them the next day.) Later I read, wrote, & was honoured by a call from my upstairs neighbour Kirk.

Saturday (vide enc. announcement) was the meeting of the Blue Pencil Club; & having been amused by the puerile character of the literary assignment—"My Favourite Character in Literature or History & Why"—I perpetrated a bit of comic verse (vide enc.) to cover the occasion. I then went to a new barber's & obtain'd a haircut which was not at all bad, after which I welcom'd Sonny & took him to see Niel, Morrow, & Ladd's bookstall—the best in Brooklyn. Here we revelled the late afternoon away, acquiring many precious volumes—Sonny got a Boccaccio, a 2-volume Dryden, an Arabian Nights, a Horace, & what not, whilst his Grandpa got Clifton Johnson's "What They Say in New England" & Horace E. Scudder's book on Old Boston. I then bought the child a pretty Egyptian idol at the 10-cent-store & put him on his homeward train, after which I returned to 169, read a bit, & started out for Columbia Heights, where I joined Kleiner & Loveman at the latter's scenick eyrie. Thence the trio proceeded to a cafeteria, gorged, & took the subway (B M T) for the B P C meeting in Flatbush beyond Parkside Avenue. It was as dull as usual, & to counteract it our trio returned afterward to Loveman's, where we argued till 2 or so a.m. Then Kleiner & I continued the discussion in a Borough Hall cafeteria, after which I returned home & read. Sunday the 1st I was up late, welcomed Kirk & Loveman, & set out with them for that delightful Italian restaurant three squares away—the Taormina, in Clinton St. Having feasted, we proceeded down town to Times Square, looked about, & settled for a session at the Double-R coffee-house in 44th St., whose nicotined atmosphere is exceeding dear to the aesthetic souls of Kleiner, Loveman, & Kirk. It moved Loveman to a poem, which he wrote on the spot, on a scrap of paper which Kirk lent him:

*Dolore*

Back to the fountain runs the flame,
  Back to the joy returns each grief;
Beauty, unhousell'd, pleads the shame
  That cries our misbelief.

Look! in the silver night & see,
  Once as the wise men saw of yore;
A radiance in the agony
  That wisdom ever bore.

Samuel Loveman[5]

I was not in poetick mood, but out of the smoke & boredom evolved a more world-weary effusion:

Amid the tap-room's reeking air
　　Where smoky clouds the candles choke,
The choicest wit is said to flare,
　　And art to shed its daily cloak.

Here may free souls forget the grind
　　Of busy hour & bustling crowd,
And sparkling brightly mind to mind
　　Display their inmost dreams aloud.

The sober stalls inspiring loom,
　　The temper'd lights a spell diffuse,
Till in the dingy panell'd room
　　Flames up—they say—the deathless Muse.

Each teeming corner echoes strong
　　With merriment of source unplac'd,
As o'er their coffee ling'ring long
　　Loaf cohorts of the vacant-fac'd.

The platitudes of yesterday
　　Between their coughs the mob repeat,
Or sated with the mental play
　　Each lounges listless in his seat.

And so they puff & sip & brood
　　With faces blank or saturnine;
Studies in emptiness & mood,
　　These patterns of a world divine.

Midst them I sit with smoke-try'd eyes,
　　Intent no flash of wit to miss;
Basking 'neath gay Bohemian skies,
　　And grateful for a shrine like this!

Speaking of verse, though—we found a *real* bit by *Dunsany* in a Sunday paper:

## EXPLICIT

In a dream I must have gone,
　　In a dream & sleeping fast,
To a city never known,
　　In a land that cannot last.

Thence these stories I have brought,
For your cities mad with steam,
That a dream from skies unthought
May be mingled with your dream.
                    Edward John Moreton Drax Plunkett,
                    XVIII Baron Dunsany.

After the Double-R we returned to Kirk's room, Loveman leaving at some undetermined hour, & I helping Georgius arrange his books. My labour was well repaid, for with his reckless generosity he insisted on presenting me with no less than 4 choice specimens—"The Story Without a Name", by D'Aurevilly, trans. by Edgar Saltus,[6] "The Line of Love", by James Branch Cabell, "City Block", by Waldo Frank, & "Daedalus", by J. B. S. Haldane—all new books from his stock! We then repaired to a cafeteria, returned & read, & retired.

I was awaked the next day by the arrival of a most unexpected guest— who under divine Pegāna but *C. M. Eddy, Jr., of The City!!* He was here on literary business, interviewing magazine editors & stopping with Houdini up in West 113th St. Let's hope he can soon do something with that extended note! I was really glad to see the poor chap—any breath from home—& showed him my room with considerable pleasure. We then called on Kirk, & with him went out to the Taormina for dinner, later shewing Eddy the illuminated skyline from the "Prospect Terrace" at the foot of Montague St.[7] Leaving Kirk at the subway, Eddy & I started out to explore the colonial mazes of Greenwich Village, when whom shou'd we meet—on the Clark St. train platform—but Samuel Loveman, Esq., nonchalantly bearing in his arms the bronze Buddha which he had purchased at last! Introductions followed, after which the three set out for Greenwich. Eddy had an engagement at Houdini's house at midnight, so we had to hustle a bit; but we managed to include the salient points by brisk walking, bidding Loveman farewell at 11:30, after which I piloted Eddy to Houdini's home via the Bronx subway. I then returned to 169 & read "Lords of the Ghostland", by Edgar Saltus. Meanwhile I had word that S H would arrive on Tuesday, so had sent L D C a card to that effect. When Tuesday dawned, L D C telephoned that she would be in town that noon, staying overnight here, (the room next mine was temporarily vacant) & proceeding to Providence Wednesday afternoon. I met her at the Grand Central, shew'd her Loveman's outfitted room & Buddha, & thence conducted her to 169 Clinton, where we met Kirk just going out & induced him to return. A telephone call now came from S H, asking me to meet her for dinner at the Milan restaurant in West 42nd St., & after an affirmative reply I got Eddy on the wire & arranged for a general party there—L D C, Eddy, Loveman, Kirk, Kleiner, S H, & H P L. Kirk went down to get S L & R K, & L D C & I rested & proceeded to the restaurant—a very attractive

Italian place which Eddy later learnt is a chosen haunt of Houdini & his wife. We all met successfully, & the dinner was delightful. Eddy then went to the Hippodrome to meet Houdini, Kirk, Loveman, & Kleiner went up to Belknap's, & S H, L D C, & I returned to 169 Clinton, where S H made lemon tea with my Sterno in Kirk's room. We then retired, S H rising early for business, whilst L D C & I observed more conservative hours. But at length all did arise, & after an exchange of amenities with Kirk I reluctantly saw L D C off on the new 4:25 train for Providence. Her seat had, through an oversight, been sold in duplicate to another, but a porter promised adjustments, & her postals from Providence indicate a safe journey & arrival. After the parting I proceeded to the Publick Library, where I met S H for dinner at a neighbouring cafeteria. Thence we proceeded to get her reservation at the Pennsylvania Station, & from there would have gone to the meeting of The Boys at Loveman's, but because she was not feeling well we went home instead—buying a copy of the new *Weird Tales* en route. Late at night a note was slipt under our door—it was from Kirk, returning from the meeting & breaking the news of Morton's achievement of the curatorship—I'll enclose it, since it's lying around here. The next day—Thursday the 5th—I was up late, & met S H at the Milan for dinner. Her health was still worse, so after sending some telegrams we came back here—covering the distance from the subway station by taxi. Her eye was now troubling acutely, & she spent the entire night perched on the edge of the bed with the electric heater trained on her face—which seemed to afford a slight relief. I read Edgar Saltus meanwhile—partly in my room & partly in Kirk's—& he very considerately made coffee for us in the morning, after which we departed for the town. Having checkt S H's things at the Penn. Station, I telephoned Dr. Long for the name & address of some good eye & nose specialist whom he could recommend, & he directed me to a friend of his—Dr. James Wilson Cassell of 40 East 41st St—who, upon our calling after a lunch at the Milan, gave considerable temporary relief by extracting a cinder which he found. We now proceeded to the train, where we found that S H's berth had been sold in duplicate, exactly as in the case of L D C's seat on a former occasion! Readjustment was promised, however, & I expect to hear that all ended well. After suitable adieux I now ambled homeward, helped Kirk rearrange his books in a set of shelves he had just made from a packing-box, & retired to rest at 7:30 for a sleep of *exactly 24 hours*—from which I was awaked by a call from Loveman at 7:30 Saturday night. Upon this awakening I spent some time with S L, Kirk, Kleiner, & young Lazare, who were holding high revels in the room above, till finally—after an adjournment to the Tiffany & return—Loveman went home, Kleiner went to bed in Kirk's room, & the rest of us set out for a walk over Brooklyn Bridge. Later Kirk & I accompanied Lazare uptown on the subway, returning in the dawn to my room, where Kirk slept on the couch whilst I did Hoag verses. When, in the afternoon, Kirk & Kleiner awaked & went out for a neighbourhood exploring trip, I wrote Hoag a long letter. Later Loveman came, & all hands went out again, but I stayed in—being monstrous sleepy. At 9:00 I retired, awaking at 8 the next morning to finish the Hoag letter, go to Belknap's for lunch, go to a cinema with the Child, & return to read Edgar Saltus & write a few odds & ends.

Today I was up at 7:00 a.m., began this letter, & received a call from Kirk, who has a guest in the person of a nice young chap named Roland Gibson. News also came from Loveman, who is giving up his expensive room & wants to move in here with our colony at 169![8] I interviewed Mrs. Burns, & she says Richardson's room is about to be vacant—he's married & going housekeeping—so that Loveman can have a fairly nice $8.00 room directly adjoining Kirk if he chooses—it's the room which L D C liked so well when we first lookt the place over on Christmas Eve. S L hasn't fully decided, but I think he'll take it—hooray for the colony! I then went up to Kirk's room, where he, Gibson, & I had lunch. That was 10 minutes ago—now Kirk & Gibson are down here, waiting for me to finish this, so that we may all fare forth to Yonkers & look over the bookstalls there. I may shew them the Van Cortlandt Mansion, too.

Such, then, is which. You'll hear more from me soon, & meanwhile—after digesting it—would you mind sending this epistle along for L D C to read? I dropped her a post card yesterday.

Be good, don't melt in the heat, & accept the paternal regards of

Yr most aff nephew & obt Servt

H P L

## Notes

1. HPL himself did not visit Charleston until 1930.

2. The Westminster Arcade, built in 1828, is an historic shopping mall in downtown Providence, built in the Greek Revival style. It was declared a National Historic Landmark in 1976.

3. H[ezekiah] Anthony Dyer (1872–1943), Providence painter and president of the Providence Art Club.

4. Morton and Merritt did not marry until 1934.

5. The poem was published in *Bacon's Essays* 1, No. 1 (Summer 1927): 8.

6. See Bibliography under Barbey d'Aurevilly.

7. HPL refers to the Brooklyn Promenade, which presents an approximately similar view of a city skyline as Providence's Prospect Terrace.

8. Loveman did not in fact move into the building.

[100]     [ALS] [HPL to LDC]

169 Clinton St.,

Brooklyn, N.Y.,

Feby. 16, 1925

My dearest daughter Lillian:—

All the things arrived, & I cannot sufficiently express my gratitude! Kirk & I are enraptured by the cardiac chocolates, whilst the card & the envelope of enclosures proved to me a source of unending delight. Those pictures of the Duncan mansion (hurrah!) & the old coffee house (alas!) I had already seen & sent to A E P G, but the view of Trinity spire—Newport—was wholly new to me, & infinitely fascinating. I have filed it for permanent preservation. The Corners & Characters, too, were prodigiously welcome.

I have lately acquired some splendid Providence material—a book on the city edited by William Kirk (very distantly related to my neighbour Georgius) & containing contributions by Pres. Faunce, Prof. James Q. Dealey, Prof. Poland, Prof. Wm. MacDonald, Prof. George Grafton Wilson,[1] &c., and that good old standby "Our Police", which I foolishly allowed to slip through my fingers after owning it all my earlier life! I acquired the new copy from honest Eddy, who got it at his uncle's bookshop. It cost $2.00, & is in *perfect* condition—more so than my old copy, since through personal disgust Grandpa had inked out all the references to Alderman Robert E. Smith. Another New England acquisition of mine is the complete works of the Connecticut poet of Colonial times—John Trumbull, author of "McFingal" & "The Progress of Dulness".[2] The edition is a reprint of the 1820 edition, & occurs in a bound volume of *The Colonnade*, which is the organ of the Andiron Club, connected with New York University. Since the works of Trumbull are out of print, the purchase was a striking bargain. I paid only a dollar, & Kleiner is green with envy. Just now I am reading another of my new acquisitions— "The New England Country", by Clifton Johnson, whom you will recall as having edited that book which A E P G gave Grandpa for Christmas 1897 & which I now have—Warren Burton's "District School As It Was".

I had noted the sale of the Arcade, & hope fervently that it will always be cherished reverently as a monument of the solid, elder Providence of the Classick Revival period. Something must be done to check the careless vandalism which—as in the case of the old coffee house—occasionally menaces the most characteristic New England landmarks. I sympathise fully with the recent remarks of H. Anthony Dyer on this subject, & hope that the survey proposed by the Colonial Dames may result in salutary preservative measures. Coincident with such a renaissance of antiquarian interest would be the larger historical museum advocated by Mr. Chapin.[3] As an illustration of what N.Y. is doing toward historical preservation, I enclose two items from the local press. I have seen the Van Pelt place, but not the so-called "Treason House".[4]

And whilst enclosing—here's a new *Tryout* with some random lines of mine, a new poem by Dunsany, & my 1925 tribute to good old Mr. Hoag, who at 94 is just as sprightly a boy as ever![5] It was hard work finding a novel form for this *eighth* performance on the same subject, but at the last moment I devised something, as you will see!

A E P G will shortly forward you some diary material, though my days on the whole are far from eventful. Yesterday I laid in a new stock of Haldeman-Julius books, which are shortly to double their price, & today I am planning a disconcertingly necessary repair siege—the sending of my Morris-Chair to the mender's for the replacement of a wooden brace which has let the bottom sag down. This householding is a fearfully responsible business!

I trust your homeward journey was pleasant, & that you are finding plenty of interesting things to do & read. S H reached Cincinnati safely, & is feeling much better than when here. A E P G seems to be having a great time in Florida—the temperature of which I heartily envy her—& she sent me a most delightfully piquant Valentine—a kittie whose eyes roll quite realistically! Last night, by the way, I wrote some verse involving cats—treating them in a somewhat Baudelairian way in connexion with the Babylonian decay of New York in the future.[6] I'll copy it for you—it was written at the Double-R Coffee-House in 44th St., where Kirk, Loveman, Kleiner & I all tried our hands in the manner of the Queen-Anne wits at Will's & Button's.

But I must desist, for Kirk is due here any minute for a trip out. Let me hear from you when you feel like writing, & meanwhile pray believe me at all times

Yr moſt aff: nephew & obt Servt

H P L

## Notes

1. William H. P. Faunce (1859–1930), president of Brown University (1899–1930); James Quayle Dealey (1861–1937), professor of political and social science at Brown (1895–1928); William Carey Poland (1846–1929), professor of classics and art at Brown (1870–1915), William Macdonald (1863–1938), professor of history at Brown (1901–17); George Grafton Wilson (1863–1951), professor of political and social science at Brown (1891–1910).

2. See Bibliography under *The Colonnade*.

3. Howard Miller Chapin (1887–1940), librarian of the Rhode Island Historical Society (1912–40) and an authority on colonial American history.

4. HPL refers to Van Pelt Manor House (c. 1882–1919) in Brooklyn, and the Joshua Hett Smith House (c. 1770) in West Haverstraw, NY, known as the Treason House because it was where Benedict Arnold met with a British officer, major John André, to plot the surrender of the fort at West Point.

5. The *Tryout* for January 1925 contained HPL's "Solstice." The poem by Dunsany was probably "Explicit," *Saturday Review of Literature* 1, No. 27 (31 January 1925): 489. HPL's birthday poem to Jonathan E. Hoag appeared in the March issue of *Tryout*.

6. "The Cats." The poem remained unpublished in HPL's lifetime.

[101]    [ALS] [HPL to AEPG]

169 Clinton St.,

Brooklyn, N.Y.,

Feby. 26, 1925

My dear Granddaughter Anne:—

I am delinquent in not having sooner acknowledged your appreciated letters & other remembrances. The Valentine is of inimitable quaintness, & I greatly relished the luscious orange full of views! I note also the scenic post cards, & must not forget to thank you for the ever-punctual cheques. Then, too, the piquant Daytona Morning Journal—whose crossword puzzle I duly clipped & presented to Our Curator.[1] Said Curator is working very hard on his new job, & is quite broke pending the receipt of his first quarter's salary. He is having to attend to all the new museum's loans & purchases, & superintend the setting up of the exhibits in an old stable—remodelled—next the Paterson Free Library. The library corporation—which is to run the museum—has purchased this adjacent tract with house & barn from an old fellow of about 85 years, who sold it with the proviso that he be allowed to inhabit the house undisturbed until his death. Thus the museum is preparing to occupy the stable at first . . . . & ghoulishly hoping! Some day in a roseate future they hope to tear down both house & barn & build a tasteful new museum building—of which good old James Ferdinand will be absolute & undisputed czar. It's a great day for him— though it will force him to leave our meetings of The Boys early, since the last Erie R.R. ferry for Paterson connexions leaves the Chambers St. slip at midnight sharp. The ride to Paterson consumes about one hour. At the end of this week Mortonius actually moves out—taking a small room near his work till he can devise more permanent plans, which (as Kleiner predicts) probably include his marriage to Miss Pearl K. Merritt.

Having thus dilated upon the prosperity of others, I am now left the melancholy duty of chronicling the exact reverse in a quarter nearer home. For, despite a marked improvement in health since her last visit here, S H has at last found the hostile & exacting atmosphere of Mabley & Carew's intolerable;[2] finally being virtually forced out of her position by quibbling executives & invidious inferiors. Her last letter to me before returning sheds so much light on the hard conditions preceding her loss of the post, that I think I will enclose it for you & L D C to read. Certainly, she is most emphatically to be commiserated; & I strongly hope she can succeed in establishing early &

permanent business connexions elsewhere. For the residue of this week she has secured a temporary engagement in the hat-designing field, which will help a bit toward tiding over. She is staying here, & managing to follow my example in inhabiting this marvellous room without destroying its perfect daytime adherence to the parlour-study atmosphere. We are, by the way, intensely sorry that you failed to receive the scarf sent from here earlier in the month. Steps will be taken toward tracing it, & I only hope you can get it soon enough to enjoy it in your present tropical setting. That setting I properly envy you—& wish you did not have to leave so early for the frigid boreal realm. Your week in Washington is vastly to be envied, too—though I myself would have chosen Charleston as better expressing the real Southern Colonial life of pre-Revolutionary days. By all means procure & study a good guide book—preferably the Rand-McNally—in advance, for one can see vastly more when one knows what to look for. But don't think of sending the book to me! You will want it as a souvenir of what you've seen—& when I go I shall want mine permanently for the same reason. Our gang plan to take the $5.00 excursion on April 12, as per circular, deciding beforehand on our exact rounds of sightseeing. In this decision Sechrist will aid us, for he knows Washington well, & has written detailedly. For my part—whatever the others do—I shall ignore all time-consuming *interiors* & make the rounds of the city proper in the dead hours betwixt the arrival of the train & the opening of the day's activity. Then I shall take the trolley & spend the bulk of the time amidst the rich colonial reliquiae across the Potomac; notably Alexandria, Va, & Gen. Washington's seat, Mt. Vernon. As I say, we've set April 12 as the date; but if you're going to be there on the 15th—another excursion date— I've a darned good mind to shift my trip to that occasion & try to serve as your guide around the famous region which I [shall, I hope, by that time] know so well [on paper]. Let me know about it—also whether or not you can stop off in N.Y. on your way home & see these quarters at 169 Clinton before some new & unexpected shock destroys them, or before I go stark mad with the uncertainty of things & the inability to continue a quiet programme of solitary nocturnal writing. I am deucedly anxious to shew you that American Wing—& you could see Milligan Place again!

I should like to see the New-Englandish kittie at your place, & trust you will give him my best regards. Last night Morton brought a catnip mouse to the Boys' meeting at Belknap's, & we all watched to see what Felis would do with it. Would that habitual reserve & imperturbability be ruffled? Felis smelled of the object, waved at it with a few graceful paw motions, rolled over once with the prize in his arms, & then calmly dropped it & walked out of the room! But humbler surroundings furnish sprightlier felines, & Kirk & I take a perennial delight in two small tiger-kittens in an Italian restaurant in Greenwich Village. They know us, & we each have one which we habitually hold. Kirk calls his Lucrezia Borgia, & I call mine Giambattista Tintoretto.

Both are playful, & although growing rapidly do not yet amount to much more than a comfortable double-handful.

I hope you will go to see St. Augustine, for that is something which not even New England can boast—a genuine *sixteenth-century* Spanish town with several (so they tell me) of the ancient buildings still standing intact.[3] I'd have to be pretty indolent indeed to forego a spectacle like that—take an old man's advice & don't miss it! I envy your new friend Miss Wheeler her colonial home in Concord—I've been to that town just once, but will never forget the charm of the central square, with the old Wright Tavern (1747) looming up in red paint on one side, & the slate-dotted slope of the ancient burying ground on the other.

About this editorial Chocorua acquaintance in N.Y.—Mrs. Fuller of *The American City*—I fancy you'd better write a letter of introduction if I try to broach the subject of journalistic affiliation.[4] There's probably about one chance in twelve vigintillion that any opening would exist—but one might as well waste time in applying as in doing anything else. Municipal betterment . . . . . applesauce! We have no bananas today! What I'd like to get is a *proof-reading* job—I think I'll ask Mrs. Miniter about those Cambridge publishers where she reads proof at odd times.

Of course they can't let niggers use the beach at a Southern resort—can you imagine sensitive persons bathing near a pack of greasy chimpanzees? The only thing that makes life endurable where blacks abound is the Jim Crow principle, & I wish they'd apply it in N.Y. both to niggers & to the more Asiatic types of puffy, rat-faced Jew. Either stow 'em out of sight or kill 'em off— anything so that a white man may walk the streets without shuddering & nausea!

As to enclosures—I can't keep everything, so you might send the Wroth article to L D C & let her dispose of it as her judgment dictates—likewise this letter. My own enclosures this time are cursory & informal, & may with one exception be consigned to the waste basket. That one exception is The Eyrie from the coming *Weird Tales* with mention of my work, which I wish you'd forward to L D C.[5] Oh, yes—& I sent you yesterday under separate cover a convenient little guide to the Metrop. Museum, which you can study at your leisure in preparation for your next sight of it. Very useful, I think, in finding out just what one wants to see.

I haven't seen the cinema "America", since I was warned in advance how Griffith had warped & distorted the facts of history in an effort to pander to the anti-British rabble. The same is true, I am told, of the similar film "Janice Meredith". Tonight S H & I will probably see "The Thief of Bagdad",[6] she for the first time & I for the second, since it is now at a local Brooklyn house with 25¢ admission. Glad you are to hear MacCormack—I like his voice.[7] Kirk, Leeds, & Loveman go to many classical concerts, but I'm too musically lowbrow to appreciate that sort of thing. Glad young Lawton is succeeding on the boards. Our Thespian friend Wheeler Dryden has just been given charge of the rehearsals of a Baltimore company of "White Cargo", the famous plagiarised play.[8] Morton & Leeds know the authoress of the book from which that play was stolen.

General events move much as usual—I'm about to write a diary letter to L D C, beginning where I left off to you Feby. 10, & will ask her to see that you get it after her. Now I must hustle & meet S H at 6.00 in front of the Tiffany Cafeteria for dinner. More anon.

Meanwhile & always I subscribe myself

  Yr aff nephew & obt Servt

    H P L

## Notes

1. James F. Morton was a devotee of crossword puzzles.

2. Mabley & Carew's was a department store in Cincinnati where Sonia had been working since the beginning of the year. She later found a position at Halle's, then the leading department store in Cleveland.

3. HPL first visited St. Augustine, FL, in 1931.

4. HPL apparently refers to the *American City* (1909–75), a monthly journal published in New York. Mrs. Fuller is unidentified.

5. HPL apparently refers either to the March 1925 issue, which contains a brief letter to the editor (by H. Warner Munn, with whom HPL was not acquainted at the time) on HPL, or the April 1925 issue, which contains letters by H. P. Tead and Howard Anderson on HPL. The magazine regularly appeared about a month before its cover date. See *A Weird Writer in Our Midst: Early Criticism of H. P. Lovecraft*, ed. S. T. Joshi (New York: Hippocampus Press, 2010), 65.

6. *America* (United Artists, 1924), directed by D. W. Griffith; starring Neil Hamilton, Everille Anderson, and Carol Dempster. Based on the novel by Robert W. Chambers (who wrote the screenplay). *Janice Meredith* (MGM, 1924), directed by E. Mason Hopper; starring Marion Davies, Harrison Ford, and Macklyn Arbuckle. Based on the novel by Paul Leicester Ford. *The Thief of Bagdad* (Douglas Fairbanks Pictures, 1924), directed by Raoul Walsh; starring Douglas Fairbanks, Snitz Edwards, and Charles Belcher. The poet George Sterling wrote some of the "captions" (i.e., scene descriptions).

7. John MacCormack (1884–1945), celebrated Irish tenor.

8. Leon Gordon (1894–1960), *White Cargo* (1923), based on the novel *Hell's Playground* (1912) by Ida Vera Simonton (1870–1931).

[102] [ALS] [HPL to LDC]

       169 Clinton St.,

        Brooklyn, N.Y.,

         April 2, 1925

My dear Daughter:—

    Pardon the ink—this rusty stuff is what I had to fill

my pen with when it ran dry up at Sonny's Tuesday. Well—Kirk is back here without having made his visit, summoned by the exigencies of his business & (ah, how my instep throbs in sympathy!!) harassed by a pair of torturesome new shoes which he purchased just before starting. His feet are covered with blisters—& he has bought another pair now! Shoes, I mean, not feet! Doubtless he wishes he could do the latter also. As for my new shoes—I sometimes try to wear them on state occasions, & mean to have them stretched again. Alas, for the universal suffering in this life of the human sole! I am tremendously sorry that you were incommoded by Kirk's shifting plans, & that you made the trip downtown in vain. He also is contrite upon hearing of it. Of Providence he saw only the 1st Baptist Steeple & the Market House—then on to Boston; where, betwixt business deals, he managed to see such things as the Old State House, Old South Church, Beacon Hill, & the like. He thinks he has successfully accomplished the object of his visit, & in Boston picked up professional "tips" which sent him successively to Springfield, Hartford, & New Haven—from which latter place he telegraphed his regrets to the meeting of The Boys assembled here. The ride from Hartford to New Haven was accomplisht by omnibus, during which trip he beheld many ancient colonial towns—a sight vastly tantalising to me, who have never beheld the interior of Connecticut. He arriv'd here about 3 p.m., & has since been engag'd in setting his room to rights, aided by the elder Burns boy.

Yes—I received all the bundles. I might like a glance at the Maine views again, but you may keep the *Weird Tales* material. It will save your purchasing the current number, unless you wish also to see Sonny's new story, "Men Who Walk Upon the Air".[1] By the way—would you care for a January number with "The Festival"? I have some extras which Wright sent me free.

One of the "Corners & Characters" you sent I had not seen before, though I had the paper each day. This leads me to think that once in a while it is left out of the early edition which out-of-towners get, but printed in the final. I wish I could keep posted—there is nothing in my yesterday's copy, though I feel uncomfortably certain that there ought to be! As to the J. Carroll Mansfield "High Lights of History"[2]—in the main it is pretty good, though necessarily incomplete & not always enlightening as to the inmost facts. It gives more information than misinformation, & for that one may be grateful. I follow it each day—more for amusement than anything else. I must get that December *Atlantic*—it must be a delightful issue! After all, I guess it's about the best of the monthlies—I'd take it if I weren't broke.

About Staples' Annals—really, you ought not to go to the expense of financing my copy! Kirk will try to get a reduction on the one he saw in a Brooklyn shop, & I really think it ought to be added to my expense account. I only wish that Dr Clark's index to it were published![3]

As to ancient Elizabethtown—I really wish you could see it in the summer at its best. I shall go there frequently, & look up many of the places in its suburbs—Liberty Hall, Wheatsheaf Tavern, &c.—which lack of time has hitherto kept me from inspecting. I may explore other New Jersey towns on walking trips when I get hold of the "New York Walk Book"—there are many near the coast, & nearly all are colonial.

Yes—I think Kirk might appreciate a miniature kittie—but I shan't let go of any of mine till I have duplicates safely in hand!! Don't go to the expense if they are costly—as Tilden & Thurber stuff generally is. During his trip G K saw many fine kittens, especially a tiny black & white pair in New Haven.

No—I wouldn't mind it a bit if I could participate in that Roosevelt Himalayan jaunt![4] As for H.R.H. & his threatened embonpoint—he ought to take lessons in reducing from his Grandpa Theobald! Diet & walking are the stuff—which reminds me that tonight I've begun my home dining programme, having spent *30¢* for a lot of food which ought to last about *3* meals:

| | | |
|---|---|---|
| 1 loaf bread———————— 0.06 | | |
| 1 medium can beans———— 0.14 | | I obtained this at the |
| ½ lb cheese————————0.10 | | James Butler chain |
| ———————————————— | | stores—like our |
| Total———————— 0.30 | | Mayflowers. |

The beans I'll heat on the sterno,[5] keeping the residue in a cup covered with a saucer. Yes—I'm getting to be a highly efficient housekeeper, & you can bet that any steep bills won't be in the direction of the larder! The rent & laundry are the large items—& a piratical concern wants to charge 35¢ each for taking in my shirt neckbands to #15! I'm letting 'em do one, but believe I'll try to see what I can do myself in that line!

Too bad you had that eye trouble—I'm constantly getting things in my eyes, but haven't yet required medical assistance. Is Capron's room changed since I saw it in May 1923? The only trouble is that the room itself— woodwork, proportions, &c.—is thoroughly & painfully Victorian. If I were going in systematically for colonial furniture, I'd first get a house of the right cast & decoration—low ceilings, small-paned windows, & appropriate mouldings, mantels, & panelling. My next decorative job will be Kirk's room again, since the arrival of his books & the prospective purchase of a bookcase will change the wall & floor scheme considerably.

As to trips—as I told A E P G, I couldn't bear to see Providence again till I can be there for ever. When I do get home, I shall hesitate about going even to Pawtucket or East Providence, whilst the thought of crossing the line into Massachusetts at Hunt's Mills will fill me with positive horror! But a temporary glimpse would be like that of a distrest mariner swept by a storm within sight of his own harbour, then washed away again into the illimitable blackness of an alien sea.

As for Washington—I don't believe I'll need any additional appropriation. Of course I never thought of staying over more than the one day, & even that much is made cheaper by the kindly offer of Mrs. Renshaw to take us to all the colonial sights in her Ford. Sechrist will meet us at the station, then when the hour gets more civilised we will proceed to Mrs. R's & start on an intelligently guided tour not only of urban Washington but of Georgetown, Alexandria, Arlington, &c. &c. &c. as well. This ought to save vast sums in carfare, & we all appreciate Mrs R's courtesy exceedingly.

Thanks for all the cuttings. Yes—I'll never call the band anything but Reeves' American! I wonder if it still exists? Fairman's Band ought to get the name & charter, for it is now the real band of the city, playing at the Park Concerts, &c.

And thanks prodigiously for that old courtyard scene! A E P G had sent one, but the duplicate is no less welcome, since I want a lending copy. It provokes me to reflect that I never saw this court—in all the thousands of times I have passed up & down College Hill! Well—such is life! It's a beastly shame the painting is hopeless—but here's to luck with the survivor!

And now for the diary, which ended—I think—(to A E P G) just as I was going up to Sonny's Tuesday noon. [Hooray—end of this impossible ink!] I duly went, had an excellent lunch, heard a fine new story & prose-poem of his, & later accompanied him & his mamma to the cinema at 95th St., where we saw that much discussed German film, "The Last Laugh".[6] It is really a very powerful & pathetic short story, presented in a highly artistic & semi-impressionistic fashion, of a poor old porter as age breaks him down to the level of a basement lavatory-cleaner in an hotel. The irony is strong but subtle, & the whole well deserving of the critical panegyrick it hath receiv'd. After the show I returned home, read, & retired; rising late the next day & cleaning my room in preparation for the Boys' meeting. Mortonius was the first to arrive, then Kleiner & Loveman together, & finally Leeds. Sonny couldn't come—but Kirk sent a telegram of regret from New Haven. The meeting was brisk, but Morton had to leave early for the last Paterson train— Loveman departing with him. Next Kleiner went—after which Leeds & I went upstairs to look over Kirk's books & pictures. Leeds left at 3 a.m., & I joined him in coffee & apricot pie at Johnson's. Then home—read—rest—& another day. Today has been a writing day—punctuated by reading. Kirk came about 3 p.m., & somewhat later I went out shopping—laundry—new bulb for my desk lamp—food—& soon returned. And here I am still. Kirk is upstairs working at his room, & later we expect a call from Loveman. I am still plugging away at my loan reading—which is complicated by a further loan from Morton—a volume of the Arabian Nights with a tale I'd never read. Well—this brings things up to the present!! Thanks in advance for the printed matter coming, & for the letter at hand. Write when convenience dictates, & accept my apologies for rousing you to receive a guest who didn't shew up!

With all those good wishes appropriate to the season,
believe me ever
Yr moſt aff nephew & obt Servt
H P L

[From envelope, In RHB's handwriting:][7] P.S. Kirk's just gone out to sell some of his newly-purchased books. I'm writing Sechrist final details of the Washington trip.

## Notes

1. *WT*, May 1925.

2 "High Lights of History" was a syndicated comic strip (1926–1942) by J. Carroll Mansfield (1896–1957). Mansfield also wrote five Big-Little Books in the High Lights of History Series (1933–34).

3. The Rhode Island Historical Society holds Franklin Chase Clark's "Index to Staples' Annals of Providence" (1904).

4. HPL refers to the James Simpson–Roosevelt Asiatic Expedition of 1925, organized by Theodore Roosevelt's sons, Kermit and Theodore Roosevelt Jr., proceeding from India over the Himalayas into China.

5. A sterno is a can containing a fuel made from denatured and jellied alcohol, used as a primitive heating device.

6. *The Last Laugh* (*Der letzte Mann*) (Universum Film [Germany], 1924), directed by F. W. Murnau; starring Emil Jannings, Maly Delschaft, and Max Hiller.

7. The note has been written at the head of the letter. The envelope is nonextant.

[103]    [ALS] [HPL to LDC]

454 Angell St.,
Providence, R.I.,
April 11, 1925.

My dear daughter Lillian:—

Abundant thanks for the letter, & for two shipments of printed matter—all thoroughly appreciated. My portfolios are growing, & I mean soon to finish the classification in those filing envelopes we purchased at Elizabethtown. The Spanish Mission picture you enclosed is exceedingly welcome—I have very few views of this type of colonial architecture—for the Pacific-Coast Spanish differed considerably from the Florida Spanish whose acquaintance I have made through a set of St. Augustine cards most considerately procured by A E P G.

As for my drawing—I'm certainly glad you thought those random sketches worth looking at! I wish I could really draw—indeed, some day I may get an elementary book on the subject & see if I can swallow one or two systematic principles. What a delight it must be to be able to crystallise, as

Laswell does, one's exact mood & impression on confronting an ancient farmhouse or Georgian street vista. I am just now highly enthusiastic over an illustrator of the nineties—one Edmund Garrett—who specialised in New England antiquarianism & wrote at least two books around his drawings of old houses & village scenes. I have his "Puritan Coast", & also a book about "Three New England Heroines" (with one article by Louise Imogen Guiney) with his illustrations; & am now on the lookout for his "Pilgrim Country."[1] He was ideally equipped—he could capture the very essence of the quaint from every angle, presenting it in a dual form which could not fail of general comprehension & appeal . . . . . & yet his prose is at times discouragingly flat & tame! So my farm landscape accidentally reproduced a Journal office display? Great minds, etc.—Rhode-Island scenery is pretty well engraven upon the souls of Rhode-Island's sons! But I'm flattered to hear that you find the attempts worth keeping—that's more than I find any of my products in this field! And I'm glad you like the silhouette—which certainly is clever for the work of a fat buck nigger![2] Yes—I had an idea that silhouettes were coming back. They certainly have a fine glamour of tradition, & one can hardly picture an early 19th century room without several of them, mostly in oval frames. Better wait till you get several—one of yourself, one of A E P G, one of W V P from his last portrait, &c—& then have them all framed. Before long, I fancy, there will be plenty of opportunities for getting them in Providence. As to the *whatnot*—yes—there was one in the corner of this room— but I have no intention of asking for it again! I am not enthusiastic about *Victorian* revivals, however much I welcome those of the Georgian period. Whatnots, shell-covered boxes, wax flowers, French roofs, heavy black-walnut, & Dundreary whiskers are among the semi-antiques which stand no chance of inclusion in my aesthetic scheme.

Under separate cover I am sending the issue of *Weird Tales* of which I have so many duplicates. I wish they'd send me some with "Randolph Carter" & "Erich Zann"—but anyway, you have the latter in the form of those detached leaves previously enclosed. Maybe I'll get some Randolph Carters soon—I recall that the Festivals arrived rather late.

As to my dietary programme—bosh! I *am* eating enough! Just you take a medium-sized loaf of bread, cut it in four equal parts, & add to each of these ¼ can (medium) Heinz beans & a goodly chunk of cheese. If the result isn't a full-sized, healthy day's quota of fodder for an Old Gentleman, I'll resign from the League of Nations' dietary committee!! It only costs 8¢—but don't let that prejudice you! It's good sound food, & many vigorous Chinamen live on vastly less. Of course, from time to time I'll vary the "meat course" by getting something instead of beans—canned spaghetti, beef stew, corned beef, &c. &c. &c.—& once in a while I'll add a dessert of cookies or some such thing. Fruit, also, is conceivable. Likewise, I shall probably get a restaurant meal once or twice a week as the occasion dictates—at Johnson's or the Automat—which may cost 25¢ or so. It would cost more to get a bread box from storage than to buy another—so I did the latter, obtaining for 75¢ a fine square white-enamell'd box with hinged lid & clasp. I keep it on the shelf of the alcove, out of reach of rodent marauders. For the latter I guess I'll keep on using the five-cent flat kind which Kirk recommended, since I can throw them away without removing the corpus delicti, a thing I should hate to do with a costlier bit of mechanism. I'm just now gunning for prowler #2, whom I heard rustling about last night.

Leeds often gives me copies of *The Writer's Digest*, & I mean to consult it often when I get the decks cleared & my main body of writing started. Future issues, too, will be welcome; & I thank you exceedingly for the helpful contribution—& extra—which I shall endeavour to put to the wisest possible use. Oh, yes—I've had my shoes stretched again, but haven't dared put them on since I got them back. Let me think for a while that they're all right—& meanwhile I shall get the old ones blacked up for the Washington trip. They'll have to be blacked pretty well to do justice to the gorgeous shirt outfits which A E P G has just sent! And speaking of shirts—I certainly will send any which need attention, although the laundry I patronise does free mending of minor breakdowns—saving you a little bother. With stockings I've been adopting a peculiar policy—wearing those which are almost ready to throw away, with hopeless gaps in the foot, & throwing them away when they are gone, thus avoiding laundry bills. I haven't had a sock laundered since I've been here—though soon I suppose I'll have run through my rag-bag & be launched on the new Christmas socks S H gave me.

S H, by the way, returned to her Saratoga retreat this noon. She is not certain just how long she will stay, having several other positions in mind; but meanwhile she is quite contented because of the refined, kindly, & scholarly atmosphere in which she finds herself—to say nothing of the intelligence & amiability of the child under her governance. She cannot, of course, contribute her originally agreed quota to the rent; but she tries to help as she can— having recently pieced out in instalments of $2.00 & $5.00 when reckoning was close.

Just at this point your *second* welcome letter has arrived. Again thanks & appreciation! Since beginning this epistle I've been out—seeing S H off on the train at the Grand Central—& tried my newly stretched shoes. Alackaday! They hurt just as before, whenever I take a step. It seems to be not because they are too *small*—in fact, they are really very *loose*—but because they are not sufficiently *flexible*. When my feet are still, they do not pain at all; but when I walk, the foot bends—*and the shoe apparently refuses to bend in unison*. Kirk suggests that I do what soldiers do with their stiff & ill-fitting army boots—coat them with neat's foot oil, soak them in water for 24 hours, & then wear them continuously for a day without previous drying. Maybe I'll try it—but what I suppose I'll have to do is to save them for occasions when I won't be walking much—such as meetings of The Boys, calls on Sonny, &c—using what is left of my old shoes for my expeditions. And when they absolutely fall off me— then may Heaven provide a path for a poor old man!! I've just taken them off & am looking at them—alas for that beauty which is only skin—i.e., leath- er—deep! They are among the *handsomest* shoes I have ever had . . . . *but!!* Now I'll get my good old Regal remnants nicely blacked up when I go out at six to meet the Boys & buy my ticket for Washington. Ouch! My feet still smart reminiscently!

Returning to yours of yesterday—bless my soul, but you-all mustn't be frightened at Grandpa's dietary programme!! Hang it all, but I *do* eat enough! All one really needs for a meal is some highly nutritious base, containing all the various food elements—proteids, vitamines, carbohydrates, &c.—in their proper balance—plus some tasty auxiliary to make it palatable—though of course it is all the better if the auxiliary can itself be of food value. In my case, the auxiliary *does* happen to be highly nourishing—being usually either baked beans or cheese or both. And incidentally—I often *do* get cocoa or chocolate instead of coffee when the gang tank up at their numerous one-arm filling stations. Enough is as good as a feast, & I certainly get enough—enough to feed a normal frame, but not such a gross excess as to build an additional burden of useless adipose tissue which is itself a debilitating drag & consumer of valuable energy. Let me assure you that I feel twice as well as when I was weighing in the vicinity of 200! As to feeding up before my trip—Great God! if you could see the engulfing plethora of needless nutriment which S H has been stuffing down me during her sojourn here!! Twice a day to—& be- yond—my capacity; pressed beef, sliced ham, bread, American & Swiss cheese, cake, lemonade, buns, cup puddings, (of her own manufacture—she brought along eight, in one of those utensils of connected cups ⟨▨▨▨▨⟩) &c. &c. &c.—indeed, I'll be shot if I don't wonder how in Pegāna's name I can get on my new 15 collars any more! Tonight I'm expected to get some spa- ghetti with the gang at the Downing St. Italian restaurant, (in Greenwich- Village—the place they have the playful tiger-kittens) but I vow, I've not a cubic millimetre of additional ventral space to spare! And in Washington I suppose I'll have to dine in style at some palatial hot-dawg lunch counter— Kirk is a fearful person for forcing one to eat, & paying for it himself if the victim refuses to purchase the nourishment voluntarily. I have, by the way, extended your regards & regrets to Kirk; & assured him that his disarranged schedule did not seriously incommode you. He reciprocates your hope of a future meeting, & trusts to be able eventually to meet A E P G.

As to a nap—I've done considerable resting this afternoon, & expect to be in fine shape for the trip. I meet the Boys at six for dinner, & later I shall return home, bathe, dress in my new finery, & prepare to set out for the con- quest of Washington. By the way—the mouse has just eaten the cheese from my trap without getting caught!

*FINAL INSTALMENT—10 P.M.*

As to cheques—I've written A E P G something anent the cashing question—more anon. Just now all is bustle—in anticipation of the Southerly hegira. Only Kirk & I can go, but we certainly propose to make a trip of it! And now—if I have time—for the diary; last brought up to Monday the 6th in a letter to A E P G.

After writing that letter I went out with Kirk to the Cairo Gardens, a coffee-house in the Arabian district near us. We had hoped to find exotic colour, but the reality was pretty cheap—fat musicians strumming Oriental chords on peculiar lutes in a tapestried alcove, but beyond that nothing but tables & chairs. Later G K treated me to some ice cream in a place across the street, after which we returned & dispersed. I did some writing, & remained up all night. The next day—Tuesday the 7th—I received word of S H's prospective advent on the following afternoon, did some writing, & later went out with Kirk to meet Loveman for dinner at the 14th St Automat, after which we all went up to O'Malley's bookstall in Columbus Ave. via elevated. Here we loafed the evening away, stopping later at a cafeteria & proceeding back to 169. S L left early, & somewhat later I excused myself from Kirk's room to descend & study my Washington guidebooks. A E P G will shew you the itinerary I evolved as the result of my study. Then I retired. Wednesday I was up late, went down to meet S H, & with her returned to Brooklyn—purchasing groceries at the shop under the Taormina & dining at home. I omitted the Boys' meeting, & instead washed dishes, read, & retired. Thursday I was up early, wrote Sechrist final Washington notes, met S H in the afternoon at the Grand Central, got my stretched shoes, & returned to Brooklyn, where we saw the cinema of "Quo Vadis" at the Strand.[3] We then purchased more groceries at bakeshop & delicatessen & proceeded home, taking dinner & receiving a short call from Loveman. Then we read & retired. Friday I was up early, wrote letters, & met S H in the subway during the afternoon, helping her get home a hat box which she had been storing with Mrs. Moran. Again we visited the grocer's, (sinful extravagance!) & again we indulged in a home meal of exquisite calibre. Later Loveman & [*sic*] called again, & after S H retired I went up to Kirk's room, where Kleiner, Loveman, & our host were assembled. After a while we all went out to the Scotch Bakery; where, after Loveman left for home, Kirk, Kleiner, & I lingered to talk about Washington. When the place closed we dispersed & went home—I to lose myself in dreams of southern colonial villages & plantations. Saturday—today—I was up early, ate a breakfast on which S H insisted, & after a period of writing saw her off for Saratoga in the 1:00 train. Pity she couldn't get to Washington! I then returned & wrote some more, & at six was down in Union Square to meet the gang for dinner. We duly met, strolled along toward the heart of Greenwich, stopped in a tropical animal store & shook hands with some inimitably droll monkeys, examined the reclaimed colonial houses in Minetta-Street, & finally reached our Downing-St. destination—where the spaghetti was superb & the kittens . . . . quite beyond words! Again the two little rascals slept & fought in their Grandpa Theobald's lap. We then returned together to 169, where Georgius & I bathed in our respective tubs, dressed in our respective outfits of least ragged clothes, & are now awaiting the approach of leaving-time. My gay Easter outfit has quite stunned the gang—I fear Kirk will never be the same again!! The four of us—Kleiner, Loveman, Kirk, & I—will sally forth together, stopping somewhere for a cup of coffee—& for me to get my old shoes professionally shined. Then the Pennsylvania Station—tickets—farewells—& Kleiner & Loveman will wave tear-stain'd handkerchiefs after the tail-lights of the coach that bears Kirk & me away. I shall probably wear my light overcoat, checking it at the Union Station in Washington, where I shall also check the book which is to beguile my hours of idleness—"Moby Dick; or, the White Whale", by Herman Melville.

And so it goes. Hooray for the early cherry-blossoms of the sunny south, & the wakening vines that entwine ancient Virginia Plantation-houses! The only devilish thing about it is the beastly short time—I expect a world of observation & antiquarian experience, yet have made an engagement for tomorrow night in this very room—with Kleiner & Loveman, who are anxious to hear at the earliest moment the tale I will have to tell.

Sechrist will meet the train in Washington; & although Mrs. Renshaw finds that she can't help us with her motor, we have calculated some very comfortable & expedient ways of getting around.

And now I must close, seal this epistle, & begin hustling up those boys— or we'll miss our train yet! You'll hear from me by card ere long—expect a fair abundance of Washington & Virginia postmarks. The night is clear, & a fair day is promised for the morrow. All's well, & sing hey for the open road!

Those 25-year-ago cuttings were very interesting. I enclose a couple of clipped poems which appealed especially to me—please return them.

More anon—thanks for innumerable kindnesses—& pray accept the sincerest consideration of

Yr aff: nephew & obt Servt

H P L

P.S. Yes—I've asked Kirk to get the Staples' Annals.

P.P.S. Hope you & A E P G recd. the Easter remembrances S H & I sent. That candy comes from the woman in whose household S H is.

[P.P.P.S.] And now *another* dollar besides that two!! *Thanks!* but don't be reckless!

## Notes

1. Garrett's book is actually titled *The Pilgrim Shore*. See Bibliography under Harriet Elizabeth (Prescott) Spofford regarding the three heroines.

2. HPL's silhouette was cut by E. J. Perry (1879?–?), a popular silhouettist in the early 20th century. His silhouette of HPL is depicted on the HPL memorial plaque outside the John Hay Library in Providence. See W. O. Thompson, "A Negro Silhouette Artist," *Voice of the Negro* (May 1905): 343–45.

3. *Quo Vadis?* (Unione Cinematografia Italiana, 1924), directed by Gabriele D'Annunzio and Georg Jacoby; starring Emil Jannings, Elena Sangro, and Rina De Liguoro. Based on the novel by Henryk Sienkiewicz.

[104]    [TL] [HPL to LDC]

169 Clinton St., Brooklyn, N.Y.,

April 21, 1925.

My dear Daughter:—

Being at last possess'd of a spare moment, I take my pen in hand to acquaint you with the particulars of my late delightful visit to the Federal City of Washington, and the adjacent parts of Virginia. Tho' my time of observation was short, I endeavour'd to employ it to the best advantage; so that I feel certain of having procur'd a very fair notion of the antient region I travers'd. The eve of my departure was markt with exceeding great bustle; Messrs. Kleiner and Loveman supping with the departing travellers—George Kirk, Esq., and my self—at the Italian ordinary in Downing-Street, and later accompanying us not only home, where we completed our final preparations, but to the station as well; bidding us adieu at midnight as we stood in line outside the gate, awaiting the readiness of the coach.

Being admitted to our seats, we found the company less promiscuous than the publick nature of the vehicle had led us to expect; and finding a pleasing bench on the left-hand side, we proceeded to make ourselves comfortable—my companion insisting that I take the seat next the window, since the route was new to me, whilst he had been over it before. I had with me the book "Moby Dick" to read in the hours before dawn, and Georgius had provided a plenitude of newspapers and literary reviews, which he very graciously shar'd with me. At a quarter to one the coach pull'd out; soon pausing at Manhattan-Transfer, in New-Jersey, to change horses, and thereafter passing in rapid succession the tall roofs of Newark, and the graceful spires of venerable Elizabethtown. In time New-Brunswick hove in sight, and before long we cross'd the Delaware at Trenton; where on Christmas Eve, 1776, during the late rebellious annoyances, Genl. Washington, crossing in the opposite direction with the aid of Genl. Glover and his Marblehead fishermen, fell upon the revelling Hessian camp under Col. Rall and atchiev'd one of his most notable victories. Once in Pennsylvania, we were not long in attaining my favourite town of Philadelphia, thro' whose northern and western parts we pass'd; and later on I observ'd the modest gables of Chester, whose archaick town-house (1724) I visited last November. We now cross'd into the Province of Delaware, where I had never before been, and were soon in the midst of Wilmington, its principal settlement, which stands near the place where the original Swedish colonists in 1638 built their Fort Christina, suffering conquest in 1654 by the Dutch from New-Amsterdam under Petrus Stuyvesant, who in turn bowed to His Britannick Majesty's forces in 1665. The region was administer'd till 1681 by the Duke of York, being then sold to William Penn, Esq., who made it part of Pennsylvania (tho' allowing it a separate legislature) till 1716, when its inhabitants proclaim'd it a separate state.

Leaving Wilmington behind, we were soon in another province as new to me as Delaware—the venerable state of Maryland, which from a small settlement of Popish gentlemen and their dependents, soon grew to be a colony of great importance. Our progress was here markt by the appearance of placid Chesapeake Bay on our left, and by a flattish topography characteristick of the immediate region, which puts it much below New-England in scenick value. The greying east shew'd us much more detail than we had been able to discern by the brilliant tho' waning moon, and it was in full light that we beheld the colonial cottages of Havre-de-Grace, a sleepy village at the mouth of the Susquehanna. From here on our course lay thro' well-till'd fields and past quiet tho' scarcely prosperous or beautiful villages; with delightful glimpses of the bay toward the east. It was over the bay and the green lowlands beyond that the sun finally rose, glowing clear and red over the drowsy landskips that led up to Baltimore. Of Baltimore itself—founded in 1729 and doubtless possessing many engrossing antiquities—we saw but little; since the route thro' most of it lay in a pair of tunnels, the space between which holds the station. What I did behold was quite promising—rows of red brick houses with marble steps and window lintels—and I hope some day to indulge in further exploration of the place. At present, however, we hurry'd on; penetrating a country of no great attractiveness and studying our guidebooks of Washington, to keep fresh in our minds the desired sights of a goal so swiftly drewing [*sic*] near. The actual arrival was abrupt and undramatick. Quite of a sudden, and whilst we were still in a region so fresh and countrified as to suggest no sign of a large town, & guard call'd out "Washington!", and everyone seized garments to prepare for alighting. No buildings of great size or frequency were visible, and I had quite begun to doubt the word of the postilion when Georgius sustain'd his contention by pointing out a misty skyward obelisk in the dim distance, which I cou'd not but recognise from pictures as the fam'd Washington Monument. Another second, and the coach was still, safe within the commodious train-shed. Gathering together our belongings, we stept down and walkt toward the more substantial bulk of the station proper—within whose gates, debonair in new grey suit and broad-brimm'd Southerner's hat, our faithful reception committee, Edward Lloyd Sechrist, Esq., cou'd be descry'd peering anxiously and twirling a polisht walking-stick of some vein'd exotick wood of his beloved South Sea Isles. Greetings were brief, and in a moment we were within the noble and impressive waiting-room of the great station—a famous domed and pillar'd triumph of purest Roman design, modell'd from the Baths of Diocletian, as the interior of New-York's Pennsylvania Station was modell'd from the Baths of Caracalla. Here plans were made for the immediate procuring of stamps, cards, and breakfast; after which we were to walk rapidly among the sights betwixt the Capitol and the Monument, meeting Mrs. Renshaw and her car at 9 o'clock at the latter point—since she had, despite the guests who previously imperill'd the plan, decided to act as chief guide after all; leaving the rival responsibilities to her try'd-and-true companion Miss Crist, who can always be rely'd upon to entertain with tact, competence, and urbane charm. These facts being communicated by Sechrist, we were led forth from the station thro' vaulted portals design'd from the triumphal arches of Rome, and set face to face at last with the city of so many lofty memories and traditions.

Washington, decided upon in 1790, survey'd in 1791, and built from 1792 onward, in accordance with the carefully predetermin'd plan of the French military designer Major Pierre L'Enfant, ought not to arouse any extravagant expectations if the reports of early observers are to be credited. Set for the most part on swampy bottom lands betwixt the Anacostia and Potomac Rivers, scarce rais'd at all above sea-level, and compleatly dominated by the plateau region on which its suburbs are situate; it was in 1800, when the government first mov'd into the few and incongruously large classick white buildings sparsely scatter'd over an almost impassable marsh, jocosely alluded to as "a backwoods settlement in the wilderness." Thomas Moore the poet, who visited there in 1804, was very outspoken in his ridicule; thus describing the town in his Epistle to Thomas Hume, M.D.:

> "In fancy now, beneath the twilight gloom,
>     Come, let me lead thee o'er this modern Rome!
>     Where tribunes rule, where dusky Davi bow,
>     And what was Goose-Creek once is Tiber now!
>     This fam'd metropolis, where fancy sees
>     Squares in morasses, obelisks in trees;
>     Which trav'ling fools and gazeteers adorn
>     With shrines unbuilt, and heroes yet unborn,
>     Tho' naught but wood and ———— they see,
>     Where streets should run, and sages ought to be!"[1]

In a prose note he speaks of the decrepitude of the hotel, the half-neglected state of the White House under Pres. Jefferson's occupancy, and of the private buildings—which, he says, "exhibit the same characteristick display of arrogant speculation and premature ruin." Less severe in intent, but equally potent as a witness to the still unsettled character of the town, is the slightly earlier traveller Weld, who pointedly remarks in his journal: "To be under the necessity of going through a deep wood for one or two miles, perhaps, in order to see a next-door neighbour, and in the same city, is a curious, and I believe a novel circumstance."[2] As late as 1839—when my good friend Mr. Hoag was a lusty and intelligent lad of eight—Washington was described as a "large straggling village reared in a drained swamp", and even more recent chroniclers have had their fling. All this I recall'd, but I also recall'd the other side—the deep love of Washington exhibited by the New-England Henry Adams in his "Education", and the much earlier praise contained in my old copy of Morse's Geography, (1814) which reads in this wise:

> "Washington city appears to contain some important improvements upon that of the best planned cities of the world; combining, in a remarkable degree, convenience, regularity, elegance of prospect, and a free circulation of air. The positions of the different publick edifices, and of the several squares and areas of different shapes, as they are laid down, were first determined on the most advantageous ground, commanding the most extensive prospects, and from their situation, susceptible of such improvements as either use or ornament may require. The capitol is situated on a most beautiful eminence commanding a compleat view of every part of the city. The President's house stands on a rising ground, possessing a delightful water prospect, together with a commanding view of the capitol, and the most material parts of the city. The grand avenues, and such streets as lead immediately to publick places, are from 130 to 160 feet wide; the other streets are from 90 to 110 feet wide."[3]

And so I emerg'd from under the Roman arch and beheld the city. The morning sun was high and brilliant, and the summerish air told me at once that I had at last set foot in that gentle Old South of which I have so often dream'd. Green and white were omnipresent—springtime leaves and grass, and delectable expanses of aethereal cherry-blossoms; which latter, indeed, were past their greatest profusion, and beginning to be replac'd by the gay and multi-colour'd flowers of the many gardens. The town, brooding quietly in the Sabbath radiance despite the herds of sightseers unloos'd upon it, does not at first impress one. The Monument is so distant, the sky so vacant of tall buildings, and the ground so devoted to parks, malls, and wide spaces, that one cannot gather the sense of compact and active life which one usually associates with large cities. Then, too, near the station are certain temporarily undeveloped tracts, and a plenitude of large, low buildings which—though having an elderly and colonial aspect—are really only the temporary lath-and-cement structures put up in war-time to house the excess of special government workers. I saw the capitol dome looming importantly through the delicate verdure of young foliage, and was on every hand conscious of a note of leisure and reposefulness at once bespeaking the austral milieu. Now came stamps—bought at a post office next the station where a grandly cloistral air animated an interior of vast size and drowsily ornate dimness—and a matutinal meal, snatched at a modest refectory but little suggestive of background and glamour. Supplies on board, we set out with buoyant step for the Capitol; observing as we went the temporary war buildings, which on closer inspection display'd some highly attractive Georgian characteristicks. The general landskip was still unimpressive, tho' a peculiar atmospherick quality induc'd a sense of mild exaltation—perhaps thro' aesthetick channels, since the sky was bluer, the foliage greener, the flowers gayer, and the marble structures whiter, than such things seem in the North. We did not omit noticing the Library of Congress, which fail'd to captivate us, or the House and Senate buildings; and once in a while a vista wou'd open up and enhance our impression of semi-rural spaciousness and freshness, whilst the charm of the low skyline grew on us each moment. At last, after traversing a delectable bit of park, we reacht the Capitol on its commanding elevation, and began to circumnavigate it till we attain'd that central and original portion whose corner-stone was laid by Genl. Washington, with Masonick ceremonies, in 1793, whose north wing was first occupy'd in 1800, and whose south wing was completed in 1811, under the architectural superintendence of Latrobe,[4] designer of the United States Bank at Philadelphia and of the Popish cathedral at Baltimore. The central or connecting part, as all know, was erected after the burning of the city in 1814 during the war, and modell'd from the plans of the mighty Boston architect Charles Bulfinch, who to his native city was a veritable Christopher Wren, and whose crowning work is the golden-domed Boston State House on Beacon Hill, put up in 1795. The original Capitol building—central portion with dome, and the two wings—was finisht in 1827; the two extensions being added during the 'fifties. The present dome, as most are aware, is not the first one; but a replacement, of stronger material, completed in 1865. As I gaz'd upon this gigantick construction, I cou'd not but compare it with other similar buildings I have seen; and I will confess that some of its rivals did not suffer by the estimate. For perfect artistry of form, delicacy of detail, and purity of material, it cannot compete with our own modern Rhode-Island State House;[5] and I am certain no true Providence man can help feeling pride when he reflects that its superior constantly looms majestick and marmoreal over his native place, giving background and dignity to Exchange-Place and Market-Square, and forming a magnificent focus for the upper end of Narragansett Bay. God Save His Majesty's Province of Rhode-Island and Providence-Plantations! The original part of the Capitol is *painted*, notwithstanding its ostensibly marble material; and a recent rumour hints at a century-old "graft" whereby an inferior stone was substituted. But let it not be thought that the building is unimpressive. Seen at a distance, the whole ensemble with dome and extensions is a stupendously noble thing, and one rejoices that it shares with the Washington Monument the distinction of being prominently visible from nearly every point in the city.

Having survey'd the celebrated structure to our full satisfaction, we descended from the elevation to the lower level of the town, following a convenient flight of steps that ran through garden-like terraces with fringing boughs. Below us lay the spreading city with venerable roofs and spires, wide park spaces, multifarious statues, and snatches of far background where the superbly slender Monument and Greek-souled Lincoln Memorial loomed white against the still more distant fragments of gleaming Potomac and templed Virginia hills. Behind and above towered the Capitol we had left, doubly majestick in the citadel-like environment furnisht by our point of view. Soon we had attain'd the bottom lands, where there burst freshly upon us the vernal charm of the place and season—the cleanness and vitality and village calm, precious things which more northerly cities seem to lose when they atchieve corresponding importance. The people, too, were infinitely less repulsive and mongrel than the crowds of New-York and its neighbours; so that the entire scene held a dreamlike glamour which titillated the spirit and made one question his own awakeness. Magnolias were in bloom, and with the fading cherry-blossoms help'd to give the air a zest and fragrance hard to describe and impossible to duplicate.

After a turn or two around the flower-fring'd paths by the Grant statue in the Publick Gardens, we proceeded to Pennsylvania Avenue and walkt along that thoroughfare toward the White House, noting as we went the many antient houses—late 18th or early 19th century—which are mostly of brick, and which have the same general outline and window-and-door arrangement as the corresponding class of colonial houses in New-York and Philadelphia—i.e., narrow facade, door at one side, symmetrically placed windows, and a pert pair of dormers jutting from a slant roof of average pitch. Doorways are seldom elaborate—the finest classick specimens, I feel, are to be found in New-England—but are often very tasteful. They are somewhat like those of Philadelphia, and do not resemble New-York doorways at all. Occasionally one sees a slanting cellar door projecting outward from the front of a house in the Philadelphia fashion—and another Philadelphia trait is the arched passageway in a solidly blocked house, leading to a garden or courtyard in the rear. Besides these distinctly urban types set solidly, there are all manner of other colonial patterns—village homes of almost farmhouse cast, more pronouncedly rectangular in facade, of brick or wood, with flaring lintels above the windows and slant roofs with or without dormers. I did not see many of the definitely Southern-Colonial type, or yet of the gambrel-roof design; both of these modes having largely vanisht before the construction of the city. Some of the more rural types, set in their own verdant and shady yards, impart a deliciously provincial tone to the town; and even the Victorian buildings scatter'd about have a certain suggestion of lazy refinement and artistick repose which accords with the major spirit of the scene. The great breadth and general level quality of the streets may subtract a bit from what would otherwise be Marbleheadish picturesqueness, but really adds something to the atmosphere of indolent Southern fascination. The bulk of the city is not—intrinsically and aesthetically—to be call'd strictly *beautiful*. It is too genteelly shabby for that—too heterogeneous in design, with Victorian jostling Georgian, and tiny wooden cottages tuck'd now and then betwixt incipient modern office buildings. But charm and personality it certainly does have; and those attributes grow on one powerfully during every minute of his sojourn, till he is finally won over as an ardent devotee. One hates to leave the restful spot when one has not a New-England to return to.

As I have intimated, we stroll'd along with eyes widely open, noting all that there was to be seen. On our right loom'd the old National Hotel, stopping-place of statesmen in the Webster–Clay–Calhoun days—and where Georgius proposed stopping that night—and on the left appear'd Centre Market—a hideous Victorian mess which probably replac'd a Georgian edifice like the Providence Market-House of 1773, the Marblehead one of 1727, and Salem's 1816 specimen. At this point we turn'd sharply south across the Mall, revelling in the beauty of the Smithsonian Institution grounds and contemplating such important buildings as the New Museum and Freer Gallery—which latter contains Whistler's famous Peacock Room, tho' we had no opportunity of seeing it.

We were to meet Mrs. Renshaw at 9 a.m. at the Monument, whose lofty summit, like the dome of the Capitol, is scarcely ever out of the tourist's sight. As the moments advanced, and lateness became imminent, Sechrist left us to keep the appointment, whilst Kirk and I absorb'd a few more impressions in the southwestern section near the riverfront, ending with the Bureau of Engraving and Printing, from which we turn'd inland directly for the Monument. We found Sechrist alone, for Mrs. R. was late—and for the moment we were transported by the magnitude of the Cyclopean white obelisk. It was closed—else I might have been tempted to essay its misty heights on foot despite the indisposition of the lift! But straightway a new wonder exalted us. On the flat lands toward the river, where in recent years the splendid expanse of Potomac Park has develop'd, the Lincoln Memorial rears its pillar'd Hellenick whiteness on an exact prolongation of the line from the Capitol to the Monument; brooding dreamlike over a limpid lily-pool on the landward side, and having beyond it the crystal river and the marble-crown'd heights of Arlington in the distance. To stand by the monument and view this sight through a delicate framework of virid vernal boughs is to succumb to a most acute aesthetick intoxication. In the mild Southern air every colour takes on an heighten'd tone—much as it must in the beloved Mediterranean world of Little Belknap's dreams—till the soul feels close to delicious swooning at the half-intolerable white beauty of the temple and its reflection, the supernal blueness of cloudless sky and tessellated pool, and the passionate verdancy of fresh foliage unwrapped from richly nourished buds—all this, and the intimations of farther sublimities convey'd by the hills beyond the river, where stand the Dorick portico of the Custis–Lee mansion and the incredible glories of the Memorial Amphitheatre. If, as the plan predicts, a marble bridge is to be built connecting the Amphitheatre with the Lincoln Memorial, the sheer and utter magnificence of the scene will be unequall'd by any wonder of that antient Grecian world from which its inspiration is derived! Our time being tragically limited, and Mrs. Renshaw not appearing, Kirk and I left Sechrist to stand on guard with instructions whilst we workt inland to continue our sightseeing. As we near'd the confines of the Executive Grounds, there dawn'd gleamingly upon us thro' the vivid foliage the riverward facade of the White House with its graceful pillar'd curve. Here at last was a basis for breathless admiration of Old Washington; for if in the Capitol Latrobe and Bulfinch did not rise to their apex, surely this splendid apotheosis of Southern colonialism and culmination of the third phase of Georgian architecture stands as the one immortal monument to the greatness of the Irishman James Hoban. Hoban, it may be recall'd, is the designer of the colonial State House at Charleston, S.C. Much of his finesse and architectural sophistication arose from his training in the British Isles, and his familiarity with the Georgian houses of Dublin, which in grace and finish are second to none. In designing the White House, his direct inspiration was the home of the Duke of Leinster in Dublin. The corner stone was laid in the presence of Genl. Washington in 1792, in David Burns' old fields by the river, and the rest slowly grew with the years; being first occupy'd by John Adams in 1800—whose wife, by the way, complain'd bitterly in her letters of its bleak, damp, uncomfortable, and imperfectly finisht condition. Jefferson is reputed to have inhabited but a part of it; and not till the time of Madison was it a seat of fashion and wit. During the War of 1812 it suffer'd with the rest of burn'd Washington, (1814) and when restor'd shortly afterward (1817) its original freestone walls were found to be so much discolour'd, that it receiv'd that famous coating of white paint from which it has ever since been known. It may be that a modern sand-blast could restore the pristine surface, yet so much a part of tradition has the name of "White House" become, that I believe it will ever retain from choice that gleaming integument which it assum'd from necessity. The park about the Executive Mansion is of the highest beauty and diversity; and on this occasion brooded with a kind of sylvan magick in the warm spring sun. I am not without envy of Mr. Coolidge for his occupancy of so stately a domain, particularly since I am sensible how well the interior now matches the exterior; all traces of the Victorian aera having long ago been eradicated. (In Pres. Grant's time the furnishing is said to have been a veritable nightmare!)

Whilst we were gazing upon this pleasing spectacle, our attention was distracted by a hail from the road, where was fast approaching the Renshaw car, with its owner, Sechrist, and a prepossessing gentlewoman of early middle age as occupants. Mrs. R. had, it seems, arriv'd at the Monument immediately after our departure; and having pickt up Sechrist, follow'd us along the course we had told him we wou'd take. With the years this lady hath become a person of much importance in Washington, being now a select teacher of dramatick and oratorical method, and prominent in female political circles. (Republican) She is, however, wholly unspoilt; and shew'd extream kindness in absenting herself from most of her guests and spending the whole day in the guidance of our party, despite the protests we mixt with our profound thanks. Mrs. Renshaw's guest, Miss Dashiel, of an antient Maryland family of French Catholick extraction which came to the colonies in 1634 with Governor Leonard Calvert, was very helpful in pointing out what sights she knew. Mrs. R. herself knew downtown Washington well, but was oblig'd to turn the guidance over to more antiquarian hands in Georgetown and Alexandria—Sechrist having a similarly partial fund of information. All did me the honour to commend the list of sights I had made, and Sechrist kept his copy for use in the piloting of other guests. The car, being small, seated just the five persons present: Mrs. R. (driving) and Miss D. in front, and myself, Sechrist, and Kirk (reading left to right) on the rear seat. We first approacht the row of spectacular publick buildings to the west of the White House park—Pan-American Union, Continental Hall, Red Cross, and Corcoran Gallery. The last three are delightfully classick—but it was the first which held us longest. This building, presented by the late Andrew Carnegie, Esq. to a society for the promotion of understanding amongst the republicks of the New World, is in the Spanish Renaissance style, and wou'd have shewn us a fine interior and patio had we been able to enter. As it was, our rambles were confin'd to the Aztec sunken garden and triple-arch'd loggia in the rear—but these were more than enough to repay our wildest hopes. Passing behind the building proper, we found ourselves in an instant translated to another world—a rare, tropick world of gleaming marble, flashing tiles, bright green hedges and terraces, multi-colour'd blossoms, and a burning blue sky which mirror'd itself in a shallow Aztec pool overhung by a full-size copy of the masterly "Sad Indian" statue[6]—perhaps the foremost bit of Indian sculpture yet unearth'd. The blazing colour and diversely gay vegetation put me in mind of the lines of Mr. Tickell (protege of Mr. Addison) on a similar display:

> "Where Kensington, high o'er the neighb'ring lands,
>  Midst greens and sweets, a regal fabrick, stands,
>  And sees each spring, luxuriant in her bow'rs,
>  A snow of blossoms, and a wild of flow'rs."[7]

The loggia in the rear is lin'd throughout—floor, walls, and ceiling—with the choicest specimens of Latin-American primitive tiling, and is adorn'd on every hand with cunning reproductions of the best Aztec, Maya, and Inca sculpture and decoration. Some of the grotesques are of unbelievable merit and vividness, and add a touch of the spectral to what is already weird enough in its Dunsanian exoticism, and in its living reproduction of a wild beauty that was old when the first Conquistador set foot on New World soil. Kirk, Sechrist, and I were the only living souls in that strange garden . . . . unless, perchance, some dim and uncanny sentience hung round that sad carven Aztec whose pensive visage brooded eternally over the blue waters of that silent lily-pool. But all things end, and we were soon back in the world we know—albeit in one of the most attractive possible phases of that world.

From this region we progress'd north and west past the Corcoran Gallery to one of the antient parts of the town, where colonial houses of all descriptions cluster'd thickly. Amongst those which we specifically noted were the Octagon House, home of the American Institute of Architects, a queerly angled brick affair where Pres. Madison dwelt in 1814 after the burning of the White House, and the former home of James Monroe (whose final home I last December shew'd you in Prince Street, New-York) and of Prof. Cleveland Abbe, founder of the U.S. Signal Service. We now turn'd up Virginia and New-Hampshire Avenues past Washington Circle into Pennsylvania Ave., crossing Rock Creek on the bridge and entering the crooked and hilly streets of archaick Georgetown, a district which, tho' now a part of Washington, was once an independent town far antedating it. Founded in 1751, the village enjoy'd a flourishing life of its own long before any mind conceiv'd the plan of an artificial Federal City at its very doorstep. In some ways, it was a relief to enter picturesque Georgetown after the broad and geometrical streets of the formally laid-out capital proper. Here, at least, was a *natural* town, where, as in such old New-England towns as Providence, Boston, Salem, and Marblehead, the narrow streets took haphazard courses in accord with fortuitous caprice and human individuality, rather than following the set patterns evolved in some doctrinaire's or mathematician's study. A E P G has characterised Georgetown as "sordid" and shabby, and this in truth may be said of M Street, its principal trunk line thoroughfare through which traffick passes from Washington to Rosslyn and Arlington via the new Key Memorial Bridge. It is, however, very rich in colonial houses of every grade—many of them far older than any Washington houses—and parts of it are still exceedingly desirable as residences for quiet folk, suggesting Power, Benevolent, or Williams Street in Providence. We threaded through it quite thoroughly, noting the old Union Hotel, stopping place of statesmen in the 'twenties, the yellow stone house where Major L'Enfant dwelt, and where Genl. Washington made his headquarters in 1791 when surveying the land for the future Federal City, and Bellvue, the Rittenhouse seat built in 1750, and now forming one of the oldest edifices in the District of Columbia. This latter is a splendid brick mansion on a terrace, trimm'd with white stone and flankt by two outbuildings like Mount Pleasant (Benedict Arnold's home) in Philadelphia. Indeed, it conforms to the Philadelphian or Middle-Colonies style rather than to the

Southern, which—together with the Germantown name of Rittenhouse as borne by its builder—makes me fancy that it was built by a Pennsylvanian who disregarded the custom of the locality. It is in the second or rococo Georgian manner characteristick of the middle eighteenth century, and is altogether one of the finest colonial houses I have ever encounter'd. When occupy'd by Jos: Nourse, first Register of the Treasury, its doors received Genl. Washington as a frequent guest.

We now turn'd toward the Key Memorial Bridge, nam'd from the author of "The Star-Spangled Banner", who dwelt at what is now its Georgetown end, and recently open'd to replace the old Aqueduct Bridge which once carry'd the venerable (1784) Chesapeake and Ohio canal across the Potomac to Virginia and which is now in process of demolition. Across the stream the wooded hills of the Old Dominion rose majestick in their springtide verdure, and we drove over the great concrete arches to the placid square of Rosslyn, where for the first time in my life I breathed bodily in that Virginian realm whose history and traditions I have ever regarded with so much veneration. I lifted my hat as a salute to Virginia's royal soil; and, appropriately mov'd, saw myself whiskt back to the District of Columbia, tho' with the assurance of a swift and prolong'd return. Once back, we turn'd northward along the old road which skirts the canal, and were regal'd with such a feast of rural scenery as few urbanites are often privileg'd to behold. At our right was a rolling country, with steep hills rising and deep vales dipping, and scatter'd here and there quaint old-time farmhouses of every type and size. On our left was the canal, shallow and placid, and dotted with the floats of such early fishermen as the springtime had brought forth to recline upon the sleepy banks. Still farther to the left, and skirted by the oddly contrasting canal, flow'd the potent Potomac at the bottom of an ever-deepening gorge. As we ascended its course, we were imprest by the deceptiveness of appearances; for whilst it seem'd to dwindle to a meer narrow, trickling stream, it was in reality profoundly deep, and fully able to sustain the enormous bulk of water which later broadens out into a gigantick tidal inlet. We now reacht Chain Bridge—so call'd, like that of similar name near Newburyport, in the Province of the Massachusetts-Bay, from its having replac'd an antient span hung from iron chains—and upon it crost over both the canal and its more natural sister stream, the Potomac. Once more in Virginia, we ascended the steep slope; pensively passing that spot, near the end of the bridge, where in another April a century ago the duel was fought betwixt Henry Clay and John Randolph, of Roanoke—a less tragick affair than the early morning rencounter at Weehawken,[8] since despite the most desperate intentions, neither principal was so much as scratcht!

And now commenc'd my real initiation into the glories of Virginia. Up and on we went, with hill, valley, and forest scenery of the most striking magnificence on every hand; great gorges with limpid streams at the bottom and oaks and willows springing from their precipitous sides; rolling plains with kine at pasture, divided by rustick rail fences and pied with occasional white blossoming trees, trim cottages, and sedate manor-houses nestling in protecting groves on the summits of numerous elevations; mystical climbs and dizzying descents of the road, the latter sometimes enabling us to trace our pathway's windings through tiers of outspread meadows below, and past many a dreaming hamlet and patient farmhouse chimney; everything, in fact, which makes New-England lovely except those stone walls, steeply-pitcht gambrel roofs, and white-steepled Puritan churches which are purely local in origin among us. Even the flora seem'd typically Novanglian, save for some abundant wild honeysuckle which I later saw at Arlington.

A brisk tho' warm wind was blowing, but it seem'd to lull as we enter'd Fairfax Court-House, seat of Fairfax County, in the vault of whose 1800 court building the original will of Genl. Washington is deposited, safe for ever in the private archives of the county clerk. This, of course, was the first Southern crossroads court-house village I had ever seen; and I was truly enraptur'd by the lazy huddle of leaf-shaded brick rising above its green lawns and dusty, rutted roadways. Court house with portico of brick arches, general store and post-office, residences of a sort—the picture was perfect in that dazzling spring sun of noontime, and I cou'd well imagine Genl. Washington himself riding slowly in on a white horse, tying the steed to the court-house portico, and disappearing within to transact his business with the queued and breech'd clerk. Mrs. R. assur'd me that Fairfax C.H. is indeed a good representative of its kind, and I felt the richer in visual experience for having seen with mine own eyes that which bulks so large in the fiction we read. Sechrist, Kirk, and I alighted and roam'd about, properly disappointed at our inability to procure a postcard of the place by reason of the Sunday closing of all emporia. Finally we re-embarkt in the chaise, and were soon darting again thro' the undulant countryside toward hoary and legend-haunted Alexandria.

As we approacht the town down a pleasing declivity we beheld on our left a very considerable eminence, whose summit held what seem'd to be the foundation of a vast and imposing future building. I was not long in comprehending that this rudiment represented the celebrated Masonick Memorial to Genl. Washington, to be set up by the Masons of the United States under the inspiration of the Alexandria-Washington Lodge of which in his day the General was an enthusiastick member and Grand Master. The structure is to reproduce in its lines one of those mighty lighthouses of antiquity, such as were set in high places near the harbours for the guidance of galley and trireme, and of which the Pharos of Alexandria, one of the seven wonders of the world, was the most noted specimen. It will be compos'd of a great marble base with classick facade, and surmounted by four receding marble terraces, the upper three embellisht with suitable columns of the Ionick order; the whole rising to an height of 200 feet and forming a not unworthy counterpart of its prototype in that other and older Alexandria by the Nile. As I survey'd this commendable enterprise, I reflected with what keen interest it wou'd be regarded by my grandfather; who in his time founded an Ionick Lodge, and adorn'd with harmonious congeniality the Commandery of St. John.

One more turn to the right, and we were in Alexandria—originally call'd Bellhaven—an antient city of 20,000 inhabitants which in Colonial times was one of the most important towns in America. This relick of Old Virginia has, by some magick known only to the gods, manag'd to keep itself in its pristine condition despite the presence of Washington only eight miles away; and still stands like Marblehead as a perfect and untarnisht specimen of the American pre-Revolutionary village. It was, as most realise, the nearest town to the estates of the Washingtons; so that it is closely connected with all stages of Genl. Washington's social, civick, military, and religious life. He was a member of its church, lodge, and fire company, rais'd his first provincial armies here, and danc'd and visited in its taverns and private houses. As it was then, so it is now; and we were struck at once with its pervasive colonial quiet, repose, and settled maturity when we enter'd its shady streets and observ'd its sedate rows of brick Georgian houses—most of them of an urban pattern, with the familiar slanting roof and pair of dormers. The town is not as old as Marblehead, and has no house anterior to 1750. It built up, however, rapidly and permanently; so that it is now much as Genl. Washington found it in his middle years, with echoes of its colonial past melodiously tintinnabulating in such names as King and Royal Streets. Enchanted by the diffusive charm of this time-hallow'd spot as it baskt in the spring Southern sun with its flowers, green grass, and delicate foliage, we alighted at Christ Church and proceeded to meditate amidst the sequester'd tombs of its verdant and picturesque churchyard. This church, the head of Fairfax Parish, was built in 1772–3, with Genl. Washington as one of its original pewholders and vestrymen. His pew, as well as that of Genl. Robert E. Lee, is markt with a silver plate. The edifice is of splendid Georgian design, plann'd by James Wren, Esq., a lineal descendant of Sir Christopher, and having a fine Palladian window in the rear. It is of brick with stone facings, surmounted by a tall wooden belfry in place of a steeple, and with its profusely shaded yard presents a poignant picture of the old-time idyllick restfulness of the South. The scene, indeed, is one of quite unexampled beauty; and so accorded with my deepest moods that I stood transported and dreaming, conscious of that mystick and illusory sensation of previous familiarity, with which I am ever affected upon beholding well-order'd reliques of the eighteenth century. The symphony of red brick, green sward and foliage, blue sky, and the subdu'd slate of the gravestones, (for here, as in New-England, the slabs are of slate instead of the brownstone of New-York and the Jerseys) all combin'd to weave a spell of singular potency, from which I broke loose with difficulty and reluctance as the party resumed its progress past more antique gables, fanlights, chimney-pots, and small-pan'd windows. Alexandria, as I have said, is another Marblehead; tho' its streets are wider and straighter, its houses finer and made of brick, and its topography less picturesquely hilly. Perhaps it is to Portsmouth, NH., that I might with greater justice compare it. The present business and social centre is on high ground a little inland from the Potomac, but the streets slope down to a very quaint and very ancient waterfront where in the days of Braddock and Washington the bustle of activity was concentrated. On the incline above the river, and now surrounded by other buildings, is the famous Carlyle house, built in 1752; at which Genl. Washington was a frequent guest, and where, at Mr. Carlyle's invitation, Genl. Braddock made his headquarters when organising his ill-fated expedition against the French and Indians in the Ohio valley. Here in 1755 assembled in the Blue Room the governors of the leading American provinces—William Shirley of the Massachusetts-Bay, James DeLancey of New-York, Morris of Pennsylvania, Sharpe of Maryland, Dobbs of North Carolina, and Dinwiddie of Virginia—and here in dungeons beneath the house were kept such prisoners as were incident to a martial venture. The building is a fine brick mansion in the second Georgian manner, with roof sloping on four sides and meeting in a ridge, where two chimneys protrude. In every slope of the roof is a dormer window, whilst the front door—opening high on a terrace above a fine formal garden with paths and sundial—is of an excellent colonial type with flattish fanlight and generous side-lights. The entrance to the dungeons is in the terrace below this. That this mansion cannot be seen from the street or waterfront, is a very great misfortune; and I am glad to hear that the Society for the Restoration of Historick Alexandria has form'd a plan to purchase and restore it, demolishing the intruding Victorian buildings which conceal its shapely bulk. Our party was guided to it by a very small and affable pickaninny with broad grin and starched and spotless Eton collar. Not far distant from the Carlyle house lie several other antiquities of prime importance, notable among which is a large structure on a corner, with cornice carried round the gable end in Middle Colonies fashion. This is Gadsby's Tavern, or the City Hotel, open'd on Feby. 20, 1793, by John Wise, who describ'd it in an advertisement as a "new and elegant three-story brick house, fronting the west end of the Market House, which was built for a tavern, and has 20 commodious well-furnisht rooms in it." John Gadsby, joint owner of a stage coach line, soon purchas'd the place; and it shelter'd many a notable man on his journey from Philadelphia to Richmond, Williamsburg, and the South generally. Its reputation was very high, and the proprietor strove to keep it so by excluding gamesters and all manner of doubtful and vicious folk. Here, in a ballroom now removed to where you saw it in the American Wing of the Metropolitan Museum, New-York, were held the dancing assemblies of the best society of the region; including many of the birthnight balls in honour of Genl. Washington, at which the eminent leader was a gracious and happy guest till the small hours of morning on each occasion from 1783 to 1798. It was in this room at Gads-by's that Washington attended his last birthnight, Feby. 22, 1798. The next year he felt the onset of time, and in November wrote as follows to the managers of the Washington Society of Alexandria:

Mount Vernon, 12 Nov. 1799.

"Gentlemen:

Mrs. Washington and I have been honoured with your polite invitation to the assemblies in Alexandria this winter, thank you for this mark of your attention. But alas! our dancing days are no more. We wish, however, all those who relish so agreeable and innocent an amusement all the pleasure the season will afford them.

Your most obedient and obliged humble servant,

G⁰· Washington."⁹

The tavern—which lies across the street from the rebuilt Masonick Lodge attended by Genl. Washington—has now every indication of desertion; and I was pain'd to see the very letters of its name fallen off from the front facade. The street at its side is infinitely picturesque and Marbleheadish. To the left of the tavern is a two-story yellow brick house with slant roof, fanlighted door, and three dormers, not mention'd in any guide-book I have seen, yet reveal'd by an historical bronze tablet to be one of the foremost relicks of the town. It is the *old* City Tavern (1752) which preceded Gadsby's and in which the young Washington in 1754 recruited provincial militia against the French, receiving also within these walls his commission as Major from the hand of Genl. Braddock. Unhappy Braddock! Hadst thou but taken the advice of thy raw Virginia subaltern, and fought in the manner of the Indians from behind the trees, thou mightest not have met that defeat and death from which thy name hath become a synonym for costly failure! What ramifications hath history! The scatter'd remnant of Braddock's army, arriving in Philadelphia with a frugal grooming including their own natural hair queued, set a fashion amongst the local dandies and macaronies which resulted in the decline of the periwig in Pennsylvania years before it vanisht elsewhere! But a short space away from the tavern—one square south and one east, toward the river front—stands the musty Ramsay house, oldest in the city, a plain, half-timber edifice with roof gambrel on the front but slanting unbroken toward the rear. This was built in 1751, and perhaps typifies the pristine Alexandria preceding the brick town of the 1760's and 1770's which still survives. But how can one describe every house of interest in a colonial centre where almost every structure merits that appellation? Suffice it to say that we did not miss the brick body and white cupola of the old engine-house of the Friendship Fire Company, organised in 1774 with Genl. Washington as a member, the country graveyard where the mysterious strange lady (thought to be a scion of British royalty) was buried by her husband in 1816 after an illness at Gadsby's Tavern, or any of the quaint scenes and street-corner effects which so perfectly preserve the Old Virginia atmosphere and align Alexandria with that solid early-American fabrick whose other phases are so well represented by Philadelphia, Elizabethtown, Greenwich-Village, Newport, Providence, Salem, Marblehead, and Portsmouth. When we did leave Alexandria it was with a regret temper'd only by the expectancy of seeing such parts of Genl. Washington's estate, Mount Vernon, as the Sunday closing of the grounds wou'd permit us to.

The ride south from Alexandria was markt by the most pleasing vistas, the road traversing a delightful rolling country with graceful meadows and valleys, stately willows, and blossoming orchard trees in agreeable abundance. At one point we crost on a bridge the wide expanse of Big Hunting Creek, an inlet of the river; and at another point the route rose to a considerable altitude; from which, looking behind and across the precipitous riverward ravines and the water itself, one might discern faintly in the distance the whole dreamy profile of Washington with its spires and Monument. On the neighbouring high ground stood many a neat estate, and toward the last the fields became sprightly with peach blooms. Then, after a downward dip, came one final rise toward the river; and we saw before us the hedges and gates of Mount Vernon, with many an alluring roof and cupola within. We had arrived, and though admittance was impossible on Sunday, we form'd a very good notion of the manor from glimpses snatcht at sundry chosen vantage-points.

Mount Vernon, originally Hunting Creek estate, was inherited by Lawrence Washington, Esq., of His Majesty's navy, half-brother to George, and first inhabited by him upon his marriage to Anne Fairfax of Belvoir—a relative to that Thomas, Lord Fairfax, who, after dwelling in the London world of mode and being counted amongst the wits of the *Spectator,* himself came to Virginia in 1746—dying, by the way, at the age of 91, of a heart broken by the fall of the British power in these colonies. The manor-house, a plain but graceful wooden affair of two stories and dormer'd attick, with vane-capt cupola and riverward portico, was constructed in 1743; when the name of the estate was chang'd in honour of Admiral Edward Vernon, under whom Lawrence Washington had serv'd against Spain, and whose great victory at Porto Bello on Nov. 22, 1739, had rais'd him to the pinnacle of fame. It is Admiral Vernon who form'd the origin of the term "grog" as apply'd to weak liquor. Having reduc'd the rum ration of the British sailor by mixing the beverage with water, he was subjected to a resentful levity which included the nicknaming of himself and his diluted drink as "Old Grog", from the grogram cloak he usually wore whilst walking his quarter-deck. Upon the death of Lawrence Washington, between whom and his young half-brother there was ever the warmest attachment, and of his small daughter shortly afterward, George inherited Mount Vernon; into whose manor-house he mov'd for the rest of his life in 1759, after his marriage with the amiable and accomplisht Mrs. Custis. His liking for the situation is well shewn in a letter written not many months after his arrival; in which he says: "I am now, I believe, fixt at this seat with an agreeable consort for life."[10] Close to the house are the usual colonnade-linkt kitchens, and in front a series of shaded lawns and deer park extend down to the river and landing. Behind are gardens, lawns, and orchards, and a summer-house which we glimpst thro' the fast-lockt gate. Here and there stand the outbuildings, and on every hand broods the undying charm of a true Virginia plantation—the first, by the way, which I ever beheld. The interior of the mansion, as we know from pictures, is furnisht throughout in proper fashion; forming an invaluable illustration of the Southern colonial manner of life. But of this we cou'd see nothing—not that, nor the tomb of the General, which lies in an appropriate part of the grounds. As we turn'd back on the highroad toward Alexandria and Arlington, my fancy held above all else a picture of a greensward sloping down to the river, and crown'd by a noble yet modest pile whose white portico, cupola, and upper story glimmer'd alluringly through the fresh foliage of a Southern spring.

The return trip was not inferior in interest and beauty to the preceding southward journey, and Alexandria dawn'd for the second time upon me with an even greater charm. This time, instead of taking the inland road to Fairfax Court House, we continued to skirt the Potomac; passing through a country of the highest loveliness on our way to the marmoreal splendours percht on the Arlington bluffs. Here and there we espy'd the city of Washington in the distance across the river, and at all times we were immers'd in a landskip of the most charming vegetation, including that profuse and bush-ingulphing wild honeysuckle which I have before mention'd as forming the only distinctively non-Northern note in the orchestra of local flora. Finally, after a sharp descent by a typical Old Virginia crossroads hamlet and a corresponding ascent beyond, we came upon the order'd legions of graves which mark the outskirts of the National Cemetery. Arlington at last!

Arlington was the manor of the Custis family, purchas'd on Christmas Day, 1778, by John Parke Custis, son of Martha Washington by her first marriage, for £1100. It had since 1669 been in the Alexander family. Mr. Custis, aide-de-camp to his illustrious stepfather Genl. Washington, died of a camp fever in 1781, his two small children being adopted by the General. George Washington Parke Custis, the elder child and later the biographer of Washington, liv'd in Gen. Washington's household till Mrs. Washington's death in 1802; thereafter residing at Arlington, which he inherited, till his own death in 1857. The present mansion he built in 1804–1812, modelling its Dorick portico after the Temple of Theseus in Athens, or as some say, one of the two Greek temples at Paestum—which was the Hellenick city of Poseidonia before the spread of the Roman power over that part of Magna Graecia. The daughter of the builder, Mary Ann Randolph Custis, became the wife of the immortal Robert Edward Lee, and to her the property descended upon her parent's death, with subsequent succession bestow'd upon her eldest son, George Washington Custis Lee. At the outbreak of the War between the States Genl. Lee (then Colonel) left Arlington with his family for Richmond to take command of Virginia's Confederate troops, and the Federal government at once took over the mansion as an headquarters, with the grounds as a camp. Later the house and grounds became respectively an hospital and military cemetery, and in 1864 were bought for such purposes by the government at a sale for delinquent taxes. In 1877 the rightful heir George W. C. Lee establisht his claim to lawful tenure, but was afterward bought out by the government, which by that time had begun to make the spot a sort of national shrine. It is now the great military cemetery of the country; collaborated by Nature, the architect, and the landskip gardner, into a spot of unsurpass'd scenick and architectural beauty. As we approacht the cluster'd splendours we remarkt each feature in turn, noting such unique devices as the Maine Memorial, which consists of the actual battle mast or conning tower of the hapless vessel, rais'd from Havana Harbour and here fixt as a perpetual exhortation to "Remember the Maine." Then, after a moment's climb, we were on the bluff above the river; and alighting, stood before one of the most prodigious and spectacular architectural triumphs of the Western World—the Memorial Amphitheatre completed in 1920.

Fancy a dream of the brightest scenes of classical antiquity suddenly crystallised into a glorious and titanick reality of glittering marble embower'd in vivid verdure and set against a sky of more than mortal blueness. This I beheld as I stood before the steps and columns and arches of the great circular concourse that loom'd up from its gardens against the celestial vault, majestick in every part, and shewing beyond it the river and the distant wonders of Washington. Words cannot describe it—they may only feel it, and become the less coherent from their awe! The amphitheatre, which follows in design the Dionysiac Theatre at Athens and the Roman theatre at Orange, France, covers 34,000 square feet and is shap'd to accomodate on its marble benches some five thousand spectators. Here are held the most solemn ceremonials of the nation, whilst in the crypt are provided suitable resting-places for the illustrious martial dead. Beyond, and on the crest of a proud marble terrace at the very edge of the bluff, lies the simple sarcophagus of the unknown American soldier of the World War, at which sages and potentates have done spontaneous homage. We ascended to the walk atop the amphitheatre's columns, and there enjoy'd the marvellous prospect on every hand; later descending and viewing the main facade that faces the river—a lovely symphony of impeccable Graeco-Roman form. Ramble as we might through the grounds, at no point cou'd the structure seem other than beautiful. Now a pillar, now an arch, now a curve of the entire colonnaded wall—always supreme and whitely ethereal grace shining thro' the pleasing coverts of green shrubs and standing out boldly against the warmly blue heavens. And so we left it—left it and forged ahead through the parklike landskip to where the old manor-house of Arlington dreams on its riverward height of Custises that are no more.

Arlington, as most persons know, is a fine Southern mansion of a style which architects might classify as hovering between the last or Adam phase of Georgian and the full classick revival—with strong leanings toward the latter in its massive and archaeological spirit. It is yellow in colour, with a portico of six immense white Dorick columns above a flight of four steps; and is said to bear much resemblance to Monticello, the seat of Tho: Jefferson, Esq., of Albemarle County, late President of the United States. The view from its front portico— the riverward end—surpasses almost any other in the civilised world; the hill stretching full half a mile down to the glimmering river, beyond which are the distant domes and delicate Monument of Washington, and the placid crests of the still more distant hills. On the south horizon Alexandria can be detected, and to the north are vistas no less beautiful if less richly historick. When Lafayette was the guest of Mr. Custis here, he vow'd the prospect from the great portico equall'd any he had ever seen; and I do not think he err'd. Arlington is unfurnisht, but has some fine woodwork worth studying. It is a museum to a limited extent, and as such open to the publick.

Time was now fleeting, and our limited schedule made our swift return to Washington quite imperative—since the New-York stage coach left at 4:35 p.m. Descending to the lowlands by the river's brink, we reacht and crost the Long Bridge or Alexandria Highway Bridge, which in the time of the Civil War was the one recognised passage to the South. Over this span—or its predecessor, no doubt—marched the Rhode Island troops under Ambrose E. Burnside and Governor William Sprague . . . . Sprague, whose horse was shot from beneath him at Bull Run, where he was gallantly and jauntily in evidence . . . . . and over it came back many a message which soon found placarding in front of the Journal Office in Washington Row, or leaded space in the newly founded Evening Bulletin. Far on the left the gentle slope of Mount St. Alban rose hazy beyond the city, its crest crown'd majestically by that stately tho' unfinisht National Cathedral to which our haste deny'd us a closer approach. Attaining the Washington side of the bridge, we cou'd not repress our admiration for the beauty of Potomac Park, a flat space beside the stream which art has transform'd from a marshy waste to a pleasing tract of drives, lawns, flowers, and verdure. At one spot we beheld a display of spouting fountains circling a pool which rivall'd the choicest glories of Versailles; whilst elsewhere there remain'd enough of the famous cherry blossoms to suggest their profuse loveliness of a week before.

Arriving on the Washington shoar at the foot of 14th Street, we again indulg'd in close glimpses of the Monument; and skirting the southerly end of the White House grounds, pass'd once more up 17th Street by the Pan-American Union, Continental Hall, Red Cross, and Corcoran Gallery on our way to Pennsylvania Avenue. There, in the mellow glow of an afternoon no longer young, Mrs. Renshaw deposited Kirk, Sechrist, and me upon the pavement for a pedestrian finale; herself driving off toward her home with Miss Dashiel, accompany'd by the most profound and sincere gratitude of the voyagers. We apologised for our inability to accompany her and meet her other guests, as she had wished; but I regret that I have so far fail'd—amidst the rush of the past week—to write her and Sechrist those expressions of thanks and pleasure which urbanity demands.

Being now on foot, our party lost no time in seeing as much as possible of Washington before the hour of my New-York stage coach. We were at this juncture in constant sight of the White House and its park, with leafy Lafayette Square at our left ahead. Turning into Jackson Place toward H St., we beheld first the building of Research University, for which I revised English themes in 1921–22, and next—on the corner of H—the old house built by Commander Stephen Decatur, who won fame as conqueror of the Tripoli pirates in 1805, and as originator of that nobly patriotick toast: "My Country—may she always be right; but my Country, right or wrong!" Here Decatur died a gentleman's death after his duel with Commodore Barron at Bladensburg in 1820, and here subsequently liv'd many celebrated persons such as Henry Clay and Martin Van Buren. Being now in H Street, we next beheld the shapely outlines of St. John's Church in 16th St. opposite Lafayette Square, a fine late Georgian specimen with Ionick portico and a belfry tower like that of Alexandria's Christ Church. It was built in 1814, and having a pew reserv'd for the President of the United States, has been variously nicknamed the "Church of State", and "President's Chapel." Amongst those who regularly attended it have been Madison, Monroe, John Quincy Adams of New-England, Jackson, Van Buren, Harrison, Tyler, Fillmore, Buchanan, and Arthur. Roosevelt and Taft were occasional visitors. Next on our route was a modest house built in 1825, at the corner of H St. and Madison Place, where the brilliant widow of Pres. Madison spent her declining years. It is now much made over, and houses that prominent social club of scientifically interested gentlemen known as the "Cosmos Club". Now doubling back past many old buildings to Pennsylvania Avenue, we observ'd the White House in closer detail; entering its grounds, passing under its port-cochere, and noting its architectural excellencies from all sides. Truly, a noble piece of work— Ave, Hobane! But time prest, so striking eastward we hasten'd to that part of Tenth Street above E where still stare across the street at each other the early-Victorian facade of Ford's Theatre, where Pres. Lincoln was shot, and the trim brick front of the old residence building where he was carried in to die. Both buildings, I fancy, will be preserv'd indefinitely as a grim reminder of a dark and calamitous passage in our history. The house is now a museum, containing the Oldroyd Collection of Lincolniana.

Our journey now became a phrensy'd race against time. Boarding an F

Street car, we were whirl'd past the Patent Office, Judiciary Square, and the Pension Office with its curious frieze of marching men, and were soon rounding the Capitol grounds in an effort to reach one more old section before the fateful starting-hour of 4:35. Christ Church (1795—oldest in Washington) we had to forego, but we did alight and glimpse the old Brick Capitol (1815) and Supreme Court building (1814) which were used by the government after the burning of Washington. This whole eastern district was deliciously quaint and archaick, and presented many tantalising vistas where venerable shade-trees guarded Georgian doorways and rail'd steps. But haste was all-important, so with brisk but sadden'd steps we trudg'd toward the Union Station through the genial gold of that Southern spring afternoon I was so soon to leave. Not a second too soon did we reach our goal. The coach-horses were pawing, and the driver's whip was cracking, and I had barely time to wave an hurry'd adieu to Sechrist and Kirk—who was staying over to transact business in Washington, Baltimore, Wilmington, Philadelphia, and Trenton—when the postilion gave his last warning cry. Creak—creak—rattle—rattle—and Washington, obscur'd by the dust of a weary highroad, became a fragrant memory and a legend.

Yr aff: Parent & Obt: Servt:

H. P. L.

## Notes

1. Thomas Moore (1779–1852), "To Thomas Hume, Esq., M.D.," ll. 9–18. HPL has misquoted Moore's text at several points. The word in the penultimate line appears as "J———n" in Moore (for Jefferson).

2. Isaac Weld (1774–1856), *Travels through the States of North America* (1806). The sentence is quoted in a note to Moore's poem.

3. Jedidiah Morse (1761–1826), *Geography Made Easy* (1784). HPL appears to have owned the 8th ed. (Boston: I. Thomas & E. T. Andrews, 1802) and the 19th ed. (Boston: Thomas & Andrews, 1818). The quotation appears on p. 184 of the latter edition.

4. Benjamin Henry Boneval Latrobe (1764–1820), a British subject and neoclassical architect.

5. Designed by McKim, Mead & White, constructed 1895–1904.

6. HPL refers to a statue at the head of an artificial pond in the sunken "Aztec Garden" in the rear of the Pan American Union Building (headquarters of the Organization of American States) in Washington DC.

7. Thomas Tickell (1685–1740), "Kensington Garden," ll. 1–4.

8. HPL refers to the duel on 11 July 1804 between Aaron Burr and Alexander Hamilton, in which Burr shot and killed Hamilton.

9. Quoted in Lossing 1.683. HPL owned Lossing's *A History of the Civil War 1861–65* (1912; *LL* 583).

10. Quoted in Harrison 122.

[105]  [AHT] [HPL to LDC]

Wednesday Morning
May 20, 1925

My dear Daughter Lillian:—

[. . .] And the diary? Let me see—I guess I left off
Saturday morning with that note scrawled on the outside of A.E.P.G.'s envelope whilst Kirk, Belknap and I were preparing to go down town to transport
some books from a disintegrating private home to the new shop at 97 Fourth
Avenue leased by Kirk and his friend from Cleveland. Well—we went down,
getting off the subway at the Grand Central, engaging *two* cabs, (for the load
was to consist of 750 books) and setting out for our loading point—the residence of the late Edward Penfold at 10 E. 40th Street—Kirk in one cab and
Sonny and I in the other. The distance was only a few squares, hence we were
soon knocking at the door and preparing to carry out armful after armful, to
be packed in the waiting machines by the two drivers. The house proved to
be a typical mid-Victorian New York home of quiet patrician type—for Penfold was a scholar and gentleman, listed in the Social Register. It was heart-
breaking to see it dismantled—beautiful Gothic and Tudor carved furniture
ticketed for auctioning, pictures coming down, *objets d'art* scattered about
or—more pathetic still—here and there remaining in their original place as
mocking reminders of the aristocratic domesticity now dissolving. The library
breathed intimately of the rich and austere personality of the deceased—oak
wainscoting with fireplace mantel, and pilasters of the Ionic order, and on
every side neat shelves reaching almost to the panelled ceiling. A shrine and
retreat of taste—now passing away for ever, to be replaced by some detestable parvenu menage or worse! Belknap and I almost shed tears, and Kirk was
the happier for his relative temperamental callousness. I could see the fall of
454 all over again, and echoed the pangs which are still fresh after twenty-one
years. Books finally loaded, we proceeded like a two-carriage funeral cortege
down Fourth Avenue to #97. Here we found carpenters' work insufficiently
progressed to permit of storage, hence had to ask the watchman of a next
door vacant shop to let us park them there. Books unloaded and cabs dis-
missed, we all drew a long breath and heaved a relieved sigh. The volumes
themselves are for the most part splendid and tasteful ones, revealing Penfold's taste and exciting my cupidity. I rather think the rashly generous Kirk
means to give me a set of Pope printed in 1760 or 1770 which took my eye—
hard as I shall try to stop him. That is, if he can find all the scattered volumes.
Our task complete, and appropriate reflections indulged in, we proceeded to
"do" the adjacent bookstalls—for as you probably know, this part of Fourth
Avenue just below Union Square is becoming the thickest of all book centres.
Here I'll have to admit a fall from grace so far as non-purchasing is concern'd, for a great volume of Bulwer-Lytton, with most of the weird novels
complete—"Zanoni", "A Strange Story", and "The House and the Brain"—

for only *ten cents,* proved a fatal bait; and I departed from the Schulte Emporium with less in my pocket and more in my hand. But only a dime, remember! Crossing the town, we were held up at Broadway by a monster police parade, from which Sonny escaped by diving into a homebound subway. Kirk and I kept on to Greenwich Village, where at #17 Downing Street (not #10!) we found the little returned tiger-kittie, who sat in Grandpa's lap just as serenely as one of those Tilden and Thurber kitties during the entire meal of native Italian spaghetti—for which Kirk insisted on paying. Now at this point—with all this chronicle of a social morning—you may smilingly doubt the genuineness of Old Theobald's retirement from the world—but look sharp! The hour was two p.m., and Kirk was ready for an afternoon of empty dawdling around bookstalls and cafeterias—already he had proposed some coffee at the Sheridan Square place, (where you got the breaded veal you didn't like) since the Downing Street joint is weak on that beverage—but what do you suppose Grandpa did? I'll tell you! The old gentleman made exceedingly polite excuses, bowed low, and took the underground stage-coach home— straight home, James!—where he sat tight reading and writing all the rest of the day, retired at night, and arose on the morrow to tuck his books under his arm and start for a solitary open-air day in nearby Fort Greene Park. There, on a bench against a secluded verdant slope, I read continuously all day; stopping only at twilight, when I wended my homeward way, pausing at John's spaghetti place for my usual Sunday dinner of meat balls and spaghetti, vanilla ice cream, and coffee. Incidentally—not many doors away, on the other side of Willoughby St., I found a restaurant which specialises in home-baked beans. It was closed on Sunday, but I shall try it some time soon. Beans, fifteen cents, with pork, twenty cents. With Frankfort sausages, twenty-five cents. Yes—here is a place which will repay investigation!

After dinner I laid in some supplies at the cheapest place open on Sunday, thence proceeding home—where I took one of our 454 dining-room chairs and went "out" for the evening—to my alcove with a pile of books! A knock came at the door—but I was not there. Windows and door-cracks show'd no light. Whose business whither I had gone? And so till bedtime, when I quietly turned in, awaking Monday noon and resuming my reading and writing. Having supplies, I didn't go out or dress, but when evening came I decided it wouldn't be politic to be "out" again. Two nights in succession would seem odd *at first,* though that will come very soon when the gang's habit is weakened a trifle more. Thus I let the light show—and surely enough, Loveman called. Now grasp the subtle work! I was cordial—but in slippers and dressing-gown, and with room not picked up. I apologised, but introduced no new or personal topics. With the sight of my writing all heaped about me, and with the burthen of conversation all thrown on him, my guest did not loll in the morris-chair by the hour as usual; but shortly adjourned to Kirk's den—though not without a promise to call on his way down. Another half-hour passes, and still I write. Now come Kirk's three familiar taps on the radiator pipe—to which I have to respond, since he knows I'm home. But my response is slow, and when I arrive I am cordial but not inventive of conversation. Another half-hour and Loveman leaves—with perfect cordiality—whilst Kirk puts himself in line for a favour—a thing I am particularly glad to grant him, since he has virtually forced so many substantial courtesies upon me. He, it appears, had also been loafing about—or working about—in his dressing-gown, and was greatly in want of a meal yet reluctant to bother to dress. Now I too was about to dine, so with the utmost hospitality I invited him down, treated him to A & P spaghetti, cheese, bread, and vanilla wafers off my best blue china, and bade him a courtly adieu almost immediately afterward—for he too felt the inadvisability of lingering in view of the obvious air of preoccupation about the place. All this while I had been lightly and banteringly alluding to my literary reform, both to Kirk and to Loveman; and speaking of the solid work ahead of me. Thus it was easy to capture the morrow by taking the initiative about when I would meet them again—saying that I would see them at the regular Boys' meeting *Wednesday,* and thus virtually exempting Tuesday. By this step, I could be sure of a quiet Tuesday night WITHOUT retiring to the alcove.

And so it was, I rested, was up again Tuesday afternoon, wrote letters undisturbed well into the night, rested again, and am now on deck once more, without having looked on a human face in the interim. Today I must do some shopping—perhaps I'll take in that grey suit and see how much it will come to, and maybe I'll be bold enough to graduate to a straw hat and let my felt be cleaned—and in the evening I shall have to be host at a Boys' Meeting. This is a McNeil meeting, and will probably be dull since Morton doubts if he can come whilst Sonny is by no means certain. These formal meetings I won't try to dodge just yet—the big thing is to get rid of the daily dropping-in and cafeteria loafing, which is death to any personal intellectual life or creative accomplishment. It'll be hard to shelve the gang, but with tact I am certainly doing it. Just now my prime difficulty is how not to offend Loveman by refusing his proposition for a Philadelphia excursion some Sunday soon. He wants to see the colonial part of the town, and wishes my services as a guide—being eager to pay my fare at the special excursion rate of three dollars. Now if I had the money, I'd be glad enough of the trip—Heaven knows I want to see a real white man's town badly enough—but unless I pay my own fare, there will be an inescapable atmosphere of obligation which will lessen my sense of independence in breaking free. It is such dubious taste to let a fellow treat one to a trip on Sunday, and refuse to open the door to him Monday evening! So I'll have to squirm out—though how to do it without offence, in view of the pressing cordiality, will certainly require allopathic doses of the subtlety I've been detailing in the past few pages! Saturday night is the Blue Pencil meeting at the Simonton studio, but I rather think I'll cut it despite the oratorical reproofs which Mortonius will heap upon my head. I may, though, take in their New Jersey picnic and "hike" Memorial Day. And in June Sechrist is coming to New York again for a day or so, bringing two of his children—an occasion on which I'll feel it a duty to repay the consideration he shew'd me in Washington.

Yr most aff: nephew & obt Servt<br>H P L

[106]    [AHT] [HPL to LDC]

Monday Evening<br>May 25, 1925

My dear Daughter Lillian:—

My current reading is Joseph Conrad's "Lord Jim", and I find it the most vital and important of any of the books on my immediate programme. I had previously read only the shorter and minor productions of Conrad, and was inclined to marvel at the depth and extent of his fame; but having read this volume I marvel no more, but join in the admiring chorus—conscious that for once the public taste has by accident failed to go wrong in its customary fashion. Conrad is at heart supremely a poet, and though his narration is often very heavy and involved, he displays an infinitely potent command of the soul of men and things, reflecting the tides of affairs in an unrivalled procession of graphic pictures which burn their imagery indelibly upon the mind. He feels and expresses as few authors can, the prodigious and inhuman tides of a blind, bland universe; at heart indifferent to mankind, but purposefully malignant if measured by the narrow and empirical standard of human teleology. Hardy, as I remarked recently, seems to me vastly overrated; being at bottom ordinary, trite, and a trifle theatrical. But Conrad's reputation is deserved—he has the sense of ultimate nothingness and the evanescence of illusions which only a master and an aristocrat can have, and he mirrors it forth with that uniqueness and individuality which are genuine art. No other artist I have yet encountered has so keen an appreciation of the essential *solitude* of the high grade personality—that solitude whose projected overtones form the mental world of each sensitively organised individual—which intrusion is powerless to assail and assalt[,] able only to intensify; which is at once the prison and protection of the proved and complex non-animal soul. Yes—Conrad is at least one idol of today which is not a "false alarm"; and I think posterity will single him out with a very few companions as one of the supreme voices of the age. It does Belknap credit that he "discovered" Conrad two years ago, and sang his praises incessantly whilst I remained ignorant and indifferent. Now I can join him, and out-shout my small child in sincere panegyric! It is to Conrad that our other sailor-novelist William McFee owes his inspiration and style. McFee—whose "Casuals of the Sea" you will recall—is no doubt the better story-teller of the two so far as facility and technical method go; but in actual poetic command of the cosmic panorama, and ruthless insight into the darkest arcana of human character, he is a child beside Conrad. To Conrad surfaces have ceased to have an intrinsic significance—he is at one with the weariness and eternal pain and horror of seas and winds and skies.

Well—more next time. After "Lord Jim"—which I fervently advise you to read—I shall turn to "The Eagle's Shadow", by James Branch Cabell.

> Yr aff: Nephew & obt Servt
> H. P. L.

Bulletin—two a.m.

I hate to add bad news—but I might as well tell you what I discovered on going to get my clothes to mail this letter. Prepare yourself for something of a shock—there may be a reversal and better news later after I get in touch with Mrs. Burns and possibly the police.

The bad news is this—that while I slept, (for it couldn't have been while I was in the alcove, on account of the sounds I'd have instantly heard) my dressing-alcove was entered, either through the door to the next room or through my door by someone having a key; and *all* my suits except the thin blue, my Flatbush overcoat, a wicker suitcase of S.H.'s, Loveman's radio material, and I know not what else, have been stolen. One circumstance—the position of a long rod in the alcove—makes me suspect the youths now inhabiting the next room, or else persons working through that room in their absence. This has occurred since Sunday morning, for at that time—as you know from my Bulletin to A.E.P.G.—I tried on the newly fixed trousers . . . . . alas! shall I ever see them again? Now I haven't been out of the house since, or even out of the room except to the bathroom. Nor could it have occurred, conceivably, whilst I was in the wash alcove. It must have happened whilst I slept—roughly, between six a.m. and eight-thirty p.m. Sunday, eight a.m. and three-thirty p.m. Monday, or nine p.m. and one-thirty a.m. (just now) Monday–Tuesday. I don't think it would serve any useful purpose to create a disturbance now, but I shall dress and be ready for a busy day to-day—alas for my programme of retirement! Nothing in the outer room appears to have been touched. The thieves were apparently professionals, knowing what was salable material. For example, they stole the newest overcoat and no other. They omitted the blue suit, no doubt, because it was hanging on a chair in the outer room.

I can't yet accustom myself to the shock—to the grim truth that I haven't a suit of clothes to my back save the thin, blue summer one. What I shall ever do if the property isn't recovered, Heaven alone knows! And after all this boxing! I can't get along on one thin suit—at least, I don't see how I can—and that near the final stage of disintegration. It certainly is a devilish mess, and I hope to Pegāna that I can recover the stuff. Unless I do—may the Gods assist me! I fear I shall have to draw some cash or something—I wear my things so long that it wouldn't be an extravagance to begin the accumulation of another stock of four suits—one good summer, and one good winter at first, and later another winter to allow of alternate wear—for the coming decade if I live that long. But then—my only really fresh-looking overcoat is gone, so what's the use? Tough luck! Here's hoping I do recover my property. No—upon my word, I don't know what to do next, with only one thin suit to my name. I suppose I must simply wear an overcoat on cool days, and wait for the gods to wake me up from the nightmare of my destitution. And— changing the phase of the subject—what shall I ever say to poor Loveman about his radio parts? Their value, I fear, is close to a hundred dollars! And I thought I was doing him a favour by storing them! His Fawcett books and paintings haven't been touched.[1]

Well—I'll seal this, and if anything new develops I'll add it on the envelope. I could curse the atmosphere blue! Just as I had decided to try to look more respectable by keeping my clothes in good order, here comes this blasted, infernal thunderbolt to deprive me of the battery of four suits and one really decent overcoat needed as a minimum of neat appearance. To Hades with everything!

Now I'll dress—scant worry about what to choose this time—and swear at the walls till somebody is up to swear at. Damnation!

Yr aff: Nephew and obt Servt<br>H P L

*Notes*

1. Edgar Fawcett (1847–1904), American novelist and poet who wrote chiefly of New York high society. Loveman was attempting to resurrect his reputation.

[107]    [ALS] [HPL to LDC]

Thursday Night<br>May 28, 1925.

My dear daughter Lillian:—

Pipe the charity paper! This is what Kirk gave me when he moved—you'll recall my shewing you the unopened package. It's an awkward size, but the surface certainly is magnificent for pen & ink. Remembering the size of the bundle, you will be prepared to receive many & many a missive of these dimensions!

Thanks prodigiously for the sympathy on the recent disaster—but don't let it worry you! Never waste emotion on the other fellow's plight—if any expressiveness is needed, I can furnish enough cuss-words to fill the suppressed part of a censored dictionary of synonymes! Yah! If I were writing a primer at this moment I'd cut out the A B C's altogether, & start in with a really vital & graphic letter—in double-size, heavy-faced, capitalised italic form! Yes—it takes real rhetoric to expound the sensation of one suddenly stript of raiment which formed not only a tasteful adornment of the present, but a relique of former youth & a legacy of past ages amounting—in the case of the older garments—to the virtual sentimental equivalent of an heirloom! Alas for the robes of my infancy, perennial in their bloom, & now cut off—or snatched off—in the finest flowering of their first few decades! They

knew the slender youth of old, & expanded to accomodate the portly citizen of middle life—aye, & condensed again to shroud the wizened shanks of old age! And now they are gone—gone—& the grey, bent wearer still lives to bemoan his nudity; gathering around his lean sides as best he may the strands of his long white beard to serve him in the office of a garment!

Yes—it certainly was quite an affair! Of course the quasi-partitional door *ought* to have been bolted & barred—& will be now that the damage is comfortably over. Loveman's pangs at his radio loss were mitigated by his joy at the fact that none of his Edgar Fawcett books was touched; but even so, he's in a position to condole with me through really subjective sympathy! He still owes $20.00 for the instalment purchase of a thing he no longer possesses, & when he reported the loss to the company in the course of finding out the serial number of the machine, the clerk seemed to suspect him of some dodge to evade payment until he reiterated his determination to come across to the very final farthing! It's a hard world! The detective, an affable, competent-looking person with the brisk voice & steely-blue eyes which belong with the part, avowed his intention of doing his very best; taking from me a minute description of each missing garment, & eliciting a thorough picture of the fugitive appropriators from Mrs. Burns—who is the only one able to identify them. What he can do has not yet appeared . . . . . . but hope & faith, the platitudinarians & fundamentalists tell us, are the twin cornerstones of orderly society! As I've just written A E P G, I really don't know the established custom of endowing the authorities with gratuities in cases of success; but I seem to have read things about passing around cigars & the like. The graceful gesture is always important. As for me—your advice is exactly what my own judgment has dictated; to wait a reasonable time & keep the home folks posted. The whole business is the most damnable sort of a blow at a time when I was mustering up the forces of optimism, industry, & reasserted individuality—but even at that, I guess the above-mentioned forces in combination are enough to give the new hydra-head a safely fractured skull. Granted a room, leisure, a book, a bathrobe, a pen, & a stack of paper, there's life left in the old man yet! But I wish to Pete those pesky pillagers had staged their Macheath act[1] before I lavished so much cash on the pressing & repair of those suits! Let us take stock of what we have & haven't:

| YES, WE HAVE NO | OTHER ABSTRACTIONS | BUT WE DO HAVE |
|---|---|---|
| new Flatbush overcoat 1924. | S H's wicker | 1918 thin blue suit |
| old 1915 thick suit | suit case | 1909 light overcoat |
| newer 1921 "   " | Loveman's | 1917  "       " |
| newest 1923 thin grey suit | radio set | 1915 winter overcoat |
| TODAY | | moth-eaten odd flannel |
| | | trousers—grey |
| | | odd grey skeleton coat |
| | | —shapeless |
| | | straw hat—clean & |
| | | shapely |
| | | newly renovated felt hat |
| | | old brown felt hat for |
| | | rainy days |
| | | all gloves, ties, & linen |
| | | all shoes & rubbers & |
| | | slippers |
| | | STILL |

Why, yes—item for item, the "still-haves" certainly do make a cheerfully impressive list—if one naively trains oneself to look at things that way. And of course the most important fact of all is that the corsairs didn't cruise into the main room at all, thus leaving unmolested the books, pictures, & other cherished objects which are—far more than any garments could be—my very life itself. The time of the event is clearly fixed as between 6 a.m. Sunday, when I retired for a deep sleep after having been up writing all night, & noon, when Mrs. Burns found the adjoining room vacant with both guests gone without paying rent. I slept till 8 or 9 that night; & having no occasion to go to the alcove till 1.30 Tuesday morning, when I went for some old stuff to slip on for posting your letter, did not discover my loss till then. Knowing the turmoil & actual uselessness of a night alarm, I waited till the household was astir before notifying Mrs. Burns & Loveman—after which things developed as outlined in my last diary-card. And that is still the last word in the case— save that in cleaning out the pirates' lair next day, Mrs. B. found three of my suit-shoulders (two that clasp the trousers by the bottom & one with horizontal bar) & the contents of S H's stolen wicker suitcase. The door had been forced by bending out the escutcheon & getting at the lock beneath. The spoilers' professional skill appears in this, for the lock was a broken one—broken whilst locked—with the shank of a broken key in it; an arrangement so baffling to ordinary skill that a month ago, when a former tenant of the next room was locked out & sought admittance through my alcove, nothing could be done to open the door despite the most careful efforts of Mrs. Burns' eldest son with the household tools at his command. These oily brigands were obviously used to mechanical problems of this sort!

Well—such is which! Business still goes on at the old stand, & I'll be delighted to receive the more generally chatty letter you were planning, as well as the promised package of papers. S H, too, will be delighted to hear from you. She is holding out well at Saratoga; & though her last small hat venture did not succeed, is still looking about for better openings—including one in Boston, at Filene's—which may justify an experimental trip thither next month over the Boston & Albany for a tentative interview. Oh, yes—& let me extend the most abundant thanks for the transmission of the two-spot—which will nobly treat the whole station-house to perfectos if the public peace's noble guardians rope the miscreants & restore the purple & ermine of state to their rightful holder! As for the reading report—finished Conrad's "Lord Jim" & started on Cabell's "Eagle's Shadow". Promises well—but Cabell is no Conrad. I'm going to read more of good ol' Joe—Belknap's given me a list of his best, which I'll follow up as opportunity permits. And to think the guy died before I began to appreciate him—only a few months ago![2]

Next on the programme comes the inevitable diary instalment—"Chapters from an Intimate Autobiography," as I'd say if I were a prominent egotist trading on fame to float a lot of dull personal detail before a jaded public. Let's see—we left off Tuesday morning as I was preparing to go down to the new Kirk–Kamin bookstall in 4th Ave. to meet Belknap & Loveman for the purpose of taking the latter on a round of the museums before his projected departure for Cleveland. Well, I went—& on time too—but found only Kamin, who reported another turn of the Lovemanic weathervane whereby the poet had been persuaded to stay here at least a little while longer, through the securing of a connexion on commission basis with a new financial & commercial magazine—or rather, a thirty-year-old one in new hands. The job began at once, so he had sat directly down to a desk (though later work will be at home) & started in, sending his regrets about the now cancelled engagement. But here is the joke—or coincidence—or confirmation of the old "small-world" saw . . . . . . for as Heaven is my judge, this enterprise, brought to Loveman's notice solely through Kamin & a relative of the latter's who is connected with it, is nothing more or less than the expansive venture of Arthur Leeds' old employer Yesley, about which we have been hearing incessantly from Leeds for the past two months! When Leeds & Loveman came face to face in the office—where Leeds now has an important executive post—both were quite properly knocked out with surprise; & each member of our gang, on subsequently learning of it, has displayed the appropriate signs of devastating astonishment. Leeds thinks he can keep Loveman nicely occupied if the latter will stick, but the poet naturally feels a certain insecurity until he can pass from a commission to a salaried basis. One moment he favours staying; another moment he favours returning to Cleveland. Kamin, who takes his fate to heart, is quite dizzy & disconcerted about it; & Kirk thinks it might perhaps be better if he returned for a while, to make a second metropolitan entry later, when he can bring his rare books to sell one by one for immediate living expenses. The work in this Yesley establishment is simple, consisting wholly of writing up complimentary articles descriptive of striking business ventures or outstanding mercantile and professional personalities; each article to be about $1\frac{1}{4}$ to $1\frac{1}{2}$ double-spaced typed pages in length.[3] This writing is all from facts supplied—"leads", as they call them, culled from press notices or advertising matter. Sometimes the writer digs up his own leads by scanning the press & picking up all the catalogues that come his way—or even watching the streets for new shops & building enterprises as they appear one by one—but generally, if he is a novice at business, he is content to write up the leads which his more commercially minded colleagues have previously selected & catalogued. His article, when done, is sent in to the office; & unless too bad to be accepted is then taken out by a trained salesman to the person or company whereof it treats. This salesman, after giving the interested party a chance to revise, urges the latter to order a quantity of the magazines mentioning him—for advertising purposes; & if he succeeds, (as he does in a surprising number of cases, since the sales force is a very expert one) the writer of the article receives 10% of the sum paid by the purchaser—amounts varying from $1.50 to over $30.00 according to the extent of the order. Thus with good luck & some ability there is here an excellent hack field for the pure writer—with trained business men to attend to the commercial details at both ends; the lead-finding at the start & the salesmanship at the finish. All that one needs is fluency & some inventiveness, plus a sense of language sufficient to capture the particular sort of atmosphere needed for each type of subject. Most of the men connected with the venture make very tolerable livings despite the commission rather than salary basis; & experts like Kamin's relative or connexion Fenton net over fifty dollars per week. Leeds is now making enough to float him but for the enormous past debts hanging over his head. A few writers work in the office, but still more do their writing at home—not only in New York, but in other cities whence they communicate by mail. Many make it a part-time venture, picking up extra cash as a side-line to other industrial endeavours. All told, it is a *speculation*, with time instead of money as the commodity staked. One writes a certain number of articles; knowing that *all* may not "take", yet feeling sure that enough will be marketed to make up for the "false alarms" & bring a tidy sum each week—not even sums but averaging a decent amount over any considerable stretch of time as fat weeks compensate for the lean. Belknap & I have talked this proposition over with Leeds before—having ourselves in mind— & he had said he would put us in touch with some work as soon as the enterprise was really under way. This is its first week, & behold! Pure chance, working through a wholly different channel, introduces it to Loveman before Leeds has a chance to meet us! But there is no question of crowding—the field is vast; & once started, Yesley (pronounced Yez′ley) can't get enough writers! Leeds & Kamin, as I have intimated, are urging Loveman to stick; but only the gods know what he will do—or for that matter has done—since last I saw him at the meeting yesterday evening! It may be, of course, that a real poet lacks the needed command of incisive business language, or the prose fluency essential to profitable quantity production where rapid hack work is demanded. Returning to the narration proper—upon learning that Loveman was busy, I called up to save Sonny the trouble of keeping the engagement in vain; getting him in time, & being asked up for lunch & the afternoon, as the child had originally asked me before I told him of our aesthetic obligation to pilot Loveman on his supposedly last farewell—in the Patti or Bernhardt sense—tour of the sights.[4] I reached there in good time, enjoyed an excellent repast, & spent some hours in a brisk discussion of Conrad, Hardy, & George Moore—from whose new book of critical & artistic comments my little host read many of the best passages aloud.[5] I then accompanied him & his mamma to a neighbouring cinema show, where one impossible film & another slightly less impossible induced a not disagreeable kind of semi-somnolence. By seven it was over; & bidding the Longs farewell at the 96th St. station I proceeded forthwith to the Public Library in 42nd St—where we saw the manuscripts—to read a new Arthur Machen tale, "The Shining Pyramid", obtainable there but not removable from the building.[6] Belknap had told me about it. In thus calling my evenings my own, to read in or do what I please in, I am achieving a sense of balance, freedom, & regained individual personality which I have long lacked. I had been asked to spend that evening around the 4th Ave. & Downing St. slums with the gang, & would have felt myself compelled by courtesy to do so a couple of months ago. Now, however, I am severely & relentlessly my own master; & politely countered the well-meant invitation with the statement that my own affairs might make it impossible, great as would be my regret, & so on. What I wanted to do I did—read "The Shining Pyramid" & found it fair though not Machen's best, took the subway home to a peaceful hearth, gave Kirk & Loveman a civil welcome (though with such indications of early retiring—opened couch, &c—as did not encourage long mooning & staring over nothing) when they called about midnight, & settled down to finish my Conrad book before finally seeking my couch. Neat? I'm getting the world in training! The old vacuously gregarious spirit is shrinking without any decrease in cordiality, & in my recaptured peace & quiet I am laying the foundations of a concentrative power which may yet enable me to do something—financially as well as artistically—& win back the more active mind & sense of humour which once upon a time I enjoyed; a power which not even the sickening shock of sudden robbery & lack of adequate wardrobe can impair.

The next day I was up at noon, surveyed the odds & ends discovered in the freebooters' nest, & did considerable writing & reading before it was time to go up to Sonny's for the meeting. Kirk had asked me to meet him at the 4th Ave. shop in the afternoon to plan one of his slum dinners, but I urbanely & regretfully—yet ah, how firmly!—pointed out that my tasks would leave not a moment vacant. Little by little the habit fades! At the proper time I took the subway for the meeting, arriving there early but finding Morton & Kleiner ahead of me. Leeds & Loveman came later, but Kirk & Kamin sent messages of regret by the latter; since the affairs of their shop had compelled them to return for an evening's toil after their prandial loaf in the Suburra.[7] The meeting was one of our best—I notice that with either Belknap or Morton present it's *likely* to be good, & that with *both* it's a sure-fire success. Morton left first, then Kleiner & Loveman, & finally Leeds & I. Leeds is a sort of sticker, but I assiduously pried him loose because of Sonny's need to retire before morning. He has to be routed out at 7 in order to turn his erstwhile bedroom into a waiting-room & parlour, & when he gets little or no sleep his stuttering is radically worse—so bad that he hates to talk with anybody or do any errands at the shops. At the last, he & Leeds & I had talked very seriously about the Yesley writing venture; & when I rode down town with Leeds I continued the conversation, getting more & more workable details from his kindly & willing lips. So keen on the trail of industrial facts did I become, indeed, that I broke my anti-loafing rule & had coffee with him at a restaurant near his hotel; absorbing the general "hang" of his proposition & learning exactly what I would & wouldn't be expected to do if I definitely decided to go in for it & "play the market" for real money with some of my new & hard-won time, energy, & independence. He agreed to shew me the ropes thoroughly, & see that my articles (which need not be signed) receive proper sales treatment; & predicted that I ought to stand as good a chance at making money as himself or anybody else who has proved he can do it. And so I told him I would tackle the thing—& he means to send me my first assignment in a week or two, when he can get together the leads best suited to me (real estate, largely) & find the right models for imitation among his old magazines. Of course, I am no longer moved or excited over any outlook of this sort. I know all these business vistas turn very swiftly to mirages before one's eyes, & make one kick oneself for any naive enthusiasm one may have shewn in advance. But it is at least no crime to indulge in frankly fantastic speculation, & I can see myself—

in an imaginatively fictional way—with an actual income & possible future for the first time in my life. My first act on achieving any really regular stipend would be to return to New England;—for location is immaterial to the venture—the Boston district (out Salem–Marblehead way) at first, till I could really acquire some solidity; & finally, after a proper Hub apprenticeship, the sacred soil of *Providence,* re-won through pain & labour, & nevermore to be quitted by a sedate old gentleman who sampled the world & found that its dearest jewel was the hearthstone he left behind! A diverting Alnaschar's dream,[8] in truth—& doubly picturesque at a moment when in all literal verity I have scarce a rag to cover my back! Well—after finishing the talk I broke away from Leeds, took the subway home, & started a giant session of reading & writing to get my deck cleared. I'm still at it*—& shall admit no one today or tomorrow if I can help it, being fully stocked with provisions. I almost hate to go to sleep for fear some one will pop in & steal the rest of my stuff! Saturday I shall also stick around home, I think, since I can't afford to risk my one suit on the "hike". Sunday my retirement will have to be postponed, since I keep open house for a highly piquant "young visiter" from classic Cambridge—none other than li'l Sandy the Slangster,[9] who's toddling over for a week-end in the petrol velocipede, & has so many other New York engagements—largely business—that he can't slip de Ole Gent a sure-thing tip as to when he'll scrape his dawgs on the 169 doormat. But he'll be welcome—& most of the gang will no doubt lounge about to assist in his reception. I haven't seen the little rascal for a year & a half, & must brush up on my syncopated patter! ¶ More bulletins later. For the present I will nudely subscribe myself

Yr most aff nephew & obt Servt

H P L

P.S. In a letter just recd., S H suggests that I drown the memory of my losses in a trip to Saratoga the middle of next month, whilst her employers are away—possibly working in a call on nice old Mr. Hoag. Sounds fine—but with neither a respectable suit nor the 14 fish for round trip I doubt its feasibility! Nevertheless, that must be a great country!

P.P.S. "Half a Century with the Journal" has come.[10] It's great!!! THANKS!

## Notes

1. An allusion to Captain Macheath, a thief in John Gay's *The Beggar's Opera* (1728).
2. Joseph Conrad died 3 August 1924.

---

*LATER—Loveman just called in, but owing to the appearance of business, went upstairs very shortly.

3. HPL wrote five such pieces; see "[Commercial Blurbs]" (*CE* 5.180–84). The Yesley venture did not materialize, and it is unlikely that HPL's pieces were ever published or that he was paid for them.

4. HPL refers to the farewell tours of the Italian-French opera singer Adelina Patti (1843–1919) and the actress Sarah Bernhardt (1844–1923).

5. Presumably *Conversations in Ebury Street* (1924) by George Moore (1852–1933), a leading Irish novelist and man of letters.

6. Probably from the volume *The Shining Pyramid* (1925). HPL later obtained the volume (*LL* 621).

7. The Suburra was the slum district of ancient Rome.

8. For Alnaschar see LDC/AEPG 2n6.

9. I.e., Albert A. Sandusky.

10. See Bibliography under Providence Sunday Journal.

[108]  [AHT] [HPL to LDC]

Friday Afternoon
June 5, 1925

My dear Daughter Lillian:—

[. . .] No—the Great Robbery is so far without a happy sequel, though I summon to my aid the choicest consolations of philosophy. That "Bend" article of platitudinous old Crane has the right idea—the fellow must necessarily stumble on a pertinent truth once in a while, since his mild second-hand observations are flung over nearly the entire field of commonplace human thought! Commiserations on the fate of the muffins—yes, depredators are certainly making the world a lively place! I don't recall that I ever laid the prevalent increase in crime to the influence of the cinema—in fact, I'm quite sure that you must be thinking of some other critic's observation—since this is a widely repeated statement which I am inclined to accept with decided reservations. I don't believe boys get many more ideas from this source than from the dime novels and coloured Sunday supplements of yesterday; and think rather that the current causes of lawlessness are much more complex—low-grade heterogeneous immigrant population, lack of home training inherent in an industrialised civilisation, unmoral sophistication due to growth of large cities, decline in religious superstition which leaves plebeians without rigid codes of conduct, and general spread of a material, pessimistic philosophy in which morals are seen to be an artificial ornament too fragile for peasants to heed in their scramble for a little joy in life before the final black extinction. In other words—it is the age itself, which one must merely accept as a fact, whether one like it or not. Personally, I am compelled to believe all the scientific facts whose public knowledge has caused this sense of unrestraint, while at the same time—out of a love of conservatism and sense of the artistic in life—deploring their inevitable consequences. There is nothing to be done—one can't reinstate a system of myth once the people know how hollow it is—and one may find consolation only in the knowledge that our civilisation is not the first to decay. Decadence is indeed the common fate of all human institutions; and protest though we may, we cannot avert the law of old age and death which sent Egypt, Babylon, Nineveh, Tyre, Persepolis, Greece, Carthage, Palmyra, Alexandria, Rome, Bagdad, and Cordova to the dust. We have passed the meridian, and henceforward may only hope that the destruction will not be too swift. Yet even that does not matter in a bland, blind cosmos.

I think you'll like "Lord Jim", though you may find it a bit rambling. Conrad's "Point of Honour"—which Daas gave me for Christmas in 1915, but which I have only just read—is not so powerful. Stephen Crane, whose stories I read yesterday, seems to me monstrously overrated. Cabell I am sure you would like—both the exquisite finish of the style and the delicate vein of gently ironic disillusion. "The Cream of the Jest" is the best thing of his I have so far seen. My next book is a re-reading of "The Gam",[1] a volume of whaling stories which A. E. P. G. gave me for Christmas 1899, and which I wish to peruse again because of the interest in New England whaling that "Moby Dick" gave me. Yes—I noticed the alien "Planets and Stars", and liked this latest one very much. The same series was syndicated in the Asheville N. C. *Gazette-News,* which I used to see in 1915. I suppose this is Currier's sabbatical year—or else that he got bored with the job and gave it up. His articles were getting much better, though they never approached Upton's.[2] As to the President of Wheaton—it struck me as significant that a *Valentine* should enjoy his dignities so close to Valentine's Corner, Chartley.[3] The Rathbone cutting I reënclose herewith, for Grandmother's red book. And by the way—in one of the books in Kirk's stock, a large illustrated folio called "The Book of American Homes", by Charles Wyllys Elliott, (1876) there is a full-page plate and long description of the great hall in the residence of one J. L. Rathbone, Menlo Park, San Francisco, California. It really shewed excellent taste for the Victorian age! Those verses "What Grandmother Wore" are very clever.[4] Lucky old lady—nowadays one is fortunate if thieves leave one anything to wear! So you also use a tip-table! One-room housekeeping makes these venerable accessories exceedingly useful.—This morning I have dutifully partaken of my whole grain wheat and maple syrup in a blue china cup in true colonial fashion! I use newspaper rather than enamel-cloth for table damask. And by the way—I'll keep the cretonne item in mind. No—I don't know the Aldrich house by sight, but am sure the inhabitants must be delightful persons. Their gift to the university has secured them lasting memory, which in truth they well deserve. As to the colossal bronze figure atop the State House—the allusion you saw was correct. It is an allegorical being entitled "The Independent Man", and typifying the spirit of civic and religious liberty which distinguished the efforts of Mr. Williams and his successors in the colony. I have heard that but few are aware of the meaning of the figure, and that it has frequently been mistaken for an Indian. Yes—I saw the Hardy cat item and delighted in it![5] I don't rate the work of Hardy quite so high as most in this generation do, but I certainly endorse his feline tastes to the uttermost limit! Which reminds me that the other day I saw and stroked quite the most delightful large maltese cat imaginable in a doorway near here. How he did rub and purr! Grandpa's big grey boy! Give my regards to the black and the white cat when you see them again. I wonder which was really the *least* clean? The School of Design graduation must have been interesting, as must also the Pettis Excursion. The preservation of antique furniture is commendable in the extreme, but why in thunder did she want to build a *Dutch* colonial cottage on *Rhode-Island* soil, when so many exquisite designs for New England colonial cottages exist? A sense of geographical fitness is rare indeed—I recall seeing several Dutch cottages in the newer part even of Marblehead, where if anywhere people ought to know better.

As to clothing—since I am keeping clear of people as much as possible, I shan't get anything quite yet. Mostly I am here in my nightshirt, (thanks for those coming—I have on the other newly mended one at this moment!) and on my solitary tramps to the park I shall (weather permitting) wear the odd limp skeleton coat and flannel trousers. When making an ordinary trip in company, I shall wear the blue coat (for truly, the other is quite absurd!) with the light flannel trousers, (a permissible combination, though not greatly to my taste) saving the blue trousers well pressed for nicer occasions—as when I go up to Sonny's house for lunch. Otherwise, the blue trousers will soon be gone; for they are grievously thin, threadbare, and shiny in the seat, and the cloth is worn off around the edges of the pockets, showing bits of a yellowish lining beneath. Like you, I wouldn't believe that one could buy a decent suit for twenty-five dollars nowadays—especially a two-trousers suit—yet here is Little Belknap with the actual, irrefutable proof. He paid just that—yet I can see how well the suit becomes him, and how finely it wears. Come to think of it, *you* saw him in a twenty-five dollar grey which he put on for the first time about the period of your call there. I have thought of trying for still cheaper bargains—old models or out-of-season goods, to which Leeds might tip me off. A *winter* suit *now* might be very cheap, or a *summer* suit *next September or October*—the latter bargain being the more likely, since winter goods have a tendency to be regarded as year-round staples, whilst summer materials occasionally go at ridiculous reductions as autumn advances. What a devil of a predicament! One can never be really at ease with less than four suits—two of each weight, so that one of the right sort can always be ready in good condition for whatever occasion may require it.

With renewed assurances of my high consideration, I am, Madam,

Yr most affec: Nephew and obt: Servt

H. P. L.

## Notes

1. See Bibliography under Charles Henry Robbins.

2. HPL refers to Clinton Harvey Currier (1876–1943) and Winslow Upton (1853–1914), both professors of astronomy at Brown University. Both had astronomy columns in the *Providence Journal.*

3. Samuel Valentine Cole (1851–1925) was president of Wheaton College (Norton, MA) from 1897 to 1925. LDC had attended Wheaton in 1872–74.

4. Minna Irving, "What Grandmother Wore," *New York Times* (26 March 1913): 10. Presumably the poem was syndicated in other newspapers.

5. Presumably a reference to Thomas Hardy's poem "Last Words to a Dumb Friend" (1904), about the death of a cat.


[109]　　[ALS] [HPL to LDC]

Monday Afternoon and Evening—
July 6, 1925

My dear Daughter Lillian:—

It is hard to believe that a week has slipt by since my last homeward epistle, but so my diary informs me. Meanwhile I have appreciated most thoroughly your notes & the package of *Atlantic Monthly* & cuttings. Just now I have received a notice from the Prov. P.O. of a newspaper awaiting me there with 6 cents of unpaid postage. This sum goes forward by the present post, & I shall expect a further treat when its results arrive.

Meanwhile—& hold your breath at this point for a decisive statement—I HAVE BOUGHT THE SUIT! It is a beauty, has 3 pieces, cost only **$25.00**, & was obtained at a well-known "chain store" called "Monroe Clothes", whose low prices have always been somewhat striking. Before long I shall send you a photograph of myself in the new outfit, & in the interim will display the exact goods by enclosing a sample. You may keep this, so as to be always familiar with the fabric of my de luxe integument, for I have prepared another for A E P G. They let me have the chopped-off cloth of both trouser-bottoms; so that I can not only be very free with samples, but can keep a useful reserve fund for patching. The fit is surprisingly excellent—39 coat— & the cut is the same absolutely plain & conservative one which my clothing has always had. The suit in general has a certain pleasing resemblance to my very first long-trouser outfit, purchased at Browning & King's in April 1904. Too bad that suit wasn't purchased earlier, so that Gramp might have seen me in long trousers!

Thanks for those Mitchell samples—which are good, though too strongly suggesting a *pattern* to please a very sedate old gentleman. You will note that the suit I did get was absolutely plain. I don't think the Mitchell firm charge differently for different sizes—didn't you notice the special appeal to fat men in the advertisement I sent? But I think the ready-made Monroe clothes are probably more satisfactory to buy, & will probably get my winter suit there also when the time comes. It is up one flight at the corner of Fulton & Willoughby Sts.—a stone's throw from here. I had always known of the system of stores, & had intended to look up one of them; but did not discover this one until last Wednesday evening when S H & I were dining at John's Italian restaurant. On that occasion we sat near the front; & I, who was facing the street, noticed through the window a clothing display on the opposite side. The price-mark *$21.50* attracted me; so that after dinner we began to investigate; & in the end—although we found nothing for $21.50—we came upon the delightful 25.00 specimen which now hangs immaculately (& I hope safely) in my clothespress. I have worn it twice—but it really seems too good to wear. Of the gang, only Leeds has seen it; but he went into ecstasies over it. Wednesday night we meet at Sonny's, & then I shall display it more widely. I told them about it at the last meeting, & have given samples to Sonny & Morton. It was finally ready on Friday evening, July 3. All told, I think I have done remarkably well, considering the price. I am sure that you will agree after studying the enclosed sample & the photograph which I hope to get shortly.

As to food these days—Great Scott! There's no need to worry about the Old Gentleman's being undernourished! The only worry I have is that S H's diet programme will get me fat again—although I haven't begun to fatten as yet. When we have home meals she insists on meat in sandwich form—ham, spiced beef, & (on one occasion) *turkey* (which I didn't know was obtainable in summer)—& of late she has been dragging me forth to veritably Neronian gorges at neighbouring restaurants—mostly John's, but once our old reliable friend Joe's. That one meal at Joe's was a classic. S H set about three good sized dinners before me at a single sitting; & since she had paid—or contracted—for them, my sense of economy compelled me to consume them! I am glad to report, however, that my weight shewed no subsequent increase. We *have* obtained some of those Scotch Bakery buns—which appear to be three cents each—& later I'll try some Campbell's Soup, which the A & P stores feature. Whole Grain Wheat is obtainable at the Scotch Bakery, as indeed I predicted from a reading of signs. S H is very fond of it, though for my part I wouldn't want to depend on it too *uninterruptedly* lest I become satiated. On the next can we're going to try some of the widely advertised Karo Corn Syrup—which was obtained by mistake, but which one might as well try as a novelty to see what it's like. Cheese continues to be a staple of mine—just now we have some of that excellent Phoenix Swiss.

Yes—it's an infernal irony that my acute taste for R.I. history did not develop till after the disposal of Dr. Clark's MSS. But such is life. I *have* a copy of the Lippitt "Battle of R.I." right here—he must have given you several. I note the duplicate Brown cutting—& will presently send the R.I. book I spoke of. All of the cuttings proved of intense interest—the flintlock, Virgil's tomb, the cloudburst, &c. &c. I'll give that *Bahai* one to Mortonius. Too bad the Sprague–Lippitt mansion is coming down—but thank Heaven it isn't a colonial house! Ugly things can well afford to go, & I wish that Providence could have some such renovation as has lately befallen Santa Barbara, Cal., where the artists mean to replace all the earthquake-tumbled buildings with harmonious structures of an architecture befitting the traditions of the locality. Oh, yes—& every time I see an ice-cream cone I think of that Middlesex kitty-cat!

I may use that dream idea of mine some day—though Pegāna knows I have more weird ideas floating around than I'll ever have a chance to crystallise into literary form. Just now I'm reading up the recent copies of *Weird Tales* to see how it's developing, & what kind of stuff Wright is mostly using. The new (August) issue is out now; with no story of mine, though I am rather flatteringly mentioned in the editor's "Eyrie". Sonny's poem, "Stallions of the Moon", is included in the contents. Next month my "Temple" & Belknap's "Were-Snake" will appear.

Thanks tremendously for that *Atlantic,* which I have read with the keenest interest. The "Visions" are certainly analogous to some of the more spectral creations of my own idle fancy, whilst the remarks on the "Fifth Estate" are indeed pertinent.[1] As I grow older & more local, the *Atlantic* has even more power than formerly to interest me. It is New England in the narrowest sense, & exactly appropriate for one who has come to be more interested in the lamp posts along Angell St. than in the nebulae of fathomless space!

Morton is "hiking" & vacationing these days, & doesn't get to the meetings; but several letters have passed between us. What will become of the Paterson plan I can't say, but if it does eventuate I shall certainly do my best to uphold my end of it![2] If I had to settle in Paterson with absolute permanence, & if I really had a steady salary to found a household on, I should exercise every art of persuasion to induce you to migrate thither. Paterson, of course, is not Providence—but I am assured by Morton & Kleiner (who has been there frequently) that it is very tolerable as such places go. I have never seen it.

Too bad A E P G got severely caught in the tempest, & fortunate your own experience was less severe. I don't believe my overshoes can be in that trunk down cellar, but I'll look when the season comes, as a matter of form. Moving is a deuced nuisance—as Kirk is finding out these days. He is really out at last—though oddly enough, three of his pictures (one of which, painted by a Cleveland friend of his, he values highly) still remain on the walls of the deserted chamber. The new lock here is much neater to work than the old one.

I wish that young Marblehead policeman could get me a berth on the force in his home town! How I'd love a post at the corner of Washington & Tucker Sts., in the midst of colonial antiquity, & with both Lee & Hooper mansions in plain sight not many yards away!! Alas! To think that all the choice things of life are wasted on the unappreciative!

Thanks in advance for whatever you may do toward getting me that Hist.

Soc. pamphlet! Get one for yourself, too, if you can—it's a perfect & detailed picture of the Westminster St. of a century ago.[3] I haven't had time yet to visit the library & read the Kimball book,[4] but am looking forward with eagerness to an opportunity.

Enclosed are three articles I have done for Leeds' paper. He likes them all, & has already sold the Paterson one—which will bring me $3.50 in a couple of weeks if nothing goes wrong. I am about to do some more—they can be handled more rapidly as one grows used to the work, & on Wednesday night Leeds has promised to give me a large batch to do. Incidentally, I have just answered the enclosed advertisement in the *N.Y. Times,* which may pertain to a proposition very like the Leeds–Yesley one. Here's hoping something at least remotely resembling cash comes out of all this vague casting about! Meanwhile I've been toiling on the United business.[5] The ballots came Thursday night, & on Friday I folded, addressed, & mailed the entire lot of about 200—some job! I enclose a sample set—two ballots & two envelopes to each voter. You may keep this, since oceans are left over. I'm sending another to A E P G.

Your mouse experience was certainly diverting! Since writing you I have caught *two* more invaders, in each case disposing of them trap & all. Traps are only 2 for 5¢, & it does not pay to bother with repulsive details when one can avoid them at 2½¢ per experience! Even so, my annual mouse bill will not bulk high in my budget! I now keep several traps in stock—I have five at the present moment—though I haven't heard an invader since Thursday. I can't find any of their holes, else I would make attempts at barricading & fortification. Of course we keep all food in tin, but even so, rodents will rove!

I hope the new Weybosset St. buildings will be decently colonial. How I hate to see the old places go! What has gone up on the site of the raised colonial house at Westminster & Eddy Sts? And is the colonial building at Westmr. & Clemence still safe? I see that the Bijou is going—I never knew that the frame of the building was Georgian! The Boston & Prov. Clothing Co. were there at one time, (before they moved across Orange St.) & before them there was another & cheaper clothing company—Jerome Kennedy & Son—(in no way connected with the present neo-Barnabic Kennedy) which used to paint advertisements on rural rocks & fences & stick posters up everywhere, proclaiming "genuine all-wool suits $9.00." That was back in the good old 'nineties when I was young. I never patronised them, though, for their appeal was distinctly plebeian.

Your envelopes are excellent—but since economy is a great desideratum these days, why not let me send you a few hundred of those which Kirk has dumped on me? The only drawback is the return address in the upper left hand corner, & that you can easily cross off as I do. I'm using the Clinton St. ones whilst I'm at Clinton St.—but most of the lot have various Cleveland addresses. Let me know if you'd like a shipment! Oh, & speaking of useful necessities—many thanks for that tube of Forhan's![6]

And now for the diary, last presented at the end of Monday, June 29. Retiring at midnight, I was up Tuesday at noon, & spent the entire day in writing & typing—including the Leeds articles herewith enclosed. Dinner was at home, & after a suitable reading interval I retired; having carefully reset a none too effective trap whose mechanism I improved with pincers. Wednesday I was up at noon, did some reading, caught the invader, & welcomed Little Sonny about 2:30 p.m. During the afternoon I discussed aesthetick & intellectual things with the Child, received a telephone call from S H asking me to meet her at John's restaurant for dinner at 6:30, & accompanied my guest to the subway; afterward—disposing en route of The Invader & his trap—keeping my appointment as per schedule. We had a full Italian dinner—& as previously related, my eyes wandered across the street to the "Monroe Clothes" sign which shortly allured our footsteps in its direction. The results I have already told you. By 8:30 I was the proud possessor of a fine new grey suit—which I left for alterations—& so elated was I that I proceeded forthwith to blow in $2.35 on a new straw hat (exactly like my last one)—the first I have purchased away from Providence. What a village dude!!

Thus suited & hatted, I bade farewell to S H at an orangeade stand & took the car for the Boys' meeting at Kleiner's. Arriving in good season, I found myself one of only four—Kleiner, Kirk, & M$^c$Neil being my colleagues—but the conversation was even brighter than at the average gathering of fuller attendance. One trivial topic which long detained us was the question of whether M$^c$Neil, in his new book, ought to have his hero say "I out with my axe & chopped a hole in the ice" when the bulk of the narrative is not in dialect. Dispersing about 1:30 a.m., the visitors repaired to their respective homes; I returning on the elevated & retiring at once. Thursday I was up early, did some writing, & set my trap for a second invader. In the afternoon S H called up from downtown asking me to meet her for dinner at Joe's; & shortly before I left, the United ballots came. At Joe's—where S H arrived ahead of me—we had the monstrous repast previously mentioned; hamburg steak, onions, spaghetti, potatoes, roast ham & dressing, ice-cream, & coffee—great God, what a diet for a stout old gentleman reducing! We then called in for a fitting of the suit, & took an open car for an evening ride to Coney Island. We had not intended to get off at all; but finding the resort phenomenally uncrowded, we did—incidentally patronising some of the assorted freak shows. In one of them there still survives P. T. Barnum's original "Zip, the What-is-It"— now probably over 90 years of age.[7] In Barnum's day "Zip" (whose profile I here reproduce) was exhibited as a semi-ape, & dressed in a furry skin supposed to be his natural hide. Now he appears in immaculate evening dress, grins amiably, & picks out simple tunes on the violin & xylophone. The age is too sophisticated for Barnum's charlatanry, & "Zip" chiefly interests people as having been part of the great showman's entourage. This creature is really a semi-idiotic Andaman Islander—one of a dwarf Malay stock inhabiting the East Indies. He was picked up as a boy by a seaman long before the Civil War, & has since vegetated in one freak show after another. Living feebly & lightly, he does not show his years; & will probably excite the smiles of still another generation. Another oddity was a new invention called "cotton candy", sold by a pair of brisk young Japanese. This is, to all external appearances, a fluffy mass of pure cotton; but upon being introduced into the mouth shrinks at once to an infinitesimal sugary dot. Still another attraction was the smart nigger Perry—the selfsame silhouettist who did our gang's portraits last winter when his habitat was the Capitol Book Shop in Broadway near 51st St. With the coming of summer he has followed the crowds—& the enclosed view of S H proves that his hand has lost nothing of its pristine cunning.[8] This is for your permanent retention. Another, with hat, will shortly go forward to A E P G. Later on you two can compare notes & decide which wants which. It was after midnight when we took the subway home—& upon our arrival we found the *second* invader caught. I took him out to the nearest rubbish container, said the burial service, & returned to retire. The next day— Friday the 3d—I was up at noon & spent the entire day folding & addressing those infernal ballots; going out with the stacked bundle at 6 p.m., stopping at a watchmaker's to leave an ailing wrist chronometer of S H's, & meeting S H for dinner at John's. From the restaurant I telephoned Leeds—who had telephoned earlier in the day & wished to make an engagement to discuss the magazine writing—& arranged to call at his office at 10 p.m.—editorial work keeping him tied until that hour. I then secured my new suit,—finished at last—laid in a stock of mousetraps, mailed my ballots, & went home to try on my new acquisition. It was perfect—& I kept it on for my expedition of the late evening; wearing also my new straw hat.

At the proper hour I sallied forth for the Leeds headquarters, which are situate on the 8th floor of a fine office building near Columbus Circle, with a striking view of Central Park. There are at least three large rooms, in one of which the solitary occupant—Leeds—was slaving away at his desk pasting pink galley proofs in an old number of the magazine to form a "printer's dummy"—which of course shews how the space is to be filled for the next issue. It is exacting work, & I didn't blame Leeds for having a headache! We talked at length, looked over the system of the establishment, & planned for future work. Then Leeds' headache got the better of him, & he insisted on dragging me off to the night performance of a dull cinema show—Loew's N.Y. Roof—whose open-air setting agreed with his malady. After drowsing over a stereotyped drama of noble Canadian Royal Mounted Policemen we descended to earth & proceeded to investigate the magazine stand in the

Times Bldg. There we found the new *Weird Tales* & *Golden Book,* paused to discuss literature in general, & lingered some few moments—till my restless guide led the expedition cafeteriaward, & pressed upon me a cherry tart & cup of coffee, for which he paid. Here we spoke once more of the business writing, rehashed details, & surveyed the field in such a way that I fancy I know about what is wanted now. Then adieux & dispersal—home & retiring.

The next day—Saturday the 4th—said to be a provincial holiday in these parts—I was up in the early afternoon & accompanied S H on an excursion to a place neither had previously visited—Pelham Bay Park, high up in the Bronx on the shore opposite Long Island. We had often heard of it, & the fact that the B.P.C.'s next meeting will be a picnic near there had called our attention to it afresh. So we went—taking the East Side Subway & changing at 125th St. It took an hour to get there; & since the train was uncrowded, we formed the highest expectations of the rural solitudes we were about to discover. Then came the end of the line—& disillusion. My Pete in Pegāna, but what crowds! And that is not the worst . . . . for upon my most solemn oath, I'll be shot if three out of every four persons—nay, full nine out of every ten—weren't flabby, pungent, grinning, chattering **niggers**! Help! It seems that the direct communication of this park with the ever thickening Harlem black belt has brought its inevitable result, & that a once lovely soundside park is from now on to be given over to Georgia camp-meetings & outings of the African Methodist Episcopal Church. Mah lawdy, but dey was some swell high-yaller spo'ts paradifyin' roun' dat afternoon! Wilted by the sight, we did no more than take a side path to the shore & back & reënter the subway for the long homeward ride—waiting to find a train not too reminiscent of the packed hold of one of John Brown's Providence merchantmen on the middle passage from the Guinea coast to Antigua or the Barbadoes. Arriving once more in Brooklyn, we raided three groceries for a home feast including sliced turkey; thereafter proceeding to consume the results thereof. After that, reading & retiring. Yesterday—Sunday—I was up at noon, had breakfast, read the Times & *Weird Tales,* & did some writing for S H. In the late afternoon we went to Prospect Park by open car, walked around three sides of that leafy realm, lingered in the delectable Vale of Cashmere, & having emerged on the Plaza, (near the Roman Arch) walked homeward along Flatbush Ave., stopping at an excellent Chinese restaurant near the Atlantic Ave. railway station for an ample Chow Mein dinner. Thence we returned home via State St. & retired. Today I was up at noon & dusted the room, & have been writing ever since, save for the time when S H prepared a home dinner. It is now evening, & I shall shortly go out to mail this epistle & get some groceries. Then I shall read in *Weird Tales* & retire—which brings this diary squarely to the end of July 6th. Tomorrow we may go on another excursion—we'll see when the time comes. And Wednesday night the Boys meet at

Sonny-Child's. Sonny, by the way, is going to the Thousand Islands with his papa & mama on the 12th—next Sunday.

In this afternoon post S H received your letter, for which she expresses the usual appreciation. Both, meanwhile, extend the sincerest assurances of distinguisht consideration; & take pride & pleasure in subscribing my self at all times as

Yr aff Nephew & obt Servt

H P L

P.S. Enclosures are so numerous I'll have to send them in a separate envelope.

## Notes

1. *Atlantic Monthly* 134, No. 6 (December 1924): Arthur D. Little, "The Fifth Estate," 771–81; Nola Connolly O'Brien, "Visions," 782–84.

2. See HPL to FBL, 2 August 1925: "Morton is all excited about this museum business—wants me to go to Paterson at the next trustee meeting and talk with the Men Higher Up. I haven't much hope of being accepted, for it's clear to me that what they want is a person with a naturalist's inclinations" (*SL* 2.20).

3. By Francis Read.

4. *Providence in Colonial Times* (1912), a significant influence on *The Case of Charles Dexter Ward.*

5. Because of dissension and apathy among its members, the United Amateur Press Association did not hold a convention in July 1925. In the mail-in election of that year, Edgar J. Davis was elected president and Victor E. Bacon official editor.

6. A dentifrice for the gums to prevent pyorrhea.

7. William Henry Johnson (1842–1926). Known also as Zip the Pinhead.

8. The silhouette of HPL has become iconic, but the silhouette of Sonia (at least one copy of which survives) is less well known. A silhouette of Rheinhart Kleiner appears in Hart and Joshi, *Lovecraft's New York Circle* 124.

[110]     [ALS] [HPL to LDC]

Monday Afternoon

July 13, 1925

My dear Daughter Lillian:—

Your postcard duly arrived—& also the delayed roll of papers, for which I thank you sincerely. The information as to early Newport physicians & medical instruction was highly absorbing, & will find a place in my permanent collection; as will also the item on the site of the old Bull Garrison house. In the same paper with the latter is an interesting article on the weird by Will Irwin,[1] whom I heard speak on Shakespeare at the Writers' Club a year ago last spring, & who—as chance would have it—helped me on with my overcoat after the lecture! The Transcripts, likewise, were highly acceptable.

As for me—the diary, last covering Monday, July 6, is as uneventful & commonplace as usual. On Tuesday the 7th I was up early, & responded to an unfamiliar tap on my Georgian brass knocker—finding the visitor to be that erratic young rover Edward Lazare—long out of touch with the gang, & bewilderedly inquiring what could possibly have become of Kirk & Loveman. I gave him the needed information, listened patiently to his doleful tale of the suburban newspaper job he was leaving in disgust, & discreetly stifled my yawns at his effervescent theatrical ambitions. Fortunately he had an early engagement elsewhere, so that I could soon buckle down to a highly necessary all-day writing siege. In the evening I prepared an adequate sandwich dinner, welcomed S H upon her return from a position-investigating trip, wrote more, read in *Weird Tales,* & eventually retired. On Wednesday the 8th I was up early, assisted S H in sweeping & cleaning the room, wrote some Leeds matter, (vide enclosures) & read considerably in one of my antique books—Dyer's "Early American Craftsmen". In the afternoon S H & I went out to a cinema show with interspersed vaudeville,—like the Emery—purchased some groceries at sundry local emporia, & returned to enjoy a hearty home dinner. I then wrote some more, & changed from my blue into my new suit—the sample of which I am very glad you endorse. After this I started for the Boys' meeting at Sonny's—which was very sparsely attended, only Leeds, Kirk, & Lazare being present besides myself & our little host. I displayed my new finery with pride, vanity, & ostentation, & was humorously congratulated upon my return from rags. Sonny read a fine new horror-tale of his,—"The Sea Thing"[2]—whilst Leeds produced a wealth of trade magazines containing topics to be written up for his publication. Since then Belknap has written six articles, but I have not found a chance—though I expect to tomorrow. The meeting dispersed at 1 a.m., & I took the subway with Leeds, bidding him adieu at 50th St., & continuing home to retire without further events. The next day—Thursday the 9th—I was up early & did some reading in *Weird Tales.* I am having to get caught up in order to deal intelligently with the editor. In the afternoon S H & I went for an extended walk toward Flatbush, carrying magazines & pausing to read at leisure in the lovely "Vale of Cashmere" in Prospect Park, near the Plaza with its Roman arch. Later we pushed on through the greenery to Flatbush itself, glancing at 259 Parkside Ave., the 1796 steeple, Albemarle Terrace, & other points of interest; & having dinner at a well-kept cafeteria. In the evening we walked back, pausing in the park to read until the twilight faded, & thereafter pounding the pavements. We meant to follow Union St. the whole way, thus traversing your route of many years ago when the horse-car carried you by the Butler residence, but were forced to quit it because of the odorous slumminess into which it has now fallen. When near home we invested in a bottle of ginger ale & some ice—imbibing the potation upon our arrival, before the melting of our refrigerant. I then read some more, & finally retired. The next day—Friday the 10th—I was up early & remembered A E P G's birthday (as I do all birthdays but Mr. Hoag's) just too late to send a timely greeting! During the early part of the day I read, & later I went out to do some shopping with S H; having an excellent dinner at Joe's. After dinner we attended a cinema, & after that we walked through some of the statelier & better-preserved byways of Brooklyn Heights. Finally returning to 169, I did some reading & retired. On Saturday the 11th I was up early, did some reading, & received a telephone call from Small Sonny—whose summer address until further notice will be Hotel Wellesley, Thousand Island Park, N.Y. He & I had both heard that morning from the mighty Alfredus-Child—who, far from coming to N.Y., is in no less an appropriate seat of Gallicism than *Paris* itself! The little rascal sailed from New Orleans (3d class) on the 14th of last month, & has since been imbibing true Parisian accent & colour whilst his wife studies at the Sorbonne. They inhabit a rather costly hotel in the Rue Madame, & Galpinius does not seem to be disappointed in the least—as yet—with the storied city of his dreams. He promises to write extensive descriptions of his impressions. Returning to Saturday, though—in the early afternoon I proceeded up to Sonny's & spent the residue of the day in literary & scientific discussion. At 6:30 we took a walk to Post Office & Library, returning to 823 for dinner & more discussion. At 9:00 all hands—Sonny, his mama, his papa, & his Grandpa Theobald—went to a local cinema show, & at 11:00 general adieux until autumn were said. I thereafter descended to the subway, sought 169, & retired. Sunday the 12th I was up early & read in my *Weird Tales* file all day. I am catching up—& soon I shall send in some more yarns, since after "The Temple" [advance sheets enclosed for your permanent retention—issue out Aug. 1] only two will remain accepted & unpublished. S H, who was out during the day, returned at night with sumptuous groceries; & we dined on beef sandwiches, pickles, pudding, ginger ale, & ice. After that I read more & retired. Today—Monday the 13th—I was up early, did some reading, & then sat down to wrestle with the flood of amateur correspondence which the postman brought. The *United Amateur* is finished, & Cook has sent a copy—very nice-looking, though crowded. It will be held till Bacon can prepare circulars to be mailed with it. The hour is now 3:30 p.m., & I will note any subsequent developments on the envelope of this epistle. S H thinks she has the Cleveland position landed—the woman is in N.Y., & they have held several conferences & hat-buying expeditions. ¶ And so it goes. Now I must write Cook, Bacon, & Conover[3]—the latter of whom has about half-agreed to accept the Secretary-Treasurership of the United. I'll be darned glad to get the whole amateur mess off my hands! Hoping to hear from you in due time, I beg to subscribe myself

Yr aff Nephew & obt Servt

H P L

[On envelope? Written at top of letter in RHB's handwriting:]

Later Diary Finishing July 13

S H return
Dinner
Out for walk around Bklyn Hts
Return & retire

*Notes*

1. See LDC/AEPG 54n3.
2. Published in *WT* (December 1925).
3. Howard R. Conover.

[111]     [ALS] [HPL to LDC]

Monday Afternoon
[20 July 1925]

My dear Daughter Lillian:—
                          Your interesting letter duly arrived, as likewise
the delightfully multifarious roll of assorted cuttings. I have literally revelled
in both, & cannot begin to comment on all the piquant topics brought up
by the varied news matter. You need not, by the way, have refunded postage for that other roll. It was, I assure you, a splendid value for the money—& would have been cheap at double the price. Herewith I return as per
request the item on Mortonius' grandfather & his hymn. Enclosed also is a
*Tryout*—which need not be returned—as well as an appealing *Bulletin* cutting
with a touch of Foster. Speaking of Foster—I am properly interested in the
Chopmist Academy, the old Coventry gambrel-roofer by the dam, the "Mr.
Cady" monument, & the orthographical achievements of our five-year-old
prodigy cousin, small Fannie J. Rathbun.[1] How unfortunate that she cannot
add her own patronymic—Rathbone—to her list of 90 perfectly spelled
words—but then, she errs in company with a prominent Justice of the Superior [*sic*] Court![2] I return the item for grandmother's red scrap book . . . as
also the Cady item. The Gabriel Bernon rattle[3] is indeed a notable object—I
presume it is in that special case of exhibits at the Hist. Soc. Anent the architectural views: I am sorry to see the Weybosset St. place come down, &
*utterly infuriated* concerning the fate of the colonial houses at College & Benefit Sts! That row on the north side of College St. has been one of the most
remarkable colonial survivals in any large city, & to see it destroyed at this
late date is absolutely beyond endurance! I should think the School of Design would have more sense, decency, & local pride—great god, what a felony
not to preserve, strengthen, & repair that corner house with its colonial door-

way & double flight of steps!! Foster's "Old Kentucky Home" is a fine late Georgian specimen—I'm glad the state is sensible enough to preserve it.[4] Hambly the smith is a finely picturesque figure—thank heaven a few of the old school are left! Oh, yes—& I was interested in the Albee reminiscences. What veritably knocked me out was the discovery that Percy Winter is William Winter's son![5] Time & again have I watched Percy sneak hypocritically about the stage at Keith's—for he specialised in "mean man" parts—yet not once did I realise that his father was the foremost dramatick critick of the age! I am glad you have kept up attendance at the Albee, & hope you will continue even when you cannot find a companion. As I have often said—regard the stage as a *book* to be looked at & read; & surely one does not need company in reading a book. Some day let's hope that Grandpa Theobald can be on deck again to take you to the Albee!

I'm glad you like the new suit—which I haven't worn again since writing you, because of the informal programme of recent days. It was showery Wednesday night when I attended the meeting at McNeil's. With this care & sparse usage, the suit ought to be good for a full decade or more, & I'm hoping that you may have a chance before it goes to see it every day for many a summer! It hangs finely, & gives me the sprucest appearance I have had in aeons. I must get a snap shot taken soon, to display all these sartorial glories! Glad you like "The Temple." No—you didn't give me the John Carter genealogy, but I read it with utmost avidity when you shew'd it to me. Hope you haven't lost it! Glad you found something of interest on the reverse side of my Leedsiana. Yes—Doc Kuntz is a nice old boy—a Presbyterian minister, but no wry-faced fundamentalist. Here's another from him—which you needn't return. He certainly does want to be a poet! It was he, you may recall, who wrote the elegy on Phillips in 1917—"He Walked With Life."[6] And speaking of letters—here's something from the immortal Alfredus which I *will* ask you to return. Grandpa's little Frenchman has come to his soul's home at last, & is duly disporting therein. He sent Belknap a post card of the Notre Dame. Belknap, by the way, is away till August 15, his present address being Hotel Wellesley, Thousand Island Park, N.Y. Just before going he imparted the agreeable news that his poem "Exotic Quest", published in Parker's *L'Alouette,* has been mentioned by that eminent brunet critick William Stanley Braithwaite in his latest anthology! Great kid! He'll be there yet! And speaking of young poets—I lately received a thin brochure of very fair verse from an amateur in Spring Valley, N.Y.—Wilfred B. Talman—& after acknowledging it learned that the poet is a Brown University student whose first lines appeared in the college paper, *The Brown Jug!* Naturally, my latest epistle to him has been full of the local colour of College Hill! Sorry the heat has bothered you—I've hardly noticed it, & latterly the days have been phenomenally cool. I'll have to look up that colonial article in *Good Housekeeping*—& as for the *Times,* I see it when S H is here, but don't otherwise. Thus any issues before June 7—including that—I wouldn't have seen; but would have seen those following. You are fortunate in having free access to it—though I'd rather have our *Sunday Journal* any day!

As for the Scopes business—it really was a revelation to me to learn how perfectly & naively mediaeval the Tennessee mind has remained. Obviously, logic & information can produce no effect upon a psychology so entrenched in its backwardness; & one might as well let the locality alone until it develops naturally in the course of succeeding generations. The only thing calling for active steps is the task of curbing poor old Bryan before he organises political machinery for stifling science in less benighted parts of the nation. Catholics & mossbacks all over the country would be only too glad to abet him in this issue.[7]

I shan't know about Paterson, of course, till autumn; but am meanwhile only too busy! The United details are slowly coming in hand—Secretary appointed & announcement bulletins about to be mailed with *The United Amateur*—& when I get the ballots counted I shall be about ready to turn the works over to younger hands for all time. As for weight & diet—don't worry about the Old Gentleman! I've been eating to repletion of late—fruit & all—for S H brings things in every evening. Sandwiches of tongue, ham, or rolled beef—apples & peaches—puffed wheat & cream—ginger ale—tea—& oftentimes *ice* in small pieces for cold drinks. Yes—& we've had canteloupe, [*sic*] too! My own programme when alone will be largely similar, save that canned beans & spaghetti will tend to replace the much more expensive delicatessen meats. Ice cream I dote upon.

Now as for the diary—my last entry was in pencil whilst out on a walk last Monday night. On the return trip we stopped at the watchmaker's for S H's watch, & there beheld the finest little black kittie that I've seen since the days of my own nigger-man! He was in a valise, about to be taken home by the watchmaker's little boy—who had found him in the street & secured his father's permission to keep him. I took him for a time in my lap—cute, playful little divvle, about ¼ grown, & with not a white hair on his shapely little body! I surely envy that watchmaker's small boy! After that we bought some fruit, ate it at home, & retired. The next day—Tuesday the 14—I was up at noon & wrote all day—having a final telephone chat with Sonny in the morning. The dinner was quite elaborate—mutton pie & apple tarts from the Scotch Bakery—pickles, tea, cookies, &c. In the evening I read & retired. Wednesday the 15th I wrote all day, & had an even more elaborate dinner—scotch ham with a salad of cucumbers, tomatoes, lettuce, mayonnaise, &c., prepared on the spot by S H. In the evening I attended the Boys' meeting at honest old McNeil's; finding only three others present—McNeil, Kirk, & Kleiner—& beholding the genial host's new book "Tonty of the Iron Hand" fresh from the Dutton presses with four fine illustrations & a gay jacket. His still later MS. has been read & approved, & he is now casting about for another subject. During the course of the evening McNeil gave me a defective copy of "Treasure Island" which he had on hand—a copy with the last page missing. This I remedied by copying the missing fragment on the rear fly leaf from a complete version which McN. had. In general, the meeting was rather dull; & no tears were shed when it broke up at 12:30. I walked with Kirk & Kleiner to the subway, then returned home & retired. The next day— Thursday the 16th—was something of a gala picnic. I was up early & read some, & at noon S H & I departed for an outing with a lunch of tongue & cheese sandwiches & peaches which she had prepared. Taking along plenty of reading matter in the form of 5¢ Haldeman-Julius booklets, (which I regret to say are published no more)[8] we proceeded by subway to Dyckman St.—up near the northern end of Manhattan—& paused for a drink of bottled orangeade before strolling to the ferry which leads across the Hudson to the N.J. palisades. Then crossing, we began the zigzag ascent of the majestic precipice by means of a winding route partly identical with the wagon road, partly a footpath through the verdant twilight of forest steeps, & partly a stone stairway which at one point tunnels under the road. The crest, which we attained in about a half-hour, commands the noblest possible view of the Hudson & its eastern shore; & along this we rambled—coming now on a patch of woods, now on a grassy pasture, & now on a chasm bordered by the jutting bed rock of the plateau itself. At one point we beheld the ruins of a noble stone house; overgrown densely with ivy & reminding one of the ruins of some sinister Rhine castle. Later we settled on a bench near the edge of the cliff & did our reading—my book being "Dr. Jekyll & Mr. Hyde", which I had not perused for 25 years. At 6 we had lunch—piecing it out with ice cream & lemonade from a neighbouring pavilion—& thereafter we descended, recrossed the ferry, & finished our walk on the N.Y. side by following Riverside Drive in its most picturesque stretch from Dyckman to 181st St. At the latter point we took the subway home—stopping at the shop under the Taormina for ginger ale & ice & drinking the former upon our arrival at 169. I then disposed of an invader I had caught beneath the sink—after which I read some & retired. The next day—Friday the 17th—I was up at noon, picked up my files & threw away bushels of needless documents, & proceeded to peruse an historical anniversary issue of the *Cambridge Tribune* which I suppose A E P G had sent to me. The account of Cambridge by Rev. Saml Eliot was superb, & ought to be republished in booklet form. S H then returned with dinner—I wrote some & went out on some errands, & finally retired. The next day—Saturday the 17th [*sic*]—I wrote all day, nearly cleaning up my correspondence. In the afternoon I went out for groceries, & in the evening I read & retired. On Sunday the 19th—yesterday—I read all day— finishing Dyer's "Early American Craftsmen", which contains much matter of marvellous interest. It seems that your bannister-back chair is a really early type—descended from the tall chairs of the restoration period & *preceding* the Windsor. There was also a great deal about Bennington pottery—telling the now high value of those fuzzy-haired little china poodles which one used to see everywhere. Didn't we have some once? I could gnash my teeth at what has been sold, given, or thrown away! I was out for grocery errands now & then, & retired fairly early. Today—Monday the 20th—I have been continuously writing except for the dinner hour, & shall end by reading & retiring. This concludes July 20. S H's position still seems good, & she is negotiating for a larger trunk.

Kleiner & Morton have been on a strenuous week's hike in the wilds west of the Hudson, far from the trails & campfires of mankind. At one point they stood simultaneously in the three states of N.Y., N.J., & Penn.—a feat surpassable only by travelling to the southwest where the four states of Utah, Colorado, Arizona, & New Mexico converge to a common focus. Oh, yes— as to the Amy Lowell poem—it is poetry, because of the imagery, but not the sort I'd try to write intentionally. And so it goes.

Yr aff Nephew & obt Servt<br>H P L

[On envelope:]

*Tuesday Night*

Letter held over. Diary for July 21—up at noon, wrote all day—S H return 6 p m with mutton pie & buns from Scotch Bakery—read all evening—Arthur Machen's delicious autobiographical volume, "Far-Off Things"—which you ought to get at library. At 10 p.m. S H felt hungry, so I'm going out for light refreshments—fruit, &c—& will mail my now mountainous stack of letters. When I return I shall read a snatch more of Machen & retire—which completes the diary for Tuesday, July 21, 1925.

Tomorrow night—a Leeds meeting at [Kle]iner's.

## Notes

1. Fannie J. Rathbun (1919–1995), daughter of Leonard I. and Grace M. Rathbun. She was HPL's fifth cousin once removed, through common descent from John Rathbun (1693–1752).
2. Elmer J. Rathbun (1870–1952), a justice of the Rhode Island Supreme Court (1919–35).
3. Gabriel Bernon (1644–1736), a Huguenot and prominent merchant. The gold rattle, owned by the Rhode Island Historical Society, is shown in Gertrude Selwyn Kimball's *Providence in Colonial Times* facing p. 160.
4. HPL refers to the Federal Hill Mansion (1795–1818), a house owned by U.S. senator John Rowan in Bardstown, Kentucky. It was the inspiration for the "My Old Kentucky Home" (1852) by Stephen Foster (1826–1874), who was a cousin of the Rowan family. It became Kentucky's first historic shrine on 4 July 1923 and a state park in 1936.

5. Percy Winter (1861–1928), stage and film actor and director, son of William Winter (1836–1917), drama critic and poet.

6. "He Walked with Life: To the Memory of Phillips Gamwell," *Little Budget* (June 1917).

7. HPL refers to the celebrated trial in Dayton, TN, in which the schoolteacher John Thomas Scopes was put on trial for teaching the theory of evolution in violation of a law recently enacted by the Tennessee State Legislature. William Jennings Bryan (1860–1925) was the prosecuting attorney; he died days after the trial was over.

7. It is not clear what HPL is referring to. The 5¢ Little Blue Book issued by the Haldeman-Julius Company continued publication until 1978.

[112]   [ALS] [HPL to LDC]

*Monday Afternoon*
July 27, 1925

My dear Daughter Lillian:—

          I take my pen in hand to say that I am well & hope you are the same. This morning the ~~enclosed~~ Journal bill came\*, & since I have no cheque-sending facilities I wonder if you could attend to it in person at the office? My banker in Ogunquit[1] will see that you receive proper reimbursement in the end, but just now it is important to keep paid up, lest the paper cease coming & entail a tedious series of post card appeals for missing issues. They are surprisingly small about stopping the paper if not fully paid on the exact date of dueness—but I suppose it is attention to details like this which has given the Journal & Bulletin its commercial supremacy & commanding position. Certainly, it is the only paper worth reading that I have ever seen.

     Last night the enterprise of the press in general set before us with startling promptness the sudden death of poor old Bryan. Unfortunate soul! He meant well, dense as was his ignorance; & I have no doubt but that his alarm at the expansion of human thought was a profound, altruistic, & genuinely frantic passion. His compact little mind was hardened into a certain primitive type of American pioneer psychology, & would not bear the strain of national cultural development. Life must have been a hell to him as all the securities of his artificial world cracked one by one under the pressure of time & scientific discovery—he was a man without a world to live in, & the strain proved too much for mortal body to bear. Now he is at rest in the eternal oblivion which he would have been the first & loudest to deny. Requiescat in Pace!

     Now as for my diary, which last ended with Tuesday, July 21st. On Wednesday I was up at noon, read all day, had dinner at home, & in the evening went to the Boys' meeting at Kleiner's. Kirk was not there, having gone

\*On second thought, I *won't* send it, but will send to A E P G, who has the cheque account. She can get a cheque to the Journal by Aug. 1st

home to Cleveland for a visit of several weeks with his brother; but his partner came—breaking (with Kleiner's permission) our stag rule to the extent of
bringing a wife along. The others were Morton & Leeds—plus the host &
Grandpa Theobald. Events progressed smoothly but scarcely brilliantly till
midnight, when the bookselling couple departed. Then, quite spontaneously,
the old-timers fell into reminiscence & retrospection, discussing youthful &
bygone things & getting so interested that the session didn't dissolve till 4
a.m.! We debated on national hymns & old songs, sang many of both, adverted to Dr. Oliver Wendell Holmes & read much of his verse aloud—& in
short had a general good time of unimpeachably literary cast till the paling
east warned us that the time had come for all honest night-hawks to be abed.
Returning home by a circuitous route which included accompanying Morton
& Leeds to the Canal St. subway station, I retired early & was up early the
next day. The one piece of bad news at the meeting was that the Leeds–
Yesley magazine venture is in difficulties & cannot pay or accept copy for
some time. Belknap & I are promised pay ultimately for what we have written, but Yesley is not very dependable at this stage. It is a question whether
he will carry on the present magazine or found another—& whether Leeds
will continue with him or seek kindred affiliations elsewhere. Thus wags the
world! Well—on Thursday I did some reading in Machen's "Things Near and
Far", wrote several letters, did some errands for S H, who was due to leave
for Cleveland on the following day, & in the evening accompanied S H for
dinner to a restaurant which neither had ever visited before—Peter's, whose
card I enclose. It is odd how widely the Brooklyn custom of using first names
for restaurants has spread. "Joe's" began it, & now we have John's, Peter's,
Jack's, Jim's, & Heaven only knows how many others! But I verily believe Peter's is the best of all—for its 80¢ table d'hote dinner was a revelation. If it
were cheaper I should patronise it often. I had breaded veal cutlet with tomato sauce, Italian spaghetti, (see enclosed editorial!) baked potato, cold [*sic*]
slaw, green corn, canteloupe, ice-cream (a delicious & unknown kind, which
probably had *maple* as an ingredient) and (excellent) coffee. After dinner we
took the open car ride to Coney Island; &, finding it not overpopulated,
alighted as we did exactly three weeks before. This time entering the so-called
"Luna Park" section, we observed many unusual things; including an open-air
circus & a "Room of Wonder" which was advertised to upset all known principles of gravitation. The latter was indeed exceedingly clever, though so simple in principle that I understood it at once. It was approached through a
series of eccentric passageways with walls futuristically painted & floor inclined in many different ways so that one had the effect of threading tortuous
rising & falling & tilting avenues in some analogue of the Mammoth Cave.
The room itself being entered, one felt at once that something must be radically wrong with the force of gravity; for although the floor was fairly level,
one was impelled irresistably [*sic*] forward & downward in a certain direc-

tion—so that hand-rails were needed to steady the traveller. On one side was a runway for a wooden ball, as in a bowling alley—& marvellous to consider, the ball ran *upward* when released, returning gently downward by another runway after the completion of its ascent—thus:

Well—in about a second I saw the trick, & drew it out in a diagram for S H. In reality, the *whole room* was steeply tilted in the direction that the balls rolled & the visitor seemed drawn; but since the walls rose at right angles to the floor, this fact was not perceived. It was like the cabin of a steeply listing ship—except that there were no hanging objects to betray the precipitous inclination. As a matter of fact, the ball in the upper runway was going *slightly downhill* in relation to the real world, though *uphill* in relation to the floor, walls, & ceiling of the tilted room. The lower runway, of course, was both really & apparently downhill. My second figure here shews the principle of the whole. The room actually stood on the steep slope YZ, at the sharp angle XYZ. But the walls MN rose perpendicular to that slope, so that the visitor—his sense of equilibrium or inclination already destroyed by the circuitous passages through which he entered—could form no direct idea of this condition. The ball ran "up" the runway AB—which, of course, in relation to the actual angle XYZ was decidedly downhill despite the apparent "uphill" angle of AB with MN. We left by passages as

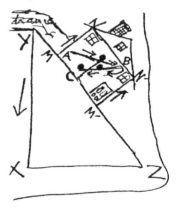

circuitous & cleverly confusing as those by which we entered—noting as we did so the amazed conjectures of other voyagers. In emerging, S H could not resist calling the attention of the gatekeeper to the fact that I had solved his ingenious riddle; & that dignitary professed a respectful surprise upon seeing my pencil diagram. He admitted that I was right, inquired what my profession was, & stated that he had seldom seen solutions produced so completely on the spot. We returned home by the elevated—the so-called "Culver Line"— & retired after a brief period of reading & writing. The next day—Friday the

24th—I was up early & ground out some doggerel for the Blue Pencil meeting of Sunday, which S H made me promise to attend out of courtesy to the Cleveland visitor Miss Schneider, (formerly Mrs. William J. Dowdell—wife of my former enemy in the United, who ran off with a chorus girl in 1922.) whom she expects to see frequently in Cleveland. I enclose the stuff—an allegedly comic response to the assigned topic "If I Had A Year Off".[2] It is worthless—but one can't be other than insipid when such insipid subjects are assigned. At 2 p.m. I met S H at the Grand Central, checked some luggage for her, & accompanied her to lunch at the Milan in 42nd St.—the place where you & the whole gang took dinner on Feby. 3, when poor Eddy was in N.Y. After an excellent repast we killed time in a dull cinema next door, later wandering to the "Little Blue Book Store", where 5¢ Haldeman-Julius books are still on sale despite their threatened discontinuance. I bought quite a supply, including some recent scientific titles. We then wandered still closer to the Grand Central, passing the Cameo Theatre & noting to our disgust—in view of the time we had wasted at the dull cinema—that there was here exhibited something we had wanted to see ever since missing it three years ago—the striking New Bedford whaling film, "Down to the Sea in Ships."[3] It was now too late for us both to see it, but *my* question of spending the evening was settled on the spot! Reaching the station & attending to parcels, I saw S H off on the 7:30 Cleveland train, thence proceeding at once to the Cameo & plunging into the reflected antiquities of New England. Nor, for once, was the presentation a disappointment. It was, indeed, the very reverse; for never had I imagined that so perfect a cinema evocation of the old whaling days could be possible. The pictures were taken either actually in New Bedford or at sea, & shew the original surviving houses, churches, wharves, ships, & accessories. To one who has lately read "Moby Dick" & "The Gam", the film was incredibly impressive. "Faking" was impossible—for one beheld the whales spouting in full splendour, the chase of the boats, the throwing & landing of the harpoon, & the subsequent struggle in which the whale overturned one boat. All this was conducted in full view of the camera, & one realised the peril faced not only by the actors but by the photographer as well. There was no substitution of the leading man when the harpooning occurred—it was the actor himself, seen full in the face, who threw the successful dart; & one may only wonder how he ever practiced an art at which novices are generally held so worthless. The whole film is of inestimable historical value as a minute & authentic record of a dying yet gorgeously glamorous phase of American life & adventure. Since the film was made, three years ago, I understand that the last whaler has gone to its eternal rest; & that the melancholy desertion of the New Bedford wharves is absolute. Yet what an industry it once was—with Providence, Bristol, & Newport in the game as well as the more definitely associated New Bedford. Now, I believe, whaling is done in steam vessels—mostly Norwegian—with auxiliary launches or ten-ders & mechanical harpoon guns. It is a weary trade—no longer a picturesque hazard. Well—that's life, hang it all! After the show I journeyed to Brooklyn, laid in some stamps & groceries, did some reading, & retired. The next day— Saturday the 25th—I was up at noon & wrote till evening; then dining on potato chips, bread, cheese, & vanilla wafers & reading Arthur Machen's "The Secret Glory". Sunday the 26th—yesterday—I was up early & set out despite dubious skies to join the picnic meeting of the Blue Pencil Club. Riding to the Pelham Bay Park subway station, I found it agreeably devoid of coons, & at once spied the waiting party of Morton, Kleiner, Wheeler Dryden, Miss Merritt, & Miss Banks. Soon afterward Miss Schneider & a friend—a Miss Semble or something of the sort—joined the expedition; which thereupon proceeded forward under Morton's orders despite my mild recommendation to wait for further stragglers. The walk to Hunter's Island lay through a very agreeable & verdant countryside, which in general lived up to Mortonius' promise of a landscape resembling New England. The island itself—or rather, a small island near it—is reached by a series of bridges; & possesses a rocky coast very palely suggestive of Newport, Marblehead Neck, Magnolia, & Ogunquit. Here we encamped—to be joined almost at once by Lewis H. Maury, who had followed us by a few seconds' margin, & who could have accompanied us had we waited. Rock-climbing, lunch-eating, snap-shotting, mineral-studying, coast-exploring, & (on my part) book-reading then followed. Kleiner withdrew to the upland woods to write a contribution for the literary programme, which he had neglected to do before; using my pencil & the back of my own contribution in lieu of other writing materials. Bread upon the waters—his verse was so good that it defeated mine by one vote when balloting for the best piece ensued—the final figures standing Kleiner 6, Grandpa Theobald 5, Ernest Adams 1. Mortonius—who might have defeated us all—discovered at the last moment that he had left his contribution at home on the bureau! After the major explorations a business meeting was held, three more members—Otto P. Knack, Miss Voelchert, & Ernest Adams—arriving just in time to participate. The party lingered till 8 p.m., then walking back to the subway (some 3 or 4 miles) singing old songs & discussing trifles. It thence proceeded to the Far East Chinese restaurant in Columbus Circle—where we dined on that other outing of Oct. 12, 1922—& filled itself with exotic colour & nourishment; my choice being beef chop suey. This rite accomplished, all hands dispersed; I seeking Brooklyn to get some post cards & magazines, & incidentally petting two delectable tiger-kitties near the P.O. (I saw, by the way, the most captivating kitten boxing-match imaginable at Hunter's Island, where a family of one mother-kittie & two children were hunting field mice in a bank wall near a creek.) But the trip was to end in still more feline fashion—for just as I was passing Borough Hall I was greeted with the sight of the loveliest little coal-black nigger-baby that ever purred or said "meow"! Bless my old bones, but what a superbly tiny atom of unalloyed night that precious rascal was! Not a non-black hair on the little devil—& his face was exactly like my vanished Nigger-Man's! Well— there was only one thing a venerable priest of Pasht[4] could do, so I picked the little imp up & held him in my lap a full hour as I sat on a bench & read about Bryan & his passing in the premature Monday morning papers. He purred & snuggled & kneaded my knees with his little paws—in fact, it was all I could do not to kidnap him forthwith! I wonder whose he is? He was obviously contented, well fed, & cared for, though he had no collar. Grand- pa's little pickaninny! Finally my young friend yawned & stretched & became uneasy, so I let him hop down to disappear in the kindred blackness of in- gulphing night & join the witches' train in unhallow'd ceremonies. After this I returned home, read a bit in Arthur Machen's "The London Adventure", & retired. Today—Monday the 27th—I was up at noon & have been writing let- ters ever since. Later I must go shopping—for groceries, & for a large tin pail in which to bring coffee from a restaurant for the next Boys' meeting, at which I shall be host. I lately learned through Sonny that honest old McNeil feels hurt because some of the members do not serve coffee despite his own conscientious preparation of that beverage when he is host; hence have de- cided to humour him this once. I can't make the darned stuff, but think I'll go out to a cafeteria & get four cups—there'll be only 4 members present— which I can serve before the fluid cools. It'll cost only 20¢—or 40 if I let each one have two. Quaint, punctilious, severe old Mac! He's a curious yet lovable character with his child psychology, sober ways, & set notions! Just what I'll do this evening I'm not sure, though I'll probably note it on the back of this letter. I may go down to the Publick Library & read that Kimball book— "Providence in Colonial Times"—or I may stick around here & finish "The London Adventure". Very shortly I shall start some businesslike writing— copying more stories for *Weird Tales* & beginning some new ones whose ideas are clamouring for expression—notably that novel or novelette of Salem hor- rors which I may be able to cast in a sufficiently 'detectivish' mould to sell to Edwin Baird for *Detective Tales*—which rejected "The Shunned House". Unit- ed matters seem to jog on successfully, & as soon as I hear that the U.A. is mailed I shall feel entitled to dismiss them from my mind. The Moe– Whitaker[5] feud continues to furnish amusement—I am told that Whitaker has issued a new & absurd anti-Moe leaflet, though it has not yet reached me. Davis is flourishing in the wilds of Maine—he has just written me on sheets of birch bark—& A E P G will shortly forward you a communication from Little Belknap, who is busy counting the Thousand Islands.

And so it goes. A comical incident occurred in connexion with the Unit- ed balloting, when Davis received in one of the printed envelopes addressed to him a card from a Brooklyn cinema theatre advertising a display of prize- fight pictures! My solution is this: that after I had dumped the surplus supply, somebody came upon the envelopes in the scrap-heap; and, moved by the aimless curiosity & pointless mischievousness of the lower orders, inserted the random card & mailed the envelope "just to see what it would do." What it did was to arouse some characteristick humour from little Davis—I'll enclose the thing with its Davisian annotation.

Well—I must close, & prepare an epistle for A E P G. I'll let some of the other correspondence go over till tomorrow, perhaps. I may postpone whatever shopping will have to be done before six, & merely lay in groceries. Whether or not I shall go to the library remains to be seen. Enclosed is an advertisement indicating that the "Miles Standish" film is coming to the Victory.[6] Don't miss it—it is full of 17th century colour, & has the greatest ocean storm scene ever recorded by the camera. And don't miss "Down to the Sea in Ships" if it is revived in Prov. as well as N.Y. A E P G says she saw it three years ago, & joins with me in praise of it. ¶ Our Wednesday meeting will be very small, since Kirk is away—as is Sonny—& Morton can't come. There may be only four present—as I said before—which will be excellent for my pocket book so far as refreshments are concern'd. Meanwhile I must get a tin or aluminum pail for the coffee. Well—so much for that. Write when the spirit moves, & in the interim pray consider me as

>              Yr aff Nephew & obt Servt
>                   H P L

[On envelope:] P.S. Will stay home & read, after a brief grocery raid on the corner store. This ends diary for Monday, July 27.

## Notes

1. I.e., AEPG.

2. HPL's poem is titled "A Year Off."

3. *Down to the Sea in Ships* (Whaling Film Corp., 1922), directed by Elmer Clifton; starring Marguerite Courtot, Raymond McKee, William Walcott, and Clara Bow.

4. Pasht is a variant spelling of Pakhet, an Egyptian goddess in the shape of a lioness.

5. HPL refers to Noah F. Whitaker, an amateur journalist and editor of the journal *Pegasus*.

6. *The Courtship of Myles Standish* (Charles Ray Productions, 1923), directed by Frederick Sullivan; starring Charles Ray, Enid Bennett, and E. Alyn Warren (as Myles Standish). Based on the poem by Henry Wadsworth Longfellow.

[113]     [ALS] [HPL to LDC]

> *Thursday–Friday Midnight*
> July 30–31, 1925

My dear Daughter Lillian:—

> I can't resist dropping a line, before receiving your promised letter, to thank you for the *Sunday Journal* & roll of cuttings,

both of which safely arrived. Among this agreeable miscellany—which I can't even begin to cover individually in comment—are many things of the very keenest interest—notably the picture of that utterly exquisite new colonial house. Thank heaven such beautiful & appropriate objects are replacing the vanishing Victorian homes—but just to pick a flaw in the almost perfect, I wonder why they chose a Connecticut-Valley type of doorway pediment for a house in *eastern* New-England? It is very beautiful—but it is not very characteristic of colonial Providence. Study of Harold Mason's photographs in the Athenaeum[1] would shew that the simple triangle is our usual pedimental treatment for a pilastered classic doorway in a house of this type. But don't let me cavil—the general effect is infinitely lovely! Those little illustrated Chapin articles are delicious—& I don't wish to miss a single one. That colonial monkey-wrench is especially interesting. The Jamestown business is interesting, but I'm disgusted by the alterations & defacements undergone by the old Clarke homesteads. What barbarous things the middle 19th century did! That's the way the old Rhodes homestead in Pawtuxet (1674) is ruined. The French-town business is also interesting—that's where the sinister Roulets in my "Shunned House" are supposed to come from![2] I see the *Christian Science Monitor* is noticing Providence a bit. They seem to take more or less geographical matter—I think I'll buy a copy some time & perhaps try an article on them if I ever get the equilibrium for miscellaneous writing. As for Ford—I certainly envy the old duffer! He's making up for lost time, & even [if] he never attains a really broad culture he'll assuredly have an excellent background of familiarity with the early American scene. The Corners & Characters, of course, are always welcome—I am especially interested in The Glebe—Dr. McSparran's residence,—since recent reading has impressed me prodigiously concerning the high civilisation of the Narragansett country in colonial times. It was rustic & almost feudal, with estates & slaves as in Virginia, & its dairy & livestock products were famous throughout the world. Narragansett cheeses equalled anything Cheshire could produce, whilst Narragansett pacers won races over the best-blooded Spanish & Arabian horses. The tearing down of that Abbott house in 1900 was a crime which ought to have brought the death-penalty on its instigators & perpetrators. It was the absolutely last relic of the *original* Providence—the 17th century agricultural village of Mr. Williams, with its feuds & Indian wars—& was in fairly decent condition when destroyed. Its demolition was sheer obtuseness & careless vandalism—may it be a shunned example to warn the publick against permitting similar vandalism in future. Speaking of change—I see that Elmgrove Ave. has been cut through to Rochambeau & is to be double-tracked. I suppose Angell was widened long ago—the company now wishes to relocate rails. I wish I could have seen that Newport pageant—I didn't study Newport as closely as I would now if I had the chance. Glad James B. Angell's Vermont college is having a new Colonial building—long live the Georgian! And I envy that club its Wedgewood teapot—I'm vastly enamoured of Wedgewood ware, though I prefer those pieces whose designs are the classical conceptions of Flaxman. As a final entry on my envy list I'll name that Kentucky lady with her 45 kitties. I endorse her move to more suitable quarters, & trust her new home will hold a good 45 more. She is in a fair way to realise the prophecy in Small Sonny's prose-poem—"some day I shall drown in a sea of cats'[']".[3] Yes, I could well appreciate 45 little black divvles like the amiable mite I held in my lap Sunday night! The Dayton–Mencken matter seems to have been conflictingly reported. Some say they want to run H. L. out of town; others say he gets on splendidly with the oafish yokels of the tank-town babbitry.[4] Who shall decide when papers disagree? Well—I'd wager a decent sum he couldn't be intensely popular in a backwoods Chautauqua centre like Dayton!

And so it goes. My diary to date has covered Monday the 27th, so I'll proceed from that point. On Tuesday, July 28, I was up at noon & stayed home all day, desperately coping with the final flood of United mail. The only thing besides write letters which I did was to get a good home dinner—but my assiduity is shewing results at last. The new board is seated, with a full official report of the election in Bacon's hands for future publication. This closes my obligations anent electoral matters, so that henceforward my labour will merely be advisory—telling one or two officers what to do, & suggesting replacements when any of the newly elected incumbents seem unresponsive or unsuitable. Bacon has finished the circular to be mailed with the *United Amateur*, & has sent the edition to Cook. Cook ought to mail the paper now in a few days—& I have asked him to send copies directly to you & A E P G. All now rests with the new board. My responsibilities are over, & the minute I can wind up this official correspondence I shall feel able to begin some real writing of my own. Wednesday the 29th I was up at noon, did some more frantic clearing-up of correspondence, & proceeded to sweep & dust my room in preparation for the Boys' meeting in the evening. This over, I went out on a shopping expedition, buying both staple groceries for myself & pastry (apple tarts & Kleiner's favourite crumb-cake) to serve as evening refreshments. I also bought a splendid aluminum pail or milk-can with a handle—like the diagram:—& holding two quarts, to use in going out for hot coffee. It cost 49¢, but will last a lifetime, & will be useful no matter where or how I am living. Heaven grant that some day I'll be bringing you home some coffee in it from the Wayland Pharmacy! Returning, I had my dinner & picked up in time to welcome the 'gang'—which turned out to be only *two*—Kleiner & McNeil— besides myself. But slim as the attendance was, it was an unusually pleasant meeting—full of really pertinent discussion. Conversation in general began with Bryan & Dayton, & took only one definite shift—when honest old McNeil uttered once more his naive & characteristic complaint that modern publick monuments have no originality, but depend on Greece & Rome for their inspiration. Try as we might, Kleiner & I couldn't make the good old duffer understand that Graeco-Roman art is an universal, definitive thing belonging to the ages—a common cultural heritage of all western civilisation, & so absolute in its perfection that aesthetics can admit of no further development in its particular direction. M^cNeil conceded that mebbe there might be suthin' in some of the things we said, but all the same he doesn't like things as they are! It's durned foolish, in his estimation, to put up Greek choragic monuments & Roman arches to American Civil War heroes! At 11 p.m. I produced my pastry & went out for coffee—getting the latter at the little joint at the corner of State & Court Sts. I ordered 6 cups—2 apiece—but with my blue china I found the amount came to *10* cups—so that we all had three helpings, & Kleiner four! They both praised my activities as an host—I brought out R.A.P.[5] forks & 454 Angell spoons, & distributed triangularly folded paper napkins. The cake I served on one Japanese tray, the tarts on another; supplying each person with a blue china plate, cup, & saucer besides his silver. Yes—all told, it was a great success, & I shall also entertain the Leeds meeting here next week. The week after that Kleiner will entertain the M^cNeil meeting—he & I are doing all the entertaining whilst Sonny is away, because the Child isn't allowed to come to Brooklyn in the evening. When he's home, we endeavour to place our gatherings where he can visit. M^cNeil, I think, was satisfied for the first time with my hospitality—for at last I pressed upon him an abundance of the coffee whose previous absence from my meetings he had noted with silent disapproval. My guests on this occasion left at 1 a.m., & I retired after one final burst of amateur writing. The next day— what was today when I commenced this epistle—was Thursday the 30th. Awaking early, & nervously exhausted with interminable amateur writing, I cut loose from all sedentary things & set out for an all-day jaunt in Prospect Park, carrying as lunches the left-over pastry of the previous night's feast. Striking into a part of the park new to me, I encountered incredible verdant marvels in the young sunlight—a rustic waterfall & tree-fring'd tarn, a hidden glen where a wild brook tumbles down unnumbered cataracts betwixt rocky banks whose fringing alders filter the glare of day to a magick cloistral twilight, a noble sweep of hill & lawn, & a forest of gigantick trees almost suggesting Machen's enchanted Gwent country near Caerleon—in short, a faery paradise with all the ethereal unreality of fiction or tapestry. Some of the choicest sights of this fantastic Eden lay just a curve or two beyond places I had visited repeatedly—potent symbol of the wonder always lurking close to the surface of life. As company I had Arthur Machen's book on critical & aesthetic theory—"Hieroglyphics", which was about the most appropriate volume I could have selected for the scene. I read it through—moving to a fresh bower of beauty for each chapter, & frequently closing it to revel in sheer enjoyment of the scenery. I shall revisit the spot, depend upon it! Evening finally came, & I ate a dinner consisting of the pastry I carried, plus a hot roast beef sandwich (with gravy on the bread) & a paper of French fried potatoes obtained at a lunch counter in Park Circle. Then I did more walking, & at 8 p.m. was seated on a bench in Music Grove, at the centre of the park, to hear the tri-weekly band concert given by the Municipal Police Band. I enclose the programme. The moment the musick commenc'd, Brooklyn faded swiftly away, & I was by the side of the lake at Roger Williams Park, seated in the old wooden auditorium & watching Bowen R. Church[6] try to lead Reeves' American Band & keep from tipping over the railing at the same time. Pretty well filled this evening—long cornet notes uncertain, face flushed, laughing pretty boisterously between pieces—well, maybe he'll last out this season, but I'll wager they have a new leader in 1903. Hear they've been negotiating with Herbert L. Clarke, who lives in Lloyd Avenue near Tommy Leeman's on the way to Slater Ave. School. Then a mist—1920—Fairman's Band—the new classick auditorium—selection from "Going Up",[7] the new musical comedy at the Shubert-Majestic this week—too bad the old Opera House is closed to leading road shows, though the Boustelle Co. is very popular & effective. Ten o'clock. "The Star-Spangled Banner". Wish I had my bicycle along as I used to have—how I'd love to scorch up Elmwood Ave. with my acetylene headlight! Well, anyway, I'll get an open car—even if I have to wait for an East Greenwich or Riverpoint inbound. Confound the nerve of the R.I. Co. putting those beastly prepayment suffocation-chambers on a line like this . . . . well, here's luck—an open inbound Buttonwoods—they're not supposed to stop to let on passengers this side of Park Ave.—that is, they didn't use to be, but who can keep track of this new business of ever-shifting zones? I'll hail it—good! He stopped. And there's an end seat! Ding-ding! . . . . Darkness—nightmares of strange underground caverns like the Boston subway—a walk under the moon past unfamiliar brick & brownstone—& then I encountered your bundles, read them, digested them, & am herewith acknowledging them! Now I shall mail this & retire—thus taking the diary completely through Thursday, July 30. Tomorrow—unless unexpected amateur developments arise—I shall endeavour to do some writing—probably fiction.

S H arrived safely in Cleveland, & has a fairly good place at 2030 East 81st St.—large room with kitchenette alcove at $45.00 per month. The east wall bulges gracefully outward with windows on the diagonal side surfaces, but unfortunately a neighbouring house cuts off most of the air & sunshine—as the Pierce house spoiled my room at 598. It's a great life! Speaking of the west—here's a prodigiously good specimen of Arabic architecture in one of the parks of St. Louis, on a card young Bacon sent me. Needn't bother to return it—I can't keep everything, & this isn't really an antiquity. No—I *do* think I'll ask for it back! I haven't many good views of Arabic scenes, & yet I mean to give several of my contemplated phantasies an Eastern—probably Bagdad—setting. I'll set aside an envelope for such, & have the colour on tap when I want to saturate myself for the writing of the story.

Latest news from the gang is that Kirk has dissolved his partnership & means to go into the business alone when he returns to N.Y. He's turned his pleasure trip into a bookbuying expedition, & means to come back profitably laden. Kleiner tells me this—I haven't had direct word.

Well, such is which. Now for a sleep, & tomorrow a day of work. One thing I must do is to copy some more old yarns of mine for *Weird Tales*. I have five or six which I'm sure they'd accept, but the MSS. are in no shape for sending. Saturday I ought to get my Mariano de Magistris cheque, but that will have to go directly to the storage company, to whom I shall owe $54.92. Poor Leeds has an even more desperate storage plight—involving the threatened sale of books he has cherished from childhood. A small *Weird Tales* cheque (for "The Unnamable") is also about due me. I'll have A E P G cash that. // Yr aff: nephew & obt Servt

H P L

## Notes

1. Harold Mason (1881–1944) was a Providence photographer whose photos of Providence domestic architecture can be found in the Providence Art Club, the Providence Athenaeum, and the Providence Public Library, among other venues.

2. Frenchtown was an early name for the city of East Greenwich, RI. In HPL's "The Shunned House" the Roulets are said to have come to Providence from East Greenwich in 1696 (*CF* 1.465).

3. From FBL's "Felis: A Prose Poem" (*Conservative*, July 1923).

4. H. L. Mencken (1880–1956) reported acerbically on the Scopes trial for the *Baltimore Evening Sun*, and his articles were syndicated nationwide. He in fact helped to arrange for Scopes to be tried as a way of pointing to the perniciousness of Tennessee's anti-evolution law.

5. Robie A. Phillips, HPL's maternal grandmother.

6. Bowen R. Church (1860–1923), cornet player and founder of the American Band in Providence. It was led by David Wallis Reeves (1838–1900).

7. *Going Up* (Liberty Theatre, New York, 25 December 1917–26 October 1918); music by Louis A. Hirsch; book and lyrics by Otto Harbach. Based on the play *The Aviator* by James Montgomery.

[114]　　[ALS] [HPL to LDC]

Thursday Night<br>August 6, 1925.

My dear Daughter Lillian:—

　　　　　　Again I will essay the diarist's part without waiting to hear from you; for if I permit too many events to mount up unrecorded, the continuous chronicle will quite exhaust both your patience & your eyesight when you are forced to peruse it entire! Therefore, having last writ you on the evening of Thursday last—the 30<sup>th</sup> of July—I will take my pen in hand to describe the occurrences of the intervening week. On Friday the 31st I arose at noon, spent the day in writing letters, & in the evening went down to the library to read in that valuable volume, "Providence in Colonial Times", by Gertrude Selwyn Kimball. A E P G knew the author of this work, who was a graduate of Mifs Abbott's & a teacher of rank in a private school; (died 1910) whilst the volume itself reveals a profound scholar & acute commentator, singularly well-vers'd in the most intimate lore of early Providence, & possesst of a style at once lucid & trenchant. The work is of the highest importance to the student of old Providence life, & I shall devour it with the keenest attention at such times as I can be present at the library. The social life of the Georgian town is amply & minutely display'd, & preceded by a graphick account of its growth from the time of its settlement by Mr. Williams. This book was intended to have been a general history of Providence, but was cut short at the age of the Revolution by the sudden & untimely demise of its author. On this occasion I read till the library clos'd—10 p.m.— after which I partook of a dinner at the Automat (meat balls—potato—apple dumpling) & return'd home to write & retire. The next day, Saturday, August 1st, I was up in the afternoon; &, responding at last to the relief occasion'd by the final transfer of amateur responsibilities to younger shoulders, commenc'd the writing of a new hideous tale, "The Horror at Red Hook", wherein I tell of hellish happenings amongst the mongrel Satan-worshippers that lurk in a slum district of Brooklyn, betwixt Clinton St. & the waterfront. A gentleman of ancient Dutch family, in Flatbush, goes down amongst these folk & becomes their leader in terrible rites—after which he meets a loathsome end. And a Dublin-born detective, who investigates the decaying rookeries of the noxious crew, sees things which shatter his nervous system & give him such a horror of old brick houses that he has to seek retirement in Chepachet, R.I., where there are no brick houses. Once, in Pascoag on a walk, he sees a brick building & falls in a convulsion! About dinner-time the telephone rang & proclaimed the return to New York of Samuel Loveman, Esq., who was stopping with Kirk's former partner, up near Columbia College. I responded with appropriate courtesies, & we defignated the morrow as a time of colloquy—he to call here in the afternoon. I then resumed my writing, which extended into the next morning, & finally—after completing the tale— retired. I was up on Sunday at noon, dusted my room, & at 4 p.m. welcom'd Loveman—who seems much improv'd, & who wore a new blue suit (with a white stripe) bought in Cleveland for *$22.50*—a greater bargain, perhaps, than my own recent pride & joy. We discours'd of literature in general, & read each other some recent work—he two poems which he had written on the train, & I the story I had just completed. The poems (which A E P G will forward to you—I made a copy) are excellent, & Loveman profess'd to regard the story as having much power & merit. You shall see the latter, by the way, as soon as I type it. In the evening we went out to John's for dinner, where I had my usual meat-balls & spaghetti, (raised from 30 to 35 cents, I mourn to say!) coffee & ice-cream. Loveman then bade me adieu to take the subway, having an engagement with his host at the Double-R coffee-house. I return'd home, wrote letters, & retired. The next day—Monday the 3d—I was up at noon, wrote letters, & went out for errands—including a 40¢ hair-cut. I then went down to the library, read more in "Providence in Colonial Times", took dinner (beef pie & peach pie) at the Automat, returned home, read the new *Weird Tales* which had just come, wrote letters, & retired. The *Weird Tales* bears on its cover the inscription "Stories by O. Henry, [a reprint] H. P. Lovecraft, Frank Belknap Long, Jr., & other authors." In writing Sonny I asked him whether he thought we ought to sue the editor or feel compli-mented! I have, by the way, received a $25.00 cheque (sent to A E P G to de-posit for my new suit in October) for "The Unnamable", & a long & cordial letter from editor Farnsworth Wright, who asks for more of my tales to keep on hand. He now has only two—"The Tomb", scheduled for January, (after a 3-month skipping of my work) & "The Moon-Bog". I must summon up my fortitude for the dreaded task of copying some junk for him—there's enough on hand to keep him supplied indefinitely. Leeds' story will appear in No-vember, & Belknap's "Sea-Thing" is due for December. Wright gives much information concerning the solidity & growth of the magazine, & says that even the old debts of the former regime will some day be paid—including $14.00 to me for "Nemesis." He praises my "Tomb" in a particularly flatter-ing way. In general, I think *Weird Tales* is improving. There have been several excellent stories in the last few issues, & most of the extremely crude matter is gradually disappearing. Belknap, Quinn, & I continue to be the only writers paid at the highest rate. Returning to the diary—on Tuesday the 4th I was up at noon, wrote letters, received a telephone call from Loveman, & went down to the 4th Ave. book shop to meet him for dinner (pot roast—ice cream) at the Automat & a trip up to his lodging to inspect his literary treasures. The latter are, as I may have mention'd when I saw them in Cleveland three years ago, exceptionally varied & valuable. Autograph letters of men as famous as Chatterton, Clare, David Gray, Browning, Dowson, Beardsley, Dermody, &c. &c., books of fabulous rarity, a complete unpublished play in MS. by Thomas Wade—&c. &c.[1] I certainly hope he will not have to part with these treasured belongings thro' œconomick necessity! He read me the completion of his prose-poem "The Sphinx", which is as dramatick & colourful as the earlier parts, & the one finished chapter of the Civil War novel, "Thracia Deane", which he has started, & which seems to promise unusual power & vividness.[2] I left at 1:30 a.m. after promising to secure him a room in Brooklyn the fol-lowing day. He dislikes the uptown atmosphere, & found the small flat im-possibly crowded because of the arrival of some relatives of his host. I then returned, read, & retired. These long subway trips I always improve by reading in the Haldeman-Julius booklets of which my pockets are full. Just now the current text is the short story material of Rudyard Kipling—who can certainly write a marvellously *weird* tale when he chooses. "The Mark of the Beast" is a little masterpiece . . . . . ugh . . . the *transformation,* & the day when the man's horses become frantically afraid of him, & the hunger for raw meat, & the long-drawn howl . . . . & the Hindoo leper-priest with no face, who mewed like an otter![3] Well—on Wednesday—yesterday—I arose at noon & went out in quest of lodgings for Loveman. After a vicissitude or two I hit on the best place of all—his own old quarters at 78 Columbia Heights, which you will recall so vividly. The kindly old lady—who is a retired Irish high-school teacher named Miss Laverty—was very sympathetic when she heard of Loveman's financial state; jobless & nearly broke, with only odd work at his host's book shop plus some odd (& Leeds-like) commercial writing secured by his host's cousin to keep him afloat till September 15th, when Brentano's great book establishment will tell him whether or not they can use him; and said she would, for five dollars a week, let him occupy temporarily the comfortable basement room of the young artist Charles Locke, who is home visiting in Cincinnati till October.[4] This was very good news, & when I communicated it to Loveman he hastened to Brooklyn to confirm it. We then moved his valises from the 4th Ave. shop, & once more established 78 Columbia Hts. as an abode of the poetic muse. That afternoon I also went to the local Federal Bldg. to arrange for the postponement of a final naturalisation formality of S H's, called for today. It was shifted to late September, when she will have to arrange to be present. Meanwhile she is doing finely in Cleveland. In the evening Loveman & I dined at a cafeteria near his place, (I had hot roast beef & peach pie. As I age, I find myself developing quite a taste for honest old English roast beef, if **very** well done) stopped at the Scotch Bakery for refreshments for the evening meeting, (apple tarts, & Kleiner's favourite crumb-cake) & returned to 169 to find Morton & Kleiner waiting outside. Admitting them, I hastened to dust my room whilst they were settling down, (thank Pegāna the bed was made!) & thereafter to change my clothes in the alcove—for I had solemnly promised Mortonius to shew him the new suit. He was properly paralysed, & after his recovery—& the arrival of Leeds—the meeting went merrily on. Loveman shew'd many of his literary treasures, which he brought in a portfolio, & the general discussion so happily developed that the meeting will go down in our records as one of the brightest. Morton, by the way, was full of expectant Paterson talk, & again urged me to be ready to appear in that town at the next meeting of the museum trustees . . . . which I shall certainly do. At 11 p.m. I served the refreshments, getting out tip-table, Japanese (10¢ store) trays, blue china, 454 Spoons, R.A.P. forks, & triangularly folded paper napkins. Using my new aluminum pail, I went out for some excellent coffee; & all hands pronounced the lunch a marked success both as a social event & dietary incident. It would be rather costly to do this regularly, but I do not frequently entertain. These two meetings here were a special summer arrangement during Sonny's absence. Most of the guests left at 12:30 a.m., though Leeds stayed till two. I then wrote & mailed some letters & retired. Today I was up late, & have been writing letters continuously ever since, except for a dinner on yesterday's feast's leavings. This excessive correspondence will thin out a bit when the new United board is fully running. A fine travelogue (to be passed around & returned to the author) came from Alfredus, & I sent it to A E P G for forwarding to you & subsequent transmission to me. The child is—at last—getting to be something of an antiquarian under the influences of mediaeval Paris! I shall now read some & retire, bringing this diary completely through Thursday. Well, such is which. Write when convenience dictates, & meanwhile pray consider me

Yr moſt aff: Nephew & obt Servt<br>H P L

P.S. Unless something intervenes, I shall tomorrow write another story.
P.P.S. In the Kimball book I learn for the first time that the Rhode-Island *Updikes* are of New-Amsterdam Dutch origin. It seems that a daughter of the Wickford trader Rich^d Smith (whose block house appeared in the Corners & Characters recently) married a certain Dr. Gysbert op Dyck—whose name soon became Anglicised to Updike.

## Notes

1. HPL refers to the British poets Thomas Chatterton (1752–1770), John Clare (1793–1864), Robert Browning (1812–1889), Ernest Dowson (1867–1900), and Thomas Dermody (1775–1802), and the British poet and playwright Thomas Wade (1805–1875). The reference to "David Gray" is unclear; it may refer to the American journalist David Gray (1836–1888) or the Scottish poet David Gray (1838–1861), but perhaps HPL intended to refer to David Grayson (pseudonym of American historian Ray Stannard Baker, 1870–1946). HPL owned a copy of Grayson's *Adventures in Contentment* (1907; *LL* 398).
2. Loveman's *The Sphinx* is in fact a prose drama. Loveman never completed *Thracia Deane.*
3. HPL mentions this specifically in "Supernatural Horror in Literature."
4. Charles Wheeler Locke (1899–1983), artist and lithographer. He taught lithography at the Art Students' League in New York from 1922 to 1937.

[115]    [ALS] [HPL to LDC]

Friday Afternoon<br>August 7, 1925

My dear Daughter Lillian:—

Your delightful letter came this morning, & I will continue my observations of yesterday in reply thereto. The daily round as you outline it is indeed time-consuming, & I manage to achieve leisure only by judicious omissions in the household programme—for example, I dust only once in three days, sweep only once a week, & eat so simply that I seldom have to do any dishwashing beyond a single plate, or cup & saucer, plus one or two metallic utensils. I appreciate the difference when I do a real job of dishwashing, such as I had to do after the meeting Wednesday, when I served six persons including myself. Today I was up late & have been writing ever since, but in the evening I have promised to accompany Leeds to a cinema of the George Eliot novel "Romola" at Loew's Circle Theatre in Columbus Circle.[1] I shall break away as soon after the show as civility permits, return hither at once, & probably start a new weird tale . . . . all of which may be said to carry the present diary entry through Friday, August 7.

The outings not only do not fatigue me, but are actually of great value both physically & psychologically. They have tanned me & given me more colour, as Loveman noticed at once after not seeing me for two months, & they put my mind increasingly in the mood for effective work & literary creation. The sight of green fields & woods & rural loveliness is absolutely essential to my temperamental well-being, & amidst the nightmare rookeries of this Babylonish metropolis I can but be thankful that a few agrestick spots like Prospect Park, or the Palisades, or Hunter's Island are still accessible. Did I mention that on Hunter's Island there is a fine old Colonial stone mansion—now occupied by the local branch of the park administration—in the third Georgian phase of architecture, & probably dating from between 1780 & 1815? Those verses "A Year Off" are for you to keep, though you might *lend* them to A E P G with the letter they accompanied. But wait—I recall her having said that she *has* seen them! Keep them, therefore, & without further responsibilities attached! As to birchbarking—you did even better than little Davis if you made *envelopes,* for his ambition stopped with the letter-sheets & kept him content to encase his remarks in the ordinary stamped product of the Federal government.

No—I must have overlooked the remarks of the Rev. Augustus M. Lord (whose venerable Georgian church I superlatively admire!) concerning the Bryanic controversies,[2] but fancy he takes about the attitude of our honest friend McNeil, who was moved to discuss these matters last week. Good old "Mac" has evolved about to the Unitarian stage, & there stopped short—since he can't understand the idea of the purposeless, unmoral, mechanistic cosmos as it is. The stamp of old-time Wisconsin Presbyterianism is too strong to be rubbed out without leaving some sort of semi-theistic impression!

Yes—I do envy old Mr. Lincoln of Foster! He is not, however, the first to employ Foster as a seat of letter'd rustication, as is well-known to those who recall the origin of the quaint name *Mount Hygeia,* as apply'd to a green elevation of much attractiveness in that pastoral domain. Before the Revolution, when Theodore Foster (the Senator from whom the town was later nam'd) & Solomon Drowne (afterward the famous Revolutionary army surgeon, some of whose effects are in the N.Y. Hist. Soc. museum, as you may recall) were intimate classmates at Rhode-Island College, (Brown Univ.) they used to plan together an elegant retirement from the world in some agreeable rural seat. The years pafs'd, & both arose to eminent positions in publick life; yet neither forgot the dream & compact of youthful days. In 1800, being able to dismifs the cares of an active career, they at last carry'd out their project; jointly purchasing a retir'd estate in that new township nam'd in 1781 for one of them, & (in deference to the salubriousness they hop'd to find) naming the elevated spot "Mount Hygiea". [*sic*] Thither they mov'd with all their families—Dr. Drowne in 1801, & Senator Foster in 1803—& there they dwelt in agrestick felicity throughout the remainder of their days, practicing the arts of rustick gentry, & dignifying the local topography by the judicious application of clafsical names. Their advent was a boon to the town as well as to themselves; for their ample means & publick spirit prompted many benevolences, & Senator Foster was ever alert to promote the growth of that region which had done him the honour to adopt his patronymick. He establisht a bank & a library, & was the chief agent in promoting the construction of a road from Providence to Hartford.

I am certainly a strong "booster" for Macaroni-Spaghetti Week, & hope to see it become a national carnival outrivalling the Saturnalia of old! No—I have not yet try'd blueberry pie, tho' your suggestion almost leads me to try for it at the Automat before meeting Leeds tonight! My favourite dessert of late has been vanilla ice-cream—a substance of which I never become wearied. Cheese—chocolate—spaghetti—ice-cream—these are my first dietetick choices!

I'll be on deck to receive such cuttings as you may send, for even though I do see the *Bulletin,* I sometimes miss an item here & there. I'm sorry you no longer see the *Times*—though I myself no longer make any attempt to be regular with anything but the *Bulletin.* There are too many papers, & time passes to[o] quickly, to make it profitable to try to keep up to date. The *past* is my province, & when I am not writing of ancient things that never were, I shall be busy considering things that used to be in Rhode Island! As to "Things Near & Far"—it is good, but not *quite* so good as its predecessor "Far-Off Things". Yes—that Room of Wonder was prodigiously clever, though as you say, it might have a tendency to make some persons dizzy. Glad you have kept up with the Albee Co., though surprised to hear that the theatre is *hot.* They have a fine ammonia cooling system installed,[3] & if they do not use it it can only be through a niggardly sense of economy. Sorry you missed Miles Standish, & hope you'll have a chance for "Down to the Sea in Ships."

That elegy of Dr. Kuntz's on Phillips was entitled "He Walked With Life"—I must try to find my copy. A E P G recalled it well, & mentioned it only recently when the author was brought to her attention. Glad you've forwarded the Alfredus-child's letter—very shortly A E P G will forward a travelogue of his, which is to be returned to me for subsequent passing-around among local amateurs & final return to the Infant himself for preservation & incorporation into his archives. He is at last becoming an antiquarian under the influence of Paris's mediaeval byways, & I surely envy him the ancient pilgrimages his situation permits him to take. A batch of postcards, also to be returned, companions the text.

Oh, yes—& here's another bright boy, Wilfred B. Talman the poet, with a long letter & a request! He is the Brown University student whose home is in Spring Valley N.Y., & his request is that I see if I can find him some spare-time job in Providence, taking about an hour or two a day, at which he can earn spending money whilst at college. He says that *writing* would be his first choice, but that he also has some degree of ability at *lettering* & *show-card writing*. He fancies that I must, from long residence, know something about Providence industries; but as an hermit I had little chance to acquire data in such fields. All I can do is to express my profound regrets—though if you hear of any opening for a bright young collegian you might let me know. Talman is a pleasant village boy, (I have never met him in person) & descended from the most ancient & considerable Dutch families of his native region. Of late he has delved much into *genealogy,* which on account of its antiquarian implications gives him several topicks to discuss with Grandpa Theobald. In Providence he boards at 256 Benefit St.—in Dr. Kalloch's former block, I believe[4]—but hears that it is coming down soon to make way for the new Court House. Be that as it may—I don't care about Victorian junk—but Pegāna preserve the Stephen Hopkins house & the Brown & Ives offices!

Well, so much for that! I must cease now, or I shall be late for my engagement with Leeds. More later—when I'll also send a copy of my new story, together with any new tales or fantasies I may write in the interim. Now that amateur stuff is fairly well disposed of, I must "get busy"—& among other things I think I'll do is to revisit some of the quaint colonial neighbourhoods I discovered last year, in order to give my mind the stimulus & fantastic impressions which later mature & take form as weird stories.

With which observation I shall close, cork the ink bottle, don street attire, & fare forth to the subway.

Yr aff: Nephew & obt: Servt:

H P L

## Notes

1. *Romola* (Inspiration Pictures, 1924), directed by Henry King; starring Lillian Gish, Dorothy Gish, William Powell, and Ronald Colman. Based on the novel by George Eliot.

2. Augustus M. Lord (1861–1941), Providence-born Unitarian minister and pastor of the First Unitarian Church (built 1816) in Providence. By "Branic controversies" HPL refers to the Scopes Trial, which was prosecuted by William Jennings Bryan. See 111n7.

3. An ammonia cooling system figures in "Cool Air," written in February 1926.

4. Lewis Howe Kalloch was HPL's dentist.

[116]     [ALS] [HPL to LDC]

Saturday Evening
Aug. 8, 1925

My dear Daughter Lillian:—

Once again I will take my pen in hand to acknowledge an appreciated communication of yours, & to extend the diary 24 hours more. Yours of the 7th duly arrived, & I noted the contents with customary interest. I am glad that the A E P G matter was promptly forwarded to you, & that you found the Morton epistle of interest. I'm not allowing myself to get excited over the Paterson matter, but am ready to take whatever comes my way. When the trustees' meeting occurs I shall be on hand with new suit & all possible eclat, & leave it to the gods what next to do. I don't think that a knowledge of art & literature counts in this position—for a long time the new museum will specialise in the natural sciences, hence experts in geology, mineralogy, entomology, ornithology, &c. are in demand. Mortonius had to qualify himself at the eleventh hour by a desperate course of study, as I shall have to do in the miraculous event of appointment. It would, I think, be possible to adopt regular hours for so important a matter as this—& I would be additionally stimulated by the fact that the work is not of itself repulsive.

I have not yet sent "The Shunned House" to *Weird Tales*, hence can't say whether or not it would be acceptable to them. I think I shall try my new story on *Detective Tales*\*, which rejected "The Sh. Ho". Shortly I shall copy several old yarns for *Weird*—but I must first cut off the flood of needless correspondence which still eats into my time: amateurs seeking advice on their new official duties, &c. Yes—*Weird Tales* is very fond of sending around cards to lists supplied by its contributors. Wright says it has proved a very effective mode of securing subscriptions. The magazine is improving, & seems at last to be firmly & reliably established despite its many previous vicissitudes. It even means to pay up the old debts of the defunct Henneberger regime—I think I said that Wright promises me $14.00 for "Nemesis" (published a year & a half ago) in the end.

About those College Hill buildings—I am sorry to say I am not mistaken, but that the School of Design intends to erect a textile building on their site.

---

\*where also I shall send my Salem novel—if ever I get the undisturbed leisure to write it. That, if accepted, would bring in a goodly sum of cash.

It may not be at once, but the knell of doom seems to have sounded—the article I read was in a recent *Bulletin,* & had an ominous stamp of authenticity. I know they are erecting other structures—among them will be a splendid art museum in which I'd give my right arm to get a job—but those have nothing to do with the textile scheme. The school is expanding into a mighty national institution—sooner or later the Dr. Carr house at Waterman & Benefit will come down . . . if it hasn't already!

Yes—on paper it is easy to say that "possessions are a burden", & that it is wisest to have nothing, but merely to live in a valise or trunk . . . . & so on . . . . fine theory indeed! But in actual fact it all depends on the person. Each individual's reason for living is different . . . i.e., to each individual there is some one thing or group of things which form the focus of all his interests & nucleus of all his emotions; & without which the mere process of survival not only means nothing whatsoever, but is often an intolerable load & anguish. Those to whom old associations & possessions do not form this single interest & life-necessity, may well sermonise on the folly of "slavery to worldly goods"—so long as they do not try to enforce their doctrines on others. They are lucky—chance has been kind to them! But to others who are so constituted as to require tangible links with their background, it is useless to preach such ideals & hypotheses. Nature has given their nervous systems other needs; & to advise them to burn their goods for freedom's sake is as silly as to advise them to cut off their legs in order to escape the burden of buying trousers. It so happens that I am unable to take pleasure or interest in anything but a mental re-creation of other & better days—for in sooth, I see no possibility of ever encountering a really congenial milieu or living among civilised people with old Yankee historic memories again—so in order to avoid the madness which leads to violence & suicide I must cling to the few shreds of old days & old ways which are left to me. Therefore no one need expect me to discard the ponderous furniture & paintings & clocks & books which help to keep 454 always in my dreams. When they go, I shall go, for they are all that make it possible for me to open my eyes in the morning or look forward to another day of consciousness without screaming in sheer desperation & pounding the walls & floor in a frenzied clamour to be waked up out of the nightmare of "reality" to my own room in Providence. Yes—such sensitivenesses of temperament are very inconvenient when one has no money— but it's easier to criticise than to cure them. When a poor fool possessing them allows himself to get exiled & sidetracked through temporarily false perspective & ignorance of the world, the only thing to do is to let him cling to his pathetic scraps as long as he can hold them. They are life for him.

Poor old Bryasinus! I fancy that he both did & didn't 'have the time of his life' in the recent Dayton business. For a while he undoubtedly enjoyed it; but when the cross-questioning of Darrow revealed his ignorance before the publick, without a chance for euphemistic rebuttal or oratorical obscuration, it is likely that he felt a mortification & peril which reacted unfavourably upon his highly-strung nerves & already weakened blood-vessels. He lacked the complete triumph he had expected, & saw enough of the determined force of scientific fact to alarm him for the security of his passionately cherished fabrick of mediaeval mythology. Like Julian the Apostate, he was frightened for a dying faith; & his invectives against modernity were animated by a feeling as strong & despairing as that which fired the "Misopogon" of that discouraged & losing champion of the Graeco-Roman gods.[1]

I shall be exceeding thankful for whatever you can do toward securing me that booklet of 1824 Westminster St. pictures at the Historical Society. Meanwhile I think you'd be interested to see the framed coloured *originals* on the top floor of the building, as Mortonius & I saw them two years ago.

St. Ronan was, if I mistake not, an early Celtick figure associated with miraculous cures; to whom a fountain in Scotland was sacred. I have sought the precise myth in vain, ransacking my library for full four hours; (a proceeding punctuated by the reading of interesting bits encounter'd on the fruitless quest) but will transmit the information as soon as I uncover it at the publick library. Sir W: Scott writ a novel bas'd upon it, intitul'd "St. Ronan's Well"; which I have not perus'd, & which is esteem'd his poorest production.

My greetings to the felines you have met—may they flourish long & gloriously! I have seen many lately, but none to equal the little black boy of two weeks ago—whom I have sought assiduously tho' in vain in the neighbourhood of Borough-Hall.

When I say that Mifs Lowell wrote *poetry*, I refer only to the essential *contents*—the isolated images which prove her to have seen the world transfigured with poetick glamour. I do not mean to say that the compleat results are to be judg'd as poems in any finish'd sense—but meerly that there is poetical vision in the broken & rhythmical prose & disconnected pictorial presentations which she gave us. She is also, of course, the author of much genuine poetry in the most perfect metres—sonnets & the like—which most have forgotten because of the greater publicity attending her eccentrick emanations.[2]

I shall view the July *Atlantick* when looking up St. Ronan at the library, noting both the poem & the article by Mr. Hall.[3] Time is so scarce of late, that I have had a chance to see but few magazines. Yes—Peter's is an excellent restaurant of the better grade, but the Automat (of which I enclose a folder) is much more nearly suited to my purse. They now have a store where some of their goods is sold, & I may occasionally patronise them for home meals. Of real restaurants, John's continues to have the greatest bargains. To-night, although I did not intend to get a restaurant meal, I was allured in by sheer astonishment at the extent of the dinner they advertised for 40¢— braised beef, spaghetti, & potato—& surely enough it was, despite the low price as modern restaurants go, almost more than I could eat! I'll get some blueberry pie the first time I see any—peaches I have had already. And I shall appreciate the roll of pictures promised in your letter.

Now for the diary, which left off yesterday as I started out to meet Leeds for a cinema show. I reached the theatre on time, & we ascended to the second balcony (20¢) where Leeds could smoke. The film—George Eliot's "Romola"—was really *magnificent,* & I strongly advise you to see it if it ever returns to Providence. It was, I think, at the Modern last spring. It is one of the finest visualisations of the Italian renaissance that I have ever seen— Belknap would go wild over it—& is absolutely correct in every detail of history & antiquarianism; photographed in Florence & Pisa on the scene of the novel, & supervised by the director of antiquities of the Florence museum—a professor of national standing in Italy. There parades before the eye all the riot & splendour of the age of the Medicis—of Savonarola, & Michelangelo, & Leonardo da Vinci—with landscapes, city panoramas, & architectural details both exterior & interior arranged with the utmost vividness & authenticity. The performers—down to the merest supernumeraries—are carefully selected with reference to the subtlest nuances of facial type, (actual Italian nobles consented to be photographed in council & banquet scenes) are adequate in acting, & are costumed with scholarly accuracy. Even the smallest properties ring true—every book displayed on shelf or table is a genuine incunabula, & a copy of Homer exhibited in one leading scene *is* actually a fourteenth or fifteenth century copy of the work in question, as shewn by a close photograph. In short, this stands with "Down to the Sea in Ships" as the best cinema display I have seen in 1925. After the performance we went to dinner at the Automat, where I had beef pie (15¢) & chocolate ice cream. (10¢) We then walked over to 6th Ave., to look in the darkened window of a marvellous shop which is selling Graeco-Roman & Egyptian antiquities at fabulously low prices. (Roman coins as low as *15¢!!*) There is glassware, pottery, &c. of the highest interest, & some of the Roman lamps & Egyptian ushabtis selling at *50¢* & up are temptations almost beyond mortal power to resist. The articles are *genuine,* & thus cheaply available because of the immense— uncountable—quantities recently uncovered by archaeologists. They impress one with the superior artistic feeling & colossal industry & productivity of the ancient world. I certainly am going to get a coin or two, & maybe one lamp or ushabti—& if I ever have a real income, I shall undoubtedly begin a collection of minor Roman antiquities. After this nocturnal window-shopping we walkt down to Bryant Park (rear of the publick library) & chatted for a while on a bench; later taking the subway for our respective lodgings & couches. The next day—today—I was up late & swamped with tail-ends of amateur correspondence. In the late afternoon I went out for some errands, ending with the braised beef at John's, as previously mentioned. In the evening Loveman called, & after some conversation I accompanied him to his house to help him move up from his $5.00 basement room to a much smaller 3d story hall room at $6.00—the change being necessitated by the noisy nature of the former, & the dampness which affects his bronchial welfare. In his new room he shew'd me more of his MSS.—some of which are exceeding rare & costly. One is of particular note & interest—a letter from the poet John Clare to his publisher, with a couplet of Keats' "Lamia" scrawled upon a vacant space *in Keats' own handwriting*—which Loveman had photographed & verified by officials of the British Museum. Loveman's theory of the matter is this: that Keats, whose publisher was the same as Clare's, had called at the office to change a couplet of "Lamia" at the last moment; & that, when he wished to write down the revised version, the publisher hastily handed him the first loose scrap he saw; which happened, by coincidence, to be the letter he had received from Clare. This is borne out by comparing the date of the letter with that of the publication of Keats' "Lamia". The couplet is this:

> "From Lycius answer'd, as heart-struck & lost,
> He sank supine beside the aching ghost."[4]

Loveman discovered the Keats item himself in a bundle of Clare letters purchased from a London autograph dealer, & after verifying it from the British Museum, described it in a letter to the *Dial*.[5] He thought of communicating it to Miss Lowell, but deferred the matter; had he been prompt about it, it would almost undoubtedly have received mention in the poetess's now celebrated Keats biography. Returning to the diary—from Loveman's room we repaired to a neighbouring cafeteria, where after a period of discussion we dispersed to our respective lodgings. Here I am still—& I think I shall stay up tonight in order to make up time lost in social amenities. Now that the festive season of Lovemanick re-welcoming is over, I must again enter that seclusion which befits an antient writer.

If I can keep my nerves in a kind of *detached* state—independent of time, space, or environment—I think I shall soon be enjoying a period of renewed literary productivity. I must slough off for a space the real & practical world, & isolate myself behind the opera-glasses of glamour & phantasy, so that I may see again that unreal world of wonder which, being seen, at once animates my pen & stamps itself on paper! To do this I may have to neglect correspondence & permit letters to pile up a bit—but this will do no harm now that United burthens are safely transferred. One may write well only after an emphatic gesture of rebellion against intrusive distractions, & an equally emphatic determination to *be oneself* in spite of all the heterogeneous advice of well-meaning multitudes. My nervous poise & aesthetic articulateness are to be attained only by telling the world to go to the deuce, & proceeding to set down the transformations which a naturally fantastic imagination makes in the visual images set before it. These visual images I shall choose with care; making solitary pilgrimages to picturesque rural spots, outlying villages, Colonial city neighbourhoods, & vistas of grotesque or beautiful skyline, in order to fill my fancy with that which most powerfully affects it & moves it to artistic utterance. As to future engagements—Tuesday night I shall probably see a fantastic cinema with Leeds & Loveman. Wednesday night there is a McNeil meeting at Kleiner's. The Wednesday after that there is a Leeds meeting at Kirk's former partner's. And the Wednesday after that a McNeil meeting at Loveman's.

More later. And in the meantime pray consider me
Yr aff. Nephew & obt Servt
H P L

P.S. I have agreed to write a prologue in verse to Loveman's prose-poem "The Sphinx."[6]

## Notes

1. Julian, Emperor of Rome (361–63 C.E.) attempted to halt the spread of Christianity throughout the Empire and to revive worship of the Graeco-Roman pantheon. His essay *Misopogon* ("Beard-Hater") is a satire on philosophers.

2. Amy Lowell (1874–1925), Imagist poet who died on 12 May 1925. HPL attacked her in "The Vers Libre Epidemic" (1917), referring to the "wholly erratic school of free poets . . . represented by Amy Lowell at her worst" (*CE* 2.20).

3. James Norman Hall, "Onward, Christian Soldiers," *Atlantic Monthly* 136, No. 1 (July 1925): 19–32. The issue also contained "Fool o' the Moon" by Amy Lowell, 47–48.

4. John Keats, *Lamia* (1820), Part II, ll. 293–94.

5. See "A Keats Discovery" (*Dial*, 18 July 1917), rpt. in *Out of the Immortal Night* 199–200.

6. No such prologue appears to survive.

[117]     [ALS] [HPL to LDC]

Thursday Night
August 13, 1925

My dear Daughter Lillian:—
                    I am revelling so gratefully in the pictures & cuttings which came this noon, that I cannot defer my thankful acknowledgment thereof. I return those so marked, & trust in Mr. Bryan's friend Yahweh for their safe receipt. Most of the extracts are of keen & permanent interest, & you can imagine the delight with which I perused the account of the Bristol House of Usher, which (but not the gravure) A E P G had also sent me. I asked her if these Finneys weren't Dr. Clark's forbears, & I now see that they were. The name Henry Finney Clark was very strong in my memory.[1] A fine old line—& I'll even forgive the worthy Archbishop for the material he supplied to the frothing Fundamentalists of a later age![2] I'd like to see that house—thank Pegāna, anyhow, that it's to be well preserved! But Holy Santa

Maria de Mt. Carmel—or whoever they select as an excuse for their fireworks displays—what a spread around la Colina Federale![3] So they're pushing through to Westminster & Cranston, as if Broadway weren't enough for them! Well, so long as Mariano pays his $37.08 regularly I've no legal pretext for starting a general massacre! Dio mio! I'm glad the bank has taken the old Cooke house. There's lots in South Main worth preserving, & I wish some of the other colonial reliquiae could be purged of their slummish decadence. What Boston did to Beacon Hill, & what N.Y. is doing to Minetta St. is worthy of careful emulation. That McSparran place interests me vastly, for only in the last few weeks have I begun to realise the feudal splendour of Narragansett country life before the Revolution, as contrasted with any other social fabric in New-England. I'm glad both the church & glebe are still standing—even tho' the former is moved to Wickford. Yes—there was an article on Goddard's postal activities in a *Sunday Journal* of some time ago. That wolf-nursing business reminds one of Romulus & Remus on the one hand, & of a good werewolf story plot on the other! As for the evolution matter—the statements in the cuttings are as sensible as can be made by those cautious speakers who pay to custom the toll of acquiescence in general theistic ideas. It takes a bolder soul to brush aside all the cobwebs of teleology & supernaturalism—even John Cowper Powys hasn't done it completely in his "Art of Happiness", which S H sent me, although he disposes of duty very nicely. Powys, you know, is Little Sonny's favourite—& he has begun to write voluminously for the Haldeman-Julius booklets, of which I've picked up a few more lately, including Poe's Marginalia. S H, by the way, will be in N.Y. next week; arriving on the evening of my birthday—Thursday the 20th—& leaving the following Sunday night.

Dates remind me of diaries—so here goes on the Old Reliable, which left off at the close of Saturday, August 8. I had meant to stay up, but retired in the morning of the 9th & slept till quite late. Then I rose, read some weird material, & retired late. The next day, Monday the 10th, I rose late, was swamped by correspondence all the afternoon & evening, & at the close of the latter turned to the business of fictional composition. I was not, however, able to produce anything—being bored with the sameness, regularity, colourlessness, & prison-like quality of the usual round & scene. Thus feeling it necessary to recover the psychology of independence & individuality—to feel that I could go where I darned please when I darned pleased, & imbibe the visual piquancy & variety of colonial sights as dictated by my mood,—I set forth on a nocturnal pilgrimage after mine own heart; beginning at Chelsea, the village overtaken by New-York in the 'forties, west of 7th Ave. between 18th & 28th Sts, & working south toward Greenwich amongst the curious houses, imagination-kindling streets, & innumerable kitty-cats whose graceful presence called back to memory the wholesome long-departed domestick life of the village. Circling round by the ancient quadrangle of the Union Theological Seminary, & dreaming dreams of the old days, I worked slowly south-ward in the light of a misty waning moon, & eventually struck the borders of Greenwich. There I threaded anew the well-loved & tortuous labyrinths which I have described in so many previous travelogues, doubling frequently on my course & saturating myself with the colonial atmosphere that means mental life for me—old iron-railed steps, Georgian knockers, or steep gables, dormers, & gambrel roofs in black silhouette against the half-clouded sky. Once I found a mother-cat with two of the tiniest imaginable black-&-white kittens—irresistibly lovely little rascals—& this time the temptation was too strong to resist . . . I put one of them in my (old blue) coat pocket, with his head out, & carried him around with me for nearly an hour; later returning to where I had found him, & depositing him on the steps from which his mamma & brother had vanished. He was the prettiest, most microscopic little rascal I've seen in years—big-eyed & alert, & prone to chew playfully at one's fingers. I saw many other small kittens during my jaunt—this must be the be-ginning of the fall crop, bless their little hearts! Grandpa's chilluns! My Greenwich peregrinations included Abingdon Square, Grove St., Grove Court, Barrow & Commerce Sts., the Minettas, Milligan & Patchin Places, Gay St., Sheridan Square, & Charlton St., & embraced many marvellous glimpses of the old times. Once I saw a colonial doorway lighted up, the trac-eries of transom & side-lights standing out softly against the mellow yellow gleams inside. From Greenwich my route led south along Hudson St. to old New York, (across Lispenard's Meadows & the filled-in swamp) & I noted the colonial square at the intersection of Canal. Later crossing to Greenwich St., I descended into the most ancient district; noting the Planters' Hotel, Tom's Chop House, & the like, & emerging on Broadway to salute St Paul's & plunge down Ann St. into the heart of Golden Hill—Irving's boyhood neighbourhood, & the seat of much disturbance during the late disastrous re-volt against His Majesty's government. I passed under the Brooklyn Bridge to Vandewater St., & noted with horror the replacement of a fine colonial row by a damnable new garage, (other excellent colonials have vanished in Greenwich, at Barrow & Hudson Sts.) & doubled back through New Cham bers & Pearl, noting beside the former a colonial smithy which has always appealed to me. Proceeding along Pearl toward the Battery, I viewed all the ancient houses & waterfront panoramas as I passed them—remarking inci-dentally that the old Harpers publishing house has been newly razed. At Hanover-Square, seat of the best British gentry before the Revolution, I lifted my hat in honour of King George the Third; then passing on by the Queen's Head Tavern—Fraunces', that is—to those regions of Battery Park where one or two colonial mansions yet linger. It was now five o' the morning, & I had so fully thrown off melancholy by my free & antique voyage, that I felt exactly in the humour for writing. The clouds were dissolving, & another day was due. Should I drag it away in New-York, & lose the keenness of my mood, or keep on in my dash for liberty—gaining fresh strength as I kicked aside the irritating fetters of the usual? The sea was before me—the clean, salt harbour beyond which lay a white man's country—& a Staten Island ferry rode at anchor. Who, possessed of any imagination whatsoever, could pause for an instant? So I planked down my nickel, boarded the ship, & in a few minutes was riding the billows under a dawn-paling sky. Whither bound? The New-Englandish soul within me suggested the nearest substitute,—ancient Elizabethtown—so upon my landing in the grey twilight I took the proper trolley & rode in ecstasy past seashores & hills turning pink & gold with the sunrise. At the Elizabethtown ferry I saw the burnished copper disc of the sun gleaming gloriously on the waters, & by 7 a.m. I was in the central district of the village, gravely saluting the old colonial spire that towers—as you will remember—above the shady churchyard. At a small shop I bought a dime composition book; & having a pencil & pencil-sharpener (in a case, which S H gave me) in my pocket, proceeded to select a site for literary creation. Scott Park—the triangular space we passed in going to look at those rooms in East Jersey St.—was the place I chose; & there, pleasantly intoxicated by the wealth of delicate un-metropolitan greenery & the yellow & white colonialism of the gambrel-roofed Scott house, I settled myself for work. Ideas welled up unbidden, as never before for years, & the sunny actual scene soon blended into the purple & red of a hellish midnight tale—a tale of cryptical horrors among tangles of antediluvian alleys in Greenwich Village—wherein I wove not a little poetick description, & the abiding terror of him who comes to New-York as to a faery flower of stone & marble, yet finds only a verminous corpse—a dead city of squinting alienage with nothing in common either with its own past or with the background of America in general. I named it "He", & had it nearly done by three, when my Leeds–Loveman engagement called me back to Babylon. Finishing the tale en route, I would have been in ample time to receive my messages had transportation been normal; but alas! at the water's edge I found a broken ferry! For an hour, amidst the profanity of draymen & other prospective passengers, the red boat was held up for tinker-ing; & when it did start I was foredoomed to lateness. The rest of the trip was pleasant, & in the evening at home I polished my story before an early retir-ing. I trust Leeds has forgiven me for my apparent remissness—Loveman has, for he telephoned this afternoon & made an engagement here for tomor-row night. He has not been feeling well, he says, & did not attend the gang meeting last night. Tomorrow I shall read him my newest story & discuss the prologue for "The Sphinx". At present, no one but myself has seen "He".

The next day—Wednesday the 12th—I was up at noon, did some Dun-sanian reading to stabilise my recovered creativeness of mood, & toward evening set out on a pilgrimage whose capricious oddity lent it the piquancy which dispels dulness. Convinced that I had waited long enough before shew-ing you the cut & outline of my new suit, & spurred on by a seaside snap-shot which A E P G lately sent me from Ogunquit, I took an open car for Coney Island to get those much-promised tintypes of the resplendent regalia—for I don't know where else to get such things except by chance, as last spring. The ride was breezy & pleasant, but when the snaps were finished I found to my displeasure that they shewed *only head & shoulders*—confounded luck, when 'twas the *suit* I wanted! However—cash was not unlimited & reinvestment were rash, so I pocketed the products & took the elevated back to Brooklyn for the meeting at Kleiner's. Here is the picture—for you to keep, permanently, since I have another to send A E P G permanently when next I write her. You can, at least, see the hang & trimness of the coat—& in September, when I can wear a waistcoat & stiff collar, I'll get a *really* full-length tintype shewing my complete outfit from new straw lid to Spartanly tamed shoes! A E P G will note, in studying this view, that I have on the fine striped shirt she gave me last April for my Washington trip, & one of the soft collars she sent in June. Suleiman ibn Daoud in all his glory! Well, as I say, I took the elevated back; & by dint of devious transference arrived on time at the Kleinerian rancho, to find Mortonius ahead of me, & M^cNeil ascending the stairs simultaneously. This proved the full quota of the evening, but discourse was natheless brisk. Paterson & poetry, evolution & Euripides, daemonology & the drama, furnished ample food for conversation; & M^cNeil's departure at 12:20 only brightened up the dialogue of the residual three. Morton still talks Paterson with a flourish—he grew quite tantalising on this occasion as he described that town's proximity to the edge of deep, mysterious forests & rural farmsteads & meadow-lands. I hold myself, of course, in readiness to appear before his tyrants whenever bidden. It was 4 a.m. ere we broke up, yet each of us would have sworn 'twas not much after two! Mortonius & I took the subway & parted at Canal St. Thence I went home—but not to bed, for I had much to write. A new story plot—perhaps a short novel—had occurred to my awakening faculties, & it was imperative to get it down in skeletonic detail whilst it was fresh. This, of course, was a matter of hours, since I adopted my complete development scheme in full. The writing itself will now be a relatively simple matter—it's to be called "The Call of Cthulhu", & I'll send you a copy as soon as it is written & typed,[4] though of course "The Horror at Red Hook" & "He" will come first. This new thing—if it turns out as long as I expect from a mere survey of the ground—ought to bring in a very decent sized cheque—it'll be in three or four parts. When the second mail came, I found myself swamped with correspondence; & have been coping with that ever since . . . . . . . . except for the time I took off for Dinner. I shall retire at a medium hour, & thus concludes Thursday the 13th of August.

I trust your *United Amateur* came safely—Cook has sent my extra copies, so I infer he is mailing the edition generally. Keep it—A E P G has another. I also received a new *Plain-Speaker*, which shews that the Moe-Whitaker feud is fiercely flourishing despite all that can be done to oil the troubled waters.

And so it goes. Now to get my mail in the box & retire to claim the somnolence of the moderately equitable. I trust that you are flourishing, & that the cooler weather is as much of a boon to you as it is a trial to me!

With every good wish, & renewed assurances of distinguished consideration, I am ever

Yr most aff Nephew & obt Servt

H P L

P.S. Tryout's cat—Thomas II, is no more. He was run over by a motor. Requiescat in pace!

## Notes

1. HPL refers to a house built by Samuel Lee in Bristol, RI, soon after his emigration from England in 1686. It stood on the site later used by the Usher brothers for a storehouse. The house was occupied for many years by Jeremiah Finney and his son Josiah. Henry Finney Clark (1790–1820) was the paternal grandfather of LDC's husband, Dr. Franklin Chase Clark.

2. HPL refers to James Ussher (1581–1656), Church of Ireland Archbishop of Armagh, who made a celebrated calculation that, based on the dates provided in the Bible, the world must have begun on 23 October 4004 B.C.E. The date is still regarded as accurate by "young-earth" creationists.

3. HPL refers to Federal Hill, the Italian district of Providence. HPL has misspelled the Italian word *collina*. But cf. "Providence in 2000 A.D." (1912): "On La Collina Federale's brow, / Near Il Passagio di Colombo" (ll. 45–46; *AT* 202).

4. HPL did not attempt to write the story until the following summer, after he had returned to Providence.

[118]    [ALS] [HPL to LDC]

Begun—Wednesday Afternoon
August 19, 1925
Ended—Sunday Afternoon
August 23, 1925

My dear Daughter Lillian:—

Your appreciated note of the 14th & card of birthday greeting safely arrived, & I must transmit without further delay the customary quota of sincere gratitude. I am glad *The United Amateur* safely arrived, & that you find it deserving of commendation. Cook crowded much material into little space, & in general assisted marvellously in furnishing the old year with a suitable & dignified close. The new board is very active & ambitious, & Bacon is already planning his opening issue—for which Belknap has written a critical review. Belknap, by the way, is staying at the Thousand Islands another month; but will call on his Grandpa Friday Sept. 21, the day after his return. The National has just asked me to accept the Chairmanship of its Bureau of Criticks, but I am refusing with all the tact & sincerity I can command.

I'm glad the Alfredus-Child's epistle proved interesting. Since that, my news of him has been exceedingly direct—direct to the extent that his wife is now in Brooklyn, in a tasteful room on the ground floor at 169 Clinton, & at the moment out looking for a job; failing which (as is of course virtually certain) she will accompany S H (who is also here, a week ahead of schedule) to Cleveland tomorrow, stop with her a week, & then proceed home to Chicago & her parents until the arrival next June of the Young Parisian. Alfredus, in short, is going in for music very deeply; has given up his professorial post in Texas, & is about to settle down to some very serious & solitary musical study in Paris—whilst his wife renews her acquaintance with the United States. She would like to get a position in New-York—which is still novel & attractive to her—if she can; but lacking any special qualifications, it would be a miracle if she did.

But now to the diary—which was partly heralded by the cards of Saturday. The last formal entry was Thursday night, & of Friday I may say that I was up at noon, wrote letters, went to see Loveman in the evening, (instead of his coming here) & after a cup of coffee with him at the Tiffany, set out on another of my soul-saving all-night-&-day rambles through ancient & rural regions. In the dark I saw again the Greenwich gables that used to be, & felt the beating of spectral wings as the waning crescent moon rose above venerable chimney-pots. By five I was at the Staten Island ferry again—& as on that previous morning I watched the pale dawn break across the bay, & the red-&-gold splendour of sunrise glorify the island & the Elizabethtown ferry. From Elizabethtown, which I reached at 7:00 a.m., I sent [*sic*] out on foot for the north along the Morris Pike; first encountering the vast white colonial bulk of "Liberty Hall", residence during the Revolution of Gov. Wᵐ Livingston. It gleamed distantly through a leafy park raised by a grassy embankment to the right of the roadway, & I tempted the wrath of the present inhabitants by ascending the drive & viewing it at close range. Tho' finely preserved, it is not in the strictest sense beautiful; & has been disfigured by many heterogeneous & inappropriate additions. It is impressive, but that is all. Not even the details are of extraordinary beauty as colonial details go. Having seen this place, I continued along the pike to observe the Revolutionary reliques at Connecticut Farms & Springfield. These two villages are the respective ends of the two British advances inland from Elizabethtown on June 7ᵗʰ & 23ᵈ, 1780. On these occasions the forces of His Majesty, encamped upon Staten-Island, crossed the sound & took Elizabethtown; thence striving to work inland along the Galloping Hill Road. The first advance was checked at Connecticut Farms, the second at Springfield; & each has left certain relicks & traditions. The Galloping Hill Road with its many twistings was long ago abandoned in favour of the Morris Pike, so that Connecticut Farms (now called Union Centre) is no longer on the main highway—tho' Springfield still is. For this reason I missed Connecticut Farms altogether on the outbound trip; encountering no historick landmark till I reached the bridge before Springfield where on June 23ᵈ the second advance was first disputed by Col. Israel *Angell* & the 2nd *Rhode Island* Regiment. Angell was at last forced to give ground to a much superior force, but his resistance was so determined that his bravery became immortal. The present Battle Bridge is dedicated to him, & bears a bronze tablet in praise of him & his loyal Rhode-Islanders, whereon is quoted a significant passage from Genl. Washington's subsequent letter to the Governor of Rhode-Island—William Greene, Esq., of Warwick. It reads:

### BATTLE BRIDGE

To the Memory of
Col. Israel Angell,
Who Commanded the 2nd R.I.
Infantry at the Battle of Springfield,
23rd June, 1780.

"– – – Headquarters, Ramapough,
29ᵗʰ June, 1780

"Sir:

– – – The gallant Behaviour of Col. Angell's Regiment on the 23rd inst. at Springfield, reflects the highest Honour upon the Officers & Men. They disputed an important Pass with so obstinate a Bravery that they lost upwards of Forty killed, wounded, & missing before they gave up their Ground to a vast Superiority of Force – – –
"Yr excellency's most obt Servt
*Gᵒ. Washington*
"To Governour Greene,
Rhode-Island."

Angell was, of course, one of the old Scituate stock; descended from Roger Williams' companion Thomas Angell & ancestor of Dr. James Burrill Angell. Having observ'd this bridge, & reflected with pride upon this tablet, I walkt on into the village of Springfield; which is an attractive Colonial place six miles northwest of Elizabethtown. Here the principal object is the Presbyterian Church of which I sent you a card, & which at the time of the battles was presided over by the celebrated Rev. James Caldwell. Parson Caldwell, upon the first approach of His Majesty's forces, had sent his wife & children to what he thought was safety at a house in Connecticut Farms. Here, however,

Mrs. Caldwell was killed by a bullet fired through the window by an irresponsible Hessian during the advance of June 7. Thus bereaved, a new fire was added to the military ardour of the Parson—who indeed preached with a pistol on each side of his Bible & a row of muskets ready for instant use in the front of the church. When Col. Angell made his resistance on June 23d, Parson Caldwell was in the very thick of the fighting among the intrepid Rhode-Islanders; & was among the first to observe the giving-out of wadding for the guns. With action as quick as thought, he rushed back to his church on the edge of the village, and entering, gathered up a vast armful of old hymn-books, whose pages would supply the necessary wadding paper. Never before did an 18th century psalmodist serve such a purpose as did the respectable Dr. Isaac Watts on that strenuous day. As Parson Caldwell delivered his precious load, he cried out to his fellow-soldiers, "Put Watts into 'em, boys! Give 'em Watts!" And they did. This incident is the subject of a rather frequently-quoted ballad by Bret Harte—"Caldwell of Springfield N.J." Having thoroughly view'd the church, survey'd the village, & obtain'd & mail'd some postcards, I started back by trolley; making inquiries as to the true location of Connecticut Farms. This information secur'd, I alighted at the proper point & struck across to the line of the old Galloping Hill Road, where on a high bluff above a sharp curving descent of the highway stands the late Georgian successor to the original Presbyterian Church (built 1730) burnt by the retreating Hessians on June 7, 1780. There is a churchyard of much picturesqueness, & nearby one may see set up a British cannon remaining from the battle. At the foot of the hill is an old colonial blacksmith shop in front of which two Hessians were buried, & close to this is the ancient Wade house, standing at the time of the battle & being just across the road from the now vanish'd house wherein Parson Caldwell's wife was shot. Connecticut-Farms (named for its original settlers, the Wades of Conn.) being now cover'd, I continued to trace the abandon'd Galloping Hill Road toward Elizabethtown, encountering here & their [*sic*] wild pastures, antique farmsteads, & venerable copses & arcades of gnarled trees which lent a weird & remote aspect to the picturesque landscape. I shall some time put these things in a tale. Finally attaining Roselle Park—a prosperous suburb—I took a car into the city & set out at once upon a fresh 6-mile walk; along the Rahway Road, in quest of a certain old Georgian mansion & tavern described in the guide-book. These I did not discover—they must have been torn down since the date (1914) of the book—but I kept on to Rahway & found the latter a blissful little city of narrow streets, occasional ancient churches, frequent wooden colonial houses, & other agreeable contrasts to the welter & chaos of New York. At length taking the omnibus back to Elizabethtown, I settled myself as on Tuesday in Scott Park—beginning a horror tale which I had in mind. This I sketched out & began filling in when my labour was interrupted by the advent of one of those curious stranger-addressing characters whom one meets every now &

then—in this case a delightful & well-dressed gentleman of about sixty-five; who, having asked a geographical direction, remained about an hour or two to converse. He was a Mr. Van Beekman of the old Dutch stock, tho' by residence a Middle-Westerner. Now visiting married children in & near New York, he had sought a boarding-place free from noise & foreign influences, & had found it nowhere save in Elizabethtown. He was a former civil engineer, had participated in the building of every transcontinental railway since the Union Pacific, was an authority on bison & other western matters both scientific & agricultural, & had been a War Correspondent in the Russo-Japanese conflict. He had helped to select the bison from whom are descended the present herd in the Bronx Zoölogical Garden, & had recently, on governmental request, made a report on the condition & distribution of the posterity of those animals. He had written many descriptive articles & means to write more, & was interested in the weird material he found me writing. Altogether, he was a fine & interesting person to encounter by chance; & I did not regret the time our conversation consumed. It was now evening, & I retraced my steps to Brooklyn over Staten Island & the ferries; observing all the glories of sunset en route, & arriving home to find myself engulfed in responsibilities of varying nature & magnitude.

Telephone calls had been vainly ringing all day. S H had returned unexpectedly & tried to find me a dozen times, Loveman had sought to catch me to cancel the engagement of Sunday night, Leeds had been ringing—& I know not how many more! Then, too, the mails were full of responsibilities. Sonny had a critique to be corrected & forwarded to Bacon *at once,* with the enclosure of a poem of his ("An Old Wife Speaketh It") of which I had the only copy, other amateur matter required instant attention, & there was a letter from Galpinius saying that his wife was returning ahead of him on the *Majestic,* sailing from Liverpool August 12, & would like to be guided about New York by the gang—with which she would get in touch by calling me up on her arrival. Some bunch of things to attend to! Well—I fixed up the mail matter, received a call from S H & arranged to meet her at the subway, & responded to the knock of Loveman, who had come over in person since he could not get me on the wire. The perplexing thing was how to receive Mrs. Galpin when the steamer came in, since the absence of my name from the telephone book would make her attempt to call me up unavailing. I finally decided to ascertain the exact time & place of landing, & send a letter to the wharf; containing the required telephone number, plus photographs of any such members as would be likely to meet her at whatever spot might be designated over the wire—so that instant identification might be possible. Of her plans & wishes beyond general sightseeing Alfredus gave us no idea. At 11 o'clock Loveman & I fared forth to the subway to meet S H, & after general greetings we dispersed; S H & I proceeding to 169 to read, write, & retire. The next day—Sunday the 16th—we were up at noon, ate an elaborate breakfast involving rich cream which S H brought in, swept & cleaned the room, called up the White Star Line & found that the *Majestic* would dock at 10 a.m. Tuesday, & set out for a scenic trip through Prospect Park. Reaching the park by open car, we observed those especially fine portions which I discovered for the first time recently; & finally worked through to Flatbush, coming out at the Parkside Ave. subway station. S H now wished to go to Sheepshead Bay & call on the Denches, whose new arrival Richard Merritt Dench was recently announced. Making the engagement over the telephone from Reed & Snyder's drug store, we took the subway & were soon at "the Bay", where before taking the Emmons Ave. 'bus S H purchased a full dinner at a delicatessen store to carry with us, in order that our call might relieve rather than increase the burthens of domestic management. Dench was absent, but Mrs. Dench & the new heir, together with Mrs. Dench's sister Miss Merritt, (who will wed Mortonius this fall) were on hand. Richard is a comely & vociferous person, in excellent health, & apparently quite resigned to the ordeal of facing a long & dull terrestrial existence. The next Blue Pencil meeting will be held at his home, & the assigned literary topic is a tribute to him— which reminds me that I must write something of the sort before it is too late. The meeting is Saturday the 29th. Dinner consisted of tongue, potato chips, olives, beets, cheese-cake, frosted cake, & other details which elude my memory. At length the visit terminated, & scorning the 'bus we walked back to the subway station, where we took an homeward train. Having arrived at 169, we now prepared a letter for Mrs. Galpin at the pier; giving our telephone number & enclosing photographs of Loveman & myself as those most likely to meet her. This completed another day. On Monday the 17th I rose early, did some reading, & in the afternoon set out to meet S H at a restaurant—Budry's, in 50th St., which A E P G will remember. After an excellent lunch of roast veal we proceeded to a cinema show & saw "The Ten Commandments",[1] whose flashing electric sign with the imitation lightning you will recall as one of the glitters of Times Square last winter. Just as Belknap said, the opening portion was artistic & impressive, whilst the later or modern part was unrelieved trash. After this we took a ride to Flatbush, about which we walked for some time, finally taking light refreshments at an excellent French bakery near Church Ave. Returning by surface car we read, wrote, & retired. The next day—Tuesday the 18th—we were up early & on the watch for Mrs. Galpin's telephone call. S H had to go out, but arranged to leave the numbers of the places she visited, so that I might reach her when Mrs. G. communicated. Meanwhile I busied myself with reading & correspondence— & framed an inquiry for the Post Office concerning an important envelope from Clark Ashton Smith, containing a letter, a story, & several poems, which was mailed to me last March & failed to reach its destination. Thus the day passed—when at three o'clock the Burns boy brought up the card of Mrs. Alfred Galpin! The steamship letter had failed to reach her; & after a five-hour search including inquiries at police stations, public libraries, & heaven knows what else, she had come upon the place through a vague remembrance that it was in Clinton Street, & that its number had three figures beginning with 1 & ending with 9. Beginning at 199, she had worked along the street northward, trying 189 & 179, & finally stumbling on the correct spot at 169. I at once telephoned S H of her arrival, & also Loveman—the latter of whom came over at once, though S H was unable to get here before he had been & gone. Mrs. G. was undecided about the duration of her stay; though waning finance dictated a very brief sojourn, whilst her trunk had already been scheduled for through transportation to her parents in Chicago. Three days seemed a logical period, though she would like to obtain a local position & settle semi-permanently till the American return of The Boy. At length she decided to plan on leaving Thursday night, on a late train. Mrs. Galpin is a small person of no especial beauty, strongly resembling the portrait of Mrs. McMullen (Lilian Middleton) which you will find in the second (green-covered) issue of *The Rainbow*.[2] She is descended from the most ancient Norman nobility domiciled in Ireland—the de Roches—& Alfredus is strongly thinking of changing his name to hers, because of its greater aristocratic significance. Some of the kin of this family, the Burke-Roches, are of international social prominence; whilst Mrs. G's own father would be the 21st Earl of Fermoy if he would renounce his American citizenship. A proper family for the reception of Grandpa's Boy—I can see him as *Alfred de Roche,* in a panelled coach with his new coat-of-arms on the door! Mrs. G. was, like Alfredus, an infant prodigy; & is a graduate of the University of Chicago. Her literary background is ample & profound, & appears to be united to an excellent taste & keen intelligence; in short, the match seems in every way a suitable one for The Child, whose genius deserves a kindred environment. Alfredus himself, I learn, is developing into a typical Parisian character. He wears his hair long—longer, in literal truth, than his wife's—& even tried to grow a beard till he found it impossible. He carries a stick, wears a small cap perched atop his shaggy locks, & affects the oldest clothes he can find—in fact, he is still wearing the old grey suit he had in Cleveland three years ago; so that if we ever have a reunion my old blue will have an appropriate companion in its memories! His resemblance to the cinema comedian Harold Lloyd has become so pronounced that small boys hail him in the streets; whilst only the other day a British official, in stamping a passport of Mrs. Galpin's on which were photographs of both, became very interested & deferential, & declared himself much honoured to meet the wife of so accomplished an actor—whose real name, Galpin, he was glad to learn! Alfredus' love for Paris is thorough & profound, & he plans to stay there studying music till June—having long ago resigned his position with the college in Texas. His plans are very vague, but his one ambition is to be a musician & composer, & I certainly believe he will succeed unless he experiences another sudden change of ambition. His scornful repudiation of literature is complete; & he not only laughs at his wife for reading, but refrained from telling her that he had ever followed letters himself—so that the Galpinian essays & critiques which I shewed her came as a complete surprise! A great boy—& believe Grandpa, he'll come out somewhere yet! His finances are very poor, for he refused to break the will whereby his father left most of his fortune to the other Alfred Galpin—son of his brother Cromwell Galpin of California. The $300.00 he did get, he was about to tear up in contempt—but his wife snatched it away before it was too late. What cash he has, comes from the estate of the mill-owner A. M. Willy, his maternal grandfather, some tangles in which his mother has just succeeded in straightening out. Alfredus sent his Grandpa a small bottle of port wine (which I shall give to Kirk) & a French cake in a sealed paper package with gay label depicting the Notre Dame. This latter I shall serve at some meeting of The Boys, in remembrance of him who is, in effect, an absent member of ours. Loveman was much impressed with the profound knowledge of Mrs. Galpin*, & with the ready classical taste which strewed her conversation with such allusions as "the wine-red sea" from Homer. S H found her interesting in the extreme, & at once invited her to stop off in Cleveland for a few days before returning to Chicago. This she will do, sharing S H's newly repapered quarters & visiting the various spots about the town which three years ago were hallowed by her scintillant spouse's presence. She will sample the unassuming delicacies of Clark's Lunch, read Baudelaire on a bench in Rockefeller Park, eat fresh fruit salad sundaes at the drug store at 105th St. & Euclid Ave., & in general retrace the steps of the Galpinian expeditions of 1922. In the evening S H led the way to the Milan, where we had an excellent Italian dinner, & afterward took all hands to the Harris Theatre, where is running a mediocre play called "White Collars"—whose dramatic adapter, Miss Edith Ellis, is an acquaintance of hers in the Gamut Club.[3] This comedy proved far from intolerable, & I will enclose one of the unique souvenir fans which were distributed to the audience—I'm sending another to A E P G. After the play we took a taxicab to the Erie ferry near the White Star dock, & fetched Mrs. Galpin's hand luggage to 169, where she took a room on the ground floor. En route we took refreshments at the Scotch Bakery. Finally we dispersed for slumber; Mrs. Galpin deciding to devote the morrow to job-hunting, & indicating her intention of rising early, perhaps before the rest of the household—returning some time in the afternoon, & attending the meeting of The Boys at Kirk's expartner's—where S H also planned to attend.

---

*she reads as rapidly as A. G. On Thursday she read Galsworthy's "White Monkey" THROUGH in odd moments.

Midnight—
Saturday–Sunday
Aug. 22–23

After a lapse I will again resume my chronicle, this time under quieter conditions which will permit me to finish it at one sitting. I last spoke of Wednesday the 19th, on which date I rose early & wrote letters till mid-afternoon, when Mrs. Galpin returned from her fruitless industrial quest. Upon her arrival she spoke of the night before—which, thanks to the negligence of busy Mrs. Burns—had not been one of rest. It seems that the downstairs room has not been kept as immaculate as some others hereabouts, & that its couch has an undesirable population of invertebrate organisms which resent the intrusion of mere mortals to a highly vindictive extent! Accordingly Mrs. G. was far from unharassed, & in the morning held an interesting conversation with Mrs. Burns—who apologised profoundly & let her have the room at a reduced rate. In the evening—S H being detained downtown—I took Mrs. G. to dinner at Peter's; where (thank Gawd) she absolutely insisted on paying for herself, as she did at subsequent meals. We then proceeded uptown to the meeting, where S H & Kleiner had already arrived, & where Mortonius, Loveman, & Leeds soon afterward put in an appearance. The presence of one direct from Paris gave a Gallick tone to the conversation, & Morton recalled with keen zest his own week there—a week which, like my five days in Philadelphia, seems to have made him acquainted with everything worth knowing, ancient & modern alike. Leeds exhibited a poem he had written on the weird novelist Algernon Blackwood, & in general the meeting was commendably brisk. Dispersal began early—about 12:30 a.m.—& the Brooklyn delegation took the subway en masse, Kleiner & Loveman dropping off as they reached their respective stations. The residual trio proceeded to 169; where Mrs. Galpin, after inspecting her room, decided she could not rest. Accordingly—& with many apologies for having delivered a guest unwittingly into an arena of sanguinary monsters—S H & I decided that Mrs. G. had better stop at some haven of undisputed immaculateness & desirability; hence I assisted in the transfer of her effects to the celebrated & dignified Hotel Bossert in Montague Street, where she obtained an excellent seventh-floor room for four dollars. I then returned, wrote, & retired. The next day—Thursday the 20th—I celebrated my oncoming senility by rising early to accompany S H to the Federal Bldg. for her final naturalisation procedure. Kirk not being due in N.Y. till afternoon, we had Loveman for a second witness. He & I were through by 10:30, but S H had to wait till 1 p.m. for ultimate details. On leaving the building we proceeded to the Montague St. branch of the Brooklyn Public Library, where I obtained a card & took out Scott's "St. Ronan's Well" in an effort to solve the problem of this holy man's identity. The effort, however, proved useless; since in the novel the name "St. Ronan's" & "St. Ronan's Well" are used merely as geographical names, without a single allusion to the legend or personage behind them. I have not given up yet, though, for I fancy there must be some clue somewhere in some library. On this occasion I proceeded home, where I found Mrs. G. already arrived after a last & unavailing early morning interview with a possible employer, & a last & earnest conversation with Mrs. Burns anent a fresh case of *robbery* in this delectable retreat! It seems that when packing in haste the previous evening she had left behind a somewhat valuable silk nightgown—which was now missing, & which has not been heard from since. Which of the sundry transient inhabitants to accuse one cannot say—but fortunately Mrs. G. is a philosopher, & able to dismiss life's casual losses with a shrug & a sigh. We now endeavoured to set out upon that course of sightseeing which malign circumstance had thus far delayed—but again the Fates interposed, & the entire morning was wasted at the Erie & White Star piers in a fruitless attempt to locate Mrs. G's trunk, for which she had failed to obtain a receipt, but which probably went through to Chicago. We did, however, recover the missing letter with its pictorial enclosures, which latter I wished to preserve. At 1:30 p.m., after telephoning S H & arranging to meet her at 169 at 6:30 to escort her to her Cleveland train, (N.Y.C. & H.R, arriving in the morning. Mrs. G., having bought a non-exchangeable Erie ticket, had to wait for a night train involving a change at Youngstown, & not reaching Cleveland till the next evening) we dined at the St. Regis in Times Square, where you & I ate so many times last winter. Since all museums close at five, it was now too late to see more than one; & this was chosen without difficulty, since Mrs. G's chief wish in N.Y. was to inspect the American Wing of the Metropolitan Museum. Arriving in good season, & previously surveying the French rooms (as you & I did) we proceeded to cover the colonial exhibits in detail; & Mrs. G. displayed a genuine interest & acute knowledge in remarking upon the objects displayed*. She purchased the dollar handbook of the collection, & means to become something of an authority on Georgian America whilst her effulgent lord & master absorbs the antique charm of mediaeval Paris. After the American Wing there was no time for general museum exploration; but we saw the architectural room with its Parthenon, Pantheon, & Notre Dame models, & the Graeco-Roman corridor with the famous athlete's head which Loveman worships as the marble embodiment of his poetic "Hermaphrodite". The museum now closing, we took an omnibus (roof) down to Washington-Square; from which we branched westward through the colonial byways of Greenwich, purchasing postcards as we went, & not omitting to observe such shrines of quaintness as Milligan Place, Patchin Place, & Gay Street. Arriving at Sheridan Square, we took the subway for Brooklyn—finding, however only a note instead of S H at 169. She had been called downtown on business, &

---

*Incidentally—we encountered a delightful old lady from Mass., now living in *Alexandria,* Va.

could be available only a brief moment at the Grand Central before train time; but would welcome any seers-off there. Mrs. Galpin, being exceedingly fatigued by continuous exertion, sent her regrets & went to her hotel to rest; but I went down & saw S H safely aboard the Cleveland train—incidentally carrying her a letter from A E P G which had just arrived. I then returned to Brooklyn & tried to get Loveman for the evening; but he had gone to discuss things with the newly-arrived Kirk at the Martinique, & could not collaborate in the triangular letter to the Alfredus-Child which I had planned. I tried to get him several times after that, but without success. Now proceeding to the Bossert, I met Mrs. G. & transferred her valises once more to 169, for later transportation to the train. She obtained some light refreshments—cheese crackers, orange marmalade, chocolate, & fruit, & served these whilst I began a letter to The Boy. In due time she added her section, & under separate cover we added the postcards obtained during the afternoon, as a supreme inducement for The Child to stop off in New York next June upon his return to the United States. I also added my one remaining copy of the new picture of myself which I sent you—to shew him what his Grandpa looks like in these days of scientifick reduction, & with his new summer finery. After completing her section, Mrs. G. rested on the couch & slept soundly whilst I finished the epistle at length. At 11:00 I fared forth to secure a taxicab, which I found only with great difficulty & alarming loss of time. Returning with it, I awaked Mrs. G. with as much gradualness & as little violence as possible, after which the expedition hastened in the cab across Brooklyn Bridge & through the town to the Erie ferry, just in time to miss the 11:50 boat which had been mentioned as the one connecting with the Cleveland–Chicago train! For a moment, dramatick despair supervened; but in another instant a clerk had cleared the skies by mentioning that according to *Daylight-Saving Time* we were a full hour early, the real boat being the *12:50* by the local clocks. Saved! We now proceeded to a neighbouring cafeteria, had coffee & read books at a table which commanded a view of the clock, & in due time returned to the ferry & sailed thereon. Reaching the other side, I assisted the luggage to the 1:25 train, & bade Mrs. Galpin convey my regards to S H upon meeting her, & to Alfredus upon writing him. Then bowing my adieux, I recrossed the river subterraneously by the Hudson Tubes, & changing at Cortlandt St. for the B.M.T., was soon in Brooklyn. Stopping to send S H a telegram as to when to expect her visitor,—7:40 p.m. standard time—(Cleveland does not save daylight) I proceeded to 169 & conducted my vain search of "St. Ronan's Well" for data on the saint. Failing, I gently laid the book aside & sought oblivion. One birthday gone! The next day—Friday the 21st—I was up at noon & attending to some imperative mail when a brisk knocking sounded on the door. Answering, I expected something no more unusual than a package, telephone message, or such-like; when lo! what vision of marvel should loom upon my aged sight but Grandpa's Littlest Lambkin himself—Sonny Belknap in actual flesh & blood, & radiating a gratifying appearance of good health! For one expected just a month later, he was certainly the most delectable of surprises; & when he saw my surprise he was himself surprised in turn—for he imagined he had been expected! As it turned out, his absent-mindedness in writing was the cause of the slip. He had *meant* to say he was returning *August* 20, but had *actually* written *Sept.* 20. All's well that ends well, of course; but I could have kicked Fate black & blue for not apprising me of the facts a day before, so that Sonny might have met Mrs. Galpin & participated in the letter to his little cousin Alfredus. She had heard all about him, for Alfredus values his letters immensely, & thinks he is about the only young fellow in existence worth writing to. But Fate is Fate; so instead of kicking at a stone wall I discussed the cosmos with Sonny & read him one of my new tales. He brought Grandpa an exquisite little Japanese picture of the sacred mount Fujiyama, by an artist he met at the Thousand Islands, & I intend very shortly to hang it in a place of honour near the door, betwixt the Salem & Marblehead plaques— which I shall spread farther apart to admit it. The Longs got two other splendid pictures by this artist, which they intend to hang in their own home, but I like mine best. In the late afternoon we decided to hold an informal meeting of The Boys that evening to readjust Belknap to metropolitan boredom— with Sonny himself as host. One of the ceremonial observances was to be the cutting & eating of the Parisian cake which Alfredus sent; & as Belknap bore it away he was careful to let the gaudy label shew, so that the world might know how complete a little Frenchman he is. We proceeded, in our efforts to round up the gang, to that now universal rendezvous, Martin's Book Store, where we found Kleiner hard at work helping the proprietor prepare a "Come in & Browse" sign. He expressed himself as all in favour of a meeting, & promised to get Loveman & Kirk for us if he could. (As it was, he got only Kirk) Our poet had just had a hair-cut, & was mourning the unaccountable disappearance of his cherished grey hairs. He thinks the barber must have used some pomade containing dye on him, & is contemplating this subtle craftsman's murder in some calm & gentlemanly way. Belknap & I now took the subway to Times Square, he going home with the precious cake, & I walking across to the Milan, where I obtained a delicious meal for *15¢* in the form of *minestrone* or Italian vegetable soup. This thick & nutritious soup is part of every full Italian dinner, & it always grieves me because I can eat so little of it before the filling courses to come. This time there were no courses to come, & I gorged myself unstintedly on a full tureen; thus obtaining a complete & incomparably fine meal for *15¢*. I shall do this whenever I am down town— though the Milan is the only place where it can be done. No other restaurant serves such fine minestrone, or such a vast quantity. I now picked my way through Hell's Kitchen in quest of honest old McNeil, who was wanted for the meeting. Luckily he was in, & very glad to accompany me to the festive homecoming. We reached Belknap's at 8:15, were cordially greeted by Mrs.

Long, & soon had Kleiner among us. Not long afterward Kirk breezed in—
my first sight of him in a month—but Loveman was on a bookbuying trip &
could not get there. Felis stalked proudly through the room now & then, & at
the proper time ice cream & cake were served—the French article proving so
unpalatable that most of us took liberal slices of the accompanying American
product to efface its memory, though we appreciated no less the sentiments
which prompted Alfredus to send it. Belknap shewed us the snap shots taken
on his travels, & altogether the meeting was highly enjoyable. About 12:30 we
dispersed, McNeil proceeding homeward, & Kirk, Kleiner & I adjourning to a
cafeteria to do honour to the Kirkian homecoming. From there we started to
walk downtown; but Kleiner dropped out at the 96th St. station, leaving just
Kirk & me—the famous pair of nocturnal ramblers of 1924. We performed
our pedestrianism in old-time fashion, covering 90 blocks & ending up at 14th
St., where, just west of 8th Ave., Kirk has hired a pair of immense Victorian
rooms as combined office & residence. This was to be his first night there, he
having just moved from the Martinique. The locality is just at the border betwixt the ancient villages of Chelsea & Greenwich; & the house, being on the
north side of the street, is probably to be accounted part of the former. It is a
typical Victorian home of New York's "Age of Innocence",[4] with tiled hall,
carved marble mantels, vast pier glasses & mantel mirrors with massive gilt
frames, incredibly high ceilings covered with stucco ornamentation, round
arched doorways with elaborate rococo pediments, & all the other earmarks
of New York's age of vast wealth & impossible taste. Kirk's rooms are the
great ground-floor parlours, connected by an open arch, & having windows
only in the front room. These two windows open to the south on 14th St., &
have the disadvantage of admitting all the babel & clangour of that great
crosstown thoroughfare with its teeming traffick & ceaseless street-cars. We
could, on inspection, find no signs of any *heating* apparatus; & if there is none,
Kirk will not keep the suite—for which he is to pay $14.00 weekly. The co-
lossal size of the rooms, together with the scant furniture supplied, will make
the problem of decoration an acute one; but the front chamber can be re-
deemed by the filling of the west wall—on either side of the mantel—with
mahogany-painted bookshelves. I drew up a detailed furnishing plan as I did
for Kirk's other rooms & for Loveman's skyey eyrie, & Georgius says he will
follow it out as far as cash & opportunity permit. He invited me to stay the
rest of the night & see the new Chaplin cinema with him on the morrow,[5] but
I was so drowsy that I thought it best to return to my own quarters. Being on
the borders of Greenwich, I walked for a while through that Colonial maze,
finally entering the subway at the Sheridan Square station. I reached home
just before dawn, & after a little writing settled down to rest—when lo! the
next thing I knew it was 9 o'clock in the evening! I suppose I have missed innumerable calls & knocks—I found fresh linen outside the door, & no doubt
Kirk tried to get me in the afternoon to go to the cinema—but to all this the

Old Gentleman was blissfully oblivious. And I think I'll let this break be the beginning of a renewed period of solitude with books & writing. The social rush was getting to be a bit too strenuous for aged bones & worn-out senile wits! My correspondence has suffered frightfully, & tonight & Sunday I must write for dear life.

Sunday Afternoon
Aug. 23

Well! I seem to be duplicating my 598 slumber record! At 6 a.m. I felt a bit tired & lay down for a second of slumber, & here it is 12:30 p.m.—6½ hours later! It's a fine day, & I'm hanged if I wouldn't go out on a trip if [I] didn't have such a beastly mess of letter-writing to do. Maybe I *will* go out on an all[-]night-&-day excursion tonight if I get the worst nuisances off my hands—Gawd knows I've had sleep enough to last me a week! I hope nobody calls up, for I want to preserve a sort of Providence mood of solitary literary creation. Just now I have a task ahead calling for extreme tact—refusing a loan of $185.00 (fancy anybody asking poor, broke old Theobald for a cash loan!) to a well-born & deserving old lady. The person in question is the mother of our poet John Ravenor Bullen, for whom last June I wrote that tedious critique;[6] & she evidently thinks—simple old soul—that Theobald is prepared to extend aid in all possible emergencies. As "security" she sends some shares of admittedly worthless stock (to which, none the less, friends advise her to hold on!) owned by her late husband, & ends her epistle with the moving phrase, '[']**Please** grant my request"! From the rambling preamble I gather that the object of the loan is to publish a book of children's jingles by the late Mr. Bullen—& I regret my inability to assist in so noble a work. I'm afraid one Bullen is all I can conveniently immortalise—& that one only through non-financial channels! Belknap tells me to adopt an exterior even more brusque & brutal than my present one, so that the unfortunate may be deterred from annoying me. He points to himself as the classic example of repellent 'toughness'.

I received the recent *Sunday Journal* & duly exulted therein. The article on Westminster St. held my notice very closely, for it is with pain that I see the old houses go one by one. I had hoped that the Putney place would remain! Now to save the Clemence St. building, the Butler mansion, AND THE ARCADE! This latter business is serious, & I wish I could stir up a body of prominent people—like Chapin of the Hist. Soc.—to write about it to the *Sunday Journal*. The mutilation of that noble pile is a blow at the soul of ancient Providence, & no fate is too black for the commercial scoundrel who dares suggest it!

But now I must cease. I'll let you know on the outside of the envelope if I start on a trip; in which case, of course, my composition-book will go along to receive the literary fruits of my rustick vagabondage. I must make the most of the warm weather, which will soon pass. Occasional touches of cold alarm me, & I fear that within a month I shall have to make one more plunge in extravagance & get a winter suit!

And so it goes! More later—& consider me at all times

Yr most aff: Nephew & obt Servt

H P L

P.S. You ought to see the KITTIE A E P G sent me for my birthday!

[P.]P.S. I enclose a sample of S H's new wall paper. Will send another to A E P G.

[P.P.P.S.] Also enclose the new TRYOUT.

## Notes

1. *The Ten Commandments* (Famous Players–Lasky Corp., 1923), directed by Cecil B. DeMille; starring Theodore Roberts, Charles de Rochefort, and Estelle Taylor. Not to be confused with DeMille's remake of 1956.

2. S[usan]. Lilian McMullen (1886–1981[?]) was an amateur writer who published poetry under the pseudonym Lilian Middleton. See HPL's essay "The Poetry of Lilian Middleton" (1922; *CE* 2.51–56). A photograph of her was published in Sonia Greene's amateur journal, the *Rainbow* No. 2 (May 1922): 10.

3. Edith Ellis (1874–1960), *White Collars* (1925), a three-act comedy adapted from a story by Edgar Franklin.

4. HPL alludes to the novel by Edith Wharton, about life in New York City in the 1870s. It won the Pulitzer Prize in 1921.

5. *The Gold Rush* (1925), in which Chaplin was the lead actor, writer, and director.

6. "The Poetry of John Ravenor Bullen"; later adapted as the introduction to Bullen's *White Fire* (1927).

[119]     [ALS] [HPL to LDC]

Monday Night
August 24, 1925.

My dear Daughter Lillian:—

Your delightful epistle came the morning after I mailed my diary, & I will not delay in extending my appreciative acknowledgment. My additional diary is simple—for I have done nothing but sleep & write letters since placing my missive to you in the box. Mail arrived in overwhelming quantities, & to cap the climax a special delivery arrived from Loveman, saying he couldn't entertain the meeting next Wednesday night. Rather than waste half a year at the telephone, I'm taking the meeting myself—& have just prepared postals for all the members. Some job, believe an old man, being a social leader! Young Talman may shew up at this meeting, for he lately expressed a wish to meet the gang. Oh, yes—& *painters* have been at work around the windows here, though I don't fancy they mean to paint the whole house—*stone* doesn't need it. Thanks for the job suggestions for Talman, but I fancy he must have tried the Brown Union & Y.M.C.A. long ago. It's a part-time *winter* job he wants, to run concurrently with his studies. But don't worry any more—we can't carry the world's responsibilities! Yes—I wish I had that motorcycle-mosquito position—I always did want a motorcycle.

As for your recollections of August 20, 1890—possibly they do eclipse mine a bit, for the Old Gentleman is getting a bit hazy after all these years. So I threw my arms about, eh, as if excited at the prospect of entering a new world? How naive! I might have known it would only be a bore. Perhaps, though, I was merely dreaming of a weird tale—in which case the enthusiasm was more pardonable. This reminds me that you shall see the new ones as soon as they are typed—lud, how I hate that job! Yes—I hope that these tales will land remuneratively somewhere, though the "Sphinx" prologue will not be a commercial venture. Glad you like the *United Amateur*—which I myself think isn't a half bad issue. Now it's Bacon's job to issue it—here's wishing him luck! As for Dr. Frank Crane—good soul—such a scatterer of general platitudes can't help saying something sensible once in a while, though ordinarily his maunderings on the obvious make me deliciously drowsy. The old duffer has no original ideas, but prosaically rehashes commonplaces from the point of view of the herd—& makes a fortune at it. I'd do it if I could! Yes— his Horn & Hardart piece is something like the late lamented Leeds–Yesley work. I wish I had a chance to cash in on such nondescript hack work!

If I ever got into the School of Design museum, my first official act would be to prohibit the tearing down of colonial houses! That entire row on College Hill ought sedulously to be preserved as a rare instance of solid survival—but look at the vandals!

Yes—Alfredus is lucky to be able to study where he likes, but there's no telling when his cash may give out. He, though, is always sure of a college position whenever he will come home & cut his hair—for his university degree & mastery of French are certain passports to an instructorship. I sent him that cutting about the leopard, & told him I hoped he wasn't gobbled up. I also warned him not to get taken in by any such fakes as that cheap Louvre gallery might try to put over on him! I'm going to send him a booklet of St. John the Divine to prove how easily a Yankee cathedral can beat his Notre-Dame & St.-Stephen-on-the-Mount! As to St. Ronan's Well—or rather, St. Ronan's identity—I'll get hold of it some day. He certainly is deucedly obscure, though, for no person can tell anything about him, whilst no reference book has any mention of him. Such is fame  & yet I'll bet the old boy thought himself quite a guy in his day! I got the Drowne–Foster data from Prof. Wilfred H. Munro's "Picturesque Rhode-Island"—which I must remember to send you. It's a fine book—& I was lucky to pick it up for a dollar at Niel, Morrow, & Ladd's. I'm interested to know that you have met one of the good doctor's hygienic descendants! Glad we can annex old Ted Foster to our family oak—& I guess these Caseys are no small potatoes. Newport was the great town of R.I. before the Revolution, just as the Narragansett region—Kingston, Wickford, &c—was the great plantation country. Those are the best soils to be descended from—Providence is relatively parvenu, not taking first place till the time of Stephen Hopkins. You must read the Kimball book if you can possibly get hold of it—which reminds me that I haven't finished it yet. I must take a whole day at the library & wind it up.

Too bad the Albee Season wasn't up to the old standard—but all things decay. It was really at its best away back—before 1910. I noticed that a cinema season is planned, & see that they're installing an organ. I hope, however, that this innovation isn't destined wholly to displace the stock company in later years. It would be a pity for so settled & excellent an institution to pass. I'm no cinema enthusiast these days, but will recommend "Romola" & "Down to the Sea in Ships" if they return. Yes—I suppose the photographing of the latter made even more of a stir in New Bedford than that of "Java Head" did in Salem![1] Oh, yes—I read that "Rip Van Winkle" thing in the *Bulletin*—but give me credit for never wasting breath on inquiries about the Grand Trunk! Willow pattern china is extremely interesting—I mean to get some if I live long enough. It is, however, widely copied at present—a very correct version being found on the tables of a popular cafeteria in 42nd St.

And so the Halsey house is haunted![2] Ugh! That's where Wild Tom Halsey kept live terrapins in the cellar—maybe it's their ghosts. Anyway, it's a magnificent old mansion, & a credit to a magnificent old town! I may treat the theme some day—& I certainly do wish Gramp could have seen some of these tales of a "deep, low, moaning sound". He *did* see some very early specimens.

No—I never even heard of Mrs. Rinehart's "Red Lamp",[3] for I have completely dropped all contact with the present. I never read a literary review, & never touch a newspaper except the *Journal & Bulletin*. It's all a bore—for the old books said all that there is to be said. None the less, I'll wager that window display was a monstrous clever thing, & that it would have vastly interested Mortonius in the days before his elevation to Museum dignity. I never heard of quite that idea before—& hope the book itself is even a tenth as ingenious! I fear Mrs. Rinehart is beginning to follow a formula & repeat herself, as other prolific detective-story writers tend to do. Still, so long as she gets paid—whose business but hers is it?

I'll get another picture soon in stiff collar & vest—full length, & shewing the whole new suit. I'm afraid I'll have to take my fine new straw hat for every-day soon, for the old Outlet straw has developed a crack or break on the side, tho' I'll swear I haven't hit it against anything. Of course it will soon be time to drag out the old Flatbush felt—but I want the new straw in prime shape for next summer. I may, too, have soon to take the new (& difficultly conquer'd) shoes for every-day, since the good old Regals are about on the brink of spectacular disintegration. Still—I've had good service from all of these, so who am I to complain? When I get a winter suit I'm going to see if I can't equal Loveman's rock-bottom figure of $22.50.

Yes—I read of the Andrews discoveries in Mongolia,[4] & regret that the expedition is meeting with governmental opposition. Primitive men found in this region would be likely to be *actual ancestors* of the existing human species, rather than stunted collateral lines like those represented by the Piltdown, Heidelberg, & Neanderthal skulls in Europe. Incidentally—there was a laughable carload of asininity about the origin of mankind by a Catholic priest in a recent *Bulletin.*

Thanks prodigiously for the stamps. I was just laying in a new stock, & these piece out nobly. I must, though, cut down some of this vestigial amateur correspondence—it is time the new board learned to stand alone! I'll enclose Mr. Hoag's latest published poem—somewhat misprinted, I regret to say. It will also appear in *Tryout* . . . . . probably misprinted just as badly. Mr. Hoag's hand is improving rapidly, so that his writing is nearly as firm as of yore. A great old boy! I'll also enclose the begging letter whose polite answering required such laborious tact. Poor Mrs. B. sent her late husband's worthless stock certificates by registry, so I suppose I'll have to register it when mailing it back. Of all damned nuisances! Oh yes—& I'm sending Sonny's "Man from Genoa" at his request to the ["]American Anthology of Newspaper Verse" in the hope that they may include it in the 1925 volume. And so it goes. My diary up to now reads "still writing", but I may go down to the Milan tonight & get that 15¢ minestrone. One occasionally gets bored with cold canned stuff.

> Yr aff nephew & obt Servt
> H P L

[On envelope? In RHB's handwriting:] P.S. Well, I'll be hanged! They *are* painting the whole house!! A rich brown like 454.

## Notes

1. HPL refers to the film *Java Head* (Famous Players–Lasky Corp. 1923), based on the novel by Joseph Hergesheimer. It was in part filmed in Salem, MA.

2. The Halsey house at 100 Prospect Street in Providence is the residence of Charles Dexter Ward in *The Case of Charles Dexter Ward* (1927), although HPL renumbered it to 140 Prospect Street.

3. Mary Roberts Rinehart (1876–1958), *The Red Lamp* (1925), a bestselling mystery novel.

4. The American explorer and naturalist Roy Chapman Andrews (1884–1960) led several expeditions to Mongolia between 1920 and 1928.

[120]    [ALS] [HPL to LDC]

Thursday Morning
August 27, 1925

My dear Daughter Lillian:—

Having received your welcome card, I take my pen in hand to keep the diary up to date. The heat, which persisted through the night, has just this moment disconcertingly abated; so that I fear we're in for a spell of chill. Brrrr . . . but how I hate autumn & winter!

My diary left off Monday night. Tuesday I was up at noon, wrote letters all the afternoon, including one to A E P G, & in the evening went to the Milan again for my minestrone—after which I imbibed another dose of the Kimball book at the publick library. Returning, I wrote some & retired late. Wednesday I was up at noon & spent the afternoon trying to prepare some verses for the Blue Pencil meeting Saturday—held at the Dench castle at Sheepshead Bay, with the newly arrived Richard Merritt Dench as the 'literary' topic. I really wish I could get out of going, but that would offend good ol' Mortonius, who wrote me especially asking me to be there with a contribution. Not knowing much to say to an infant without triteness & insipidity I decided to go in for the heavily didactic—telling the poor kid what a tough world he had stumbled into, & advising him to cling fast to dreams & imagination if he expected to have even a tolerable time of it. For this harangue a long Swinburnian metre with internal rhyme seemed to me most appropriate, so I started in thus tuned. I enclose the disappointing result—which you can keep, since I have another carbon for A E P G.[1]

In the late afternoon I went out shopping for the meeting which I had so suddenly taken upon myself, & purchased good quantities of paper napkins, raspberry tarts, & Kleiner's beloved crumb-cake. Returning in good season, I prepared to entertain my guests; & was quite ready when good old McNeil blew in as advance guard. Morton & Loveman had written that they couldn't come, but I was quite surprised & disappointed when Kleiner & Kirk failed to put in an appearance. I don't know yet what happened to them—for my card to Kleiner was very plainly addressed. My second guest was the Brown University student Wilfred B. Talman, whom I now met in person for the first time. He is a splendid young chap—tall, lean, light, & aristocratically clean-cut, with light brown hair & excellent taste in dress. He gave me extra copies of his poetical brochure for you & A E P G, inscribing them with his regards. I enclose yours in a sort of dual envelope which I have constructed in lieu of anything on hand of the right size. Talman ought to call on you & A E P G this autumn—I'm sure you'd both like him very much. He is descended from the most ancient Dutch families of lower New York state, & has recently become a genealogical enthusiast. He is, incidentally, one of the Annetje Jans heirs who claim the valuable Trinity Church property—but who will never get it. There was an article on this subject in the Bulletin a day or two ago, which I cut out for Talman. You will note that Talman's booklet was printed in Providence by the Bear Press—one of the adjuncts of the Brown Union in Rockefeller Hall. They quoted him special rates as a student, & now he's going to see if he can't use his 'pull' to get something printed there for Belknap—how appropriate that Grandpa's Child should have his first collection of poems printed in Old Providence! Said Child was the third & last arrival of the evening, though limited numbers put no curb or damper on discussion. Sonny & Talman took readily to each other, & we hope to have the young Brunonian at subsequent meetings—tho' he can't attend next week, which is a Leeds meeting up at Belknap's. When refreshment time came around I set the tip-table & went out for coffee, but the small gathering couldn't begin to consume all the fare I had provided in expectation of a larger quota. The amount of crumb-cake remaining is prodigious, & there are four apple tarts—in fact, I can see my meals mapped out for me for two days!! Ironic circumstance—I got the crumb-cake especially for Kleiner, who adores it, & in the end he was absent; so that I, who don't particularly care for it at all, must swallow unending quantities in the interest of œconomy! Talman had to leave immediately after the refreshments to get an accomodation-train for Spring Valley, but Sonny & old Mac stayed on a bit & discussed weird stories. They they [sic], too, bowed their adieux, & Grandpa was left to dishwashing & subsequent letter-writing. I'm still at the latter occupation, but mean to lie down & rest before noon; getting up later & attending to more writing. I guess I'll mail this first—& you can consider the diary as ending with the period roughly classifiable as Wednesday the 27th. Before retiring I shall eat a breakfast-supper of crumb-cake—ah, me!

Had a letter from S H yesterday, saying that Mrs. Galpin didn't shew up in Cleveland at all! She's quite worried, imagining all sorts of kidnappings, wrecks, & such like; but I fancy Mrs. G. was merely too tired out to relish the Youngstown change of cars, so went straight home to Chicago. Sonny took a great trip up the Hudson with his mamma & papa Tuesday—note the card. This "day line" trip costs only $1.80, & I've a darned good mind to get wild & blow in on it some day, for the scenery it reveals is truly tremendous—Palisades, West Point, Catskills, &c. Today, though, my wildest wandering will probably stop short at Prospect Park, if indeed it gets that far. Heard from little Davis yesterday—he has a prospective United recruit in the person of a Maine high school principal named H. N. Roundy, upon whose trail I am now setting Moe. The young folks certainly seem determined to get going, & it looks as though the old United were going to get back on the map again. I've just sent Roundy an application blank & copy of the official organ—it's hard to get used to the fact that I'm an elderly gentleman just retired completely from amateur journalism!

Well, such is which. I'm having to find a place here for Sonny's rubbers, which he left here by mistake Friday, & by intention last night, when he absolutely refused to encumber his feet with them. How freakish these children are getting to be! More later. Meanwhile pray consider me at all times

Yr most aff Nephew & obt Servt

H P L

[On envelope? In RHB's handwriting:] This dump, newly-painted, doesn't look half bad!

*Notes*

1. "To an Infant."

[121]     [ALS] [HPL to LDC]

Septr. 1, 1925

My dear Daughter Lillian:—

I will open the melancholy-sounding month of September by taking my pen in hand to continue the diary last extended through Friday, August 28th. You have meanwhile received my postcard from Paterson, which on Sunday I beheld for the first time. No business was involved, for financial adjustments regarding the alterations on the museum building (an ex-stable) have kept the trustees busy & deferred action on the matter of a staff; but as you will see in the ensuing diary, I had a highly enjoyable trip. Meanwhile I hope the Talman booklet reached you without the falling-to-pieces of the home-spliced envelope. He has just written me to say that he will probably be unable to attend further meetings this summer unless Mortonius holds one in Paterson, since his health is such that the train ride from Spring Valley forms too great a tax upon his stomach. He was ill for a time when here last week—having to retire to the bathroom & being unable to participate in refreshments. In his letter he encloses two stories of weirdish cast, which he wrote years ago, & which appeared in his high-school paper. Both have crudities, yet are undeniably promising in atmosphere. Oh, yes—& I heard from S H, who will next be here on or around the 15th. Last Saturday she sent by *air mail* the text of a circular she wished revised & returned in haste by the same route—in doing which I patronised that especial branch of the postal service for the first time.

And as for the diary—on Saturday the 29th I rose at noon, wrote letters, & at 2 o'clock received a very welcome call from my small grandchild Belknap. After some discussion which included a reading of my new story "He", (which my auditor praised highly, & considered much better than "The Horror at Red Hook") we went out to look at the Roman antiquities in that 6th Ave. shop window & to see if honest old McNeil was in. The antiquities—lamps, vases, glassware, coins, & the like—properly tantalised us; & after we had rung unavailingly at McNeil's bell, we crossed over to Madison Ave. to enjoy the numerous antique windows along that thoroughfare. Having made a canvass of this region, we paused at the Plaza (59th St. & 5th Ave.) to delight in the alluring array of old-time hansoms & barouches, which bring up such delicious memories of the nineties' departed elegance. Some day we are going to pool our surplus funds & take a ride in a hansom—just to catch a last surviving thrill from a tasteful, bygone age whose glories are sinking irrecoverably into the hideous abyss of mongrel modernity. After this we strolled northward through Central Park, responding to the charm of the greenery & discoursing of beauty. At the 72nd street entrance we diverged to the subway; the Child going home, & his Grandpa repairing to Brooklyn to dress for the evening's B.P.C. meeting at Sheepshead Bay. I reached that meeting about 9 o'clock, & found the small Dench abode exceedingly well filled. A fair quota of members were present, together with several visitors. Richard Merritt was not on exhibition till the very last of the evening, but was an almost constant topick of conversation, & the theme of all the literary contributions. Nearly everyone had something to say—indeed, I can scarce recall a meeting with fewer silent participants! When the literary programme was reached, we found the offerings quite evenly divided betwixt verse & prose; & in the end, despite metrical flights from Kleiner, Morton, & Ernest Adams, my piece (sent you in my preceding epistle) was honoured by electoral pronouncement as the best verse of the evening. Miss Merritt—the future Mrs. Morton—won the first mention for prose. After the reading & voting, & the serving of excellent refreshments, discussion became general. Kleiner, Dench, Morton & I considered the prospects for the morrow, when a special Nature-study "hike" was scheduled for the Paterson Rambling Club; & despite the 62¢ fare to Paterson I determined to go, since the route was to be through some of the wildest & most beautiful scenery in all the New-York area. Mortonius left the meeting early to catch a train, but I left with the majority at midnight, walking to the station & thence employing the subway. Then 169 & bed. The next day—Sunday the 30th—I arose at 6:00 a.m., dressed in haste, (old blue suit, old shoes, battered straw hat) and prepared to meet Kleiner at the Chambers St. ferry at 7:45. Knowing how persistently picnickers pester a lunchless person with insistent offers of donated nourishment, I omitted breakfast & took along a lunch instead—two sandwiches, one ham & one cheese, neatly done up in waxed paper to fit the pocket—which I obtained at the Bickford cafeteria near Borough Hall. Kleiner was on hand at the ferry, but Dench had chosen another route, so that we did not meet him until our arrival in Paterson. From the boat the morning skyline of Manhattan took on a mystic & ethereal aspect, the new skyscraper in West St. having a weird Babylonish charm with its terraced silhouette & original architecture of vertical lines. The train ride to Paterson was for the most part very dull, though livened by a glimpse of a very interesting Georgian steeple in Hackensack, which I must some time visit. Finally Paterson was reached—a suburban station which necessitated something of a walk to the Club's accustomed rendezvous in front of the City Hall. Of the "beauty" of the town, nothing could be said without liberal draughts on the imagination—for it is certainly one of the dreariest, shabbiest, & most nondescript places it has ever been my misfortune to see. Fall River is worse, but Pawtucket & Woonsocket would give it some close voting. Most of its buildings are Victorian, though a few specimens of the later Georgian survive; & the general seediness & weariness are partly atoned for by the narrow, curving, & hilly streets, & the geographical location of the place on the windings & falls of the Passaic in a natural bowl rimmed by virgin wooded hills visible at the end of every vista. There is one good publick edifice—the domed county court house; whilst the late Victorian structures of pseudo-Renaissance design at the civick centre have something of a continental aspect if viewed from the proper angles. The residential districts have, as a usual thing, separate wooden houses of Victorian vintage & incredible ugliness. One good section which Kleiner described I did not have a chance to see. Near the many-bridged river in the business section one finds occasional late-colonial structures—wooden dwellings & brick business blocks with small-paned windows. Of the latter there is quite a row in Broadway—a row really deserving of a postcard, though it would never occur to the existing denizens to select it as a subject. The general atmosphere is not in the least like that of New-York, (from which it is 17 miles distant) a certain touch of the rural everywhere predominating. Life seems mostly in the hands of Yankees & Germans, though a mongrel Italian & Slav element is indicated by the physiognomies of the repulsive rabble—the mill folk. One very bad feature is the city water—flat, muddy, & polluted; though still considered fit to drink despite its obnoxious qualities. It comes from a river fouled by countless factories. There exist in Paterson many distinctive local customs & peculiarities, such as the survival of the ancient publick market system, with live fowl & fresh vegetables sold from wayside booths as we sell them on Dyer St. & Market Square in the early morning, & a self-conscious emphasis on the traffick problem which gives birth to omnipresent "Respect-the-cross-walk" placards, & to an universal array of red & green lights at all the street intersections, even in the residential district. The street-cars are—except for the great interurbans—of the small one-man type such as that which makes the run from Mathewson St. over North Main & Olney to Camp St., & are painted orange-yellow, the general colour of Northern New-Jersey cars belonging to the extensive "Publick Service" system. Omnibuses are very numerous, including both local & interurban lines, & one route de luxe which goes directly to the heart of New York City over the Weehawken ferry. The town is said to have good parks, though I beheld none of them. Its hideous factory section is fortunately out of sight, across the river from the ordinary parts. The publick library in Broadway is an excellent & rather new classical edifice of marble, with great Ionick columns on the facade. It is soon to be enlarged by a wing in the rear. Adjoining it on the east is the estate on which the museum will stand—the ugly Victorian house for whose aged owner's death the trustees impatiently wait, & the stable in which the collection will meanwhile be displayed. It is about the alterations to this latter building that the delay is now occurring. The accompanying diagram—executed just now from memory alone—shews the general arrangement of the buildings involved in the library-museum enterprise. Eventually the trustees hope to tear down both

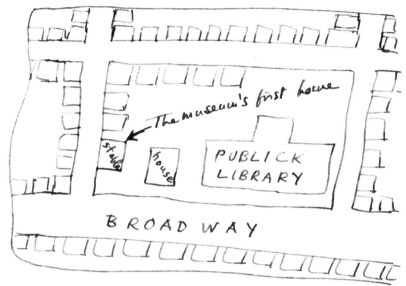

house & stable & erect a modern museum building in the classical style. Paterson, whose present population is about 140,000, was founded in 1792 by a company of cotton manufacturers headed by the illustrious Alexander Hamilton, whose name & statues are seen everywhere in the vicinity, & who occupies in its annals the place which good old Roger Williams occupies in ours. The other local celebrity is McKinley's vice-president, Garrett A. Hobart, who was a lifelong resident, & whose venerable widow still survives there. Its selection as a manufacturing centre was determined by two causes—the fifty-foot falls of the Passaic with their wealth of water-power, & the proximity of the region to the port & metropolis of New-York. Its name was taken from the Governor of New-Jersey at the time of its creation—the Honourable William Paterson, Esq., who signed its charter as a township. As time passed, the industries of silk, iron, & cotton gained pre-eminence in its life—especially the first named, which has caused it to be known as the "Lyons of America." This dominance of industry has brought in discouraging hordes of peasant foreigners, & introduced repellent sentiments of treason & radicalism. For this mess the factory owners are to a great degree responsible, for in their desire to obtain cheap & submissive help they shew an utter disregard of the biological complexion of the city; importing dreary hordes of inferior Syrians, Jews, Poles, & Southern Italians whose sluggish minds & broken spirits cause them to work for starvation wages till aroused by agitators. Mortonius lives in a very decent neighbourhood at 211 Carroll St.—his second boarding-place in the city—in a Victorian wooden corner house with upper & lower verandahs. His second-floor room, with two west windows on the front upper verandah & a large bow-window on the side, is very neat & tasteful; & occupies the same relative place in the house that mine does in 169 Clinton. He has bought an office desk which stands in the bow-window, & brought a mineral cabinet from his darktown quarters to house his immediate collection. A large wardrobe cupboard contains his culinary apparatus, & each morning he pre-pares his breakfast on a large-sized Sterno stove. Altogether, he seems very comfortable & contented, & will retain the room until spring, when he hopes to set up housekeeping with his more or less radiant bride-to-be. Returning from description to narration—Kleiner & I walked to the City Hall & found Mortonius with a considerable aggregation of the Ramblers. The latter are somewhat heterogeneous in personnel, with comparatively little of the ma-turely civilised element which I would find congenial; but most of them are bright & downright folk of solid Nordic origin, with much natural intelligence & an appealing touch of the provincial. Their president, a wholesome but not grammatically impeccable man of early middle age named Ernest, (odd for a *last* name) is connected with the principal local newspaper,—*The Paterson Call*—& the leader on the present expedition, a solemn-faced, eccentrically dressed character named Regan, is a veterinary surgeon. As their guest of honour they had a man named Swift,[1] affiliated with the *N.Y. World,* who lec-tured informally on different Nature topicks—botany, geology, Indian antiq-uities, &c. &c.—as the numerous assemblage (some 20, perhaps, of all types & ages) passed from object to object. Soon after our arrival Dench came; & whilst the party tarried for late-comers & watched a queer white-bearded man distribute religious tracts (one enclosed) with much muttering against the worldliness of Sunday "hikers", Mortonius took me for a scenic walk through the principal streets of the central district. At length the outfit embarked on a Haledon car & rode to the end of the line, thence walking along the road to where a woodland path debouched uphill at the left toward the slopes of High Mountain. The day was magnificent both in sky & temperature, & as we entered the woods our lecturer proved exceedingly interesting. The ultimate destination was Buttermilk Falls, a lovely cascade in the heart of the primal forest; which, though presenting no actual torrent save at the season of spring rains, has at all times a wildly beautiful appearance arising from the numerous pools & terraces, & from the seismic rocks which border it—octagonally crystallised basalt whose crowded pillars suggest a monstrous pipe-organ or a reduced replica of such formations as the Giants' Causeway in Ireland. To reach this scenick Mecca we traversed some of the finest woodland country I have ever seen—unlimited acres of stately forest untouched by the wood-man's axe; hill & dale, brooklet & glen, ravine & precipice, rock ledge & pin-nacle, marsh & brake, glade & hidden meadow, landscape & prospect, spring & cleft, bower & berry-patch, bird-paradise & mineral treasury. Mortonius found a splendid pair of fossils for his collection, & many others accumulated unwieldy loads of strange flowers & vegetable forms—the skunk-cabbage & mandrake, thistle & chicory, fern & fungus, & all sorts of things but dimly familiar to the urban soul. Never before had I seen so vast a stretch of con-tinuous woods. It was the wilderness in earnest, despite such occasional signs of man as a tumble-down stone wall or a rusty barbed-wire fence to be climbed with difficulty or scrambled under with sacrificed dignity. One might become lost with delicious ease—the expedition kept together by means of shrill & powerful whistles, & even with this precaution a separation occurred once, whereby we were split into two roughly equal parties which could not rejoin for over an hour & a half. During this division our Blue Pencil contin-gent had equal representation on both sides—Kleiner & Dench being in the hasty faction which had forged ahead with Regan, whilst Mortonius & I were in the more studious & leisurely group with Swift, which finally—after cross-ing an open tract with some breathless vistas of distant lines of mountains—overtook the advance section on a hillside where the fainting of an elderly la-dy had caused them to pause for lunch. Upon this reunion our section also ate lunch, though a resumption of travel was ordered before Mortonius had finished, thus arousing many a growl from that amiable bear. In one fenny valley we encountered enormous clumps of blueberry bushes, which the trav-ellers stripped with voracious avidity. Shortly afterward we struck a glen of tremendous majesty, whose slopes were so strown with octagonal fragments of the brittle volcanick rock of the region, that walking became a matter of the greatest precariousness & difficulty,—& a cruel tax upon expensive shoe-leather. At last Buttermilk Falls hove in sight, in no wise disappointing the fondest expectations of those who had never seen it. There is a glorious pic-turesqueness & an ineffable majesty in such a spectacle—the precipitous cliff, the rifted rock, the limpid stream, & the titanic tiers of terraces flanked by massed slender columns of immemorial stone; all bathed in the abysmal hush & magical green twilight of the deep woods, where filtered sunlight dapples the leafy earth & transfigures the great wild boles into a thousand forms of subtle & evanescent wonder. The falls in the forest—sacred to the gravest Manitou of the red folk, & rich in the aura of their accumulated traditions! Here all the party rested, & commenced an orgy of thirst-slaking wherein the cumulative drouth of the preceding journey (earlier brooks had no potable water) discharged its fury upon the raniferous crystal of the deep, cool pool on the midmost terrace. The pilgrimage being resumed, we turned to the left through "The Clove", a strange & impressive valley of great depth; whose narrowness forced us to walk in single file, & whose sides were littered with unbelievable heaps of octagonal basalt fragments detached by water & weather from the outcropping rock ledges. Just before our emergence from this place we encountered two striking phenomena—a towering pinnacle of heaped rocks which the slenderer among us climbed, (thanks to my reducing, I climbed with Kleiner instead of moping below with Mortonius!) & a liberal patch of blackberry bushes at which most of the lately-slaked thirsts were greedily revived. At length we came out into a small tract of sunlight & rolling meadow, where the shell of a deserted Colonial farmhouse crowned a grassy knoll. Here a group photograph was taken, & many a draught absorbed from the silent stone-curbed well. After this the tramping was over more tempered ground, though here & there a rugged feature spiced the way—especially one verdant chasm to the right of the path, where the sheer drop to bottomless spaces was so vast & abrupt as almost to intoxicate the sensitive spectator. Then the woods grew thinner, & we came out upon a sunny hillside with half the world spread out before us in a gorgeous panorama of far violet peaks, vivid expanses of forest & mead, graceful coils of white ribbon-like road, & a piquant sprinkling of ancient farmhouse roofs peeping out from the midst of gentle hill gaps & embowering greenery. It was the climax & finale of a jaunt of just ten miles by the leader's pedometer, for after that we descended to a modern highway & partook of ice cream at an omnibus station called the "Hillside Rest". Here again a division of forces occurred—for whilst Morton & I were willing to leap up coffeeless & catch the 'bus which suddenly appeared, Kleiner & Dench remained to sip at leisure with a minority of the party. Back in Paterson, we bade the disintegrating group farewell, & Mortonius again played the guide to what there is of an ancient section there. At length we repaired to the rendezvous which we had set for Kleiner & Dench—Westerman's Restaurant, near the City Hall,—& there passed the time by consuming dinner. I ate only because Mortonius couldn't rest content till I did—taking my favourite spaghetti, which luckily was very good despite the non-Italian nature of the refectory. During the meal James Ferdinand tipped me off as to where I might obtain data on *St. Ronan*—the Catholick Encyclopaedia at the publick library. It seems that there were *twelve* St. Ronans, all good Irishmen, but I'll see if one among 'em wasn't a little more distinguished than the rest, so as to form a fairly probable subject of the painting which started the present quest. Two of the Ronans, it would appear, are venerated in Scotland as well as in Ireland. In time Kleiner & Dench shewed up, & discussion was increased whilst they ate their dinner. Then all hands adjourned to Morton's room in Carroll St., were introduced to his pleasant elderly landlady—a Mrs. Greene, of the central middle class, apparently—& indulged in conversation prior to Dench's departure for the 8:09 train he had selected. We then saw Dench to the station—the main Susquehanna station, & not the outlying one at which we had landed in the morning—& embarked upon an evening exploration of residential Paterson;

noting the impossible Victorian houses, & studying the publick library with its soon-to-be-museumised neighbours. Mortonius pointed out the hellishly ugly Hobart dwelling—where the vice-president's aged widow still makes her home. She is a local benefactress of much prominence, & has given many things to the library & museum—especially a set of paintings including several of value. Later we returned to Morton's room, where we discussed future "hikes" until the time came for Kleiner & me to bolt for the 10:00 train. Our host accompanied us to the station—only a 7-minute walk—& waved adieux as we boarded the train & sank into our seats munching the chocolate Kleiner had bought & insisted that I share. The return trip was by a route other than that we had traversed on the outbound journey, giving us lamplit glimpses of Passaic & Rutherford instead of Hackensack. It must have been the route followed by A E P G in reaching Hohokus. As we struck the seaward marshes a dank, cold breeze blew through the cars, & prepared us for the change of vehicle at Jersey City. Then came the ferry, a landing at the N.Y. wharf in a district still redolent of the past, & a walk up Chambers St. to the City Hall, where Kleiner & I repaired to our respective B.M.T. entrances. A brief ride, & I was in Brooklyn—proceeding at once to 169 & retiring for a slumber which did not terminate till 3:30 the next afternoon. All yesterday I wrote letters, retiring late & rising again today at noon. Since then I have likewise been wrestling with mountains of mail, & shall probably do nothing else before another sleep—which will carry this diary squarely through Tuesday the 1st. If I do break loose & go to Staten Island or Elizabethtown or somewhere with my composition-book I'll let you know. Tomorrow night Sonny wants me to come early to the meeting at his house—note his card, with its graphic reaction to Clark Ashton Smith's "Abominations of Yondo", which I lent him in MS.

Since beginning this epistle I have received much mail—including your prodigiously welcome missive, & the enclosed doleful chronicle from S H, which records the change of her Cleveland address to 1912 E. 86th St. Too bad about the flatiron incident—hope the landlady doesn't impose an exorbitant & disproportionate charge! And just after the tasteful repapering of the room, too!

Your letter & enclosures proved as delightful as usual—& how can I thank you sufficiently for the verdant passports to the Hudson River trip!? I shall make inquiries about the boats at once, & hope to present you ere long with a travelogue of scenick beauty for which your generosity will be responsible! I trust the line is still running despite the approach of dreaded autumn. The cuttings are eminently interesting—& that anent the national anthem reminds me of a recent conversation with Mortonius on the subject. He says that the account in the cutting you recently lent me is altogether erroneous—his grandfather came on the tune whilst in college, among some old Norman hymns he was translating; & he *never knew it was the air of "God Save the King" till after he had written "America"*. Myths grow up about everything of this kind—&

one doesn't always have a grandson handy to clear away the barnacles! About High St.—if I understand aright, it included not only Weybosset above Broad, but Westminster all the way to Olneyville. Am I not right? I'd also like to know just what part of the present Weybosset St. was once *Broad*. It certainly was not the *whole*—was it the section above Dorrance? Or above Mathewson? That rampageous Washington kittie was certainly not as nice as the little black-&-white boy I petted in Paterson Sunday—& as for memory, I can beat that nonagenarian, for I have a perfectly clear recollection of things which happened centuries before I was born!

Don't worry about my lending money. If I have been a friend of Arthur Leeds a year & a half without handing him a penny, I am absolutely proof against the great genus of panhandlers! Mrs. Bullen sent her husband's book to M^cNeil, & he thinks there are real possibilities in it! He wants to talk it over with me before writing her, so I'll have to set a date to call on him. Probably Sonny will want to come along, too. As to the eccentric will of Alfredus' father—that was probably due to wheedling & pressure brought to bear on the old gentleman during his very last days by the family of his brother. He was, at that late period, very easily influenced; & he was not allowed to forget that he had once (before his second marriage, & at a time when no one thought he would ever have a child of his own) promised to leave the bulk of his fortune to his *nephew* Alfred Galpin, (Cromwell Galpin's son) who was named for him. He never had the least friction with Alfredus the Mighty, & that superboy was quite dumbfounded when a reading of the will disclosed the state of things. All lawyers agreed that The Child could break the document without any real difficulty—but here his pride stepped in & forbade him to take action. He even purposed to tear up the trifling cheque he did receive—but was prevented by his wife. Now he is deucedly hard up—as he admits in a letter just received by Sonny. Belknap has ordered some art postcards from the Louvre & other museums through him, & I am doing the same. We are sending him 50¢ a piece—which goes far in France—& trusting to his judgment & knowledge of our respective tastes to select appropriate things for each. I trust the Young Parisian has escaped the fox as well as the leopard—perhaps he is too ethereally slender to be seen by their dazzled eyes. He has lately *grown an inch*, now standing 6 feet 2 & weighing only 130. He is, like his Grandpa, experimenting with cheap eating; & has brought many a meal down to 7 or 8 cents. His method is to cook large quantities of fresh vegetables—especially cabbage. I doubt if I could endure such a menu.

Not knowing the names or present address of that small "Tom——meeee!!!!" who owned my one-time furry visitor William Stanley Braithwaite, I can't even conjecture whether or not this lad is the Thomas Mills now appointed to West Point. It is not by any means impossible, for he would be just about the right age at present. If so, I congratulate him, & hope he will find just as nice kitties up the Hudson as the black boy who used to come over & call on Grandpa Theobald! And I trust that little Prescott Pierce is still tunefully enjoying his saxophone! Yes—Mrs. Burns should be reprimanded concerning her superfluous & carnivorous tenants. So Dr. Clark also encountered them? Poe did, too—do you recall my pointing out the Planters' Hotel (then Mrs. Morrison's boarding-house) where he stopped upon moving hither from Philadelphia? It is the old brick colonial house with the curve—at the corner of Greenwich & Albany Sts., behind Trinity Church. No use talking, N.Y. is a tough place! Too bad you found the heat oppressive—I suffered when the temperature dropped last Friday, & was glad enough when Saturday brought more genial conditions! Glad you like Talman's poems, & will tell him so. We all think they shew great promise, & look to him to be one of the future high lights of amateurdom. I guess I'll send you those early stories of his—asking you to send them to A E P G & tell her to return them to me, since he wishes them back. Note that he did the art heading to the literary department of his high-school paper. I'm sure he'll enjoy a call on you & A E P G when he returns to Brown this month, & I'm equally sure you'll both pronounce him a fine boy. I'll enjoy seeing your annotated Doolittle cutting—it was at the Bixby Silver Co. that he used to repair my watch. My first two watches came from there, & I still have the tasteful silver case of the absolutely first . . . . . a case much nicer, it soon developed, than the works it so ornately enclosed! Glad you like the new United Amateur, & hope Bacon will do his best to keep up the literary standard. Yes—amateur journalism is good exercise for those out of touch with more formal aesthetic influences, & has certainly been a major influence with me since my entrance to it in April 1914. Pleased to hear that you liked my lines to young Richard Merritt Dench—I wasn't tremendously fond of them myself, & was genuinely surprised when they won first mention over Kleiner's very ingenious humorous offering. The verses of Mortonius & Ernest Adams had obvious weaknesses, but Kleiner's seemed to me the best & smoothest of the evening. Deuced odd how a person of taste like James Ferdinand falls into banality the moment he attempts metre—one would think his critical faculty would save him.

Yes—I noticed about the working hours of the Countess de Chambrun, but that is nothing novel or unusual.[2] Amy Lowell was similarly nocturnal, & so have been a large percentage of all creative writers. One simply can't think in the daytime, with all the clatter of the world outside one's windows, & with the possibility of being disturbed by knocker or telephone any moment. At night, when the objective world has slunk back into its cavern & left dreamers to their own, there come inspirations & capabilities impossible at any less magical & quiet hour. No one knows whether or not he is an author unless he has tried writing at night. Many a mind closed & sluggish in sunlight, opens up rare & magnificently exotic vistas in the beams of the moon.

So you have Paterson speakers in Providence? Great Scott! how can they ever go back after having seen a real city? Glad Mrs. Herron is such an ideal landlady—apparently there are very few such! I was interested to hear all the Tillinghast data, & wish I had seen the burial ground. I know how Colonial that section is, though I have been through it but *once*—in November 1923, with A E P G, Mortonius, & C. M. Eddy Jr., after a visit to the Shepley museum. I believe that Pardon Tillinghast is generally listed as a 1st Baptist pastor; though he was probably more of an organiser & business manager than an actual wielder of pulpit eloquence. At all events, he was one of the most powerful of all the 17ᵗʰ century local Baptists. Yes—I seem to recall this later Pardon Tillinghast, the jurist.[3] Of the Gortons I have heard much—from the Coventry valetudinarian Wilbur Gorton—who wore a *stock* long after his contemporaries had adopted the prosaic collar & tie—back to the famed Samuel Gorton, prince of eccentrics, upholder of the English common law, & general thorn in the flesh of estimable Mr. Williams. Old Sam was the founder of Warwick, & a very great deal besides! I'd like to see that Austen [*sic*] book again—I think I read it once, but that was very long ago, before I could appreciate it as much as I can now. Didn't he write another, also—called "Philip & Philippa", or something of the sort?[4] Very shortly I'm going to lend you some of my pet historical works—especially the Munro & Richman volumes. You can find "Lamia" in any edition of Keats at any library; but if you'd like to take your time reading it, I'll send you my copy of Keats. And I must look up that Hall article in the July *Atlantic*—I'll do it the day I embark on my quest of the twelve Irishmen—the Saint Ronans. Speaking of Rons—I'm glad Ronald K. is still as debonair as of old.[5] I'll wager he looks twice as prepossessing after reducing—that's the great movement of the age! He & I were both uncomfortably elephantine when last we met. Glad Capron has had a good European jaunt, & hope he continues to enjoy his antique furniture despite its Victorian setting.

I groan to think of the passing of colonial Westminster St.—may Heaven preserve the Butler mansion AND THE ARCADE! You ought to see those drawings at the historical society made in 1824—the originals of those in the pamphlet I want so much. They are on the very top floor, off the gallery in a book stack, & there is a special electric light enabling one to study them in detail. I hope that some day, since Westminster is doomed, a wholesale reclamation may take place in South Main St., where so many ancient houses survive in a hoisted state above the slum shops. These are in many cases much older than the Westminster St. houses, including gambrel-roofed specimens; & if cleaned, renovated, & lowered to the ground, would produce an effect almost like that of Salem's Essex-St. Would that Providence were a smaller place; so that, like Salem & Portsmouth, it might retain more of its primal Colonial charm!

Septr. 2

Well, here's another day! I retired at midnight, & am up again at 9 a.m.—ought to be able to clean up my letters by afternoon & get down to the library

to read that Atlantic & find St. Ronan & have a whack at "Providence in Colonial Times" before going up to Sonny's for the meeting. Or maybe—if it
seems decently warm—I'll take some work to Prospect Park & enjoy what
little is left of the summer. The day seems fair enough so far. Monday's *Bulletin* hasn't come yet, though Tuesday's has. I'll give 'em another day, & then
drop a postal if I don't get it. The last time I did that, they sent the missing
copy promptly with a very courteous note of apology. Oh, yes—& I must do
some shopping, too. I'm all out of provisions, & some laundry is awaiting me
at the institution around the corner. Life is prosaic. And I must pay my rent,
too—how perennial is boredom! I'm taking quite a bundle up to the meeting—Talman booklets for those absent last week, an American Mercury
Belknap lent me, & the Child's rubbers—which will be a responsibility on
both sides till they are returned to their proper habitat.

And so it goes. I'll thank you in advance for the bundle of cuttings you
mention, though it has not yet arrived. Now I'll proceed to write A E P G &
some others, & see what the afternoon brings forth. I can't tell in here about
the temperature, but my trip to the shops & laundry will give me a sample.

With every good wish & testimonial of esteem, believe me,
Yr most aff Nephew & obt Servt
H P L

## Notes

1. Howard W. Swift, author of *Getting Acquainted with Nature* (1969) and other books
on plant life.
2. Clara Eleanor Longworth de Chambrun, Countess of Chambrun (1873–1954),
American-born novelist and Shakespeare scholar. She married a French count who
was a direct descendant of the Marquis de Lafayette.
3. HPL refers to Pardon Tillinghast (1622?–1718), one of the early settlers of Providence and a pastor of the Baptist Church in Providence, and his descendant Pardon
Elisha Tillinghast (1836–1905), associate justice of the Rhode Island Supreme Court
(1881–1904).
4. HPL refers to the Rhode Island writer John Osborne Austin (1849–1918). HPL
owned three of his books: *The Journal of William Jefferay, Gentleman* (1899), *More Seven
Club Tales* (1900), and *Philip and Philippa* (1901) (*LL* 63–65).
5. Ronald K. Upham, HPL's boyhood friend.

[122]     [ALS] [HPL to LDC]

Before Dawn Tuesday
Septr. 8, 1925

My dear Daughter Lillian:—

I duly receiv'd the roll of interesting newspaper
material, & cannot forbear from expreſsing my thanks at once. All the items

are of keenly absorbing quality, & I shall not fail to look up the *Atlantic* articles mention'd on the margin of that philosophical "Minute Movie". That
French lead boundary plate is indeed a find—I recall reading about them
three years ago. Of equal—& to me greater—interest is the Newport infantry
cap—which ought some day to go to the R.I. Hist. Soc. either by exchange or
purchase. The Doolittle item is a breath of old times, & the account of the
abandoned Tingley place has infinite appeal—I had already cut it out & filed
it for preservation. I am glad, too, that the Hazards continue to sustain the
colonial tradition of Narragansett culture. They are apparently the only great
house of that region to survive the Revolutionary decline with undiminished
splendour, & I trust that their prominence may last through many a generation to come. I'd like to get hold of a copy of that novel, "College Tom",[1] for
its hero is a character I have frequently met in my summer's reading.

My own enclosing must perforce be of lesser interest. Letters from S H
relate the somewhat felicitous aftermath of her moving, whilst the set of
Greenwich cards will remind you of our explorations last winter. These are
for you to keep—a duplicate set having gone to A E P G. As a loan—to be
passed on to A E P G for ultimate return to me—I am sending the new Clark
Ashton Smith tale—"The Abominations of Yondo", which I trust you will
enjoy to the accompaniment of appropriate shivers. It will eventually go to
*Weird Tales*—& I surely hope the editor will accept it.

As for my diary—which ended last Wednesday noon—I didn't have a
chance to go out except for local errands before the time came to start for the
meeting at Belknap's. Morton, Leeds, Kleiner, & Kirk were there; Loveman absenting himself because of a financial quarrel with Kirk which threatens to develop into a second McNeil–Leeds feud. The session was one of our best;
everything under the sun being discussed, & the hideous "Yondo" read amidst
the shudders of all. Leeds then had us read two short tales by Algernon Blackwood as preparation for the reading of his long blank-verse tribute to that author—this latter reading exciting varied critical comment. We dissolved at 2
a.m., Kirk & I walking all the way down town to 14th St.—& Leeds with us as
far as his 49th St. region, where we paused for coffee & ice-cream. The rest of
the night was spent at Kirk's, talking & reading the new books he had about.
When morning came, the session continued; & although we went out for an
Italian dinner at noon, (Kirk insisting on treating) we still did not dissolve.
Twice in the afternoon & evening we fared forth for ice-cream, yet not till 10
p.m. did I finally take my leave for Brooklyn. In that session I read three
books through—an antiquarian treatise on Broadway, a study of H. L.
Mencken by Ernest Boyd, & a volume on the literary movement of the
1890's—& digested many a current magazine article, such as that by George
Sterling on Ambrose Bierce in the new *American Mercury*. After reaching 169 I
did some writing, & finally retired at some hour of indeterminate lateness.
The next day—Friday the 4th—I was awaked by the vigorous knocking of 'It-

tle-Sonny, who had come over to accompany his Grandpa to the 6th Ave. antique shop, (where Mortonius had commissioned me to buy him a dollar's worth of Roman coins) & to honest old M^cNeil's to discuss the MS. which poor Mrs. Bullen had sent him for examination. The antique place was a veritable fairyland of Greek, Roman, & Egyptian wonders at astonishingly low prices, & Sonny & I were both tempted into buying a few of the 15¢ Roman coins after we had filled Mortonius' modest order. I also 'fell for' one of the ancient pottery lamps whose cheapness is due to the limitless quantities lately excavated—a Grecian affair of about *500 B.C.* It sits before me now, enchanting in its glamour, & has already suggested at least one weird story plot to my imagination; a plot in which it will figure as an *Atlantean* rather than Hellenic survival. What primordially vague & godlessly archaic scenes hath that strange lamp illumin'd—that strange lamp which now broods on my desk awaiting oil & flame to revive its secret memories? Will it ever tell?[2] Thus preciously laden, Sonny & I left the shop with reluctance, & sought the noisome expanses of Hell's Kitchen. M^cNeil was out, so we took the subway down to Union Square to call on Loveman at his shop. We found him about to leave; & after shewing him our newly acquired antiquities & waiting for the end of a sudden thunderstorm, accompanied him to a fine new Italian restaurant he had discovered in a side street opposite Grace Church—the Roman Spaghetti Place, whose card I enclose. Belknap

greek lamp as seen from above - Exact size.

side view - greatly reduced - shewing location of flame.

now left, whilst Loveman & I indulged in nutriment; after which we proceeded westward toward Greenwich to loiter until time to meet Leeds at Columbus Circle for a cinema to which he had invited us—"The Unholy Three".[3] The atmosphere, oddly affected by the late afternoon storm, had by this time acquired a very peculiar tinge of spectral yellow; which lent to the scene an agreeable unreality & aspect of antiquity. The venerable houses & crooked streets of Greenwich took on a singular glamour & archaic vividness; so that the past seemed risen & omnipresent, as if emanating vaporously from every brass knocker, colonial doorway, & Georgian gable in the whole fascinating wilderness of time-touched roofs & chimney-pots. In the midst of this odd & unexpected spectacle an added feature introduced itself when, at Sheridan Square, we were witnesses to a rather picturesque eviction—a dumpy-looking woman (whether peasant or pseudo-artist we could not decide) having been turned out on the sidewalk with all her domestic furniture, whilst an aesthetic-looking youth with wavy brown hair, dreamy eyes, a black-&-red checked flannel shirt, & a crimson silk sash supporting flaring trousers, brought her a pail of coffee from a neighbouring cafeteria to dilute the saline streams from her unhappy eyes. A curious crowd supplied the requisite background for this infelicitous idyll. At length we took the subway for Columbus Circle, met Leeds, & entered the Circle Theatre—20¢ seats in the 2nd balcony. The film was good—an underworld study of unusual character, involving some decidedly weird & gruesome effects—& I advise you to see it if it returns to Providence. It ran last week at the Victory. We then repaired to a cafeteria for the usual fluid, after which we walked down to the 49th St. B.M.T. station & bade Loveman adieu. Leeds & I then proceeded to Bryant Park—back of the Public Library—to watch the moon over the Babylonish black bulk of the American Radiator Bldg. (which a Pawtucket architect design'd) & to discuss such topics as the sight might suggest—afterward walking to sundry points of perspective & eventually bowing farewells. I then proceeded homeward & retired. The next day—Saturday the 5th—I was up at 2:30 p.m. & proceeded at once to McNeil's to discuss the Bullen MS. I found the juvenile jingles very good, but since neither McNeil nor I could do anything about them, we sealed them carefully up for transportation back to Canada. McNeil will write Mrs. Bullen an encouraging letter, & both he & I will hope to hear no more of the matter. We are through with being philanthropists! At 5:45 I left for Union Square, since I had an appointment with Loveman to go on an exploring expedition in Brooklyn. Upon meeting, we at once entrained for that placid borough; dining at John's & thence proceeding to Loveman's room to discuss the big news—the forthcoming publication of "The Hermaphrodite" & about 30 other poems in a 100-page book to be financed by some friend in the Bronx.[4] We tentatively selected a group of shorter poems for inclusion in the much-to-be-desired volume, & at about 9:30 set out for the nocturnal exploration we had planned. Starting among the dim streets under Brooklyn Bridge, we first encountered a tiny black-&-white kitten whose graces threatened to detain us indefinitely, & whose kidnapping we quite seriously discussed. *Such* a *little* kitty-cat! At length breaking away, we were drawn by a neighbouring glare of lights & blare of brasses; & turning a corner into hilly Main St. came suddenly upon the most delightful & unexpected scene of teeming Italian festivity—a feast of St. Joseph, with its festooning of flags & coloured lanterns, its showers of confetti, its gaily bannered bandstands, & its curious old-time customs such as wholesale mock-flagellation with little whips purchased from smiling vendors. We lingered long at this idyllic spectacle under the mellow moon—a spectacle whose provincial simplicity would not have been possible in any of the larger Italian quarters like Federal Hill—but finally moved onward through the black & sinister streets toward De Kalb Avenue. Pausing on the steps of the Brooklyn Hospital (which I came to know so well last year) for Loveman to rest—for he is no such hiker as most of us—we decided to take a car for the singular spot he wished most especially to shew me; which we did—alighting at Classon Avenue & turning a few steps to the left along that thoroughfare. The general neighbourhood was much like Kleiner's—ugly wooden houses of Victorian date & Germanic implications—but at one point the facade of a sprawling flat was pierced by an archway of considerable magnitude bearing the name of "Union Place". Through this we passed; treading old-fashioned cobblestones that boasted more than one friendly grass-blade, & peering ahead at the vista of verdure which promised such an escape from the prosy metropolitan world. And what an escape it was! Litten only by the gibbous moon, & by a solitary lamp-post that flickered fantastically, there lay beyond that wooden tunnel a little realm apart—a brooding backwater of the 1850's, where in a quadrangle facing a central iron-railed bit of park stood side by side the high-stooped homes of elder days, each in its iron-fenced yard with garden or grass-plot, & totally innocent of the injudicious restorer's vandal touch. Silence rested soothingly on every hand, & the outer universe faded from consciousness as it retreated from sight. Here dreamed the past inviolate—leisurely, graceful & unperturbed; defying all that might occur in the seething hell of life beyond that protecting archway. The moon looked gently in & approved what it saw—old-fashion'd flowers & shrubs within the iron enclosure, carelessly cobbled roadway returning on itself in rectangular bends, little wooden dwellings with brick basements & tall front steps, turf or blossoms in the railed front yards, quaint iron railings & swinging gates which rust could not conquer—all the quiet, lovely things of calmer, healthier times which made the world beautiful before progress & machinery & mongrelism turned it to a mocking madhouse. I know not how long we stood gazing upon this blessed sight, but at length we bade it a reluctant farewell. Purchasing some provisions at a shop nearby, we took the car for Borough Hall & proceeded to 169; where, after a period of rest & discussion, Loveman removed his Fawcett books from storage & prepared them for transportation to his quarters. We then set out with bookstrap & valise, but so heavy was the burthen that Loveman summoned a taxicab before we had traversed many blocks. Reaching Columbia Heights in this fashion, we conveyed the books upstairs, arranged them on the mantelpiece, & indulged in epilogical comment till 2 a.m. or thereabouts. I then returned to 169 with the empty valise, & have not been out of the house since. Loveman, finding several duplicates among the Fawcett books, insisted upon giving them to me; but I tell him he must not consider the transfer of ownership final, since a Fawcett 'boom' would impart to the volumes a considerable market value. Edgar Fawcett, you may recall, is the forgotten N.Y. author whom Loveman wishes to popularise as soon as he is done with the other & less obscure Edgar—Saltus. Until Sunday morning I wrote letters continuously,—including one to A E P G—then retiring & sleeping till late in the day. On being up again I wrote more letters & retired at 10 p.m., not awaking till 1:30 p.m.

Monday. Since then, too, I have been writing letters, & I don't know when I shall be through—but when I am I'll read some in the new *Weird Tales* & retire again. Tomorrow night—Tuesday—I have an engagement with Loveman either here or elsewhere to look once more over his poetry prior to its publication. He is very lucky to find a backer—the volume will be a nice one; probably with Sonny's "Pirates and Hamadryads" as an introduction,[5] & with the imprint of some fictitious but high-sounding publishing-house on the title-page—perhaps "The Ferris Thone Company", using the name of the hero of that excellent tale of Loveman's in the *National Amateur* a few years ago.[6] These are great days for Samuelus—for what thrill in life can equal the expectancy of having one's first real book published & placed on the market? On Wednesday, unless weather prohibits, I'm going to spend that generous two fish of yours & take the Hudson River scenic trip with Belknap & his parents; enjoying some of the finest cliff & mountain vistas that I shall ever have seen. In the evening we shall be back in time for the meeting, (a McNeiler) held at Kirk's new joint in 14th St. Kirk also has the next (Leedsian) meeting.

I hope to write some more stories shortly—but I must get rid of my superfluous amateur letter-writing. Any incubi or responsibilities detract disastrously from one's creative imagination, & I must cultivate the stimulating impressions of freedom, novelty, & strangeness. Meanwhile I must finish the two stories I sketched out roughly last month—the short thing developed from C. W. Smith's tomb notion, & the longish novelette involving antique horrors risen from the sea.[7] The new *Weird Tales* is out, though with nothing in it by our gang. Young Talman just sent me a story to look over—mediocre, but I trust I've found a tactful way to tell him so whilst suggesting improvements.[8]

And so it goes. I'm not dressed now, hence unless I decide to slip on an old coat & trousers over my nightshirt & dodge out in the dark to the letter box, I'll be mailing this tomorrow with whatever external annotations developments may call for. It's possible that I may go to the library in the afternoon, but I rather doubt it. More likely I'll give this room a good sweeping & dusting, faring forth only to attend to such trivial commonplaces as laundry & grocery shopping. I've a new staple for my home meals—*Cheese Tidbits,* which are tiny National Biscuit crackers with very strong cheese flavour, retailed in 5¢ packages by local grocers. For dessert I also have a new dish—Marshmallow Sandwich, consisting of marshmallow betwixt little vanilla wafers, & likewise coming in 5¢ packages. These & potato chips have lately won a prominent place on my diet list—though I often eat out, mostly at Italian places. It's odd how superlatively fond I am of Italian dishes—though the omnipresence of my beloved CHEESE motif may go far toward accounting for it. Well—such is which. I'll close for the nonce, extending the usual compliments & courtesies, & subscribing myself, as at all times,

Yr most aff: Nephew & obt Servt

H P L

[On envelope:]

Tuesday Evening

8 p.m.

Diary—continued

Retired at dawn—up again 4 p.m.—cleaned room—went out shopping & to barber's—now am going over to Loveman's for discussion of book. Loveman is going on the Hudson trip tomorrow.

———

Just heard from S H—who has at last received the delayed letter from me mentioned in enclosed note.

## Notes

1. By Caroline Hazard. The work is not a novel but a historical study.

2. The lamp probably inspired *CB* 146: "Ancient lamp found in tomb—when filled and used, its light reveals strange world." HPL used this idea for "VI. The Lamp" in *Fungi from Yuggoth*.

3. *The Unholy Three* (MGM, 1925), directed by Tod Browning; starring Lon Chaney, Mae Bush, and Matt Moore. Based on a story by Tod Robbins. The film is a crime drama with weird overtones.

4. W. Paul Cook published the long poem *The Hermaphrodite* (with no additional poems) in 1926. The Caxton Press published an edition that contained the poem and also some of Loveman's shorter lyrics.

5. FBL's "Pirates and Hamadryads" (*United Amateur*, July 1925) was an essay on Samuel Loveman's poetry.

6. "Ferris Thone." *National Amateur* 46 (*sic* =44), No. 3 (January 1922): 26–27.

7. "In the Vault" (written on 18 September) and "The Call of Cthulhu" (not written until summer 1926, after HPL's return to Providence).

8. "Izrim," *United Amateur* 25, No. 2 (May 1926): 3. See HPL to Talman (7 September 1925), in which he praises the story.

[123]    [ALS] [HPL to LDC]

Saturday–Sunday Midnight

Septr. 12–13, 1925

My dear Daughter Lillian:—

Your card duly arrived, & pending receipt of the promised letter I will take my pen in hand to bring my diary down to date. Let me see—I think I left off Tuesday evening; when, having returned from the barber's, I set out for Loveman's to confer about his poetry book & go exploring. Well—I went, found my host in, conferred, & duly set out on the nocturnal expedition; stopping at Loveman's favourite Spanish restaurant to get a 25¢ dinner (enormous value) of beef, spiced & stuffed in the piquant manner of old Castile & Arragon. We then fared eastward, following the Brooklyn shore through the overtaken ex-villages of Wallabout & Williamsburg to Greenpoint, in an effort to discover the landmarks mentioned in one of Fawcett's books. Fawcett, you may recall, is the forgotten N.Y. author whom Loveman is trying to popularise. Williamsburg seemed to present an aspect considerably different from that of Brooklyn proper, & includes an enormous publick market district (like Dyer or Canal Sts) whose existence I had never before suspected. Greenpoint—which is the section across the river from 14th St. Manhattan—turned out to be almost exactly the same as when Fawcett so vividly described its unrelieved dreariness. It is a tedious, semi-squalid region of incredibly ugly wooden houses; & though the piles of cedar lumber which the author locates near the waterfront have given place to warehouses & factories, it cannot be said that the change has contributed anything to the aesthetic tone of the region. In one block we came across the glare of an Italian fiesta much like that which we saw near Brooklyn Bridge the Saturday before, but on the whole less picturesque. Finally we took the car back to Borough Hall & dispersed—agreeing to meet at 8 on the morrow, since Loveman decided at the last moment to join the Hudson River outing of the Longs. Sonny, by the way, sent his Grandpa a final cautionary notice of such quaint picturesqueness that I will enclose it for you. I returned home, wrote letters, read some, & started out again at 7:45 a.m., arriving at Loveman's on time & taking the subway with him for Belknap's. Reaching 96th St. long before the appointed hour of 9:15, we stopt at a cafeteria for light refreshments; finally reaching the Long establishment on time & chatting with Sonny till the entire party was ready. About 9:30 all hands sallied forth—Dr. Long, Mrs. Long, Belknap, Loveman, & I; laden with lunches & blessed with a sunny day despite a coolness I would hardly have chosen. Taking a street-car to the Fort Lee (129th St.) wharf, we purchased round trip Newburgh tickets & waited for the boat—which soon arrived & received us. It was the new steamer *De Witt Clinton,* & seeking the uppermost deck we all ensconced ourselves along the western rail, prepared to assimilate as much scenery as possible in a trip of three hours each way. It was my first real view of the Hudson country, since on my Cleveland trip I was unfavourably situated in the train both going & coming. The Palisades rose in their accustomed beauty, & in time gave place to the domed & rolling hills typical of the river's upper reaches. Here & there appeared panoramas of striking magnificence— mountains glimpsed through gaps in mountains, & violet lines of distant peaks rising above & beyond vast green clusters of nearer peaks. Headlands jutted boldly into the river, & the sparkling blue of water & sky lent a profound & dramatick vitality to the whole gorgeous spectacle. Towns occurred now & then—Yonkers, Tarrytown, Nyack, Ossining, & Haverstraw—& fancy repeopled the region with the characters of its myriad myths & rich history. It is, par excellence, the Irving country, & I regretted that I could not catch a glimpse of Sunnyside from the boat. Below Haverstraw is the spot where poor Maj. Andre landed when he conferred with Genl. Arnold, & higher up is Stony Point, where Genl. Wayne achieved so great a celebrity.[1] In time we reached a scene of poignant wonder & beauty, where lofty hills rose boldly & profusely from the river's very edge on both sides, forming a picture worthy of the Rhine or any of the world's great inland water paradises. This was the Indian Point & Bear Mountain region, where picnickers are wont to stop & explore—& where I must take a closer look about some day. As if moved by the thought of picnickers, we here commenced to consume our sumptuous lunch; nibbling as we passed under the new Bear Mountain bridge, & past the impressive fortified battlements of West Point. Soon there arose on the left the lordly heights of Crow's Nest & Storm King, whilst on the right Breakneck Mountain appeared fully capable of living up to its name. Having passed these, one obtained the most majestic view imaginable by looking back & considering the whole vista of the river & both banks. Many persons photographed it, & we all regretted that we had not brought cameras. There now appeared on the left, crowning a terraced height, the ancient spires & roofs of Newburgh; flanked by colonial houses & country-seats of the greatest possible attractiveness. On one green eminence stood the head-quarters of Genl. Washington when he was in that region—the house shewn in one of the views in the folder I mailed you—& I was glad I studied it well, since we had not time to visit it by land. Then came the landing, & the dizzy & ecstatic ascent of Newburgh's narrow climbing lanes, where colonial gables & twisting byways supply an atmosphere hardly to be duplicated this side of Marblehead. Of this wonderland we could hope only to enjoy the slenderest glimpse, since the return boat left in forty minutes. What we did was to climb to the main street, (which runs ledgewise like Benefit St. along the precipitous river-bank) buy & mail some folders & postcards, glance up regretfully at un-visited higher terraces, & saunter back toward the landing. Dr. Long obtained a bag of candy at the ten-cent store, & Loveman purchased at the same em-porium a pad & pencil to draw & write with on the return trip. Thus fortified, we sought the wharf; arriving in ample time to board the proper boat—the *Albany*, an ornate but by no means repulsive relick of the Victorian age. Of Newburgh I shall say more when I see it again—as I most certainly must! The return trip was spent in reading, drawing, writing, & literary discussion; all set off to advantage by the superlative scenic background. Arriving at the 129th St. pier somewhat before six, we all proceeded to the Longs' for dinner. At 7:30 Loveman & I left; he for his shop & I for the meeting of the gang at Kirk's. Sonny was too tired to attend the meeting, whilst Loveman preferred to wait another week & let his quarrel with Kirk cool off a bit. I reached Kirk's in good season, finding Kleiner already there. Very soon Morton & McNeil arrived, & the session duly developed. I gave Mortonius the Roman coins I had bought for him, & he displayed a large variety of new museum minerals. Magazine articles were read, reminiscences exchanged, & every effort made to brighten things up—yet in spite of all the proceedings dragged intolerably, with everyone thoroughly bored. Then M<sup>c</sup>Neil went home & the rest adjourned to a cafeteria—since Kirk had supplied no refreshments—when lo! something about the coffee seemed to act as a stimulant to jaded wits, & we all commenced to converse as brilliantly as can be imagined! Kleiner left first, but Kirk, Mortonius & I stayed on till 2:30 a.m.—James Ferdinand finding this possible because he was stopping in darktown with his former housemate Walker at 138<sup>th</sup> St. I then returned to 169, read the Bulletin, & retired. Awaking late on Thursday the 10<sup>th</sup>, I received a call from Leeds inviting me to see the great film of "Siegfried"[2] at the Century—a stupendous German spectacle in which the scattered myths of the Nibelung ring from the early Volsung saga to the Wagnerian tetralogy are fused into one concise & coherent whole, & shewn to the accompaniment of a mighty orchestral composite of Wagnerian musick. Balcony seats were 50¢, & Leeds insisted on treating even though he can ill afford it. I tried to stop him, but he is as bad as all the rest of the gang for generosity—I can never catch up with all the donations they seem determined to shower about! Having written some letters, I took the subway & arrived at Columbus Circle (the theatre is a few doors north of this in Central Park West) on time, finding Leeds in front of the theatre & at once going in with him. The sumptuousness of the house—which I had never before entered—pleased me exceedingly, even though there is something a trifle over-ornate—Byzantine, as it were, in suggestion—about the stucco relief decorations of the main auditorium. I presume you may recall from the newspapers that this house—first called the "New Theatre"—was built about fifteen years ago as a sort of experiment in an endowed classic theatre like the Comedie Francaise in Paris, but that the failure of the original venture soon threw it on the market for miscellaneous productions. As for the film—it was an ecstasy & a delight to be remembered for ever! It was the very inmost soul of the immortal & unconquerable blond Nordic, embodied in the shining warrior of light, great Siegfried, slayer of monsters & enslaver of Kings. The central figure was acted by a German of perfectly adapted colouring & physique—Paul Richter—& the scenery was an absolute triumph of Northern phantasy worthy of Dunsany. Great & mysterious forests spread out with their titan trees, creeping roots, & fantastick play of light & shadow. Castles of mystery crowned haunted crags, & in the Icelandick scenes the abode of Brunhilde was a portentous wonder in colossal lava, brooding spectral & desolate under never-dying auroras. The musick, too, was of ineffable inspiration. Insensible as I am to musick in general, I cannot escape the majesty of Wagner, whose genius caught the deepest spirit of those ancestral yellow-bearded gods of war & dominion before whom my own soul bows as before no others—Woden, Thor, Freyr, & the vast Alfadur—frosty blue-eyed giants worthy of the adoration of a conquering people! I am certain that Wagner is the supreme musical genius of the last hundred years, at least; & perhaps the creator of the second-greatest artistick monument of the whole Nordic race, the Gothick cathedral being the greatest. Exalted beyond words, we left the theatre at last, as the funeral march of the golden-haired young demigod pealed from the orchestra. Nothing had so inspired me in weeks, & I believe a masterful daemon-tale could be founded upon the sinister bass musick from "Rheingold" (played when Siegfried overpowers the King of the Nibelungs & seizes their treasure) alone! After this we proceeded to the Automat for dinner & thence to Bryant Park to chat of literature a while. At last we divided, & I returned home to write some & retire. Friday I was up at 4 p.m. & wrote throughout the afternoon & night, retiring at 3 a.m. Saturday the 12th I was up at 2:30 p.m., wrote some, went out shopping, & finally went down to the Milan for my beloved minestrone dinner, preparatory to a session at the publick library—where I read those Atlantick articles, found all there was to be found about St. Ronan, & digested more of the rather voluminous & richly informative Kimball book, "Providence in Colonial Times." At 10 p.m.—when the library closes—I returned to 169 & wrote some more—which I am still doing. I doubt if I shall retire tonight—at most, I shall only recline on top of the couch in my clothes. (Naturally, the old blue!) Tomorrow—or *today,* if the clock tells aright— Loveman says he is coming over, & we shall probably visit that quaint Brooklyn fishing village, the "Old Mill", which Sonny & I saw in 1922. The next gang meeting is a Leeds one at Kirk's. After that is a McNeil meeting at McNeil's. Further than that my social programme is indeterminate, though I want infernally to get in another Hudson River trip if possible before the cold weather. As for things auctorial—Farnsworth Wright of *Weird Tales* has just written me again, outlining his plans for a book of spooky short stories, culled from his magazine, to be published in the spring. In this collection he means to include my "Rats in the Walls" as well as Sonny's "Ocean Leech"; & since the royalties (if any!) are to be divided amongst the authors represented, I may derive a few cents in the end.[3] Wright says that Henneberger was in Brooklyn recently, & tried unsuccessfully to find me. I am rather glad he failed! I'll shew you Wright's letter when I've answered it. Another interesting letter is from the Alfredus-child, who sent his Grandpa some fine cards (free ones, mailed before he received the sum I sent through 'Ittle-Sonny) of Paris, & promises to send some more. He has moved from the Rue Madame to the ancient dormitory of the academy where he is studying musick—the Schola Cantorum—& inhabits an edifice which once housed the austere monks of the Benedictine order—address, 269 Rue St. Jacques, Paris (Vᵉ). One of his cards shews the Roman ruins in the Parc Monceau—a noble Corinthian colonnade of which many columns are yet standing in good preservation. Certainly, Paris is a marvellous place, & the abode of unending antique wonder. Now as to St. Ronan—how scarce is all material! I have, however, by dint of comparing several Popish treatises & encyclopaedias, been able to narrow down to one holy man of that name who seems to stand out above the rest in area of devotion & frequency of mention. This is a Ronan born in Scotland at some time in the 8th century A.D., & migrating to Ireland later on, where he became the Bishop of Lismore. He is venerated in both countries, but on what ground I'll be hanged if I can tell, since the above skeletonick data is all that anybody seems to know—or seems inclined to relate—about him. What legend the French painter got hold of is a mystery to me, though there may be such things current in the lesser literature of the Papists. Some time I'll make a more exhaustive search—the thing begins to assume the alluring aspect of a game! As for the Atlantic articles—there is much sense in what Miss Repplier so piquantly relates, though her acute & humorous analysis will not stop the psychological phenomenon she describes.[4] Mr. Hall's article is also eminently sensible, though a bit diffuse in approach. As I have always said, missionaries are infernal nuisances who ought to be kept at home—dull, solemn asses without scientific acumen or historical perspective; & cursed with an eternal blindness to the obvious fact that different lands, races, & conditions naturally develop & demand different cultural standards & usages & different ethical & social codes. In the Providence book I came across much material that was new & interesting to me. It seems that between about 1673 or 4 & 1711–13 there was no Great or Weybosset Bridge, the structure erected in 1660 having fallen to pieces for want of care despite the best efforts of Mr. Williams to arouse the citizens to the need of its maintenance. Wagons either forded the shallow (near Steeple St.) or went half a mile up stream to the old bridge (1642) by Smith's grist mill, whilst cattle sometimes forded & sometimes swam, & unmounted pedestrians employed canoes. When the river was high & the current swift, crossing was very difficult, & it was almost impossible to pick a given landing place on the shore. One had to alight where chance & tide took him—& for this reason the town board kept the whole Town St. shore clear from Crawford St to Thomas Olney Sr.'s lot, forbidding the construction of wharves & warehouses betwixt these two points. I learned also that there used to be a churchyard **in front** of St. John's, on the Town St., as well as behind up the hill toward Back St. It seems to have disappeared in 1810, when the original structure (built 1723 as King's Church) gave place to the present stone edifice. All the graves & their markers are lost. But more anon. For the present I must get some other letters off, subscribing myself as at all times,

Yr most aff Nephew & obt Servt

H P L

## Notes

1. Major John André (1750–1780) was a British intelligence officer who was hanged

for collaborating with American general Benedict Arnold in his plan to hand over West Point to the British. General Anthony Wayne (1745–1796) was a United States army officer who defeated the British at the Battle of Stony Point (16 July 1779).

2. *Die Nibelungen: Siegfried* (Decla-Bioscop, 1924), directed by Fritz Lang; starring Gertrud Arnold, Margarete Schon, Hanna Ralph, and Paul Richter.

3. The volume was never published, although a somewhat similar volume, *The Moon Terror,* with stories by A. G. Birch, Anthony M. Rud, Vincent Starrett, and Farnsworth Wright, appeared in 1927. FBL's "The Ocean Leech" appeared in *WT* (January 1925).

4. Agnes Repplier, "Cure-Alls," 12–18 in the July issue referred to earlier.

[124]     [ALS] [HPL to LDC]

Monday Morning
Septr. 14, 1925

My dear Daughter Lillian:—

Being about to plunge into a period of story work to last till the Wednesday meeting, I will continue my diary to the present time, that I may embark upon my composition with a clean slate. I left off Saturday night or Sunday morning; when, having returned from the publick library, I was immersed in writing. Omitting bed, I rested on the couch in my clothes Sunday noon, & was awaked at 5 p.m. by the arrival of Loveman for the Old Mill trip. We started at once, dining at John's & taking the elevated for Crescent St., at the extreme eastern rim of Brooklyn, whence the road leads south to Jamaica Bay; on whose shore reposes the quaint, out-of-the-world fishing village we sought. You may recall my mentioning a visit to this place with Sonny in 1922. I have planned a thousand times to revisit it, but continually deferred the process. Mortonius is the original discoverer so far as our gang is concerned—he took the B.P.C. there, & upon their report the voyage of Belknap & myself was undertaken. On this occasion the sun was low when we reached Crescent St., yet we decided to walk rather than take the omnibus—since the twilight would only add a greater glamour & beauty to the spot. For a long distance the road was merely a squalid Italian street, but at last came the mystic salt breeze, the sight of spreading salt marshes, & the colonial bulk of the Old Mill rising at the left—with another colonial building on the right. Betwixt these two, as through a gateway of the past, shimmered the sunset-lighted inlet along whose banks the wooden-hut village straggled like a lowly Venice of remote provincial coasts. Cabins of every sort clustered thickly, with here & there a frame house of more pretentious construction. Plank sidewalks on piles bordered the street of water, on which small boats with tall masts rode at anchor, & here & there a lofty little wooden bridge spanned the aqueous highway—permitting the vessels to glide beneath whilst pedestrians crossed from shore to shore. A glamour unspeakable, as of far Maine sea days, pervaded the scene, & could not be destroyed even by the denizens we encountered. Following the lead of Sonny & myself three years ago, we pursued the alluring street around many a picturesque turn as it clung to the sinuous inlet, now & then pausing to look backward or ahead as some peculiarly enticing panorama presented itself; some haunting, old-world effect of roofs & chimneys & masts & flagpoles, or some quaint vista of wharf & hull, doorway & yard, or steps & garden-plot. When I saw it before, I had never seen Marblehead; so I wondered whether the second glimpse would lose any of the pungent effect of the first. It did not, for this place heads a genre of its own, like to nothing I have encountered elsewhere. It is now, apparently, more given over to cottage colonists of the lower middle class than to its original fisheries; but has suffered no decay in aspect or atmosphere. Outsiders seem to group it with its foremost landmark & call it all "The Old Mill"; but local bulletins on walls apprised us that it boasts the native appellation of *Kiendahville¹*—perhaps dating back to original Dutch times, though I cannot vouch for it at the moment. At length we came to the place where Belknap & I ceased our bygone travels, & where the village appears to end; but looking out over the endless salt marsh I noticed a high plank bridge & plank walk which seemed to lead away to a second huddle of huts nearer the sea. Adventuringly we sampled the suggestion of remoter worlds, & in due time were rewarded by the sight of another twilit creek settlement exactly like the first, & forming indeed a part of the same village—an outpost flung out to face the rim of the desolate waste! Here again were the plank sidewalks & bridges, the huts & little gardens, the shining waters & the nodding boats, the waving masts & the weaving sea-winds—all this lure & fantasy in a tiny hamlet far away from any noisome haunt of crowds & trade! Night fell, & across the marshes lights twinkled out. Strange birds flew over us, hinting distant maritime secrets they did not tell. Jupiter blazed out in the southwest, poising itself for a while above the roof of the uttermost house of the village—the last, cryptical house whose near windows look upon the world of men but whose far windows look away over the dun, unpeopled marshes where only the eerie fireflies bob & wink. A black cat brushed by our feet, & we dreamt of profounder vistas than the marshes gave us. At last we turned away & came back to the haunts of fevered, futile, & furtive folk—but with a memory of fascinations close akin to the soul of the sea & of old desolate places. I must take Sonny-Child to see the part we did not find three years ago. Riding back to the elevated in the omnibus, we took a Broadway–B M T (Williamsburg Bridge) train whose ultimate destination was the subway; & changing at Canal St., eventually landed at the 8th St. station, near the tangled lanes of old Greenwich. This proved the starting-point for another antiquarian ramble; & although we saw nothing new, it was a boon to revel again amidst familiar & age-mellowed byways. All the ancient roofs & dormers & doorways greeted us with the friendly mien which only long acquaintance can foster, & before we were through we left unvisited not a single scene shewn in the cards I mailed you last week. As usual, the Minettas, Milligan Place, Patchin Place, Gay St., & the bend in Grove St. proved the supreme Meccas. Grove Court was attractive, but the destruction of the neighbouring colonial houses in Barrow & Hudson Sts. threw a cast of melancholy over it. At last, after a ghoulish glance into the walled & barred bit of graveyard in the shadows at 11th St. & 6th Ave., we departed for the 14th St. subway station & were soon back in our respective lodgings. Now I mean to wipe aside all answerable correspondence & buckle down to fictional work. Let's hope nothing imperative comes in the morning, (it is now 5 a.m.) for I want to keep on plugging & have something really done before the meeting Wednesday night. I doubt if I shall retire this morning, though I may lie down briefly as I did yesterday. It is raining—but that does not worry an indoor workman with an ample stock of provisions on hand. My favourite new staple is Cheese Tid-Bit—you must taste some, for they are truly rapturous in pungent appeal! The *Times* was so full of antiquarian material today that Loveman brought me a copy. One article I enclose—which need not be returned. Two others will reach you thro' A E P G—& these I would like to see again some time. More anon.

               Yr aff Nephew & obt Servt

               H P L

## Notes

1. Actually *Kiendlville*, a stilt community on an inlet of Jamaica Bay near Spring Creek and the Brooklyn–Queens border.

[125]    [ALS] [HPL to LDC]

               Tuesday Morning

               Septr. 15, 1925

My dear Daughter Lillian:—

               Let me thank you for the letter with pictorial enclosures which arrived yesterday afternoon, & express my delight in the familiar scenes evoked by the camera & colourist. Every time I see the Flatiron Building in Madison Square I think of its architectural offspring, the Turk's Head; & without any local partiality I am able to say that our Providence edifice is the handsomer & better-proportioned of the two. The view of the John Hay Library is delightful, & the artist-photographer chose an ideal vantage-point. The Van Wickle gates shew up well—& opportunely, too, for I was only recently discussing them with Talman, who admires them particularly. Yes—that postal with the grotesque figures is from Small Sonny, as I thought I mentioned in the letter. "Yondo" moved him to more eloquence than words could express—which reminds me to ask you if you liked it? No—the letters from S H which I enclosed need not be returned. She is not yet here, but yesterday sent a box of assorted Viennese candies which evidently came from the woman with whom she stayed in Saratoga last spring. It is now safe to forward anything you wish to A E P G—addressing it "The Northfield, East Northfield, Mass." Too bad you are bothered by social greeters at the open door—I simply won't keep my door open here, with assorted canaille inhabiting the contiguous regions. Cold or hot, this room has to be a separate entity—a little Angell-Street in the midst of chaos! No—I shan't bother to seek other quarters unless the heating problem precipitates open warfare, but I may have to get a cheap oil heater for the winter days. Mrs. Burns becomes quite rabid on the electric problem, & took Kirk's heater away from him by main force! I hope like you that this beastly strike business may not extend to the bituminous field—industry is a hideous drag, & it is unfortunate that society ever allowed itself to become so interdependent that it must hang on the whims of a pack of dirty peasants![1] One thing I'll have to do soon, & that is to get a man to fix my alcove light. Mrs. B. won't do it, & the nuisance gets me nervous—I can't bathe myself, wash dishes, or black my boots in any comfort with only the feeble rays of outside illumination filtering in. And yet the room as a whole is so admirable in proportion & design, & so perfectly in harmony with my type of furniture & ornaments, that I wouldn't give it up except under the most extreme pressure. Fitted up as it is, it is an ideal haven for a person of my tastes, & all who see it unite in praising its homelike & reposeful atmosphere.

Well—it's the 15th of September, & when I next go out I must omit my straw hat! I had the last year's felt re-blocked in the spring, so that it will present a very smart appearance when it appears above my new suit. Monday the streets hereabouts were littered with old & broken straws—sad annual hecatomb!

Yesterday I answered the enclosed *Times* advertisement for commercial writers, which Sonny-Child sent me after having answered it himself. Here's hoping for an early fortune, which I shall spend on buying 454 & the barn, tearing down Angell Court & putting back the stone wall, & rebuilding my "engine house" & "New-Anvik".[2] I shall place an early order for brown paint. Oh, yes—& I'm again trying to get my "Three Impostors" back from poor old Hancock.[3] He said the editor of the *Coney Island Times* had it, but when (after a delay) I wrote the editor, the latter said he had given it back. Now I'm writing Hancock again. Hope he won't acquire the habit of dropping in here, as he threatened to do last spring—probably he won't when he sees I've no money to lend him. Poor old duffer—& he comes of one of the most aristocratic families in England!

I'm collecting notes from the Kimball book at the library. The style is so diffuse & so much a mosaic of quoted phrases, that I think there may be after all a place for a shorter & more direct book on Old Providence. Some day, if I live, I shall write such a volume—in which the dear steepled hill town of the 18th century—the town of Stephen Hopkins, Abraham Whipple, John Carter, & the four Brown brothers, "John & Jo, Nick & Mo", will live again in all its quaintness. I find many interesting things about it in the book—for example, that the Joseph Jenckes, Jr. prominent about 1740–1750 was a *giant* 7[ft] 2[in] in height—& that in the cold winter of 1740–41 the bay was completely frozen over, so that people drove to Newport in their sledges over its solid surface. The first coach in town was owned by John Merritt, Esq., an English gentleman who came by way of Newport & built in 1746 a country-seat on a spot just east of the *old* Pawtucket Road. (the present Arlington Ave.) His estates reached clear to the Seekonk, & probably comprised the sites of both 454 & 598. His library was the finest in town except that of his friend Dr. Checkley of King's (St. John's) Church, & by all accounts he seems to have been a man of rare taste & geniality. The Rev. John Checkley (b. Boston 1680) was himself a delightful character, liberally educated in England, & famous as a wit & man of the world. He dwelt sometimes in the glebe house, (present Morris Ave.) & sometimes in an urban residence at the S.E. corner of Presbyterian or Rosemary Lane (College St) & the Town Street. It becomes very obvious to the historical student that the foundations of elegance, luxury, & taste in Providence were *not* laid by the early Baptist home-lot families at all, but by the more polished Episcopalians from Newport, Boston, or England, who came after 1700 & were largely communicants of King's Church. When Obadiah & Nicholas Brown were grasping for money & writing ill-spelled, ungrammatical letters to their sea-captains, gentlemen like Mr. Merritt & Dr. Checkley were reading Addison, Pope, & the Latin classicks, & indulging in polished conversation. It is the influence of Stephen Hopkins & a few like him which broke down the barriers & founded an universal & homogeneous social fabric of taste, learning, & accomplished living.

> Yr aff: Nephew & obt Servt
> H P L

P.S. There is no especial diary matter to record since yesterday. I've been indoors reading & writing, & hope to get some stories copied for Weird Tales.

[On envelope:]
Since sealing this I have received from young Talman a set of 3 pictures of the house at the corner of Angell & Benefit which he painted in pastel crayon last year. One of them has been in a School of Design exhibit, though to me they all look pretty amateurish. Still—they're Providence!

Just received notice of next Blue Pencil meeting, held at the Adams residence Sept. 26, in Plainfield, N.J. Some railway fare! Guess I'll risk offending 'em & not go!

P.S. Well I'll be hanged! Loveman just called up & wanted to spend the evening in discussion! But I wouldn't give up the library, & told him to come along if he wanted to. His own fault if he's bored!

[P.]P.S.—Diary extended through Tuesday the 15th

Read up some on old Paris to answer things in Galpinius' letter—rested on couch—up again & wrote letters—and am now going down to library to read "Providence in Colonial Times". I shall then return & write some more—which will finish Tuesday wholly. New diary will start with the morning of Wednesday the 16th.

will get minestrone dinner at the Milan

Talman leaves for Prov. this week—I'm suggesting that he call on you.

[P.P.]P.S. Loveman has just sent me a poem based on that "Old Mill" which we visited Sunday!

*Notes*

1. A nationwide coal strike organized by the United Mine Workers lasted from September 1925 to February 1926.

2. These were features that HPL had constructed in a lot next to 454 Angell St. that he used as a playground. See HPL to the Gallomo, 3 September 1920; *Letters to Alfred Galpin* 93–95.

3. *The Three Impostors* is an episodic novel by Arthur Machen.

[126]    [ALS] [HPL to LDC]

Friday Morning
Septr. 18, 1925

My dear Daughter Lillian:—

Again I will take my pen in hand to bring my diary down to date before plunging into some story work. The last entry was Tuesday evening, when Loveman telephoned just as I was going to the library, wishing to come over & discuss matters in general. Now that he has quarrelled with Kirk & developed a restrained coolness toward his present friend-employer Kamin, (Kirk's former partner—whom he leaves on Monday to take a cataloguing job with Dauber & Pine, rival booksellers on the same street; the Brentano prospect having fallen through) he is inclined to vent his overdeveloped instinct of gregariousness upon me, which would rather disrupt my own programme & inner life if I permitted it to the fullest extent. But I am maintaining my independence as much as politely possible, & on this occasion told him that I was going to the library—so that if he wished to see me he would have to come along! And so he did, asking me to stop for him en route at his shop. Having thus met, we proceeded to my favourite Milan for dinner, & thence crossed over to the library. Turning Loveman loose in the outer rooms, I now entered my favourite 328 (the American genealogy & history room) & obtained "Providence in Colonial Times", reading a couple of chapters which brought me well down into the 18th century. I noted with amusement the Congregational secession movement which founded the branch now adhering to the Round Top church. In 1742 the New Light movement split the congregation of Rev. Thos: Cotton, whose church was on the site of the present Superior Court House, & caused one of the dissenting elders, an ignorant carpenter, son of a blacksmith, named Joseph Snow, to establish a church on a site once thought of for the mother church—on land lately bought from Zechariah Mathewson far across the Great Bridge on the Plainfield road. Here the new edifice was built, & here Snow preached with more volume than scholarship—it being said that he could be heard of a Sunday by the idlers & fishermen on the Bridge & the Market-Parade. But whatever his limitations, he was a good business man, & dabbled very profitably in real estate around his church, so that houses began to spring up thickly on the West Side. Acquiring most of the Mathewson estate, he had the foresight to link it with the Bridge by a new straight highway across the salt marsh & Muddy Ford, raising the needed money by a lottery & calling the new road (or shell & gravel causeway) Back St. (a common name applied five years later to the road on the hill—Benefit St.) This *original* Back Street, prospering beyond Elder Snow's wildest dreams, is our Westminster St. of today. The original Congregational church, oddly enough, proved in the end more unorthodox than the seceding church of Elder Snow; for whereas the latter became the Beneficent Congregational,—still nominally Trinitarian, tho' the Rev. Asbury Krom[1] may think his own thoughts—the mother congregation turned Unitarian, & after a move southward along Benefit is now prospering in its 1814 edifice under the Rev. Augustus M. Lord. This original church was founded by the gifts of citizens & other Congregational churches—notably one in *Marblehead*. When it was built, in 1728, at a point half way up Rosemary-Lane, the name of this narrow passage was changed to Presbyterian-Lane, (Presbyterian being synonymous with Congregational in those days) a title which it bore till it was widened after 1770 & renamed College-Street. The educational notes in the book are interesting—& Whipple descendants will be pleased to see that the best school in town was Whipple Hall, in the North End, a one-story brick building erected 1768 with hipped roof & belfry. I also got a date I had been unable to get before—that of the building of the *original* colony-house—where Stephen Hopkins kept the publick library he founded—which burned down in 1758. It was 1732. This ill-fated structure was in Gaol Lane opposite Shakespear's Head; but the *spot* was certainly no unlucky one, since the next building erected there—the schoolhouse of 1769—is still firmly standing with every prospect of a long life before it! When the gong announced the library's closing at ten, I picked up Loveman at the door & we proceeded to the subway & our respective homes, stopping at the Automat for coffee & ice-cream. I stayed up, reading on architecture since I found it impossible to write. About 11 the telephone rang to announce S H's arrival in town for the very briefest of trips—return being at 1 p.m. the next day—& I proceeded to change into my good suit & shoes (& newly blocked felt hat) to meet her at Budry's Restaurant in 50th St—which A E P G will remember. The dinner was excellent, & after it S H attended to some business whilst I went down to 14th St. to see Kirk & tell him I would not be at the evening meeting—since it seemed most proper to devote the day to S H, it being her only one here this month. I found Kirk busy with arranging, whilst niggers unloaded vast stocks of new books from a dray. The place was in the wildest disorder, but held promises of better things. And more—the proprietor had just indulged in the luxury of an assistant! This new employe was none other than our poor old pal Arthur Leeds, who had approached Kirk in desperation a couple of days before, asking for a loan which would keep him from being turned out of his room for non-payment—an event to happen that very night. Kirk, knowing that a "loan" to Leeds is the equivalent of a gift, was about to bid farewell to sixteen dollars when it occurred to him that he might be able to use an office-boy in his new enterprise—somebody to answer the telephone & receive goods whilst he himself is out on buying expeditions. Accordingly he offered Leeds the job at a pittance of a salary—just enough to keep him his hotel room & get his meals until he finds something better. (He had been unable to get the Capitol Book Store job which he had in sight.) Leeds jumped at the chance, & was very much in evidence when I called. Giving Kirk the matter I had meant to present to the meeting—Mortonius' crossword puzzles, Galpinius' letter & cards, &c. &c.—I entrusted to him my sincerest regrets for the evening, & withdrew as the time approached for me to meet S H at 5th Ave. & 57th St. I'll enclose his new business cards—the large one for dealers from whom he wishes to buy, & the small one for the publick to whom he wishes to sell. He certainly believes in the roughness! Having duly met S H, I accompanied her on a walk toward Times Square, in which we studied theatre facades with a view to the evening's entertainment. We at length chose the new *weird* cinema, "The Phantom of the Opera", for which we obtained 1st Balcony tickets.[2] This has been extensively advertised, & I knew it must be good. We now proceeded to the Grand Central to get S H's valise, checked it at the Hotel Astor near the theatre, & walked some more before the opening of the performance at 8:30. Then came the cinema (ticket stub enclosed)—& what a spectacle it was!! It was about a *presence* haunting the great Paris opera house—a Second-Empire (i.e., mid-Victorian) structure built by the architect Charles Garnier on a site honeycom[b]ed with mediaeval vaults—but developed so slowly that I actually fell asleep several times during the first part. Then the second part began—horror lifted its grisly visage—& I could not have been made drowsy by all the opiates under heaven! Ugh!!! The *face* that was revealed when the mask was pulled off . . . . . & the nameless legion of *things* that cloudily appeared beside & behind the owner of that face when the mob chased him into the river at the last! You *must* see it if it comes to Providence. That face is the one definitive triumph of the art of makeup—nothing so horrible has ever existed before, save unexpressed in the brain of such an one as Clark Ashton Smith. At 10:30 it was over, & having obtained the luggage at the Astor, we proceeded to the St. Regis (where you & I dined so often) for supper. I ordered Welsh rarebit, hoping it might coöperate with the terror-cinema & give me a nightmare of literary value[3]—though it didn't. At length we took the subway for 169, but found on quitting the station that a brisk rain had set in. S H had an umbrella, so leaving her in the station I took it & obtained a taxicab, in which we both rode the few though potentially soaking blocks to the door of this humble abode. Once arrived, I wrote some & eventually retired, sleeping so soundly that I was only semi-conscious when S H arose & left for down town errands & Cleveland. At 4 p.m. I was up & about, & examined with delight an immense packet of postcards which The Boy sent from Paris. Most of them were of Notre Dame & the Hôtel de Cluny—the latter a mediaeval monastery now transformed to a museum. I at once proceeded to pen him my thanks. At 8:00 p.m. Loveman came over—I shall have to get an alcove light & be "out" evenings as I was last spring if I expect to write uninterruptedly—& at 9:00 we issued forth for dinner at John's & a nocturnal walk. The walk was down Broadway, Brooklyn, from the Gates Ave. car line (which we took) to & across the Williamsburg Bridge, & thence to the James Monroe house, which I had just found in the Bulletin to have been saved at the last moment, instead of demolished as Kleiner reported. (See enclosed) As we saw it, it was raised on piles preparatory to its removal to the parklike space provided for it; & we pickt up small souvenirs in the form of brick fragments from the foundation. I enclose one as a possible object of interest. Loveman now took the subway home, whilst I prolonged my walk in my favourite state of solitude. Proceeding up to Astor Place, I viewed the colonial oasis of St. Marks-in-the-Bouwerie, & kept on to Stuyvesant Square, where the decaying old mansions & Quaker Meeting-house look pensively upon an iron-railed enclosure, grass-plot, & fountain once every inch as select as Gramercy Park. Here I paused to write, & completed a letter to John Russell, who had just sent me three splendid postcards of gabled Tudor houses in Ipswich, England. At 2 a.m. I rose for more walking, ambled through Gramercy Park up Lexington Ave. to 42nd St, & crossed to Times Square for the homeward subway—arriving here at 4:00. Since then I have been writing, & I'm doubtful about what I'll do today. I may stay home & type, or I may go out to the park & write on a bench. It's sunny, tho' not as warm as I'd like it to be. And if anybody calls me on the telephone, confound it, I'm out anyhow! Sunday Loveman wants me to guide him around antique Elizabethtown, which I've agreed to do; but until then I mean to keep my time my own! And so it goes. Now I'm going downstairs for the morning mail—fervently praying I'll find nothing which will demand technical or extended attention. Just now I'm working on the tomb story whose plot I developed from a germ supplied by honest old Smithy of the Tryout. More later.

Yr aff Nephew & obt Servt<br>
H P L

P.S. Found the enclosed letter from Sonny, enclosing another writing advertisement (which I'll answer) & asking me if I have tomorrow free. I guess I'll admit this one additional encroachment, for unlike everybody else, The Child always has something actual to say.

## Notes

1. Asbury Krom (1880–?), pastor of the Beneficent Congregational Church.

2. *The Phantom of the Opera* (Universal, 1925), directed by Rupert Julian; starring Lon Chaney, Mary Philbin, and Norman Kerry. Based on the novel by Gaston Leroux.

3. The notion that one will have nightmares after eating Welsh rarebit late at night is of long standing. HPL may be alluding specifically to the newspaper comic strip by American cartoonist Winsor McCay (1869–1934), *Dream of the Rarebit Fiend,* begun in September 1904. Its recurring theme was that a character had a nightmare or other bizarre dream, usually after eating Welsh rarebit.

[127]    [ALS] [HPL to LDC]

169 Clinton St.,<br>
Brooklyn, N.Y.,<br>
Friday Evening<br>
Septr. 18, 1925.

My dear daughter Lillian:—

Your epistle arrived after the sealing of the one which you will receive simultaneously with this, so I'll start a fresh one rather than disturb the serenity of the James Monroe brick. The diary has not much to add—I didn't go out, but rested on the couch instead, & shall probably not go out till I start for Sonny's tomorrow. A telephone call just (6 p.m.) came from that rascal Henneberger, who is in town again for over a week. He wanted to make an appointment for lunch, but I told him that tomorrow & Sunday are taken. He then said he'd call me up again later. I shall meet him, & see if there's any hope of getting the $40.00 he has owed me for over a year. There is no fathoming a queer duck of his type—all I know is that I shall never do any more work for him except on a strictly cash-in-advance basis! The poor fish is in a playful mood this evening, apparently—he announced himself over the wire as "the shade of Edgar Allan Poe"—but I recognised his slap-dash mumbling accent at once. It'll be curious to see him, but if he has any more magazine schemes he can take them elsewhere.

Glad you liked the Newburgh views & Greenwich cards—no, they weren't especially expensive, & I'll send the later Greenwich cards as soon as they're issued. I must see Newburgh alone, when I can explore at will, although it'll require diplomacy to manage it, since Loveman said he wanted to accompany me when I made the trip. He is too easily exhausted to make a good explorer—when I study a town in limited time I must be free to walk interminably. No—A E P G didn't send the Northfield menu, but instead recommended some N.Y. restaurants of which she heard from fellow-guests. I'll investigate them in due time, though I believe I've already discovered the dietetic gems best suited to one of my purse—John's in Brooklyn, & the Milan & Automat in Manhattan.

I didn't see the *Times* for Septr. 6, but will undoubtedly read much of this Solomonic temple later on—besides seeing it next year in Philadelphia, as you must also. That exposition will be a notable thing, & I mean to drink my fill of it. I hope, though, they won't move the Longfellow house from Portland as threatened. That would be an inexcusable incongruity! As to Solomon's temple,—any reconstruction must of necessity be highly conjectural, since the Biblical description is so ambiguous that different architects draw widely different conclusions. An excellent reduced model is to be found in the Semitic Museum of Harvard—a thing analogous to the models of the Karnak temple, Parthenon, & Pantheon which I shewed you in the Metropolitan Museum here.

I didn't see the Old 5th Ave. article, but have doubtless seen many similar things elsewhere. I note in the Bulletin that the 100th anniversary of 42nd St. is now to be observed—in which I ought to join, since 42nd St is the site of the publick library where I discovered "Providence in Colonial Times!" I *did* see the Times of the 13th, as you know, & put several cuttings in circulation. Don't bother to send Gilboa back—one can't keep *everything!* Yes—I recall your sending the article on the planner of the N.Y. water system—a marvellous planner, yet ruthless in wiping out whole villages of real people to keep alive the stinking mongrel vermin of this chaotic metropolitan mess! As for this Prof. Charles Richet—he is an odd character. A sincere scientific spirit, without doubt, but with a vein of credulity which has led him to countenance spiritualistic notions & become a sort of French counterpart of poor old Sir Oliver Lodge.[1] Yes—I saw the *American Mercury* at Kirk's & read the Bierce article. Ambrose was an odd egg, but he certainly did write some potent & unforgettable tales!

A hitch seems to be developing in the publication of the Loveman book, (as Sonny says, nothing ever comes of anything!) but all hope is not yet abandoned. I am too old & cynical & world-weary to be interested in books of my junk—I wouldn't go to the bother of typing the stuff unless I knew it would bring financial returns. The Grecian lamp reposes on my museum shelf & lends a very distinctive touch to the atmosphere. Shortly I shall base a tale upon it, in which horror & phantasy will mix in equal proportions. The Blue Book store in 42nd St. closed last week, & I have not as yet found any successor. Henceforward, I fancy, one will have to return to the old method of ordering the volumes directly from the Haldeman-Julius plant in Kansas. This new vegetable refectory in Washington St. must be quite an establishment—it is well that a varied taste is so broadly supplied. You certainly have a discriminating & Epicurean menu—though I read of the piscine items without envy. My taste has become so prodigiously Italianated that I never order anything but spaghetti & minestrone except when those are not to be had—& they really contain an almost ideal balance of active nutritive elements, considering the wheaten base of spaghetti, the abundant vitamines in tomato sauce, the assorted vegetables in minestrone, & the profusion of powdered cheese common to both. My most universal dessert, when I get any, is vanilla ice cream, which surpasses anything else of reasonable price. I do, however, often indulge in huckleberry pie when that appealing commodity is procurable. I'm afraid its season is beginning to wane now.

I shall have to be thinking about an oil heater next month or later. I know they are very effective, for the one lent by Mrs. Burns kept me alive through the night preceding that memorable eclipse morning! Here's hoping that you encounter no frigidity yourself—get a heater if you do. As for my alcove light—of course the trouble is in the fixture, else I would have bought a new bulb & been done with it aeons ago. The thing never was right, but a man fixed it up provisionally when I came—& now it has gone wholly to the devil. Two minute pieces of brass have dropped out—& in general, the thing has gone far beyond the stage of easy or amateur repair. It'll take a man from the lighting company, & I'll have to get one soon—especially if I am to use the alcove in being "out" evenings when well-meaning company would interrupt my activities. I've only renewed one bulb—my desk light—since I've been here. Of course I did it myself, for the feeble bulbs Mrs. B. furnishes are wholly unfit to read by. Kirk & I both had to use our own bulbs in setting up housekeeping. Yes—you spelled *Watt* right. It is a term taken directly from a man's name.

I'd like to see that Maltese kittie you mention. Last night I stroked the most delightful Maltese imaginable in front of the James Monroe house—he was about half-grown, & purred & arched his back in a manner truly captivating. He seemed impressed with the antiquity & sanctity of his surroundings. Then on the homeward trip I saw a magnificent little black & white boy by the subway entrance. Kirk is going to keep a kitty-cat in his new quarters, & has already picked out his companion—a tiny black fellow with a little white, now too young to leave his foster-mother, but to be delivered as soon as sufficiently grown. Needless to say, I am awaiting his advent with the keenest expectancy—he is an orphaned waif, who strayed into Kirk's favourite Downing St. restaurant just at the time when the old lady cat there was nursing her own tiger brood. Madam Tabitha, in a generous mood, added the forlorn mite to her household without the least hesitation; & there he now abides, awaiting the time when his Grandpa Georgius will be able to bear him away. Those Downing St. Italians cherish their felidae with an almost Egyptian tenderness which warms the heart! No kitten has ever been killed in that restaurant, but with each new brood a canvass of patrons is made with a view to providing homes. And not only have the homes been always forthcoming, but at one time the two kittens which the proprietor kept were *stolen*—one finding his way back, (well-nourished & evidently after a stay with kindly thieves) but the other remaining to this day a mourned & unsolved mystery.

Did you see the article in the Bulletin (one of Ashmun Brown's series) on the exiled Rhode-Island loyalists who went to New Brunswick in 1783? If not, I will lend you my cutting; for one ought not to miss it. It shews that the Revolution was by no means an unanimous movement of one territory against another, but a Civil War in the fullest sense of the term, with neighbourhoods & families tragically divided. The best people in Rhode-Island, as elsewhere, were loyal to His Majesty's rightful government, (as they would be loyal today to the U.S. government if New England tried to revolt & secede) & at the close of the war migrated en masse either to England or to Canada, where some Yankees were already settled. Newport & Narragansett were especially well represented in these migrations, since culture in those parts was considerable, & attachment to our proper Sovereign & Parliament correspondingly deep. The churchyard at St. John's, N.B., is full of tombs with Rhode-Island names—but you've probably seen this already in the paper.

Speaking of the motherland—I can't resist shewing you the alluring Ipswich (England) cards which Russell sent me. Please return them—or send them to A E P G with instructions that she return them. You can easily see in these ancient Tudor houses the architectural spirit which dictated the first wave of building in New England. Wolsey's birthplace & Salem's House of the Seven Gables are blood brothers, & although they are all gone now, we once had long rows of them on our own Towne St. In such an abode honest Pardon Tillinghast dwelt, & in such good Mr. Williams departed this life for a glorious immortality. There are few indeed remaining in New England, though mother Britain still teems with them. One of ours, oddly enough, is in *Ipswich*, Massachusetts. You'll recall the room taken from it for the Metropolitan Museum's American Wing. Yes—& there's another such gabled house in the Massachusetts Ipswich—a *Whipple* house into the bargain! I wish I could get postcards of these Massachusetts houses to send Russell in exchange for the views of *his* Ipswich. I've seen the Whipple house from the train betwixt Salem & Newburyport, but never stopped off as I wish I had. I'd love to inspect the British Ipswich, too! But I must desist, & save further topics for my answer to the second letter which you say you are about to write. This ends the diary for Friday, September 18th, 1925.

   Yr aff Nephew & obt Servt

    H P L

## Notes

1. Charles Richet (1850–1935), French physiologist who won the Nobel Prize in 1913, but who later became interested in spiritualism and coined the term "ectoplasm." Sir Oliver Lodge (1851–1940), British physicist who became attracted to psychic phenomena and spiritualism.

[128]    [ALS] [HPL to LDC]

Wednesday Afternoon
Septr. 23, 1925
Finish'd Thursday Morning—Septr. 24

My dear daughter Lillian:—

I received your delightful note, & will take my pen in hand to reply, even tho' I may have to leave for the meeting before I get very far. Let me see—I last wrote Friday night, after finishing my new story "In the Vault" (based on old Tryout's idea) & receiving a telephone call from Henneberger, whom I have not yet seen. I stayed up, & the next day went to Sonny's for lunch; holding with him a very doleful session on the financial crisis which has overtaken the Alfredus-Child, & of which we had been simultaneously apprised by a series of pensive epistles that very morning. It seems that unless a miracle occurs, our young wonder will have to quit the delights of Paris & forfeit all the musical advantages his present position there gives him—& this just as he had moved to those delightfully mediaeval monastic quarters in the Rue St. Jacques, with flagstone floor, cement walls, & a section of a great stone arch for a roof! His latest & most desperate letter dwelt on the utter necessity of his staying in Paris, & asked me to lend him (if my own finances, of which he knew nothing, permitted) from $200. to $500., to be repaid as soon as he is remuneratively occupied. Naturally I can scarcely do this, but Sonny & I are infernally sorry none the less. If he has to return at once, (by steerage, he fears, & without the railway fare to Wisconsin!) we shall try to entertain him as royally as possible in New York. He could sleep on Kirk's spare cot, & the Longs say they will be glad to have him as a table guest as long as he can arrange to stay. Loveman thinks he could arrange to contribute substantially to a fund for his carfare home to Appleton. We'll certainly be monstrous glad to see the sassy little divvle, though we mourn the tragick interruption of the Parisian studies upon which he had so firmly set his heart. Having thus appropriately mourned, Sonny & I went down to see honest old McNeil; to whom we shewed the wealth of Parisian cards which the mail had brought us both. I'll enclose a duplicate of my favourite for you to keep—isn't that urban panorama utterly exquisite? Paris, despite the mistakes of many well-meaning but tasteless architects & city-planners, has never been unfaithful in the worship of sheer beauty; & has never allowed its lovely skyline of ethereal spires to become contaminated with the vile climbing structures of commerce. To turn from this view to the skyline of Brooklyn, whose forest of once beautiful spires is hopelessly polluted by factory tanks & tall apartment houses, is to envisage one of art's most sordid tragedies. Ugh! Sonny went home at six, but McNeil kept detaining me with an hospitality I could scarcely evade—pressing upon me his frugal supper (of Campbell's vegetable-beef soup, which I don't like & will take care never to buy for my own larder!) & not permitting me to get away till midnight. When I did break away I came directly home & wrote, retiring at 5 a.m. The next day at noon I was awaked by the knock of Loveman, who wished me to guide him about antique Elizabethtown. Getting ready as soon as possible, I duly sallied forth with him, proceeding via the Atlantic Ave. & Staten Island ferries. In Elizabethtown we took the longest ordinary sightseeing route, which includes one or two points you didn't pass last December. Pausing in both the Presbyterian (old brick church with steeple) & St. John's (Gothic church with yard of earlier date) churchyards, we obtained in the latter some fragments of red Colonial gravestone which were scattered about the ground. I have one now for a paperweight—appropriate ornament for a weird writer. It bears some chiselled letters—— *embr / er fr* & is clearly recognisable for what it is. I will enclose a much smaller & mailable specimen. At one point Loveman discovered an alley which led to a miniature rural world of grassy lanes in the middle of a city block—a sight which impressed me exceedingly. We returned via Newark, dined at John's, & dispersed about 9:30; after which I finished typing my new story ("In the Vault", which you will shortly receive through A E P G, & which is to be returned to me) & did some writing, resting about 6 a.m. At two that afternoon—Monday—I was awaked by the knock of Sonny-Child*, who came to have Grandpa guide him to the Old Mill. This the Old Gentleman was glad to do, & we at once took the Fulton St. elevated—the Child reading "In the Vault" en route, & expressing his mature approval. At Crescent St. we changed to an omnibus atrociously crowded with small schoolchildren, & were soon at the fascinating seacoast village described in my former epistle. It was exactly the same, as it always is, & we revelled in each mark of quaintness from the ships' figureheads above the cottage doors to the delectable array of small kitty-cats playing in the sun beside the sea. Belknap was enraptured by the swarms of fiddler crabs darting in & out of their holes in the mud flats exposed by the tide, & took one home in a cigarette box as a reminder of his old naturalist days, when he collected beetles & butterflies. He aims to preserve the crab in alcohol & eventually give it to Mortonius for his museum. At length bidding a reluctant farewell to these enchanted scenes—& pausing

---

*minus, thank Heaven, that attempted moustache, tho' he says the omission is merely temporary.

for a cherry drink in a colonial shop with low ceilings, exposed beams, & small-paned windows—we took the omnibus for the Lexington Ave. elevated, there taking a subway—Williamsburg Bridge B.M.T. train & changing at Canal St. for Times Square. From this point Sonny went directly home, whilst I crossed over to the library to read "Providence in Colonial Times", the end of which I am now approaching. When the library closed at ten I proceeded to the Automat for dinner—the one high up in Times Square at 47th St., which alone has a certain potato salad (10¢) whereof I have become exceeding fond—& thence home to type "He" (which I enclose herewith, asking you to send it on to A E P G & tell her to return it to me) & write letters. I have gathered together all the material I must copy for Wright, (who has, by the way, rejected "The Shunned House" as beginning too gradually, though he extends it high personal praise) & will try to get some of this beastly typing done in the next few days. Since then I have done nothing but type & write— for correspondence piles up discouragingly. It is now Wednesday evening, & I am about to leave for the gang meeting at McNeil's. This will probably be a dull affair, for Belknap won't be there—although he will be host for the next (Leeds) meeting. The weather is now distressingly cold—I have on my thick wrap over vest & trousers. When I go out I don't know what I'll do, since I've no thick suit, & an overcoat would look devilish odd. I guess I'll shiver & bear it! I shall dine on minestrone at the Milan tonight. And so I leave—to resume again as soon as I return, at which time the diary will continue.

Thursday 1. a.m.

Dull affair? Holy Pete, but the term is too mild! Nobody was there but Kleiner & our host, & I never saw an evening drag so before. I had not time to stop at the Milan, but that proved just as well; since Kleiner handed me two large cans of baked beans which Mortonius had asked him to deliver. These are of a special brand made in Melrose, Mass., & not sold outside New-England, & have the peculiar tang of New-England cookery which all other beans lack. Mortonius orders them from the factory & continually keeps a stock on hand; & recently I told him to order me two cans as a sample. On this occasion, after a suitable period of pointless discussion, I suggested that our host add a can of the beans to his evening's refreshment, thus affording us all an opportunity of testing Mortonius' judgment. This he did, & I found the unique delicacy very passable—having indeed an authentick Novanglian flavour not to be detected in the average canned product. They would have been better had catsup been present, but McNeil—simple soul— keeps none of these worldly, highly-spiced devices in his primitive & ascetick larder. Whether or not I shall order more of these beans, the second can will decide. The meeting dispersed at 12:00, & here I am an hour later, prepared to write till tomorrow—when I may take a trip to library & museum, & may stay home typing MSS. I'll let you know later what I did. Saturday night the

B.P.C. meets at the Adams home in Plainfield, N.J., but on account of the carfare I am not likely to attend. Next Wednesday the (Leeds) meeting is at Sonny's, & the week after that I shall entertain the McNeil meeting myself. Next Monday Loveman wants me to take the Hudson River trip again with him & "do" Newburgh thoroughly—& I shall if my purse permits. Such, then, is my diary complete to the morning of Thursday, Septr. 24, 1925.

I shall read with interest the article on Solomon's Temple—& I wonder if you are aware that we had such a thing (on a much smaller scale) in Providence once? Yes indeed—in Mr. Hacker's Aſsembly-Room, in Town-Street, in September 1764 there was on exhibition a most distinguiſh'd spectacle manufactur'd by the clever Moravian mechanicks of Germantown, in Pennsylvania, & thus advertis'd in the Providence Gazette & Country-Journal: "View of the Famous City of *Jeruſalem*, in which are Repreſented *Jeruſalem*, the *Temple of Solomon*, his Royal Throne, the noted Towers, and Hills, likewiſe the Sufferings of Our SAVIOUR from the Garden of *Gethſemane* to the Croſs on the Hill of Golgotha; an Artful Piece of Statuary, worthy to be ſeen by the Curious."[1] Thus Philadelphia, or its quaint northwestern neighbour, Germantown, has long & solid experience in the making of singular Biblical antiquities; so that we have reason to expect much of next year's performance. Good old Hacker's Hall—what vary'd events it knew! Here in 1768 the accompliſht dancing-master John Baptist Tioli taught the minuet to young Browns & Crawfords & Carringtons & Powers & Tillinghasts, & here in the following year a fluent & animated elocutionist gave a spirited reading (with songs)* of that very Beggar's-Opera[2] which we later witness'd so advantageously in Infantry-Hall. Amusements were not frequent in those days—& how naively did the thrifty burghers legislate out of town the New-York theatrical company which began performances in a quick-made wooden building in Town-St! The sheriff stopped to enjoy the performance first, then gave them their marching orders. This was in 1762, the year Morro Castle was taken. Staid old days—no wonder the West Side wanted to set up a separate township in Feby. 1770, under the name of Westminster . . . . though they compromised by merely giving the name to their main street, which Elder Joseph Snow of the New Light Presbyterian (later Beneficent Congregational = Round Top) church had cut through & built up.

Yes—I read of the death of Miss Moon, & shewed it to Loveman, who was deeply interested on account of his Civil War novel.[3] He believes he will mention her in it, though as a very subordinate character. The Canada article you read was undoubtedly the best—with the account of Rhode-Island loyalists—& it is the only one I am saving. Surely, Foster folk have lost most of their external quaintness, tho' I doubt not but what their diction & ideas may

---

*It began at 7 p.m., & admission was *half a dollar*—the Spanish dollar being even then a common local unit of currency.

retain certain delightful traces of residual rusticity. It is too bad that a wide-spread mechanical civilisation has wiped away the colourful individualities which once gave to the divers parts of the country so fresh & vary'd a charm. The Nooseneck old home day, too, must have been refreshing. I return the cutting for grandmother's red scrap-book. Wish I could have heard the Rev. John Tillinghast at one of his June meetings—& regret to say that my Columbia grandson doesn't know his Columbia grandson, since colleges these days are such vast affairs. "Yondo" was to have been sent to A E P G, but I can do that myself. Later Smith wants me to send it to Weird Tales for him. The Talman matter was also to be shewn to A E P G, tho' if you don't think it would interest her you might return it to me. It is Talman himself who wants it back, so if he calls on you, you can give it him. His address is now 256 Benefit St. So the old Bijou is gone! I didn't attend it often, for the pictures were generally old & indistinct, but its garish facade was indeed familiar to me! I think the upper part of the building was colonial, but of course was only the merest shell in latter years. I first recall it as the home of Jerome Kennedy & Co's cheap clothing store—the one that used to tack advertisements of *$9.00 all-wool suits* on all the trees, rocks, fences, & barns of the countryside. This was no progenitor of the present Kennedy's in the Barnaby building. Another theatre in a metamorphosed colonial building was the Nickel, on the site of the present Albee. The old house was raised high above the auditorium which was built in Victorian times. In my heyday this place was a burlesque show called the "Olympic"—as bad as the Westminster—but I need not add that I was not a patron. I hate to see the old places go, & welcome any news of preservation or restoration. The Slater Mill business delights me, & I wish I could inspect the place for antiquity's sake, even though my interest in textiles is closely bound to the zero-mark. I enclose a pair of cuttings on other restorations—that of the Colony-House at Newport being the more notable. This noble structure was design'd by the great Newport architect Peter Harrison, Esq., whose work was in demand all over the colonies, & who at one time was a pupil of Gibbs, (whose steeple design was taken for our 1st Baptist) & an assistant to Sir John Vanbrugh.

The limits of the former High St. would be easy to discover from any antique street directory, & such the Hist. Soc. must certainly have in abundance. Too bad the Gov. Greene house is not open to the publick. Had you not sent me its picture in Corners & Characters, I should have missed it; for my Bulletin of Aug. 31 did not come, & the supply was exhausted when I wrote. I have noticed the sketches of Miss Dyer & deem them exceedingly clever.[4] I have not, however, saved them; since my interest in *faces* is relatively slight. Should the artist turn to landscape effects, or portray the narrow streets of the quaint Italian towns which must be so familiar to her, I should at once begin a collection. No—I have bought no shoe trees, but I would have some if I had new shoes. I think my old ones must be somewhere around here. As for lights—as I have said, the trouble with my alcove affair is far within the wall fixture, & utterly unreachable by any simple means. I see in the latest Times, which Loveman brought me Sunday, that the Metropolitan Museum is about to move the old Gardner–Wentworth mansion from Portsmouth N.H. to New York, setting it up in the museum grounds. This is too much! To ruin a colonial town by taking the very houses away is as bad as ruining it through mere commercial vandalism, & I strongly hope the city of Portsmouth & state of New Hampshire will protest. With Longfellow's house captured by Philadelphia & this one by N.Y., a very dangerous precedent will be set; so that one may fear the ultimate despoiling of all lovely New England towns for the benefit of wealthy distant cities. The admiration which would snatch a lovely building from its natural setting seems to me more disastrous than no admiration at all! Great God, but when they set up the 1st Baptist Church in Times Square & the old Market House in Lincoln Park, Chicago, it will be time for me to end it all in the deep Seekonk! Still worse vandalism is planned in London; where according to a Transcript cutting sent by A E P G there is a move to tear down Adelphi Terrace, built by the brothers Adam & inhabited by Garrick & other Georgian celebrities, to make way for a vile apartment house. This is sheer felony—for Adelphi Terrace is the finest existing monument of the refined architectural style which crowned the 18th century, & which in America was upheld by such giants as Charles Bulfinch & Samuel McIntire.

I shall probably finish "Providence in Colonial Times" at my next long library session. As I peruse, I regret more & more furiously that I did not read Dr. Clark's MSS. on old Providence whilst they were accessible—the fire department one, for instance, would be very apposite in supplementing what I have just read in the Kimball book. It seems that our first fire-engine, ordered in 1754, was deliver'd in 1756 & extensively repair'd in 1758. That year the old Colony House burned down, (& with it all the books of the Providence Library [founded by Stephen Hopkins & now the Athenaeum] which were not out in the hands of borrowers) & called the attention of all to the need of better protection. In 1760 a new large engine was order'd in London, & kept at the house opposite Judge Jenckes at the Great Bridge, the smaller & older one being kept in the gangway to the south of the Baptist Meeting House. (Smith & N. Main) Fire procedure involved the whole town, all able-body'd householders being expected to keep two fire buckets, & attend each fire fully clothed & bearing the buckets. Lines—"bucket brigades"—were formed to fill the tank of the engine, & all the workers were under the superintendance of a fire warden whose badge of office was a large red speaking-trumpet. The fire district comprised the compact part of the town, & in defining it the old documents reveal some quaint & now forgotten sectional names. It seems that the section betwixt Smith & Orms St. was (in 1760) call'd "Charlestown", whilst the Turk's Head region—Weybosset Point—was known simply as "The Point". The West Side was stridently parvenu but progressive, & as early as 1754 had a schoolhouse at the corner of Mathewson & Chapel Sts. Another thing I got straight was the descent of the Browns from Pardon Tillinghast. It seems that Pardon's daughter Mercy married Nicholas Power*, & that her daughter Hope Power married James Brown the younger, by him becoming mother of Capt. James, Nicholas, John, Joseph, & Moses Brown. Thus the famous brothers Brown were Pardon Tillinghast's great-grandchildren. I found a quaint picture of Moses Brown in his old age, & find that he dressed in the full Quaker fashion. Possibly you have seen it, but in case you haven't I'll append a rough sketch. He certainly had a good share of chin—I wonder if any of the surviving Browns in any way resemble him! This book also contains much romantick data on the Hopkins family & their bold seafaring ex-

ploits, & bluff Abraham Whipple figures quite extensively in the chronicle of local doings. You certainly ought to read this book, & I sincerely hope it's in the publick library. Which reminds me that I can't find here a book I want very much—Augustus Hoppin's "Memories of Auton House"—tho' I shall look for it in the Brooklyn library. Another thing I want to read is the diary of the Rev. Ezra Stiles of Newport—full of intimate colonial data. Stiles was later president of Yale.

I shall, I think, see "The Lost World" two weeks hence, for it is coming to the Strand at fairly popular prices.[5] This palaeontological phantasy charmed me as a story some fifteen or more years ago, & I have wanted to see it ever since it was presented as a cinema. What a writer Doyle was before he went to seed as a dupe of spirit-mediums! Lost worlds have always been a favourite theme of mine, & I shall treat of them more than once before I lay down my fictional pen for ever. The novelette I have mapped out, & which will probably be the next thing I shall write, deals largely with strange vestiges of a past primordial & horrible beyond expression. To me there is no one subject in literature so fascinating as chronological disarrangement—the conquest of time & Nature, & the momentary bringing together of two ages infinities apart.

Another thing I plan is a tale of other planets—perhaps of other universes. Letters from readers to the editor of *Weird Tales* shew a great demand for this sort of narrative, & applaud with an amusing lack of discrimination the unbelievably puerile ravings of an author who signs himself "Nictzin Dyalhis", & whose utter ignorance of astronomy is equalled only by his fatuous determination to write about nothing else.[6] When I get worked up to the mood, I mean to do some interplanetary stuff, but mine shall not violate any

---

*I suppose this Power is an ancestor of Mrs. Whitman, the poetess, whose father was also named Nicholas Power.

known fact or law of celestial science as known at the present time. I am slow in getting to these things, but the gradual winding up of other matters is liberating me little by little for work. Bad as my pile of correspondence is, it isn't as bad as formerly; & the United burthen is definitely off my shoulders. Now I must get my old stories copied off for *Weird Tales*, & then I'll feel free to go ahead. Did I say that I'd just sent Wright a large batch to look over? Most of them he won't want, because they are exceedingly fantastic; but a few may take his eye. They are:

| | |
|---|---|
| The Doom that came to Sarnath | Nyarlathotep |
| The Cats of Ulthar | The Tree |
| The Terrible Old Man | The White Ship |
| The Quest of Iranon | Celephaïs |
| He | The Other Gods |

Those I shall presently type are "Beyond the Wall of Sleep", "From Beyond", "The Horror at Red Hook", & "Polaris". And I shall send the newly-typed "In the Vault" as soon as you & A E P G have read it. A E P G, as I have said, will shortly send it to you.[7]

But I will close for the present, resuming the chronicle in due time. I hope you like this cooler weather—it ought to please somebody to compensate for the way it knocks me out! With every exprefsion of efteem, believe me, Madam,

Yr most aff Nephew & obt Servt<br>H P L

[On envelope:]

*Later*

Telephone call from Sonny—he's coming over to read Grandpa a story of his which Detective Tales returned after having accepted it—the magazine is about to fail. Thank heaven, Weird Tales is on a better basis!

¶                                                  *2 p.m.*

Sonny has arrived, & his story is splendidly clever! That child will "arrive" yet!

¶

And now—3:30—we are going out to call on Kirk.

## Notes

1. Cited verbatim in *The Case of Charles Dexter Ward* (*CF* 2.244).

2. John Gay (1685–1732), *The Beggar's Opera* (1728), a satirical ballad opera.

3. Virginia Bethel "Ginnie" Moon (1844–1925), a Confederate spy during the Civil War. She died on 11 September 1925.

4. Nancy Dyer (1903–1979), daughter of H. Anthony Dyer and a painter and sculptor in her own right.

5. *The Lost World* (First National Pictures, 1925), directed by Harry O. Hoyt; starring Bessie Love, Lewis Stone, and Wallace Beery. Based on the novel by Sir Arthur Conan Doyle. The film (about dinosaurs roaming the jungles of present-day South America) was a landmark in the use of special effects.

6. Nictzin Dyalhis (1879?–1942) published eight stories in *WT* between 1925 and 1940.

7. Of the stories listed here, "The Doom That Came to Sarnath," "Nyarlathotep," "The Tree," "The Quest of Iranon," "Celephaïs," "The Other Gods," "Beyond the Wall of Sleep," "From Beyond," and "Polaris" were rejected by *WT,* although nearly all of them were published after HPL's death.


[129]    [ALS] [HPL to LDC]

Sunday Morning—

Septr. 27, 1925

My dear Daughter Lillian:—

Having (as I hope) got ahead of me some little time without engagements, I take my pen in hand to bring my diary down to date. I shall *not* be making the Newburgh trip tomorrow, since Loveman finds that his new position will occupy him—therefore I am as free as correspondence will allow, for whatever reading or writing the cold weather will permit me to indulge in. Autumn has sapped at the root of my activity, & I am having to use the electrick stove, come what may of it! An oil heater is, I fear, an imminent necessity; so that when I send my next *Weird Tales* cheque to A E P G for cashing, I fancy I shall have to ask her for ten dollars of it in cash at once, to buy me the device itself, & a good supply of fuel. It will, of course, be useful wherever the winds of fortune may in future waft me—& being independent of household power connexions, will be happily immune from controversies with practical-minded landladies. I have heard that the "Perfection" brand, manufactured by the Standard Oil Co., is the best & most effective; though perhaps not the cheapest in initial cost. My present household costume is (a) vest & trousers, plus (b) thick wrap, plus (c) heavy blanket. This seems more effective than full suit & overcoat, tho' I shall further experiment with both before deciding on an official regalia. Ugh, but cold weather is hades!!

As for my diary—I last writ you of my departure with Little Belknap on Thursday afternoon to call on Kirk. He was out, so we went over to Fourth Avenue to see Loveman in his new job. Here our guest was in—& we found him in full charge of the small "annex" store which the firm of Dauber & Pine has opened a few doors north of their main establishment. He seemed well contented, & asked me to guide him on a sightseeing trip the following Saturday night—a thing I readily agreed to do, since it forms an easy way of repaying in part his many gifts & favours to me. He enjoys exploration acutely, yet has not the initiative to look up points of interest for himself—hence is keenly grateful to anyone who will plan & lead tours for him. Having paid him our respects, Sonny & I walked north to Madison Square to look at overcoats for the Child—who had admired one in a shop window there. A closer look did not disillusion him, & I rather think he will invest when he has the cash in hand. It is a much more youthful garment than his old Grandpa would be seen in! Belknap now took an omnibus home, whilst the Old Gentleman kept on walking toward the Publick Library. Having reacht that haven, I proceeded to the lair of the Kimball book, & was soon in the blessed refuge of Old Providence. This time I finished the volume & passed on to others of kindred subject—& what a wealth was at my command! The library does not, however, (& neither does the Bklyn lib., confound it!) have Augustus Hoppin's "Memories of Auton House" or Rev. Ezra Stiles [*sic*] colonial diary. The chiefest treasure I unearth'd, and something which brought before me with absolute & minute authenticity the ancient town of my heart, was a series of maps by Henry R. Chace, shewing in detail *every* street, road, & house in Providence at four different periods—1650, 1765, 1770, & 1798—as compil'd from the most fundamental legal & governmental documents & collated with the most approv'd historical accounts.[1] The value of these maps is scarcely to be overestimated, & they will certainly play a great part in whatever I may in future write upon the subject. The author indeed deserves well of his fellow-Rhodinsularians—I suppose he is not a relative of Dr. Clark, since he spells his name *Chace*. Most of his work seems to have been accomplisht betwixt 1904 & 1914—fruitful decade! Another thing I found was the maundering in prose & verse of that worthy Six-Principle Baptist James Brown the Elder, grandson of Chad Brown & grandfather of the immortal brothers Nicholas, John, Joseph & Moses. His outpourings were undilutedly theological, & I will append a stanza of his verse with the original spelling, punctuation, & capitalisation:

> "Therefore I pray you bee ſo kind
> in theſe fu lines profeed
> and ſumthing in them you ſhall find
> thats worth your whiel to reed."

In the Kimball book I found much concerning our early shopkeepers & their signs; the latter being of infinite quaintness, & adding a delicious touch of variety to the facades along the Town Street. In the North the Brazen Lion sway'd nobly in the wind that blew o'er Constitution Hill, whilst not far off the Sign of the Boot proclaim'd the neat cordwainer's* shop of Robert Perri-

---

*a curiously derived old word meaning *shoemaker.* It comes from the Spanish town of *Cordova,* which yielded the finest shoe leather.

go. Capt. Joseph Olney's hardware & rum shop had the Sign of the Golden Ball, (later transferr'd to the new tavern which still survives as the Mansion House) & Nathaniel Balch (who was a young blood of the Moses Brown, Jabez Bowen, & Jonathan Clarke set) kept "stoneware & decanters, pipes, pepper, spices, &c., cheshire cheese, also hats, flour, chocolate, also a few lottery tickets" at the Sign of the Hat. Clark & Nightingale (the latter, builder of Benefit St. house now known as John Carter Brown ho.) kept stationery at the Sign of the Frying-Pan & Fish, whilst Knight Dexter (father of the Ebenezer who still keeps our attorneys busy[)] retail'd dry goods at the Sign of the Boy & Book. The Gladding Bunch of Grapes was on hand, as was the Sign of the Elephant at which James Green kept brassware, rum, flax, indigo, & tea. The boys painted out the tea legend on Green's sign with lampblack when the rebels burnt the offending herb in the Market-Parade before the new Market House. John & William Russell kept dry goods at the Sign of the Golden Eagle, whilst their younger brother Jonathan on the West Side (in Deacon Snow's section) had a grocery-store at the Sign of the Black Boy. Old Jabez Bowen (young Jabez's father) had an apothecary shop at the Sign of the Unicorn & Mortar, & Smith & Sabin—dry-goods, sported the Sultan's Head—colourful old days; would that they might return! Just before the revolution the tone of the colony & the town attain'd a new smartness, & old institutions receiv'd new names. Towne St. began to be call'd Main St., & in certain parts, Cheapside; whilst Olney's Tavern (where the Boston Stage stopt till the new Golden Ball supplanted it) assum'd the title of the Crown Coffee House. The coming of the college with its learned professors, sprightly students, & enlivening ceremonials & processions was a very salutary influence. Presbyterian-Lane, once Rosemary-Lane, was widen'd & call'd College-Street; & up & down its precipitous length mov'd a very cultivated train, of whom one must first mention the august *Praeses*—Rev^d. James Manning, who wore a fine white wig "of the largest dimensions in the country." His house is still standing—& curst be the School of Design if it tears it down! [Which reminds me—yesterday I awak'd muttering over & over again the phrase "Save the Arcade—save the Arcade—save the Arcade—&c.", though I did not recall the dream which gave rise to the utterance.] In the last chapter of the Kimball book I learnt of the spectre which haunts the Halsey Mansion in Prospect St. It is a *thing* which plays the piano during the sinister small hours . . . . & there is a bloodstain on the floor which cannot be washt out. Niggers from the neighbouring darktown will not pass the place after dark—or at least, would not at one time. Ask Delilah about it. Of the supposed cause of this haunting—the identity of the murder'd person & the spectral pianist—Mifs Kimball says nothing; tho' no doubt deeper investigation would find the appropriate legend in local folklore. This was the home of wild young Tom Halsey, who kept live terrapins in his cellar. And oh—by the way—I find that the Benefit St. house (sadly alter'd) undermined & occupied by the tunnel workers in 1906–7–8 was built by honest Ebenezer Knight Dexter in 1796. As for other pleasing odds & ends—Mathewson St. was originally School St., (so nam'd from the schoolhouse of 1754) & the West Side's town well was situate where it joins Broad St.—just where the comfort station is now. Broad St. extended down to Muddy Dock Bridge, (Dorrance St.) below which the name Weybosset existed as now. The compact part of the town was very rapid in extending, all that we today recognise as "downtown" being built up fully by 1800, except where later fillings were made in Cove & harbour. One interesting point would be to find when the old Towne St. began to decay & give place to Westminster as a main business thoroughfare. Personally, I think it must have been in the decade 1830–40—or more broadly the twenty years betwixt 1830 & 1850. The painting of 1824 (the Francis Read view, whose reproduction in the Hist. Soc. pamphlet I want so intensely) shews most of the houses still residential; but the coming of the Arcade (which God now save!) must have turned the tide. By the fifties we find lower Westminster *the* business street, though a residential cast seems to have persevered above Union & Mathewson till one or two decades later. Ah, me! The closing bell drove me forth from Providence to the garish terraces of Babylon at 10 p.m., & I had dinner at a new spaghetti place I discovered in 43d St.—card enclosed. Very good spaghetti, & the only place of the sort in the immediate neighbourhood open after the library's closing-time. I thence proceeded to 169, & devoted the night to reading up borrowed books—disposing of three; two of Sechrist's & one of Cook's, which I subsequently prepared for shipment back to their respective owners. Retiring in the morning, I rose late that Friday night; then doing some more reading—of local borrowed books—& retiring late. Saturday the 26th I was up at noon, read & wrote some, & did several errands. Later I typed some more of my old stories—hateful task! [And this reminds me to enclose for your perusal Wright's latest letter to me.] At 7 p.m. Loveman came to be guided about—incidentally exhibiting an excellent lyrick he had just written, to which I supply'd a title. We dined at John's, thence proceeding to the Brooklyn Publick Library to look things over. On Loveman's recommendation I drew out a volume of tales by an author of the 1890 period—one W. C. Morrow, a San Franciscan—supposed to be weird; carrying it about with me during the evening & finishing it after my return home. It was clever—but no more than that. Full of the vivid melodrama & smooth mechanics of the 'nineties, but lacking (save in one splendid case) the intimations of ultimate cosmic horrors found in Poe & Machen. After a trip to Loveman's room for changes in his costume, we set out on the subway for our chosen theatre of exploration—the upper end of Manhattan Island. Emerging at 181st st., (deepest point of the whole subway system, by the way) we struck westward toward Riverside Drive to observe the imitation mediaeval castle with its massive & towering walls—which Loveman had never before seen save from a boat. Under the slightly gibbous moon it loomed impressively up, & all hands declar'd it well worth travelling to see. Now returning inland, we struck northward along Fort Washington Ave., now spoilt with parvenu apartment houses, but with the battle ground of Washington Heights on our left, & a sheer precipice on our right, below which the lights of the upper city glimmer'd. In time we passed the old French cloister sold by George Grey Barnard to the Metropolitan Museum— noting incidentally that it is not yet open to the publick after its purchase. Farther on rose the pretentious stone castle of the late "Boss" Tweed—now housing a boys' school—& eventually the avenue descended to Broadway in a series of gentle curves. This route, indeed, was the same as that traversed by daylight last June with S H & Sonny—& by twilight in Nov. 1922 with Sonny & Mortonius. Arriv'd at Broadway, we struck north to see the Dyckman cottage by moonlight—Loveman never having seen it at all. He was vastly impressed, & will later visit it by day when he can get in. After a northward turn to see the old 1769 milestone—"12 miles from N. York",—we proceeded through the bleakly squalid streets of what was once the village of Inwood to the subway, (there an elevated) taking a southbound train for 96th St. to observe the final feature of the evening's programme—the secluded but very modern "Pomander Walk", a quaint court of imitation Elizabethan houses hidden amidst the towering garishness of parvenu apartment buildings. This artificial bit of antiquity (which Sonny first shew'd me about a year ago) was very pleasing, but not altogether convincing. Having fully survey'd it, we took the subway for Brooklyn—Loveman alighting at Clark St., & I proceeding hither, where I still am. I have now finished the Morrow book—most of which I read on the subway—& shall now try to get some writing & copying off my hands, if the cold weather will permit. A few minutes ago I set back my clocks as directed by the Evening Bulletin, so that the grey of the dawn will steal up apparently an hour earlier than it did yestermorn. And I shall notice the early twilight next evening.

I hope I'll have the next couple of days uninterrupted for work. With proper seclusion, I ought to be able to work up an atmosphere for creation— & if I do go out, it will be to quaint scenes which I can invest with *my own* imaginative overtones, undisturbed by the necessarily different impressions & mental reactions of others. Really, the only way to appreciate quaint sights is in perfect solitude. I may, if it's clear, go to Jamaica; which is only a 5¢ fare on the Brooklyn elevated, yet which is said to contain many old houses. Oddly, I have never visited any of the Long Island villages north & east of those in the Borough of Brooklyn. But I may not, after all. I have a good stock of provisions here, & if I can work, I guess I shall. If it's warm, though, I might take my composition-book to Jamaica & (if that village proves to be any good) work in the open on some bench. But probably it won't be warm, so the chances are, I'll remain right here. I'll let you know, in all probability, on the back of this epistle, exactly what I shall have decided upon. Now that summer has deserted these melancholy fields, I am keeping an ampler larder—of things that hot weather spoilt. Yesterday I obtained my favourite chocolate squares at Roulston's, & I shall restore bread & cheese very shortly. Having indulged in a fairly Epicurean diet for some time, I may be able to return to the very cheap home routine until it again bores me & becomes difficult to eat—the saving is enormous if one can keep it up!

And so it goes! Just now, before I attempt any serious labour, I think I will peruse some old-fashion'd poet on the subject of *autumn,* that I may the more gracefully reconcile myself to the rigours of an unwelcome season. By hearing the glamorous things writ by periwigg'd observers of the harvest-time, & hunter's-moon, & other various manifestations of rural English life at this time of year, I may achieve a state of mind productive of that artificial warmth which comes from enjoyment & aesthetick appreciation. I shall glance at Thomson, Bloomfield, Pope, & Somerville, nor omit any others that may occur to me. And a perusal of the Farmer's Calendar in the Old Farmer's Almanack ought to conjure up a picture of New England farmhouses & teeming barns & hilly fields lined with sheaves under the mellow harvest moon, well calculated to allay the pangs of a merely physical frigidity. More anon.

Yr aff: Nephew & obt Servt<br>H P L

[On envelope:]

Later—Sunday noon.

Gloria Dei in excelsis! It's grown *warmer!* A reprieve!!! I had lain down—dressed—to get a snatch of rest, & slept till now. Now I shall decide whether to type or take my composition-book & go to Jamaica or somewhere & write in the open. Gather ye rosebuds while ye may, says old Herrick . . . . . . . I guess I'll get one letter disposed of & see how the good weather holds out.

¶ 2 p.m.

Got my correspondence *all* done! Don't owe a letter in the world! Now if I don't get a flood of 'em tomorrow, I shall be reasonably free for fiction. And now I guess I'll start for Jamaica—too good a day to miss! More bulletins later—& if Jamaica has any good post cards, I'll see that you & A E P G are supply'd. Heaven preserve this milder weather a few days!!

## Notes

1. Henry R. Chace (1838–1916), who, after his retirement as a Providence banker, became interested in Rhode Island history. HPL refers to *Maps of Providence, R.I.: 1650–1765–1770* (Providence, RI: Nelson E. Osterberg, 1914), and *Owners of the Lots, Houses and Shops in the Town of Providence, Rhode Island, in 1798* ([Providence, RI: Livermore & Knight, 1914]).

[130]    [ALS] [HPL to LDC]

> Monday Morning
> Septr. 28, 1925
> Ended Septr. 30, 1925

My dear Daughter Lillian:—

           I cannot forbear extending my diary a day more, to recount the trip whereof you have had a postcard bulletin. Truly, it is amusing to reflect that so rich a region hath till now lain unnotic'd at my very door; but a five-cent fare from either Times Square or Borough Hall. It is, however, a very generous journey for the money—lying well out in the Borough of Queens, & having little or nothing to do with New-York, tho' (like rural Staten Island) technically within its corporate limits.

           Proceeding by elevated to Jamaica, L.I., I was utterly astonisht at what I beheld upon quitting the train. There, all about me, lay a veritable New-England village; with wooden colonial houses, Georgian churches, & deliciously sleepy & shady streets where giant elms & maples stood in dense & luxurious rows. To deem it near New York was well-nigh impossible—& I was strongly tempted to hire a room & move out on the instant! Jamaica is an English colonial village, hence has no Dutch houses. Such Long Island towns were virtually overflows from the Connecticut region, hence are really New England in all but name. The houses lack the classick doorways of New England proper, but have the general outlines & symmetries of Novanglian architecture—hence you can imagine the effect upon me of a long row of them seen in the afternoon sunshine behind their guardian trees! Jamaica appears to be still American in population, though doubtless doomed through accessibility to N.Y. It already has a few apartment houses, though most of the non-colonial architecture seems to be Victorian or Edwardian. Many shady back streets with spreading lawns & wooden houses of the 1890 or 1900 period remind one of certain sections of Providence—say Cooke or Governor St. near Waterman. The streets have lately been numbered to conform to the Brooklyn–Queens city plan, but the signs condescend to give the original names as well in small letters below the numerals. The main thoroughfare—Jamaica Avenue—has become a thriving business section with new buildings in excellent taste—mostly classic, & fortunately not tall. The postcards on sale display'd only modern subjects, hence I purchas'd none at all. There certainly ought to be views of the two old churches, though, for they are really notable objects. The Presbyterian (whose date I could not find) is white & shingled, & has a belfry tower & clock. Its facade has unhappily been defaced by ornate Victorian additions, though these could easily be remov'd. The best church, though, is the brick Methodist affair in the same street, mainly built in 1807, tho' with many rambling additions. (all, however, in good Georgian taste) There is a magnificent Ionick portico with massive wooden columns, & a very tastefully proportion'd white steeple of the Christopher Wren type.

Another notable Georgian church is the brick 1st Baptist, whose only flaw is a steeple of excessive plainness & insufficient size. It was with a shock of surprise that I read the date *1922* on the corner-stone—surely the finest piece of modern imitation I have ever seen, save the Packer House at Perth Amboy, N.J. After tasting liberally of this *Jamaica ginger*—a draught I shall many times repeat—I resolved to enlarge my explorations by visiting its sister town of *Flushing*, on the N. shore of the island, of which I had heard much. This also is an overflow of Connecticut, though a Dutch hamlet had existed on the spot long enough to give it its name—an Anglicisation of *Vlissingen**. Taking the car, I was whirl'd thro' a gratifying succession of woods & fields, till at length I arriv'd in the midst of what lookt like a small & venerable city. It was Flushing—& with its many colonial houses it suggested some such place as Newport, where a respectable segment of the past has been join'd to something of progress & wealth. It is not now directly connected with New York by subway or elevated, tho' a line is being pushed thither & will reach it within a year. It will then, like Jamaica, be only a five-cent fare from Manhattan & Brooklyn. The first thing that took my eye was a great white gambrel-roof'd house with ell & large grounds, apparently of the 1740 or 1750 period, & having a railing around the roof at the break of the incline. It was labell'd "The Homestead", & advertised furnished rooms—& again I was tempted to hire on the spot! I next visited a shop & obtain'd some post cards, finding only two old house subjects. The best was the one I sent you—the old Bowne house of 1661—& upon emerging from the shop (where I writ the message) I began at once to shew my duplicate card to various policemen, inquiring of them the whereabouts of the original. They were not very good antiquarians, for none of them had either seen or heard of the place; but one of them knew where a *Bowne St.* lay, & on the chance of finding the house there I followed his directions. I was wise—for the guess proved a good one. The house was there, in a huge & shady yard; & whilst I was seeking it I saw a gratifying profusion of Georgian gambrel-roofers, some of them very ornate, & having finely pilaster'd classick doorways. They resembled the houses of Elizabethtown in having a gable in front, projecting from the slope of the roof's lower pitch. (see picture of Carteret Arms, Eliz. which you liked so well.) Finally I came upon the Bowne house, & a fine old pre-Georgian relick it proved to be! I recognised it at once, even tho' it was uniformly painted a slate colour (apparently a favourite in Flushing) instead of the yellow shewn in the view. The roof has a very queer pitch not uncommon amongst the 17th century houses of the Middle Colonies—a pitch which I will here illustrate by a sketch of the gable end—This place was built by John Bowne in 1661, & housed the first Quaker meeting ever held in Flushing.

*named from Vlissingen (call'd in English Flushing) in Flanders.

Its appearance I need not detail, since you have the view; but I might sadly & iconoclastically add that there are now two brand new brick apartment houses just across the street from it! But vast slices of the old Flushing remain. St. George's parish has a new Gothick church; but the churchyard is old, & the original Georgian belfried building stands deserted around the corner facing a side street, its crowning golden cock still doing good service as a weathervane. I explored Flushing till twilight, then returning to town, dining on spaghetti at the Milan, & proceeding to 169, where I typed on a story till late, & have since been enjoying the Georgian couplets of Bloomfield's "Farmer's Boy", of which I have the 1803 edition. Now—before sealing this—I shall rest a bit; & after I arise I'll see what I'll do. I want to explore more of this fascinating eastern terrain—so near & yet so far—but the weather has turned dubious, so I can't tell how it will be. If I go, I'll leave this epistle unfinisht & continue after I return—but of that later.

Tuesday Morning

Well—the second postcard has ere now appris'd you that I did go. Meanwhile your appreciated letter came, & I perused it with customary enjoyment & gratitude. I rested a bit in the morning, & in the afternoon started out on the second day of my travels; taking "The Farmer's Boy" along & proceeding on the subway to Queens Plaza, where I changed to an elevated train bound for Astoria, on the northwest corner of Long Island. I thought this would be new territory to me, but as it turned out, it was the very first spot on Long Island that I ever saw; being at the portal of the great Hell Gate railway bridge, over which rolled my train on my initial metropolitan advent of April 1922. I had noticed then a huddle of nondescript wooden houses— & now I learned that this was the old-time (early XIX cent—not colonial) village of Astoria, founded by the first John Jacob Astor. Returning to Queens Plaza, [the elevated centre for northern Long Island—a rather dismal square across the Queensboro Bridge from 59th St Manhattan] I noticed en route a very attractive sight—the misty skyline of distant New York all grey & fairy-like as on the first occasion of my seeing it, three years & a half ago. The Queensboro Bridge loomed up deliciously in the middle distance, belying the ugliness apparent on a nearer view; & the whole was glorified by slanting shafts of sunlight (as in a John Martin[1] engraving—you recall those of Kirk's I shew'd you) which dropt from an opening cloud to the vaporous regions of earth. At Queens Plaza I took the train bound toward Flushing—which now runs as far as Corona & transfers to a surface car. The route included some far from unattractive suburbs, with several new publick buildings of deliciously colonial design. At length Corona—a nondescript but hardly repulsive village—was reached, & I took the yellow trolley for Flushing. Along the way I saw evidences of the new elevated as it is rising arch by arch across the salt marshes bordering Flushing Creek & Flushing Bay; & ahead there loomed the modest & graceful skyline of the town—unspoilt by tall buildings, & still dominated by chimneys & steeples & treetops as a city's skyline ought to be. The object which will eventually dominate it is the belfry of the Sloane furniture factory—a select establishment which makes the highest & most artistic grade of reproduced antiques. Fortunately the firm is true to its antiquarian tradition, & is shaping the future belfry in the most authentic colonial pattern. Flushing is indeed very beautiful, & I hope it may long stay so. Soon across the bridge, I alighted from the car & proceeded on my pedestrian rambles— purchasing cards & mailing them at the P.O. when opportunity offer'd. I revisited the scenes of the day before, & discovered still better ones—including a shady hill street close to the main thoroughfare & the station, whose white colonial houses & bank walls savour magnificently of that rural New England of which they are in reality the overflow. Life in Flushing seems normal, village-like, & wholly untouched by N.Y. It has its own conservative daily paper, the *Journal,* (founded 1842) & its advertisers tend largely to ignore their technical absorption by New York City; giving their addresses as "Flushing, L.I." or "Flushing, Queens Co., N.Y." Till twilight I roamed about, pausing near the P.O. to stroke a delightful kitty-cat, (tiger) & finally taking the trolley for my first discovery of the day before—Jamaica. Arriv'd in Jamaica, I found exploring useless after dark, so took the elevated-subway back to New York—omitting, of course, the side-trip to Canarsie (a village in Brooklyn, on the S. shore of L.I., a little this side of the Old Mill) which I mention'd on my card. Changing cars at Canal St., I rode up to 49th & dined at the cheap spaghetti place (25¢ for a liberal order) at 47th & 8th Ave. which Leeds introduced to me, (it was after 9, so the Milan was closed) after which I returned to 169 & typed till quite late. I then read to the end of "The Farmer's Boy", (a great pastoral written in 1798—do you know it?) began my hundredth or thousandth re-reading of Thomson's "Seasons", (whose 2nd centennial is nearly due, since the first part was publisht in 1726) & answered the mail which had arriv'd during my absence. Now I am continuing this epistle, & shall probably conclude & mail before setting out on my third day of delightful & solitary exploration. The day is clear, & seems decently warm. Taking Thomson (of whom I've bought a new & very tiny copy on a 5¢ counter, since my 1819 edition is wearing out from much pocket carrying) along to beguile odd moments, I shall go first to see what Canarsie is like; after which I shall proceed to Jamaica & take the trolley for Mineola. When there, my course will map itself out—& I only hope there are good & cheap electric connexions for Huntington, which I greatly want to see, though I fear the regular railway fare is considerable. I'll let you know of the stages of my trip by postcard bulletins—if I can find any decent cards. But meanwhile I'll go downstairs & see if the postman has brought any stuff which I must answer.

—Yes, hang it, he did! Stuff from my old United enemies, which must be answered with bland tact & suave irony, though the brunt of their fight will henceforward devolve upon young Bacon instead of on me. Bacon—lucky child—will probably move back to Boston next year, perhaps stopping in Philadelphia (for the sesquicentennial & the Natl. Am. Press Assn. convention) & New York en route, & accepting my guidance to ancient places. A E P G also sent a nice letter, following an exquisite set of Deerfield colonial cards which sent me into virtual ecstasies yesterday. And then there was the new *Netopian,* with some fearful & wonderful inaccuracies about good old Moses Brown.[2] It calls him the *son* of *Chad* Brown, (instead of Capt. James Brown, Jr., Chad's great-grandson) & imputes to him a knowledge of *astronomy;* in this matter probably confusing him with his brother Joseph— Providence's first man of taste & elegant accomplishments to spring from the rugged, grasping old home-lot stock. Joseph Brown was a fine figure—I'd like to write his biography. As an astronomer he assisted Dr. Benjamin West (*not* the painter of same name) in observing the 1769 transit of Venus, as an architect he designed University Hall, collaborated on the 1st Baptist church, & conceived his truly exquisite house in Towne St.—still standing as home of the Providence National Bank—, & as a general man of science he ended his well-spent days as professor of natural philosophy in the college so soon to assume the name of his illustrious family. Of all the Browns he is my favourite, tho' John may have been more capable, & Moses more amiably overflowing with publick spirit. Only lately I read of the quiet tragedy of these boys' uncle, Elisha Brown, who built the first brick house (still standing in N. Main St. & shewn early in the Corners & Characters series) in the compact part of the town; a tragedy of collapsing fortunes as poignant as the later collapse of the Spragues. Elisha was a man of wealth & (for his time) taste, with a fine new house, fair library, excellent furniture, & sumptuous china & silver plate—but he made the political mistake of espousing the Ward party during the bitter Hopkins–Ward feud of 1750–1768; being once Deputy-Governor under Ward. All the other Browns—& all the rest of Providence, in fact— were more violently Hopkins than Stephen Hopkins himself; but Elisha, having set ideas & strong sympathies with a cultivated pro-Ward group in Newport (Newport, except for the Wanton faction, was solidly Ward) refused to align himself, & was consequently made the prey of the local commercial oligarchy over which his own flesh & blood dominated. He was financially ruined & driven from society, reaching the nadir of poverty & dying in virtual indigence after the sale of his house & personal effects at publick vendue. How few who today behold that trim old brick gambrel-roofer in N. Main St. realise the melancholy tale that lies behind it! Here a good but stubborn man of the best blood met with defeat & exile, & hence he departed from affluence to suffer the asperities of a penury for which his birth & breeding had but ill adapted him. *The Netopian* is quite a paper for an advertising venture, but I wish it would condescend to be just a trifle more careful about its facts. It has the Hospital Trust behind it, so ought to be able to buy & study the

Kimball book, costly tho' that volume must be with only 550 copies printed.

And now after all I think I'll defer the completion of this missive till after my trip. This Long Island exploring has a coherence which ought to gain it presentation in one continuous document. I shall, then, answer A E P G & clean up other correspondence, then take the elevated for regions my feet have never trod before! More anon.

Tuesday–Wednesday Midnight<br>Septr 29–30, 1925

Was my third expedition a success? Well, just glance over the third or Hempstead postcard again & draw your own conclusions! I can hardly wax coherent over it yet, but know in the meantime that I have seen a sort of combined Bristol, East Greenwich, Newport, Salem, Gloucester, Wickford, & what not, large as life, no dream to flee in a flash, & all within a brief afternoon's journey. That was the climax—but meanwhile let us consider events in chronological order. My trip differ'd widely from what I had plann'd, but its apex prov'd so much more than I expected, that no regrets attend the striking deviation. I embarkt upon the elevated in quest of *Canarsie*, a settlement on the south shore of Brooklyn just this side of the Old Mill, but found at the end of the line only a gridiron of sandy, squalid streets with the air of a run-down seaside resort of the 1880's. Subsequent study of the map convinces me that I miss'd the heart of the village; but I am fairly certain it amounts to nothing. I shall see some time. Quitting this spot, I changed cars for Jamaica, & was soon in that fascinating town awaiting the Mineola car. My intention was to go from Mineola to Roslyn, & there seek a connecting line to Huntington, if there be any; but in all this travel outside the boundaries of N.Y.* I am handicapped by want of a suitable map. None is sold in the stationery shops, & tho' I saw by an advertisement that there is an ornamental map of Long Island in the September number of *Country Life*, I have so far been unable to secure a copy of that magazine. I am thus forc'd to a very primitive species of blundering till I can afford to lay out two dollars for the "N.Y. Walk Book." The route to Mineola was markt by no striking beauties, but lined almost continuously with modern real-estate developments testifying mournfully alike to the spread of the city & to the want of taste & ingenuity in the architects of small dwellings. Endless rows of dull, duplicate dolls' houses—grotesque in malproportion, & often with just enough of the Georgian & colonial about them to furnish futile parodies of the real article. At last, though, an open space was reached, where many signs proclaim'd the fields of the Curtiss aeroplane factory. On the horizon ahead & to the right

---

*Mineola, Garden City, Hempstead, & Freeport are all in Nassau township—*not* part of N.Y. City. I hope they will never be overtaken & annexed—but who can tell what the evil years will bring?

appear'd som[e] alluring steeples, roofs, & belfries, tho' it was long before I came to their midst. Mineola itself was reach'd very suddenly, & prov'd to be a straggling, uninteresting village, mainly modern & having no conceivable attraction save a county fair—which I did not visit. I stay'd only because of the steeples & belfries I had seen in the distance, & began to explore the fields & roads southward in quest of the dream-city or mirage (whichever it might be) whose presence they indicated. After all, it was not a mirage, but the exceedingly scenick & well-kept suburb of *Garden City,* now fam'd as the seat of the publishers Doubleday, Page, & Co. It is a modern town, but rather pretty withal; with a railway station in feeble imitation of a Dutch colonial house, & a post office block which really succeeds in suggesting a Georgian business building of the later period, with marble base, grey brick superstructure, & the correct ornaments & cornices of the Adam period. (God save Adelphi Terrace!) The streets are a veritable maple forest, dense rows of giant maples lining either side & keeping the town all summer in a pleasing green twilight, & the houses are generally attractive in the insipid modern manner. There is a notable Popish cathedral of Gothick design, & several other publick edifices apparently dating from Victoria's placid reign. The works of Doubleday, Page, & Co. are hous'd in a series of brick buildings resembling an university, set back from the main highway behind an attractive wall with shapely gates. They must form a very tolerable place to labour in, & I envy those who are able to secure posts as readers, revisers, or proofreaders with the firm. But one would tire of seeing Garden City too much, so I kept on southward in the expectation of some quainter village. Remember that I had no map, & knew nothing of the country—trusting to chance with a very agreeable sense of adventure into the unknown; just as I used to enjoy getting "lost" on walks around Cat Swamp, East Providence, or somewhere, with you, Gramp, or my mother in the early & middle 'nineties. The southbound cars said "Freeport", & that sounded good enough for me. I knew there was a Hempstead somewhere, reached by trolley from Jamaica; but had no idea of its direction or nature. Not until I encountered some roadside signs did I realise that I had stumbled into it. Then came scattered houses, some of them colonial, & a delicious old yellow farmhouse with a spacious sheep-pasture across the road, where grazed a woolly flock which might have sprung bodily out of the 18th century pastoral poems I carry'd in my pocket! I had reached Hempstead! There now stretcht ahead of me a narrow, winding main street much like that of Gloucester, with old houses on every hand, & occasional white spires, towers, & belfries rising into the sky. Enchantment reign'd supreme, for here dwelt the soul of antique New-England in all its fulness, unimpair'd by the tainting presence of a foreign Babylon some twenty or twenty-five miles to the east. How can one describe it all? The churches alone a[re] worth a cycle of sonnets! There was St. George's in full Episcopal dignity near the principal square, with snowy belfry & venerable churchyard. This parish was founded in 1704, & receiv'd from Her Gracious Majefty, Queen Anne, a fine prayer-book & communion service. It was formally charter'd by George the Second, & appears still to be the leading house of worship of the town. The building is a plain, neat Georgian affair, & the churchyard is enclosed by an excellent 18th century picket fence with white wooden urns atop all the posts. God Save the King! The Methodist church in Front St. is white & steepled in the best New England manner, recalling such things as the Barrington white church. It is marr'd, however, by painted windows of the Romanesque design, which clash with the general type & outline. Christ's First Presbyterian Church (to quote its ambitious title) has a white square-tower'd building* put up in 1846, & somewhat incongruously ornamented in the Gothick fashion. It stands beside the railway station on a site us'd for over two centuries. This is the oldest Presbyterian church in these colonies, the organisation having been founded in 1644 by the Rev. Rich^d Denton, who came from Halifax, England, to secure greater latitude for his dissenting theological notions. The first church edifice, put up in 1648, serv'd also as a stockade wherein the settlers might gather in case of attack by the redskin salvages. Certain Hempstead thoroughfares, notably Greenwich-St., are truly extatick dreams of colonial loveliness with their great white houses, gambrell'd, peaked, or pillar'd, set back from the highway in their verdant, shady yards. I could gnash my teeth & spit in disgust at the apathy which prevents the local stationers from providing postcards of them—the one I sent you being the only specimen available, & even this shewing the house only as an incidental background for the Spanish War cannon. But if the stationers are apathetick, the same most happily cannot be said of the townsmen in general; for all the new publick buildings are in the finest colonial style. The High School (just completed) is of brick, finely porticoed & pilastered in the third or Adam phase of Georgian, & shewing traces of the classick revival sponsor'd by Bulfinch. The Town-Hall, whose rear abuts on a fine little park travers'd by a creek with rustick bridges, was built in 1918, & is of the belfried Georgian type like its fellow town-hall at Apponaug. The *gilding* of the belfry's dome may be in a little dubious taste, but 'tis a fault most easy of remedy. Long did I wander about the winding ways of Hempstead, lost in rapt observation & admiring reflection, & sending to a select circle the one type of colonial postcard I could find. When next I visit it—& that will not be far in the future!—I shall go directly from Jamaica; for of course the approach thro' Mineola & Garden City is but a senseless digression unrepay'd by fitting sights, & follow'd by me only because of my compleat ignorance of the country. Hempstead lies 9½ miles due east of Jamaica.† Afternoon had now advanc'd very far; so abandoning all thought of Huntington & the northeast, I

---

*like the Newman or white church where the car line turns in Rumford.
†The running time of electrick cars being normally 48 minutes.

continu'd south on foot in quest of that *Freeport* whither all the cars were bound. The walk was longer than I had expected, hence it was twilight before I approacht the village & was inform'd of its history by a roadside sign. This sign declar'd that the town was founded in colonial times by one Daniel Raynor, who built a grist mill upon that stream now known as the Freeport River. The settlement, at first call'd *Raynortown*, grew from small beginnings to one of the principal towns of Long-Island; lying on the southern shore beyond Long Beach. As I enter'd the main street I beheld an orgy of illumination which shew'd the presence of the "White Way" germ; & noted every earmark of a prosperous & complacent city. The houses are of varying age & condition, but very few are colonial—in fact, there is scarcely anything antique in the atmosphere of this second Attleboro or Long-Island Pawtucket. Much of the residential district is modernly pretty, but of distinctiveness there is little. I shall not bother to visit it again—indeed, what would not be tame beside immortal Hempstead? I now took the car for Jamaica—for there is a direct line proceeding through Lynbrook & not involving a return to Hempstead—& in due time (after a delay caused by a stone in the roadway which made the motorman think he had jumped the track) reached that traffick centre; there taking the elevated (sickly anticlimax) for Borough-Hall. Arrived thither, I dined at John's & return'd to 169, where I am now engag'd in my accustom'd epistolary diversions. Eventually I may retire, taking care to be up tomorrow night in time to attend the meeting of the gang at Sonny's.

I must not give over this chronicle without mention of another Hempstead ecclesiastical item which I omitted in the main account. Not only did I encounter the Episcopal, Methodist, & Presbyterian faiths, but the good old Baptist persuasion as well; & indeed, in a manner much more personal than that of the others! As I was writing my cards in the drug store & thinking of *white churches*, there enter'd an impo'tant frock-coated pusson what des nachelly exudified de atmosphere ob chucches, tho' I can't say his complexion suggested the concomitant New-England adjective. Yassuh, he might hab come straight fom de Congdon St. Baptist Chuch,[3] where dey done got de 'rig'nal 1775 clock what used to be in our steeple—for lawdy bress us, he was such a strong & orthodox Baptist! He was selling hymn-verses—salvation-poems, breddern!—whut he done make up hisse'f; he, de Evangelist Revun St. Jawn, pastor ob de Little St. James United Baptist Chu'ch ob Hempstead! De money done go inter a hawspittle fo' de po' li'l' chilluns ob de parish; & Revun St. Jawn he sling out de eloquention in des de smoovest, insinuatin'est, musicallest voice yo' ebber did hyar! Well, suh, ah done look at de pome, & ah done gib Brudder St. Jawn a dime right straight away—fo' lawsy me, dem rhymes was wuff it!! Ah send 'em 'long fo' y'all to see—yo' might gib 'em to Sistah Anne, whut am a good Baptist herse'f, but be sho' yo' tells her to sen' 'em back to Deacon Theobald; cause ah wants to pass 'em roun' some mo'! Ah guess ah shew 'em to de prayah-meetin' tonight, w'en de breddern am all assemblified, & Deacon

Mo'ton am right awn de spot wiv de true 138th St. Baptist orfodoxology. Den ah put 'em in de lettah & seal it up fo' de mail-man. Now le's all sing togedder, breddern & sistern, & jine in de chorus a-praisin' ob de Lawd:

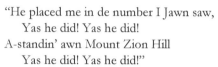

"Yo kin tell de worl' 'bout dis,
Yo kin tell de nations ah'm blessed,
Tell 'em whut Jesus hab done
Since de Comfo'ter he done come
    An' brung joy to mah soul.

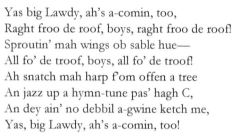

"He placed me in de number I Jawn saw,
    Yas he did! Yas he did!
A-standin' awn Mount Zion Hill
    Yas he did! Yas he did!"

Yas big Lawdy, ah's a-comin, too,
Raght froo de roof, boys, raght froo de roof!
Sproutin' mah wings ob sable hue—
All fo' de troof, boys, all fo' de troof!
Ah snatch mah harp f'om offen a tree
An jazz up a hymn-tune pas' hagh C,
An dey ain' no debbil a-gwine ketch me,
Yas, big Lawdy, ah's a-comin, too!

Well—so much for the diary. Any needed extensions or additions can be inserted later, or supply'd in my customary fashion on the outside of the envelope. I think I shall rest around here tomorrow—or *type* around here, which sounds more industrious—but later I shall have more travelogue material, since I must visit Hempstead repeatedly, & get at least one glimpse of the more remote Huntington, which by all accounts is the premier colonial town of western Long Island.

And now permit me to advert with pleasure to your welcome epistle & its enclosures. I recall Willie Lynn as a little boy—he lived in Humboldt Ave., & played very intelligently & vividly. He always liked the drama, & took children's parts with the Albee Stock Co. in 1901 & 2. I never saw him on the stage after that till 1918, when he was with the light opera company playing a short summer season at the Shubert-Majestic. He took comic parts—& I think I saw him four or five times. Very capable & effective in his field, he seemed to me; though in youth I used to think his voice & accent a bit affected & sissified as a result of his elocutionary training.

Permit me to sympathise with you regarding the cold! If the winter turns out as rigorous as some prophets threaten, you will need an oil stove yourself—for depend upon it, the entire tribe of landladies will employ the current coal strike as an excuse for underheating their establishments as badly as the law allows! Mrs. Burns has already become eloquent on the subject—Loveman says she gave him quite an impromptu dissertation on the uncertainties of fuel prospects the last time she answered the bell for him! I shall get my stove with the *Weird Tales* cheque which is due here tomorrow or thereabouts—letting A E P G cash it & return me the visible simoleons. That ought to leave some toward the suit—which I shall have to get soon, tho' S H wanted me to let her help select it if possible. I think I can get one for as little as I paid for the summer outfit—$25.00—for this "Monroe Clothes" system is truly remarkable. Leeds, though, advises me to look at another firm even cheaper—$22.50—whose name I'll have him give me again tonight. I have an idea that clothing may be slightly cheaper in N.Y. than elsewhere, since it is nearly all made on the spot. Surplus supplies are constantly thrown on the local market cheaply, to avoid cost of transportation elsewhere. My summer suit has proved eminently satisfactory, & I shall probably patronise the same chain store for the winter outfit. I shall get my usual cut in navy blue, if possible; though I wouldn't utterly reject a dark grey or oxford mixture like the 1915 suit that was stolen. Of course I'll send you samples—& a photograph as soon as possible. As for overcoats—I am all right there, with one winter & two spring garments. In fact, I have exactly the same array as I had in Providence; since the only one the thieves touched was the new & nice-looking one which S H Gave me in the spring of 1924. And my re-blocked hat will probably do throughout the season. One thing I regret is the final passing of my old Regal shoes, which I fear this last 3-day series of "hikes" has definitely finished. The patches are gone, & the holes too greatly enlarged to warrant mending; whilst all the cracks seem about to start open. There is a still older pair of Pierce shoes which might last for three or four more trips, but after that I fear I shall have to take the now finely conquered new shoes of last February for every-day, which will spoil their present shapeliness all too soon. As an alternative I might experiment with a pair of three-dollar "Thom McAn" shoes which Leeds recommends—taking those directly for rough wear & keeping the others for best—but I'll see later. For a while the Pierce relics will keep me afloat. One-suitedness will also embarrass me on fall & winter "hikes", though possibly I can keep on wearing the thin blue under an overcoat. I'd hate to use a new winter suit roughly. Confound those thieves! What a mess they made, just as I'd got my wardrobe back to the 4-suit normalcy necessary for really comfortable & effective getting-along!

Poor little Alfredus is having his financial troubles, too, & is wearing the same suit he wore in Cleveland three years ago! I hope he can get his loan from somebody, though of course I was forced to tell him at once of my own regretted inability to play the Macaenas [*sic*].[4] If he comes to N.Y. our gang will harbour & entertain him gratis—so that he may be assured of our benevolent intentions despite the fact that no actual sums of cash are at our command. Yes—S H sent a ten-spot this month to treat me to a Philadelphia trip, (tho' it went gradually for small trips, postcards, & laundry instead) & left a five-spot upon her departure a week ago last Thursday. Extra laundry occasion'd by my many long walks & active trips, & restaurant meals occasion'd by my mild revolt against canned nourishment, have somewhat impair'd the rigid œconomy I achieved last spring; but I think I can return to those austerities as the cooler weather permits me to wear linen longer & keep bread & cheese without early moulding. I have been recklessly disposing of five a week lately, but believe that during the winter I can so reduce things as to keep within that sum despite the added oil bill which my heater will unfortunately create. With *bread* as a basis, I can certainly keep food down to 15¢ per day, except for a weekly spaghetti-meal at John's to break the monotony. One thing that alienated me from continuous home eating was the breakdown of the alcove light—I have the deuce of a time with dishes, & hate to cut bread in the room itself where all the crumbs complicate the sweeping problem. I don't believe a repair man would charge over a couple of dollars to fix that bracket wiring, & I think I'll have one come when I get that cheque. I guess a new cord for the desk lamp would cost about as much, besides being most diabolically awkward—not only to use in the alcove, but to flop around when the lamp is in its normal place on my table.

I'm glad you like my new tales, & hope you'll also like "The Horror at Red Hook" when I get it typed. Just now I'm spending all my spare energy typing old material, so that I can once more get *Weird Tales* supplied well in advance. As soon as that is out of the way, I shall go ahead with the new story—a sort of novelette—which I mapped out in such close detail last August. Yes—varied experience is generally of much value to the fictionist—of paramount value if his work be realistick, & of substantial incidental value even if it is of another sort. It corrects the commoner psychological misapprehensions & extravagances of the immature writer by impArting a healthy cynicism & teaching that nothing in the world is of value save one's early dreams & perspectives, lightly taken—yet such is the stupidity of the average human animal that vast herds continue to write naively & absurdly even after undergoing the utmost vicissitudes that life can furnish! This "So Big"[5] was very popular last year—Mrs. Moran lent it to S H, tho' I wouldn't waste my time on it. Popular fiction is usually of no literary significance whatever. I saw the cinema of the tale,[6] & imagine that the book may be perhaps a trifle less asinine than most current stuff. As for me—I have retired conclusively from the present age. In a cosmos of aimless chaos & upon a planet of futility & decay, nothing but fancy is of any importance. Time & space are the sheerest incidentals; & when one lives in a decadent & disillusioned age which has nothing of moment to say, it becomes a man of sense to stop wasting his time on contemporary fumbling, & to turn back to a period whose utterances have something in them to which his own psychology responds. All ages & places are alike of no significance in the ultimate void—therefore let each man pick from the sorry jumble of chronology & cosmography whatever milieu is least repugnant to his imagination & aesthetick faculty. I belong back with the Georgians in point of time, & in point of space take most readily to the English or New-English rural realm—the meadow, the wood, the farm, & the village—when I am not roaming the universe at large in quest of unique horrors. So the affairs of 1925 et seq. are not likely to make any considerable impression upon me. They are not the especial section of the endless kaleidoscope-display of useless patterns which most happens to interest me.

Yes—those Ipswich houses are delightful, & I wish I might some day see them. As for footscrapers—I should say I *have* seen them, & studied them in detail in Providence, Boston, Salem, Marblehead, Newburyport, Portsmouth, New York, Philadelphia, Elizabethtown, & everywhere else I have been! Only this past day I have been studying them in Hempstead! And now I'll desist a while, retiring for a little slumber. I'm leaving this unsealed, & may or may not make additions as new material presents itself. Either inside or outside I'll probably carry the diary through Wednesday the 30th.

Yr aff Nephew & obt Servt

H P L

P.S. One of my bedroom shoes has begun to unravel at the top. I haven't cut off the unwinding yarn—would repair be reasonably easy if I sent the ailing article by parcel post?

[P.P.S. (from envelope?) copied by another hand:] GOOD MEETNG—EVERYBODY PRESENT

## Notes

1. John Martin (1789–1854), British painter and illustrator whose work HPL admired for its cosmic qualities. HPL discusses him at length in a letter to Vincent Starrett.

2. "The Moses Brown School: A Very Modern Descendant of a School System Instituted in the 17th Century," *Netopian* 6, No. 6 (September 1925): 7–12.

3. At 17 Congdon Street in Providence.

4. HPL means "Maecenas," referring to C. Maecenas (68–8 B.C.E.), a celebrated Roman patron of the arts and literature.

5. A novel by Edna Ferber. It won the Pulitzer Prize in 1925.

6. *So Big* (First National Pictures, 1924), directed by Charles Brabin; starring Colleen Moore, Joseph De Grasse, and John Bowers.

[131]    [ALS] [HPL to LDC]

Friday Evening

Octr. 2, 1925

My dear Daughter Lillian:—

As I take my pen in hand to continue my diary, I am about to start down to 14th St. to attend the reception in honour of the homecoming of our gang's official mascot—Edgar Evertsen Saltus Kirk, who this morning left his foster-mamma at the Downing St. restaurant & took up his abode with Uncle Georgius in Chelsea! He is black & white & exceedingly playful, so I am apprised over the telephone, & his master is going to round up as many of our circle as possible to welcome him & make him feel as much at home as a very small kitty-cat can feel in a vast pair of early-Victorian apartments. I shall stop somewhere en route & get Edgar some catnip—which I trust he is old enough to appreciate. Verily, I am all impatience to behold this diminutive personage, & envy Kirk his ability in devising a working plan for harbouring a feline member of the family. I saw loads of fascinating kitties in Jamaica, Flushing, & Hempstead!

As I said, the meeting was a good one with all present. It broke up at 12:30, & all hands took the subway—Kleiner & I keeping on to the Nevins St. station in Brooklyn, & thence walking out to his home, since he wished to shew me the Bushwick Reformed Dutch church, which he used to attend. It was built in the 'fifties, but by some divine miracle was cast in an earlier & lovelier model; so that R K was sure it would interest me. Our walk was brisk & pleasant—out Fulton St. & Lafayette Ave.—& at length the desiderate fane hove in sight—a white wooden edifice with Corinthian pilasters & Wren type of steeple, which I would have sworn could not be later than 1820 at the most! Certainly, one Victorian architect mercifully escaped the taint of his time! Congratulating Kleiner on the scene of his long-past theological instruction, I took the elevated for 169 & spent the rest of the night—& the next day too—in straightening out my correspondence. Thursday night I went out shopping & retired at midnight after some reading in the new *Weird Tales* I obtained; awaking today at 1 p.m., just in time to receive the telephone call from Kirk (via Leeds, for Kirk doesn't dare call up here in person on account of his unpaid bill!) anent the homecoming of microscopic Edgar Evertsen Saltus Kirk. Since then I have been writing letters, & now I must dress & go down to see the young lion of the evening. Tomorrow I must do some typing, & Sunday I have promised to shew Loveman some of the Long Island country—Hempstead above all. The next (McNeil) meeting will be held here, & Loveman will entertain the Leeds meeting the week after that. That's all I can predict of my social programme except that S H (of whose retain'd position the enclosures will tell) will be here next week or the week after, including a Sunday during which I shall shew her Jamaica, Flushing, & Hempstead—or Hempstead & as much else as a single day will allow.

The new *Weird Tales* is out, & contains Leeds' vampire story. That is a great tale, despite a few touches of the diffuseness, prosaicism, & conventionality which always make his work not quite so satisfying as it might be. The atmosphere & climax are ideal—& I'll congratulate the author this evening when I see him! He still works for Kirk, tho' Georgius complains of his tendency to "loaf on the job" & absent himself unduly at will. This month's

*Weird Tales* also has material by H. G. Wells & Edward Lucas White, (author of "Andivius Hedulio") shewing rather a gratifying rise in general standing.[1] I don't care for Wells' story, though; & White's is so illogically grotesque that I wonder Wright accepted it (tho' of course it was White's fame which counted) after his rejection of Little Sonny's very similar & much better motivated "Shrunken Man" tale. (which W. Paul Cook will probably print in the *Recluse* which he contemplates.)[2] On the whole, I fancy this issue of *Weird Tales* may be accounted as very fair indeed.

Enclosed is all the matter bearing on the threatened loss of S H's position, & the happy aftermath by which that loss was averted. These notes needn't be returned, tho' A E P G might be interested to see them. I also send a note of commendation which S H received from a customer, & which she may possibly wish to preserve, tho' she did not expressly say so. She will next be in New York, it seems, about the 10th or 15th of this month. Also enclosed is another of the pathetick Galpiniana—the one just preceding the one you saw before. Poor little rascal, I hope some eleventh-hour Providence may preserve for him the continued Paris study he so acutely requires! I send—for your permanent retention—another of the Paris cards; shewing the rural quiet of the gardens of the ancient Hôtel de Cluny—a mediaeval monastery now a museum.

The current "Corners & Characters" item—the Daniel Petty farmhouse in upper Westminster St.—is of double interest to me this week, since its gable set in the front of a gambrel roof is exactly what I have been seeing in the Long Island region lately. The same type is also common around Elizabethtown. The only difference is that in the N.Y.–N.J. region the gable is not blunted—being like this ⌂ rather than this: ⌂. And you will always notice that New England houses have a longer *upper* pitch of the gambrel than do the houses of N.Y. & N.Y.[*sic*]* Not till one gets to Germantown, Pa. does one find the N.E. proportions again.

But now I must desist, & get on my clothes preparatory to visiting Edgar Evertsen Saltus Kirk. Loveman will be there, his quarrel with Kirk having healed. He's had rather bad luck about his books—the backer withdrew from his poetry venture, & after all this time the Phila. publishers have decided not to issue his Saltus critique! More anon—& I'll tell you all about tiny Edgar Evertsen. Meanwhile I am ever

Yr most aff Nephew & obt Servt

H P L

\*

## Notes

1. *WT* (November 1925): Arthur Leeds, "The Return of the Undead"; H. G. Wells, "The Stolen Body"; Edward Lucas White, "Lukundoo." HPL later revised his opinion

of "Lukundoo" when he came to write "Supernatural Horror in Literature," praising it as a tale that "rouse[s] darker apprehensions" (71).
2. "The Creeper in Darkness," later published in *Strange Stories* (April 1939). Cook did not print the tale in the *Recluse*.

[132]    [ALS] [HPL to LDC]

Sunday Morning
Octr. 4, 1925

My dear Daughter Lillian:—

Your appreciated letter arriv'd yesterday afternoon, & in replying to it I cannot forbear beginning with my diary—which chronicles the pensive sequel to the affair of small Edgar Evertsen Saltus Kirk, to meet whom I was going down town when last I writ you. As outlined in that former communication, I indeed went down to 14th St., stopping on the way to purchase a catnip ball at a chemist's shop; & upon my arrival was greeted by Kirk, Loveman, & Leeds, together with an amiable & appealing stripling of the feline species, about ¾ grown, & white except for grey markings on ears, feet, & tail.

Now this alert & sophisticated specimen was obviously not the black & white atom from Downing St., who had been too small to leave his foster-mother; & my host at once proceeded to explain the discrepancy. It seems that the Downing St. nursling is still too young to be taken, & that Kirk—out walking Thursday night with Loveman—saw this larger kitten in a Greenwich alley, becoming so captivated with him that he took him home & adopted him forthwith, on the principle that a cat in the home is worth two in the restaurant. The little rascal was delightfully playful & friendly, & revelled gracefully with the catnip ball I brought him before hopping up to sleep in Grandpa's lap. After a time all hands went out to dinner at a neighbouring cafeteria, shortly returning & resuming play with Edgar Evertsen, & later welcoming Kleiner, who completed the evening's quota. We then all pitched in to help Kirk address envelopes for his coming catalogue of books for sale, (there will be 8000 envelopes in all) taking comfortable seats & singing old songs to enliven the hours. I hope it will not be esteem'd boastful in me when I say that I turn'd out the largest number—Kleiner standing at the other extreme with the smallest, since he chose to experiment with a new kind of handwriting he is adopting—the mediaeval broad-stroke uncial, which greatly resembles printing. It has lately been foisted upon the children of most of the free schools in England, & N.Y. has just taken it up. An article in McClure's Magazine[1] got Kleiner started, & he is now creating considerable amusement by his experiments & practicing. It must be own'd, however, that the results seem rather attractive—one young student's signature now looking somewhat like    ℛheinhart Kleiner.    this: As for the rest of us—one can't teach old dogs new tricks, besides which we are by no means convinc'd that the innovation really affords that glib rapidity which is claim'd for it. So Grandpa Theobald—weathering this fad as he weather'd the vertical writing of the late nineties, will continue to perpetrate his 18th century scrawl, trusting to his readers' cryptographical skill to decipher the messages he wou'd fain convey. And now the tragedy intervenes! About midway in our labours young Edgar Evertsen politely asked to be excused for a time, so that Kirk let him out the window. Moments pass'd, & he did not return—nor were any of the various searching-parties which we dispatch'd able to find him. Eheu! He had melted into that engulfing & uncommunicative night which had so lately yielded him up, & it is to be fear'd we shall never behold him more! The catnip ball rolls listlessly & mournfully about, & the piece of play-string pines for a little paw to chase it. I tell Kirk that Edgar probably had a good home to begin with, & has doubtless returned to it. Now he'll have to wait till that Downing-St. kitty-cat is old enough to leave his foster-mamma! Leeds was in his glory, & I saw no signs of loafing on his part. Indeed, his version of the deal places all the culpability elsewhere. It seems that Kirk is unwilling to pay him enough to keep his $8.00-per-week hotel room, & that he has instead insisted on his economising by moving down to the bleak & litter'd pair of rooms in 14th St., so that rent will be eliminated. Then he can dole poor Leeds out a few pennies at a time for food & laundry, & be absolved of the necessity of paying a regular stipend. Leeds is quite heartbroken, for he does not know what he can ever do without the privacy, clean linen, & bath privileges of the hotel—but stark poverty offers no alternative. He was to move yesterday, & the event loomed ahead in his mind like a coming funeral. What adds to the confusion is the fact that Kirk himself may shortly move, since his boarding-house has become the "Hotel Hispano-Americano." Well—our session lasted till 1 a.m., & even the loss of Edgar Evertsen was insufficient to choke the flow of alleged melody. We then returned to the cafeteria & dispersed, tho' Leeds long detain'd us in the subway with a chronicle of his misfortunes past, present, & future. Proceeding at once to 169, I read considerably in *Weird Tales*, wrote some, &—having stay'd up—went out shopping about 10 a.m. Then I rested a bit & rose late, writing some letters & doing some more reading. Now Sunday is about to dawn, & at 1 p.m. I have promised to take Loveman to Hempstead. In the interim I may do some typing, or may—if the weather is clear—take a solitary trip to some rural or village spot to calm my nerves with that New England consciousness which only the isolated contemplation of old-fashion'd sights can produce. The weather is medium—just now my electric stove is not lighted, tho' I have a blanket pinned around me.

Permit me to commiserate you most sincerely upon your cold. I haven't one yet, but shall no doubt fall a victim before long. My life from October to June is generally one continuous cold of varying severity. I trust that your landlady may not prove too chary with heat, & hope you will always have gas or oil facilities at hand to piece out whatever deficiencies may occur. Be especially careful whilst your cold lasts—though no doubt you will be, without any gratuitous cautioning from me!

We haven't had any further news from the Alfredus-child, but constantly hope for the best. As you will by this time have seen from his other note, the immediate cause of his difficulty is his mother's ill-advised real estate move—trying to remodel the house for renting. We all hope the little rascal can pull through somehow, & are preparing to entertain him royally whenever he passes through here. As to my tales—I haven't yet sent "In the Vault", but fancy it ought to be as acceptable to Wright as anything of mine. "He" is among a batch already sent but not yet passed upon. I shan't spoil "The Shunned House" by abridging the introductory parts—it's easier to write a new story for the magazine & keep this one in what I consider its more artistic form. About the Paterson Museum—that card I sent is *not* its building. The picture is of the *publick library*, which has charge of the new venture, & at which Morton is now working—but the museum will be housed in a brick ex-stable to the left of the library as shewn in the card. It is the remodelling of this barn into a museum building that is creating all the delay—but Morton still says it will be ready by the middle of winter, at which time the engaging of an assistant will become a matter for immediate consideration. I'll look through the September *Atlantick* when next I am at the library, & shall no doubt enjoy the "Two Peas in a Pod" article if it reflects my own disgust at standardisation & monotony. I'll read that other one, too—"Hey Diddle Diddle".[2] Yes—you might keep the Talman stories to shew A E P G—& sometime I'll send you his crayon sketches of the house at Angell & Benefit Sts. I haven't heard from him since his arrival in Providence, & suppose the task of getting settled at college is keeping him busy. He ought to be glad to get to Providence, as I am sure A E P G will. Hurrah for the riddance of Butler Exchange & Infantry Hall! It would be a good idea, though, to call the new structures by the same names; thus preserving a continuity of tradition whilst escaping the ugliness of the Victorian edifices. All I hope is that the coming buildings won't be too *tall*. Tall buildings belong only in certain geographical locations, where limited surface compels expansion upward, & where there can be enough of them to provide a continuous horizon of fairy-like pinnacles. In a small New England city this sort of construction & horizon must be held distinctly out of place; the proper skyline being one of traditional steeples, belfries, domes, trees, chimneys, & low roofs. Thank heaven that in Providence the hill provides a dominance of old-time features which even the Turk's Head & Biltmore cannot overthrow. The Christian Science dome in Prospect St., a purely classical object, is likely to crown our urban silhouette for many generations. After N.Y. it is a relief to come upon skylines of the old type as I did in Flushing & Hempstead. Again I envy the skill of a Laswell, who can draw such things with animated pen, & for ever preserve his choicest impressions of them. I shall certainly be most effusively grateful if you can get me that set of Westminster St. views at the Hist. Soc. In case you have mislaid the letter in which I described the booklet, I will again quote the title in full: "Westminster St., Providence, as it was in 1824, Drawings of Francis Read, Presented by his Daughter, Mrs. Marinus Willett Gardner.[3] R.I. Historical Society, 1917." As I said before—get one for your-self too, & don't fail to look at the coloured originals as display'd on the top floor of the building. Morton & I saw them in 1923. And by the way—if you can get Hoppin's "Auton House" or Ezra Stiles' diary at any local library, I'd be infinitely oblig'd for a glance by parcel post—prompt & safe return guar-anteed! I'm greatly interested to hear that Dr. Clark knew Henry R. Chace so well. Chace's contributions to our knowledge of Old Providence are truly tremendous, & must have involved a degree of laborious research & collation beyond any layman's power to estimate. Oh, yes—I recall now that a Mrs. Chace had something to do with that volume of Poe letters to Mrs. Whit-man,[4] & that she presented a lock of Poe's hair (originally in Mrs. W's keep-ing) to the Poe Cottage in Fordham. Very shortly I shall send you by parcel post some of my favourite R.I. books—ones belonging to me, which you can read & return at leisure. Meanwhile it would pay you to see if you can get the Kimball book anywhere—Pub. Lib., Athenaeum, College Library, &c. &c. Yes—I shall see "The Lost World" this week, & know I shall enjoy it. Those of our gang who saw it are still marvelling over the impressive cleverness of the mechanical effects. Meanwhile don't miss "Siegfried" or "The Phantom of the Opera" when they come. I wish I might have seen that white kittie with whom you conversed in Angell St., & am sure he was much cleaner than the lamented Edgar Evertsen Saltus Kirk. Edgar would have had an early bath had he stayed with his Uncle Georgius—maybe that's why, with a kind of eery prescience, he did not stay! The New School of Design building, I take it, is the *museum,* which will henceforward supplant the awkward & inad-equate basement of the main building, so long the sole abode of the collec-tion. This change is greatly to be welcomed, & yet I shall regret to see the passing of that basement museum, which in 1897–8–9 was an enchanted world for me—a true magick grotto where unfolded before me the glory that was Greece & the grandeur that was Rome. I have since seen many other mu-seums of art, & am now sojourning but a five-cent fare from the next-greatest in the world; yet I vow that none has ever moved me so much, or given me so close & vivid a sense of contact with the ancient world, as that modest basement on Waterman St. hill with its meagre plaster casts! I hope the new building does not mar the graceful lines of the Pendleton House.

Very shortly—thanks to your kind offer—I shall forward my grey shoes by parcel post for repairs; tho' I dread being without them in the interim. There's no other kind of any real good in winter, & if their construction is not a matter of arduous labour, I must say I'd appreciate few things more keenly in the future! But these present ones still have a good long life ahead, since I sedulously save them all summer by wearing bath sandals instead. As for suits—I still think 25 fish will see me through, tho' I may let A E P G send thirty in case I can find nothing for less. I've so far seen absolutely nothing in the windows that I'd wear, since what isn't faddish is double-breasted, & unsuitable for a man of middle age; but I know there must be some conservative models in large chain stores like the "Monroe Clothes" system. My summer outfit satisfies me in every way, & I'm sure I can do as well for a winter suit. If I decide—as you advise—to wear it every day, I shall get absolutely the cheapest thing which I can wear with any degree of decorum, so that I may feel justified in obtaining another a year hence & thus getting back to my normal outfit of four. What you say of higher prices for winter suits because of additional wool sounds logical, tho' I have never found it to be so in practice. Neither is it a fact that ready-made suits for fat men cost more than suits for lean—apparently the vital item in suit cost is not material but workmanship. About shoes—I find my 1918 Pierce pair in better shape than I expected, hence may be able to postpone further investments in this direction a while. The later 1922 pair wore out first, & were thrown away at Parkside; but these old war-horses, which I wore all around Gloucester, Magnolia, Cleveland, &c., still hold together without any actual holes. Since the approach of winter may limit my long "hikes", it is quite possible that these resurrected relicks may tide me over till spring if I live that long.

You might shew A E P G the *Weird Tales* letter & send it back some time—& meanwhile I will send you Wright's latest as soon as I get it answered. I'm going to send him a large additional batch of tales as soon as I get them typed in the course of my present Remingtonian siege. And I am going, also, to begin a series of new tales after I get all this old business settled. I hope my cheque for "The Temple" will come soon—it's due any time now, & ought to be for quite a fair amount since the story is of considerable length as short stories go. That cheque ought to get me an oil heater & fuel, & see to the repairing of my alcove light—about which matter I shall shortly enquire at the Brooklyn Edison Co. I have resumed the use of bread, but have to do the cutting on my writing table—which I dislike very much to do. And I eat from newspapers rather than try to struggle with dishes in an unlighted cavern!

I'm glad you agree with me about the removal of historic houses to new locations—the enclosed cutting relates the latest piece of vandalism in this line. What an idea! To tear down a fine original manor-house merely to build a reproduction in a distant land, when new material could have been used with almost equal success! Well—that is life, & nothing will ever stop it. All civilisations end with the same kind of decadence, & this incident is only a repetition of what happened in declining Rome, when Constantinus stripped the arches of Titus & Trajanus to adorn his own, & filled his new capital of

Constantinopolis with sculpture & architectural details filched from all over the Hellenic world.

Both the small cuttings in your letter are of great interest, as was the roll which came Wednesday. I shall welcome the additional matter when it comes. Some day soon I shall undertake the long-promised clarification & classification of my files, so that I can find old cuttings when I want them. So far I have followed only the crudest & most empirical of systems, wherein the degree of "order" is little better than stark chaos! By the way—it seems to me the Old Farmer's Almanack ought to be out pretty soon. Let me know when you see it on the stands, & when you do, I'll look for it at the Grand Central Station—which appears to be the only place in N.Y. where it is sold. How anybody can get through the year without the Old Farmer's is a mystery to me!

And now let me exprefs the hope that your cold has taken a turn for the better! Spare no remedies or precautions, & don't exert yourself save when absolutely necessary. I am sure you could arrange with your landlady to obtain good dinners in the house without braving the raw fall air these days— try it! Enclosed is a *Tryout*—shewing that the amateur world continues to plod along. Soon I hope to send you the first *United Amateur* of young Bacon's regime. More soon—

Yr aff Nephew & obt Servt

H P L

[On envelope? In RHB's handwriting:] 12:30 p.m. Special—Last Moment. ¶ Loveman is here—I stayed in all the morning & now we're going on the trip. He brings news that *Edgar Evertsen has been back* to Kirk's & run away *again!!*

## Notes

1. [Unsigned], "Poems in the New Handwriting," *McClure's Magazine* NS 1, No. 6 (October 1925): 940–41.

2. *Atlantic Monthly* 136, No. 3 (September 1925): Earnest Elmo Calkins, "Twin Peas in a Pod," 311–18; [Unsigned,] "Hey Diddle Diddle!" 426–28. The Calkins article is a lament that the advance of mechanization and international business is causing the European nations to lose their unique and distinctive cultures. "Hey Diddle Diddle!" is a defense of Mother Goose as appropriate reading matter for small children.

3. Note the name of the character Marinus Bicknell Willett in *The Case of Charles Dexter Ward*.

4. *Last Letters of Edgar Allan Poe to Sarah Helen Whitman*, ed. James A. Harrison (New York: G. P. Putnam's Sons, 1909). One of the benefactors of the volume was Mrs. Henry R. Chace.

[133]    [ALS] [HPL to LDC]

Friday Morning
Octr 9, 1925

My dear Daughter Lillian:—

Well, here we are with the other story, typed at last! I don't believe *Weird Tales* will take it, but I shall send it along just the same to make sure. This copy is to be read, shewn to A E P G, & ultimately returned for my files. I heard from Wright yesterday, & out of the batch of tales I had sent him he accepted "He" & "The Cats of Ulthar". I am now about to send him a fresh batch, composed of this "Red Hook" tale, "From Beyond", "Beyond the Wall of Sleep", "Polaris", & "In the Vault". Along with those I shall also send S H's "Four O'Clock" & Clark Ashton Smith's "Yondo".[1] Speaking of Smith—I heard from him again this morning, & he enclosed a new drawing—which I'll send along for you & A E P G to admire & return. I trust, by the way, that you've duly welcomed the returned prodigal—from whom I received a brief announcement this morning, saying that she's cashed my $50.00 *Weird Tales* cheque & will send the proceeds by registered mail. That will solve my autumn clothing & fuel problem. I also had a card from Talman lately—which I'll enclose. It seems that he has found in our Prov. Publick Library some material of vital importance to his Dutch genealogical work—he being one of the countless heirs of Annetje Jans of New Amsterdam, whose claim to the Manhattan lands owned by Trinity Church is historic. I hope the Sunday Journal will use his material. He is stopping at 256 Benefit St.

By this time A E P G will have shewn you the letter & card which bring my diary up to Wednesday afternoon. On that occasion I did some local shopping & welcomed Mortonius as first of my evening guests—he accompanying me to the Scotch Bakery to buy refreshments. (crumb cake for Kleiner, cup cakes for all) Kleiner was next to arrive, & then McNeil, but no more came. Loveman had an engagement with the widow of Edgar Saltus, who may aid him in publishing the Saltus book which the Philadelphia firm so treacherously abandoned. The meeting was very fair, Morton shewing off some new minerals & imposing upon us the task of reading a dull book of poems by the amateur James Larkin Pearson, who wants help in selecting the best ones for a smaller volume.[2] He asked Morton's aid, & Jacobus Ferdinandus wants us all to submit a symposium of verdicts. Anything to please—but I do dread wading through those 400-odd pages! At 11:00 Mortonius & I went out for coffee, which I thereafter served in proper fashion with cake, blue china, 454 Angell silver, & triangularly folded paper napkins. All hands left at 12:30, after which I washed dishes & did typing till into the next day—finishing the ponderous MS. which I now enclose. I then rested, did some writing in the evening, rested again, & am now at my correspondence once more. After mailing this & going shopping I shall try to get rid of the Morton-Pearson business—& then I shall buckle down to writing some fiction. I have no engagements till Sunday, when I've promised to shew Loveman around Hempstead again if the weather is good.

Enclosed is a flippant modernisation of Martial by Sonny-Child. In spirit it is probably not far from the spirit of the original as applicable to the Rome of Domitian's reign. And here's a cutting to shew what sad work the flames were doing only a few blocks away whilst the Wednesday night meeting was going on!! More later.

Yr aff: Nephew & obt Servt<br>H P L

[On envelope:]
P.S. Wright wants "The Outsider", which I let him read, tho' it's promised to W. Paul Cook.[3] I've half a mind to ask Cook to let me give him something else instead—tho' of course I can furnish Wright with all the tales he can use without doing so.

[P.]P.S. Evening—
Diary continued—

Tel. message from Kirk inviting me over to help him with envelope-addressing. Am going, since I owe him many favours for books he has given me.

## Notes

1. *WT* rejected both stories. It was once believed that HPL revised "Four O'Clock," but in a letter to Winfield Townley Scott (11 December 1948; ms., JHL), Sonia states that HPL only suggested changes in the tale. It was first published in *The Horror in the Museum and Other Revisions* (Arkham House, 1970) and is now included in an appendix to *CF* 4.

2. *Pearson's Poems* appeared in 1924. Pearson (1879–1981) later published other collections. *My Fingers and My Toes* (Nashville, TN: Ingram Books Co., 1971) was his one non-self-published title. (It was subtitled "complete poems" but is actually a selection.)

3. Cook had accepted the story for the first issue of the *Recluse*.

[134]  [ALS] [HPL to LDC]

begun—Wednesday Afternoon<br>Octr. 14, 1925<br>finish'd—Thursday Evening<br>Octr. 15, 1925

My dear Daughter Lillian:—

By this time A E P G will doubtless have told you of the safe arrival of my registered letter, & of my immediate notification of her. I am sorry she had such a time inquiring at the post-office, & wish now that I hadn't written so promptly & alarmingly when Saturday failed to bring the expected envelope. For all I know the safeguards of registry may delay a letter somewhat—at any rate, it arrived safely Monday morning & I duly signed for it. Had it gone astray I am sure the P.O. would have done something decided about it—for that fee of 15¢ (so lately rais'd from 8) can hardly be for an oversight merely nominal. But all's well that ends well, & when the postman leaves the official card asking me whether the reported-missing item has come or not, I shall be happy to report its receipt.

Now as to the scattering of the golden hoard so lately received, let me assure you that I am faithfully waiting about the oil stove till all of your instructions & advice shall be assembled before me. The "Perfection" is what Mrs. Burns recommended, & what Loveman also says has a very fine reputation in Cleveland, where it is made. Yes—I shall obtain the larger or regular size if I choose this make, though I am waiting to hear of the alternative type which your landlady recommends. I'll leave it to you—as you may decide from what you learn—whether the stove had better be bought in Providence or Brooklyn; & if the latter, I'll promise not to let any *oily* clerk palm off a more expensive model on me. As you say, one always hopes that one won't need such an emergency device another year—tho' they are handy things to have wherever one is. I shouldn't throw one away under any circumstances. As to their care—of course I know absolutely nothing; but I shall make the salesman give me the very minutest instructions, & follow implicitly whatever printed directions there may be. I didn't know they demanded a base, although such a thing seems eminently logical. If a tray is very cheap I might get one; otherwise I presume the oilcloth mats you mention are the thing. What are they—linoleum? I know nothing about them, but will look for them at the ten-cent-store. I'm glad the heater will burn seven hours or so, for there are times I've needed it fully that much at a stretch. I hope to economise as much as possible, though, for oil (at its cheapest, ordered through Mrs. Burns's dealer) is 16¢ per gallon. I've just ordered 5 gallons for next week—the wagon coming around Tuesday—giving Mrs. B. $1.30; 80¢ for the oil, & 50¢ for the containers. The latter will be refunded to me when I stop taking oil & return the cans. They are 1-gallon tins, on each of which the deposit is ten cents.

Today I don't *quite* need extra heat, but the place is seldom continuously warm over any long period. It certainly put its best foot forward when you were there! Mrs. B. has the British idea of underheating; & unfortunately this is the one British custom that I can't share with enthusiasm, since Nature chanced to give me a physiological organisation which completely crumples & withers when the mercury gets much below 74° or 76°. I simply can't guide a pen, & shake every now & then with involuntary contractions of the shoulder muscles. I was certainly made for the tropics, as my airy love of the most sizzling summer days shews, & would try to settle in Florida or somewhere if that didn't mean an even worse distance from the Colonial New England which has come to mean my only surviving interest in life. Coal in N.Y. is $18.50 per ton, & very hard to obtain. Prof. Watson's excellent advice would be of no avail here; for on account of the effects of bituminous soot & grime in so densely populated a region, the use of soft coal is prohibited by the city ordinances. Householders, therefore, must freeze or turn to gas & oil if they cannot get either anthracite or coke.

As for my diary, previously brought to Monday–Tuesday midnight, you will find it chronologically brief but important—for *I have bought a suit!* Of this more anon—but I may reach that part of the diary by saying that before dawn Tuesday I wrote a weird piece of verse prompted by the season,[1] (copy enclosed) & that I thereafter sailed into the Saltus typing for Loveman, getting the stuff done by the middle of the morning & thanking Gawd for the finish. The more closely I examined the MSS., the less I liked them. Tinsel cleverness only—Saltus assuredly petered out after his golden heyday of the late 'eighties & early 'nineties. But it all helps Loveman toward the recognition he desires. If Mrs. Saltus gets Brentano's to publish the book, the presence in it of two hitherto unpublished Saltus items will promote its bibliographic interest & ensure it a somewhat wide circulation. Upon completing this task I did up some correspondence & arranged with Mrs. Burns for my oil. So pleased was the Gorgon at the prospect of my not using the electrick heater, that she became almost civil; detailing the evils of the coal situation, & incidentally promising once more to have a man fix my alcove light. Then, buckling on my armour & going through the advertisements in all the local newspapers I could get, I prepared to sally forth in quest of a winter suit.

And what a quest! From shop to shop I went, but to buy a decent suit of winter weight for anything less than $35.00 seemed for a time an impossibility; & when I finally did achieve it I could denominate it as nothing less than a miracle. I shall try it on tomorrow after alterations, & will send you a sample unless the tailor forgot to save some as I told him to.

To keep track of all the emporia I visited would require an intellect more statistical than mine. "Monroe Clothes", where I got my fine summer suit & on which I had rather depended, had nothing at all except flimsy things no thicker than that aestival outfit itself—& that, I soon found, is well-nigh the universal rule today. In this age of well-heated houses men have stopped wearing the heavy clothing they used to wear (just as winter underwear is practically obsolete)—so that the unhappy victim of a menage in which the name *Burns* applies to the family instead of the fuel is very literally left out in the cold! Moreover, a three-button coat is virtually unobtainable except in the more costly grades. Even the most conservative of the cheaper suits have the two-button sack—which is just the same as the older style except that the top button (usually left unbuttoned anyway & rolled under the lapel) is absent. Kirk's spring suit (which you'll recall my admiring last April) is of this sort— which reminds me that he's had two fine ones since then: a blue with white pencil stripe* (like Loveman's new one*) bought in Cleveland, & a fine new grey* just purchased in N.Y. Like me, he wants four always on hand for all weathers. I wonder if he'll get a Prince-Albert or morning-coat for the wedding which may take place in December?

Returning to my yesterday's quest—it were tedious to enumerate the places I visited—& the more I saw the more bleak the prospect appeared. Anything under about $35.00 was either thin & slimpsy, or sportily cut, or of undesirable pattern, or of abominable texture & workmanship. This last was the great objection against my first choice—the blue serge type. Fabricks were of plebeian coarseness, & lapels & other individual features seemed hewn with a blunt axe or hacked by a blind man with dull shears! At only one place did I find anything of three buttons with a decent design, & even this had a pattern (tho' a subdued one) & was so thin & crinkly that it suggested mid-July when it didn't suggest the poorhouse.

But ere long my quest became complicated by a new problem. I *did* find a suit of *exactly* the right goods, weight, grade of tailoring, & conservatism of cut—EXCEPT that the coat was two-button instead of three. It is true that its aspect was exactly like that of my present clothes, since the top button of a three-button sack is always rolled under the lapel; but the fact that the button was *absent* instead of merely *hidden* rankled. I could not help thinking that I *might possibly* find something somewhere else which would surpass it; so I told the salesman that I might or might not be back. This establishment was one into whose windows I had looked last summer—the Borough Clothiers in Fulton St. Bklyn. They had first shewed me cheap goods like the rest, but when I told them that I could not take such material—& also that I could not pay more, since this suit was to be but a provisional affair awaiting a better—they began to be doubly courteous through the possibility of selling me a second suit when the time came . . . . . for I did not mention that that time would be at least a year from now. And so the zealous salesman consulted a man higher up, & proceeded to make a raid on the higher-priced cases; offering to let me have a better suit for the rigid twenty-five than this figure would ordinarily procure—all in the interest of securing my further custom. There were no three-buttons, but from the $34.50† case (after many trials of $27.50's, $30.00's, $32.50's, & other $34.50's) the man finally produced the suit which gave me pause. It was a dark, rich grey without any pattern, & had the cut & tone of a gentleman's attire. After the anaemic fabricks I had been disgustedly inspecting it was a relief & a revelation, & I had almost pounced upon it with savage fierceness after a trial of the coat (which fitted perfectly &

---

*all of these of the new-fangled 2-button sort!

†I regard this price as bona-fide, because it was printed on the tags sewn on the suit; whereas the suits the salesman had previously shewn me as twenty-five dollar suits had that smaller sum printed & sewn on in just the same way.

was exceptionally becoming) when I started to button up the garment that so vastly delighted me. Then I discovered that, although its outward appearance was just like that of my usual coats, (of which I fasten the top button only about twice or three times in all the decade of wear I get out of them) this coat was of the despised & new-fangled two-button type! Hell!! It certainly was a problem. Here was virtually my only chance to get a really good & becoming suit for twenty-five dollars—& all spoiled by a hidden detail of which I might be conscious as many as two times in the next ten years! The salesman warningly told me that I could find no such opportunity elsewhere, & advised me not to miss the chance of getting a suit so conclusively of a higher grade than that for which I felt able to pay—yet it seemed as if some perfect three-button outfit might just *possibly* be lurking undiscover'd around the corner.

And so I moved on, & resumed the weary quest—visiting fully as many shops as I had visited before, & finding always the same story—of nothing suitable under the 35-dollar grade. But as I went from place to place I became a realist. Studying cuts & fabrics of all prices, I began to see clearly that the suit I had admired & rejected on a technicality certainly *was* of the $34.50 grade, & most definitely so. The texture & drape, tailoring & style, all corresponded to what other dealers shewed me only at a price well over thirty dollars—added to which was the important fact that it was one of the very few which seemed to be of sufficient warmth & thickness. And so—as the preceding paragraphs have perhaps suggested—I went back & bought it!

What I have is assuredly a marvellous value for $25.00, yet not a farthing more did I pay. It is precisely of the shade, type, & texture I most desire—except that that hidden top button is not there. And after all—would it have been worth while to pay nearly a ten-spot more for the psychological consolation of an invisible presence which I never use? With my present lean purse—now forced to bear a steady oil bill besides all its former burthens—I did not feel justified in spending a tenth of an hundred dollars for an unseen button! I doubt if I shall tell the gang that the extra button isn't there—& I'm sure they'll never suspect it if I don't. As for me—I shall forget it myself, & exult in the truly phenomenal turn of Fate which has given me a really tasteful & becoming suit for a price so small. I am sure you will be delighted when you see the sample & the photograph I shall have taken. Really—the longer I reflect, the more astonishing seems my luck in the matter! Having made this momentous purchase, I performed minor errands & returned to 169—so fatigued

that I was forced to retire almost at once; awaking again early this morning. I did, however, receive a telephone call from Loveman, saying that Kirk's ex-partner has a typewriting job to be done, which I can get if my rates are low enough. Typing is a terrible ordeal for me, but I shall accept the order if the fellow is willing to pay the best rates (75¢ per 1000 wds) as just ascertained by me in the advertising columns of the *Writer's Digest*. I am going to see him about the matter late this afternoon, before proceeding to the (Leeds) meeting at Loveman's. Meanwhile I shall wrestle with correspondence, & possibly get out to the barber's if I have time. I'm not sure whether or not I can get this letter ready for mailing before the meeting. Friday S H will be in town—perhaps to stay 2 or 3 days—calling me up at noon & arranging to meet me about 5:30 p.m. for dinner. Meanwhile I shall go for the new suit—wearing it if it is all right, but leaving it for further alterations if (as is more likely) the first set of changes prove not quite enough. I never knew a suit to be right with only one round of "fixings-over".

And now let me thank you for all the interesting cuttings—both the few enclosed in letters & the varied wealth of treasure sent under separate cover. The rolls came yesterday afternoon, & have furnished me with an abundant feast of piquant mental diversion. My files have visibly expanded after receiving the additions to various departments, & to thank you individually item for item were a fruitless attempt, much as I should like to achieve it! The pictures are delightful. Cologne's skyline reminds me once again how tawdry the average American city is with its ugly business structures as opposed to a really beautiful town with peaked gables & Gothick spires. The cathedral at Cologne is Morton's favourite building, though others profess to find German Gothick relatively crude as compared with that of France & England. And Newburyport! How well I recall my first sight of that square![2] Little Davis & I rode through on the car, confidently expecting to come *later* on the main business section, when it turned out presently that this *is* the main business section! It is just about as old Tim Dexter saw it—which reminds me that this new biography of Tim[3] seems to differ with the authorities that I looked up, in that it credits the accounts of the whalebone, coal, & warming-pan ventures, whereas other authorities have been inclined to relegate them to the domain of myth as fictional boasts fostered by the fanciful & egotistical eccentrick. Some day I must get that large print of Tim's mansion framed! Speaking of Little Davis—he has just entered Harvard, & now lives at 50 Newport St., Arlington, Mass. (N. of Cambridge, on the way to Lexington & Concord—the former Indian "Monotomy") He will have plenty of competition now in the matter of brains, but I'm confident the little rascal will hold his own amongst the best of 'em! He was seventeen last April—some boy! But it's too bad (to go toward the other chronological extreme) that honest old Bicknell has departed this life.[4] He was such a delicious & colourful link with the past that I had

hoped to see him live on indefinitely. To be cut off at only 91 is provoking—
& yet he had accomplisht much in the brief span which the Lord allow'd him.

About the return of the Elgin Marbles to the Acropolis—I'm in favour
of it if the Greek government proves its intention to embark on a really bona
fide restoration of the Parthenon. The place for ancient beauty is on the spot
where it flourished, & the British Museum would best prove its true patronage of art & beauty by seeing that the sculptures are fixed in the most appropriate setting, wherever that may be. You'll recall that Lord Byron mercilessly
attacked Lord Elgin in 1811 for bringing over the marbles—writing an unpublished satire called "The Curse of Minerva" which was printed after his
death.[5] He has Minerva appear in scorn & tears by her ruined temple & thus
address the despoiler:

> "'Mortal'—'twas thus she spake—'that blush of shame
> Proclaims the Briton, once a noble name:
> First of the mighty, foremost of the free,
> Now honour'd *less* by all, & *least* by me:
> Chief of thy foes shall Pallas still be found.
> Seek'st thou the cause of loathing?—look around.
> Lo! here, despite of war & wasting fire,
> I saw successive tyrannies expire.
> 'Scaped from the ravage of the Turk & Goth,
> Thy country sends a spoiler worse than both.
> Survey this vacant, violated fane;
> Recount the relicks torn that yet remain;
> *These* Cecrops plac'd, *this* Pericles adorn'd,
> *That* Adrian rear'd when drooping Science mourn'd.
> What more I owe, let gratitude attest—
> Know Alaric & Elgin did the rest.'"

And speaking of restoration—I am indeed glad to hear of the coming renaissance of the old Arlington estate, which I visited last April & found in a
state of discouraging bareness. The article, though, is amusingly erroneous in
associating this house so intimately with the *Lees*, (whose ancestral estate was
*Stratford*, in Westmoreland County) since it is a *Custis* home, & only came to
Robert E. Lee through his wife, who was a Custis. Thus one might add to the
ignorant writer's statement that Genl. Lee 'was the last of his line to possess
Arlington', the equally correct statement that he was likewise the *first* to do so!
As for Dr. Bartram's garden & house—I saw them in Philadelphia last November, & wish the season had been such that I might have tasted pears from
a tree which has regaled Lord Cornwallis, Genl. Washington, & Dr. Franklin!
The house itself—built by the botanist's own hands—is a pretentious mansion of stone put up in 1731, but has many crudities of detail & immaturities

of proportion owing to the amateurish education & ability of its somewhat eccentrick builder & owner. (vide my travelogues of that period) But of course the articles touching on Rhode-Island were of greatest interest to me. I have often seen the old *Warwick* in the harbour of New-York when crossing the ferry to Staten-Island, & invariably lift my hat to it. And to think that the ancient *What Cheer* is here, too—scrapped & stranded in the mud like Grandpa Theobald! And the familiar *Islander,* too, upon which I made my only trip to Seaconnet in July, 1902![6] I recall the frightful headache I had whilst driving about Seaconnet, & how the 155234 prescription cured it during the return trip, & what a thunderstorm sprang up whilst we were off Prudence Island, & how it cleared up gloriously before we hove in sight of Bristol's gleaming steeples . . . . . And the old *Pontiac,* that I used to see going through Red Bridge on its way to or from Pawtucket—great God! I'm going to take a ride in it out to the Statue of Liberty! And more—as coincidence would have it— my outbound trip on that Hudson River excursion of last month was in the *DeWitt Clinton,* built by the Grand Trunk with PROVIDENCE in mind! I'm glad to note the growth of the Athenaeum, which is an unbroken continuation of the old Providence Library founded by Stephen Hopkins in 1754. May it live for ever & prosper! And that Siamese kitty-cat poem is delicious—I must shew it to Kirk when he gets his second Edgar Evertsen Saltus Kirklet from the Downing St. restaurant! And now I must declare a recess & get out to the barber's. Will continue the diary later, beginning at this place.

*Thursday Evening, 7:15 p.m.*

   Well, *the suit is here!* The coat & trousers fitted like a dream, & the tailor altered the waistcoat whilst I waited. And what a result! The thing is absolutely *sumptuous,* & I don't believe I'll dare to take it for every-day. It is certainly no mere $25.00 suit, for as I inspect all the details of tailoring I can see that it is a more finished garment (as to lining, buttonholes, &c) than even my delightful bargain of last June. With its luxurious texture, impeccable cut, & perfect fit, it fairly radiates comfort, restfulness, & good breeding; & is certainly every inch as much a gentleman's garment as the new suits for which Kirk has been paying so much more. I have, in truth, every reason to believe that the price-mark of $34.50 was a *bona fide* one; & shall assuredly give to this firm (whose card I enclose) whatever future patronage circumstances may allow. I know that S H will be enthusiastick over it tomorrow, & have half a mind to go down to Kirk's tonight (where the gang are addressing envelopes) to shew it off! The only trouble is that it is too nice to get mussed up by wearing—I ought to keep it in a glass case & get a cheap suit to wear! Yes—I certainly do enjoy good clothes—of the quiet & rich variety. It is a form of aesthetic pleasure which I should indulge to the full if possessed of the proper resources; being always dressed in the height of sedate luxury & immaculateness, & having an immense wardrobe of sober, aristocratic garments to provide that tasteful & unostentatious variety from day to day which becomes a gentleman. And now for the disappointment. I could *not* get *samples,* & don't know what I shall do to convey you the proper idea of the suit's exquisite dark fabrick! I have half a mind to send you the waistcoat by parcel post, to be returned as soon as possible. By Jove, I'll do it! Just as soon as I've shew'd it off to S H & the gang! In taking in the garments the tailor could find no good left-over pieces, & did not realise that I wanted specimens so much that I'd have been satisfied with any old scraps & inch-wide fragments. And I must get photographed! The fit is delightful—very loose, & suggesting my present 1918 blue suit in cut & atmosphere. And one would never suspect the absence of the third & top button. I haven't put it on yet—it is really quite too utterly good to wear!

But now for my diary, left off on sheet III as I was about to depart for the tonsorial artist's. I got a better man than last month, (one has to take what chance brings in these 40¢ places. A regular shop like the nice Flatbush one I patronised last year charges 60¢) so that I have a trim & splendidly balanced cut to match my new suit. From there I went down town to see this chap about the typing job, & may get the order in a week or so—which will help out finely with my oil bill if it materialises, though the work is peculiarly nerve-racking & exhausting to me, & impossible to keep up long at a stretch. From there I went over to the shop where Loveman works, meeting him & Kleiner, & going out with the two to the Automat (the 14th St. one) for din-ner. (I had beef & mince pie) We then turned up our coat collars (for a rain had set in) & proceeded to the subway; entraining for 169, where we packed up my crockery, silver, trays, & coffee-pail in the valise to take over to Loveman's—I having offered to act as caterer, since he is peculiarly helpless in matters of domestick management. En route we stopt at the Scotch Bakery for crumb-cake & apple tarts, which I carried under my coat (the 1909 one) whilst Loveman toted the valise. Arriving at Loveman's, we found Mortonius already there; admitted by the amiable old landlady (the one you saw) & mak-ing himself at home. Then followed a very entertaining session, during which Morton shewed off his newest minerals, whilst general discussion flow'd free & fast. At one time Loveman had a caller in the person of his bibulous fel-low-poet Hart Crane, (formerly of Cleveland) who was just back from the country & only about ¼ "lit up" by his beloved booze. Poor Crane! A real poet & man of taste, descendant of an ancient Connecticut family & a gentleman to the finger-tips, but the slave of dissipated habits which will soon ruin both his constitution & his still striking handsomeness! Crane left after about an hour, & the meeting proceeded. At 11 I went out for coffee, splashing through the rain & finding at the cafeteria an exquisite & tiny black-&-white kitty-cat whose graceful anticks detained me a considerable while. Then I returned & served the refreshments, (I had brought paper napkins) later washing & repacking the dishes & silver whilst the gang talked poetry. Kleiner—drat his clumsiness!—

broke one of my blue china cups; which makes two broken, counting the one Kirk broke last February. I must get a couple more at the 10¢ store to complete my set. *I* have not broken *any*, despite my constant use of the articles! Well—we broke up about 1:00 a.m., & I returned to 169. Fatigued, I retired at once; & slept till quite late today. Today I have been wrestling with correspondence & shopping—& in the late afternoon I got the memorable suit. The evening is still young, & the more I think of that impeccable cut, fit, & texture the more I am moved to put the suit on & go down to crow over Kirk & his two new suits, neither of which has the subtle tone & elegance of mine, despite the greater price he paid for them. ($37.50 for the blue & $40.00 for the grey) Anyway I'll put it on now & admire myself in the glass— & I *must* send you that waistcoat to give you an idea of the thing! Oh, yes—& I must make room for the newcomer in the clothespress; where, I trust, it may long rest undisturb'd by the covetous & the predatory!

*15 minutes later*

It's on! And what a beauty it is! Really, it is almost incongruous on such an ugly hulk as Grandpa Theobald! Elegance—dignity—decorum—these qualities stick out all over it! Certainly I am going down to shew off—& if the new kitten is there I shall cover myself with newspapers before daring to play with him! As I study the vest with the coat on I find a bit of residual looseness in the neck, which I may let the tailor amend later, but for the present I needn't bother. It's a great buy, & I shall exult properly in it!

Here's hoping your cold is better, & that A E P G had a good trip to Boston. I'm sorry she was so worried about the registered letter, & have sent her renewed assurance of its safety. With every good wish,

Yr most aff Nephew & obt Servt

H P L

## Notes

1. Either "October" or "Hallowe'en in a Suburb."

2. HPL first visited Newburyport, MA, in the company of the young Edgar J. Davis, in the spring of 1923. He would later draw upon it for the setting of "The Shadow over Innsmouth" (1931).

3. John P. Marquand, *Lord Timothy Dexter of Newburyport, Massachusetts.*

4. Thomas W. Bicknell (1834–1925), Rhode Island historian, died on 6 October 1925.

5. In fact, *The Curse of Minerva* was written in 1807 and published as a pamphlet in 1820, four years before Byron's death.

6. HPL apparently refers to Seaconnet Point, RI, a peninsula on the northern tip of Aquidneck Island in Narragansett Bay. Nothing is known of his 1902 trip there.

[135]  [ANS postcard][1] [HPL to LDC]

> [Postmarked Brooklyn, N.Y.,
> 16 October 1925]
> FRIDAY NOON
> Octr. 16, 1925

Diary, Continued:—

Didn't go to Kirk's last night after all. Tired, so just mailed letter & retired. Up early today & went to see about my vest. The tailor had plenty of spare time, so worked while I waited, & after three fittings the vest is letter perfect. En route I laid in a new collar supply—my neck being now down to 14½ even. Fortunately I had not even unwrapped my last batch of 14¾ stiff collars, so changed them. And more—I came across a special sale of *fountain pens* at *$1.28,* & bought the one I have needed for so long—am writing with it now. It is a self-filler, & has the large barrel I need for holding loads of ink. It is of the new popular orange colour—I didn't want it, but they had no black rubber ones, & the sale was too good to miss. Kirk has one & it works finely. ¶ Am at P.O. now, but must hasten home to receive call from S H. Yrmmmm H P L

P.S. The new suit looks great by daylight!!

*Notes*

1. *Front:* Blank.

[136]  [ANS postcard][1] [HPL to LDC]

> [Postmarked Brooklyn, N.Y.,
> 19 October 1925]
> *Monday*

Talk about *your* moving—listen to this bad news!

Mrs. Burns is raising my rent to $10.00 per wk. *even*—instead of $40.00 per month. Would you stay if you were I, or would you look around for something else? It will amount to about $3.00 per month more, I fancy, though of course the weekly cheque from A E P G will still cover it. Faucet just fixed in the alcove, & she promises to fix the light soon—although in crude attempts to do this she has broken the plug feeding the tall lamp & shews no disposition to fix this up. I'll wait for your advice before getting my heater.

You have my sympathy on your own household upheaval!

More very soon—

> Yr aff Nephew & obt Servt
> H P L

## Notes

1. *Front:* Blank.

[137]     [ALS] [HPL to LDC]

Tuesday Afternoon
Octr. 20, 1925

My dear daughter Lillian:—

Here's a farewell communication to old 188,[1] & a sequel to the bombardment of sketchy postcards which recent days have brought forth. Heaven knows that moving *is* a lottery—& in this weather a painful nuisance—so that in spite of my rage of yesterday at the slight rent increase I am now, after mature reflection, inclined to cast my vote on the side of pacific acquiescence. After all—the weekly cheque of ten fish will still cover the matter, & I shall by remaining be spared the far from negligible expense of furniture transportation. Moreover—once settled in a new place, I might have the same trouble repeated before long—to say nothing of a possible increase when S H stays there, as she may next month if Cleveland does not turn out well. So, despite the fact that I have postponed the purchase of my oil-stove till I have your final opinion & advice, I am now inclined toward the policy of hanging on for the present at an even ten per week (abt. 43 per month instead of the former 40 per month) rather than risk the uncertainties & vicissitudes of a sudden move. I have made use of this occasion to tell Mrs. B. what I think of the shortcomings of the place, & she has promised better linen service—whatever that promise may be worth. If I do stay, I'll have to get my oil stove at once; for if Mrs. B. ever finds me with this electric heater going, you may look for my brief obituary in the *N.Y. Times* & *Brooklyn Eagle*. Let me know as soon as possible how you vote—for I've impanelled you as foreman of a hastily assembled family jury!

Concerning your own household crisis—again I exprefs my profoundest sympathy, temper'd with gratification at the thought that you have Delilah's effective aid in the locomotive process. Tomorrow I shall be offering up prayers to Pegāna for the safe transference of your lares & penates, & shortly afterward I shall hope to hear of your complete satisfaction with the quarters at 115 Waterman—a row of houses I recall very well, & whose exterior Victorianism I hope is aton'd for by the comfort & spaciousness of the interior. Don't work too hard at your moving—remember that Delilah is on hand to do all the heavy lifting. And let me know what the place is like when you're settled.

Yes—Alfredus is out of his worries. His wife succeeded in convincing his mother that the fiscal debacle wasn't as bad as it might be, so he received a $250.00 cheque which—with the exercise of frugality—will solve all his problems. Yesterday I received two more communications from him which were actually mailed several days *before* the one I received first, & in them was a vast new batch of scenick & antiquarian cards for which the little rascal (besides returning the cash Grandpa sent him for the former cards) absolutely refuses to accept remuneration! I enclose a duplicate for your collection—this is the Place de la Concorde, with the Egyptian obelisk in the centre, & the Madeleine & Sacre-Coeur in various parts of the background. Some of the new *gargoyle* cards are hideously impressive—ghouls & chimaeras which lend to Notre Dame a touch of the sinister. They are so well done that one can forgive the modernity of most of them—for in cruel truth most of them are the work of the modern architect Viollet-le-Duc, who restored the cathedral to its mediaeval state betwixt 1847 & 1876. Very few of the original gargoyles survived intact. M. le Duc's work on Notre Dame quite atones for some of the Second-Empire atrocities he perpetrated on other publick buildings of Paris. The Boy wrote a long travelogue this time, & illustrated it with judiciously chosen cards of ancient streets & buildings. He is certainly getting to be Grandpa's little antiquarian—& he certainly has struck the right city to be an antiquarian in! Among this quota of views are some of the few surviving *Roman* ruins in Paris—the baths of the Imperator Julianus, & an arena of even earlier date. It was Julianus (Julian the Apostate, so-called) whose liking for Lutetia Parisiorum raised it from obscurity to the position of an important provincial town. During his reign it discarded the ancient name of Lutetia & adopted formally the appellation of *Parisii*.

Yes—I shall get Regal shoes, but not *exactly* the same as the last ones, since I want them *high*. I plan to obtain *Style 2021*, which you can see for yourself in any Regal window. Let me know whether or not you deem my choice wise! As for the sending of the new vest—hang it all, but *how* am I to let you know *just* what I've got? It is the precise *texture* I wish you to see—the smooth yet not hard surface, the well-bred darkness of a patternless mixture wherein light & dark grey threads are made to fuse aristocratically to an homogeneous whole in which the diversity or "pepper-&-saltness" is only faintly suggested as the eye strives to judge whether the fabrick is black, navy-blue, or very dark grey. It is, as becomes a winter suit, vastly darker than the summer one. I've just been over it again (for I'm in my wrap) to see if there is a single inside piece that I can snip off, but am hang'd if I can find one! It's so confoundedly well tailor'd that everything is neatly even & sewed down! I'll see what I can do— but meanwhile you shall shortly behold full-length snap-shots of me in both my new suits—summer & winter—these having been taken by S H Sunday noon. I'll have the film developed as soon as I take up the remaining exposures in Hempstead.

As for my diary—I think it ended in the P.O. Friday noon as I was going home to get S H's call. The call came, & after some finishing touches on the dusting I went down to Budry's restaurant to meet the arriving guest. Meanwhile I noticed with rage that Mrs. Burns had broken the tall lamp connexion in her efforts to fix the alcove light—& that she shew'd no disposition to repair her damage; averring that there were enough other lights for one room! Having found S H at Budry's in a new brown dress as tasteful in its way as my new suit, we dined & went to a cinema of Harold Lloyd—"The Freshman", which I think is now at the Victory.[2] We had then meant to attend still another, but a sudden drizzle caused us to abandon the design & proceed to 169. En route we stopped at the Grand Central for S H's valise & at the Clinton Delicatessen for provisions. Arriv'd at 169, we ate supper, read, & retired; arising early on Saturday the 17th. S H is reading for the first time that semiclassick of a few years ago—"If Winter Comes", & wanted me to read it in order to discufs it with her.[3] This I did—beginning it Friday night & finishing it Saturday night. It is not bad—almost literature, in fact—but deadly dull & very overstrain'd & melodramatick in character-drawing toward the last. Saturday morning I set out early on several errands—among them the obtaining of a fountain pen for S H like the one I had bought the day before. This time they *did* have dark ones, & of course I got one. Later, reflecting on the aestheticks of the matter, I changed my orange one for a dark one—but as luck would have it, the new one has an unsatisfactory point! Now I must change it again if they'll let me—large pens for $1.28 are not a bargain to be sneezed at! On this occasion I also bought 2 cups at Woolworth's to replace the broken ones. I had to take saucers too, but since the pair cost but a dime I couldn't object. Now I have two extra saucers to break! But the most important event of all was the shortening (whilst I waited) of the new trousers, which S H thought too long. Now the suit is *perfect*—as I hope you'll agree from the snapshot. Returning to 169 I read diligently in "If Winter Comes", & at 7 p.m. met S H downtown for dinner at the Automat & a search for a good cinema or play. I say *search* advisedly—for the crowding of everything was incredible, & we couldn't find a thing offer'd save standing-room. Accordingly we didn't go anywhere, but return'd to 169 to read—stopping en route for some more provisions—crackers, raspberry jelly, apples, pears, grapes, a lemon, a grapefruit, & some of that exquisite Swiss Gruyere cheese. That evening I finished "If Winter Comes" before retiring—being excellently sooth'd to sleep by it. The next day—Sunday the 18th—we were up early, ate breakfast & wash'd the dishes, took snapshots, & in general wasted so much time that we had to abandon the Hempstead trip. At noon we proceeded to the Grand Central to arrange for S H's trip that evening, & from there we repaired to the Penn. Sta., where we made some futile inquiries anent Hempstead trains. Seeing that we couldn't tour Long Island, we proceeded toward Times Square, selecting Regal shoes in a window, & finally stopping at a Keith theatre to see the vaudeville—the usual weary round of singing, dancing, trained dogs, & acrobaticks. The 2nd balcony was only 50¢. After this we proceeded to the Grand Central & loiter'd till S H's train left. I then went to the Milan for a minestrone & spaghetti dinner, & thence return'd to 169 to read & re-tire—arising Monday at noon to admit Mrs. B. & a faucet repair man, & to receive the bad news anent rent. I then wrote some, & in the mid-afternoon received a call from Sonny-Child, who wanted to shew Grandpa his big new double-breasted winter overcoat. He liked the Old Gentleman's suit, & said it was just like all of my things—sedate & quiet. In the evening I saw the Child to the subway—stopping en route for my disastrous change of pen. Then I return'd to 169 to write till 3 a.m. & then retire. Today I was awak'd at 10:30 a.m. by a telephone call from Kirk & Loveman, who want me to go to Kirk's this evening. Georgius has a new kitty-cat named Priscilla, & I shall buy him a catnip ball when I go. I shall go down to Loveman's shop at six, dine with him, & then proceed to Kirk's. I have written letters all day, & must now dress for my engagement. I've never seen Kirk's new 15th St place, & he's never seen my new suit! I hope the gang will like the garment. Tomorrow night there's a McNeil meeting at Sonny's. The locale of the following Leeds meeting is undetermined. Hallowe'en the Blue Pencil Club meets at the home of some friends in New Jersey across the 125th St ferry, (literary topick, "Oc-tober Days") but it's such a nuisance getting there that I don't believe I'll go. And S H will next be here early in November, as present plans look. Such is my diary—past & to come—to the best of my knowledge.

And so it goes. Here's the best of luck on your moving, & a hope for your early vote on my household question. More later—I'll tell you about Kirk's kittie.

Yr aff Nephew & obt Servt—

H P L

P.S. Sonny may let the amateur Parker publish him a thin book of poems (abt. 30 pp—board cover) for $125. or $150.—his aunt to defray half the cost. Kirk & Loveman will help him sell it in N.Y.[4]

P.P.S. Marvellous bundle just came from A E P G. I must rhapsodically thank her.

## Notes

1. At the time, LDC was living at 188 Waterman Street.

2. *The Freshman* (Harold Lloyd Entertainment, 1925), directed by Fred Newmeyer and Sam Taylor; starring Harold Lloyd, Jobyna Ralston, and Brooks Benedict.

3. By A. S. M. Hutchinson. The novel, dealing with domestic conflict in which a woman divorces and, as an unwed mother, commits suicide, was the best-selling book of 1922.

4. Parker did not publish the book, but a similar volume, *The Man from Genoa and Other Poems,* appeared in 1926 from W. Paul Cook.

[138]     [ANS postcard]¹ [HPL to LDC]

[Postmarked Brooklyn, NY,
21 October 1925]
*Wednesday Evening*

Welcome to fresh woods & pastures new! A E P G transmitted your house-hold verdict to me. I stay—& tomorrow I buy my oil stove! The oil came yes-terday.

¶ As I left for a late afternoon shopping tour today I mailed A E P G a diary letter—which you will see presently. It now remains for me to add the results of that tour.

¶ I changed the pen for the one I'm now writing with—black fluted bar-rel with gold trimmings. It seems to flow very well, & is certainly a bargain at $1.28.

¶ And I got my Regals! No. 2021, as I told you I would. They are Vici kid, & feel as comfortable as the knit bedroom shoes which I'm about to send you for repairs! I have them on now, but shan't wear them for every-day after this. The man said they ought to be kept on *shoe-trees,* but when I went to look for mine I couldn't find them. Do you recall my bringing them to 169?

¶ Loveman was going to call for me here before the meeting, but tele-phones that he is detained. Therefore I'll start right out for Sonny's now. More later.

¶ Hope you had an easy moving, & that you find 115 tolerable.

Yr aff nephew & obt Servt
H P L

*Notes*

1. *Front:* Blank.

[139]     [ALS] [HPL to LDC]

Thursday Afternoon
Octr. 22, 1925

My dear daughter Lillian:—

Well! So my card of welcome to 115 was a bit premature after all! I wonder if you got it? It told of changing my fountain pen for a black one which I like, of getting my new 2021 Regals, & of starting out for the McNeil meeting at Sonny's. I reach'd Belknap's in safety, & en-joy'd what was almost an ideal meeting; with all hands present, & everybody happy except honest old McNeil, over whose puzzled head most of the conver-sation flew. The business of the evening was the reading   by Mortonius—of all the poems Sonny has pickt out for his coming book, & the minute criticism of every point by everyone present. It was certainly a splendid batch of poetry, & the items adversely criticised very few; so that the session was really a highly instructive exposition of the poetick principle. I hope the literal-minded & timorously silent M^cNeil profited by what he heard going on around him! My suit made the same hit that it did the night before at Kirk's, whilst my new 2021 Regals were a veritable knockout! Mortonius says he's getting a new suit too—in Paterson—but admitted that it'll be hardly the egregious bargain mine was! The meeting dissolv'd at 1 a.m., Morton & M^cNeil proceeding at once to the elevated, & the rest of the visiting delegation walking down Broadway to 72^nd St. for the air. At this latter point all hands took the subway, dispersing eventually to their final destinations. Having reacht 169, I read a little & retired; arising this noon & spending the time since then writing letters. I doubt if I'll have time to get the oil stove today—& if I don't I shan't go out at all, I guess, but stay in, read, & write. By the way—we've shifted the seat of the next (Leeds) meeting from Kirk's to Morton's Paterson hangout. And the week after that I entertain the M^cNeil meeting. So much for the immediate future.

Enclosed is a *Journal* bill which I hope you or A E P G can attend to in time to avoid the stoppage of the *Bulletin* at the end of the month. Pardon my bothering you, but I seem to recall that either you or she advised me to let the business be done at the Providence end. Since you're so busy, you'd better let her attend to the matter—handing her the enclosed bill the next time you see her. The more I see of other papers, the better I like the *Bulletin*. I don't think there's any other journal in existence so well-balanced!

Enclosed is the latest from S H, (I've answered it, so it needn't be returned) shewing the situation in Cleveland & announcing the final melancholy tidings of position-loss. The trouble with the new position is that it is only on a commission basis, so that during slack seasons the remuneration is next to nothing. I have just written, expressing my profoundest sympathy.

Sympathy, too, is due to you anent your chaotic week. I hope the delay to Monday comes as a respite rather than as an added inconvenience. Am I to infer that your landlady has sold the house, so that all the tenants must migrate? What a beastly nuisance!

*Evening*

Good news! A fire has been started in the furnace! How long it'll last, I don't know; but I shall enjoy it whilst I may. If they'd deferred it much longer, there'd have been legal complaints. I didn't go out, but have been reading & writing letters. Now I shall retire—without dressing & going out to mail this. I shall mail it in the morning as I go out on my quest of the oil stove, adding such tidings as the morning mail may bring. The five gallons of oil rest peacefully in their cans under my sink, & I hope shortly to have something to burn them in. I mean to start early & do considerable looking, for I may find a bargain like the one in the enclosed cutting—a real Perfection at $5.49, at our City Hall Hardware Co., 150 Washington St. Corresponding bargains ought to be lurking somewhere around Brooklyn or N.Y., if one have the patience to ferret them out. I may go to Flatbush—it's deuced odd, but the business section along Flatbush Ave. (so lately a mere country village Main St.) strikes me as a much better place to get what one wants than the business section of Brooklyn proper or any corresponding area in New York. It is more like Westminster St., I think, than any other one thoroughfare hereabouts. Before night I hope to have a heater ordered—for delivery Saturday. Kirk invited me over to the place tomorrow night, but I don't think I shall go. When I get proper heat again, I shall be exceedingly domestick, & cut out many of the features of my social programme. S H left a lot of provisions here last week, including a *lemon*—so tonight I have been emulating W. V. Phillips in his vespertine glass of the citrick beverage. This is, I think, the *second* glass of lemonade I have ever made in my life, & it tastes quite acceptable—tho' not nearly so piquant & good as that which you make. I don't think I used enough lemon—only half a small one in a tumbler. But I will desist & turn in. Good luck with your moving, & may you find 115 comfortable & *WARM*.

More later—

Yr aff Nephew & obt Servt

H P L

[On envelope:]
Friday Afternoon—continuation of diary.

Slept till noon today, when I rose & wrestled with letters. Next, a local tour of grocery shopping. And now I'm starting off on the quest of the oil stove—wish me luck!

Another letter from S H, whose prospects seem unfortunately black. Conditions in new place are uncongenial owing to rivalry of those who sell on commission. She advises me to move—but I stand by my vote & the results of the election & stay! More soon.

P.S. I find that the hapless *Mackinac* is moored in Erie Basin not three blocks from this house! Guess I'll go down to the waterfront & look the poor old thing over. This is certainly the meeting place of superannuated R.I. wrecks & unnavigable hulks!

[140]  [ALS] [HPL to LDC]

Saturday Night
Octr. 24, 1925
Finiſh'd, Tues., October 27th.

My dear daughter Lillian:—

I received your welcome letter this morning, & perused with utmost interest the news it contained. What a beastly shame that you are put to all this bother & expense of moving—& that you now have to pay more rent! So you still have things in Mrs. Glazen's stable? I thought the tragick fate of the paintings had made you wary of that centre of mouldiness—but perhaps for certain non-perishable things it is as good as any haven. Confound the fate that prevents us from having a civilised home & furnishings somewhere in Angell St.! So it takes a Tilden–Thurber man to move your delicate French clock? That is where I have the advantage of you; for my ponderous onyx affair has sturdy American works, & seems none the worse for all the promiscuous knockings-about it has had. It was bought in St. Louis, shipped to Auburndale, transferred to 454, (or 194, as it then was) shunted to 598, exiled to Flatbush, condemned to Clinton St.—& still runs quite excellently! No doubt it will long outlive me & be sold as junk by my heirs. Glad you got my postal of welcome, & hope to hear later of your detailed experiences, including recent feline conversations. Yesterday I had a very entertaining colloquy with a tiger-&-white kitty-cat in the grocery near here—& only wish I could contract for one of the small heirs which the proprietor tells me are expected in a few weeks. If ever we have a home, a coal-black little Thomas with yellow eyes must be one of the first acquisitions!

As to house heat—I can't tell yet whether I'd call Mrs. Burns worse than the average. She has had heat just *twice* this year so far, & on many days the temperature has been so low that no one but a Norseman or Esquimau could live without some independent heat of his own. I honestly believe that is why, as a general rule, only Scandinavians stick here! Besides the impudent old Syrian below me—whose name I find to be Alexander Messayeh[1] & who is apparently an importer of Syrian merchandise—the only two names I see steadily on mail here are Claus Petersen & Hjalmar Ericson . . . hardy sons of the Arctic, as they need to be unless they invest in oil heaters! On the other hand, Kirk has had no heat either—& I think he pays $14.00 for the two rooms as he did at the other place. He means to use all the gas & electricity he wants, & tell the landlady to go to a place where extra heat is unnecessary if she objects! What perhaps spoils me for an impartial judgment is the fact that aside from Kirk's the only other boarding-house with which I am familiar is Loveman's—where conditions are probably exceptional. It makes me laugh to think that we did not especially like the place when we first looked at it, (tho' of course the reason was that we had been looking at some particularly fine places) for in truth it appears to be about as nearly ideal as a boarding-house could be. The Laverty sisters are elderly Irish gentlewomen, spinsters, & neat & conscientious to an almost finical degree. The house is blazing hot from the first chill of fall to the last raw day of spring—day & night, without variation—& the abundant linen & spotless bathrooms are a delight to consider. No tenants are taken without references, & whilst most of them are Irish papists, they are all persons of refinement & standing—responsible & decorous intellectual workers & artists. Yes—boarding-houses are a lottery, & Loveman certainly drew a prize. And it was sheer *luck,* for I vow that neither he nor I could have told at the outset just which of the various places would be good & which poor! If I left 169 tomorrow I might do just as badly again—or worse. Kirk's place, for example, I think distinctly worse. But all the same, Mrs. Burns could be legally prosecuted for not having a fire now, for there is a N.Y. city ordinance that the temperature of rented houses, when heat is understood to be furnished, must be kept at 68° or over between October 15 & May (or is it April?) 15. Leeds says that inspectors are quite zealous in following up complaints—tho' of course, as Kirk says, to complain would be merely to antagonise one's landlady & render moving inevitable. Perhaps, too, in this strike season the legal machinery may be partly suspended, as is the ban against bituminous coal. Anyway, I guess the wise man "lies low" unless he is really in a position to move.

So it is to you that I owe those cuttings in A E P G's pre-season Christmas box! Thanks! As I told her, they were all prodigiously interesting—& I'm doubly interested now that I learn that Dr. Clark was the M^cCabe family physician. M^cCabe must be a highly interesting character—is he still flourishing at the Historical Society, whither the item said he had gone? I've looked again for the shoe-trees, but nothing doing! The trunk is down cellar, but of course I wouldn't have been ass enough to leave just those in after taking everything else out. They are certainly not in the two logical places—chiffonier or cupboard shelf—so I fancy I must have let them go in storage. I had no good shoes then, so was not reminded of my need of them. Yes—I'll get some of those ten-centers you mention—in fact, I meant to get them whilst shopping today, but didn't think of it till re-reading your letter just now. Maybe they're what S H uses—your description & diagram seem to fit. I have not worn the Regals at all except that one night to shew them off to the gang, & shall not till the old shoes shew visible signs of deterioration. The only reason I got them now was to have them ready—& to get them whilst I had the cash from my *Weird Tales* cheque. It's just as well to get one's heavy shopping over with in one fell swoop, & then settle down to placid frugality again. Have you looked in the Regal window at #2021 to see just what I got? This model has the old-fashion'd catches at the top to obviate unlacing & lacing—a thing my ease-loving soul always seeks in a high shoe. I don't believe I'll ever get any more low ones, for they are a tremendous nuisance on "hikes", letting in sand & stones so that I have to empty them a dozen times in a single afternoon's trip.

¶ And now, having answered your epistle, I will proceed to the gorgeous chronicle of shopping triumphs which I was going to send you anyway to-night—whether or not I heard from you. Let us begin (for I may as well weave in the diary also) with the Perfection heater which I was starting out to get yesterday afternoon when last I wrote. Though I had been advised to go to Macy's, I thought I might as well start nearer home—especially since there is a very high-grade hardware store just around the block in Court St.; a dignified old place with real Yankee clerks, remaining from the time when the neighbourhood was a first-class & undecayed business street. Thither I went—& found the place a veritable headquarters for Perfection stoves!

There were two sizes, one $5.49 & the other $6.20, of which I chose the latter because of its greater oil capacity. This is undoubtedly the one you have seen at $7.00—reputed to hold a gallon, tho' not quite doing so unless one crowds the tank a bit perilously . . . which I don't. The obliging clerk had a brand new stove uncrated for me in the cellar, & after bringing it up, instructed me in whatever points were not included in the generous & accurate card of minute directions—about the oil gauge, &c. His advice coincided with yours except that he insisted that no *mat* or *tray* is necessary. The tank, being filled & wiped elsewhere, (I shall always do it in the alcove when I get a light there—now I do it on a pile of newspapers in the room proper) never drips, whilst the base & legs never become hot. And since it does not always stand in the same spot, it is not likely to wear a hole in the carpet very soon. Accordingly I have not yet obtained this article—tho' I will if your experience & observation indicate its extreme desirability. So far the contraption seems most delightfully cleanly & practical—& I followed all your advice in starting it, even tho' your latest bulletin did not arrive till I had begun operations. The printed instructions, you see, agreed with you. I see that the top has a damper to open when the stove is used for heating vessels, & note what you say about keeping water there. I have not yet resorted to this expedient, because I dislike the looks of a saucepan in a gentleman's study, & doubt if the hygienic advantage can be so *very* vast. But I may come to it yet if I can find a sufficiently aesthetick bowl capable of enduring the blaze. What I *shall* use the stove-top for is the preparation of *hot dinners*. No more cold beans & spaghetti for me—& today I bought a canned goulash-&-macaroni dinner for 35¢, which will make me two piping hot meals. In winter I dare keep the second half in a Mason Jar till the next day. You know what these complete canned dinners are—remember when we got the beef stew? The grocery in Clinton St. under the Taormina restaurant keeps a prodigious variety, (beef & lamb stew, goulash, boiled dinner, frankfurt & beans, kidney stew, &c. &c. &c.) & I shall be a consistent patron throughout the winter. The *variety* prevents that turning of the palate which beans & canned spaghetti (cold) produced early this autumn. 35¢ for 2 meals means 17½ cents a meal—& adding 5¢ for bread & cookies, the sum total (22½¢) is not at all formidable as such things go. *Goulash* is brazed [*sic*] beef covered with a highly seasoned sauce—an Hungarian dish very popular in restaurants, & a prodigious favourite of mine. You may recall my ordering it at the St. Regis one evening last winter. I'll let you know how this canned edition of it tastes when I use the one I've just obtained. But returning to my store purchase . . . Since the shop was only a block from this door, I decided to carry the stove myself & avoid the delay of delivery; hence had it safely beside my desk in less than half an hour after my super-envelope postscript to you. The afternoon was still open, & I debated whether to go down & look over the Mackinac or embark on that quest of a Leedsian cheap suit which the welfare of my splendid acquisition seemed almost to force on me. Daily wear had already done much to blunt those knife-edge knee creases, & I could only groan at thinking of what the months of constant friction would inflict on those elbows & that seat—for in this weather the use of the thin blue has become impossible, & the new triumph was doomed to take the brunt of daily knockabout wear—"hiking" & around the house—unless I could find a $5.00 or $10.00 alternative covering like Leeds' emergency outfit. Of course, I meant to take my time & employ all the patience in the world, for that is the only way to obtain a real *bargain*. What I had done in the realm of a good suit I resolved to do in the realm of emergency covering—& to find some remnant or odd & end at no price at all & with no fine material at all, but which might nevertheless surpass Leeds' $5.00 suit in having at least the cut & colour of a gentleman's garment. Leeds' thing roughly fits him, & wears excellently—but its texture & style are frankly impossible. It is a constant humiliation to him, but he was forced to buy in haste without widely looking around, since his former suit was actually falling to pieces at the time of the purchase. As he told me, one must in seeking such a thing look for one or the other of two types of garment: manufacturer's remnants, which one finds only by chance at sales, & staple workmen's suits, which are in stock all the time & one of which he was obliged to get. The centre for all such junk is 14th St & 7th Ave., rather near where Kirk lives now, & in this section I planned to look (after a preliminary Brooklyn survey) until I found a really *decent* looking rag or had to give up. I *wouldn't* be seen in publick with an outfit like Leeds'—& in case of finding nothing I decided to see what I could do in matching my suit with some cheap, coarse trousers for "hikes", house, & rainy days. These would be better than nothing, for it is always the trousers that get the worst of things. Anything to prevent the instant ruination of what ought to be a best suit for dignified wear to the Longs', the museum, & such places as give a shabby person a sense of embarrassment. Well, as I say, I debated whether I'd haunt the waterfront or go on this perhaps hopeless quest. At first I decided on the waterfront, but was deterred by the raw, cold blasts that swept up State St. as I turned down it. So, reversing my direction, I headed up Fulton St & Flatbush Ave. on a slightly modified search for that alchemic goal of all the ages—something for nothing!

Brooklyn was a flat failure. There were no "cheap joints" in the sense my present condition required, & I'll vow the $20.00 things they displayed were about as bad as Leeds' $5.00 catastrophe! At the same time I enjoyed myself tremendously—& for this reason: that *every* salesman I interviewed mistook my new suit for an expensive made-to-order product of a first-class tailor. As one man they remarked upon the choice quality of the goods, & deprecatingly expressed fears that their humble products were not very well calculated to meet the taste of a man accustomed to such a manner of dressing. It was, as the cant phrase runs, "pretty rich"; & I could not bear to shatter their peace of mind & sense of congruity by telling them that the radiantly aristocratic ensemble had cost me but 25 plunks! It confirms my original belief that I have secured a very rare bargain, & further confirms my belief in my own taste where clothing is concerned. You'll recall my saying how I pounced on that suit the minute I saw its fabric & cut (before I discovered it was only 2-button)—& in general I think I have developed an eye for the difference between the clothing a gentleman wears & that which a gentleman doesn't. What has sharpened this sense is the constant sight of these accursed filthy rabbles that infest the N.Y. streets, & whose clothing presents such systematic differences from the normal clothing of real people along Angell St. & in Butler Ave. or Elmgrove Ave. cars that the eye comes to feel a tremendous homesickness & to pounce avidly on any gentleman whose clothes are proper & tasteful & suggestive of Blackstone Boulevard rather than Borough Hall or Hell's Kitchen. Belknap wears the right sort, & so does Kirk. Loveman usually does, tho' his taste is not perfect. But Morton, Kleiner, Leeds, & McNeil are frankly impossible. And so, pining for the sight of a Swan Point car full of regular men, I have resolved to dress like Butler Ave. or not at all. Confound it, I'll be either in good Providence taste or in a bally bathrobe!! Certain lapel cuts, textures, & fits tell the story. It amuses me to see how some of these flashy young 'boobs' & foreigners spend fortunes on various kinds of expensive clothes which they regard as evidences of meritorious taste, but which in reality are their absolute social & aesthetick damnation—being little short of placards shrieking in bold letters: *"I am an ignorant peasant"*, *"I am a mongrel gutter-rat"*, or *"I am a tasteless & unsophisticated yokel."* And yet perhaps these creatures are not, after all, seeking to conform to the absolute artistic standard of gentlefolk. Possibly their object is entirely different; involving a recognition of their non-membership in the cultivated part of the community, & a desire simply to dress in accordance with the frankly different standard of their own candidly acknowledged type & class—as a Breton or Catalan peasant affects the grotesque finery of his kind, regardless of the attire of general European society. Sonny & I have frequently discussed the possible rise of a definite American plebeian costume, & we think we can already see evidences of it. Its present visible signs are tight, waist-fitting coats, with narrow lapels & buttons near together; extremely low-cut waistcoats, approximating evening waistcoats & probably derived from the rabble's ignorant admiration of the dress-suited heroes of their favourite cinemas; & exotick & effeminate "pastel" tones of colour—purple, lavender, & the like. The whole general trend of this growing peasant garb is toward the conspicuous & the feminine—infallible marks of a decadent slave-stock as opposed to the classically subdued & loosely but finely hung garments characteristic of a genuinely refined & wholesomely masculine ruling or conquering class or race-stock. The phenomenon, as Belknap noted even before I reminded him, is a perfect parallel of the degradation of the virile Roman toga into the fussy gaudinesses of the Byzantine mob. Eventually, as the whole civilisation decays, this artistic corruption will spread to the upper classes as well as the herd; but for the present it is possible to divide clothing pretty clearly into what gentlemen wear & what they don't. Better far to wear the frayed & tattered rags of something with taste, than to sport the newest & freshest suit whose cut & texture bear the ineffaceable stigmata of plebeianism & decadence. But sententious reflection hath taken me far from my diary! I was saying that the Brooklyn dealers, whilst having nothing of Leedsian cheapness, all pleased me by confirming my taste & exalting my new suit—a thing, by the way, they would never have done had they known it was ready-made; since *clothiers* as apart from *tailors* pursue a policy of deadly rivalry & mutual derogation. How assiduously I concealed the label on the inside coat-pocket! I enclose a couple of the cards they were all so anxious to give me—souvenirs of the professional regard commanded by the truly well-drest man! Well—having exhausted Brooklyn, I descended to the depths, & took the subway for the 14th St–7th Ave. colony. Pegāna, what a gauntlet to run! Indescribable scum pulling one into holes in the wall where flamboyant monstrosities ululate their impossibility beneath price-cards of $4.95, $7.50, $10.00, $12.50, $15.00, $17.00, $18.00 . . . . . puffy rat-eyed vermin hurling taunts when one does not buy & airing spleen in dialects so mercifully broken that white men can't understand them . . . . . crazinesses in cloth hanging in fantastic attitudes & displaying unheard-of anomalies—before Heaven I vow that despite the horrors I've seen *on* people, I never saw the like of these fungous freaks *off* people! Perhaps the human form inside a suit fills it out to some semblance of Nature—certainly these empty nightmares swinging in the winds like gallows-birds had nothing of Nature in them! Once I came on a shop that handled remnants, & saw some very tolerable things which I would have barely consented to wear—but none that were of my size were of the desired winter weight. Once, again, I saw something in a "bargain basement" that caused my heart to flutter . . . . but I found it was *second-hand*, & fled!

And now approaches the moment of a success so miraculous that I cannot believe it without looking down at the garment I am wearing. For I am saved, by all the Powers that be! Saved, & restored to my pre-robbery four-suit status by a "find" so titanic that I need have no trepidation in shewing my "alternative covering" to the four winds & all the world! Safe on its shoulders ready for the museum or the Long's [*sic*] is my cherished triumph, (whose trousers I shall now have pressed after their week of hard & steady wear) whilst on my aged form as I sprawl carelessly about is a garment of dark, rich brown (sample enclosed—if your memory is good you will recall that it is closely similar to my winter suit of *just 20 years ago*—my heavy brown of 1905, which was the first suit I ever bought at the Outlet) whose weight & cut are exactly the same as those of my best suit, (for I have a *best* suit now!) whose fit is *perfect*, whose general aspect is *exactly* the same as that of all my usual clothes, (*nothing* off-colour or indicative of cheapness) which has (as if in answer to the one probable objection of cheap goods which the salesman so volubly denied) *two pairs of trousers,* & which—to come to a fitting climax at last—cost me (with the extra trousers) just **$11.95!!!**

Look at the sample & see if you believe it! Look also at the snap-shot which I will later have taken of myself in it! The point is, that it is really a gentleman's garment in design, material, & fit; which will enable me to wear it to ordinary meetings & on the street as well as on "hikes" & around the house, thus saving the "triumph" & conclusively removing the need of getting another good suit a year from now. Of course I don't know how it will wear—but even that matter is of minor importance in view of the extra trousers. The remnant salesman claimed it was a Rogers-Peet suit—or one originally designed for that firm & later sidetracked & shopworn—but since it lacks a label I reserve my right to be healthily sceptical on that point.

As for details of acquisition—these are singularly undramatick. I had come upon merely another one of the myriad sales of misfits & left-overs in 14th St, & had donned about a dozen coats of varying degrees of impossibility, when I suddenly knew that I was suited. The coat was a limp rag; crushed, dusty, twisted, & out-of-press, but I saw that cut, fabric, & fit were just right. There was no mistaking it. Other coats I might have worn on rough trips under the spur of necessity,—all in the great cause of saving the "triumph"—but here was the sort of thing I might conceivably *choose* in buying a good suit; a garment of my own general style & atmosphere, (despite the now unavoidable 2-buttonism) sober & aristocratic, & suggesting a mellow background which not even its mussed & distorted condition or its pauperish price (for this was a *$9.95* sale) could obscure to my now trained eye. The suggestion of 'pattern' or *mixture* (for there is no *pattern* beyond the blend of dark shades as you may see it) which the sample displays, is scarcely noticeable in the broad surfaces of the fabric as a whole; the massed effect being a plain dark brown even more in my style than my only other brown suit of 20 years ago—which had a definite stripe. The coat was a 42; but chancing to run small, fitted me to perfection except where the neck was crushed—& I could easily envisage the rectification of this feature. The salesman was doubtful of matching it with trousers, since of the three pairs he had (there was no other coat & vest) one was too big & two were too small. He was selling the extra ones separately at $4.00, & trusting to luck & the tailor to piece out a suit when the coat sold. Well—I let him shew me other things; crinkly & repulsive fabricks, crude cuts, & shapeless things with coarsely sewed edges, as well as fairly decent things which were too thin or didn't fit; but eventually I brought him back to this one. He wanted me to take the too-small trousers & have them let out rather than the too-big ones & have them taken in; but I balked, since I saw that the former would in any case have to sit low on the hips instead of coming high as mine always do. Here a dispute threatened to intervene, & (although I *would* have taken the suit anyway) I signified my unwillingness to accept the garment unless the roomy trousers were included. He, on his part, evinced a corresponding reluctance to include those trousers; when suddenly there appeared what was probably his original plan, but which was really just as agreeable to me as to him. He would, he said, include the larger trousers if I would also buy the smaller ones as an extra pair—"two-trouser suits" being quite the thing now, as you know. Good Oriental guile, but I had not read the Arabian Nights in my youth for nothing. "Season, O excellent Hafiz," I said, (in effect) "the rice of good enterprise with the salt of philosophy, & reflect that he sells most amongst the merchants of Bagdad's bazaars who most bounteously meets the purses of the caravans from Ormus & Samarcand & Bokhara. I have come far across the golden sands; my camels are weary & my drachmae of Indian gold are nearly spent. I must away to the caravanserai at the Bab-el-Tilism except I be well suited; for I am in no mind for a bad bargain, & my camel-drivers clamour to be free to royster in the taverns beyond the Mosque of Almansor. Hei! I have no thirst for your extra breeches. I should not know what to do with them. Think you I am like my camels, or yonder donkey pulled by the water-boy, that I have four legs to be clothed? Why should I give you four pieces of gold for that which I do not wish? Turban of the Prophet! It were better fitting that I buy no garments at all, but give my few coins to the poor & make the pilgrimage to Holy Mecca's Kaaba Stone, that my grandsons in Samarcand may bless my beard & call me an Hadji! It is not thus that the merchants of Balsarah & Damascus rob an aged pilgrim—consider what generosity is due to venerable years, & what generosity will sell that which else would not be sold! But fie! I am not without pity for a worthy merchant. Let us say that you are poor, & saddled with that which none will buy. I will be generous, & pour the balsam of compassion on the wounds of indigence. Your robes I will buy, & the extra breeches too—if for those breeches you will demand but less. Perhaps my son can wear them, for he is small & slim. Hear, merchant! To the jaws of avarice I offer the meat of compromise—take these *two* pieces of gold for the breeches & I will buy your garments, even tho' they be worn & dusty & altogether unfit save to sell at a loss to the brown coral-traders from the Indian Sea!" And so it went— suit $9.95, extra trousers $2.00! The tailor at once measured me, & when I returned the next day I found everything absolutely perfect except the larger trousers, which were too long, but which were capably shortened to exact perfection whilst I waited. The coat was utterly perfect without alteration; hugging my collar tightly, & bearing no mark of its former crushed condition; whilst the vest became neat & trim with the first fixing. The larger trousers are very loose in the seat, but not at all baggy; & of course the coat comes far below any place where the bagginess would be manifest. The smaller trousers, despite my objection, really hang excellently; & the vest meets them with safety & to spare even when they are at their lowest. I shall divide wear betwixt the two pairs of trousers, thus avoiding the holy seats of the two stolen garments; whose repeated repair cost me so much trouble & expense, as you'll recall. The smaller ones shall be devoted to roughest purposes—country walks, rainy days, & around the house—whilst the larger ones will serve for those middling occasions like ordinary meetings or library trips when I can't be my toughest, yet oughtn't to be wearing the "triumph" out. Of course I don't know how long the cloth will last—but it's a safe bet that I get a good $11.95 value out of the outfit! Really, when you see the snapshot you'll understand how surprised I am at my good luck. The enclosed sample, too, ought to tell its own tale of wonder. I clipped it—with another for S H—off the immense surplus doubled inside the larger trousers after taking in. [At this point I gave a start, finding the other sample gone—although I could easily clip many more—but I've just found it again on the floor. I only wish I could get you a sample of the *other* suit, which of course is obviously much finer in texture & lining. I'll send you that vest yet, by insured parcel post, now that I've got another warm suit to wear!] The fact is, that whereas two weeks ago I almost despaired of getting *one* good suit for $35.00, I have for about that very sum obtained not only a superlatively fine garment which arouses the marked & favourable comment of experts, but *another* whose outward aspect is every inch as good as that of any suit (except the "prize", & perhaps my 1904 & 1912 grey mixed suits) I have ever owned—& this with *two trousers*. I can't yet account for the excellence of design in so cheap a thing—it is *exactly* correct, even in the smallest matters of lapels or buttons on the sleeves, whereas virtually all the other 14th St. junk bore obvious & visible crudities, & marks of the plebeian in design. The suit has, to all appearances, those intangible refinements of outline & composition which cheap suits *never* have—& at the moment, while it is fresh, I'd willingly wear it anywhere. Whatever be its material in point of wear, & whatever be the cause of its appearance in a $9.95 sale, it was certainly cut to a very aristocratic pattern having absolutely nothing in common with the shape & style of cheap suits as sold at $5.00 to $18.00 in 14th St. Naturally, I don't believe the Rogers-Peet legend; but I think it may possibly be a stray $22.50 suit from one of those chain manufacturers who assiduously copy the best models—like the "Richmond Clothes" of Cleveland, where Loveman obtained his present delightful bargain.

Well—such is which! In my prime I could never have gotten so excited over clothes, but exile & old age make trifles dear to one. With my nervous hatred of slovenly & plebeian dressing, & after the maddening robbery which threatened to reduce *me* to exactly the thing I hate, you'll admit that apparel became very legitimately a "touchy" subject with me till such a time as I might again possess the four suits necessary for balanced dressing both in summer & in winter. But all things pass—& after one more letter descriptive of the reaction of the gang to my "alternative covering" I shall cease for evermore to discuss or think of suits. A gentleman should be always attired in good taste, but he should never be actively conscious of his clothes. They should be to him integral outgrowths of his personality & aesthetick sense; matters of course, & never artificial bedizenments to be flaunted. They become an active issue only when they disappear & leave one stranded—& now I have my four again & am good for another ten years if I live that long. Praisèd be Pegāna, say I—& praisèd be Hish, (the Dunsanian god of silence) say'st thou!

Oh—& my poor diary! Where *did* I leave off? Ah, yes—still in a clothing shop! Well—by that time it was evening, & I hopped a Butler Ave. car (alias the subway) for home & proceeded to examine my other new acquisition—the Perfection heater. I studied the directions, looked over the device itself, & became thoroughly familiar with the elementary operations—though I shall have to look at the directions afresh when the installation of a new *wick* becomes necessary. I am, of course, keeping the printed card of instructions most religiously. At length I mastered likewise the operation of the individual 1-gallon oil cans from the dealer, & filled the tank preparatory to lighting up—when lo! It dawned upon me that I had not such a thing as a *match* in the place! That's what the electricity habit does to one—& all my nice 454 match safes in storage! So I went to the corner grocery & got some M T safety matches, made in Finland & not in Heaven where they say matches are made, & at length touched off the fuse. No explosion—but bless me, what a genial heat! I thawed out for the first time this fall; & by dint of frequently extinguishing the stove, have managed to keep decently warm on only a gallon & a half of oil up to this midnight. The stuff, at rock-bottom local prices, costs 16¢ per gallon, & the amount to be used will vary as the temperature outside—plus Mrs. Burns' caprice—may vary. As for the heater—believe me, it's a bird! Tonight it keeps the room *too warm* unless extinguished at intervals, (it's rainy & *damply* raw rather than biting) & last night despite a stinging frigidity outside & no steam heat inside it did not by any means have to burn continuously. It is, for its size, an amazing banisher of the Arctic daemons—& its portability renders it indispensably useful. I shall never be without one again—for one can take it into corners where gas won't go. Here, for example, I can avoid the horrors of bathing in that cold alcove—cold even when the distant steam radiator is in action—by bringing the stove to its very door & imparting a genial glow to the scene of ablution. What is more, I can heat small amounts of water on its top when the local flow is lukewarm or less. And of course its culinary possibilities are manifold, as I shall endeavour to prove when I serve that goulash. Bless me—why don't I serve it *now*, since I haven't eaten heavily during the day? I guess I will—& report on it in this very epistle! I'll light up & get it hot, then prepare the dish, (I hope the can opens easily!) & have dinner over before I seal this document . . . . . Well—now the old boy's lit! Open goes the damper! . . . . Now to tackle the dinner-pail—or can. I'll put on my wrap for that, for even if this new suit is a device to save the best one I don't want to spatter it up at the outset . . . . . . . Can's open—stuff looks gorgeously savoury—cold scrapings taste so, too. Gravy's all congealed to jelly—will have to heat whole thing before dividing into to-night's & tomorrow's portion—Mason Jar for latter . . . . . .

¶ Well—dinner's over, & a great old feast it was! Fancy having a hot meat dinner right here in my study, where so many quarts of cold beans & bread have been consum'd! Little Vulcan (for so I will call my Perfection for old times' sake) heated up the material in less than no time, & gave me a most gratifying sense of culinary importance. I haven't done so much cooking since just a year ago—when S H was in the hospital & I prepared my own spaghetti with Tucco sauce. Of course the stuff wasn't equal to restaurant goulash—canned stuff is never up to the fresh article—but there's all the advantage in the world in having it at home, & the price is exactly ½ of the restaurant price—35¢ covering *one* order at most joints, whereas this 35¢ can furnishes *two* orders. May Heaven & Mr. Mason preserve the second portion! For dessert I had raspberry jelly on Uneeda lunch biscuit. But hold on! Where's my diary? Oh, yes—last night & the test of the stove. I forgot to add that when I went out for matches a political meeting was buzzing on the street corner, with bugles, band wagon, & hot air going full blast. A very small boy was distributing campaign cards, & pressed the enclosed into my cynical palm.

Vote for Nova! Hip, hip, hooray! Nova! Nova! Nova Persei! Nova Scotia, Nova Carthago, Nova Zembla! He's an Algeron, boys, but no Algernon! An Algeron, but not an Algerine*! Born & bred in Brook-a-lyn, & jurned the bar as an attoiney XXIII years ago! I'll jern verces & sing these voises:

> Nova, Nova,
> Second Grover!
> Pass the hat
> Fer a Dimmy-crat!
> He's no rover,
> Brooklyn all over—
> Nova, Nova,
> We want Nova!
> Vote for Nova
> An' live in clover—
> Butcher, beggar,
> Barber, bootlegger;
> Don't weaken or soften,
> Vote early & often!
>     = oily

---

*Algerine = Barbary coast pirate, of *Algiers*, of later 18th century. Name applied by Dorrites to Gov. King's legitimist adherents in the Dorr War.

He may be no Casa-nova with the peepul, but he'll hand out the right Nova-caine to soothe the transit problem. We want more subways—we want cheap coal—we want free drinks—we want Nova! Rrrhrah! rrrraaa . . . Nova! Boom, bah! Well—I spent the evening reading; re-reading Marco Polo for the first time in thirty years, since I felt like encountering something strange & remote & naive*. Retiring later, I was up at noon today, went down town for the super-new suit, observed the start of a rain & accordingly wore my latest acquisition home, (with its smaller trousers) set out again shopping, going to Flatbush† for my special Old English cheese & getting the goulash at the local grocery, & finally ended up here at about 5:30 p.m., since when I've been reading, writing this epistle, & eating the goulash dinner as mention'd on t'other side of the sheet. Ere long—& before mailing this document—I shall retire; being up again tomorrow in time to dust the room before 1:30, when Loveman comes to secure my services as guide to the art museum. Wednesday the gang (Leeds) meets at Morton's joint in Paterson. Saturday there's a Blue Pencil meeting—which I doubt if I'll attend, but to which I'll wear the "triumph" if I do go—& if the weather's fair. By the way—if the weather's still rainy tomorrow I shall wear the "alternative covering" to the museum—for as I have intimated, it can't be told from a first rate suit! Oh, yes—& I think I said that I entertain the McNeil meeting a week from next Wednesday. So much for the diary, past, present, & future . . . . quite a full instalment, this, though it marks the finish of the spectacular buying season. Today in a subway car I saw the following inane doggerel advertisement:

> Rooms for rent,            READ THE
> Prices right;             WANT ADS IN
> Dandy rooms—              THE NEW YORK
> Large & light!            AMERICAN

to which I mentally address the following reply:

> At size & light
>     I'll cavil not,
> But here's MY fight—
>     ARE THOSE ROOMS HOT?

> Yr aff Nephew & obt Servt—
>         H P L

---

*Loveman's going to found a poem on an especially colourful passage I pointed out to him.

†a branch of a bank is about to open up in that long-vacant Parkside Ave. corner—the new brick apartment house & its shop-space on the Flatbush Ave side of the ground floor.

Monday Afternoon
Octr. 26, 1925

Well—I didn't seal & mail this Sunday after all! I was up early, but so busy with dusting & sweeping till Loveman's arrival that I had no chance to attend to anything else. So now I'll continue the diary. As I say, I was up early; & since the morning was rainy I donned my new "alternative covering" despite my museum destination. When Loveman came & saw it he became quite ecstatic & delirious with admiration—averring that it looks just as well & becoming on me as my best suit, & vowing it can't be less than a $35.00 garment originally. He even accepts the Rogers-Peet legend, though I cautioned him against being gullible. Now he is going to try for something of the sort himself—devoting an evening to traversing the rounds of cheap shops, though well aware of the heartbreaking gauntlet he will have to run before finding anything fit to wear. On this occasion I donned my old brown hat & 1909 spring overcoat & fared forth with my guest to John's—where, after a meat-ball-&-spaghetti lunch, (confound it, their coffee has gone up to 10¢!) we took the East Side subway for 86th St—the nearest express stop to the Metropolitan Museum. Upon emerging we found that the rain had given place to a furious wind & increasing cold, & that the sun shone through a sky mottled with swift-scudding clouds. Glad enough to gain the museum's shelter, we checked our hats & overcoats & proceeded to digest once more the familiar scenes of beauty—American Wing, Egyptian rooms, the George Bellows paintings, & the Graeco-Roman hall—from which latter, to my horror, I found all the *Roman* statuary gone; tho' I hope this means only a happy transference to some superior setting. At five we left, returning to the subway & proceeding to Kirk's; where we found him & Leeds & the cat without a furnace fire, but running gas-stove & electrick grill and exceedingly busy painting the bookshelves which Leeds' carpentering skill had just set triumphantly in place. The colour will be a cream-white to match the woodwork & the greater part of the kitty-cat. Kirk spilled some paint on his best new grey suit—but *not* on *mine,* which both he & Leeds inspected with admiration. Kirk shared Loveman's profound astonishment, but Leeds—latterly train'd in adversity's hard school—declared that he had sometimes done as well when possessed of plenty of time to search, & added that he now has his eye on an even more spectacular bargain for only *$8.00\**—a blue suit with white pencil stripe which he is having saved for him till he can scrape up the eight iron men. Well—we lounged & worked & sang old songs & played Leeds' phonograph & stroked the kittie till 9 o'clock, when all hands adjourned to a cafeteria for dinner. Having eat at noon, I took only a little corned beef & potato salad. Loveman now went home, but I returned to 15th St. with Kirk & Leeds; who were staying up all night. During the hours I read through some absorbing weird stories from Leeds' pile of books & magazines, & at 4

---

*without extra trousers

a.m. we again adjourned to the cafeteria*, where I took only coffee. Dispersal now ensued, & I return'd to 169 & retired.

Today I was up at noon & have been wrestling with correspondence (aided by Little Vulcan's equatorial emanations) ever since—pausing for a telephone message from Belknap's mamma inviting me over at 5:30 p.m. for dinner & the evening. Loveman is invited also. Though the Longs' is a place where I shall usually wear my best suit, I shall tonight wear the new alternative covering (which really looks quite nice & rich enough to wear anywhere!) to shew it off to Sonnykins. Maybe he'll try for one like it himself—tho' as a general thing he hates the slum shops as venomously as I do.

Your letter of Sunday has now arrived, & I am today invoking all of Pegāna's gods in behalf of your prosperous transference to 117. As you will see by the preceding pages, I am spectacularly well able to endorse & confirm all that you say on the oil-stove question—& am glad you have had a chance to see just what I am using. Get one for yourself, by all means, if your new room betrays the slightest tendency toward coldness—but my directions advise keeping the top *closed* except when heating or cooking. At night I often turn off the light to watch the cheery twinkle from the front—fire & the hearth are, next to a cat, the greatest of all symbols of felicitous domesticity. No—I won't press in the stopper too tightly—& I fill the tank on a heavy old newspaper . . . . not that I mean the *Bulletin* is *stylistically* heavy! I enjoyed both the cuttings, & had previously noted the one about "Manna". His face looks like that of Oscar, a delightful neighbour of Kirk's, who occasionally drops in to call on the Kirk feline.[2] I held Oscar in my lap yesterday. I've seen the Bourne painting at the museum—great stuff, & I'm glad J. B. French won't have to pay the agent's commiſsion! ¶ Well—now I must start for Sonny's. More bulletins later, & I certainly hope you'll like the suit sample. I *must* send that vest of the best outfit if I can't find a stray seam or inside trouser-bottom to clip! ¶ And so it goes. Hope 117 proves satisfactory, & that you will be able to rest up finely after your strenuous migration. Let me know how the new place seems. ¶ Oh, yes! And pray tell A E P G that her latest cash & cheque mixture came through safely! ¶ Yr aff Nephew & obt Servt H P L

*Tuesday Night—Octr. 27*

Another instalment! But tonight I vow I *will* mail this express package— or freight consignment! We last beheld me starting for Sonny's yesterday afternoon, & may continue from that point. Reaching my destination in safety, I found the Child in, & properly imprest him with the splendour of my new & inexpensive acquisition—he says it is the most becoming thing he's ever seen on his aged Grandpa; & agrees that the cut is definitely aristocratick, whilst the fit is graceful & impeccable. He has a new navy blue suit of precise-

---

*The Chatham, at 8th Ave & 14th St, where the man is beginning to know us.

ly the same style, for which he pay'd $30.00. (with 2 trousers) Well—ere long Loveman arrived, & all sat down to dinner whilst the radio did its best to drown conversation. After the meal Belknap read aloud a new poem he had just finished—a ballad of about 120 lines entitled "The Marriage of Sir Jehan de Mandeville", which provided discussion for the rest of the evening. It is the finest piece of work the Child has ever done, & fairly teems with that glamour & strangeness which make his "Man from Genoa" notable. He, like his Grandpa, has lately had a spell of reading in the naive old travellers with their colourful wonders, but has happened to light on Herodotus & Mandeville instead of Marco Polo. In this poem he speaks of the wedding-day of the great legendary voyager, when Mandeville is about to exchange the freedom of far places for the placid round of domestick retirement. The bishop being delay'd, Mandeville regales the assembled guests with recollections of the strange things he has known; & the ballad becomes a vivid chronicle of distant deserts & incredible valleys of monstrous beauties or deformities; of marvels & monstrosities—

> "And of the Cannibals that each other eat,
> The Anthropophagi & men whose heads
> Do grow beneath their shoulders."

The long catalogue of prodigies is handled with ineffable freshness & dexterity, & makes me eager to read through Mandeville again when I have finisht the re-reading of Marco Polo. Sonny, I find, has never read Marco Polo; but he means to do so now. He has read the recent book founded on it— "Messer Marco Polo", by Donn Byrne—which I have not read, although I believe either you or A E P G or both have. Another feature of the evening was a series of readings from Loveman's Saltus book, whose MS. he had with him. Rejected by Brentano's, it will appear thro' a publisher named Laurent, & with a bibliography which Loveman will compile from data in the possession of Saltus' daughter—to whom the widow will give him an introduction. All this will be a great asset to his progress, placing him in touch with just the persons he needs. He has already found a valuable admirer & ally in the person of the critic Benjamin de Casseres, to whom Mrs. Saltus introduced him. The MS., as typed by a friend, is in execrable condition as regards punctuation; & I have offered to straighten it out for the printer. I took it home with me & have it here now to work on—being about to return it Wednesday night at the gang meeting in Paterson. It is certainly a marvellous piece of work, & well merits the ecstatic—even effusive—encomium accorded to it by de Casseres. Well—the meeting dissolved at midnight, & after walking down to 72nd St. for the air the visiting delegation took the subway for its respective homes. Sonny won't be at the Paterson meeting tomorrow night, & may after this attend only once in two weeks or so; for his physician thinks that the excitement of general debates, as when the whole gang is assembled, works havock with his nerves &

causes him to stutter more violently than usual. This trouble has increased lately, so that the child often has to help himself out with pad & pencil. Instead of the meetings, he will entertain one or two friends quietly on the "off" weeks. It is certainly a shame that so brilliant a boy is bothered with poor health—yet fortunately the latter does not interfere with his work. The new poem is the greatest thing he has ever written, & I certainly think he is progressing rapidly toward a real place in literature. Having reacht 169 I was charmed to find a furnace fire going, so that I did not have to light Little Vulcan. I wrote some, & then retired; rising at 10 this morning & going on with the writing. It was a fine day, but work kept me from going to Hempstead as I had wish'd. I promised to have that MS. for Loveman tomorrow evening, & it comes to 75 pages or so. The house still has a fire, & this evening I do not need the oil stove, tho' I did for one brief interval during the day. Yesterday I ordered 2 gallons more of oil—for the man makes his rounds on Tuesdays.

And so it goes. Tonight I shall finish up (if possible) my letters & begin the Saltus MS.—then resting & finishing the MS. during tomorrow. Tomorrow evening I meet the gang for the (Leeds) meeting in Paterson at Morton's. Some day later in the week a few of us may go to see a cinema called "The Peak of Fate",[3] which Leeds recommends as scenically impressive & distinctly out of the ordinary. Saturday I may or may not attend the B.P.C. Sunday there may be an Hempstead trip, & the following Wednesday I entertain a (McNeil) meeting here. Such is the social programme—tho' I trust it may prove subordinate to a programme of writing actively made possible through my new stove & the mentally tranquillising influence of a restored wardrobe.

This afternoon I heard from Farnsworth Wright of *Weird Tales*. He accepts "The Horror at Red Hook" & writes enthusiastically of it, & may later on accept "From Beyond", tho' he can't decide now. The other three he definitely rejects—"In the Vault" as being too horrible for the censors, "Polaris" as being a prose-poem rather than a story, & "Beyond the Wall of Sleep" without explanation. He wants "The Outsider" very much, & I may try to get it back from Cook. I'm glad he accepts "Red Hook", for it is so long that it will bring in a glorious cheque some time next year. As for the rest—I guess I can always keep him supplied with all the new matter of ordinary length he can logically use. I'll send you his letter when I've answered it.

Today A E P G's second envelope came—with the delightful Trinity Church matter. I shall write her tonight, but in any case pray extend her my profoundest gratitude. I explored Trinity thoroughly with her & P. G. in 1916 on the final family trip to Newport. It's a great old place, though of course from the strictly artistick point of view cannot be compar'd with our own 1st Baptist.

Well—such is which. I trust that by the time you get this you will be fully & comfortably settled at 117—with a Perfection heater if you need one. And here's wishing you an undisturb'd & prosperous tenancy of the new abode! More later, as additional news events develop. Meanwhile I am ever

Yr aff: Nephew & obt Servt

H P L

P.S. I guess this epistle will be your *genuine* welcome to 117! Hope you're having as easy a moving as possible!

## Notes

1. Alexander D. Messayeh (c.1875–?).
2. A cat owned by a neighbor of Kirk. When it was killed by an automobile later in the year, HPL wrote "In Memoriam: Oscar Incoul Verelst of Manhattan."
3. *Der Berg von Schicksals* (Berg- und Sportfilm, 1924), directed by Arnold Fanck; starring Hannes Schneider, Frida Richard, and Erna Morena. Alternately titled *The Mountaineers* and *The Peak of Fate* in English/American theatres.

[141]    [ALS] [HPL to LDC]

Saturday Morning
Novr. 7, 1925

My dear Daughter Lillian:—

Your delightful missive duly arrived, & I am exceedingly pleased to know that your new room promises comfort & cheer. Southern exposure is a great asset—something I have not had since 454, though in summer this room gets a bit of sunlight & would get more but for the tall block across the street. My alcove & tall lights are not yet fixed, though new promises have been made. The one real improvement is in linen service—my quota arriving regularly each Friday, & without the lapses of former weeks. As you observe, this business is as hard on the renters as on the rentees—& one could sympathise considerably with Mrs. Burns in her tussle with shifting & promiscuous canaille were it not for her careful blindness where matters of equitable adjustment are concerned. It is amusing to notice her alert concern for the amount of electricity I use, as contrasted with her refusal to recognise the poor heating, spasmodic linen service, squalid bathrooms, dwindling facilities, transient & low-grade lodgers,—& such advantages to her as accrue from my continuous occupancy & complete care of my room; the latter feature exempting her from all responsibilities in the way of cleaning & chamber work. But such are the average conditions, I presume, of boarding-house life—& apparently Mrs. B. has corresponding struggles with the owner of the house; the shrewd Irish wife of a local police lieutenant who herself conducts a boarding-house in Columbia Heights. Good-sized rooms at Loveman's average about $12.00 per week, though elsewhere there are lower prices . . . if one could only be sure about the heat. Mortonius, in Paterson, pays only *$8.00* for a finely heated room—but his luck is exceptional. The most tremendous expense is that of *moving*, hence I shall stick close to my present seat of hibernation for the nonce. I think I said that the movers charged Kirk $40.00 for a trip of only two blocks.

As for my bargains—one gets such things only by looking for them at great length & with infinite patience. Of all my clothing bargains these last two are the best; for I gave the matter my very closest attention & care, whereas I was more reckless in some of my earlier ventures in Providence & Pawtucket—knowing, no doubt, that I did not have to rely on the results as my only existing garments. In that former epoch of bargain-hunting—which I definitely abandoned in 1915—I was often saddled with really impracticable material such as that shapeless bluish thing whose collar rode above all over-coat collars; though now & then I had a real bargain like the summer grey of 1911, (one exactly like the new stolen grey that we bought in 1923) which fitted very tolerably, & which was by no means worn out when I grew too fat for it in 1916. I gave it to poor Herbert—but if I had kept it, it would be just right for me now . . . as would likewise the blue summer suit of 1913 & the light grey of 1914, both given away, alas, for the selfsame reason. Oh, for the gift of prophecy! The sole survivor of my old-time bargains is that light-grey pair of flannel trousers which I wear for absolute *worst* in midsummer. I think I got them for a dollar or two in 1910. They have always been too long—& sometimes I think I'll have 'em shortened for luck after fifteen years!

Kirk seems to be doing fairly well with his books, & I'll ask him to be on the lookout for a good Bulfinch. Meanwhile I believe I have some things around here which, tho' by no means so fine, are at least better than nothing. I'll send 'em along if they look worth it. Loveman will probably get no profits from his book, but is eager for the literary standing its publication will bring. Kleiner's new penmanship has still further approached artistic perfection, so that his best efforts are marvellous & beautiful things to see. Truly, he equals the average mediaeval monk in his general text; & he will now devote himself diligently to the great initial letters, illuminated in many colours. He plans shortly to print out a booklet containing specimens of verse by all the members of our circle—& of mine he will probably choose the brief lines "To A Dreamer" which appeared in *Weird Tales*. As for the latter—there is no fear that celebrities will crowd out the old contributors. I have *six* accepted in advance*, & the editor wants still more; whilst Sonny has one accepted & has just sent in another. His "Sea-Thing" in the current issue is great. The Wells tales—so far very mediocre, as I view them—are very early work, & appeared in obscure British magazines in the '90's. They never appeared in book form or in America, so Wright thought them a good investment when *Weird Tales'* London agent brought them to his notice. The Edward Lucas White tale appears to have been a regular contribution—whether or not through a literary agent I can't say. The William *Penn* sale must have been quite an event—why

---

*Including "The Outsider", which Cook relinquished very gracefully.

didn't you get one? Pen sales are very frequent in Brooklyn, but the one I patronised looked the best to me. It is still going on, & if you'll tell me what kind
of a point you'd like I'll get you one. They are very good about *changing*, & I
think S H will send hers back to be changed, since the feed seems slow. Mine
is the 4th I tried. No—Sonny's "Yondo" drawing need not be returned; tho' I
*would* like back the horrible face by Smith himself which I enclosed some time
ago. Too bad *Weird Tales* rejected "Yondo"—Wright is provokingly finical
about having the *plot* element in what he takes.

Glad you had a good chance to see the Petty homestead, & hope it may
long be preserved. The James Monroe house in N.Y. is still in process of
moving—a very slow process—& we can't yet figure out what "park-like
space" it's headed for. In Hicks St. near the Clark St. (Brooklyn Heights)
subway station, a whole row of late Georgian houses is coming down; &
many are my tears thereat.

Good luck with your clock regulation—& may you & Delilah work wonders in giving the new room a settled aspect. She certainly is a valuable nigger,
& ought to bring a good $900 or $1000 in any fair market north of Savannah.
Sorry you don't like the lap dogs—I think I like them the best of all dogs,
since they are the most like cats. But I always prefer the real article, hence am
much more interested in your bobtailed Maine neighbour with the sable coat
& yellow eyes. Is his *decauditation* a natural feature, or has accident play'd its
tragick role with him? If the former, I should say he had a strain of Manx
blood—Maine cats are very mixed, a strong strain of Persian being responsible for the celebrated "coon cat" of which Belknap's "Felis" is the specimen
*par excellence*. Hope the beans & rolls were palatable. I had beef stew last night,
& will take the rest this morning. Like you, I heated all at the outset—the extra heating doing the second portion no harm. Since I am not wedded to the
convention of *certain* foods at *certain* hours, I only keep my second portions a
*half*-day; letting them form my *next* meal instead of the meal after next. In this
way I have avoided all deterioration of meaty material. Beans & canned spaghetti are twice as good when hot, but my favourite canned things are the complete dinners which I described some time ago, & of which I think I like beef
stew best. I can also heat the mutton pies I get at the Scotch Bakery. Some time
I'll try canned succotash—indeed, I have acquired a new interest in canned
goods now that I possess heating facilities. Now & then I get Heinz beans instead of Atlantic & Pacific, since although the cost is greater, the flavour is finer. I may try various brands of *canned spaghetti*, too. As to leaving the top of the
heater open—I tried it, but didn't seem to get any very definite results. Sometimes I turn the blaze down to save oil, for I never wish to exceed 5 gallons
(80¢) per week. By the way—ought the oil gauge to work without any assistance such as tapping or moving the stove? I find that mine seems to require
such an incentive now & then, tho' the process involves no difficulty at all.

"Beyond the Wall of Sleep", written in 1919, was a tale of a murderous

Catskill Mountain degenerate, confined in an asylum, & found to have strange qualities by the physician who tells the story. He was, it turns out, the earthly abode of a powerful celestial spirit, from whom the doctor gets a communication through an electrical apparatus at the moment of the poor creature's death. This spirit is bound on a strange mission in the skies, & its liberation is marked by the appearance of the star Nova Persei—which presumably results from its conflict with an inveterate enemy. The narration is set in the year 1901 to coincide with the appearance of the well-known Nova. Most of the amateurs liked the tale very much, & I was surprised at its rejection by Wright. The one thing that encourages me is the fact that two of my *new* tales ("He" & "Red Hook") have been accepted; a circumstance which indicates that age has not as yet considerably impaired my powers of authorship. "If Winter Comes" bored me vastly, yet the trouble was not that it lacked a happy ending. The real fault was a certain strained quality & falsity to human nature which appeared increasingly as the action progressed. I must read this "Messer Marco Polo". Sonny-Child is enthusiastick over it, tho' I doubt if I shall like it as well as Marco's genuine narrative, which has all the naive force of Herodotus. Mandeville gets boresome, I find. Yes—it's too bad old Fulton fed the flames at the ferry, but such indeed is life! He ought to have been in a museum—which reminds me anew that I must investigate the new municipal museum in the old Gracie Mansion (1813) in East River Park, of which the well-known antiquarian Henry Collins Brown is curator. It ought to have been open for months, yet I have deferred explorations. East R. Pk. is an open space at the foot of 86th St., with an excellent view of the islands & of the Hell Gate & Queensboro Bridges. Yes—Dr. Chapin is a great character.[1] In England I believe he would not only have gained fame, but achieved knighthood—fancy the proper dignity of the title *Sir Charles Chapin!* I hope your cold is over, & can still report that I have not yet entered on my winter cold of 1925–26. Leeds, Kirk, & Loveman have been the sufferers, & are hardly out of the woods even now. Yes—I noticed the secretary in the cuttings. The urn was one of the standard forms of 18th century ornamentation, & is coming to be again as Georgian designs regain their ascendancy.

I appreciated the new cuttings you enclosed. No—I haven't yet read "Sylvestre Bonnard",[2] tho' I well recall Alfredus' enthusiasm over it in 1919. The lament on Victorian architecture is well merited. New York suburbs can shew even worse, especially in the foreign colonies where every species of blasphemous bedizenment insults the observing eye. Now that the elements of colonial design are revived, it is an infinite pity that they are so extensively misapplied. The old Georgian sense of balance & proportion seems hopelessly lost.

This Brougher is doubtless a highly amusing person, & is not likely to do any permanent harm. Comparatively few nonconformist clergymen are mellowly cultivated—save perhaps those of the best churches of the Eastern cities. The most likeable of all clerics are those of the Church of England, most of whom have mature taste, a ready sense of humour, & a healthy tendency to indulge in aesthetic & intellectual interests outside their parish routine. I see that one of Elder Brougher's sons holds forth in Mortonius' new burg—Paterson.

As for my current diary—I think my last Providence despatch extended to Monday afternoon, as I was starting down to Kirk's at 5:30 to help him address some more envelopes. Arriving in good time, I found Kirk, Kleiner, Loveman & Leeds all assembled; & shortly afterward the gang started out to dinner at the Chatham Cafeteria—its new loafing headquarters at 8th Ave. & 14th St. When we returned, the addressing began; & as before, I made a record for speed & quantity. Loveman left early & Kleiner slept on the couch, but Kirk, Leeds, & I toiled on till 2 a.m., when the supply of envelopes gave out. We then adjourned to the Chatham again, Kleiner leaving us shortly, & Leeds following his example somewhat thereafter. Kirk walked with me to the Union Square station of the B.M.T., where I bowed my adieux & took the train for 169. Arriving at 4 a.m., I read a little & retired. Tuesday I was up late & welcomed the arrival of Clark Ashton Smith's new book "Sandalwood", which is composed half of original verse & half of Baudelaire translations. The verse is not equal to Smith's older work, but this may be because he has transcended his natural province & tried to write amatory instead of weird poetry. I have an idea he will be more his old self in the forthcoming weird volume entitled "Incantations."[3] Just as I had finished the book Loveman appeared, bearing as gifts two odd volumes of Jacob Brucker's "Historia Critica Philosophiae", printed at Leipzig in Latin in 1766, & containing chapters on the Cabbala & Pythagorean mysteries. He thought they might have weird potentialities, tho' they turn'd out to be full of academic & historical matter rather than colourful formulae for evoking daemons. Loveman wished me to dine with him at John's & discuss books later on in his room, & this I did; observing incidentally his delightful new Remington portable typewriter—which seems to me by far to outclass the widely known Corona. Returning at midnight, I read my new philosophical books & stay'd up thro' the night—attacking new correspondence when the morning mail came. About noon I cleaned the room in expectation of the evening McNeil meeting, & shortly thereafter welcomed a call from Little Sonny, who had come to shew his Grandpa a new story & extend his regrets about the meeting—from which he was forced to be absent thro' the duty of seeing his aunt off on the Florida train. The story was very well done—the martyrdom of St. Vincent at Valentia treated in a weird fashion—& we sealed & mailed it to Wright forthwith.[4] I shewed the Child my Smith book, & he order'd one for himself. Plans for his own volume of verse go steadily forward, tho' he finds it hard to decide on a binding. About 5:30 p.m. Sonny left, & I went out with him on a shopping tour. Returning soon with the evening's refreshments—crumb-cake & raspberry tarts—I read desultorily as I awaited the guests; who proved to be successively Kleiner, Mortonius, & honest old McNeil. Discussion began quickly, & the event turned out to be one of our most enjoyable sessions—Dr. Johnson, Germany, & the Civil War being the main topicks debated. At 11:00 Mortonius & I went out for coffee, which with other refreshments was forthwith serv'd on the tip table with blue china & 454 silver. We disbanded—not without reluctance—at 1:30 a.m., after which I washed dishes, read, & retired in the morning. Thursday I was up late, went out shopping, & read miscellaneously thro' the night, retiring at 7 a.m. Friday I rose at 6 p.m. & read proofs of my story in *Tryout*,[5] later attacking correspondence & resting a while about the middle of the night. Now I am up & about my correspondence again, & shall go shopping as soon as I am through—which will be very soon if the morning mail does not swamp me with letters. The warmth & clearness of the day tempts me Hempsteadward—but if I don't go I'll do some work on the horror-novelette which I have so minutely planned out. As for future events—tomorrow Loveman wants to plan a trip somewhere, Wednesday there's a Leeds meeting at Kirk's, & the Wednesday after that nice old McNeil entertains the gathering at his slum roost. Beyond that I am uninform'd. I must keep my programme freer of outside events in order to preserve an equilibrium for writing, but politeness impels me to submit to many social demands till I can devise a diplomatick means of diminishing them. And so it goes. Last Tuesday I had a leaky can of oil from the dealer, which might have made a very pretty mess had I not discover'd it before it soak'd thro' the paper on which my supply rests. As it was, I borrowed an empty can from the Gorgon & transferr'd the contents of the offending vessel, so was speedily all right again. ¶ S H seems to be faring better than former reports indicate, & may spend Christmas week here on a vacation. ¶ Morning mail just came, bringing only the Bulletin. Good work—now I'll have today free! First shopping, & then I'll see whether I'll take an outing or work on the story. ¶ I've been trying some *very strong* cheese in order to economise on bulk, but like it so little that I don't think I'll get any more. ¶ More soon. ¶ Yr aff Nephew & obt Servt

H P L

P.S. What's your absolutely final & definitive house number—115 or 117 Waterman? The back of your recent epistle leaves room for speculation.

## Notes

1. Charles Value Chapin (1856–1941), superintendent of health in Providence (1884–1932) and author of *The Sources and Modes of Infection* (1910) and other treatises on medicine. His son was H. M. Chapin (see LDC/AEPG 100n3).

2. Anatole France (1844–1924), *Le Crime de Sylvestre Bonnard* (1881), translated as *The Crime of Sylvestre Bonnard*. France won the Nobel Prize for Literature in 1921.

3. No book titled *Incantations* was ever published, but the poems intended for it are contained in the subsection "Incantations" in Smith's *Selected Poems* (1971). In 1936,

R. H. Barlow had contemplated publishing it but typesetting never began.
3. The FBL story is unidentified. It may not have been published.
4. "In the Vault."

[142]    [ALS] [HPL to LDC]

Saturday Evening—<br>
Novr. 14, 1925<br>
Ended        Thursday Night<br>
Novr. 19, 1925

My dear Daughter Lillian:—

Yours of the 12th duly arrived, & I note with interest the intricate causes behind your elusive address. When A E P G first wrote me of the change, she gave the number as *115;* & I duly entered that figure in the "In-case-of-accident-notify" column of my diary. Then came a correction, & I carefully changed the 115—already carefully changed from 188—to 117. Later I noted 115 in your return address on an envelope, & inquired concerning it. Now I trust it's settled—& I've again carefully entered *115* in my book! The entrance arrangement is certainly complex enough—it must be odd not to know what door one's going home through! Sorry you find more dirt than at 188—but I'll wager your very worst isn't half as bad as the coarse, gritty dust that filters into my windows here! And there are places, no doubt, even worse than this. Yes—it wouldn't take much to have a place brighter & better than the Burns average . . . look at the enclosed, which is the latest downhill move! Now I have to heat water on my stove when I need it—for I can't be rushing up & down stairs constantly asking for the hot water to be turned on. If I were a realist I'd get revenge by writing the place up in a story—maybe I will anyway. If I do, I'll have the house represented as a den of cutthroats, & let the landlady end up on the gallows! Moving, though, certainly is a devil of a mess & expense; & I fancy you did better than one could do here. Here's hoping you get your window-ropes & shades before I get my alcove & tall lights—promises are wonderful things! Glad you have plenty of light & a good view—that marvellous neo-Colonial Metcalf Laboratory ought to add a dollar a week to the price of the room! I don't think I've noticed the garden you mention, but I can imagine how attractive it must be. And isn't Hathaway & Douglas' carpenter shop somewhere around there? Hope the neighbouring phonograph plays attractive tunes—or at least, refrains from playing obtrusively unattractive ones. I'll wager you hear nothing as weird as I get from my neighbour Abdul Firouz ben Hussein Ali—or whoever he is. In the morning I hear him strangely chanting—& shouldn't wonder if he is saying his prayers to Allah in Arabic. I wonder if he wears a turban? More likely his headgear comes from Truly Warner!

Thanks for the Corner & Character. Like you, I have noticed the hiatus in the Laswell series, & hope fervently that it may prove but temporary. Many as have already appeared, the artist has hardly begun really to cover the state; legions of vividly interesting old buildings existing in Newport, Warren, Bristol, Wickford, Providence, & scores of other places. He ought to do some of the houses on the hill—Star St. for example. I wish, too, that he would publish another book. All too few of his delightful drawings are given this definitive permanence, & it would be a monstrous crime for any of them to sink into the usual neglect & oblivion attending newspaper features. I noticed that paragraph about cheese, & am glad that Gramp's allusion has found such open & illustrious verification. One might remark, however, that Liszt's belief in the *indigestibility* of cheese is the merest popular superstition; since most real authorities— including him who ought to be Sir Charles Chapin—agree that to the average stomach cheese is both highly nutritious & properly digestible. It is certainly my favourite article of nourishment—&, I fear, my chief source of extravagance; since those 39¢ pound lots do vanish with unconscionable swiftness. A couple of weeks ago I tried getting very strong cheese for economy's sake— so that a little would go far—but didn't like it very well, so have gone back to my regular brands. Certainly, if Liszt be right, my beans & bread ought to digest well tonight! Undoubtedly my liking for caseous[1] delicacies comes from W V P—& it has lost nothing in strength during the process of transmission! Whilst on the subject of diet, though, let me add a note for your benefit in case you ever buy ginger-snaps. Don't let anybody substitute *Yum-Yum* (Sunshine) for *Zu-Zu* (Natl. Bisc. Co.) I got some the other day at a James Butler store whose brands of bread & cheese I like, & when I tasted them I was disgusted by their abysmal inferiority. They have absolutely none of the wholesome flavour of the older & better known product—& even if the specimens I encountered were sub-normal ones, they argue a degree of variation from which the NBC product is happily free. This is not a paid NBC advertisement, but a spontaneous & wholly non-professional pointer from one who (confound it!) still has two packages of Yum-Yums to get rid of. After that, only NBC products, you can bet! Another diet note—*when heated,* the cheap Atlantic & Pacific beans taste exactly as good as the costlier Heinz ones. Cold, the Heinz commodity is incomparably superior; but heat proves the great leveller. I think I have said that the A & P 9¢ can is larger than the Heinz 14¢ can.

Glad you like the October lines. The ones you enclosed are very clever— & their author, Robinson, mentioned me in his column once when Loveman's Colophon Club (now defunct) voted my "Hypnos" (most ludicrously) among the six or ten or twelve "best short stories of the world". You may recall my shewing you the cutting two years or so ago.[2] As to the metre being 'long & lazy'—it is so as he uses it, but you will note that in "October" I brighten'd it up with an internal double rhyme—thus—

> Never say I chose this metre just to skimp on things like rhyme;
> What indeed could e'er be neater, or more fitted to the time?

This infant poetess Nathalia Crane[3] lives only a few blocks from here, I am told—in Hicks St. Her father is suspected of writing the verse himself because he once attempted poetry in youth, & even had a book of verse published at his own expense. It was derided widely by the critics, & some have thought that he is now taking a quiet & humorous revenge by getting them to praise his verse when signed with a child's name. This, however, is only a minority opinion; the majority* of responsible reviewers seeming to regard Nathalia as a genuine prodigy. I haven't read any of the stuff, but others of the gang have—& of them only Belknap & Loveman incline toward the cynical theory of paternal or other adult authorship. All the other cuttings were of interest, too—& about the Smith horror-head—I *may* have received it back & lost it, but certainly can't find it now. My files are getting chaotic—I must have a day of general cleaning & classification shortly. As for "Beyond the Wall of Sleep"— since you don't recall reading it in 1919, when it was written, I'll enclose a copy herewith; asking its ultimate return. You may wonder how the term "radio" can occur in something written six years ago—but the answer of course is that I interpolated it just now when making the new copy to try on *Weird Tales*.[4] As it happened, I copied it for nothing; since Wright rejected it. When you read it, you'll probably recall having seen it before. Yes—that submerged city in the Caspian is much like the sunken towns which I & other fantastic authors love to write about. I hope to read further reports on it—though I am quite certain they will reveal none of the horrors which will come out of my submerged Pacific city of L'yeh—which is older than mankind![5]

Glad you've looked up my Regals & seen the sample of my best suit. Now you know about how I look—tho' the snapshots are yet to come. It certainly is a vast relief to have a proper stock of clothes again, & I can only hope that no future thief may stage a repetition of last May's tragedy. All observers agree on the excellence of my present wardrobe; & what you say of overcoats is quite true, tho' S H has occasionally recommended my getting a fresh one. I'll send the bedroom shoes shortly—tho' I hate to be without them! Oh, yes—I have plenty of assorted slippers & sandals, but nothing is ever comparable to the real, old-time, home-knit bedroom shoe. I have them on now. When I send them I may also send a shirt or two (if it isn't an imposition) to see what you can do toward taking in the neckband to *14½*†. To wear a collar over a too-large band is a constant source of annoyance—it is always slipping off at the sides—& if my supply could be suitably contracted I would feel infinitely more comfortable. The way to do it would be to get a *14½* collar (Arrow-Devon) at the Boston Store & fit the bands beneath it. Stiff collars seem to run larger than soft—the Devon 14½ apparently being

*the principal dissenter is Edwin Markham, who claims that the work of six different adults is grouped together under a juvenile signature.
†I'll also ask you to darn a small hole in one of them, if you don't mind.

of just the same size as the 14¾ soft Tide collars which A E P G sent me last June. Perhaps the secret is that a soft collar is strongly contracted at the top by the tie, so that one can wear a larger size so far as band is concerned. The regular stiff 14½ is a very loose fit—Belknap advises me to go down to 14¼ for neatness' sake, but I don't think I will just yet. I wear all my clothing very loose. As for fountain pens—use your own judgment, but if you're looking for a real bargain, here's the place to get one. At this $1.28 sale both large & small specimens are shewn. I got the large, but the small might appeal more to you. The make is *Keene*—which you may or may not have seen or heard of before. Speaking of writing—I must get hold of a specimen of Kleiner's lettering to shew you. It is truly masterly work, & I don't see how on earth he manages to do it. He has lately engrossed a copy of Loveman's lines on Kirk's new shop, which Kirk has hung up in the main room of the emporium.[6]

I am interested to hear that the Maine kitty-cat is an acknowledged Manx. Bless me, but I'd like to see him! And too, I'd like to see the visiting black kittie of more longicaudate proportions. The dogs must be fairly interesting—& I agree that the black Pomeranian is to be preferred to the (theoretically) white poodle. But to me, a good—or even a fairly good—cat is to be preferr'd to both!

That Village Blacksmith Shop must be deliciously interesting, & I'm sure I never saw anything of like ingenuity in N.Y.—tho' of course I don't see much of the town & its windows these days. My mental life is really at home, & the image evoked casually by the phrase "down town" is always Market Square, Turk's Head, Exchange Place, Mathewson, Dorrance, Westminster or Weybosset. The complex mechanism needed to produce the varied simultaneous motions you describe must be intricate & ingenious to the ultimate degree, & I don't wonder at the crowds who stand & admire it. Trust the Journal to discover all the latest marvels & devices! The Shepard Baby Roger must also be a spectacle worthy of a glance. I didn't realise that the Christmas season was so close—I suppose all the shop windows must be putting on their annual holiday dress. Glad the Petty house retains something of its original state despite mercantile defacements—& speaking of defacements, is it not poetick justice that Edward Redding, who threatened the facade of the Arcade, should now be a fugitive from justice with two forgery indictments hanging over his head? I knew he must be a rascal—any person capable of planning such beastly vandalism must lack some important element of character! I hope he gets 25 years or more at Cranston, & that the Arcade may remain always in its pristine purity—staring with untainted classicism a quarter-century hence at the man who planned its mutilation, as he will stagger out of the grey stone crypts of Warden Linscott's summer hotel, haggard & prematurely broken, & remorseful over his contemplated architectural profanation if not over his dubious financial machinations. Poor Redding—he had *alteration* on the brain, & thought he'd try it on both buildings & cheques.

Now may a similar or worse fate befall any pusillanimous dastard who dares lift a finger toward the demolition of the Stephen Hopkins house & the Brown & Ives counting house. That court building does *not* need to go thro' to Hopkins St.!

About my oil gauge—I asked at the hardware shop, but the salesman said the company would take so long to adjust the matter that I'd lose all the use of the stove when I need it most! The matter is not important—for the least jarring of the stove will set the gauge working—& I doubt if I shall bother about it till spring. Maybe the thing will limber up anyhow in time, as it gets more & more saturated with oily vapours. I might try, by the way, the oiling of the pivot where the indicating hand swings round. The stove works to perfection, & so far I have secured that most agreeable combination—perfect comfort & small oil bills. Its culinary value is an added asset—& I can assure you that no more delicious meals were ever served beneath this roof! No more leaky cans so far—I fancy Mrs. Burns gave the oil man a highly pertinent series of remarks, spiced with that emphasis which only she can wield! I don't think I'll need a mat for the cans—a good thick layer of Evening Bulletins seems to serve admirably.

Don't go to any inconvenience about that Historical Society thing—but if chance makes it easy for you to get hold of that booklet, I shall prodigiously appreciate a copy. As I think I mentioned, the title is: "Westminster St., Providence, as it was about 1824. Drawings of Francis Read, Presented by his Daughter, Mrs. Marinus W. Gardner. R.I. Hist. Soc. 1917." The originals, as I have probably said before, are on display at the museum; Mortonius & I having seen them in 1923. If you can get two copies, we ought to have one apiece—for I know you'd enjoy having one for inspection when you wish.

S H seems to be doing better in the new place, though an incipient attack of bronchial pneumonia—nipped in the bud by a competent physician & by a several days' stay in bed—has kept her from business recently, tho' she expects to be back at it soon. She has made a decided "hit" in the educational department of the store with one of her old articles on salesmanship, & has just written another & longer one (very effective, it seems to me) which I revised & returned by air mail Friday. I enclose the cards sent her by her business associates—accompanying a bouquet of flowers.

As for my own diary—I think I left off Tuesday morning, whilst deciding whether to go on a trip or write on my story. As it turned out, I did neither; for S H's letter arrived with the long article for revision, & I knew that I would have to attend to that for some time to come. Accordingly I worked on it till afternoon, rested & rose, worked thro' the night & thro' Wednesday, & on Wednesday evening attended the meeting (Leedsian) at Kirk's. This gathering was a decided success—all hands being present, tho' Morton pensively predicted that it might mark the end of his *regular* attendance, since increased—or at least changed—duties will henceforward keep him more &

more in Paterson. Kirk served refreshments on some new pink china (in exe-crable taste—why didn't he get an old-fashion'd looking blue like mine?) & with some excellent new imitation-Colonial silver he had bought, & afterward the whole company gathered around the fireplace in the front room—the room with the shelves, which constitutes the shop as distinguished from the living quarters. Discussion first centred around Dr. Erasmus Darwin, (Charles's grandfather) & Mortonius read aloud selections from "The Botan-ick Garden". We then drifted on to the subject of *quotations,* & Morton & Loveman started their favourite pastime of trying to have the gang place cer-tain quoted passages. Of course they carried off all the honours, for I have no rote memory at all; but I took revenge by "sticking" them on some odd points—mostly homely verse from Colonial sources, such as the lines on the title-page of the first number of the Farmer's Almanack—

> "While the bright radiant fun in centre glows,
> The earth in annual motion round it goes;
> At the fame time on its own axis reels,
> And gives us change of feafons as it wheels."

Sonny was the first to leave; Loveman next. The rest lingered till 3 a.m., when a regretful dispersal took place. I took the subway to 169, did a bit of writing, & retired at 5 a.m. Rising Thursday at 1:30 p.m., I worked on S H's article all day; & being fatigued by matter so much out of my own line, retired at 7 p.m. Friday, though, I was up at 1:30 a.m., & had the article done by dawn. I then went out for a cup of coffee, getting as I did so an utterly gorgeous view of the great copper disc of the rising sun, as it hove in sight at the very end of the long, narrow, old-fashion'd vista of State St., down which I was walking toward Court. The rest of the morning I spent in typing; & at 2 p.m. sallied forth to the post office to get the article off by air mail. The day being fair, (despite a transient shower later, which found me, however, safe within a car) & of such delicious warmth that I wore no overcoat, I decided to devote it to an exploring trip; so took the elevated for the former fishing village of Ca-narsie, on the south shore of Brooklyn east of Sheepshead Bay, to see what it was like. I may have mentioned that I missed this place during my early ex-plorations, since I thought I had reached it when I came to the end of the el-evated; whereas in truth one changes (without extra fare) to a surface car to finish the trip. This time I did change—but without seeing anything quaint enough to justify the excursion. Merely a few scattered & nondescript wood-en houses, plus a shabby-looking amusement park—a frayed & seedy Rocky Point, as it were—closed for the winter. But I lost nothing financially—since by staying on whilst the car looped about I continued to ride back on my original nickel. At Eastern Parkway—still on the same nickel—I changed for Jamaica, & was there rewarded by one of the major discoveries of all my

New-York explorations—a thing of which I had heard vague rumours from Kleiner, but which he could not precisely recall or definitely place. I allude to the spacious King Mansion,[7] built in 1750, a vast white gambrel-roofer* with a series of two "ells" behind, set in an exceedingly tasteful little park fronting the main street (Jamaica Ave.) just before one reaches the village on the trip from Brooklyn. It is perhaps the largest gambrel-roofer I have ever seen—the idea of the builder having evidently been the odd one of sticking to the architectural traditions of the medium-sized house whilst actually achieving the vastness which others sought only in the stately square Georgian type with flat or hipped roof—like the Jumel Mansion or Van Cortlandt manor, for example. It stands intact with its outbuildings amidst the white-flagged walks & green lawns, with Georgian village spires visible to the east, & many another quaint old house in sight—only the elevated marring the peaceful village effect. It is owned by the city of N.Y., & tended by representatives of various organisations such as D.A.R., Jamaica Village Society, &c., being open Mondays, Wednesdays, & Saturdays from 1 to 5 p.m. As you may imagine, I at once planned a visit on the following day, when I might get in; & it was with reluctance that I quitted the scene at last—the quiet rural green glorified in the ruddy radiance of the late afternoon sun, with white steeples & ancient white farmhouse walls flushed with a delicate & evanescent pink. But leave I did, & struck west & north along Jamaica Ave. & Queens Boulevard in quest of a place I had heard much about, & had located on the map—the modern suburban development called "Kew Gardens", planned & built in very close imitation of a mediaeval or Elizabethan English village. The way led up a hill away from Jamaica into some very pretty rolling woodland, & when I encountered Maple Grove Cemetery I struck due westward among the tombs (not ancient ones, I regret to say) up a fairly steep hill toward the opposite side which, according to the map, bordered on Kew Gardens. At length I attain'd the crest, travers'd a level space, & emerg'd upon a high road overlooking a valley—where, magnificent in its reproduced antiquity, stretched a Chaucerian village of dream; with sunset-gilded chimney-pots & steep half-timber'd gables peeping out from a lavish wealth of trees whose autumn branches were scarcely yet bare. Then for a scenick revel! The place is beauty personified, & has a very Providence-like air suggestive of Orchard Ave. or the new streets beyond Paterson that border on Blackstone Park & the Seekonkward slope of Angell St. The residential houses are of two sorts— Tudor English & American Colonial; & the architectural scheme of everything in the village is safeguarded by the restrictions of the developing corporation. The ground is very uneven, which creates a picturesqueness of the loveliest sort; & the business centre is built up in the mediaeval English man-

---

*of the N.Y. pitch—upper part of roof narrower

ner with great blocks of ancient-looking houses—some half-timbered, some brick & plaster with *artificial* peelings & discolourations to give the effect of immemorial antiquity, & some of the elaborate many-gabled type with carved oak timbers, red tiles, diamond-paned lattice windows, & exposed beams alternating with plaster—everything being perfectly true to type, even to the gables overhanging the street & supported on grotesquely carven corbels. One row of this sort, on a sweeping hilly curve which suggests for all the world the high street of some drowsy Kent hamlet that King Richard the Third might have known, is an almost perfect image of one of the really old Ipswich (Eng.) houses shewn in the cards John Russell sent me, & which I believe I sent you for inspection. The one I mean is that called "The Ancient House"—which you may or may not recall. The fact is, that those three cards give an excellent idea of what the nucleus of Kew Gardens is like; & the imitation is so perfect that—at least in the glamour of sunset—one gains no jarring sense of spuriousness or modernity. One secret is that the houses fit the landscape so surpassingly well. Having drunk my aesthetick fill for the day, I embarkt upon the long 'trek' to the elevated by another route, & was in less than an hour back at 169, getting supper & retiring at 7:30 p.m. The trip, despite all its vivid splendours & diverse scenery, had cost me exactly *ten cents!*

Saturday I was up very early, grappled with my correspondence, & at 2 p.m. started on my second exploring trip. The day was equally warm & delightfully fair, & I took the elevated at once for Jamaica & the old King Mansion. This time the mansion was open, & I stept within to a realm of golden memories & quiet, beautiful old traditions which quite banished New-York from the field of consciousness & reality, & made me fancy I was in America again. Here were rooms furnished gracefully in the olden way; with colonial pieces of rare loveliness, & an occasional Victorian relique whose ugliness was quite forgotten amidst its power of evoking simple, homely recollections of untainted American yesterdays, when life flowed normally & continuously in channels whose fountain-head was the past. Cases of relicks perpetuated the unbroken local traditions of Jamaica Village, where from early colonial times there existed a wholesome rural civilisation headed down from generation to generation of cultivated residents, & comparable to the local civilisations of places like Marblehead or Portsmouth. In the old days, indeed, Jamaica was as separate & remote from New York as Salem itself—hardly realising the existence of the busy town so many miles away. It was a Yankee overflow from Connecticut, & had its own great families, unique customs, legends, & touches of individuality as pronouncedly as any isolated New-England village. Now, of course, it is being absorbed into the New-York fabrick as Flatbush was—linked to the maelstrom by the elevated & its five-cent fare. Flushing will go the same way when the elevated is completed thither, & I suppose even Hempstead (now outside the New York city limits) will be in peril 25 or 50 years hence. But meanwhile Jamaica retains some sunset spark of its old American village life, & as I entered the peaceful portals of the old gambrel-roofer I felt a sense of homecoming—of treading ground that has something in common with the old places of New England with their mellow ancestral memories—of being in touch with a holy & venerable sacrament kept alive amidst chaos & decay, & standing at one with the soul of Providence & Newport, Boston & Concord, Salem & Marblehead, Portsmouth & Newburyport, & the Shepley Library & R.I. Historical Society & Essex Institute & Lee Mansion & Moffatt-Ladd house & Haverhill Historical Society . . . . . . . It was a breath of life from the sources that inspire my being! Among the *Victorian* relicks was an old haircloth rocker **exactly** like the one my mother used to rock me to sleep in—the one that cracked when it rocked, & that had the little projections planed off the arms for fear I'd get hurt on them. This Jamaica specimen had the projections still on. There was no question of mere *similarity*—the two chairs were *absolutely identical*—beyond a doubt the products of the same maker or factory—& I shall go often to see this one. I wonder if the rocker cracks when it rocks? Well—at last I left the place, & proceeded again up Queens Boulevard & across the cemetery to Kew Gardens, which I saw again in the light of a glorious sunset. All the charm of the previous day remain'd with me, & I explored the region with delighted thoroughness, revelling in the delicate impressions of Old England which the buildings & topography afforded. Soon I am going again, & mean to explore a neighbouring tract call'd *Forest Park,* which looms up very alluringly on the map. As dusk fell I again sought the elevated via Metropolitan Ave., & as I turned into Jamaica Ave.—the ancient colonial post road—I found a farmhouse of the keenest antiquarian interest, now falling into melancholy decay with a sickly coat of yellowish-brown paint. The original house was a New England farm type of the early & middle seventeenth century—it must have been built betwixt 1630 & 1670—with front facing the south & roof sloping down almost to the ground in the rear; (exactly like the Rebekah Nurse house [1636] in Danvers, of which I've shewn you pictures) but at some time during the later colonial period a Dutch purchaser added a porch & gave the front roof the characteristick New-Netherland curve & dormer windows—producing one of the oddest hybrids which colonial architecture can boast—like this: (Shaded part is original New England farmhouse) The grounds are run to utter decay, & I suppose the house will soon be torn down to make way for the endless rows of cheap wooden villas which are transforming this once lovely countryside—the Richmond Hill district—into a dreary & semi-squalid waste of lower middle-class stagnation.

Now taking the elevated, I was home again at 6:00 p.m. & began this letter. I shall now retire, be up early tomorrow, & accompany Loveman on still another exploring trip.

*Monday Evening*

True to my determination, I was up early Sunday, & after some writing met Loveman at John's at 1:30 p.m. Deciding on Flushing as an objective, we took the East Side subway to the Grand Central & transferred to the Queensboro subway-elevated; this time riding on to the end & avoiding the slip-up of the previous week. The new line is rapidly drawing near Flushing, & when it reaches there, the separateness of the village will be doomed. Even now real estate men are beginning to fill & build on the salt marshes around Flushing Creek—the last bit of open country separating the village from New York's expanding fringe. Reaching Flushing by the now very slight surface-car link, we threaded up & down the shady, hilly streets with their quaint colonial houses & alluring New Englandish panoramas; drinking to the full an atmosphere so different from that of New York that one can hardly believe Times Square is less than an hour away. The new colonial belfry of the Sloane furniture factory is approaching completion, & will dominate the skyline exquisitely when painted white & adorn'd with a suitable clock. We saw again the 1661 Bowne House whose picture you like, the 1694 Quaker Meeting-House with its hay-cap roof & churchyard with tiny white stones, the stone marking the spot where George Fox (whom Roger Williams "Diggd out of his Burrovves") preached on June 7th, 1672, & all the little sights & atmospherick touches which took on new glories & rous'd misty ancestral memories amidst the golden radiance of a magical & transfiguring sunset. But at length we took the car & elevated back to Babylon; proceeding to a cinema which Loveman wanted to see & which bored me nearly to sleep, & afterward dining at the Times Square Automat. It being still early, we dropt around to see honest old McNeil, who is to have the meeting next Wednesday after all on account of Sonny's fatigue with other engagements. He proved an amiable host, & we did not leave till midnight, after which we dispersed homeward. I wrote a little, & retired about 4:15 a.m. This morning—Monday—I was up about 11 a.m., did some writing & proofreading, (of my hideous tale "In the Vault" in honest old Smithy's coming *Tryout*) & am still at my desk. But of course, I have been glancing over the Sunday Journal, as any good Rhode-Islander ought. A E P G's letter arrived safely with cheque & bill, & I was charmed by the Weybosset St. postcard she enclosed—shewing that old building at the corner of Mathewson with the Reed & Barton jewellery shop. As for the future—I shall probably be in all of today except for shopping. Tomorrow evening Loveman & I are invited to dinner at Sonny-Child's, & the next night is a McNeil meeting at McNeil's—probably a dreary affair, since Morton, Sonny, & Kirk are almost certain to be absent. The Wednesday after that is a Leeds meeting at Kirk's—on Kirk's birthday—& on the following day I shall eat my Thanksgiving dinner at the Dench home; Morton, Miss Merritt, Kleiner, & honest old McNeil being also present beside the hosts. The following Saturday—the 28th—is a Blue Pencil meeting at Miss Banks'—far uptown—with Wheeler Dryden as nominal host & "Embarrassing Moments" as "literary" topick. I doubt very much if I shall go. Beyond this I have no authentick data, save that I hope to take much time for my own fiction during the ensuing days. I am once again trying to cut down both on correspondence & on the social programme, & think I am succeeding somewhat in both fields. The United is maddeningly held up by the delay of the official printer, Harry R. Marlowe;[8] but I feel that the responsibility is really no longer mine, so that I may honourably rest back & avoid getting into any new whirl of negotiation & letter-writing. I'm sure young Bacon is perfectly competent to deal with the situation himself.

Oh—by the way—apropos of nothing—my brown suit had a rain test last night & came out with flying colours in the figurative rather than literal sense. In other words, the colours stayed fast instead of running fast, & the shape remained unshrunken & undistorted. After all, it must be pretty decent wool; & I possess a renewed respect for my felicitous bargain! I enclose something about the Philadelphia exposition, which I certainly want to see next year. That town utterly captivated me with its delicious Colonialism, & it's hard to realise that a year & several days has elapsed since my memorable five-day series of explorations. Some time when I feel I can blow in three dollars I mean to take a Sunday excursion thither—& some other time when I feel really *wildly* extravagant I mean to take another five-fish excursion to Washington. Philadelphia & Alexandria are the pleasantest recollections I have outside New England.

The current Sunday Journal has some highly interesting things, including an account by H. M. Chapin of the "Sign of the Bunch of Grapes". The old Providence signs must have been delightful—Jabez Bowen Sr.'s Unicorn & Mortar, Joseph & William Russell's Golden Eagle, Jonathan Russell's Black Boy, James Green's Elephant, Smith & Sabin's Sultan's Head, Knight Dexter's Boy & Book, Clark & Nightingale's Frying-Pan & Fish, Joseph Olney's Crown, John Carter's Shakespear's Head, Jonathan Cady's Boot & Shoe, Jacob Whitman's Turk's Head, Thurber's Bunch of Grapes, & such things as the Brigantine, Golden Fox, & Painter's Arms. Old times! Old times! And there is a delightfully alluring thing about the mysterious antiquities of Pemaquid, Me., which I will enclose in case you've missed it by any chance. The idea of a Roman settlement in America is something which occurred to me years ago—in fact, I began a story with that theme (only it was about Central America & not U.S.) in 1906 or 1907, tho' I never finish'd it. I must see the *Adventure* article on which this cutting is based—Leeds probably has it, since A. is his favourite magazine.[9] I think, too, that I'll do some looking-up about Pemaquid at the publick library. The theme is certainly a golden one for mystery! I'd like to write a tale of the digging of a Westminster St. subway—or a Providence–Pawtucket subway—& the incidental discovery of broken Corinthian columns bespeaking the forum of some unknown Roman town at the head of Narragansett Bay. A trireme under Cn. Pomponius Falco during the war against the Mediterranean pirates in Cicero's time is hurled by a storm thro' the pillars [*sic*] of Hercules & into the vast Atlanticus. At length it reaches a pleasant bay inhabited by copper-skinned barbarians, & after a treaty is drawn up, a town is built on the side of a pleasing hill & named MVSO-SICVM—as the settlers interpret the name *Moshassuck*, which they hear from the barbarians. Wars arise, & for a time the Romans are victorious, conquering considerable outlying territory & founding the towns of PATVCITIVM, SOVAMIVM, PATVXETIVM, POCASITIVM, MOSVANSICVTVM,[10] &c. &c., till at length a disastrous reverse—or perhaps an earthquake or something—occurs & wipes the colony from the face of creation.

But I must cease. It's a bitter cold & windy day—Injun summer's over—& I probably shan't mail this till tomorrow—Tuesday. But I'll piece out the diary with notations on the envelope or somewhere. I shall probably stay in & read or write tomorrow, till it is time to go up to Belknap's. On that occasion I think I'll wear the best grey suit for the first time since I bought the brown. More later.

Yr aff Nephew & obt Servt<br>H P L

P.S. *Tuesday Evening.* Not going to Belknap's tonight after all. He's laid up with a severe bronchial cold & has postponed the engagement till Friday. His mother just called up to impart the news. Have been in all today, & guess I'll stay so till the meeting at McNeil's tomorrow night. ¶ *10 p.m.* Loveman called & has just gone.

P.P.S. I enclose sheets of Belknap's "Sea Thing". Please shew to A E P G & return.

P.P.P.S. I think that restriction of hot water must have been rescinded. Somebody probably complained with exceptional vigour. Within the last three days it has been turned on at all times, which looks like a genuine resumption of service.

[P.P.P.]P.S. Just revised a new poem for Mr. Hoag.

Thursday Morning—<br>Novr. 19, 1925

Well, well! This epistle has been lying around so long that I'll add a sheet to bring it down to date. I was in writing letters all day Wednesday except for a shopping trip, & in the evening started out for the meeting at McNeil's—very early, in order to warn McN. not to go up to Belknap's. There was considerable confusion as to locale, since Sonny forgot to notify everybody that he was unable to entertain the gang. Tuesday night Loveman said he had not been notified, so I knew that there was danger of Kleiner & McNeil's having been likewise neglected. Rather than send them up to Belknap's on a fruitless er-rand, I took it upon myself to see that each had the information correctly. Kleiner I telephoned—& found that he had not been notified. M<sup>c</sup>Neil has no telephone, but by getting there early I would be able to prepare him for the change if he had not previously been notified. I found, however, that Sonny *had* thought to write him; so that he was preparing to receive the bunch. But what a small bunch! Mortonius kept in Paterson by new duties, Sonny ill, Kirk & Loveman at an imperative book auction—only Kleiner & I to form the visiting delegation! Kleiner arrived about an hour after I did, & discussion became quite interesting. He brought a book quite well known three years ago—"The Undertaker's Garland", by John Peale Bishop & Edmund Wilson, Jr.—which contains several ironic variations on the theme of death & decay as treated from the standpoint of post-war pessimism, disillusionment, & melancholy. I read it through during the session, & found some of the items of extreme cleverness. Bishop is the greater poet of the two authors, whilst Wilson is the subtler intellectual & analyst.[11] Both are youngish chaps, graduates of Princeton around 1917. Later on honest old M<sup>c</sup>Neil served his simple refreshments—tea & cookies—& discussion continued; poetry, monastick lettering, & scores of other subjects being covered. Kleiner gave me[12] one of his broad pens in an effort to convert me to his style of calligraphy; but I gravely fear I was not born for such effete refinements. He promises, however, to prepare a fine specimen of his own work for me to send to you in order to fhew (now we come again to my more natural, or *Rhode-Ifland Journal of Aftronomy* Style of Printing!)[13] the proficient Sort of Work he is accomplifhing in this Field of artiftick Endeavour. I am confident you will agree, that he excels any other Calligrapher you ever obferv'd, not excepting the renown'd Doctor *Warren Tillinghaft,* whofe aviform Flourifhes once adorn'd the Pages of many a young Gentlewoman's Album. His Efforts are now bent to the Perfection of illuminated Initials, in which Province there is no doubt but he will brilliantly fucceed. The meeting dissolv'd at midnight, & I proceeded to 169 at once; there taking my pen in hand to complete some epistles. With intervals of rest I shall keep on thro' today—tho' the moderating weather tempts one forth to the rural realm. Tomorrow night, unless Belknap's health continues bad, I shall dine up at 823. Sunday Loveman wants to go on a trip under my guidance. Next Wednesday there is a Leeds meeting at Kirk's on the latter's birthday. The day after that I take Thanksgiving dinner at Dench's. The next Saturday (28<sup>th</sup>) is a B.P.C. meeting which I shall omit if I can politely do so. And the next Wednesday Sonny has the M<sup>c</sup>Neil meeting. This is all I know of the future social programme. W. Paul Cook wants an article from me on the element of terror & weirdness in literature, but I shall take my time about preparing it.[14] Meanwhile I hope to get aloof & composed enough to do some writing on my own hook. I've just revised a poem for Mr. Hoag, which goes like this:

## ALONE

Oft have I wander'd, mute and lone,
　　Where Autumn turns the green to gold,
And froſted Leaves are downward blown
　　To feed the coming Springtide's Mould.

Oft have I trod thoſe Realms of Mind
　　Where Silence breathes with voiceleſs Breath,
And Footſteps ſcarce an Echo find
　　In Solitudes of Dream and Death.

Oft have I view'd from Lands apart
　　The myriad Scenes long gone before,
The Childhood Days of happy Heart,
　　And all the Light and Life of yore.

So ſeek I ſtill dim Vales where far
　　The Thruſh and Waterfall are heard;
Where worldly Cares may never mar,
　　Nor Folly found o'er Wiſdom's Word.
　　　　　JONATHAN HOAG, GENᵀ·

Viſta-Buena,
Greenwich, N.Y., Novʳ· 14, 1925.

And so it goes. Unless something turns up, you may consider this diary as running thro' Thursday to an uneventful retiring—anything to the contrary being duly noted. If I get my correspondence well dispos'd of by noon, I shall hope to devote the afternoon to a reading of Machen, in order to get my mind into a mood for composition. Or if it were very warm I might think about some rural exploration within the radius of a nickel fare. And some time I want to get down to the publick library & read that Timothy Dexter book, (of which Tryout has just sent me another fine review) as well as Gemmill's new work on the Salem witch trials, & a volume of two or three years ago on the tale of terror.[15]

Well—such is which. Some time soon I'll send a package of shirts—2 or 3—whose necks need taking in to fit a 14½ collar, & one of whose necks needs darning in a visible spot. That's the shirt I bought in Boston in April 1923 after a 3-weeks-old kitty cat tore the neck of an older shirt in exactly the same place! And with the shirts will come the bedroom shoes. Superabundant thanks in advance for all repairs! And more later.
　　　　　Yr aff Nephew & obt Servt
　　　　　H P L

P.S. Glad to see that Fred C. Perry is getting more & more *historical* in his "These Plantations" column. It quite atones for the absence of F. H. Young.[16]

P.P.S. Hot water still turned on! I guess that one curtailment didn't work!

[P.P.P.S.] *NIGHT* I've been writing at home all day. Now I'm going to retire.

[On envelope:]

P.S. It's hard to keep my days to myself! Kirk just telephoned & invited me so urgently for Saturday night that I couldn't find any way of giving a polite refusal!

FRIDAY—

I retired at midnight, rising today at 9 a.m. Engagement at Belknap's cancelled—he has a form of grippe. Now I shall do some writing.

6 p.m.—Mrs. Long has just telephoned that Belknap is better, & wants me to take lunch there tomorrow. I shall—going from there to Kirk's in the evening. Have been writing all of today, & shall do the same throughout the evening.

*Last Word*

Shall mail this & retire—about 11 p.m. New diary will start with Saturday, Nov. 21st.

## Notes

1. I.e., cheeselike.

2. See Edwin Meade Robinson (1878–1946), "The Philosopher of Folly: A Journalistic Journal," *Cleveland Plain Dealer* (13 March 1923): 10: "At a recent meeting of the Colophon Club, the ten members present were asked to write lists of what, in their opinion, were the six greatest short stories ever printed. It might have been expected that (since there was no collaboration in the lists) the result would be a list of sixty good short stories. But one story appeared in four lists, and seven other stories appeared more than once. The result, then, was a good list of eight short stories, as follows: [¶] "'The Procurator of Judea,' by Anatole France (four votes); 'The Necklace,' by De Maupassant; 'Youth,' by Conrad; 'Without Benefit of Clergy,' by Kipling; 'Marjorie Daw,' by Aldrich; 'The Girl With the Golden Eyes,' by Balzac; 'The Gentleman from San Francisco,' by Bunin; 'Hypnos,' by Lovecraft. To make a list of six only, the last two mentioned were discarded; Bunin's story because several considered it a sketch rather than a short story in the strictest sense; and Lovecraft's because it has not yet been published, but is still in manuscript form."

3. Nathalia Crane (1913–1998), who wrote a book of poetry, *The Janitor's Boy*, at the age of ten (it was published in 1924). By 1942 she had published eight more volumes of poetry, and a novel in 1926.

4. HPL refers to the phrase "my cosmic 'radio'" in "Beyond the Wall of Sleep." The original publication of the story (*Pine Cones*, October 1919) read "my ether-wave appa-

ratus." See *CF* 1.80. Although the term "radio" was coined as early as 1881, it did not come into widespread usage until the 1920s.

5. L'yeh presumably became R'lyeh, the underwater city in "The Call of Cthulhu" (1926).

6. Presumably one of the two poems titled "For the Chelsea Bookshop" (see *Out of the Immortal Night* 119–20). The first was printed as a bookmark. To *engross* is to produce a (legal) document in its final or definitive form.

7. The home of Rufus King (1755–1827), youngest signer of the U.S. Constitution. U.S. Senator (1789–86, 1813–25), and ambassador to Great Britain (1796–1801, 1925–26), at 153rd Street and Jamaica Avenue in Jamaica, Long Island.

8. Marlowe was Official Editor of the NAPA in 1924 and President in 1929.

9. It is not clear what article in *Adventure* HPL is referring to.

10. HPL has coined putative Latin names for Pawtucket, RI; Swansea, MA; Pawtuxet, RI; Pocasset, MA; and Moosup Valley, RI.

11. Wilson later wrote a notoriously hostile review of HPL's work, "Tales of the Marvellous and the Ridiculous" (*New Yorker,* 24 November 1945), that significantly affected HPL's reputation for decades.

12. With this word, and extending to "shew," HPL demonstrates the style of calligraphy that Kleiner was advocating.

13. HPL refers to the hand-drawn weekly (later monthly) magazine that HPL hectographed during the period 1903–09. This passage—from "(now we come . . ." to "fucceed" is written in the style HPL has just mentioned.

14. This would become "Supernatural Horror in Literature."

15. HPL refers to William Nelson Gemmill's *The Salem Witch Trials* and Edith Birkhead's *The Tale of Terror.*

16. Fred C. Perry and F. H. Young were both editors at the Providence *Journal.* The column "These Plantations," edited by W. Chesley Worthington (1903–2002), appeared in the Wednesday edition. Five of HPL's *Fungi from Yuggoth* sonnets appeared in the column in early 1930.

[143]     [ANS postcard][1] [HPL to LDC]

[Postmarked Brooklyn, N.Y.,
25 November 1925]
*Wednesday night*

Oh . . . ah . . . upon my soul! Is this Christmas or Thanksgiving? Well—you might say it's both—Christmas on your part & thanksgiving [*sic*] on mine! Here are the thanks, anyway! Blessed Westminster St! Did you study it carefully? And can't you get another for yourself? Wasn't it a great old street in 1824? And *Maple Grove!* Bless me, but it does give *some* brand of sap! I shall treat the gang tonight at Kirk's birthday festivities. ¶ Diary since my last night's card to A E P G—went out to the Bklyn. library, got Birkhead's history of "The Tale of Terror", came home & read it through, & retired 7 a.m. Up tonight 4 p.m. It's a miserable day—snow that's half rain—so Sonny can't go to the meeting; but his mother just telephoned, asking me to come up now for dinner & carry his present & verses to Kirk when I go. I shall do so—& am now about to start forth. ¶ And to think I have that Westminster St. at last! You must go to the Hist. Soc. & see the large *coloured originals* on the top floor! And thanks again for the candy! More later.

Yr aff Nephew & obt Servt<br>H P L

P.S. [*on front*] Good idea—this annexation of Edgewood & Pawtucket which I see proposed in the paper. We ought to take in much of E. Prov. also.

## Notes

1. *Front:* Blank.

[144]     [ANS postcard][1] [HPL to LDC]

[Postmarked Brooklyn, N.Y.,<br>27 November 1925]

Well—the King still lives, & it looks as though Heaven had its eye on the good old Arcade even if that rascally vandal is out on bail! Hope you got the specimen of Kleiner's lettering we sent you—he chose a poem of Housman's as a medium for the display of his art. ¶ As for my diary—I went up to Sonny's Wednesday night, had a good beef pie dinner, discussed poetry, then took his birthday gift down to the meeting at Kirk's where Kleiner, Morton, Loveman, Leeds, & our host were assembled. Verses to Kirk were read, spirited discussion rose, & Kleiner's lettering was wrapt up for you. Morton & Loveman left at 3, Kleiner & I at 4:30. Then home & to bed. Thursday I was up at 9 a.m., & had reached the Dench estate at Sheepshead Bay by 1 p.m., finding Morton, Miss Merritt, & honest old McNeil there. At once Dench, Morton, McNeil & I started out on a "hike" thro' the flat marshes around— getting exercise if not scenery, & seeing 2 colonial houses. Returning at 5, we were soon join'd by Kleiner, & a marvellous repast of turkey—with all accessories including cranberry sauce & mince pie—ensued. After that, discussion, word games, & inspection of the infant—now 4 mo. old & very prepossessing. Morton & Miss M. left at 11 p.m., Kleiner, McN. & I at 1 a.m. Upon leaving the Dench castle I proceeded at once to 169, wrote a bit, & retired at 4 a.m. Up today at 3 p.m., & intend to write all day unless I go to library. Tomorrow Morton wants me to attend the B.P.C. meeting—I'll see about it. Yr aff Nephew & obt Servt H P L

## Notes

1. *Front:* A color drawing of a Pilgrim couple with a landscape and a cabin in the background, and printed verse titled "Thanksgiving Greetings."

[145]     [ALS] [HPL to LDC]

Wednesday Morning—
Decr. 2, 1925

My dear Daughter Lillian:—

I was delighted to receive your two recent communications with their piquant news & apt enclosures, & take my pen in hand to exprefs my appreciation. I will send along the shirts for alteration very shortly—tho' one I see I have never worn, (a 15 which I purchased rather early in my reducing campaign) hence I will try to change that if I can recall at which of several similar & contiguous Borough Hall shops I bought it. As for the shoes—the unravelled part broke off lately, & since no more seems to be unravelling, I wonder if I hadn't better defer repairs till the time (which can't be so remote) when new soles will be needed? I'll study them again & think it over—but meanwhile I'll collect a shipment of shirts for attention. In doing so I'll also see if the *sleeves* need attention as well as the neck. My reducing, having subtracted from the fatty regions of the shoulder & upper arm, has made most of the 35 sleeves too long—indeed, I should say that my proper size is now permanently 14½ neck & 34 sleeve.

I am indeed glad that you liked the specimen of Kleiner's new lettering, & gave him your thanks at the meeting last night. Yes—it's really to keep! Next week, when we have a fuller quota, I'll transmit to the entire gang your acknowledgment of their collective Thanksgiving greeting. Meanwhile let me thank you for the delightful little turkey which now struts gobbling before me on my desk. By not making his appearance till after Thanksgiving he escaped the customary fate of his kind—& Christmas holds no terrors for him, since I am invited to Sonny's for the feast! Speaking of birds & feasts—I shall be anxious to learn what became of the rooster found on the City Hall roof!

Your experience with *heat* has certainly been picturesque—& I think you were wise not to give the presiding powers any loophole for future frigidity by mentioning the unwonted plethora of Thursday. I wonder if I shall ever be driven out of 169 by too much heat? Something tells me that my danger in this direction is not violent—tho' I get delightful comfort with my faithful Little Vulcan. He burned only 3 gallons this last week, tho' I suppose the figure will mount up in the really bitter weather. The Gorgon was raving yesterday about the price of *coke*, which she is getting in preference to bituminous coal, & which is now $22.00 per ton in New York. No doubt she'll use as little as she can—but she can't cut off heat entirely if she expects to obtain even as stable lodgers as weekly transients!

What you say of the Peck garden interests me profoundly. To think that such a thing should have existed all my life without my even suspecting its hidden presence—a cryptic paradise lurking in the heart of modernity & revealing itself only to the chosen few! I've patronised Hathaway & Douglas ever since I was born—mother used to get stocking stretchers (for drying) carved out of boards there—yet never dream'd that its prosaick domain stood next door to a land of enchantment. This garden, together with the colonial buildings of Brown, ought to make your vista a veritable pageant of beauty; & I think you are singularly fortunate to find such a spot.

Glad you liked "Beyond the Wall of Sleep", which I was quite sure you had seen. Enclosed (to keep) are those sheets from the current *Weird Tales* which pertain to me & my work. "The Tomb" has minor misprints but is decently legible, whilst I appreciate very much the favourable publicity given to my future tales. That "Red Hook" thing, which runs to 24 pages of MS., ought to bring me in a deliciously fat cheque some time next spring or summer. Cash for "The Tomb" is due February 1st., & the next month I'll have a smaller cheque for "The Cats of Ulthar", which is due to follow in the "February" issue out Jany 1st. Payment, as you see, follows publication by two months. I enclose a *Tryout* with my "In the Vault" so badly printed as to be almost illegible. You may keep this or throw it away, just as you choose. This is the tale which *Weird Tales* rejected on the ground (foolishly, I think) that its extreme gruesomeness would not pass the Indiana censorship. Sonny has just sent in another tale, of whose acceptance he remains doubtful. Glad you liked his "Sea Thing". My "Shunned House" will be published next spring in W. Paul Cook's proposed magazine, *The Recluse,* which he may or may not try to launch professionally. Cook, after cancelling all his obligations toward amateurdom by the issuance of a **312-page** *Vagrant,* (the largest publication to appear in the entire history of amateur journalism)[1] will commence an experiment in *book* publishing; handling first a volume of Belknap's poems & next a volume of Loveman's. He will try to market the books through regular channels, & gain for himself & quiet Athol a reputation in the literary field. He may visit New-York in the winter or spring, in which case the gang will take pleasure in shewing him the sights & directing him to all the rare book emporia. It seems likely, from various chance remarks of his, that he possesses the finest private library of any person ever connected with amateur journalism—a thing one would hardly suspect upon beholding his slight, malaria-racked, & obviously rustic form faltering hesitantly & bewilderedly along the crowded & engulfing streets of a city. I haven't see him face to face since 1921, & shall be glad to do so.

By the way—I'll enclose a carbon of my birthday lines to Kirk, which you may retain if you wish.[2] The "village" allusion perpetuates the fact that the section of N.Y. west of 7th Ave. & between 14th & 30th Sts. was formerly the separate hamlet of *Chelsea,* which sprang up in the early 19th century. Its streets are not crooked, like those of Greenwich, because at the time of its building the formal plan of the future city extension (adopted 1811) was already known, so that the blocks were laid out by surveyors according to the lines of New York highways yet to come. When the city did overtake Chelsea, early in the 1840's, its expanding streets simply joined neatly with the village streets which had been prepared in expectation of their coming. The allusion to Clement C. Moore, author of "The Night Before Christmas",[3] reminds one that this popular literary figure lived on this territory—inheriting it from his ancestors as a country-seat even before Chelsea was built. *Wharves* are mentioned because the piers of all the principal liners occur on Chelsea soil—the Cunard at 14th St. & the White Star at 23d. As for "sequester'd quads"—this refers to the original quadrangle of the Union Theological Seminary, still to be seen where Ninth & Tenth Avenues intersect the 'twenties.

Since you don't see the *Sunday Journal* now, I'll enclose the current Chapin article—very interesting in its indication of *square panes* at a date when I had thought all panes were diamond. Please return it. Under separate cover (& in company with a *duplicate* Washington book which you may keep) I send part of a section with a highly absorbing article on the Plainfield Pike—of vital concern to anybody with Foster–Greene–Rice City associations—& a description of steamboat days on the Bay. Maybe I'll send *all* the printed enclosures under separate cover—but I'll see. By the way—you oughtn't to be deprived of the *Journal* regularly. Why not switch the subscription to yourself, & send me the paper after you've read it? Let me know what you think of the plan. There's a fine view of the head of the Bay, with east & west sides outspread, in the rotogravure section. And speaking of enclosures—I send also an extract from the *N.Y. Tribune* which Morton gave me, & which tells of the coming renaissance of that Alexander Hamilton house I took you to see a year ago. Do you recall it? I'm vastly glad to learn of its future safety & importance—with that & the James Monroe house safely moved, one can justly say that history is not quite dead. And by the way—look at the enclosed announcement of a new Rhode Island book! Is it any good? I fancy they'd have it at the publick library.

I was indeed glad to see the added mention of Dr. Chapin, who is certainly coming into his own at last. During the influenza epidemic he began his emergence into national publicity, for it was upon his advice that Dr. Copeland, then Supt. of Health of N.Y. City, (now a Senator at Washington)[4] made his momentous recommendation that no places of publick assemblage be closed. This recommendation was adopted in New York, but according to the old rule of the prophet's honour in his own country was *not* adopted in Providence—where, as you will recall, schools & theatres were closed for a considerable period. Chapin maintained that as much congestion & contagion—& perhaps *more*—occurs when people are excluded from their usual haunts, as when they are suffered to go their own way without interference. I trust that the younger Chapin may some day be as famous an antiquarian as his father is a medical authority! Speaking of the younger Chapin—I am jubilant at the finding of that one Westminster St. booklet, & have been imaginatively walking up & down that expanse of colonial houses ever since I received it! More than one of those houses have I seen in my day—tho' only a few are left now. May the gods long preserve the Butler mansion, the place at the corner of Clemence, the "Auton House" (*how* I'd like to get hold of Hoppin's book, which isn't in either N.Y. or Bklyn. library!) & the brick mansions high up near Jackson & Franklin. Glad you saw the coloured originals upstairs—I discover'd these when shewing Mortonius about in 1923, but had no idea there was a booklet reproduction of them. The closing of the Shepley museum is utterly barbarous—upon my soul, I don't think much of the old boy if he didn't provide for the permanent exhibition of his collection. He ought to have deeded it to the Historical Society, or to Brown University, or to some foundation established in his name. Egad! But it's a publick crime to keep a treasure-house like that closed!! The prospect of "Old Grimes" & "John Jeffrey [*sic*], Gent."[5] fills me with ecstasies of commingled gratitude & avidity. What a shame their bindings were ruined! I recall so well the neat, trim red of "Jeffrey", which I read with much interest some twenty years ago! Did "Philip & Philippa" also suffer? Eheu! But this stable mould seems to have wrought more damage to antiquarian heirlooms than did the great flood of 1815! I still grit my teeth & see red when I think of that exquisite great painting!! That cutting about the "motorless age" struck an answering chord in my aged bosom. I wonder if there are still any hamlets free from the clangour of traffick? A few at least are physically unchanged—the same venerable buildings delighting the passing eye, as in such places as Greenville, Chepachet, &c—whilst I am inclined to think that the back roads of New Hampshire & Vermont must afford examples still less infected with the taint & ugliness of modernity. I think I shall use that Pemaquid idea sometime—& meanwhile here's another item apparently rich in possibilities—the De Prorock–Beloit discoveries in the Sahara.[6] The ancient & the unknown form a spectre perpetually luring & beckoning, & he who cannot be an archaeologist may enjoy scarcely inferior thrills by weaving into the waste places of earth sundry fancies of his own. De Prorock has been happy, from the dramatic point of view, in his chosen territory of exploration. Whilst Egypt & Mesopotamia have been repeatedly worked over till few major revelations are left to be made, the rich lands of Northern & Western Africa have languished virtually untouched since the fall of the Roman Empire. There brood side by side the secrets of immemorial pasts, & the equally hidden lore of historick Carthage & Mauretania. Suspense inheres in every turn of the shovel, & whilst one day we learn of the imprint of Egypt on a colony of Phoenicia, we next day pause awestruck at archaic intimations which dwarf the Pyramids to modernity & rattle at forbidden doors of unimaginable elder worlds. 'Tis a thing of infinite fascination, & I can but wish I might get a job under some of these adventurous leaders. Tropick skies—primordial mysteries—what more could one ask?

And now for a confession of reprehensible ignorance. I do not know a blessed thing about the legend of the rowan-tree, any more than I did about St. Ronan, & must proceed to look the entire matter up at the publick library.

Not a single dictionary or encyclopaedia in my possession hints that there is such a thing as a rowan-tree legend, tho' it is well known that the wood of the ash (the rowan is a mountain ash) has always been esteem'd in popular mythology. Furthermore, we find the name "Rowan" frequently used as a given name, whilst the surname *Roantree* (variation of *rowan-tree*) is exceedingly common. The plumber in State St. who attends to this house is named *Daniel V. Roantree*. Obviously, according to the cutting, the rowan must be the centre of some highly picturesque bit of mediaeval folklore; but of this I never had the slightest previous notion. I shall make inquiries of the gang, (which I forgot to do last night) & shall leave no resource of the local libraries unexhausted. Mediaeval legendry always was a weak point with me—I must reform.

Too bad you haven't continuous hot water, but glad you have some at all. The arrangement you have is the same as that at 9231 Birchdale Ave., Cleveland, where Galpinius & I stopped in 1922. The Child used to go down cellar & light the heater for his Grandpa when the Old Gentleman rose at an odd hour—which he generally did—& all the time, of course, when the family went away on their vacation leaving us in full charge. Too bad you didn't get a regular Thanksgiving feast at some restaurant—you could have had some festive dish even if you don't care for turkey. Last Christmas you had *roast duck* at Joe's, & I hope you'll do no less this year. Yes—I recall the boy at the Journal office, & trust he may be able to unearth hopeful news concerning Laswell's Corners & Characters. It must be rather pleasant to be as near down town as you are, so that you can have the exercise of walking one way. And as for window displays—I'm sure I never see anything in N.Y. to equal the spectacles you describe! Dench ought to move to Providence if he expects to remain an authority on the subject! Glad Delilah is still a valuable commodity— I wish I could present you with a deed of sale to such a prime piece of property for Christmas, but these pesky abolitionists have wrought havock with the trade, & my purse isn't what it ought to be! As for your other black friends—I'd like to see that precious kitty-dog & puppy-cat! I petted some delightful kitties last Sunday, including one of the brightest little maltese-&-white creatures I've ever seen. Yes—a whole show of Houdini must be extremely interesting. That's more than I ever saw. I wonder if poor Eddy still does revision for him?

As for my diary—carried up to last night in my epistle to A E P G—I duly went up to Sonny's, had a fine roast pork dinner, heard a new poem of the Child's, & was on hand when the gang began to arrive—Kleiner, McNeil, & Loveman, in the order named. We raised honest old Mac to the 7th Heaven by shewing him the effusively laudatory article on his "Tonty of the Iron Hand" syndicated by Angelo Patri in the *N.Y. Evening Post.* Now since Patri's stuff appears on the Woman's Page of the *Bulletin,* I wonder if you've seen it? It must have been printed there, but I generally omit it. This is a great "boost" for MᶜNeil, for the articles appear in all first class papers & enter the best homes throughout the nation. Otherwise the meeting was deadly dull. Loveman slept most of the time, & a general exodus began at 11:30 p.m. after some delightful refreshments. I returned hither at once & started to dispose of my correspondence, so that now, at 7 a.m. Wednesday, I don't owe a letter in the world. No telling, tho', what the postman will bring an hour from now. I shall retire about 7:30 & be up tonight. Next (Leeds) meeting at Belknap's, & the one after that (MᶜNeil) at Kleiner's. More news as it develops, & meanwhile I have yᵉ honour to subscribe myself as

Yr moſt aff: Nephew & obt Servt

H P L

P.S. Would it be any trouble to get me *two* 1926 calendar pads exactly like the enclosed at Davis' Card Store—Buffington's—in the Arcade?

[P.P.S.] I shall look in the 10¢ store for another diary exactly like my present one, which we bought last December in colonial Elizabethtown, as you'll remember.

## Notes

1. The issue appeared in Spring 1927 and contained HPL's poems "A Garden" and "Nathicana" and the collaborative tale "The Green Meadow" (written with Winifred Virginia Jackson).

2. "To George Willard Kirk, Gent., of Chelsea-Village, in New-York, upon His Birthday, Novr. 25, 1925."

3. Clement Clark Moore (1779–1863), an American professor, published the poem "A Visit from St. Nicholas" in 1923. It later became known as "The Night Before Christmas." HPL refers to Moore's poem in his birthday ode to Kirk (ll. 17–20).

5. Royal S. Copeland (1868–1938), president of the New York Board of Health (1918–23) and U.S. Senator (D) from New York (1923–38).

5. Books by Albert Gorton Greene and John Osborne Austin (the latter properly titled *The Journal of William Jefferay, Gent.*). *Philip and Philippa,* mentioned later, is also by Austin.

6. "Count" Byron Khun de Prorok (1896–1954), Hungarian-American amateur archaeologist, anthropologist, and author of four heroic travelogues. In the late 1920s and early 1930s, he undertook expeditions in Africa pursuing ancient legends and eventually claimed to have found evidence that Atlantis lay in North Africa and the location of the Biblical land of Ophir.

[146]     [ALS] [HPL to LDC]

Thursday Noon
Dec. 10, 1925

My dear Daughter Lillian:—

Thanks prodigiously for the calendars & for the note accompanying them. You oughtn't to have destroyed the corrected sheets of the letter you mention; for I don't mind erasures at all, & am sure that my own epistles are full of the ugliest conceivable interlineations, amendments, & scratchings-out. When your longer letter does come, I shall accord it the delighted perusal which all such documents invariably receive.

That Gibson utilisation of the rooster incident is certainly clever in the extreme—so clever, indeed, that one tends almost to wonder whether the appearance of the bird himself was not due to some Machiavellian manoeuvre of an advertising man! However, evidence lacking, we may perhaps be justified in accepting a less sophisticated explanation, & assuming that Dan Chanticleer indeed proceeded from Biltmorean altitudes.

I saw that article on the Wendel mansion, & am under the impression that I pointed the house itself out from an omnibus when you were here. Do you recall that cold day's ride up 5th Avenue? The article neglects to state one fact which the lecturers on the "rubberneck wagons" mention—namely, that the Wendel sisters are still among the shrewdest & most active buyers of real estate in N.Y., accumulating land in all the choicest parts of the town, & *never* selling what they once acquire. They only *lease*—& when they depart this life their distant heirs will have a titanic fortune to revel in. The Wendel or Wendell family is one of the oldest & greatest of the original Dutch stock, & is further notable for its illustrious New England offshoot; which produced not only Dr. Oliver Wendell Holmes, but the Portsmouth N.H. branch of which the late Prof. Barrett Wendell was the greatest scion.[1] I have seen the Wendell house in Portsmouth—a fine old Georgian mansion of the hip-roofed type built in 1760 by Capt. Jacob Wendell & still inhabited by the family.

Speaking of Portsmouth—I've just had a note from the State St. Trust Co. thanking me for calling their attention to the mistake in their book whereby the Langdon ho. was shewn as the Warner ho. They had, however, been apprised of the matter before.

Enclosed for you to keep is a Chelsea bookmark like that I sent A E P G, & a recent Tryout with my story. I also send a letter of honest old Tryout Smith, shewing how pluckily he has just fought off the trickery of some mortgage sharks who have been trying to take his hard-bought house away from him. He's 74—but nobody can impose on him, bless his heart! The incident has not a little drama in it, & illustrates the widespread diffusion of financial worry.

As for my current diary—I think I last concluded it Tuesday evening in my epistle to A E P G. After mailing that missive I retired at 7:30 p.m., sleeping till 8 a.m. Wednesday. Upon arising Wednesday I read some in Machen & the new *Weird Tales*, later receiving a call from Sonny's mamma inviting me up at 5 p.m. for dinner before the meeting. Accepting, I put on my best grey suit & sallied forth; stopping off at the publick library for a two-hours' reading of the Marquand book on Lord Timothy Dexter. You & A E P G *must* somehow get hold of a copy of that delectable thing—for it breathes within its pages all the piquant life of Old Newburyport! Arriving at Sonny's on time, I found the Child in a towering rage over Wright's rejection of his latest tale, "Legions of Lemuria";[2] but soon pacified him by pointing out how insignificant a cheap editor's opinion is. I read some of his latest material, & supplied a "surprise twist" ending for his very newest story, which he adopted with avidity & mailed forthwith to the *Frontier* magazine. A masterful dinner now ensued, after which the guests began to arrive in the following order: Morton, Kleiner & Loveman together, & Kirk & Leeds together. With this full quota we had a very brisk & pleasant meeting; & did full justice to the superb Welsh Rarebit which Mrs. Long prepared for us. Dispersing at midnight, I was home by 1 a.m., & thereafter read in a book of weird stories by Algernon Blackwood which Leeds had lent me. This was rather long, & was still unfinished when the morning mail arrived at 8 a.m. Since the latter hour I've been writing letters, & this afternoon may go to the library to finish the Dexter book since tomorrow I must stay in to receive a telephone call from Sechrist. The next (McNeil) meeting will be at Kleiner's, Sechrist probably attending. The next (Leeds) one—Dec. 23—will be at Kirk's & have something of a Yuletide character. Christmas I dine at Belknap's. Mortonius won't be in on any of this, since he gives a lecture next Wednesday night & will be in South Sudbury with his father & family for Christmas. ¶ More later ¶ Wait till you see the snapshot of me in my new brown suit with a little grey kitty-cat, taken last Sunday!

Yr aff Nephew & obt Servt

H P L

## Notes

1. The Wendel family was among the wealthiest in New York City during the 19th and early 20th centuries. It owned a large mansion at Fifth Avenue and 39th Street, remaining in it even as other houses in the area were torn down to make way for office buildings. Oliver Wendell Holmes (1809–1894), novelist and poet, purportedly dandled the young HPL on his knees around 1893 (see *SL* 1.296). Barrett Wendell (1855–1921) was a well-known literary scholar who taught at Harvard from 1888 to 1917.

2. The tale does not appear to be extant.

[147]     [ALS] [HPL to LDC]

Sunday Night
Decr. 13, 1925

My dear Daughter Lillian:—

I was delighted to receive your interesting communication; & can, as you say, hardly believe that a year has elapsed since your thousand-times welcome visit here! I wish you might repeat the event now, for there are scores of sights you could not get to see, & which fairly clamour to be inspected!

I thought you'd find that Plainfield Pike item interesting, but hardly realised how many of the described points you had actually seen. Yes—I half fancied that the McGregor homestead was connected with the immortal & literarily flamboyant Jeremiah—& it is interesting to note that a scion of that stock still remains, with whom one may discuss old times. Some of those old towns must have delightful colonial reliquiae, & I envy the bland Dr. Tillinghast his sojourn at a place so venerable as the Plainfield Academy. I have never seen Plainfield, but know it must be delightfully Georgian. Dr. Tillinghast was certainly a character! Ordinarily I would be inclined to censure you severely for depriving our family of a connexion with the tradition of Pardon Tillinghast—& thro' his granddaughter, with that of the illustrious Browns—but since you brought us one whose tradition was no less noble & whose self was so immeasurably greater, I can at this date afford to be very lenient, & recognise in your rejection of the chirographical tooth-tinker a prescience & discrimination of the soundest sort!

I'm glad you find the R.I. book interesting, & think I'll try to see if it's available at any library here. The Kimball book deals only with *Providence*, & concludes (owing to the author's death) shortly before the Revolution. Have you tried to get that at the library? It's really a tremendous item—a better source-book for Providence than any other I know. That & the Henry R. Chace maps re-create in every detail the ancient town—& adding to these the Francis Read drawings which you so kindly procured for me, one has an absolute picture of the Providence of yesterday, as though one were set bodily backward through the years in the midst of it. This reminds me that I must lend you some of the R.I. books I promised—the Richman history, & Prof. Wilfred H. Munro's "Picturesque Rhode Island".

I note the amusing editorial on the City Hall rooster, & enclose another one of more recent date. It certainly was a picturesque incident, & press & public were not slow to rise to the occasion! Glad you are noting Venus & Jupiter—if I had any decent observing place I'd get my telescope out of storage & study their discs. Yes—Jupiter will be in conjunction on Jany. 25, reappearing shortly in the morning sky. Venus is already past greatest elongation, will be at greatest brilliancy Jany. 2nd., & will disappear during that month, coming to inferior conjunction Feby. 7th & reappearing in the morning sky during February. In March, when Venus is again at greatest brilliancy & Jupiter has become visible again, the two planets will be associated together in the morning sky as they now are in the evening sky—a highly interesting proximity in view of their refulgent prominence. By the way—did you see the astronomical article in the Bulletin for Decr. 1st? I missed that issue, & when I wrote to the Journal office they informed me that the supply was exhausted. I don't need the article, though, for the Old Farmer's tells me all I require. These articles aren't what they were in Prof. Upton's time! It's a shame that your star book should be damaged, & I hope that it—as well as the Abbott volume—can be salvaged somehow.

As for this Redding—I hope he won't choose a *colonial* town for his next real-estate machinations! I'd better send out bulletins warning Salem, Marblehead, Portsmouth, & Newburyport against him! And some sort of campaign ought to be started to save the Arcade as it is—to tamper with that noble relique would be vandalism in its most noxiously virulent form! Yes—I had heard that one of the fragments of the Arcade column broken in transportation was set by the original & well-secluded grave of Roger Williams. The other fragment is set in the Field lot in the North Burial Ground. By the way—I never explored the latter, tho' its oldest sections must have some marvellously historic stones. But it lacks the picturesqueness of such places as St. John's churchyard. I like churchyards more than common cemeteries, for they are so gracefully linked with tradition—the edifice well balancing the venerable slabs in the composition. So far as I know, St. John's is the only real churchyard we have. Oh, yes! I knew that the Boston Store occupied the site of the old Universalist church. The one shewn in the Read drawing was the first—built in 1822—but the year after the drawing was made (1825) it burnt down, & was immediately replaced by another. That lasted, I think, till the present home of Callendar, McAuslan, & Troup was built—whereupon the church erected the present Washington & Greene St. edifice, where I delivered the astronomical lecture with my lantern in 1913.[1]

Yes—I'll wager that the shop windows are attractive this time of year! Shepard's handkerchief display ought to be written up by Dench—& maybe it has, for all I know, since he has correspondents in most important cities, who send him closely detailed descriptions of all the unusual windows they see, from which he formulates his articles. It was for him that Mortonius was so anxious to collect window data a couple of years ago. That Journal home window must be exquisite; and, as you suggest, rather tantalising to those who must remember old homes at long-distance from the barren shades of a boarding-house room. I'm interested to hear of the popularity of black overcoats—tho' as a matter of fact they were always the most approved thing for conservative old gentlemen. I'd never buy anything widely different—that or dark oxford grey are the shades for the dignified & the elderly. My 1917 spring coat is dark oxford with satin facing, & my 1915 winter coat is black with velvet collar. My 1909 spring coat—the old one which I use as a raincoat—is black with plain collar. The only sartorial acquisition I'm now contemplating is a Truly Warner lid—the seedy state of my present roofing being responsible for such reflections. If I do get one, it'll be a brown one like the older one you recall—which still does duty in violent rainstorms. So those Viennese candies are becoming popular in Providence? 'Twas ever so. Even in the days of Stephen Hopkins, the Browns, & the Crawfords, all manner of important gewgaws were sold in the shops along Cheapside & Towne Street. I'm sure Gladding's advertising lettering must be highly attractive if it resembles Kleiner's work. Yes—Kleiner is devoted to the art, & could probably commercialise it if he wished—but he doesn't wish. He has his one Fairbanks Scale Co. job—but outside of that he is absolutely the gentleman & dilettante. What he does, he does because he likes to do it; & never does he see the fruits thereof. All his verse goes into the witty "columns" of the N.Y. dailies, where nothing is paid, & all his lettering goes into the engrossing of pleasing texts for himself & his friends.

Glad you like "In the Vault". Wright's rejection of that was sheer nonsense—I don't believe any censor would have objected to it, but ever since the Indiana senate took action about poor Eddy's "Loved Dead", he has been in a continual panic about censorship. As for "The Tomb"—I'm not especially fond of that, for to my mind it's distinctly stiff & crude. It was the first tale I wrote after an hiatus of 9 years—1908 to 1917—& shews a distinct cumbrousness & rustiness.

I certainly would like to see "Nig", & hope you find him pleasant company. He seems to be a reprehensibly shrewd gentleman, & I must say I don't approve at all of his depredations on his helpless neighbour—clever tho' they be! But the best kitty I've seen lately is the lively little divvle that I came across a week ago—& whose picture you'll see when my camera film is developed. Glad you find Sayles Hall vespers entertaining, & that the speakers are others than extreme mossbacks. Yes—I noted Mrs. Gilman's speech & think it was eminently sound.[2] I certainly hope to see promiscuous immigration permanently curtailed soon—Heaven knows enough harm has already been done by the admission of limitless hordes of the ignorant, superstitious, & biologically inferior scum of Southern Europe & Western Asia. Interested to hear that you read Patri's puff without knowing that honest old McNeil's book was meant. We all hope it will promote sales for the worthy & amiable author—for certainly he needs cash badly enough! As for the girls' book which Patri hopes to see written—I fear neither Mac nor I will be the author. Our pens run in different channels!

As for my hours—whilst I hate being tied down, I must say that during the present week I've been sleeping a great deal in ordinary hours. Monday I retired at 4 p.m. & slept through till Tuesday morning. Tuesday I retired at 7:30 & slept till 8 a.m. Wednesday. Wednesday I didn't retire, but Thursday I retired at 11:30 p.m. & slept till 10:30 Friday—or rather, *lay* till that time, for I didn't sleep soundly. Friday I hit the hay again at 2:30 p.m. & slept through till 6 a.m. Saturday, & Saturday I retired at 1 a.m. & slept till 8:30 a.m. today. How's that for bourgeois regularity? What's more, I'm going to retire *now*, at quarter past midnight, before finishing this epistle! Still, I can't always promise such model hours; for if I'm writing anything important, I must be absolutely unhampered by chronological restrictions. Kirk's business is mostly done by mail; & with Leeds & a boy to attend to the shop, he manages to do just about as he chooses. He frequently omits a night's sleep altogether—yet never seems any the worse for it. But speaking of sleep—I guess I'll snatch mine now. I must be up early tomorrow & get the room dusted; for at noon Edward L. Sechrist—now in town—will call me on the telephone, & is likely to be here in person shortly afterward. So for the present, good night!

*Monday Morning—10:30 a.m.*

Well, here I am up again! Morning mail came with A E P G's letter & remittance, (tell her so if I don't get a chance to answer her at once) & with an interesting Sunday Journal containing an account of the Great Swamp Fight by H. M. Chapin. Also brought a note from Farnsworth Wright with advance sheets of my "Cats of Ulthar", which will be published next month. I re-enclose these for you to keep—it will save you buying a February *Weird Tales*. I shall be skipped in the next issue, but in the one after that (dated April, out March 1st) my "Outsider" will appear. By the way—did I mention in my last diary that Morton discovered one of the tales in the current issue to be a direct plagiarism of an old ballad in Percy's Reliques?[3] Whilst I am enclosing, I note some things of pictorial nature which I had saved to shew you. That view of an English village displays delightfully the source of the colonial house's general lines—& as for that square-rigger, if it's on exhibition anywhere in N.Y. I certainly must see it! I doubt if it is accessible to the publick as yet.

I shall certainly appreciate most profoundly the rebound books which—whether or not they can arrive on schedule time—will form such an eminently appropriate holiday remembrance. And pray don't think of anything more than that—for surely those alone ought to make a Christmas of the most gorgeous sort! I hope indeed that you still have Dr. Holmes' letter regarding the malaria article. I wish the article might be prominently published in lasting book form—indeed, I wish that all of Dr. Clark's works could be issued—the classical translations & Providence historical matter among the rest. If ever I have any cash, I'm going to make the R.I. Hist. Soc. issue those tavern & sanitation & fire department &c. books in a set—they would form an invaluable asset to the study of local history, & would tend to make the subject easily accessible, instead of remaining as the esoteric property of a few Chapins, Riders, & Bicknells.[4]

I trust you enjoyed your call on your former modiste & hostess—am I to understand that her new habitat is Olneyville? You mention proximity to one of the heirs of the late Jeremiah Phillips,[5] & I can't associate his family with anything but Olneyville. As to my overburthen'd correspondence—the new hitch in the United (delay in official organ caused by a faithless printer) is the prime cause of the excess load. I have hopes of being able to whittle it down again, just as I am again making a determined campaign to clear away needless social engagements. Yesterday was the first Sunday I have had to myself since November 1st!

*2:10 p.m.*

As I conclude this document, I am awaiting Sechrist's ring at the bell; for he was to come at 2:00. I telephoned Sonny, but he was out—so he'll have to wait for a later session if he wants to meet Sechrist. There now remains to be added my diary—but since my postcard to A E P G brought it down to Saturday evening, the chronicle will not this time be an extensive one. After mailing the card to A E P G I did some grocery shopping & returned to 169, spending the rest of the evening writing. Retiring at 1 a.m., I was up again at 8:30 a.m. Sunday, & spent the entire day getting my correspondence cleaned up—so that when this epistle is in the box I shan't owe a letter in the world except one to A E P G acknowledging the current weekly remittance. I retired at 12:30 p.m., & was up this morning at 9 a.m., since which time I have written letters, been out shopping, & cleaned the room in expectation of my guest. This afternoon I shall be discussing things in general with Sechrist. Tonight, when he has another engagement, I shall probably go to the library & finish the Timothy Dexter book. Tomorrow & Wednesday I shall probably be guiding Sechrist around, & Wednesday night I shall take him to the M^cNeil meeting at Kleiner's & see him aboard his night train to Washington. From that time till the next Wednesday I hope I shall be free from engagements & able to concentrate on home things. Then will occur a Leeds meeting at Kirk's—with a Christmas tree. Christmas day I shall dine at Belknap's unless S H comes during the day—for she will probably be here Christmas week & see all the new sights I've been discovering since October. If she does not arrive till Christmas *night,* I shall dine at Longs' just the same. Well—such is which. Now I'll get this sealed & stamped, & sit back with folded hands & lighted oil-stove awaiting the Guest of Honour. // Yr aff Nephew & obt Servt H P L

[On envelope:]

P.S. Note Clark Ashton Smith's Baudelaire translation in *Weird Tales* sheets directly after my "Cats of Ulthar".[6]

P.P.S. Mon.–Tues. Midnight. Didn't get this mailed after all! Sechrist came about 3 & stayed till 6—interesting conversation. We talked with Belknap over the telephone, but the Child had been down town with his mother & was too tired to come over. At 6 Sechrist left, & I escorted him to the car needed to bear him to his dinner engagement. His business here is very pressing, & he won't be able to see sights Tuesday or Wednesday; but he may stay over Thursday & see the American Wing of the Museum &c. And he'll attend the meeting at Kleiner's Wednesday night. After seeing Sechrist on his car I went to the library, found the Dexter book inaccessible, & read the ghost stories of Montague Rhodes James. Came back when the library closed, am writing a few lines, & will be in bed before very long. So the next diary will begin Tuesday morning. Haven't bought the new hat yet, but am wavering.

P.P.P.S. Tuesday Morning. Retired 2 a.m., now up 9 a.m. Shall write letters & go to library. Am dangerously inclined toward the new hat question. Just had nice note from A E P G.

## Notes

1. Around the time of this lecture, HPL wrote "The Members of the Men's Club of the First Universalist Church of Providence, R.I., to Its President, About to Leave for Florida on Account of His Health." Perhaps SSL had urged HPL to join the club as a way of getting him out of the house during his "recluse" period of 1908–13.
2. Apparently a lecture by author and sociologist Charlotte Perkins Gilman (1860–1935). She spoke out frequently on the dangers of immigration, which she felt was diluting the "Anglo-Saxon" character of the nation.
3. "The Fair Pastie Pye," "edited by" Arthur Edwards Chapman, *WT* 7, No. 1 (January 1926): 63–68. It is a prose retelling of "The Lady Isabella's Tragedy."
4. For Chapin, see LDC/AEPG 100n3. For Bicknell, see LDC/AEPG 134n4. Sidney S. Rider (1833–1917) was a bookseller who published numerous books and magazines on Rhode Island history.
5. Jeremiah E. Phillips (1800–1848), HPL's great-grandfather (father of Whipple Van Buren Phillips).
6. CAS's translation of Baudelaire's "Spleen" (*Les Fleurs du mal,* no. 80) appeared in *WT* (February 1926).

[148]    [ANS postcard][1] [HPL to LDC]

[Postmarked Brooklyn, N.Y.,
21 December 1925]
Monday Afternoon

Well, this *is* a Christmas! The rolled map has just come, & I am revelling in it!! What a clever pageant of historical geography!!! The artist is the same one who drew the map on the back cover of the new Miner book, which I am perusing with ecstatic appreciation.[2] Certainly, our local history is getting some belated attention which it has long deserved! How can I sufficiently express my thanks? ¶ As for my diary since the Saturday night card to A E P G—I retired Sunday morning at 6 a.m. after perusing the Rhode Island book, & was up again at 3 p.m. From that time till midnight I addressed cards for Christmas; then mailing them & retiring. Today I was up at noon, & received a *telegram* from Cook's friend Orton saying he's coming over tomorrow just after 5. I'd forgotten to give him my telephone number—for which I am apologising in a hasty Xmas postcard. Just now I've been reading the Sunday Journal & glancing again at the R.I. history & Old Grimes. I used to *sing* Old Grimes to the tune of "Auld Lang Syne". Now I'm going out to the library—diary continued later. ¶ See by the paper Dr. Seabury—slick rogue!—has gone down to his last reward.[3] ¶ Yr aff Nephew & obt Servt H P L

[P.P.S.] Interesting article in the Sunday Journal on newspaper published by French fleet in Newport in 1780—La Gazette Francaise. [P.P.P.S.] YOUR LETTER JUST CAME. WILL ANSWER VERY SOON

[*On front:*] P.S. I never saw those Narragansett Indian village models (shewn in the book) at the Park Museum! I miss everything good!!

P.P.S. Wish I could get that guide book to R.I. park reservations—published in 1922—which the Miner book mentions!

## Notes

1. *Front:* Blank.
2. *Our State: Rhode Island* by Lilian Burleigh Miner. The map referred to was drawn by Eugene E. Witherell of the Rhode Island School of Design.
3. Frederick Wheaton Seabury (b. 1857), a dentist in Providence, had died 19 December.

[149]     [ALS] [HPL to LDC]

Begun—Early Tuesday Evening—
December 22, 1925
Finiſh'd—Wednesday Morning
December 23, 1925

My dear Daughter Lillian:—

        I was delighted to receive your epistle just as I had finished a postcard to you in acknowledgment of that marvellous map, & will lose no time in translating my appreciation into a reply. Fortunately my correspondence is well in hand just now, tho' Heaven only knows how it will be after the arrival of the next morning mail! Yesterday I wrote fifty Christmas cards—stamping & mailing them before midnight. Only a few, of course, had verses—& these were all brief & not very brilliant. To Sonny I said:

> Precocious Sir, who draw'ſt with wizardry
> Charm from the sky, & horror from the sea;
> Whose airy soul explores with lyric art
> All space & time where Beauty hath a part;
> From fields of Fame one moment deign to gaze
> On lower realms, whence rise inferior lays:
> Mark ancient Theobald—prosy, stiff, & drear,
> Yet warm as any in his Christmas cheer!

The book I got for him was a symposium of modern criticism—in the "Modern Library" series.[1] On the flyleaf of this I wrote:

> A plain old soul, nor sharp nor analytical,
> 　　Seeks here in all sincerity to please
> A modern child, sophisticate & critical,
> 　　Who finds our world a wearisome disease.
>
> Take then this volume, lofty & fastidious,
> 　　Where disillusion shakes its scornful head;
> Ne'er will the donor frown with glance invidious,
> 　　Tho' deep thou study what he hath not read!

That last line is literally true—I couldn't be hired to wade thro' the confounded mess. I might have three or four years ago, but nowadays I'm too old-fashioned & provincial to give a hang about critical modernities. I belong in the Thomas W. Bicknell class now! But in saluting the House of Long I did not forget the regal & temperamental Felis—tawny aristocrat & thoroughgoing Yankee from Maine. To him I said:

> Haughty Sphinx, whose amber eyes
> Hold the secrets of the skies,
> As thou ripplest in thy grace
> Round the chairs & chimney-place,
> Scorn on thy patrician face:
> Hiss not harsh, nor use thy claws
> On the hand that gives applause—
> Good-will only doth abide
> In these lines at Christmastide!

To Kleiner, remembering his newly-practiced calligraphick art, I sent the following message:

> A wreath to thee, whose double art
> Can play the bard's and draughtsman's part,
> And give to what thy visions trace
> A setting worthy of their grace!
> The monkish scribe, beat by thy hand,
> Shares envy with the poet band;
> Nor will th'impartial judge allow
> That any do as well as thou.
> Thus humbled, let us all draw near
> To wish our Victor Christmas cheer!

To Loveman—& also to Mr. Hoag & Dr. Kuntz, for I am economical in my metrical flights—I said

> Son of the Muse, may Yuletide bear
>    A thousand joys to crown thy worth,
> Whilst Fame supplies her curule chair
>    To seat thee with the great of earth.
>
> Sweet as the musick of thy lyre
>    Be all the coming year shall bring,
> And with thine own Aonian fire
>    May life to thee of Beauty sing.

In addressing Kirk, I again adverted to the close association betwixt Chelsea & Christmas, due to Clement C. Moore, author of "The Night Before Christmas" (whose *real* title, by the way, is "A Visit from St. Nicholas".)

> Since Chelsea is Old SANTA'S home,
> I trust he'll call before he starts to roam,
> And find in KIRK a worthy youth to crown
> With all the fame that MOORE of old laid down.

To Leeds I gave a couple of allusions to the old-time musical comedies of which we were so fond, & whose airs we are still wont to hum upon occasions; "The Prince of Pilsen" & "The Burgomaster":[2]

> May Yuletide such beneficence evince
> That thou mayst walk as gay as Pilsen's Prince;
> Let wealth come fast, & sweet content still faster,
> Till thou'rt as placid as a Burgomaster!

To Honest old McNeil I gave an allusion to his work & success in writing boys' novels about the French pioneers:

> May Gallick shades thy Yuletide bless,
> And all their pleasing lore express,
>    Of wilderness & stream;
> TONTY*, successful, bids thee raise
> For bold CHAMPLAIN† thy potent praise,
>    And revel in the theme!

In writing Sechrist I alluded to his Polynesian & African travels, & to the hellish play—"The Dybbuk"[3]—to which he so generously treated me last week:

---

*Henri de Tonty, companion of La Salle, & subject of the book lauded by Angelo Patri
†on whom he is now writing a book. His intermediate book, about the Sieur Du Luth, for whom Duluth, Minn. was named, is now in the press.

May Polynesian skies thy Yuletide bless,
And primal gods impart thee happiness;
Zimbabwe's* wonders hint mysterious themes,
And ne'er a Dybbuk lurk to mar thy dreams!

To good old Mortonius I gave some allusions to his museum business &
mineral collecting:

From mines celestial Santa digs a gem
To deck your proud Museum's diadem;
A common stone, yet worthy of a place
In some dark alcove, or inferior case:
'Tis Christmas Cheer—swell'd livelier & greater
By him who bears it to a sage Curator!

To John Russell, in England, I sent this:

To old Britannia's story'd strand
    My Yuletide greetings glide,
As with a warm extended hand
    I brush the seas aside!

New England, too, naturally received not a few of my effusions; that to little
Davis being as follows.

May Santa bring to Harvard's brightest son
A Pickle for a Very Knowing One,†
Whilst Father Charles & red-crown'd Merrimack‡
Unite to swell with praise his gen'rous pack.

Good old W. Paul Cook received this:

May Yule to thee all blessings swift impart,
Artist, & patron of each soaring art;

---

*Zimbabwe is the native name of a great walled city in the African jungle—ruined
& uninhabited, of course—of whose origin the blacks know nothing. It seems to
have been the centre of great gold mining operations thousands of years ago, &
has been associated with the "Ophir" of the Bible. Sechrist has seen it with his
own eyes.
†"A Pickle for the Knowing Ones" is the title of the absurd book published by
"Lord" Timothy Dexter of Newburyport; whose house Davis & I went to see in
1923, & whom Davis humorously alleges himself to resemble.
‡Davis' original home is in Merrimac, on the river of that name. It was there, you
will recall, that I went to see him.

> Long live thy house, & may the future know
> Athol as nucleus of the Muses' glow:
> Let foremost stand; for ornament & use,
> Thy tasteful volumes\*, & thy bright *Recluse!*†

And here is what greeted li'l' Bimbo Sandy:[4]

> Run out of slang, & far from fresh supplies,
> I pen this feeble message to the wise:
> Forgive the style, & grasp the good intent,
> For ne'er was Christmas cheer more truly meant!

Parker,[5] (now living in Cliftondale) who calls his magazine *L'Alouette,* (The Lark) heard from a dark & Poesque bird:

> Let Cliftondale to Yuletide croakings hark,
> As the dull Raven greets the sprightly Lark!

To Mrs. Miniter, who finds humour in my predilection for Colonial graveyards, I despatched these lines:

> From distant churchyards hear a Yuletide groan
> As ghoulish Theobald heaves his heaps of bone;
> Each ancient slab the festive holly wears,
> And all the worms disclaim their earthly cares:
> Mayst thou, 'neath sprightlier skies, no less rejoice,
> And hail the season with exulting voice!

But bless my soul! I can't expect to quote the whole mediocre assortment! The foregoing are typical, & shew how little genuine inspiration I have in my old age. And of course full half the cards went out without verses. So far I've received none from those I haven't sent to—but probably I shall before the siege is over, & shall have to reciprocate with exclusively New-Year cards.

Yes indeed—I certainly wish that you could be a Wendell heir, so that you might be here for the Christmas dinner; or that *I* could be; so that 454 Angell St. might be the home of both, & the dinner prepared by Norah or Delia (sober, I trust) or Svea or Jennie or Bridget under your own direction, & served by honest Delilah in proper uniform & apron! I trust your feast at the Ripley plantation will not prove a bore—anyhow, it will save the price of a meal, which means something nowadays. I shall certainly get a good two dollar's [*sic*] worth of nourishment up at Sonny's—even tho' I am taking him

---

\*Books he will be publishing for Belknap, Loveman, etc.
†Title of the select private magazine he intends to start in the spring.

only a 95¢ book! Thus do the poor become calculative. Yes—I will give
Belknap's mamma your regards, & am sure she will appreciate them. As for
S H's proposed N Y trip—I indeed warned her of its enormous expense, but
she argues that as a holiday extravagance it is worth it; so it will probably take
place unless I receive very sudden telegraphic word to the contrary. The five-
spot which she sent, & which A E P G cashed, will go well as an entertainment fund—for in spite of the gratuitousness of museums, a few carfares &
cinema admissions soon make an outing of this sort no cheap affair! As for
the matter of permanent locations—bless my soul! but S H would only too
gladly coöperate in establishing me wherever my mind would be most tranquil & effective! What I meant by 'a threat of having to return to N.Y.' was
the matter of industrial opportunity, as exemplified in the Paterson possibility; for in my lean financial state almost any remunerative opening would con-
stitute something which I could not with any degree of good sense or
propriety refuse. Now if I were still in N.Y., I could perhaps bear such a thing
with philosophical resignation; but if I were back home, I could not possibly
contemplate the prospect of leaving again. Once in New England, I must be
able to stick there—thenceforward scanning Boston or Providence or Salem
or Portsmouth for openings, rather than having my eyes on Manhattan or
Brooklyn or Paterson or such distant & unfamiliar realms. I may remark, incidentally, that the Paterson matter stands exactly as before. The work on the
museum building is held up, & until then all expansion is in abeyance—
Morton being meanwhile instructed to hold small displays & exhibitions in
the library building. But, he says, the work will almost certainly begin in the
spring; & at that time an assistant will almost certainly be required—so there
one is! I could stand the prospect (for the work itself would be congenial) if I
had not meanwhile had sight of a real white man's country—but if I once saw
New England again, with her hilly streets leading down to the sea, & her avenues of ancient elms, & her clustered gambrel roofs, & her white steeples rising over centuried churchyards, I could nevermore bring myself to venture
outside her confines. S H's attitude on all such matters is so kindly & magnanimous that any design of permanent isolation on my part would seem little short of barbaric, & wholly contrary to the principles of taste which impel
one to recognise & revere a devotion of the most unselfish quality & uncommon intensity. I have never beheld a more admirable attitude of disinterested & solicitous regard; in which each financial shortcoming of mine is
accepted & condoned as soon as it is proved inevitable, & in which acquiescence is extended even to my statements (as determined by my observation of
the effect of varying conditions on my nerves) that the one *essential* ingredient
of my life is a certain amount of quiet & freedom for creative literary composition—to be snatched whether or not I am otherwise employed, & whether
or not it conflicts with that schedule of early hours & regularity which a more
simply industrial regime stamps as normal. A devotion which can accept this

combination of incompetence & aesthetic selfishness without a murmur, contrary tho' it must be to all expectations originally entertained; is assuredly a phenomenon so rare, & so akin to the historic quality of saintliness, that no one with the least sense of artistic proportion could possibly meet it with other than the keenest reciprocal esteem, respect, admiration, & affection—as indeed it was met at first, when manifested under less trying circumstances & with far less comprehension of the chronicle of failure stretching ahead. It is one of the marks of an old-fashion'd gentleman, as distinguished from the herd of crude & careless moderns, that he recognises his harmonious relation to the pattern in which Fate has set him, & never ceases to live up as fully as he may to such aesthetic responsibilities as may arise from his previous decisions. Ineffective & injudicious I may be, but I trust I may never be inartistic or ill-bred in my course of conduct. Harsh or sudden revolts & repudiations are alien to an Englishman of taste; & when one's profoundest admiration, deference, & regard are elicited by the conditions one encounters, it is not difficult to follow that conservative course which all the canons of art & all the precepts of gentle breeding map out as the only proper one. But to turn from abstractions to the concrete—S H fully endorses my design of an ultimate return to New England, & herself intends to seek industrial openings in the Boston district after a time—tho' for the present this second Cleveland position seems to present great advantages & to offer conditions which are unusually congenial for a thing of the sort. The remuneration is not great, but the prospects of advancement are considerable; & the prevailing spirit of fairness & forbearance shewn alike by management & employees is an incalculable relief after the nerve-racking friction of the former position—with flashy upstart scum as employers. (although even there the *employees* were tolerable) This Halle establishment is the leading department-store of Cleveland; perhaps equivalent to our Shepard's. And so you may be assured that only the Paterson possibility holds me in New York. The slightest chance of a position in New England would being me home at any minute with a haste almost comical to a spectator; & indeed, the definite disappearance of the Paterson possibility would cause me to migrate anyhow—to secure quarters near Boston & begin a systematic hunt for work through *Transcript* advertisements much (tho' I hope not as vainly!) as I hunted in New York through *Times* advertisements during the first year. In Boston, indeed, I might be able to put more inward heart (tho' I certainly could put no more patience & diligence!) into the quest; for there would be around me a world to which I bear at least some semblance of relation, instead of the alien desert that is the Gotham of today.

Glad you enjoyed the enclosures & the Washington booklet. Yes—the recent progress of both science & archaeology is certainly staggering in the extreme; & I am avid with curiosity to learn what comes of the Prorock discoveries in the Sahara. The uncovering of a totally unknown civilisation, distinct from any previously known, & perhaps antedating all others, is indeed a thing to excite the keenest attention of anyone with the slightest inclination toward the strange, the weird, & the ancient. I was intensely interested to hear Sechrist last week when he described his own personal observations of the great Zimbabwe ruins in Africa. Mighty walls with herring-bone friezes, great monoliths in the public squares, spacious vaults with steps of well-wrought stone, gold mines with traces of vast shafts & sluices—here, where for thousands of years only the wandering blacks grimaced & danced, there was once a mighty city of miners & traders—perhaps an outpost of the Babylonian or Assyrian empire, a colony of Meroë or Æthiopia, a dominion of the lordly Minoans or forgotten Hittites, or that distant & mysterious land of Ophir whence the galleys of King Solomon brought gold, apes, peacocks, spices, ivory, ebony, & almug trees. Its patched & uncertain walls tell a strange story of decay—repairs shewing less & less skill as the white man faded & mixed with the black tribes of the hinterland. For some reason commerce with the outside & northern world (for the city is in Rhodesia, far down the Red Sea coast) must have been cut off—perhaps the mines gave out, so far as ancient methods could reach, tho' modern machinery is reopening & working them now. At any rate, the city at last fell into disrepair & decay, till crude heaps of stone & obeah-altars tell of the white man's passing & the black's long reign. The jungle had come back, & monkeys & negroes chattered in the ruins of temples where Solomon's captains once made sacrifice. Vines choked the gates of ancient treasuries, & around the city gates bats & ghosts fluttered as the Bantu's chants & tom-toms sounded from afar. Thus for thousands of years it lay—& then the white man came again!

But something tells me that when future explorers excavate the site of Providence, the present Washington Bridge will not be among the enduring relics they will find! Truly, it is a miserable makeshift, & I agree with Mr. Williams (whose picture at it I beheld) that it calls for a very early replacement. I hope a form at once stable & artistic will be selected, & that a statue of Genl. Washington will be set at the Providence end, as John Brown set one when he built the original bridge there in 1790. Point St. Bridge also needs replacement—in fact our only decent non-railway drawbridge is good old Red Bridge—may it have a prompt & successful convalescence! That is an admirable structure—it would bear a railway train. Yes—I noticed the spelling-match winner. Orthographical aptitude is usually a native gift—some, like Paul J. Campbell & honest old McNeil, can never spell. Probably I shall begin to slip up pretty soon, for my memory is not what it used to be. I note the revised location of Mrs. Herron & our kinsfolk—but Cranston St. means much the same as Olneyville to me. It is all in the unknown West—that undiscover'd country from whose bourn few travellers return—& seems very remote from good old Angell St. & the ancient hill. No—I didn't know that a brother of old Jerry McGregor was a famous surgeon, Civil War veteran, & accident victim in Providence! We live & learn. By this time you'll have seen from my letter to A E P G that

I not only read but cut out the Edward Arnold obituary.[6] Too bad my mother didn't snap him up—I can see myself this minute basking in elegant leisure at my Coventry country-seat, & driving into Providence now & then with a smart coach-and-four & liveried grooms! As for the new R.I. book—I fairly devoured it, & am yet looking at the pictures over & over again. Did you ever see those Narragansett village models in the Park Museum which are reproduced as cuts? I never did, & fancy they must be fairly new. And that marvellous pictorial & historical map! I'd frame & hang it if it weren't that the key is on the other side. At that, though, one might *copy* the key! As for the Arcade, I wish somebody would start some definite campaign to save it! With all this talk about the new memorial, nobody takes steps to preserve the riches we already have! I've a mind to write a letter to the Sunday Journal!

Glad you have a nicely curtained alcove like those you helped me to prepare. It must look delightful with the red drapery! Most unfortunately, Sechrist couldn't see the American Wing. You'll recall that it closed at 4:00 last year because of lack of artificial lighting, but I never suspected that this temporary unreadiness would last all these months. It has lasted, however, & when we reached the scene at about 4:05 last Thursday the Wing had just closed! I felt exceedingly mortified, & cursed fate in English, Latin, & Sanscrit; but may only hope that on some future trip Sechrist may taste the pleasure so far denied him. His brother has just sold the ancestral home in Maryland, & a fearful amount of antique material of his family seems imperilled unless he himself can take quick action. I was interested & amused by the cuttings you enclosed—& edified by the timely Yuletide greeting. Good old Tilley—he still plods along in his simple faith despite the scientific leanings of earlier years! Glad his wife has such a fine new set of chimes to play on—tho' I'll bet they can't beat our St. Martin's in Orchard Ave. I now hear St. Anne's chimes in Clinton St. each Sunday morning, & they are *immeasurably* inferior to the St. Martin set. Times have changed since the old Brattle St. Church in Boston rejected a gift of an organ (which was finally given to St. John's of Portsmouth N.H. & is still in use there) on the ground that it was 'an ungodly chest of whistles'. And speaking of godliness—I can fully appreciate the items on commandments & on Ananias! Yes—& the fine Yuletide 1st Baptist programme with the good old Gibbs steeple! The astronomical article was very welcome—I used to see those Brainin articles in the Asheville (N.C.) Gazette-News. They aren't as good as Upton's, though. In 42nd St. near the publick library a man has a telescope trained on Venus & the moon at so much (a nickel, I think) per look. I may patronise him just for old times' sake—I wish I had a place to use my own telescope! And speaking of the library—I've not yet given up my search for the Rowan-tree legend, & hope to shew you results before long. These mediaeval myths are multifarious & elusive, & form a branch of folklore into which I have delved singularly little.

Yes—I am revelling in Old Grimes, & am so glad to have the Hoppin conceptions as well as the text. I'd give anything to get hold of Hoppin's book—"Memories of Auton House"—which seems absent from all N.Y. libraries, tho' they have others of his books. About poor Eddy's tale—it certainly did achieve fame of a sort! His name must have rung in tones of fiery denunciation all through the corridors & beneath the classic rotunda (if it has a rotunda) of the Indiana State Capitol! But I agree that his financial laxity is something much more deserving of legal & judicial attention, & wish some appeal to his adversity-blunted conscience might be devised. Did A E P G tell you that she saw him looking into a Washington St. shop window & placidly puffing a pipe? She thinks he recognised her but didn't dare speak. Strange case—but as I just wrote A E P G on a card, I'm through with freaks & paupers & plebeians & odd fish at last. It took a long time to shew me how profitless they all are—Arthur Fredlund,[7] Herbert Benson,[8] Eddy,[9] &c—but I now see how asinine it is to bother with them. They give no pleasure in the end, & become an intolerable nuisance & parasitic pest.

As for my diary since yesterday's postal—I went to the library, failed to get most of the stuff I wanted, & settled down to some interesting witch books. Returning when the place closed, I did some writing & retired at midnight. Up about noon today, I did more writing & am now awaiting the arrival of Cook's friend Orton, who is due here any moment now. I'll tell you what he's like in my next communication—but I feel sure he'll prove pleasant. I shall take him out to dinner at John's. As for ordering cocoa instead of coffee—I do sometimes, but they don't have it at John's. Automat chocolate is a favourite potation of mine. ¶ And now I must pause & get the room dusted before Orton comes. I hate to let anybody get a bad first impression of the place, & was careful to have everything spick & span when Sechrist blew in. The newly cleaned window & laundered curtains make things very pleasant just now—indeed, at this moment, looking around the room, I can hardly realise what a poor neighbourhood & house I'm in! I won't seal this now, but will add more later & tell you what Orton's like.

Early Wednesday Morning
Decr. 23, 1925

Well—Orton has been & gone; & as I predicted beforehand, he's a great chap! He came ahead of time, before I had finished dusting; but fortunately I had covered the principal pieces—so hiding the rag I at once answered the door. No more likeable, breezy, & magnetic person ever existed than he. In person of smallish size; dark, slender, handsome, & dashing, he is clean-shaven of face & jauntily fastidious of dress—light grey suit of faultless cut, tasteful light shirt, wing collar with dark bow tie, light overcoat, & light felt hat with variegated though quiet band. He confessed to 30 years, but does not look more than 22 or 23. His voice is mellow & pleasant, tho' just now a trifle husky with the bronchial trouble which has affected him ever since his advent to N.Y.; & his manner of delivery sprightly & masculine—the careless heartiness of a well-bred young man of the world. When I noticed his occasional adjectival use of "damn" I feared for a moment that he would turn out to be profane; but soon discovered that this word is absolutely his *only* form of swearing, & that he is wholly free from any trace of vulgarity. His general bearing is hyper-alert & easy, involving facile gestures & graceful lounging postures. He smokes cigarettes with an air, but owns that he really prefers a pipe. A thorough Yankee to the bone, he hails from central Vermont, adores his native state and means to return thither in a year, & detests N.Y. as heartily as I do. His ancestry is uniformly aristocratic—old New England on his father's side, & on his mother's side New England, Knickerbocker Dutch, & French Huguenot. His uncle, with whom he is now staying in Yonkers, is a professor of some note. Orton was educated in Vermont, where he was born; in Athol, Mass., where his immediate family now live; & at several different colleges—the latter diversity being due to a wandering instinct which is very strong within him. Harvard is his principal university, but I was delighted to learn that he has spent a year at **Brown** (1920–21)—so that he knows Providence quite well. When in Providence he tried McNeil's stunt of slum-dwelling to save cash for incidentals & bookbuying, & had a room in *South Main St!* Orton's wandering began very early, & has taken him all over the United States, Mexico, Europe, & North Africa. It has been intermittent rather than continuous, & has punctuated his college years quite pleasantly. Part of it was war service in France, which he truly enjoyed as an exciting adventure despite the attendant squalor. His business is *advertising*, but he hates & despises it, & plans to leave it as soon as he can raise the capital to return to his native state & carry out the pet project of his life—the founding of a Vermont magazine of large size & high literary merit, which may have a nation-wide as well as local appeal. He hopes to do this in a year, & has bought a home in the rural interior of the state, where he will try to assemble around him a congenial coterie of Vermont-born literary men. One of his pet schemes is to induce W. Paul Cook—his best friend despite the almost ludicrous external differences* between them—to come & live with him, also acting as managing editor of his new magazine. But for the present he is enjoying what is almost a sinecure job in the advertising department of H. L. Mencken's† American Mercury—soliciting advertising from book publishers who would give it whether or not he solicited it! He wants to move to Brooklyn, & when he returns from his holiday trip to Athol (he starts tomorrow noon) I shall help him find a room in Columbia Heights. Despite his affable sociability I don't think he'll become a nuisance, for persons as well-born &

---

*i.e.—temperamental, cultural, & sartorial differences. In face & physique they are quite similar—the dark, wiry Yankee type.
†he knows Mencken personally

well-bred as he never carry familiarity & gregariousness to excess. He is the real goods—"regular people" like Belknap. Of Athol he talked much. Cook he regards as one of the finest & most extraordinary characters he ever met— a man of high intellect & keen taste despite the rusticity which poverty for two or three generations behind him has imparted to his speech, dress, & manners. I knew, of course, that Cook came of excellent stock—a direct descendant of the Rt. Honourable Benning Wentworth, Esquire, His Majesty's Governor of the Province of New-Hampshire in the good old days. Orton also spoke of C. [*sic*] Warner Munn—youthful weird author whom Cook has encouraged, & who made such a spectacular entrance into *Weird Tales* with his very first fictional attempt. This young Atholite (age 23) is very well connected, being a cousin of the owner of the *Scientific American;* but is not extensively cultivated or well-read himself. His erudition seems confined wholly to weird matters, & he shews no disposition to broaden in literary taste. As coincidence would have it, a letter from Cook arrived whilst Orton was here, (I'll answer & enclose it herewith) & the latter was amused by the reference to him as "intensely modern". In actual fact, he is independent & eclectic; having no use for the extreme moderns, & seeming modern to Cook only because the good old *Vagrant* is getting a bit antiquarian & fossilised like Grandpa Theobald. It took only a few moments' conversation to shew me that Orton is profoundly well-informed & gifted with acute intelligence & taste. Despite our spectacular oppositeness of manner & experience, we have that common ground which belongs to those of the same Yankee heritage & of the same essential point of view & opinions on the human scene. He is, in the most delightful sense, congenial & even stimulating—I can't conceive of anyone's being bored in the company of one so buoyant, expansive, & urbanely affable. I know that the gang will 'take to him' instantly when he attends the meeting tonight. He hopes to pass through Providence at some time within a year, & when he does I shall certainly have him call on you & A E P G. Of New York he has seen singularly little—& of its colonial antiquities almost nothing. In these matters he shews an eager appreciativeness which will make it a pleasure to act as his guide. His health is not good, being impaired by a bronchial weakness which some time ago developed tuberculous tendencies—though an ample sojourn in Arizona, New Mexico, & Mexico itself seems to have killed the latter danger completely. When in Mexico he explored with intense interest many Aztec & Maya ruins—indeed, I fancy he could swap yarns very interestingly with his fellow-wanderer Sechrist.

Well—to return to the diary—about 6 o'clock I took Orton out to dinner at John's, detouring en route to the Montague St. parapet, where I shewed him the faery city of towering flame that is the Manhattan of early evening. He had never before seen this marvellous spectacle, & was quite overcome by its unparallelled majesty & bizarrerie—a magic to which Lord Dunsany was keenly & appreciatively sensitive during his American visit of 1919. Orton at once announced his intention of getting a room in Columbia Heights over-looking the bay, & in that process I shall no doubt be able to assist him. We now completed our trip to John's, consumed a fine dinner of braised beef, potato, spaghetti, & apple pie with ice cream, & returned to 169; where we talked & looked at books till after ten o'clock. He was scheduled for the 11:40 train to Yonkers, & we allowed time for a walk over Brooklyn Bridge—which he had never before crossed in any fashion whatsoever, & which delighted him greatly. He had, indeed, never before set foot in Brooklyn; though he has been in N.Y. continuously since early October, & has visited it frequently throughout his life. Reaching the Manhattan side rather early, & still having much to discuss, we did not at once disperse; but instead, I accompanied him by subway to the Grand Central, where we lounged about that luxurious lower waiting-room next the restaurant (the one you & I waited in one evening before you took the Mt. Vernon train) till the time of his train's departure. As it turned out, we got so deep in conversation that he almost missed his train—the last of that night—& certainly would have if it hadn't been a minute or two late in starting. Today—in the afternoon—he will call me up & arrange for a meeting before the time of the gang's gathering; probably coming over here about six & taking dinner with me. He will try to get off early from work & pack for his Thursday trip to Athol in time to get over here in good season tonight—his worst bother is his distance from town, which makes it impossible for him to go home after office hours & return to N.Y. for the evening. That's why he wants to move in. Well—after seeing Orton safely on his train I returned to 169 & have been writing ever since. Among the letters I am answering is one from Mr. Hoag, containing the melancholy news that the Greenwich High School (not an ancient or historic building, thank Heaven) has just burned to the ground*! It was the Alma Mater of most of his grandchildren. I shall continue to write till well into the morning; then I shall rest & be ready for Orton about six. In attending the meeting I think I'll wear my good suit & get the brown pressed.

Just now it's getting beastly cold—though Tuesday was warm till evening. I've had to keep the oil stove going continuously ever since my return from the Grand Central. The meeting tonight will have a distinctly Yuletidish cast, & promises to be a good one. Everybody except Morton is expected to be there, & with Orton as a guest the festivities ought to be pretty brisk. Oh—by the way, one of Orton's plans—in case his Vermont magazine doesn't materialise next year—is to join a scientific expedition to unknown Mongolia, which is planning a thorough canvass of the regions not touched by the expeditions of the American Museum of Natural History. He thinks he has the "pull" necessary to land a berth. Great life—wish I had the ambition & enterprise to work my way around the globe & into strange, far places! //

---

*school now temporarily housed in the old Colonial academy building—now an Odd Fellows' Hall.

Yr aff Nephew & obt Servt

H P L

P.S. Orton is intensely captivated by the work of Clark Ashton Smith, & wants to order all his books.

[P.]P.S. Wednesday Afternoon—Cold has become hideous & paralysing—almost as terrible as on that eclipse morning last January. Couldn't sleep because of it—have to have oil stove every second!
*Evening:* Shall go out shopping & then to the meeting.
[P.]P.P.S. In my next letter I will enclose earlier Cook letter describing Orton. These needn't be returned.
[P.]P.P.P.S. It's so beastly cold near the windows, I think I'll take the stove & tip table far into the room & write there!
[P.]P.P.P.P.&c.S.—Orton just telephoned that he can't get to the meeting tonight after all!
N.B. I now have on (a) brown vest & trousers, (b) thick wrap over them, & (c) winter overcoat over the wrap!
¶ But my oil stove is nobly behaving. It is fighting single-handed, with not a speck of heat in the radiator!
¶ I think I'll try wearing a blanket over the overcoat.
EXTRA—FINAL EDITION—a little heat in the radiator! I can take off the blanket!

## Notes

1. By Ludwig Lewisohn.
2. *The Prince of Pilsen* (1903) and *The Burgomaster* (1900), both with music by Gustav Luders, book and lyrics by Frank S. Pixley.
3. S. Ansky (pseud. of Solomon Rappoport, 1863–1920), *The Dybbuk* (Neighborhood Playhouse, New York, 15 December 1925–c. March 1926). HPL cited the play in "Supernatural Horror in Literature" (54).
4. Albert A. Sandusky, amateur journalist in the Boston area. Sandusky printed some issues of HPL's *Conservative*.
5. Charles A. A. Parker, amateur journalist and editor of the poetry magazine *L'Alouette*.
6. Edward Everett Arnold (1853–15 December 1925), a descendant of William Arnold, one of the original thirteen proprietors of Providence and prominent in the drug and chemical businesses. He also served three years in the Rhode Island senate.
7. Arthur Fredlund (1892–?) was a Swedish youth whom HPL attempted to educate when he was about sixteen (see *SL* 1.70).
8. HPL may be referring to Herbert Benson (1891–?), an English emigrant who in 1917 was residing at 151 Jewett Street and working at the Narragansett Hotel.
9. HPL refers to C. M. Eddy, Jr. (see LDC/AEPG 153).

[150]   [ANS Christmas card] [HPL to AEPG]

[23 December 1925]

As when a Pigeon, loos'd in Realms remote,
Takes inſtant Wing, and ſeeks his native Cote,
So ſpeed my Bleſſings from a barb'rous Clime
To thee and Providence at Chriſtmas-time!

――――

Yr aff: Nephew & Obt Servt

1925                                                    H P L

[Printed message:] Wishing you a Merry Christmas and a Happy New Year

[151]   [ALS] [HPL to LDC]

Early Saturday Morning
Decr. 26, 1925

My dear daughter Lillian:——

I cannot forbear setting down without further delay my diary for the past three days, involving as it does such a delightful Yuletide. You last heard from me Wednesday, as I was setting out for the (Leeds) meeting at Kirk's, so that the chronicle must begin with my arrival at the Chelsea Book Shop. I found all present except Loveman, who is detained at work these evenings because of the opening of his employers' new shop; & was equally pleased & surprised to see good old *Mortonius,* whom I had thought on his way home to Sudbury. It seems that he had deferred his departure till Thursday, in order that he might be with us on this occasion—& he signalised his presence most nobly by acting as Santa Claus to the entire group—giving each member some appropriate gift from the ten-cent store, with accompanying verses by himself. Mine was a bizarre paperweight* of exactly the sort to appeal to a Dunsanian fantaisiste—a globe of glass about three inches in diameter, set on a black base & containing within it a *castle* with white walls & red roof, whose open door & windows yawn weirdly &

 alluringly. The entire globe is filled with water—or some analogous fluid—& when shaken becomes permeated with white flakes, as if a snowstorm were raging about the lone tower. I, however, prefer to regard the tower as a strange edifice of forgotten Atlantis, long sunken under the sea, & inhabited by sinister & terrible polypous *things,* which float

―――――――――――――――――――

*The presentation verses were as follows:
When of great Lovecraft's merits I would write,
My Muse in vain essays the lofty flight;
But then I see his wit with kindness blend,
And straight forget the genius in the friend!

ghoulishly about in the cryptic currents of the deep. The device only cost a dime, but Mortonius certainly hit my taste to a T! I keep it before me on my desk, atop the fascinating cedar chest which came in my Providence bundle. The meeting on the whole was pretty lively & interesting. Sonny had to leave at 11:30, but the rest stayed on till about 2 a.m. Kirk's refreshments were very good—he really makes surprisingly excellent coffee. Upon the general dispersal I returned to 169, wrote a bit, & retired at 3:30 a.m. Thursday I was up at 3 p.m. & wrote letters all day. In the afternoon mail a generous Christmas bundle came from S H—containing 2 white shirts, 1 suit of underwear, 6 collars, & 1 exquisite cravat—a mixed affair with grey predominating, & harmonising with my best grey suit as well as the brown tie harmonises with the brown suit. The undervest has long sleeves—which I don't like—but I suppose these can be cut off. The shirts, however, are too large; tho' they are indeed 14½. I guess a neckband has to be definitely smaller than the collar worn over it, so that straight *14* is the proper shirt for me nowadays. Of course, I could have had no idea before trying one on, for I have bought no shirts since my reducing attained its stabilised form late in May. Among my mail on this day was a letter from an ex-amateur in London—Nigel Van Biene[1]—who wants me to act as American agent for a literary bureau which he established last August & which he says is succeeding finely. The work would mainly involve the placing of MSS. in professional magazines, & would be on a commission basis. Before I commit myself either toward acceptance or declination I shall seek a variety of opinions from those whom I deem competent—in fact, I have already begun to do so, with conflicting results so far. McNeil advises against, Loveman is rather neutral, & Sonny is mildly in favour. But of this more in a future diary. Well—I retired at 3 a.m. & was up at 1:30 p.m. on Christmas Day. Proceeding at once to Sonny's in my best grey suit & new grey mixed tie, I found Loveman & honest old McNeil there before me; all prepared for a record-breaking Yuletide celebration. And record-breaking it certainly turned out to be! Gifts showered profuse—Sonny breaking the ice by handing his Grandpa a festive package the very moment the Old Gentleman handed him his book. This package contained an *exquisite* dark blue tie, of *exactly* the sort I would have selected myself, together with a piece of rock from the strange Arctic land of Spitzbergen—which the Child knew would appeal to Grandpa's fantastic imagination. Shortly afterward we adjourned from the parlour to the dining-room, where the table was set in sumptuous & artistic fashion with a white colonial house—roof laden with snow—in the centre. Holly, poinsettias, & lighted red candles vied with the fully ornamented Christmas tree in the corner to produce glamour; & on the table beside the colonial house was a lifelike Santa Claus—pipe in mouth—about a foot high, with bulging red pack upon his stalwart shoulders. From this pack, at the conclusion of the meal, presents were distributed to all; each gift being a silk handkerchief with borders adapted to the age & taste of the recipient. Thus honest old M<sup>c</sup>Neil—whose only presentable suit is brown— received one with a brown border; whilst I, who am elderly & conservative, drew a modest grey. Belknap, as a young decadent, was allotted a passionate purple; & others were outfitted with equal taste & congruity. The meal itself surpassed description, & was eat to the accompaniment of the radio. Turkey was the base, but every imaginable accessory was provided, till the banquets of Lucullus sink to tameness in comparison. For dessert one had the choice of plum-pudding or mince pie—I choosing the pudding because of its ancient & honourable association with the Yule. The feast concluded, all hands adjourned once more to the parlour, where an enormous red stocking was seen to be suspended from the archway leading to the dental office. This was a *grab-bag*, filled with little useful articles, & meant to be passed around till the contents was exhausted. So ample was its load, that it made *nine* circuits before the five recipients—Honest old M<sup>c</sup>Neil, Loveman, Belknap & his papa, & Grandpa Theobald—succeeded in emptying it. My own "haul" was as follows:

> 1 stick Williams' Shaving Soap
> 1 tin Mavis Talcum Powder
> 1 toothbrush
> 1 ivory handled nail file
> 1 pair sleeve garters—to hold cuffs out of dirt's way.
> 1 pair "gold" collar buttons
> 1 penholder with rubber grip
> 1 spring tape measure in red celluloid case
> 1 package long envelopes

Had I been arrested on my way home, I am sure the police would have found in my pockets strong presumptive evidence of my having robbed a Woolworth or Kresge emporium! This grabbing being completed, all hands adjourned to the dining room again; & where we found around the walls an array of 25 advertising illustrations, clipped from magazines, but without identifying text. This was a game of identification—the idea being to test one's familiarity with the current advertising of the day. As a prize, a box of chocolate creams was offered—the box being a circular tin affair with a delightful peacock & crescent moon on the cover. Now since I *never* read the popular magazines, & scarcely so much as glance at the advertising cards in the street-cars, I did not expect to count at all in this competition. In fact, I announced without hesitation that I might as well not even try. But being at last persuaded, I cast my blundering eye over the array & did about as badly as I expected—identifying only *six* out of the twenty-five. But here is the joke. Incredible as it may seem, the others were just as bad & worse than myself! Sonny could pick only three, & Loveman & M<sup>c</sup>Neil only five each—so that in spite of my abysmally poor showing & utter ignorance of modern advertising I won the prize! The chocolates are magnificent—I offered to treat the crowd, but Mrs. Long wouldn't let me, since there was a great bowl of assorted chocolates on hand throughout the day, from which everybody was expected to help himself. I've only just now made the taste which permits me to pronounce an opinion on my prize. The game being over, & the prize awarded, all hands adjourned to the nearest cinema show; where an excellent orchestra made up for any mediocrity which may have resided in the two long films—both Western dramas. Upon our return to 823, more discussion ensued; & later on an exquisite supper of chicken salad & some sweet dessert in tall tumblers was served. All this time Felis was gliding & rippling about in a big red bow; & so amiable did the season make him, that he only hissed—neither scratching nor biting—when Grandpa Theobald tried to stroke his luxurious wealth of fur. The only cloud on the general gaiety was the illness of Mrs. Long's father at his hotel downtown; an illness which has taken a turn for the worse during the past week. His mind seems to fail at times, though he is only 81; & during the course of the evening Dr. Long was called down to see him, although he returned to report that the sufferer was no worse. Mr. Doty will not have a regular physician or nurse about, but the attendants at the Touraine know his needs very well, & either Dr. or Mrs. Long goes to see him every day, bringing him food of the dainty sort he most relishes. At supper each plate was garnished by a "lollypop" set on a pedestal & covered with a paper effigy of Santa Claus—a device I brought home & now have on the desk before me. Well—after still more discussion the party dispersed & all hands went home. I arrived about midnight & have since been writing this—after which I shall read Rhode Island material, write on my weird article, or do something till I can get sleepy enough to retire. As for the future programme—I don't know yet exactly when S H is coming, but will probably find out in the morning mail. Next Wednesday there is a McNeil meeting at McNeil's, & the Wednesday after that a Leeds meeting at Morton's place in Paterson. Beyond this my engagement file has no entries. I may send this along during Saturday, or I may wait & add something—I'll see what turns up in the morning. Meanwhile let me hope that your own Yuletide was far from unpicturesque!

     Yr aff Nephew & obt Servt

       H P L

P.S. Retired 4 a.m. up [*sic*] Sat. at 2 p.m. Shall go shopping & perhaps library, then will probably return & write.

P.P.S. 6 p.m. Afternoon mail swamped me, so haven't been out yet. Hope to get out before shops close—must get suit at tailor's & go to the barber's.

[Addendum on p. II recto:] S H isn't sure of date of arrival. If dropped from Halle's after the Christmas rush, she will be back in Jany. for an indefinite time.

[*On envelope:*]      Saturday Night—7 p.m.

Didn't get out much of any where, but am going to dodge down & see if the tailor is still open. Then I shall write again & retire about midnight. This finishes Saturday—next diary will begin Sunday morning.

## Notes

1. Nigel Van Biene (1905–1986) was the author of two short story collections, *The Sibilant Whisper* (Shanghai: Shanghai Sports, 1923) and *Ragged Tales* (Shanghai: Lettercraft, 1924), and a poetry collection, *Miscellanea* (Shanghai: Lettercraft, 1924). He wrote the "Sports & Stage" column for the *China Press*.

CPSIA information can be obtained
at www.ICGtesting.com
Printed in the USA
BVHW041648200821
614848BV00014B/170

9 781614 982470